I wanted to tell the story of an atom.
Primo Levi

Do not define today. Define backward and forward, spatial
and many-sided. A defined today is over and done for.
Paul Klee

DUST & DATA

Traces of the Bauhaus
across 100 Years

Ines Weizman (ed.)
Spector Books

Contents

Part 2
**Hospital, Library, Drafting Rooms, Absent Silence:
The Bauhaus in Weimar**

Onward:
Turning Dust to Data

Ines Weizman

Introduction: When Pixels Meet Grains of Dust

The conceptual matrix that organizes this book is framed by two material concepts: *dust* and *data*. It is along these two axes that I sought to filter, commission, and collect a series of essays, presentations, and conversations that deal with the 100-year history of the Bauhaus. While *dust* organizes my attempt to foreground new approaches to the material analysis of objects and ruins pertaining to the school, *data* designates new approaches to managing the enormous amount of information accumulated about the subject over the years, of which the size of this book is only a faint echo. Indeed, the contemporary challenge in historical research is simultaneously concerned with finding new access to the physical materiality of the objects of our analysis—artifacts, buildings, environments—as well as charting the web of relations, connections, and patterns in which these objects are nested. The latter challenge might benefit from a digital historiography. In doing this, I attempt to connect two current theoretical strands of thought. Object-oriented theories help us to understand materials as being infused with vibrancy and the power of agency, while critical digital culture opens the door to a discussion of codes and algorithms, invisible infrastructures, networks, and databases.

Writer Brian Dillon has pointed out the paradox of dust in modernity. "In the public sphere," he says, "it signifies the depredations of industrial innovation or rising population on buildings and bodies, while in the private realm it continues to denote one's very lack of modernity, to point to an archaic or shameful inheritance, to signify lassitude or decay."[1] Modernism promoted buildings without ornament, with clear, smooth, and polished surfaces, and marshaled everything from traditional brooms to vacuum cleaners against the accumulation of dust. Modernism's preoccupation with hygiene was also its attempt to escape the historicist pomp of the nineteenth century, and the purging of dust was a move against the entropic temporality of history.[2] This, as Anselm Wagner shows in this volume, was exemplified in Le Corbusier's instruction in *Toward an Architecture* to "demand a vacuum cleaner," and a discourse on hygiene that Walter Gropius was concerned with when he started the school in Weimar, and which remained specific to the Weimar years of the Bauhaus.[3]

Though modernism sought to generate the eternal present of the brand-new, nothing escapes the tyranny of time, and the shiny surfaces of then are now themselves dust. So the dust that modernism fought against, returned to haunt it. Today, I believe, one of the important means available to us when we return to a reading of modernism is through the dust it disintegrated into and left behind.

In the material world of architecture, dust is also data. Dust is never a single object. Dust is an environment, the thickness of our air. Its material contents are dry human tissue, biological and mineral substances, and of course architectural residue and building matter. We could see in it the sedimented layers of history. Dust undoes the singular, fetish-like qualities of objects. Architectural history is too often only engaged with the history of architects, of styles and internal debates, and not enough with the materiality of architecture or the history of its materiality. A building not only has a history, but is an object *in* history. We can thus read a building as a recording device that registers its users and its environment.

This book will come out as the centenary celebrations of the founding of the Staatliches Bauhaus in Weimar in 1919 draw to a close. These events for the Bauhaus school, the "Bauhaus style" and "move-ment"—once considered edgy, controversial, politically radical, and even dangerous—were generously supported by state and mainstream institutions in countless conferences, exhibitions, and publications. The German government, a coalition of conservatives and social demo-crats, decided in 2015 to invest almost eighty million euros to celebrate the Bauhaus nationally and internationally.[4]

Not only was the political sting taken out of the Bauhaus project; the physical products of the school have also gone through a gradual process of commercialization. Looking today at the prices fetched by furniture, textiles, light fittings, and even door handles derived from the school, it is clear that Bauhaus has become a luxury brand.

Ines Weizman

When Pixels Meet Grains of Dust

9

In spite of this, the turmoil and transformation of the period in which the school was established might remind us of our own period. In an ironic turn of history, Sachsen-Anhalt, the state in which the most important Bauhaus building—Gropius's Bauhaus school in Dessau—is located, is today one of the strongholds of the radical right-wing party, which promotes traditionalism, localism, and nationalism.[5]

One of the problems may be that those sponsoring the celebrations would prefer to separate the objects of modernism from the ideology that produced it. But in fact, this ideology was not homogeneous: although most members of the Bauhaus were not aligned with the Nazis, some were; and whereas Gropius and Ludwig Mies van der Rohe eventually emigrated to the United States, Hannes Meyer, Gropius's successor as director of the Bauhaus from 1928 to 1930, found himself on the opposite end of the political scale, which was as complicated to live as it was to narrate later, when the political boundaries of the Cold War shifted. After being forced to leave his position in Dessau, he moved to the Soviet Union, where he joined the Swiss Communist Party; then in 1936, he briefly moved back to Switzerland, then to Mexico, eventually to return to Europe, where he found himself caught in limbo between the political frontlines of the East-West divide. As Thomas Flierl writes here, Meyer was "too communist for the one, too bourgeois for the other."[6] Other teachers and students, as Daniel Talesnik discusses here, were also caught in the political storm of the history to come. It is this complexity of Bauhaus history—the ideological interpretations under which it was located, relocated, relocated again, silenced, dispersed, rediscovered, and eventually celebrated—that are investigated in this collection. The ambiguous political legacy of the school made it difficult to discuss before the Cold War had ended and the dividing line between East and West Germany had been erased. But even now, not all borders have been dissolved, and new ones have recently been created.

This book originated within the XIII. International Bauhaus-Kolloquium, a conference that I organized at the Bauhaus-Universität Weimar in 2016, titled, like this book, *Dust & Data*. It brought together an internationally diverse community of scholars, theorists, artists, and audiences of various backgrounds and interests. A few of the pieces come from related presentations and events that I organized in the run-up to the Bauhaus year and the subsequent International Bauhaus-Kolloquium I organized in 2019. Some of the authors of the essays in this book are both established and young Bauhaus scholars, while others are architectural historians, theorists, and writers who have discovered new perspectives on their work by focusing on the Bauhaus.

The book has three parts. The first deals with the products of the school, be they material artifacts, codes, or ideas; the second with the way its history unfolded in Weimar and was told there, that is, with its historiography; and the third deals with the migration of the school's ideas and protagonists around the world. These parts are interspersed with transcripts including documents, conversations, and interviews.

Part I, titled *Objects, Pattern, Textures, Codes: Theories of Bauhaus Materiality*, explores the different material and immaterial products of the Bauhaus: objects, concepts, ideas, media, and buildings. The Bauhaus sought to transform society through the introduction of new types of objects, mass-produced and readily at hand. Its protagonists believed, each in her or his own way, that through these objects a new form of life and society could be organized.

Part I starts with an essay by Alina Payne. It starts the book because it reflects upon current discussions regarding Big Data and the agency of objects through the mid-19th century writings of architect and critic Gottfried Semper. In her reading of Semper's *Der Stil*, Payne distinguishes four issues that reverberate everywhere in this book: *materiality*, *agency*, *the migration of objects*, and *objects as data*. Leading out of this theoretical meditation on history, Anselm Wagner, as mentioned above, looks at the public discussion of hygiene in the Weimar Republic and its ideological exaltation of hygienic cleanliness that entered architectural and urban design. Pep Avilés offers an intriguing account of arguments between teachers at the school concerning another topic that's very current these days: media materiality. His discussion of the term *Faktura* is going through debates about the material properties of different media, painting, photography, and film. Jörg Paulus's essay deals with textures, primarily those imprinted on different media—here it is the thin paper of an academic journal printed in 1977 that documented the papers presented at the first International Bauhaus-Kolloquium. From the imprint of a text from the inverse page on a photograph, he reads the entanglement of optical and haptic perception micro-historiographically.

Ines Weizman

When Pixels Meet Grains of Dust

11

Essays by Elizabeth Otto and Persephone Allen explore female members of the Bauhaus school as well as the voices of lesbian, gay, and transgender members. Christopher T. Green explores the notion of code through the work of Josef and later also Anni Albers as they tried to find a transitional phase between analogue abstractions and digital thinking. Green intriguingly links their explorations, aimed initially at restructuring, painting, weaving, and collaging, to architectural drawings and even to buildings.

Anna-Maria Meister looks at the material history of the Masters' Houses in Dessau and their discontinuities, both to the Weimar experiments with new housing typologies such as the Haus Am Horn and to each other, which prevented them from forming an architectural series. The differences between them, she argues, have also determined the trajectory of their preservation and reconstruction from the postwar years to the present.

Robin Schuldenfrei, beginning her analysis with the Director's House in Dessau, looks at yet another dimension of the exploration of materials by Mies van der Rohe and Lilly Reich at a time before Mies took over the directorship of the Bauhaus in 1930. She traces their attempt to play down form in favor of materiality. In the absence of decoration, the material surfaces themselves—marble, travertine, wood, wool carpets, deep leather—were given the task of providing pattern and form.

Indeed, ornamentation might be a crime, but material luxury seemed to be a necessity for modernism, and sometimes only the best would do: zebrawood for furniture and partitions, top-quality onyx, Carrara marble, green calf leather sofas, silver spoons, and polished aluminum of lamps and chrome-covered columns.[7] Modernism no longer had time for the artisan labor fossilized in details and decoration, as in the arts and crafts movement, and turned to the deep time of nature itself. Yet the luxury of modernism exposed its multiple temporalities: the annual rainy periods resulting in the striped patterns of oak, teak, Makassar or other tropical woods, the life of the beast that went into the leather, the millennia of minerals congealing into shape on the marble, and the million years of fossils in the travertine— geology turning into architecture. The proposition of luxury thus gives our understanding of the contemporary yet another crucial dimension: it shifts our gaze to the planet itself.

Ending this first part of the book, Nicholas de Monchaux takes on this wider scale of analysis when relating Bauhaus ideas about industrial objects to the famous Schlemmer figures and the space suits developed by NASA in the 1960s, making explicit the connection between the Bauhaus and the Moon landing, which celebrated its 50th anniversary in 2019.

Part II, titled *Hospital, Library, Drafting Rooms, Absent Silence: The Bauhaus in Weimar*, starts in Weimar in 1919 with the founding of the Bauhaus. It collects essays that look at the political and social context from the immediate aftermath of World War I, when the school was founded in Weimar, to its demise on the eve of World War II.

The essays in this part have been compiled in order to undertake something of a *microhistory* of the school. Microhistory is a concept developed in the 1970s by the "Italian school," which included Giovanni Levi and Carlo Ginzburg.[8] These historians sought to depart from a history of kings and queens, presidents and prime ministers, the so-called *"histoire événementielle"* in which the important documents are official letters or transcripts of courts and summits. Microhistory was also pit against the history of the *longue durée* that the Marxist historians of the Annales school—Marc Bloch, Lucien Febvre, and Fernand Braudel—had developed in the interwar period. The history of the *longue durée* is the impersonal history of processes, of undercurrent, the history of capital, the history of trades, a history of large territories such as the Mediterranean. Instead they concentrated on a history of artisans, the outliers of those not conforming to what was considered the norm, of those who had left almost no traces.

The moment of foundation in 1919 was already folding the future into itself. Countless and hardly traceable micro-events that happened in Weimar—a debate in one of the workshops, an argument in Gropius's office, students folding up telephone books, or a moment in a collaging exercise when students put together photographs they had cut out of magazines in the school's library, a story told by Frank Simon-Ritz—were leading to effects that were geographically wide and temporally extended. This happened along the trajectories of migration of the school's protagonists.

In 1919, in the aftermath of the war, the Kaiser was gone and the old order shuttered. This allowed a period of unprecedented innovation and radical changes in science, industry, technology, and consumer patterns, as well as a fundamental break with traditional art forms.

Photography, print media, radio, and film were becoming increasingly important instruments of artistic expression as well as of political propaganda. Weimar was chosen as the meeting point for the National Assembly because Berlin was too volatile. It was here that the ideas of left and right, conservatives and liberals, reformers and modernists, laborers and capitalists confronted each other.

These political circumstances, but also the history of Weimar as a cultural center of literature, music, arts, and philosophy, influenced the constitution and orientation of the Bauhaus as an institution and as a mode of production. It attracted people drawn to the promise of experimentation and conviviality with a group of the most modern artists and architects, as well as those who simply arrived because there was no other place for them. The desire of the *Bauhäusler* to create a new world might have been because everything they were taught to know, along with the value system they'd inherited, was liquefying. "All that was solid *had* melted in the air"—as Goethe wrote in *Faust* (he might have written this line only a few dozen meters from where the Bauhaus was founded a hundred years later), inspiring *The Communist Manifesto* of Marx and Engels about four decades later.[9]

Although we now perceive the Bauhaus professors and some of the school's graduates to be the old sages of our practice, they were quite young when they established the school and began to teach there: Walter Gropius was 36, Josef Albers and Johannes Itten were 31, Gerhard Marcks 30, Georg Muche 26. Moreover, the entire endeavor was to some degree improvised, unaware of its destiny.

This second part of the book begins with an essay by Zeynep Çelik Alexander in which she gives more texture to the image of rupture and the historical "turning point" that 1919 was, but she is also aware of the continuities between the Bauhaus and previous schools of thought and pedagogy that influenced and became radicalized at the Bauhaus.[10] In his essay, Peter Bernhard shows how, in lectures on literature, dance, philosophy, and even archaeology,[11] the school tried to find allies in fighting off the conservative forces attacking the Bauhaus. Anna Bokov presents new research about the relation between the Bauhaus and the Vkhutemas school in Moscow, established shortly after the Bauhaus. She goes on to question why the story of the Vkhutemas school remained in the shadow of the Bauhaus, and to ask what the role of historians of modernism was in doing so.

Important details about the inauguration of the school are revealed by Norbert Korrek. When the Bauhaus was founded, the upper floors of the building were still used as a hospital for wounded soldiers returning from the trenches of World War I. Indeed, many members of the staff and students had only just returned from the front. Gunta Stölzl, who began her studies in Weimar and would later become the master of the weaving workshop, had volunteered during the war as a nurse with the Red Cross. Paul Klee was designing aircraft camouflage for the Royal Bavarian Flight School—which is related to the aviators who took the first aerial images of the Middle East and Africa. Walter Gropius served in the signal corps. When his airplane was shot down, a parachute allowed him to escape with his life.[12] László Moholy-Nagy was also wounded in the war, which as Joyce Tsai shows in her essay, had an impact on his practice.[13] We need to understand the emergence of the Bauhaus in relation to these young people returning from war, the sound of cannons still ringing in their ears, the death and destruction that they had seen in their minds, perhaps some with a condition we might now understand to be post-traumatic stress disorder, or PTSD. To add another dimension to the modernists' obsession with dust, it is also because of the trauma of the war that the architecture promoted by Bauhaus teachers sought a clinical hygiene that evoked the quality of a hospital.

While wounded soldiers were still confined to their beds and being wheeled through the corridors of the van de Velde building, special rapid air and rail links were established between Berlin and Weimar to provide transportation to the meetings of the National Assembly in Weimar. Walter Gropius landed in Weimar a few times rather than arrive by coach or train. Different eras bumped against each other. To paraphrase the writer William Gibson, "the future was already there; it was just not evenly distributed."[14]

This part also charts a number of debates about the legacy of the school undertaken in East Germany during the Cold War in the context of the International Bauhaus-Kolloquium. This is dealt with in a subsection titled *The Legacy of the Bauhaus in East Germany: Debates at the School of Architecture and Construction (HAB) in Weimar.*[15] One would think that in the East, the Bauhaus would be readily embraced by the communist regime, but, on the contrary, it was initially rejected, then neglected, and the material remnants of the school building were left to rot. Bauhaus history was largely taboo in the architecture schools of the GDR as in other places throughout the Eastern Bloc; the school was considered too avant-gardist, too experimental, too "cosmopolitan," too free-thinking to be harnessed by the stale state communism and its pedagogical dogmatism. In her essay, Kathrin Siebert discusses the bureaucratic and ideological obstacles that Western architectural historians faced when invited to teach as visiting professors at the Hochschule für Architektur und Bauwesen (HAB) Weimar. The timeline presented by Christiane Wolf and Norbert Korrek shows how, in the late 1950s, discussions of Bauhaus history slowly emerged at the HAB Weimar, but were suppressed. They show that Karl-Heinz Hüter, a researcher at the department of architectural history and theory, published the first comprehensive book about the Bauhaus in Weimar (*Das Bauhaus in Weimar*), which was censored in 1964. Hüter's story and that of his book are also discussed in a selection of transcribed interviews with himself and with former organizers and participants of the International Bauhaus-Kolloquien, which in 2016 were part of an exhibition in Weimar and are now available as an online archive of the history of the International Bauhaus-Kolloquien between 1976 and 2019.[16]

From 1976 until the political transformation of 1989, as this subsection reveals, the International Bauhaus-Kolloquium, the conference series from which also this book originates, was an important institution in which Bauhaus history was slowly being established as a field of research. The conference, inaugurated in Weimar to correspond with the opening of the Bauhaus building in Dessau, has emerged as a place in which the expanding limits of what could be said under a slowly melting authoritarian regime could be tested. The colloquium has also offered a unique forum for international architectural historians and theorists from both sides of the Iron Curtain.

Part III, titled *Refugees, Migrants, Returnees, Travelers: Bauhaus Architects in Exile*, deals with the migration of teachers and students from the Bauhaus, the dissemination of its ideas into various cultural contexts, and the circulation of objects—the products and artifacts produced by Bauhaus protagonists.

The essays here present new archival research that unearthed new details about the worldwide web of exchange and collaboration that Bauhaus protagonists had after leaving Germany.

Marija Drėmaitė tells the story of Vladas Švipas, a Bauhaus architecture graduate from Kaunas who returned to Lithuania and lived through both German and the Soviet occupations. During the war, he was brought back to Germany as a prisoner of war. After the war, he emigrated to the US, where he reestablished the connection to Gropius through written correspondence, but his architectural career in a foreign environment never really regained its momentum.

Ines Sonder follows the incredible path of Bosnian architect Selman Selmanagić, probably the only Muslim at the Bauhaus, who during his studies in Dessau became an active communist. Forced to leave Germany with the arrival of the Hitler regime, he initially arrived in Palestine, where he worked at the office of Richard Kauffmann. With the mounting national struggle in Palestine, he was involuntarily forced to find commissions with Arab clients in Jerusalem and Gaza.

Veronica Bremer tells the story of the Design Centre in Sydney, inspired by a collaboration between Australian artists and designers with László Moholy-Nagy and Marcel Breuer, whom they had met in London. London was a frequent stopover for Bauhaus teachers on their way to the US. From there, Moholy-Nagy traveled to Chicago, where he became director of the "New Bauhaus," and Breuer joined Walter Gropius at Harvard.

Anna Vallye looks at the difficulties Gropius and Martin Wagner had in adapting some of the social reform and urban planning agendas they'd developed in the 1920s for a German context to the postwar climate at Harvard. Through a close analysis of their teaching curriculum, she shows how different European and US conceptions of modernism remained irreconcilable and how it was impossible to realize social agendas in urban design projects in the US.

In a related essay, Michael Kubo looks at Walter Gropius's architectural office, TAC. Gropius hoped to realize ambitious projects in Iraq, including a university campus in Baghdad. His plans for the university are a rare glimpse of how Bauhaus ideas were adapted to postwar reality and how he sought to export them to the Middle East.

Hamed Khosravi's essay concentrates on architect Gabriel Guevrekian, a contemporary of the Bauhaus, who worked in France. Originally from Tehran, he started in the office of Adolf Loos in Vienna, participated in some of the CIAM meetings, and eventually arrived in Chicago, where he worked as an architect, taught, and

Ines
Weizman

When
Pixels
Meet
Grains
of
Dust

17

potentially could still have met with Moholy-Nagy. Brought together, the individual stories collected in this part shed new light on the wider network of Bauhaus members and their contemporaries after the closure of the school.

My essay on the so-called "Bauhaus in the Golan," a former customhouse located in the Syrian, Israeli-occupied, Golan Heights, shows that the history of the Bauhaus—and that of international modernism, of which it is part—intersects, uncomfortably, with the history of colonialism. A hundred years on, architecture is again entangled in geopolitical transformations with global repercussions. Refugees are arriving in Europe in numbers not seen since the end of World War II. The horrible wars in Syria, Iraq, and elsewhere seem, at least in part, to be a reaction to the European order imposed on the Middle East in the aftermath of World War I. The spectacular violence of barrel bombs and suicide vests echoes a slower violence whose roots bore through the ground of the colonial history and occupation to which this area was subjected.

In an *Onward* section, which both closes and revisits the context of "dust and data," Bernhard Siegert's essay refers to the recent European perception of a "refugee crisis." In his talk at the conference in 2016 in which his essay here originates, he noted that traces of Bauhaus sensitivity could be found in the work of research architects who are using contemporary media to produce innovative new spatial and data analyses to counter dominant policies toward migrants. Their combination of aesthetic and scientific strategies adds to the required toolbox of the contemporary historian, while opening new avenues for making history operational. His essay smoothly leads into a conversation between novelist and spatial thinker Tom McCarthy and architect Eyal Weizman. In their respective works, both deal with the way that memory, space, and media interact. Sometimes it is merely a crack in the surface of a building, captured in a grainy image, that holds the key to a lost memory (as such, they draw a connection back to the carbon atom with which Primo Levi so epically concludes his *The Periodic Table* and which inspired this book).[17] But the task of the historian, they agree, is no longer concerned with a single trace, often lost, nor with information scarcity, but rather in dealing with an overabundance of information. The contemporary historian (novelist and forensic expert for this matter) needs to find "more than human" approaches and prosthetic algorithms for dealing with contemporary history. Just like the detective, the historian can no longer afford to concentrate on searching for the needle in the haystack, but must rather study the haystack itself, its disposition, and patterns within it. Although written in the context of the 100th anniversary of the Bauhaus, the ideas in this collection belong not only to our present, to the year 2019, but also to our immediate future in which other important Bauhaus dates and milestones of Bauhaus history and the history of modernism will be revisited. It is only through updating our historical methods that we can "re-scan" historical details and see in them heretofore invisible details. By mapping the relation between a huge multiplicity of objects, we can also discover invisible patterns. Indeed, if we look at it close enough, Bauhaus history could function as a prism through which future scholars might continue to find traces of the future in the biographies of the school's protagonists and in the stories of its artifacts, objects and ideas—that is, its dust of data.

1   Brian Dillon, "A Dry Black Veil," *Cabinet* magazine, no. 35: *Dust* (Fall 2009): 59–65.
2   Caroline A. Jones, "Dusting," in *Jorge Otero-Pailos: The Ethics of Dust*, Thyssen-Bornemisza Art Contemporary, ed. Eva Ebersberger and Daniela Zyman (Cologne: Walter König, 2009), 34.
3   Le Corbusier, *Toward an Architecture* (Los Angeles: Getty Research Institute, 2007), 172.
4   "Das Bauhaus gehört der Welt, aber es kommt aus Deutschland und ist einer der erfolgreichsten Exportartikel unserer Kulturgeschichte. Deutschland ist daher nicht nur sich selbst, sondern auch der Welt verpflichtet das Bauhaus zu bewahren und zu fördern." From the press release of the parliamentary decision to fund the Bauhaus Jubilee: SPD Bundestagsfraktion, "Bundestag verabschiedet Antrag zum Bauhaus-Jubiläum 2019," press release no. 79/2015, February 5, 2015, www.spdfraktion.de/node/36068/pdf (accessed July 1, 2019).
5   In this tense atmosphere, political pressure forced the Bauhaus Dessau Foundation to cancel a concert by a left-leaning punk band at the Bauhaus Foundation Dessau in October 2018, demonstrating that the political tensions surrounding the school and its legacy have endured. The cancellation was largely argued on the basis that the building, a UNESCO World Heritage Site, could become a space of political agitation and aggression between far-right and leftist activists. Politicians and cultural groups have largely criticized this decision. See "Open Letter to the Bauhaus Dessau Foundation," e-flux Architecture, October 24, 2018, www.e-flux.com/announcements/224013/open-letter-to-the-bauhaus-dessau-foundation/ (accessed June 6, 2019).
6   Thomas Flierl, "Migrant with a Conflicted Sense of Home: Hannes Meyer after the Bauhaus" in this volume. See also Thomas Flierl and Philipp Oswalt, eds., *Hannes Meyer und das Bauhaus im Streit der Deutungen* (Leipzig: Spector Books, 2019).
7   See also Robin Schuldenfrei, *Luxury and Modernism: Architecture and the Object in Germany 1900–1933* (Princeton: Princeton University Press, 2019).
8   Carlo Ginzburg, "Microhistory: Two or Three Things That I Know about It," in *Thread and Traces: True False Fictive*, trans. Anne C. Tedeschi and John Tedeschi (Berkeley: University of California Press, 2012), 193–214.
9   *All That Is Solid Melts into Air* is also the title of the famous book by Marshall Berman (New York: Verso Books, 1982).

10 See also John V. Maciuika, *Before the Bauhaus: Architecture, Politics, and the German State, 1890–1920* (Cambridge, UK: Cambridge University Press, 2008).

11 On the lecture of Egyptologist Hermann Ranke at the Bauhaus in 1921, see Peter Bernhard, "Ich hörte eine gewaltige Vorlesung aus dem Gilgameschepos," in *Bauhaus Vorträge. Gastredner am Weimarer Bauhaus 1919–1925* (Berlin: Gebrüder Mann Verlag, 2019), 197–200.

12 On Walter Gropius's war service on the Western Front, see Deborah Ascher Barnstone, *The Break with the Past: Avant-Garde Architecture in Germany, 1910–1925* (London: Routledge, 2019), 80–88.

13 As Robin Schuldenfrei showed in her research, when László Moholy-Nagy became the director of the New Bauhaus in Chicago in 1937, and especially at the beginning of World War II when he was considered an "enemy alien" in the US, he taught and designed for the "war industry," developing alternative construction materials for the military in times of scarcity, as well as protective equipment for soldiers and wounded veterans. Robin Schuldenfrei, "Assimilating Unease: Moholy-Nagy and the Wartime/Postwar Bauhaus in Chicago," in *Atomic Dwelling: Anxiety, Domesticity, and Postwar Architecture* (London: Routledge, 2012), 87–93.

14 According to Wikiquote, Gibson is reported to have first said this in an interview on August 31, 1993 on the NPR radio program *Fresh Air* {unverified}. He repeated it, prefacing it with "As I've said many times ...," in "The Science in Science Fiction" on *Talk of the Nation*, NPR (November 30, 1999, timecode 11:55), en.wikiquote.org/wiki/William_Gibson (accessed June 16, 2019).

15 With respect to existing research, the years of the National Socialist direction of the school that followed under Paul Schultze-Naumburg, and the immediate postwar years in Weimar, are omitted here in order to outline the story of the difficult reevaluation of the Bauhaus history in the GDR.

16 bauhaus-kolloquium.de/archiv/

17 Primo Levi, *The Periodic Table*, Penguin Modern Classics (London: Penguin, 1986 (1975)). Also, Tom McCarthy's novel C explores carbon as the basic element of life. Tom McCarthy, C (London: Jonathan Cape, 2010).

Introduction

Part 1

Objects, Pattern, Textures, Codes: Theories of Bauhaus Materiality

Alina Payne

The Agency of Objects: From Semper to the Bauhaus and Beyond

Materiality/immateriality, agency, the archive, big data, and migration may seem contemporary issues, yet, like the Bauhaus, they, too, have a long genealogy. And how each generation discovers its issues is never entirely removed from a past with which it has a palimpsest relationship. In this sense, Gottfried Semper (1803–79) activated many paths that artists and architects later traveled, and his work sparked important later developments. The excess of objects at the Great Exhibition of 1851 in London, which he had witnessed, called for a coming to grips with many new concepts. [fig.1] "Big data" was one such concept, due to the sheer quantity and almost endless variety of displayed wares; the circulation of objects so dramatically felt there for the first time also raised the issue of the traces of their passage. Their very materiality emerged as a nerve ending of art-making because the materials themselves were entering the threatening if expansive world of industrialization; finally, given the exhibition environment in which these objects were presented, how objects might be framed and processed (be it in museum vitrines or photographic atlases, etc.) became an urgent cultural and political act. Semper offered commentary in all these areas: departure points and insight that decisively marked the thinking about architecture for subsequent generations, from the immediate responses in reconceiving the relationship between architecture and objects (as its indexing agents) in the nineteenth-century *Gewerbeschulen* (craft schools) to the Bauhaus and beyond. If the best art theory comes from history (as Friedrich Schlegel put it in 1812), what then might a look back at Semper from the perspective of the Bauhaus teach us about problems latent in our own current architecture culture?

Confronting the world of objects:
Semper in 1851

Although each of the above issues was culturally pertinent in its own right to an architect like Semper, perhaps they all nevertheless revolved around one central problem — that of agency — and one question: what is the origin of architecture? It is to this topic, then, that Semper turned in his monumental treatise *Der Stil* (1860–63), and it is there that he put the object on the map ahead of architecture as a cultural index and ground zero of art-making. From the perspective of the object, this was its coming of age. Unexpectedly from the vantage point of traditional architecture treatises, volume one of *Der Stil* focused on the textile arts (carpets, fabric, upholstery); ceramics (pots, vessels, and other containers) followed in volume two, then wood-working (furniture), and only as of page 344 *Stereotomie* or stone construction, i. e. architecture.[1] For Semper, tattoos, textiles, carpets, wattles, reed fencing, ceramic vessels, woodcarvings, and the gestures involved in their making were the ancestors of architecture and its meaningful forms. [fig.2]

To be sure, the nineteenth century marked a climax in preoccupation with the objects of daily use, and in that sense Semper's reorientation was not entirely surprising. Everything from luxury to everyday items—furniture, pottery, silverware, textiles, wall coverings, hardware, and dress—had come under sustained scrutiny. However, unlike previously when such concerns, if voiced at all, remained within the province of artists, artisans, and decorator/architects, this discussion now drew into its orbit historians, politicians, museum administrators, and education officials. This was the world of *Sachkultur* (the culture of objects) that Semper grew into, yet even here his ideas before 1851, the date of his involvement with the Great Exhibition in London, and after 1851, though they may seem similar, were worlds apart. Most important was the fact that making/production became his principal theme—it had been there before, but now it became articulated and developed in a consistent and in-depth way, with tangible examples and ideas rooted in actual experience, and therefore also much more convincing. Whereas earlier, Semper had drawn examples of primitive objects that (in his view) lay at the origin of complex artworks from books, from atlases and ethnographic accounts, now he was actually seeing the Maori, the Trinidadians, the North American "Indians," and their artifacts. As an author, he also had an added unique

Fig. 1. Interior perspective of the Crystal Palace at London's Great Exhibition, 1851. Color lithograph from *Dickinson's Comprehensive Pictures of the Great Exhibition* (London, 1851). **Fig. 2.** Gottfried Semper, "The Tomb of Midas" from *Der Stil in den technischen und tektonischen Künsten*, 1878 edition, 429.

advantage: he and his reader shared the same experience— the experience of the Great Exhibition. It is rare for both author and reader to have been overwhelmed in the same way, yet in London this is precisely what happened and it gave his work even greater power and urgency. What he had encountered was what we today might call "big data": an excess of visual information, of objects and hence of potential relationships between them that somehow connected canoes with steam engines, China with America and India and beyond. Indeed, one of the catchphrases of the time was "all the world comes to London" and it was associated with an image of a genuine global event that overloaded all data banks. The impact was such that it caused Semper and others to experience a sense of collapse and of crisis: a collapse of traditional (European-based) architectural theory and a crisis of understanding and processing.

Such an encounter had significant consequences. Although Semper has been read as a defender of ornament, its champion, he may be more rightly seen as the defender of artistic agency in architecture. In Semper's post-1851 writings, fabrication and the fabricator are his two main coordinates, not the artwork in and of itself. To the extent that he focused on fabrication, Semper was in complete synchrony with the Exhibition, whose main theme was precisely "Manufacturing." The maps of the displays at the Crystal Palace illustrate clearly how the Exhibition was understood: the focus was certainly on the object and the machinery needed for its fabrication, the materials new and old, and what could be achieved with them by way of new processes. Yet the fabricator—the artisan, the worker, the machine operator— was not showcased as such. The physical act of making was not placed under scrutiny here (it would be several decades later, as result of Semper's influence, at the Paris Exhibition of 1889 as *l'histoire du travail*, but not here, not now). Inevitably this became one of Semper's main themes, concerned as he was with the disconnect he observed between form and making (which he addresses at some length in his 1852 essay "Wissenschaft, Industrie und Kunst"). His example is eloquent: the

Durchschnitt, Untersicht und Details eines Joches der getäfelten Decke des Theseustempels zu Athen.

cutting of granite into lace-like forms is possible only because the machine can do it, but not because the material lends itself to such doily-like treatment.[2]

By focusing on crafting, Semper showcased the fundamental role of the maker, of the human body—wielding tools, working materials, representing itself. His empathy theory (here in its infancy) moved in the same direction, recognizing not only a detached viewer experiencing the crafted object as would be the case in Heinrich Wölfflin's work several decades later, but also the maker as key participant, as a fundamental link between object and viewer/user.[3] Thus, in the process of rethinking the very basis of artistic creation, Semper confronted four issues that had deep nerve endings and that are not coincidentally resurfacing today: materiality (that which is being fabricated or manufactured); agency (the role of the tools and of the maker's hand and body); migration or mobility of objects (without which the Exhibition would not have been possible, nor Semper's confrontation with the excess of objects, simultaneously displayed); and the ensuing enormous amount of data that he makes a superhuman effort to process and synthesize into a single theory. Drawing upon anthropology, ethnography, museography, archaeology, art history, psychology, geology, and linguistics, Semper fashioned a response to what he identified as the challenges of the Industrial Revolution to society and civilization.[fig.3] This was a titanic effort, the last of its kind in architecture, to systematize "big data" coming from so many perspectives. And it was possible only because the various disciplines had not yet gelled into distinct areas of academic study but still presented overlaps and shared domains that allowed a trespasser to attempt a grand theory.

Alina Payne

The Agency of Objects

27

In a world that was rapidly moving toward commodification, Semper thought to reinvest making with meaning: the agency of the objects was in fact the agency of the maker. Indeed, Semper could not have missed the loss of value experienced by labor. Peter Stallybrass's essay on Karl Marx's coat is relevant as a parallel here and deserves a brief parenthesis.[4] While Marx was writing *Das Kapital*, so Stallybrass recounts, he had no money and depended on handouts either from his friend Engels or from his wife's family (who were, on the whole, fairly reluctant). As a result, he had to pawn his coat very frequently, yet if he pawned it, he could not go to the British Library to work—without a proper coat, he could not look the scholar and be admitted into the reading room. For this reason, he could only return to the library once he had redeemed his coat. So, on the one hand, his coat was part of his identity—as a scholar who could be admitted into the library—and on the other, it was also a simple commodity, something that had no intrinsic meaning and could be traded for money, an abstract economic device. And, as Stallybrass argues, that it is precisely this constant back and forth between the coat on his back in close touch with his body and his identity on the one hand, and the money it could garner as an object of exchange on the other, that rought home to Marx the reality of labor voided of meaning and the damaging consequences of commodification through a loss of the self.

One could perhaps make a similar argument for Semper. Exiled, constantly on the breadline, without a job and seeking even menial ones without success, living from handouts (from Henry Cole in his case), involved in the 1848 revolution, and part of the same German expat political group as Marx (though not nearly as radical as Marx would have wished), Semper must have realized the consequences of a capitalist global economy. He may or may not have pawned his coat, but just as Marx writes about his coat in *Das Kapital*, so Semper fo- cused on the human body and its *Bekleidung* (clothing; transferring the concept to architecture, whose "body" is likewise "clothed"). In so doing, he placed the body of the maker back in the center of things. The symbolism of form he proposed (as a visualization of essential functions)—just like the close bodily connection between the hand of the maker, its tools, and materials, and the fabrication process that he stressed—allowed objects to be reinvested with meaning and resisted the evacuation of meaning from objects treated as commodities.

¹Muthmaszlichen Ansesichten eines alten Pfahldorfs. ²Gegenwärtiger Zustand eines Pfahlbaues. ³Pfahlbau von oben gesehen. ⁴Pfahlbau von Bauhvolle. ⁵⁻⁷⁰Aus den Pfahlbauten im Bodensee. ⁷¹⁻⁸⁰Aus dem Neufchatelersee und andern schweizer Seen. ⁸¹⁻⁸⁸Aus den Pfahlbauten bei Wismar. ⁸¹⁻⁸⁰Aus dem Finersee bei Vicenza.

Given this context, it is perhaps not that surprising to read the injunction of Henry Cole (one of the masterminds of the London Exhibition) after the 1855 Exhibition in Paris: "The tendency of future Exhibitions [after 1851], in their foreign departments, will be to exhibit not rare and costly production, required by very few purchasers, but manufactures; and especially those manufactures the use of which is universal, and not merely national or peculiar."[5] Basically, Cole describes consumable goods. The great Exhibitions generated much thinking along these lines, but it was not always clear-cut, and the value of the exhibited objects oscillated just like Marx's coat between commodity and meaningful artistic products. One example of such oscillation is the Orient Museum in Vienna created in 1875 by the then director of the Vienna Museum für Kunst und Industrie, Arthur von Scala. The newly created museum collection was based on his own collection of East and Central Asian artifacts, which was first displayed at the 1873 Exhibition in Vienna. The collection achieved great success as a pavilion, and the museum was created in its aftermath with the selfsame objects so as to fulfill an educational role. Thereafter, Scala kept adding to the collection; he had representatives everywhere buying objects (from the Bosporus to Japan, from Mongolia to India), but these were not only historical art objects: they were increasingly modern ones. And thus by 1886, the museum had been fully transformed into a *Handelsmuseum* (a trade museum) on the model of the Central African museum in Brussels. In fact, this oscillation between objects belonging in an art museum and a commercial display was inherent from the onset—from their appearance at the Great Exhibition.

Alina Payne

The Agency of Objects

29

The Museum für Kunst und Industrie in Vienna also oscillated between these two poles, as indeed all such decorative arts museums were intended to do. To be sure, the collection was meant to be of valuable objects, but also of models for industry. Alois Riegl, the museum's curator of textiles, challenged this contradiction at its very root in his *Volkskunst, Hausfleiss und Hausindustrie* (1894).[6] It was precisely the museum's and government's will to commodify a simple barter system (objects made at home for personal consumption and personal meaning were traditionally exchanged for other homemade products in rural areas) that caused his reaction and deep disapproval. The entire existing eco-system of work and life would be destroyed, he felt, and he said so in no uncertain terms. Yet Vienna was not alone in its eagerness to trans-form lifestyles into commodities. In Dresden, Semper's early career stomping ground, the mission of the Kunstgewerbemuseum, was to develop models for industrial production and to develop the taste of the buying public[7]—in short, to create objects for consumption.

Still, Semper's reaction was not that of the British artists / reformers who either took a political stance or simply rejected the machine by trying to turn the clock back to the Middle Ages. Instead, his response was "his" museum.[8] [fig.4] And his answer to the big data of the Exhibition and to the proliferation and circulation of objects it displayed was his *vergleichende Ästhetik* (comparative aesthetics): as objects from all over the world came together, he proposed to com-pare them. Indeed, he conceived of a museum that would be about materials and fabrication processes, not about objects as such, neither as models for industry nor for anything else: a museum in which the memory of making, the successive stages in this metabolic chain (*Stoffwechsel*), was embedded in exhibits and organized their arrange-ment and their taxonomy. The four corners of his ideal museum plan were the four primary materials from soft and pliable to hard and breakable. They connected to each other in a spiral movement as one form of making (based on one material) gave way to the next by way of an increased complexity of crafting required by the increased complexity of the material. If one were to read Semper's treatise into this museum (as he fully expected one to do), then these materials, whose essential formal characteristics are manipulated by the human hand and tools, translated from one to the other in an upward sequence from soft (textile) to hard (stone) and ultimately produced monumental art, that is, architecture. In short, at the center of this museum, architecture itself was on display. But it was an unusual museum: for one, architecture could not be seen even if the path along the ascending spiral added up to architecture; for another, it was the fabrication of objects that took up center stage, not their ultimate evolutionary arrival point. Thus, Semper's museum put the worker and labor back in focus. It was about fabrication, agency, and reinvesting objects with meaning. In a way, it was a natural response to the Industrial Revolution and the emphasis on manufacture at the Great Exhibitions. But it was also their thoughtful critique.

Semper's lesson

Needless to say, this was not a definitive answer for how to display material data (and the need to display it). Eventually Semper's museum methodology of comparative aesthetics (*vergleichende Ästhetik*) also lost ground in anthropological collections, where it had been applied with much success. Franz Boas, for example, moved away from a Semperian organization of displays to showcase objects in cultural contexts. In 1887, he fought against the classification and display (in the museum setting) of objects according to physical resemblance across cultures and instead argued for their placement within the setting of their own eco-culture in order to understand their real meaning. It was he who pioneered the vitrines-as-display strategy—the reenactment of a moment in time: a stage-like display that framed and collected data, that contained and gave it cultural meaning. This approach, perceived as novel and radical at the time, led to a well-publicized debate between Boas and Otis T. Mason, a curator at the US National Museum in New York.[9] Perhaps it is not surprising that Boas, educated in the German environment, where the history of culture was a prominent concern across disciplines, pioneered it for anthropology. His vitrines, so illustrative and visually appealing, spoke equally to the scientific concerns of the field and to the exhibition-as-show (or as panoramas) mentality that pervaded the museum world. Indeed, Boas conceived his *vitrines* as panoramas, where sculpture and painting blended into each other to create lifelikeness, with figures and objects

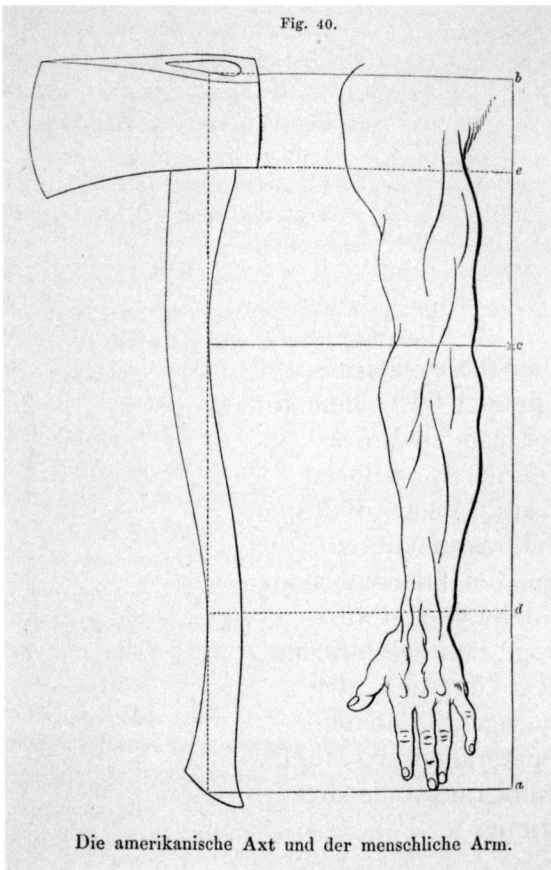

Fig. 40.

Die amerikanische Axt und der menschliche Arm.

Fig.5. Ernst Kapp. *The American Ax and the Human Arm* from *Grundlinien einer Philosophie der Technik*, 1877, fig. 40.

emerging from a chiaroscuro background. But if his display ran counter to Semper's proto-structuralist model, it did nevertheless retain his focus on man as maker of tools, objects, and artifacts.

Semper was not alone in identifying agency as a problem for his time. Another clear statement on the discomfort with the changing nature of artistic agency came from a contemporary of Semper's whose efforts to theorize the machine indicate the problems it posed. In his 1877 work *Grundlinien einer Philosophie der Technik*,[10] Ernst Kapp argued that if the machine is to replace man's work, then logically it has to correspond to the organism it is going to replace. [fig.5] Basing his central argument on a definition of the machine that he borrowed from physicist and physiologist Hermann von Helmholtz, Kapp defined all objects made by man as extensions of his body, unselfconsciously conceptualized as such through *Organprojektion* (organ projection), a term he introduced. Though he admitted that compared to tools, the machine as a whole reflects the body less, Kapp insisted nonetheless that there are parts of the machine that resemble various organs. His organ projection theory thus presented the body as consistent with its tools—be they hammers or machines, but also clothes or architecture—since they were all outward extensions of the body. The continuity between objects and architecture across the body is one implication here; the other is the possibility that the body leaves an imprint (and hence its agency) even on machine-made objects.

Perhaps the principal lesson Semper bequeathed later generations is that the objects of daily use are so many nerve endings of culture. When held, they are in direct physical contact with the user, as opposed to being exclusively ocular devices, and thus their capacity for agency is far greater. Objects of daily use—whether luxury or commonplace—that were seen as miniature industrially made sculptures whose materials and forms could be held, caressed, carried, and manipulated were, in the decades that followed, also seen to facilitate a link and a bodily acculturation to the alien forms and aesthetic that new modern technologies produced. [fig.6] This was, in any event, the claim of

Fig. 6. Ceramic and porcelain exhibits from the Weimar Bauhaus. *Form ohne Ornament*, 1924, 77.

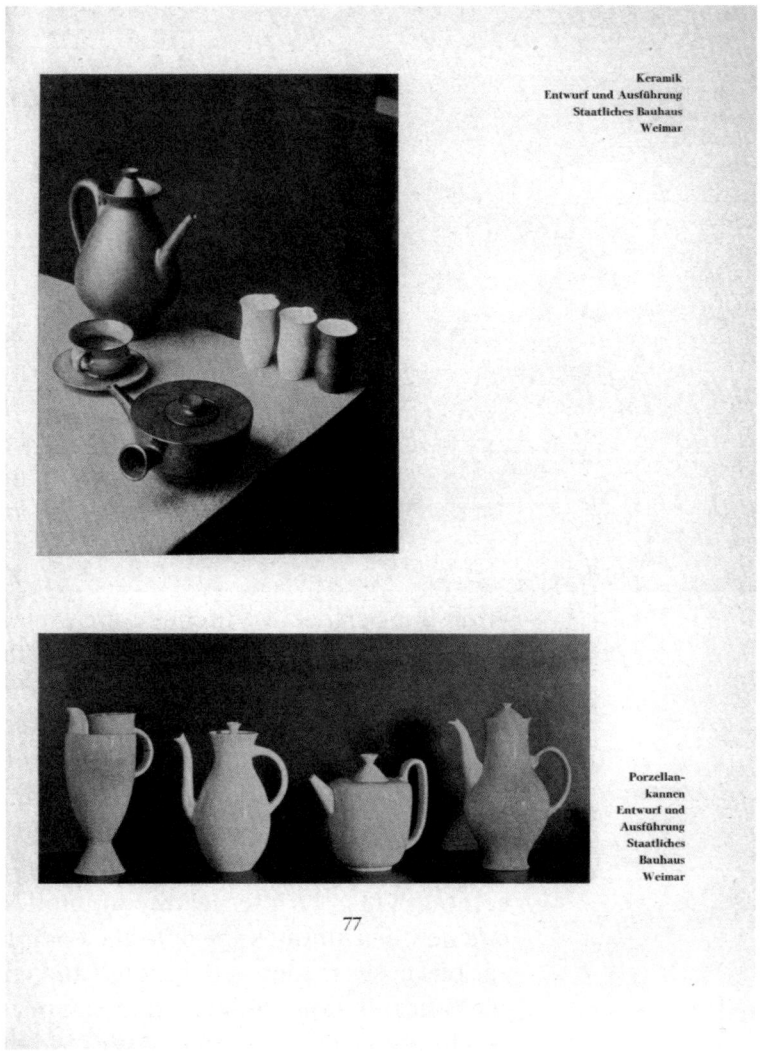

Keramik
Entwurf und Ausführung
Staatliches Bauhaus
Weimar

Porzellan-
kannen
Entwurf und
Ausführung
Staatliches
Bauhaus
Weimar

77

contemporary theorists, starting with Richard Streiter (professor at the Polytechnikum in Munich in the 1880s) to Le Corbusier in the 1920s.[11] Architects and critics looked at objects as a class of intermediary devices—"limb-objects" in Le Corbusier's words—that acted upon the body and allowed it to relate and respond, and most importantly to appreciate the aesthetics of the new. Indeed, Streiter argued that the conduit toward a new style is the physical experience of objects of daily use; through constant exposure (of sight and touch) to the qualities of technology-based objects, he argues further, we have become accustomed to them, and thus our *Formgefühl* (sense of form) has been affected correspondingly. The same is true of our body sense (*Körpergefühl*), which has become sensitized to mobility and speed through the steep rise of means of transportation. As a result, he concludes, we are impatient with any "ballast" that interferes with this movement, and it is here, he concludes, in this new sense of self and of objects that the origins of the new style will be found.[12]

The 1910s and 1920s saw an explosion of objects as subjects—this time not in academic disciplines or museums, nor in the popularizing literature of manuals, but as sites of intense artistic exploration, foregrounded in a number of media: in art, architecture and film, by Cubists and Dadaists, in the context of the Bauhaus and Soviet revolutionary art, in magazines such as *Veshch/Objet/Gegenstand* (thing/object) and *G*.[13] Also in candid statements by such artists as Fernand Léger, who stated that "[t]he most significant event of our times is the rise in importance of the object."[14] Even if conceived a century later, the door handle prototype illustrated here from the

Alina
Payne

The
Agency
of
Objects

33

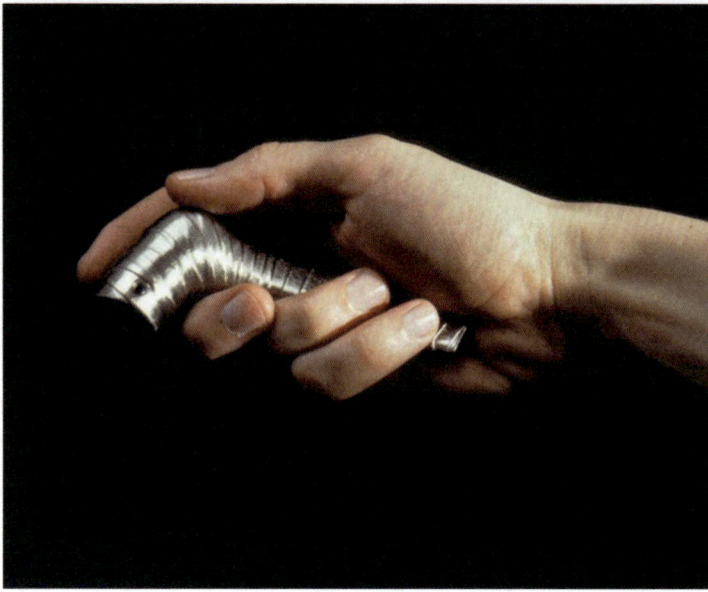

New York architectural office of Adam Yarinski conveys the inherent agency in objects that modernists recognized and deliberately exploited and then passed on to subsequent generations of designers. [fig. 7] From this perspective, architecture's relationship to objects may seem to be one more rivulet swelling the vast flow of this stream. Yet each one of the arts arrived here along its own riverbank that shaped its course as well as its character. In architecture, this turn to the object has been most often associated with the Bauhaus, the iconic modernist site that took up the baton from Hermann Muthesius's brainchild, the Deutscher Werkbund. Yet, as I hope to have demonstrated here, the Bauhaus was the endgame of a long history that had started in earnest in 1851. Its internal discontinuities and disagreements, crises, and new orientations speak to the complexity of the issues and the various answers that were intuited and tried because the Bauhaus lived the contradictions embedded in Semper's model. Semper posited two levels of agency: of the maker (and the maker's hand working the materials) and of the object in all its materiality (affecting both the maker and the viewer). The reciprocity of this agency was the inherent problem, for it assumed an evolutionary process (a constant back-and-forth between making and increasingly complex materials); yet the mode he proposed to enforce it was actually revolutionary, that is, top-down rather than bottom-up. The dogmatic aspects that slowly creep into the Bauhaus over the years, the enmities and exclusions, the departures and breakups, attest to this travail that has its origin in Semper: they are expressions of worry, insecurity, and a fear of instability that needs to be prevented and avoided at all costs.[15]

To the Bauhaus

The immediate inheritor of a highly developed discourse on the object, the Bauhaus thus became the site of a collision of two impulses: on the one hand, the impulse to see the object as an economic embodiment or commodity and on the other, the impulse to preserve artistic (the fabricator's) agency in a world of mass production and standardization. [fig. 8] Thus, the specter of Marx's coat that likewise straddled the world of the body and of commodification arose once again. For some

time—and the Werkbund certainly marked a climax—collaborations between artists and manufacturers toward artist-designed goods had developed into the main issue surrounding objects. This was the most economically relevant discussion, and it was therefore also the most sustained one. Thus, the Bauhaus, especially under Walter Gropius, sought to produce a generation of designers who could create a society of consumers in step with modernity—understood not only as an aesthetic but also a political phenomenon. In so doing, the Bauhaus merged a century-long engagement with the object with the new idea of the avant-garde that pressed upon it from outside, from the other, more radicalized sister arts—from painting, from sculpture, from photography. Yet although the Bauhaus seemed to have opened a new chapter, all the while it was building upon the ruins of what had come before it. For the Bauhaus did not spring fully formed from Walter Gropius's mind; rather, the school that he recovered from its ashes after World War I was built upon the foundations of a Kunstgewerbe-schule conceived in the full sense of the nineteenth-century post-Great Exhibition reforms. The didactic mission that underpinned the Bauhaus from its inception was a throwback to the nineteenth-century strategy to process and control "big data" or the infinite proliferation of things. In this case, though, the solution was to rethink it all from zero, to clean house, to create a tabula rasa.

It is important to recall a basic fact: that at the Bauhaus, what was made had to have been taught. Semper had already promoted education as the solution to the dangers the Industrial Revolution posed to civilization. Yet not all art is discursive or systematic. Adolf Loos did not teach, nor did Le Corbusier. Both wrote, but did not devise a pedagogically systematic method of conveying ideas to others so that they, too, could develop their own. Le Corbusier wanted to find modern life in its unselfconscious and spontaneous products—in the tennis racket covers, dentist's equipment, laboratory beakers, and petri dishes—and use it as such. [fig.9] The Bauhaus wanted to design those products. The teaching mission at the Bauhaus meant that a didactic stance also suffused its output. This is not the same as proselytizing for one's ideas—which architects had done since time immemorial. Rather, it meant that when the model house was conceived, so was the model life, and both were presented as "lessons." This stance was deeply tied to a *Gesamtkunstwerk* (total artwork) mentality, and with it to a commitment to crafting all details, to leaving nothing to chance.

Fig. 9. *Ad. Hermès, Paris*
from Le Corbusier, *L'art
décoratif d'aujourd'hui* (Paris,
1925), 91.

des tables à fumer turques, des parapluies japonais, des vases
de nuit ou bidets en Lunéville ou en Rouen, des parfums façon
Bichara, des abat-jour façon lupanar, des coussins forme potiron,
des divans où s'étalent les lamés d'or et d'argent, les velours noirs
avec flocs de Grand-Turc, des carpettes avec corbeilles de fleurs
et colombes entre-baisées, des linoléums imprimés de rubans
Louis XVI. La belle petite bergère midinette en cretonne fleurie,
fraîche comme un printemps, semble, dans ce bazar, quelque

Ad. Hermès, Paris.

apparition écœurante de ces vitrines à costumes historiques des
musées ethnographiques.

Non seulement cet afflux de fausse richesse est malpropre,
mais surtout et avant tout cet esprit de décorer tout autour de
soi est un esprit faux, une abominable petite perversion. Je re-
tourne le tableau; la bergère midinette est dans une gentille chambre
claire et limpide, mur blanc, bonne chaise de paille ou de Thonet;
table de bazar de l'Hôtel-de-Ville (tradition Louis XIII, très belle
table) peinte au ripolin. Une bonne lampe bien astiquée, de la
vaisselle de porcelaine blanche; et sur la table on s'aperçoit que
trois tulipes dans un vase sont une présence princière. C'est sain,
net, décent. Et pour faire gentil, il suffit de si peu.

True to its didactic mission, then, the entire ensemble in which modern life unfolded was preconceived at the Bauhaus—from cups and spoons to furniture and carpets. The interior of the Haus Am Horn, the exhibition house of 1923, was entirely fitted out with objects manufactured by the school workshops, from the Pyrex dishes (Jena glass) in the kitchen to the light fixtures in the sitting room. Although it looked simpler, less visually cluttered, almost ascetic, it was not substantially different from the earliest architecture projects associated with the Bauhaus such as the Sommerfeld House of 1921—a commission of Gropius's but executed by the Bauhaus workshops and students.

Nothing was left to chance; nothing penetrated from outside. Clearly, this was not an Art Nouveau approach; the objects were proclaiming machine production and submitting to its visual vocabulary. Nor were they site-specific, rooted to their spot, built into walls and fastened to the floor as they were in Victor Horta's and Hector Guimard's houses. But the complete environment that they formed and the desire to intervene at the smallest level was reminiscent of Muthesius's and Peter Behrens's Darmstadt "artistic houses," where the objects belonged together far more tightly than their movable quality suggested. In short, the Bauhaus 1923 prototype was a socially aware version of the aestheticized house of 1900: not spontaneously produced by contemporary forces, but the result of top-down intervention. As such, the Bauhaus was not really a seismograph of modernity and mass culture, but rather an inventor of modernity, as the *Gesamtkunstwerk* lay hidden behind the appearance of spontaneous mass production that the Bauhaus objects proclaimed. Likewise, artistic agency was still the driving mechanism behind this production-line appearance—reinforced by the Bauhaus GmbH limited company founded by Gropius in November 1925, complete with a catalogue of its products.[16]

*Alina
Payne*

The
Agency
of
Objects

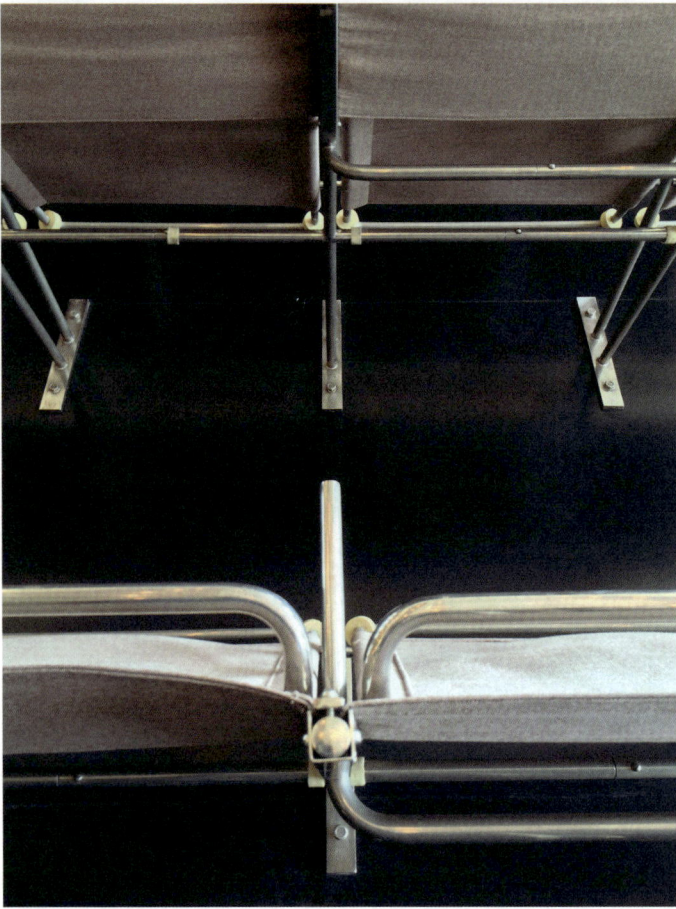

Fig. 10. Auditorium chairs, Bauhaus Dessau. Photograph by Alina Payne.

Nothing reveals the role of artistic agency at the Bauhaus better than the arguments about authorship, brought to a head by Marcel Breuer, who rebelled against Gropius and insisted on signing his furniture pieces.[17] Indeed, all objects were carefully designed by artists purposely trained to identify the "essence" of modernity; the "total work of art" of modernity was totally controlled. Thus, for all the talk at the Bauhaus against artistic agency and its programmatic rejection— the experiments with chance, paper-cutting, photography which distances the hand of the maker, the imperative not to sign work—it remained a top-down system of artistic intervention.

If the agency of the artist was ostensibly yet unsuccessfully rejected at the Bauhaus, the agency of the object was sought, was deliberate and was fundamental: in a world of few possessions and maximum mobility, each object had to be fully effective. As theorists like Streiter had argued a generation earlier, the object's less overt function was that of mediator or bridge between viewer and house-machine and house-metropolis. For one thing, it allowed scale to be comprehended and overcome, facilitating a direct and physical interaction with the products of industry that resembled in miniature those of architecture. The reason the object acquired significance to architecture—at the Bauhaus and elsewhere—was that it was made of the materials and according to the methods of industry, and as such allowed the users to become familiar with these novel forms through intimate handling. [fig.10] A steel-frame chair, like a glass coffee table or lamp, suggested elliptically that the house was made from the same materials as the object and in the same way, as a mechanical, production-line assemblage. By extension, or analogy then, the house becomes not only an object, but is understood to be the result of the same industrial, mass-production process. Yet this was more often than not a fiction: a piece of rhetoric, an eloquent gesture, of which the object was the agent.[18]

Indeed, this was the essential factor that recommended the object to the attention of modernist architects. It is primarily through the object that the house and with it all other architecture could participate in the standardization and mass-production visual rhetoric, since at the time, both the building site and the construction technology were far behind the aesthetic imagination.

Steel and metals more generally—nickel, brass, and other alloys—were the materials of machines, of objects and of large-scale, precisely engineered structures. Working in masonry and concrete in the 1920s may be why Le Corbusier invented and was so keen on pilotis, which recalled the tubular steel and leather vocabulary of his armchairs. Through their agency, his concrete and stucco houses could be perceived as partaking of the lightness and levitating language of steel and of industrially assembled buildings like bridges. This also might explain why for all modernists it was imperative to throw out the forms and objects associated with a different, pre-modernist aesthetic inside the house. They recognized that the new buildings could not be comprehended without the appropriate tools, since the buildings themselves did not yet participate in the new systems of production and consumption as visibly as they could have wished.

Where does this, then, leave agency? And what sort of agency? Perhaps the best way to understand it is to say that the Bauhaus experiences and struggles with the problems of agency—of the maker, of the objects—were first set out by Semper. According to anthropologist Alfred Gell—the voice behind the recent turn to the issue of agency in art history—agency means "securing the acquiescence of individuals in the network of intentionalities in which they are enmeshed."[19] In that sense, the Bauhaus objects were intended as active agents. Gell continues that in order to be efficacious, "agents tantalize, they frustrate the viewer, they display a certain cognitive indecipherability"—in short, they contain "an ideal of magical efficacy." In this scenario, technology is enchanting (or magical) because it is enchanted, and the objects illustrated in *Form ohne Ornament* (the 1924 Werkbund exhibition), many of which were from the Weimar Bauhaus, partake of and create this magic (as does the publication and the exhibition). The irony was that although the Bauhaus pushed hard for the agency of the object, detaching it from the maker, it was imposing a strong and supremely controlling maker in the background all the while.

This, then—the story of artistic agency and of objects—was a *longue durée* story. What had driven Semper toward rescuing the agency of the maker, of the hand, of the tool, was the Industrial Revolution, the anxiety over the artisan's hand being replaced by a machine. Yet, his was not a nostalgic William Morris-like concern, but rather a concern that the evacuation of making from the production of objects broke the chain of layered meanings of materials succeeding each other in time (of the continuous *Stoffwechsel*) and therefore also meant the evacuation of meaning *tout court*. Today we suffer a similar anxiety. The dematerialization of the object world into virtuality has moved us with some urgency to reconnect with materials and hence with making. What, after all, is the agency of objects or things if apprehended through evanescent images on screens rather than through their real physical presence? This may explain the rising interest in Semper, the material turn, and the concern with agency (and presumably its loss), with the archive and the hard data it contains. As I hope I have argued, the Bauhaus stands halfway between Semper and the now, a carrier of old perplexities and of complex ways to engage them— a manifestation of those anxieties brought out into the open and conveyed to us—as both dust and data.

1 Gottfried Semper, *Der Stil in den technischen und tektonischen Künsten oder Praktische Aesthetik*, vol. 2 (Munich: Fr. Bruckmann Verlag, 1878, 1st ed. Frankfurt am Main: Verlag für Kunst und Wissenschaft, 1860–63). On Semper and the Great Exhibition as a marketplace for objects, see especially Alina Payne, *From Ornament to Object* (New Haven: Yale University Press, 2012).

2 Gottfried Semper, *Wissenschaft, Industrie und Kunst und andere Schriften*, ed. Hans Wingler (Mainz and Berlin: Florian Kupferberg, 1966; previously published 1852).

3 On Wölfflin and his empathy theory seen within the context of turn-of-the-century empathy-based aesthetics, see Harry Mallgrave, ed., *Empathy, Form and Space: Problems in German Aesthetics, 1873–1893* (Santa Monica: Getty Center, 1994).

4 Peter Stallybrass, "Marx's Coat," in Patricia Spyer, ed., *Border Fetishism: Material Objects in Unstable Places* (London: Routledge, 1998), 183–207.

5 Henry Cole, *Fifty Years of Public Work*, vol. 2 (London: George Bell and Sons, 1884), 258.

6 Alois Riegl, *Volkskunst, Hausfleiss und Hausindustrie* (Berlin, 1894).

7 Klaus-Peter Arnold, *Geschichte der deutschen Werkstätten und der Gartenstadt Hellerau* (Dresden, 1993).

8 Semper's text on the museum was "Ideales Museum für Metalltechnik." Written in 1852 and dedicated by Semper in 1867 to Rudolf von Eitelberger, the first director of the Vienna Museum für Industrie und Kunst, it was first published in Julius Leisching, "Gottfried Semper und die Museen," *Mitteilungen des Mährischen Gewerbemuseums* (Brünn [Brno]: Burkart, 1903).

9 George W. Stocking, Jr., *Victorian Anthropology* (New York: The Free Press, 1987).

10 Ernst Kapp, *Grundlinien einer Philosophie der Technik. Zur Entstehungsgeschichte der Kultur aus neuen Gesichtspunkten* (Braunschweig: George Westermann, 1877).

11 Richard Streiter, *Ausgewählte Schriften* (Munich: Delphin, 1913); Le Corbusier, *L'art* *décoratif d'aujourd'hui*, 1st ed. (Paris: Cres, 1925; English translation by James Dunnett, *The Decorative Art of Today*, 1987), xxii–xxvi.

12 "[h]aben sich durch das beständige Sehen und Benutzen jener Erzeugnisse [der modernen Technik] unsere Augen und unser Tastgefühl mehr und mehr an die struktiv-technische Sachlichkeit gewöhnt und unser tektonisches Formgefühl dementsprechend beeinflusst, so ist zudem noch unser Körper-gefühl durch die ausserordentliche Steigerung der Verkehrsmittel für eine grössere Bewegungs-fähigkeit sehr empfänglich und demnach für allen hemmenden und beschwerenden Ballast sehr empfindlich geworden." Streiter, *Ausgewählte Schriften*, 81–82.

13 The Dadaist magazine *G. Material zur elementaren Gestaltung*, founded with filmmaker Viking Eggeling, appeared intermittently between 1923 and 1926 (only six issues). It was produced and edited by Hans Richter in Berlin. Articles dealt with emergent culture; they covered car engines, men's clothing, poems, film, and so on. *Veshch / Objet / Gegenstand* appeared in 1922 (only three issues); it was conceived and edited by Ilya Ehrenburg and El Lissitzky, also in Berlin. On the Soviet revolu-tionary objects, see Christina Kiaer, *Imagine No Possessions: The Socialist Objects of Russian Constructivism* (Cambridge, MA: MIT Press, 2005) and Maria Gough, *The Artist as Producer: Russian Constructivism in Revolution* (Berkeley: University of California Press, 2005); Detlef Mertins,

"Architecture of Becoming: Mies and the Avant-Garde," in *Mies in Berlin*, exh. cat., B. Bergdoll and T. Riley, eds. (New York: Museum of Modern Art, 2001), 106–133.

14 Fernand Léger, "Actualités," in *Variétés*, February 15, 1929, p. 522, X 1-08, FLC (Fondation Le Corbusier).

15 Alina Payne, "Bauhaus Endgame: Ambiguity, Anxiety and Discomfort," in Robin Schuldenfrei and Jeffrey Saletnik, eds., *Bauhaus Construct: Fashioning Identity Discourse and Modernism* (London: Routledge, 2009), 247–66.

16 There was a growing interest at the Bauhaus to commercialize the objects produced in the workshops: those from the furniture workshop since 1922, those from the ceramics workshop from November 1923 onward. Droste, *Bauhaus 1919–1933* (Bauhaus-Archiv and Taschen: Berlin, 1990), 134.

17 See, for example, most recently the discussion of Marcel Breuer's and Mies van der Rohe's efforts to sign their chairs against Walter Gropius's directives. See Magadalena Droste, "The Bauhaus Object between Authorship and Anonymity," in *Bauhaus Construct*, 205–25.

18 On Le Corbusier's machine-produced furniture designed by himself for the Pavillon de l'Esprit Nouveau in 1925, see Nancy Troy, *Modernism and the Decorative Arts in France* (New Haven: Yale, 1991).

19 Alfred Gell, *Art and Agency: An Anthro-pological Theory* (Oxford: Oxford University Press, 1998).

*Alina
Payne*

The
Agency
of
Objects

Anselm Wagner

The Bauhaus and the Vacuum Cleaner

From a semiotic point of view, there is nothing antithetical about dust and data. Dust can be categorized among the indexical signs that are a trace of past events. Hence, in spite of its supposed worthlessness and meaninglessness, dust is a historical repository of the first order. For since practically everything will turn to dust one day, dust contains practically everything.

In his essay exploring dust as a medium of traces, Roland Meyer writes, "Dust ... is an environment in miniature: a physical archive, an encyclopedic image of our material surroundings."[1] "Dust," he continues, "invariably consists of residues, material traces of the past. Traces point to a past event, an erstwhile presence, to bodies that are absent or corrupted, and because of this referential context, these traces can be regarded as signs."[2] Dust is thus not only an index in the sense proposed by Charles S. Pierce but also a clue: detectives can uncover a felony by analyzing the dust at the scene of a crime. Meyer makes reference to one of the first forensic experts, the doctor and attorney Edmond Locard, who dedicated himself to the analysis of dust in the police laboratory he set up in Lyon. To start with, his colleagues did not take him seriously, but his big breakthrough came in 1911 when he supplied the crucial evidence needed to convict a gang of counterfeiters. Locard had discovered that the metal dust found on the clothes of the gang members had exactly the same chemical composition as the counterfeit coins.[fig.1] In the wake of this, Locard applied himself to the analysis of the "microscopically tiny particles that cover our clothes and bodies," and which he regarded as "the only proofs that never deceive or lie, ... if one can only interpret them."[3] Forensics thus became a hermeneutic science, similar to literary studies, art history, or psychoanalysis, which developed at the same time, following in the footsteps of philology and archaeology.

Fig.1. Lead dust on the sleeve of a coin counterfeiter, from Edmond Locard, *Traité de criminalistique: Les empreintes et les traces dans l'enquête criminelle* (Lyon: Joannès Desvigne et ses fils, 1931), 898.

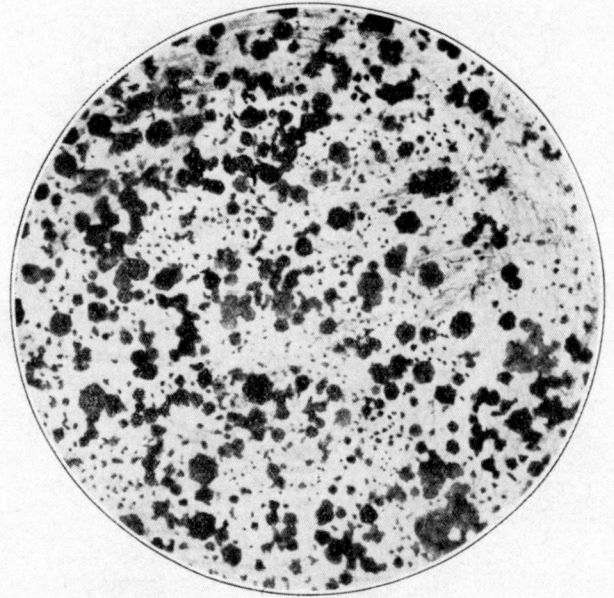

Fig. 254

Poussière de plomb sur la manche d'un faux-monnayeur.

The following essay sets out to apply this forensic method on a literal and metaphorical level to the Bauhaus and its milieu of architectural theory. Here it is not about the dust left behind by the Bauhaus but rather the attitude, first of all, that the Bauhaus and its adherents adopted, both directly and indirectly, toward this seemingly marginal issue. This process is then used, in a second step, to glean "circumstantial evidence" about the advance of modernization and even perhaps to help profile the Bauhaus era as a whole.

"Demand a vacuum cleaner"

In November 1930, at the 3rd International Congress of Modern Architecture (Neues Bauen) in Brussels, Walter Gropius gave a lecture on the question "Low-, medium-, or high-rise?,"[4] a subject of some controversy in urban development. The Weimar Republic's "Imperial Guidelines on Housing," issued the previous year, had singled out, based on hygienic considerations, the "single-family house with garden" as the goal to be aspired to and codified the limit of "a maximum of three stories for medium-sized cities and four stories for larger cities."[5] On economic grounds—and in a departure from the original Bauhaus ideas and the ideology of the Werkbund housing projects—Gropius opted to take up the cudgels on behalf of residential high-rises, knowing that he could never argue against hygiene, the undisputed guiding principle of modernism. Gropius thus had to work *with* hygienic arguments—in other words, by demonstrating that the "essential preconditions for healthy human thriving ..., light, air, and the opportunity for exercise,"[6] were better available in high-rise rather than low-rise structures. Initially, he laid this proof at the door of Professor Ernst Friedberger, director of the Research Institute for Hygiene and Immunology at the Kaiser-Wilhelm-Institut Berlin. Friedberger was a prominent hygienist who, as such, was unassailable and had the (actual) economic argument in place: In 1923 he had contended that the financial strain on commuters spoke against suburbanization,[7] postulating "high-rise construction as the only suitable form of

Anselm Wagner

The Bauhaus and the Vacuum Cleaner

43

Fig.2. Le Corbusier, "Tower-Cities," 1920, from Le Corbusier, *Toward an Architecture* (Los Angeles: Getty Publications, 2007), 124.

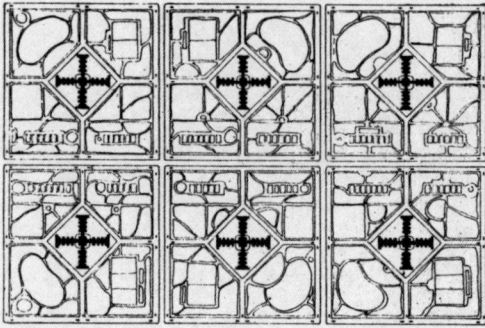

L.-C. 1920. TOWER-CITIES. Land subdivision proposal. Sixty floors, height 220 meters; distance between the towers 250 to 300 m (equivalent to the width of the Tuileries Gardens). Width of the towers, 150 to 200 meters. Despite the large area of the parks, normal urban density is increased 5 to 10 times. It seems that such constructions should be devoted exclusively to business (offices) and thus erected in the center of large cities whose arteries would be relieved of congestion; family life would not adapt well to the astounding machinery of elevators. The figures are stunning and pitiless, magnificent: if every employee were allotted a surface of 10 m², a skyscraper 200 m wide would accommodate 40,000 people. Haussmann, instead of making narrow thoroughfares in Paris, would have demolished entire neighborhoods and condensed them vertically; then he would have planted parks more beautiful than those of the Grand Roy.

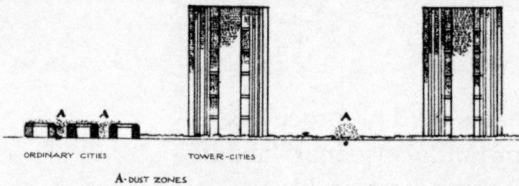

TOWER-CITIES. This cross section shows at left the suffocating dust, stench, and noise of present-day cities. The towers, on the other hand, are far apart, in healthy air, among greenery. The whole city is covered with greenery.

architecture with as much green space as possible in the immediate vicinity."[8] While Friedberger had called into question the popular thesis regarding the supposed unhealthiness of metropolitan life, Gropius went a step further and declared that living in a single-family house was unhealthy for the bulk of the population, because with it came the "risk of infection in overcrowded public transport."[9] And he pointed out that "it is still very questionable whether the villa owner, located in the midst of the natural noise, stench, and dust of roadways, will live more peacefully and healthily than his much poorer fellow citizen on the tenth floor of a well-planned and well-equipped high-rise estate."[10]

The contrast of dust-laden villa and healthy high-rise constitutes the radicalization of a similar antithetical pairing from Le Corbusier's *Vers une architecture*. This polemic, which was published in a German edition in 1926 under the title *Kommende Baukunst*, had already sparked Gropius's interest back in 1923 and fully confirmed him in the stance he took.[11] In the chapter "Three Reminders to Architects: Plan," Le Corbusier contrasts "ordinary cities" with "tower-cities": [fig.2] on the left, you can see the "ordinary city"—in the form not of a suburban single-family housing estate but rather of a perimeter block development of the kind that was typical in Germany in the second half of the nineteenth century and was to become the "bête noire" of all modernist critiques of the city. Between the buildings and just above them, one can see clusters of dots marked with the letter A, which are identified in the key as "dust zones." On the right, the "tower-city" rises up beside it: set at a distance to one another, its sixty-story skyscrapers completely dwarf the "ordinary city." The zone of street dust midway between them is limited to a relatively narrow lane of traffic. The caption reads, "This cross section shows at left the suffocating dust, stench, and noise of present-day cities. The towers, on the other hand, are far apart, in healthy air, among greenery. The whole

Fig. 3. "Hoch die Hygiene!"
(Here's to Hygiene!), postcard
for the International Hygiene
Exhibition in Dresden, 1911.

city is covered with greenery."[12]
Le Corbusier here follows the view
shared by all modernist architects
that the dense metropolitan centers
of the nineteenth century are
inimical to health and to life itself.
Like Gropius, he conflates "dust,
stench, and noise"; they dominated
the streets and, in his opinion,
polluted these houses, which were
built much too low and much too
close to the road. The fact that
Gropius replaces the perimeter
block development with the villa,
contingent on his line of argument,
seems somewhat artificial and
obliges him to turn Le Corbusier's
traffic "noise" into the less logical
"natural noise" (dogs barking? birds twittering?). However, it is likely
that the "road dust" which, in Gropius's opinion, marred the villa
settlements was not exclusively airborne—rural or suburban roads
were typically unpaved in his day so that the cars that drove on them
regularly left pedestrians shrouded in clouds of dust. This was pointed
up as early as 1911 in a caricature produced in conjunction with the
Dresden Hygiene Exhibition. [fig.3] Yet Le Corbusier's solution is
identical to Gropius's: the buildings are set back from the street so as
to increase the population density necessary for the economic life of
a city. Huge parks neutralize the dusty roadways—the houses of the
future remain undisturbed by them. Keeping house and (street) dust
apart was to heal the city and its inhabitants. Like monuments to a
religion of the future centered on hygiene, the skyscrapers tower above
the cruciform(!) plan, stretching up into the sky: "Beginning with the
fourteenth floor, there is absolute calm, there is pure air."[13]

To prevent the small amounts of dust that might nevertheless find
their way into the apartments from establishing themselves, Le Corbusier recommended that property owners be required to make the
following provision: "In your big room, storage units to protect your
books from dust as well as your collection of paintings and works of
art, and in such fashion that the walls of your room are bare."[14]

*Anselm
Wagner*

The
Bauhaus
and
the
Vacuum
Cleaner

45

The free walls and built-in cupboards were designed to give the dust no place to settle. The housing manual, which was to be printed by the "temperance societies and the league for repopulation" and distributed among the "mothers of families," included many measures for combating and avoiding dust. It began by tackling dusty street clothing ("Don't undress in your bedroom. It's untidy."), went on to recommend bare walls, wooden floors that can easily be cleaned, unencumbered by furniture and oriental rugs, and culminated in the call to "demand a vacuum cleaner."[15] This last appeal should probably be seen as more symbolic, because vacuum cleaners were still very much a luxury in Europe in the early 1920s and if they were to be found at all, it was only in fine hotels and upper-class homes.[16] This meant that there were probably no vacuum cleaners either in Haus Am Horn, the building in Weimar that exemplified the Bauhaus ethos, or in the Dessau Bauhaus and its Master's Houses. However, their rubber flooring, minimal carpeting, bare walls, and unprofiled furniture made of steel, glass, and varnished wood—"smooth and washable,"[17] according to Gropius—ensured that the dust was easily manageable even without the help of a machine.

In *Bau und Wohnung*, the book on the Weissenhof Estate published to accompany the Stuttgart Werkbund exhibition organized by Ludwig Mies van der Rohe, several of the architects involved refer to the lengths they had gone to in their building designs to make it easier to combat dust: Hans Poelzig notes that his house, which is intended to serve the "mind worker," whose wife probably "also has a career or would prefer not to be exclusively focused on keeping house," is "designed as rationally as possible." To this end there are "built-in closets, and the movable furniture is arranged in such a way that it is an easy task to thoroughly clean the space."[18] Mart Stam presents a similar argument: "The work in the house is to be kept to a minimum, which means reducing the number of rooms, the amount of furniture, and the sum total of corners that can collect dust."[19] Josef Frank contrasts the "neutrality, simplicity, and authenticity" of modern design with the "clutter of bygone days," the "monuments to tasteless-ness, witnesses of impotency, dust collectors."[20] And J. J. P. Oud concludes the "explanatory report" on his row houses with the follow-ing statement: "The frames and windows are made of iron, both inside and out. For practical reasons (dust), this is ideally machined to a completely smooth finish."[21]

Fig. 4. Plate I from Erna Meyer, *Der neue Haushalt. Ein Wegweiser zu wirtschaftlicher Hausführung* (Stuttgart: Franckh'sche Verlagshandlung, 1929), 38.

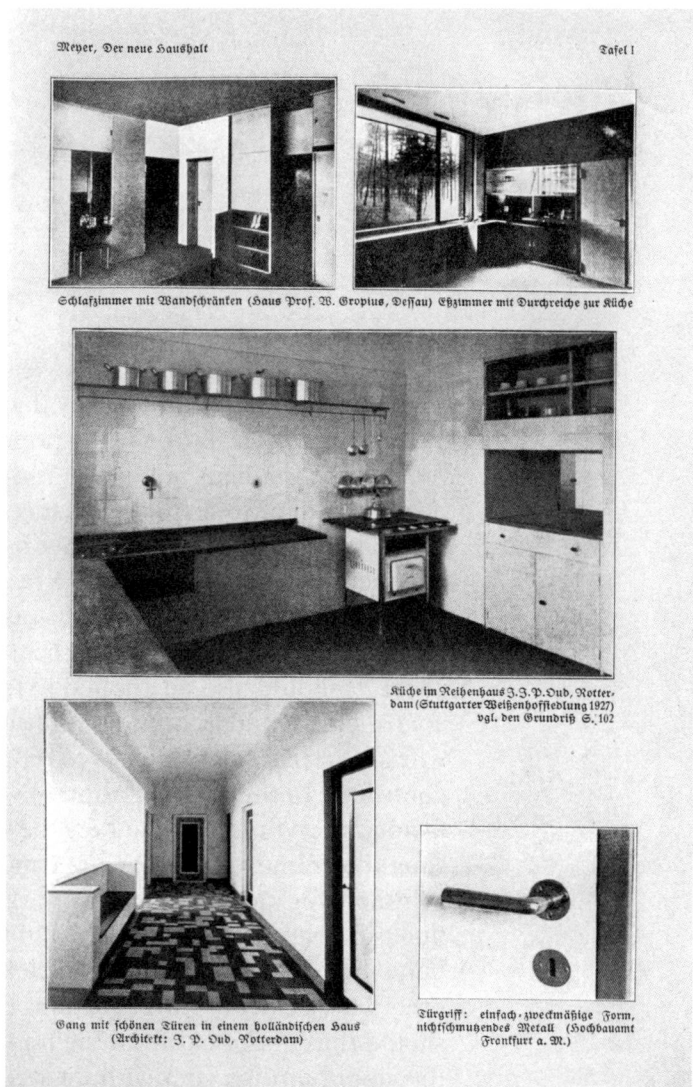

Schlafzimmer mit Wandschränken (Haus Prof. W. Gropius, Dessau)   Eßzimmer mit Durchreiche zur Küche

Küche im Reihenhaus J. J. P. Oud, Rotterdam (Stuttgarter Weißenhofsiedlung 1927) vgl. den Grundriß S. 102

Gang mit schönen Türen in einem holländischen Haus (Architekt: J. P. Oud, Rotterdam)

Türgriff: einfach-zweckmäßige Form, nichtschmutzendes Metall (Hochbauamt Frankfurt a. M.)

Oud, who in other contexts also speaks out against pitched roofs, because the "useless triangular spaces they generate within are only good for producing dust,"[22] adds his remark that the suggestions made by Dr. Erna Meyer have been "extremely useful." The Munich economist had produced a set of guidelines with a particular focus on rational designs for the kitchen: these had been sent by Mies van der Rohe to all the participating architects,[23] and Mies had gone through an intensive process of sharing ideas on the planning of the Werkbund estate.[24] Together with Hilde Zimmermann, Meyer had also curated the accompanying exhibition of model kitchens in the Gewerbehalle in Stuttgart.[25] Besides Adolf Gustav Schneck's single-family houses, the only building complex in the Werkbund estate that she is almost completely persuaded by is Oud's row of houses.[26] The kitchen in house no. 8 [fig. 4], clinically clean and akin to a laboratory with tiled floor and walls, was entirely in keeping with her guidelines: "Most of the available wall surfaces of the kitchen," she wrote in a review, "are taken up with cupboards, so that all the hand tools can be housed in the place where they are to be used on a daily basis, truly 'handy' and yet still protected from dust."[27]

Oud and Meyer had known each other since 1925,[28] when Meyer was working on her book *Der neue Haushalt* (The New Household), which appeared in 1926 and immediately went on to become a bestseller with thirty-eight(!) repeatedly updated and expanded editions in the period up to 1929. The first edition of Meyer's *Wegweiser zu wirtschaftlicher Hausführung* (A Guide to Economical Housekeeping), as the book's subtitle ran, was illustrated with residential buildings by Oud, Gerrit Rietveld, Bruno Taut, and the Bauhaus that she presented as exemplary.[29] In the later editions, Oud's kitchen on the Werkbund

Anselm Wagner

The Bauhaus and the Vacuum Cleaner

47

estate and Mies van der Rohe's Weissenhof chair are added.[30] It would be no exaggeration to say that Meyer's guide to housekeeping did incomparably more for the popularization of the Bauhaus ideas than all the Bauhaus publications put together. This also applies to no lesser extent to the Bauhaus reception in Israel: in 1933 Meyer emigrated to Palestine, where her housekeeping book was translated and met with an equally positive response.

The battle against house dust is a key consideration for Meyer. Her arguments here are strictly economic: the "principle of least effort"[31] should also be applied to the private household, and an apartment should be seen not only as a dwelling but also as a "house-wife's workplace,"[32] a means to reduce her workload and ultimately contribute to the emancipation of women. Thus, as in a Taylorist factory, everything that hinders the well-functioning flow of work should be removed from an apartment: "How is it [the apartment] to be usable for quick, smooth work if everywhere we bump into super-fluous objects that we put here and there hundreds of times a year quite unnecessarily and need to clean from dust?!"[33] Knick-knacks, oriental rugs, heavy velvet curtains ("the worst dust collectors"),[34] etc., should thus disappear from the home. Pictures should also be reduced to a minimum. "It goes without saying that the frames of these salvaged favorites should have no embellishments or any other decora-tive features that would attract dust."[35] In the case of furniture, either the ornamentation should be sawn off, as recommended by Bruno Taut,[36] or products designed by the Bauhaus or the Deutsche Werk-stätten Hellerau should be selected: these offered a "combination of practicality (high legs that allow the area under the furniture to be mopped, no paneling that can collect dust but rather smooth plywood surfaces, absolutely no unnecessary edges, molding, or any kind of 'ornamentation') and beauty."[37]

According to Meyer, the smooth, washable, minimalist Bauhaus- and Weissenhof-style interior is more or less self-cleaning: "Where neither the floor paint or surfacing nor the decorative features of the furniture or the countless objects hanging on the walls or standing around catch the dust with octopus tentacles, where the space only contains a few smooth items and light materials, the work is almost completely done before you set foot in the room."[38] Meyer knew, however, that the path from the "coziness" of the Wilhelmine parlor to the cool austerity of the New Objectivity was a long one and that her readers would only be able to adapt to this atmosphere of severity step by step. For those who have not yet reached the ideal state, Meyer recommends the vacuum cleaner: "As long as one remains in the transitional stage, the vacuum cleaner is the greatest source of relief—now that it can be purchased in installments ... the process of acquiring one has become considerably easier ... If one uses it regularly and not only every couple of weeks or even months, one can reduce the levels of dust throughout the apartment to almost nothing."[39] The restriction of the vacuum cleaner to those who had not yet completely converted to the modern apartment may have had to do with the costs involved (in the Weimar Republic, you would have had to shell out the equivalent of an average monthly salary to buy one),[40] which deterred the socially engaged economist from assenting to Le Corbusier's "Demand a vacuum cleaner." What is striking, though, is Meyer's conviction that the "dust problem" can be solved simply by means of the proper (interior) architecture.

Erna Meyer's belief in the cleansing power of architecture had probably been awakened by Bruno Taut, whose ideas and designs from his manifesto *Die neue Wohnung: Die Frau als Schöpferin* (The New Dwelling: The Woman as Creator) afforded her broad scope. The idea of contributing to the emancipation of women by reducing and simplifying the furnishings and household effects can be found there, as can the iconoclastic recommendation of sawing the decorative trim off furniture and removing, along with the knick-knacks and embellishments, all the pictures from the walls.[41] Taut expected this to provide not only a reduction in the housework required but also a mental and spiritual catharsis: "Physical hygiene must be supplemented by mental hygiene."[42] The "crammed living spaces"[43] typical of the mid-nineteenth century turned women into thralls "enslaved by dusting,"[44] negatively affecting their intellectual development, while the "lucidity, clarity, and cogency"[45] of the modern house "in themselves already have a major salutary influence"[46] and automatically contribute to the enlightenment of the housewife. She will "see that her fetishism is as nothing and that the 'bare' apartment without little pictures and ... without souvenirs—in short, 'without'—is, after all, ultimately more beautiful; quite apart from the fact that the workload taken from her also gives her the energy to rid herself of the fetishism and superstition."[47] Taut puts forward a number of examples to illustrate this kind of "salutary" space: aside from his own designs, he also cites the Bauhaus prototype Haus Am Horn in Weimar (1923), which had just been completed at the time Taut was writing his essay— its high skylight room, unadorned with pictures, perfectly conveyed Taut's ideal of spiritual purity.[fig.5] Taut's own unrealized design for a circular dining room with glass wall and ceiling [fig.6] seems to have even more sacred associations. In this Grail Temple, the moral impact of "pristine" architecture is made explicit when Taut writes that "the entrance to the hall ... [might] remain open, as conversations held in a clean environment need not be conducted in seclusion."[48]

The ideological exaltation of hygienic cleanliness through moral and cultic purity, as evoked in Taut's work, was a far cry from the preoccupations of the Dessau phase of the Bauhaus, although it played a certain role in the design of Haus Am Horn in Weimar. Le Corbusier had recourse to it relatively often ("We would perform a moral act: *to love purity!*" he writes in the "Law of Ripolin," and "Whitewash is extremely moral"),[49] and Henry Ford also remarks in his autobiography, which was widely read in Germany, that in his factories, "the dark corners which invite expectoration are painted white," following this with "One cannot have morale without cleanliness"[50]—a sentence that architecture critic Adolf Behne cites in *The Modern Functional Building* to corroborate the exemplary quality of industrial construction for modern architecture.[51]

Dust and disease[52]

However, the campaign against dust waged by the Neues Bauen movement was driven not so much by moral concerns nor solely by economic considerations but rather, first and foremost, by a rationale that was hygiene-oriented and can thus be inserted into modernism's biopolitical mission.[53] In *Urbanisme* Le Corbusier cites, for example, the garden architect Jean-Claude Nicolas Forestier, stating that exhaust gases and tar dust weaken the human faculty to procreate and it is thus postulated that "the third generation to live in a town is sterile."[54] The toxic nature of dust was also a pervasive theme in the hygiene discourse of the Weimar Republic: "Dust ... is deleterious to the health, a carrier of bacteria, a transmitter of disease, inimical to all living creatures, quite apart from its other ill-favored properties," warned engineer Eduard Pfeiffer in his popular work *Technik des Haushalts* (Household Technology), which is otherwise written in an objective scientific tone.[55] In her *Buch der Hausfrau* (Housewife's Book),

Fig. 5. Georg Muche, Haus Am Horn, Weimar, 1923, living room, from Bruno Taut, *Die neue Wohnung. Die Frau als Schöpferin* (Leipzig: Verlag von Klinkhardt & Biermann, 1924), 41.

Fig. 6. Bruno Taut, "Entwurf für ein reicheres Landhaus bei Berlin" (design for a more luxurious country house near Berlin), dining room, 1923, from Bruno Taut: *Die neue Wohnung. Die Frau als Schöpferin* (Leipzig: Verlag von Klinkhardt & Biermann, 1924), 54.

Abb. 28. Staatl. Bauhaus Weimar:
Wohnzimmer im Haus am Horn

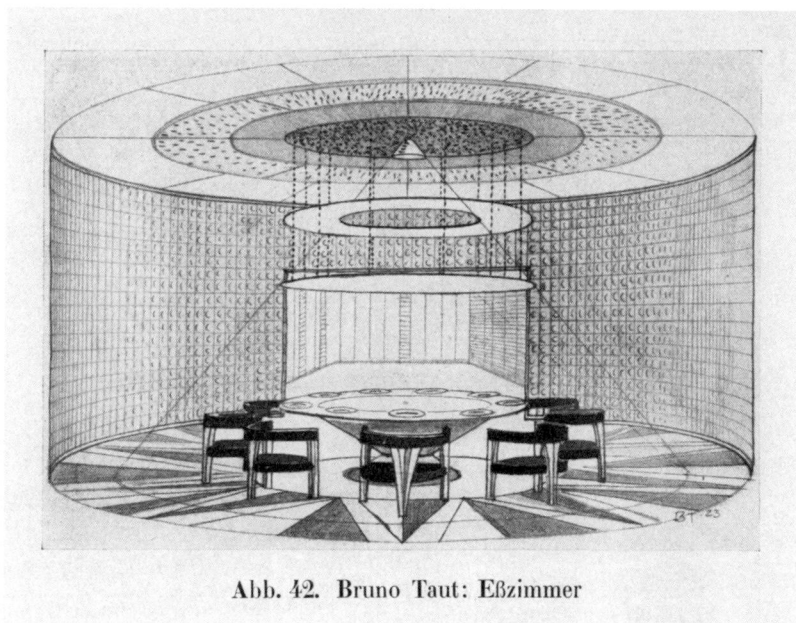

Abb. 42. Bruno Taut: Eßzimmer

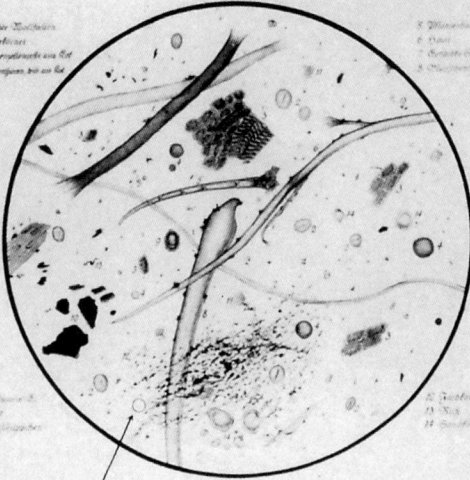

Eine Spur Zimmerstaub
— 300 fach vergrößert —

Der Zimmerstaub besteht aus allerlei
Abfällen – z. B. Erde, Sand, Kohle, Holz- und Leder-
mehl, Metallstaub, Kleidungsfasern, Speiseresten,
Abscheidungen von Pflanzen, Tieren und Menschen
– z. B. Hautschüppchen, Haaren, Fettteilchen –,
pflanzlichen und tierischen Lebewesen – z. B.
Sporen, Schimmel, Samenkörnern, Eiern (auch
Schmarotzereiern), Larven und Dauerformen nie-
derer Tiere – und schließlich einer Unmenge von
Bakterien, darunter auch oft Krankheitserregern.

Der Zimmerstaub und ebenso der Straßenstaub ist sehr gesundheitsgefährlich.
Die Berührung mit ihm ist möglichst zu verringern.

Lebensfähigkeit von Krankheitserregern im Kehricht

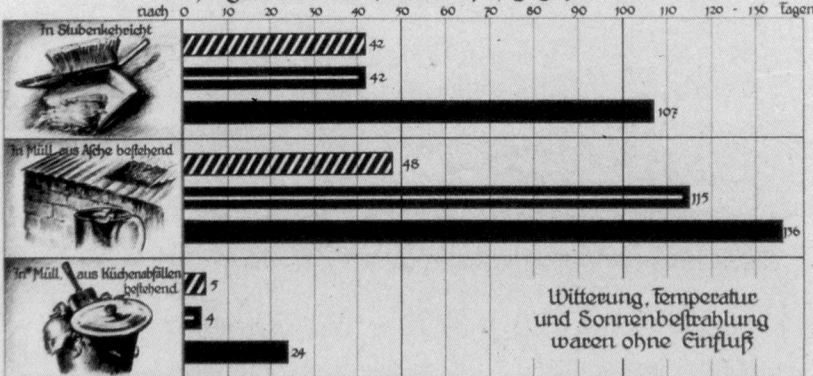

Fig.7. A trace of house dust at 300× magnification, glass-plate slide produced as a teaching aid by the Deutsches Hygiene-Museum (Image 6 from slide series 43: "Industrial Hygiene"), circa 1927.

Fig.8. "Lebensfähigkeit von Krankheitserregern im Kehricht (nach Hilgermann)" (ability of pathogens to survive in sweepings, according to Hilgermann), glass-plate slide produced as a teaching aid by the Deutsches Hygiene-Museum (Image 24 from slide series 43: "Invasion of Flies: a Health Hazard"), circa 1928.

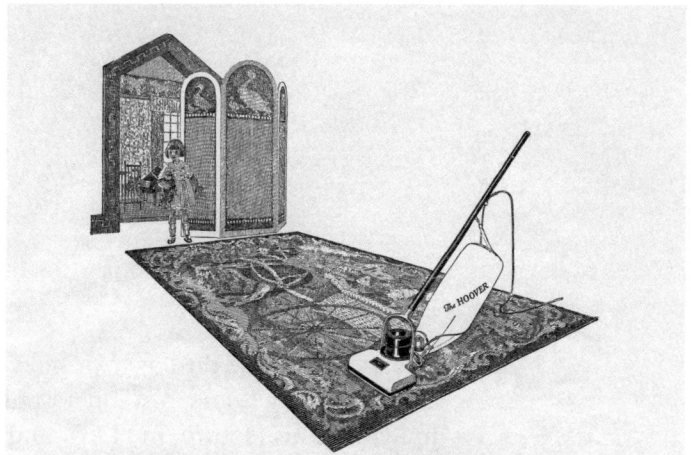

If Only For Your Children's Sake

More and more as winter comes your children must play indoors—with the nursery carpet as their playground.

And often little hands and knees will be in close contact with that carpet ; and sometimes little fingers that have pressed deep into its pile will make dangerous acquaintance with their owner's mouth.

Are you sure of the absolute, hygienic cleanliness of your carpets ?

Surface sweeping will not effect that. Only the Hoover can guarantee it, because only the Hoover *beats* out all the dangerous, germ-harbouring dirt, from the depths of carpets, as it sweeps them electrically and suctions away all this loosened, swept-up dirt and dust into its dust-proof bag.

And the Hoover does all this in one easy,

rapid operation which scatters no dust, to filter into your children's lungs, and cause mysterious illnesses.

A "Servant to the Home," the Hoover's thorough, sanitary cleaning is needed most of all in the nursery. Act now. Any Hoover dealer will gladly give you a demonstration of the Hoover on your own carpets. It commits you to nothing—that is understood—but you will be amazed at the quantity of dirt, dangerous dirt, the Hoover extracts from a carpet usually cleaned by other methods.

Only £3. 19s. down and 31s. a month for a short time pays for the Hoover while you use it. There is also a larger model for hotels, clubs, offices and large residences. Write for illustrated booklet and names of nearest Hoover dealers.

Hoover Limited, 288, Regent Street, London, W. 1,
and at Birmingham, Manchester, Leeds and Glasgow

The HOOVER

It BEATS.... as it Sweeps   as it Cleans   Reg. TRADE MARK

Clara Ebert-Stockinger of the life reform movement claimed that "the harmful dust [consists] of millions of microbes and pathogens ... and anyone who has seen it under the microscope will likely be convinced of the tremendous importance of daily dust removal."[56] It was this microscopic view that was shown to the German people at "300x magnification" in educational campaigns [fig. 7, 8] to illustrate how many pathogens are "contained in a trace of room dust" and that this, like the dust in the street, is "very damaging to the health" and "contact with it ... is to be reduced as much as possible." The first vacuum cleaner advertisements relied primarily on arguments of hygiene: in 1902, for example, the British Vacuum Cleaner Company proclaimed that in an ounce of dust from the corridor carpets of the House of Commons in London over 425 million bacilli had been found, including many pathogens of deadly diseases: in a word, dust was a danger to the British Empire![57] And what is, according to Sigfried Giedion, the first full-page advertisement promoting an electric vacuum cleaner from the year 1909 bluntly observes, "Dust is full of disease."[58] In the 1920s—as Christoph Glauser writes in his *Geschichte des Staubsaugers* (History of the Vacuum Cleaner)—manufacturers engaged in a veritable race to see "who could install the most effective bacteria filter in the vacuum cleaner. In order to effectively kill the bacteria as well, substances like DDT were frequently used in these filters as well."[59] Advertising by the Swedish firm Electrolux[60] and the US manufacturer Hoover [fig. 9] liked to appeal to the parental sense of responsibility for protecting the health of their children playing on the floor:

> *Only the Hoover* beats *out all the dangerous, germ-harboring dirt from the depths of carpets, as it sweeps them electrically and suctions away all this loosened, swept-up dirt and dust into its dust-proof bag. And the Hoover does all this in one easy, rapid operation which scatters no dust to filter into your children's lungs and cause mysterious illnesses.*

Anselm Wagner

The Bauhaus and the Vacuum Cleaner

53

The idea of house dust as toxic goes back to the practice of bacteriology established by Louis Pasteur, Joseph Lister, and Robert Koch. Back in 1870, in his lecture on "Dust and Disease," Irish physicist John Tyndall presented the finding that the dust floating in the air consists of organic material and contains microbes that can also transmit diseases, using this to confirm Lister theories[61]—in particular, that if you burn the floating dust, the air becomes sterile. Dust had now been discovered as a medium for (airborne) bacteria; unlike the bacteria themselves, it had the advantage of being visible to the naked eye. This dust, which had hitherto either been considered a mere nuisance or classed as materially or historically valuable,[62] now came within the purview of biopoliticial hygiene measures. The act of dusting and dust removal was thus no longer just a matter of creating order but was given the lofty status of a preventive measure to combat disease and epidemics.

Dust control was now not simply the concern of physical culture, commerce, and production; the question needed to be directed, above all, to the built world. Hygiene was given an elevated role in the fields of architecture and design, and its effects cannot be overstated. To put it crudely, we might say that it is dust and the fight against it that over a long period gave birth to the modern age of environmental design.

Already the hygienists of the late nineteenth century criticized the Victorian residential architecture and its interior furnishings cluttered with ornamentation, knick-knacks, plants, and textiles as unhealthy "dust collectors." Doctors received unexpected support from avant-garde architects, who rejected the retrograde illusory contrivance of the bourgeois interior and advocated a modern design adapted to the industrial age.[63] According to my thesis, such a design could only be pushed through with the help of the tailwind generated by the discourse on health and hygiene, which (still) constitutes a main ideological mainstay of the modern age. Smooth unprofiled surfaces and easy-to-clean, nonporous materials like steel and glass were considered healthy long before they came to be appreciated—as shown in the last section—as labor-saving and attractive in their own right.[64] This is corroborated, among other things, by the fact that hospital architecture and furniture preceded the general development of this trend;[65] in a retrospective look at the years leading up to World War I, Robert Musil reflects ironically on this phenomenon: "Modern man is born in a hospital and dies in a hospital, so he should make his home like a clinic. So claimed a leading architect of the moment."[66]

An early example of the close alliance between reformers in the realms of health and design is Scottish architect Colonel Robert W. Edis. His contribution to the 1883 book *Our Homes and How to Make Them Healthy* included these reflections: "For many years, we have been content to cover the whole floor surface of the rooms with carpets, under which dirt and filth naturally accumulated, to exclude light and air by heavy fluffy curtains, to form resting places for blacks and dust by the use of internal Venetian blinds, and to fill our rooms with lumbering old-fashioned furniture, with flat or sunken tops, which formed dirt and dust traps, rarely cleaned out."[67] Edis's prescription was interior architecture without cornices and redundant textiles and ornamentation so that dust would not collect. He thus prefigured the identical demands made by Taut, Meyer, and Le Corbusier, forty years in advance of them! But Edis was by no means the first to arrive at these conclusions. As far back as 1859, Florence Nightingale had described the ideal sickbay in very similar fashion in her influential book *Notes on Nursing*. To facilitate cleaning, it should have lacquered floors, oil-based paint on the walls, polished and varnished furniture, and as few profiles, hangings, and rugs as possible to avoid creating any dust traps.[68] For today's reader, Nightingale seems to be describing a kind of Bauhaus apartment *avant la lettre*. In any case, her text provides the first definition of a "sanitary style" in which interior architecture validated by the insights of bacteriology begins to spread beyond the sickbay.

The battle of the bacteriologist against the "invasion of bacteria"[69] could not, of course, be confined to the interior; rather, the house itself had to develop into a fortress that could repel dust and germs. This was a particular issue in industrial cities that were heavily contaminated with dust and smog. In 1887, for example, Chicago architect Daniel H. Burnham had the visionary idea of building high-rises completely from glass to create "impenetrable surfaces of floors, ceilings and walls." The justification for this complete transparency, which was still entirely utopian at the time, coupled with impenetrability, was the fight against the harmful effects of air pollution: "A house thus built will protect its occupant more thoroughly than any other from dust, dirt and permeation of gases, and thus from the seeds of disease and death."[70]

Anselm
Wagner

The
Bauhaus
and
the
Vacuum
Cleaner

55

The "sanitary style" developed in the US and UK in the late nineteenth century provided a model for central Europe, where there had been an architectural shift to aesthetic modernism in the early twentieth century: this turned out to be much more radical than in the Anglo-Saxon countries. In 1908 Hermann Muthesius could look back at a process of development that was apparently already complete. It was clear to him that the hygiene coming out of the hospital system had helped author modern residential architecture and that what had been initially accepted as healthy was ultimately also seen as beautiful:

> The need for cleanliness removed all heavy textile hangings; dark paintwork gave way to light; dust-prone decorative reliefs and architectural articulations gave way to smooth unadorned surfaces. What happened in Germany in the design of the sickbay in large hospitals, where rooms were completely geared to hygienic considerations, was part of a general process in England (the country that had led the way in all matters of hygiene in the nineteenth century) of formally structuring the house and its contents. This marked the birth of a new design principle ... The ostentatious room [typical of the boom years of the second half of the nineteenth century] was now replaced by a bright, unadorned, hygienic space. Here a modern science, hygiene, had provided a new foundation for architectural design ... The new forms led by degrees to the creation of new conventions ... The bright, the smooth, and the sanitary soon took on an aesthetic appeal. The receptive sense was gradually given artistic stimulus ... by the new spaces ... The bright, airy, smooth room became the ideal of coziness and elegance.[71]

Like many apologists of modernism, Muthesius used the argument of hygiene to substantiate the medical necessity of the new, clean formal language. To him, too, this was not simply a question of interior design; rather, it related to the way the space was constructed and thus had a genuine architectural dimension.[72]

Living without leaving traces

After World War I, "white modernism" set out to give a thorough "dusting" to the way the city looked. The primary victims here were historicist buildings, which the modernists never tired of lashing out at and whose sculpturally designed plaster façades had numerous seams, cornices, and molded features in which substantial amounts of dust could build up. The idea of "undecorating" or "de-façading" thus became the watchword in the 1920s—i.e., removing the stucco that was condemned as dishonest and unhygienic, and rendering the exterior walls smooth.[fig. 10] Even such people as Bruno Taut and Erich Mendelsohn promoted such measures, which were carried out in West Germany up until the 1970s and in the GDR until the fall of the Wall.[73] These buildings can now no longer be assigned to a historical period by the lay observer—they seem somehow modern but strangely characterless and, above all, timeless. Perhaps the "dust allergy" of the modernists had to do with their antipathy not only to historicism but to history in general; it related to their idea of beginning at ground zero and living in an eternal present in which the past does not exist. The constant decay of matter, which indicates the passage of time, must be halted by any and every means and any trace of it eliminated. The hygiene of modernity may cause the dust to disappear, but with it, in a sense, goes history, too.

This is particularly apparent in the modernist predilection for glass, the proverbial clarity of which was invoked by Taut, Le Corbusier, Gropius, Mies,[74] and many others, and on which—at least when it is used vertically—dust has great difficulty in settling. Glass is timeless: it does not take on a patina and appreciates having all traces removed. No less a figure than Walter Benjamin pinned the modern wish to leave no trace on glass architecture: "It is not for nothing that glass is such a hard, smooth material to which nothing can be fixed ... If you enter a bourgeois room of the 1880s, for all the coziness it radiates, the strongest impression you receive may well be, 'You've got no business here.' ... For there is no spot on which the owner has not left his mark ... A neat phrase by Brecht helps us out here: 'Erase the traces!' ... This has now been achieved by [Paul] Scheerbart, with his glass, and by the Bauhaus, with its steel. They have created rooms in which it is hard to leave traces."[75] In Bruno Taut's and Erna Meyer's campaign against the fetishism of sentimental mementos, which are "all too often things that have flown in from outside,"[76] like specks of dust that float through the window and themselves become dust catchers, we can recognize, with Benjamin, the reflex of a war generation, who returned from the battlefield "not richer, but poorer in communicable experience" and had to clear a "tabula rasa" in "barbaric fashion."[77] In this reading, an entire generation of actors

Anselm Wagner

The Bauhaus and the Vacuum Cleaner

57

sought to take a resolute stand against Edmond Locard's forensic principle that every form of contact leaves behind a trace and in the process produced, as if under compulsion, the smooth world of things of the New Objectivity.

A new social class that established itself in the 1920s followed this urge to achieve a purity that left no trace. Siegfried Kracauer devoted an entire monograph to this phenomenon: *The Salaried Masses.* Here, workers dream of rising within society to become salaried and declare "that they want their children one day to have better, easier and 'cleaner' work than they perform themselves."[78] For this salaried class, it is the traces not only of their work but also of their very origins that should become invisible. In the glamorous world of department stores and in the cabarets that carried the New Objectivity to an extreme, where the salaried masses "for not much money can get a breath of the wide world,"[79] this world is shown to them "not as it is, but as it appears in popular hits": "a world, every last corner of which is cleansed, as though with a vacuum cleaner, of the dust of everyday existence."[80]

The attractiveness of a cleanliness that leaves no trace can be found in a kind of secularized promise of salvation, which is part of modernism's progressive paradigm. The success of the Bauhaus purism, which has persisted into the present, has a great deal to do with the way it manages to interconnect medical, aesthetic, and religious discourses on purity in a process that is mutually reinforcing. The hygienic cleanliness of dust-free surfaces is not only suited to the expression of social advancement in the form of an object fetishism removed from history and from day-to-day life; it can also be related to the spirituality of "pure elementary representation"[81] espoused by the likes of Paul Klee. When Mies van der Rohe extols the glass skin of steel-frame buildings, because "the purity of the material ... [bears] the sheen of pristine beauty,"[82] cleanliness is ennobled as the mystic heart of modernism that has shaken off the dust of the past and promises an eternal "innocent" future.

1   Roland Meyer, "Flüchtige Verteilungen: Staub als Medium von Spuren," in *Staub: Eine interdisziplinäre Perspektive*, ed. Daniel Gethmann and Anselm Wagner (Vienna and Berlin, 2013), 142.

2   Meyer, 140–41.
3   Edmond Locard, cited in Meyer, 139.
4   See Walter Gropius, "Flach-, Mittel- oder Hochbau?," in *Ausgewählte Schriften*, ed. Hartmut Probst and Christian Schädlich,

Sektion Architektur der Hochschule für Architektur und Bauwesen Weimar (Berlin, 1987), 123–30.

5 Gropius, 123.

6 Gropius, 124.

7 Ernst Friedberger, *Untersuchungen über Wohnungsverhältnisse, insbes. über Kleinwohnungen und deren Mieter in Greifswald* (Jena, 1923).

8 Cited in Gropius, "Flach-, Mittel- oder Hochbau?" (see note 4), 124.

9 Gropius, 125.

10 Gropius, 126.

11 See Jean-Louis Cohen, introduction to Le Corbusier: *Toward an Architecture* (Los Angeles, 2007), 1–78, here: 45, 47, 52.

12 Le Corbusier: *Toward an Architecture*, 124.

13 Le Corbusier, 125.

14 Le Corbusier, 167.

15 Le Corbusier, 172.

16 See Christoph Glauser, *Einfach blitzsauber: Die Geschichte des Staubsaugers* (Zurich, 2001), 164.

17 Walter Gropius, "'Sparsamer Haushalt' und falsche Dürftigkeit" (1919), in Probst and Schädlich, *Ausgewählte Schriften* (see note 4), 76.

18 Hans Poelzig, "Erläuterungen," in *Bau und Wohnung*, ed. Deutscher Werkbund (Stuttgart, 1927), 97–98, here: 97.

19 Mart Stam, "Wie bauen?," in Deutscher Werkbund, 125–26, here: 126.

20 Josef Frank, "Der Gschnas fürs G'müt und der Gschnas als Problem," in Deutscher Werkbund, 49–55, here: 49.

21 J. J. P. Oud, "Erläuterungsbericht," in Deutscher Werkbund, 87–94, here: 94.

22 J. J. P. Oud in a letter to Edgar Wedepohl, ca. September/October 1927, cited in Karin Kirsch, *Die Weißenhofsiedlung: Werkbund-Ausstellung "Die Wohnung" – Stuttgart 1927* (Stuttgart, 1987), 99.

23 See Kirsch, 67, 69, 81.

24 See Kirsch, 59–61.

25 See Kirsch, 35.

26 See Kirsch, 92.

27 Erna Meyer, "Wohnungsbau und Hausführung," *Der Baumeister* 25, no. 6, supplement (1927): 89–95, here: 93.

28 See Kirsch, *Die Weißenhofsiedlung* (see note 22), 91.

29 See Kirsch, 34.

30 Erna Meyer, *Der neue Haushalt: Ein Wegweiser zu wirtschaftlicher Hausführung*, 38th ed.

(Stuttgart, 1929), 102, plate I (ill. 86) and 103, plate VII (ill. 87).

31 Meyer, 12.

32 Meyer, 71.

33 Meyer, 79.

34 Meyer, 82.

35 Meyer, 81.

36 See Meyer, 89–90.

37 Meyer, 90; see also 169.

38 Meyer, 137.

39 Meyer, 137.

40 See Glauser, *Einfach blitzsauber* (see note 16), 86.

41 See Bruno Taut, *Die neue Wohnung: Die Frau als Schöpferin* (Leipzig, 1924), 60–61.

42 Taut, 60.

43 Taut, 58.

44 Taut, 60.

45 Taut, 95.

46 Taut, 70.

47 Taut, 87.

48 Taut, 50.

49 Le Corbusier, *The Decorative Art of Today* (Cambridge, MA, 1987), 188, 192. Originally published as *L'Art decoratif d'aujourd'hui* (Paris, 1925). See also Janet Ward, *Weimar Surfaces: Urban Visual Culture in 1920s Germany* (Berkeley, CA, 2001), 80; Mark Wigley, *White Walls, Designer Dresses: The Fashioning of Modern Architecture* (Cambridge, MA, 1995), xvi, 3.

50 Henry Ford, *My Life & Work* (1922; Lockport, NY, 2012), 79–80; see also Ward, 80.

51 Adolf Behne, *The Modern Functional Building* (1923; Santa Monica, CA, 1996), 41, 104. Originally published as *Der moderne Zweckbau* (Munich, 1923).

52 The following section is an abbreviated and amended version of "Moderne Architektur als Mittel zur und Resultat von Staubbekämpfung," which formed part of my essay "Historie versus Hygiene: Staub in der Architektur(theorie)," in Gethmann and Wagner, *Staub* (see note 1), 75–106, here: 91–104.

53 See Christof Kübler, "Die architektonische Moderne: Formgewordene Hygiene!," in *Schweiz*, ed. Anna Meseure, Martin Tschanz, and Wilfried Wang (Munich, 1998), 98–103; Stanislaus von Moos, "Das Prinzip Toilette: Über Loos, Le Corbusier und die Reinlichkeit," in *Verlangen nach Reinheit oder Lust auf Schmutz? Gestaltungskonzepte zwischen rein und unrein*, ed. Roger Fayet (Vienna, 2003), 41–58; Anselm

Wagner, "Otto Wagners Straßenkehrer: Zum Reinigungsdiskurs der modernen Stadtplanung," bricolage: Innsbrucker Zeitschrift für Europäische Ethnologie 6 (2010): 36–61.

54 Le Corbusier, *The City of To-morrow and Its Planning* (New York, 1987), 199. Translated from the 8th French edition of *Urbanisme* by Frederick Etchells.

55 Eduard Pfeiffer, *Die Technik des Haushalts*, 8th ed. (Stuttgart, 1928), 70.

56 Clara Ebert-Stockinger, *Das Buch der Hausfrau: Eine neuzeitliche Haushaltungskunde*, 2nd ed. (Basel, 1929), 92.

57 See Glauser, *Einfach blitzsauber* (see note 16), 118.

58 Siegfried [sic] Giedion, *Mechanization Takes Command: A Contribution to Anonymous History* (New York, 1948), 593.

59 Glauser, *Einfach blitzsauber* (see note 16), 168.

60 See Glauser, 168.

61 See John Tyndall, "On Dust and Disease," in *Essays on the Floating Matter in the Air in Relation to Putrefaction and Infection* (London, 1881), 1–43, here: 2, 6ff., 29, 38.

62 See Wagner, "Historie versus Hygiene" (see note 52), 75–90.

63 See Aileen Cleere, "Victorian Dust Traps," in *Filth: Dirt, Disgust, and Modern Life*, ed. William A. Cohen and Ryan Johnson (Minneapolis, 2005), 133–54.

64 See Joanna Merwood-Salisbury, *Chicago 1890: The Skyscraper and the Modern City* (Chicago, 2009), 106–7; Adrian Forty, *Objects of Desire: Design & Society from Wedgwood to IBM* (New York, 1986), 180–81.

65 See Kübler, "Die architektonische Moderne" (see note 53).

66 Robert Musil, *The Man without Qualities*, vol. 1 (New York, 1996), 15. Originally published as *Der Mann ohne Eigenschaften* (Berlin, 1930).

67 Robert Edis, "Internal Decoration," cited in Cleere, "Victorian Dust Traps" (see note 63), 138. See Forty, *Objects of Desire* (see note 63), 172.

68 See Florence Nightingale, *On Nursing: What It Is, and What It Is Not*, 2nd ed. (New York, 1860), 91.

69 Christoph Gradmann, "'Krieg den Bakterien!' Wunsch und Wirklichkeit der medizinischen Bakteriologie und der Labormedizin am Ende des 19. Jahrhunderts," in *"Sei sauber ...!"*

Eine Geschichte der Hygiene und öffentlichen Gesundheitsvorsorge in Europa, exh. cat., Musée d'Histoire de la Ville de Luxembourg (Cologne, 2004), 228–37, here: 231.

70 Daniel H. Burnham, S. M. Randolph, and Normand S. Patton, "Illinois State Association of Architects," *The Inland Architect and News Record* 9, no. 9 (June 1887): 88–90, here: 89–90; see Merwood-Salisbury, *Chicago 1890* (see note 64), 111–12.

71 Hermann Muthesius, *Die Einheit der Architektur: Betrachtungen über Baukunst, Ingenieurbau und Kunstgewerbe; Vortrag, gehalten am 13. Februar 1908 im Verein für Kunst in Berlin* (Berlin, 1908), 42ff.

72 Muthesius, 47–48.

73 See Hans Georg Hiller von Gaertringen, *Schnörkellos: Die Umgestaltung von Bauten des Historismus im Berlin des 20. Jahrhunderts* (Berlin, 2012).

74 See Bruno Taut, "Nieder den Seriosismus!," *Frühlicht* 1 (1920): 1; Le Corbusier, *The City of To-morrow* (see note 54), 280; Walter Gropius, "glasbau" (1926), in Probst and Schädlich, *Ausgewählte Schriften* (see note 4), 103–6, here: 103; Ludwig Mies van der Rohe, "Was wäre Beton, was Stahl ohne Spiegelglas?" (1933), in Fritz Neumeyer, *Mies van der Rohe: Das kunstlose Wort; Gedanken zur Baukunst* (Berlin, 1986), 378.

75 Walter Benjamin, "Experience and Poverty" (1933), in *Selected Writings: 1927–1934*, ed. Michael W. Jennings, Howard Eiland, and Gary Smith, trans. Rodney Livingstone et al. (Cambridge, MA, 2005), 731–36, here: 733–34; see Ward, *Weimar Surfaces* (see note 49), 73–74.

76 Meyer, *Der neue Haushalt* (see note 30), 76.

77 Benjamin, "Experience and Poverty" (see note 75), 731–33.

78 Siegfried Kracauer, *The Salaried Masses: Duty and Distraction in Weimar Germany* (1929; London, 1998), 84. Originally published in 1929 as *Die Angestellten*.

79 Kracauer, 91.

80 Kracauer, 93; see Ward, *Weimar Surfaces* (see note 49), 81.

81 Paul Klee, "On Modern Art" (1924), in *Art in Theory 1900–1990: An Anthology of Changing Ideas*, ed. Charles Harrison and Paul Wood (Cambridge, MA, 1992), 343–50, here: 349.

82 Mies van der Rohe, "Was wäre Beton?" (see note 74), 378.

Pep Avilés

Faktur, Photography, and the Image of Labor: On Moholy-Nagy's Textures

If one cannot get the feeling for the new sense of space, the treatment of textures and plane surfaces, the studies of the Bauhaus fall to pieces.
Sigfried Giedion, *Focus*, 1939

Wherever I looked, I saw myself surrounded by folding screens, cushions, and pedestals which craved my image much as the shades of Hades craved the blood of the sacrificial animal.
Walter Benjamin, "Die Mummerehlen," 1932–34

The prevalence of visual values in modernity arrived at the expense of subordinating the other senses to the effective and affective dialectic between human eye and images. In this context, the sense of tact found a smooth, more desirable integration into vision in art and architecture's discourse than did the others, thanks in part to a new understanding of the material and aesthetic qualities that the modern industrial form of labor introduced:[1] textures acted as catalysts and signifiers of the synthesis of hand and mechanical labor throughout the multiple stages of the avant-gardes, reclaiming a space between sight and tact that could stage an aesthetic project corresponding with the impact industrialization was having in modern societies.[2] The new territories that the permeation of tactile aspects in materials and consumer goods increasingly conquered became explicit in the literature reacting to the Second World War, once textures began to be portrayed as substitutes for past ornamental practices that modern artists and architects emphatically discredited. It was László Moholy-Nagy who in his *Vision in Motion*, published posthumously in 1947, described texture as "the legitimate successor of ornament."[3] Moholy-Nagy ascribed representational values to texture that went beyond mere aesthetic materialism: the emphasis on textured surfaces was associated with agreements and relationships, i.e., with a new social contract procured by and channeled through technologies of reproduction (and production) of images. In the postwar years, after being abandoned, banished, and resented for decades—this mainly applied to academic ornament, but also to any expression that could be stigmatized as a superficial or banal form of subjectivity—textures were to serve as the proper substitute for ornament in modernity to overcome a moment of stagnation in design.[4]

Texture:
A legitimate surrogate

During the first two decades after the Second World War, textures were among architects' favorite forms of expression to enhance the external appearance of buildings: examples in the architecture of Marcel Breuer, Paul Rudolph, and Eero Saarinen—just to name a few—are common. Walter Gropius, for instance, described texture as a prelude to future developments in an individual's "form language," and Marcel Breuer understood it as fulfilling an "instinct for décor" instrumental in avoiding the dangers of a "sterile architecture."[5] How was it possible that the use of textures became increasingly important to the development of a modern architecture once described as an ornamental form? How did this apparently seamless substitution take place? According to Moholy-Nagy, the creative power that had formerly gone into the production of ornament was "transferred now into materials, tool-formed textures, and surface treatments."[6] What did he mean by "transferred"? How was this psychoanalytical tool, transference, operating in postwar production beyond the identification of formal replacements for underlying old concerns? I would argue that there was actually a triple transference: semantic, techno-material, and ideological. As we will see, the incorporation of texture in Moholy-Nagy's work as a valid mechanism for invigorating design through materials followed a very convoluted path, full of meanders, misunderstandings, mistranslations, and conflicting personal agendas. In postwar architecture, textures stood as a socially legitimate and technologically opportune alternative to the applied ornament that modern architects and designers repudiated; textures were a form of

*Pep
Avilés*

Faktur,
Photography,
and
the
Image
of
Labor

63

abstract, mechanical subjectivity that perfectly suited capitalism's need for the division of labor and yet fostered the rapid circulation of commodities as image. Concealed behind the term's phenomenological patina lie specific meanings acquired and transmitted by direct osmosis among various members of the European artistic avant-garde in the 1920s.

Traveling concepts: structure, texture, surface aspect, massing

Let's begin by considering what Moholy-Nagy called "surface treatments." The book *Vision in Motion* illustrated and expanded the pedagogical curriculum followed during Moholy-Nagy's nine years as director of the economically and politically unstable Institute of Design in Chicago.[7] In *Vision in Motion*, Moholy-Nagy continued and evolved the observations and experiments from both the Weimar and Dessau period but also from his time in exile in London. The word "texture" became central to the understanding of Moholy-Nagy's articulation between human sensory experience and industrial production—and perhaps even already emerging digital technologies— appearing way more often in the book than concepts traditionally associated with modern culture such as space or time.[8] Although never explicitly or precisely defined in *Vision in Motion*, the word "texture" became central for the understanding of Moholy-Nagy's interests at the intersection of technology and biological experience.[9] The publication closed a period of more than twenty years of the continuous presence of Moholy-Nagy's work in the United States that had begun with the publication of his photograms in 1923 in *Broom*, a cultural magazine that distanced itself from dusty prior conventions in art by promoting new topics, concepts, and media.[fig.1][10] A major landmark in this relationship was the translation in 1932 of his pedagogical book *Von Material zu Architektur* as *The New Vision: From Material to Architecture*.[11] *The New Vision* introduced Moholy-Nagy's *Vorkurs* (preliminary course) from the former Bauhaus to the English-speaking audience. The book's impact on interwar and postwar culture was due to the normalization and canonization of a pedagogical method that would soon be associated with *pars pro toto*. The book was literally viewed as a treatise for the depersonalization of the modern designer: Walter Gropius, for instance, assigned universal legitimacy to the publication when he stated that it was less "a personal credo" than "a standard

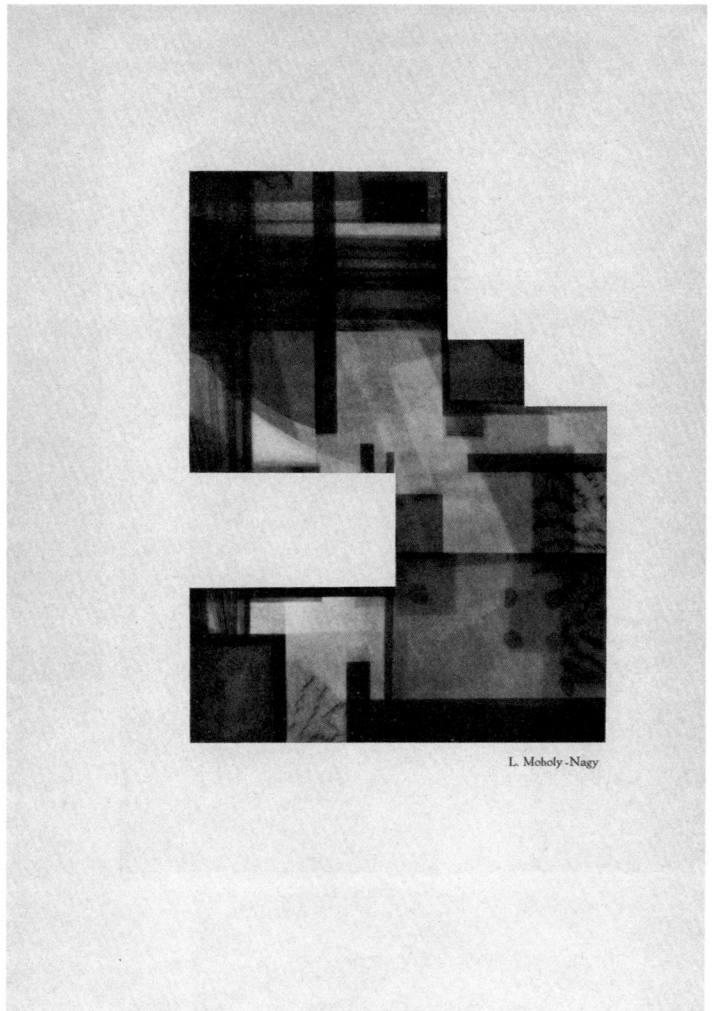

L. Moholy-Nagy

grammar of modern design."[12] The book itself could be understood as a technological apparatus—a *dispositif* in Foucault's terminology—that was meant to describe, organize, and fundamentally alter the visual environment at the intersection of technologies of mechanization and new media of reproduction. Unsurprisingly, the point of departure for that understanding lay neither in easel painting nor in traditional art forms, but in material—its use, transformation, manipulation, and tactile assimilation.

The New Vision systematized the visual classification of manufactured and raw materials according to four different categories: structure, texture, surface aspect, and massing. Structure represented the visible inner physical and chemical properties of materials, often appreciated through technology (microscopic photography, metallography, aerial photography, etc.). Massing responded to the modern fascination with the visual impact of serial organization, a material interpretation recalling the social critique that Siegfried Kracauer so wittingly put forward in his contributions to the *Frankfurter Zeitung*.[13] Yet the difference between texture and surface aspect—the latter often and symptomatically interchangeable with surface treatment or surface appearance—was a more difficult one in etymological and historical terms. Texture, defined by Moholy-Nagy as "the organically resulting outward surface," was the visual result of biological processes, as illustrated by cats' fur, rotten apples, or the well-known image of a hundred-year-old wrinkled man.[fig.2][14] In the original definition of texture, we cannot find a single trace of industrial agency. Surface aspect, on the other hand, was the result of the working process, hand- or machine-made.[fig.3, 4] Illustrated by the accumulation of dust in a machine filter, the term was used to signify the aesthetic appraisal of the traces of the modern industrial mode of

Pep Avilés

Faktur, Photography, and the Image of Labor

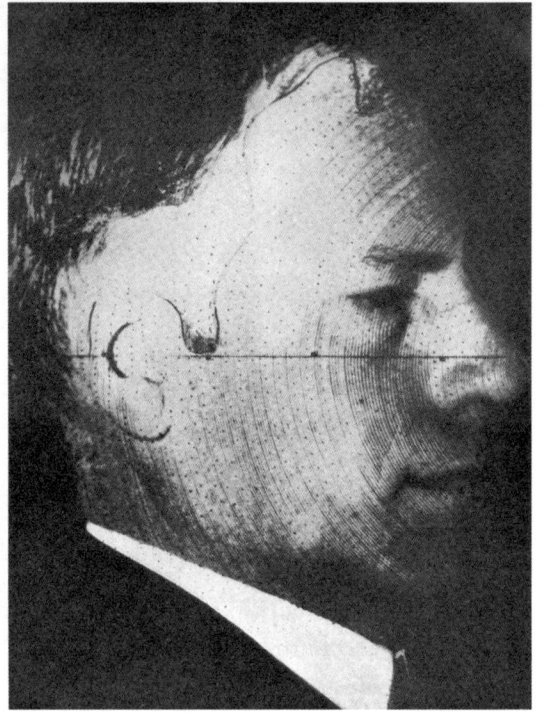

Fig.2. Texture of the skin of a 130-year-old man from Minnesota, from László Moholy-Nagy, *Von Material zu Architektur*, 1929.

Fig.3. *Faktur.* Early stages of a relief photograph, from László Moholy-Nagy, *Von Material zu Architektur*, 1929.

Fig.4. Massing (*Faktur*). Dust filter in a machine room, from László Moholy-Nagy, *Von Material zu Architektur*, 1929.

production in materials as captured by the lenses of the photographic camera—traces that already predict the rapid aging of what has only recently been understood as ultramodern.

These four concepts belonged to the lexicon that emerged from the famous *Vorkurs* that Moholy-Nagy and Josef Albers taught during the mid-1920s at the Bauhaus in Weimar and Dessau. Among the most significant features of this first English version printed in 1932 was the mistranslation of some of the original terms of Moholy's conceptual armature. In it, these had been presented to German readers as *Struktur*, *Textur*, *Faktur*, and *Häufung* (or *Haufwerk*).[15] The fact that the word *Faktur* was translated as "surface aspect" or "surface treatment" suggested, on the one hand, a yielding attitude towards the superficial qualities that Moholy-Nagy wanted to underscore. On the other, it anticipated the kind of ornament that he envisaged by transferring the agency driving its production to human-operated machinery. The presence of the word *Faktur* in Weimar Germany was not unproblematic: the capacity of the term to indicate working processes dates back to the avant-gardes of the 1920s, and more precisely, to Russian literary Futurism and Constructivism, in which the concept *Faktura* (фактура) became an ideological Trojan horse used to debunk easel painting in favor of modern art forms that could stage the socioeconomic changes prompted by industrial production. Eventually, *Faktura* also became a political concept that referred to the social organization of labor within a communist state.

In Russian Constructivism, *Faktura* had appeared not as a surrogate of ornament, as Moholy-Nagy had announced, but as the form that ornament could take within a society in which the means of production had been radically altered by modern industry. Under the banner of the artist as producer, the issue of ornament in modernity seemed to vanish once the industrial object became materially and conceptually more sophisticated. Moholy-Nagy seems to have been aware of technical and epistemological discrepancies when he decided to draw a distinction between both categories (*Textur* and *Faktur*) in *Von Material zu Architektur*. However, ultimately accepting the word "texture" as the English equivalent in *Vision in Motion*, the concept in which he was interested in the late 1920s and 1930s was, in fact, *Faktur*.[16] To Russian Constructivism, as well as to Moholy-Nagy, *Faktura* entailed a practice but also a place, a locus in which material ideology, social and political aspirations, and artistic expression finally met.

Pep Avilés

Faktur, Photography, and the Image of Labor

67

Russian *faktura* (фактура): genealogies
of a common subjectivity

Signifying the manual capacity of the artist to control the final aspect of the canvas's surface, *Faktura* belonged to the tradition of Orthodox iconography and easel painting. From the outset, it was an intrinsic quality of the work of art, a fundamental aspect of its expressiveness. It was linked to the painting's mode of production and as such remained co-substantial to its being. The modern use of the term *Faktura* emerged in Russian literary circles of the 1910s, specifically around Futurist liaisons, highlighting a shift towards abstraction in prose and poetry, whose material qualities—i.e. a graphic representation of sounds and words—served as point of departure for a renewal of meaning. The term soon became crucial within the avant-garde for the assimilation of alien technologies, as it stood in direct opposition to traditional easel painting as well as their corresponding themes and contents. After Russian artists such as Kazimir Malevich became interested in non-representation, *Faktura* also helped enhance the palette for abstract painting as it incorporated as-found industrial materials. The existence of new industrial techniques increasingly came to be identified with the precision, smoothness, or roughness of machine-manufactured surfaces.

It was David Burliuk, a regular contributor to the Munich-based art magazine *Der Blaue Reiter* and a member of the Futurist literary group *Hylaea*, who, in an addendum to the collective manifesto "A Slap in the Public Face" signed by Alexander Kruchenykh, Victor (or Velimir) Khlebnikov, and Vladimir Mayakovsky, began to grant the term a central place in the Russian avant-garde.[17] Burliuk proposed a taxonomy of surface properties that initially distinguished between smooth and rough but then went further into the capacity of materials to retain or reflect light: strongly shining, shining, weakly shining, glowing, and dull. Voldemars Matvejs (writing under the pseudonym Vladimir Markov) went further in developing this concept for the pre-revolutionary Russian avant-garde in his short book entitled *Faktura*, published in 1914 for the Saint Petersburg Union of Youth. In this text, Matvejs situated *Faktura* as an interdisciplinary concern, equally valid and apt for assessing painting, sculpture, and architecture. He did so by resorting to the psychological effects of materials on any work of art, highlighting the "'noise' perceived by our consciousness in one way or another." By "noise," Matvejs meant the pleasant surplus information derived from the creative use of materials, equally valid in all art forms. His definition resorted to anthropological accounts of the use of ornament in past tribes and societies, but also in contemporary society: from hair to tattoos, from bones to feathers, from perfumes to clothing, from dusty to polished surfaces, any material could be appropriated for surface decoration.[18] To Matvejs, *Faktura* entailed "the method of processing and blending" those objects, a method that tried to grasp the effects generated by traditional ornaments, among other connotations.[19] His material determinism offered an alternative to what was commonly known as *maniera*, that is, style, by removing agency from the artist and immediately granting it to society as a productive collective. Although Matvejs' influential piece opened up the term to new associations, his universal description through multiple categories eventually rendered the term all-encompassing; *Faktura* came to mean every surface—be it natural or artificial, handmade or machine-made—that was capable of producing an effect, and with greater stress placed on the subjective aspect set into play by the reception of art than on the objective and precise industrial mode of production.

Individual subjectivity was challenged by the collective effort required by revolution and supported by Constructivism. Through the years of World War I, an emerging group of artists including Vladimir Tatlin and Gustav Klutsis, who were influenced by the writings of Matvejs and the works of Picasso, began paying attention to the surfaces of industrially produced materials, incorporating them into their "constructions" as indexical of their origins. In Constructivist circles, *Faktura*—together with *Tektonika* and *Konstruktsiya*—became central to the "communistic expression of material structures."[20] Alexander Rodchenko, Varvara Stepanova, and Lyubov Popova, among others, considered the term useful for addressing the new aesthetic's relation to the industrial qualities of materials, and so it became explicit in the Vkhutemas studios during the mid-1920s. But if there is anyone who ought to be credited for incorporating the word *Faktura* into the vocabulary of architecture and linking it to transnational debates such as those taking place at *L'Esprit Nouveau* or *De Stijl*, it was the artist Aleksei Gan. In his book *Constructivism* (1922), Gan identified *Tectonics*, *Faktura*, and *Construction* as concepts that were instrumental to the departure from traditional art and the achievement of a proper material expression for Soviet Marxism.[21] To serve this end, *Faktura* had to acquire a representational and epistemological role and thus to illustrate the full production process that was taking place in this newly organized society. Yet while *Tectonics* and *Construction* appeared in Gan's book as imprecise concepts that bore a direct relation to the formation of a communist society, the word *Faktura* assumed a very sharp industrial meaning that organically linked "base" and "superstructure:" to Gan, *Faktura* was not only the final appearance of an object but also the final image of a complex socio-technological mode of production in a communist state:

> *Let us take, for example, cast iron—an industrial material. To make an article of it, a complicated production process is conducted. Cast iron is melted, i.e., transformed into a burning liquid mass, then it is cast into a shaped mould, goes through the emery department or is simply cut around, and then goes to the mechanical department to lathes, after which one can say that the cast iron has become an article.* This entire process is facture, i. e., the processing of metal in general, not of its surface only. *Here the material is perceived in status as a raw material. The purposeful use of material means selection and processing, and the nature of purpose-oriented processing is facture.* More precisely, facture is an organic condition of the material processed or a new condition of its organism. ... *Facture is a reminder of the fact itself.*[22]

By the early 1920s, *Faktura* became a reminder, a signifier, of the entire political and social organization of the mode of production. The ideological impetus of the term lay in its representational content, transforming materials into litmus papers on which traces of the political organization of labor could be appreciated.

Textural pedagogies

It remains unclear how the term *Faktura* was received at the Bauhaus. It is unlikely that *Faktur*—especially with all the political nuances that it assumed after his departure—was among Kandinsky's catchwords; he was, after all, a totally different kind of artist from the type promoted by Russian Constructivism and the Soviets during the early 1920s. As a Constructivist artist himself, Moholy-Nagy was acquainted with the debates emerging in Russia, particularly through the works and writings of Rodchenko, Popova, and Tatlin.[23] There were many sources from which he may have been influenced by the Constructivist term: through his former colleagues at the journal MA, where the word *Faktura* was associated with Malevich's work already in 1923; through his own

Russian students, who had migrated to Weimar to study; and through personal osmosis from his association with his friend El Lissitzky during the 1922 Constructivist-Dadaist congress in Weimar and his knowledge of the topics covered by the magazine *Veshch/Gegenstand/Objet*. Although Aleksei Gan excoriated El Lissitzky for his inability to detach himself from aesthetic practices, the latter definitely partook of Constructivist circles and methodologies; his *Raum für konstruktive Kunst* at the International Art Exhibition in Dresden in 1926 and his *Schwebender Körper* (1919) installed in Hannover in 1928 show a conspicuous sensibility for the aesthetic appropriation of the supporting wall, a sensibility echoed later in some of Marcel Breuer's early works.

Within the Bauhaus milieu, the provenance of the term *Faktura* was, in fact, disputed; in a 1967 interview, Josef Albers, who had been jointly responsible for the Bauhaus *Vorkurs*, complained bitterly of the historical developments that had led to the publication of *Von Material zu Architektur*.[24] The reason for his dismay was the book's embrace of the aforementioned division of *Struktur*, *Faktur*, and *Textur*. In the fall of 1928, Albers was invited to lecture on his pedagogical methods at the *Berliner Kunstgewerbe Museum*, coincidentally the building that Martin Gropius, Walter Gropius' great uncle, had built between 1877 and 1881.[25] After the lecture, Moholy-Nagy's first wife, Lucia, who served as his German editor and played a crucial role in his technical understanding of the photographic medium, approached Albers to ask him for definitions of the concepts that he had just presented, and apparently he complied with her request.[26] According to Albers, the definitions were afterwards "misappropriated" by Lucia Moholy-Nagy for her husband's book. At the time, Moholy-Nagy's second Bauhaus book, whose anticipated title at the time was *Von Kunst zu Leben*, had not yet been published. But Malevich's *Die gegenstandslose Welt*, in which the word *Faktur* appears at the very beginning of the German translation (edited by Moholy-Nagy and translated by Hans von Riesen), had been.[27] The images that Malevich used may have influenced Moholy-Nagy's visual rhetoric, but the word *Faktur*, though it appeared several times in the text in reference to photography, was not central to Malevich's theory of Suprematism, which was discussed towards the end of the book. A year later, in the 1929 issue of the *Bauhaus* journal, dedicated almost entirely to Oskar Schlemmer's experiments in the theater, Moholy-Nagy's *Von Material zu Architektur* was announced. The author decided to change the title of the book from *Von Kunst zu Leben* at the

Pep
Avilés

Faktur,
Photography,
and
the
Image
of
Labor

71

last minute, right before it was published and almost two years after
he had left the school and moved to Berlin. This detachment from the
final events held at the school after his presumably unethical appropriation of Bauhaus methodology infuriated some of the professors.
According to Albers, Klee and Kandinsky had initially hidden Moholy-
Nagy's publication from Albers since they both agreed that his adoption of Albers' methods and pedagogical theory had been dishonest.
Klee's animosity towards Moholy-Nagy went beyond the latter's rejection of his mechanic-dynamic project; he actually described Moholy-
Nagy as "the prefabricated spirit of our time."[28] However, though
Albers might be granted responsibility for classifying the manipulation
and visualization of matter—as he stated in his postwar complaint—
no exhaustive and progressive explanation of the various terms was
evident in the literature available by 1928. Nonetheless, this episode of
personal rivalry reveals the relevance that these concepts acquired in
the decades following Moholy-Nagy's publication.

To be precise, the use of textures in the preliminary course had
already become significant prior to Albers and Moholy-Nagy's leadership.[29] Johannes Itten's previous work seems to have been responsible
for the frenzied taste for textures among Bauhaus students, as Marcel
Breuer's famous 1922 caricature of Josef Albers illustrates. Itten fostered the production of "ornamental abstraction" through textural
exercises as a way of exploring intuitive perception—a pedagogical
method that he retained at his later appointments in Berlin and
Krefeld in the 1930s.[30] By using handheld tools, utensils, objects, and
even human and non-human organs, students printed traces on matter
in different positions. These exercises were meant to liberate students
from previous aesthetic influences in order to better assimilate future
workshops. Looking back at his pedagogical career and particularly
his Bauhaus years in 1963, Itten noted that in working on these
exercises on texture, students caught a "real design fever":

> They began to rummage through the drawers of thrifty grandmothers,
> their kitchen and cellars; they ransacked the workshops of craftsmen and
> the rubbish heaps of factories and building sites. A whole new world was
> discovered: lumber and wood shavings, steel wool, wires, strings, polished
> wood, and sheep's wool, feathers, glass, and tin foil, grids and weaves of
> all kinds, leather, furs, and shiny cans. Manual abilities were discovered
> and new textures invented. They started a mad tinkering, and their
> awakened instincts discovered the inexhaustible wealth of textures and

their combinations. The student observed that wood could be fibrous, dry, rough, smooth, or furrowed; that iron could be hard, heavy, shiny, or dull. Finally they investigated how these textural qualities could be represented. These studies were of great value to the future architects, craftsmen, photographers, graphic artists, and industrial designers.[31]

Indeed, this environmental expansion of design tools along with research on the "wealth of textures" continued under Albers and Moholy-Nagy's leadership. However, minor but significant differences arose when the two faced the challenge of replacing Itten's curriculum before and after the school moved to Dessau.[32] Leaving behind Itten's pedagogical version of Mazdanism and its worship of self-expression, students concentrated in abstract material repetition and perception. From the very outset, Albers, who ended up having the longest affiliation with the Bauhaus school, showed a deep concern for as-found industrial materials and their compositional possibilities. The techniques used in exercises by Albers's students demonstrate a close sensibility to painting, as brushes were used to mimic textiles and surfaces. Moholy-Nagy, in contrast, was attracted to the capacity of art—through its alliance with new media—to generate new forms transmitting social organization and subjectivity.[33] If to Albers, the agency of the artist was paramount—we can simply recall, among other things, his series of glass compositions for Gropius's Haus Sommerfeld—then to Moholy-Nagy, technology enabled a mediated subjectivity in production that was nonetheless incorporated into the final object.[34] His tactile rhetoric with respect to surfaces and materials followed Constructivist experiments and emphasized the production of devices and taxonomies in order to enhance and master human perception, that is, to produce new tactile experiences. Walter Kaminsky (1927) and Gerda Marx's (1928) famous *Tasttafeln*, as well as Rudolf Marvitz (1928) and Willy Zierath's (circa 1927) exercises illustrate this point.[fig.5] Art and industrial techniques—and science during his final years teaching in the US—constituted the pivotal axis around which society and subjects could be improved. In Rainer Wick's words, Moholy-Nagy's functionalism was based on illustrating "the new social content of material production," that is, producing the proper image for the new set of economic relations.[35] From that point of view, both pedagogical curricula were complementary rather than contradictory. It is in this intellectual context that *Faktur* appears as central. Although in *Von Material zu Architektur* Moholy-Nagy had

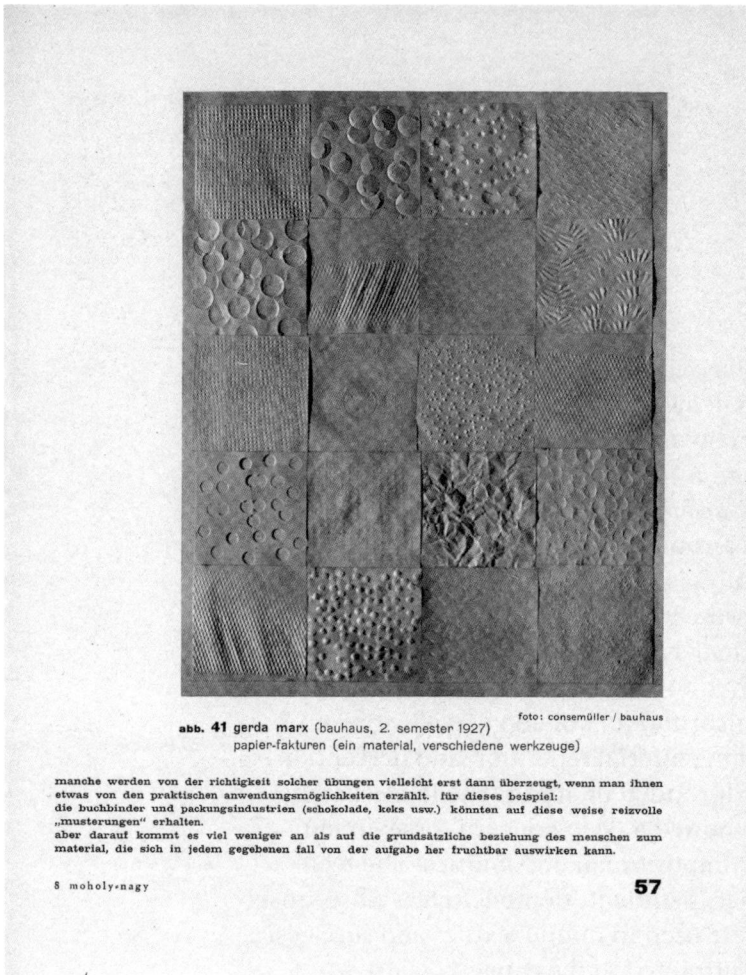

foto: consemüller / bauhaus

abb. 41 gerda marx (bauhaus, 2. semester 1927)
papier-fakturen (ein material, verschiedene werkzeuge)

manche werden von der richtigkeit solcher übungen vielleicht erst dann überzeugt, wenn man ihnen etwas von den praktischen anwendungsmöglichkeiten erzählt. für dieses beispiel: die buchbinder und packungsindustrien (schokolade, keks usw.) könnten auf diese weise reizvolle „musterungen" erhalten.
aber darauf kommt es viel weniger an als auf die grundsätzliche beziehung des menschen zum material, die sich in jedem gegebenen fall von der aufgabe her fruchtbar auswirken kann.

8 moholy-nagy   57

exemplified the concept of *Faktur* through exercises done by students before 1927—Ulrich Klawun, 1924—the absence of the term in archival sources makes me think that the triple classification—*Struktur, Faktur, Textur*—was a post-conceptualization made by Albers during the spring of 1928 after Moholy-Nagy's departure. It seems that *Faktur* as a category was certainly alien to Moholy-Nagy's teaching methodology in relation to matter during his years at the Bauhaus and, to some extent, to the Bauhaus itself as it appeared on the fringes of the activities practiced by the different masters in the various fields in which they had been involved prior to 1928.[36]

Regarding pedagogical methods at the Bauhaus, only Paul Klee—*Pädagogisches Skizzenbuch* (1926)—and Wassily Kandinsky—*Punkt und Linie zu Fläche* (1926)—had published their teaching agendas by the end of the decade. In 1927, El Lissitzky had contributed to the publication of the pedagogical results of the Vkhutemas with a design cover.[37] By the mid-1920s, the concept of *Faktura* was being used at the Vkhutemas in a formalistic yet pedagogical manner to train future architects in how to master the expressive capacities of materials. This publication, in fact, reveals an understanding of the word that is very similar to the one that Albers had used in the preliminary phase of the *Vorkurs* that he had taught in Dessau. Actually, Albers was the next person to be interested in presenting his pedagogical methods at the Bauhaus. In 1928, he published an article in the second issue of the school's magazine entitled *"Werklicher Formunterricht"*—"Formal Exercises in Craftworks"—in which he illustrated his teaching methodology with work by his students.[38] In it, Albers used the term inconsistently and rather conservatively, associating the surface appearance of materials with formal painting techniques in which "intersections, mixings and interpenetration occur by illusion."[39] Albers exemplified the compositional and quasi-textile aspect of materials by including in the article works by Bauhaus *Meisterin* Gunta Stölzl and students Ilse Voigt and Anni Fleischmann—later known as Anni Albers—from the knitting division of the school.[40] Albers's article is significant, since it marks the first time that the triad—*Struktur*, *Faktur*, and *Textur*—appeared within the context of the Bauhaus in written form. However, it appeared here in a highly specific manner, its *raison d'être* being to change the surface appearance of materials once their surfaces were treated as paintings:

> *We classify the appearances of the material epidermis (outer layer) as essentially different in structure, facture, and texture. Their utilization is done through painting as construction, so that spatiality, overlaps and penetration occur more as an illusion. Special interest in questions of appearance is a manifestation of particular constructive-mindset epochs. This aspect has been very well kept by the gothic, as it was neglected subsequently, when façade and space, equipment and clothes were made in just one material, when walls, furniture and floors were coated with color.*[41]

Materials as media

Despite Albers's complaints in 1967, he never fully described in the article the systematization of the *Vorkurs* and the role that these concepts—*Struktur, Faktur, Textur*—played in the episteme of the class. However, the analogy between façades and dressings suggested by the article is certainly not a surprise. Nor is the relation between surface aspects and painting techniques in Albers's work. In contrast, Moholy-Nagy's genealogy and interest in the term arose from the sharp dialectic over the aesthetic legitimization of a different medium: photography. In the late 1920s, the term *Faktur* was not unknown to Moholy-Nagy; it appeared for the first time under his name in the book *Malerei, Photografie, Film*, published in 1925.[fig.6] Here it was associated with film photography and illustrated with stills showing dresses, textile patterns, and make-up worn by actresses Fern Andra and Gloria Swanson. Moholy-Nagy had also used the concept two years later, before the appearance of Albers's teaching statement in the *Bauhaus* magazine, in an article he wrote in 1927 for the German photography journal *Das Deutsche Lichtbild*, in which he unraveled topics of his epoch-making "Production-Reproduction," published in 1922.[42] It was only after the re-publication of the former article—

Pep
Avilés

Faktur,
Photography,
and
the
Image
of
Labor

75

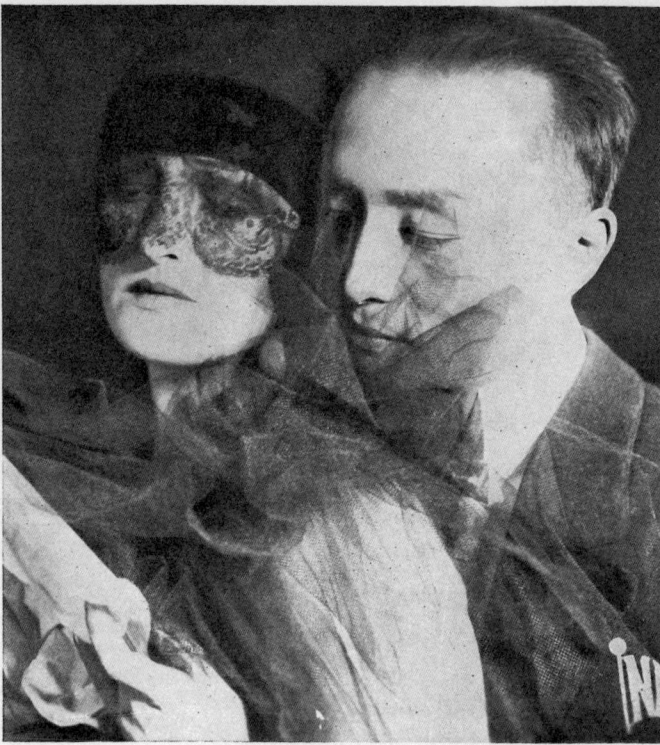

Aus dem Nationalfilm: „ZALAMORT".

Porträtaufnahme mit Fakturenwirkungen.

84

"Die beispiellose Fotografie"—in the Amsterdam-based art magazine *i10* that the word *Faktur* became the epicenter of a dispute between Ernö Kallai on the one hand, and Adolf Behne, Willi Baumeister, and Moholy-Nagy on the other.[43] Kallai criticized photography for its inability to produce *Faktur*, an aesthetic constituent limited to easel painting. Moholy-Nagy, in turn, echoing Constructivism, denied that the understanding of *Faktur* had only to do with tactile qualities. To him, *Faktur* in photographs portrayed the entire process of photographic production in addition to the surface aspects of the image's content, and therefore it represented a legitimate artistic form as valid as traditional easel painting. We can understand the term's growing relevance to Moholy-Nagy's work by looking closely at the 1927 edition of *Malerei, Fotografie, Film*, in which the title is not the only difference we can find. In this new edition, Moholy offered the first definition (to my knowledge) of *Faktur* within the context of the Bauhaus: "the manner and appearance of the manufacturing process."[fig. 7] In 1929 he expanded on this in *Von Material zu Architektur*:

> *Faktur ist die Art und Erscheinung, der sinnlich wahrnehmbare Niederschlag (die Einwirkung) des Werkprozesses, der sich bei jeder Bearbeitung am Material zeigt. Also die Oberfläche des von außen her veränderten Materials (Epidermis, künstlich). Diese äußere Einwirkung kann sowohl elementar (durch Natureinfluß), als auch mechanisch, z. B. durch die Maschine usw. erfolgen. Fakturen können an einem Objekt verschiedenerweise vorkommen, z. B. bei einer Metallschale als: Musterungen (Hammerschläge), vollkommene Glätte (gedrückt und poliert), Lichterscheinung (Spiegelung, Reflexion, Farbbrechung) und als je nach Material und Kraft variierte Niederschläge.*[44]

Part 1

Theories
of
Bauhaus
Materiality

76

Fig.7. First definition of *Faktur*: manner and appearance of the manufacturing process, László Moholy-Nagy, *Malerei, Fotografie, Film*, 1927.

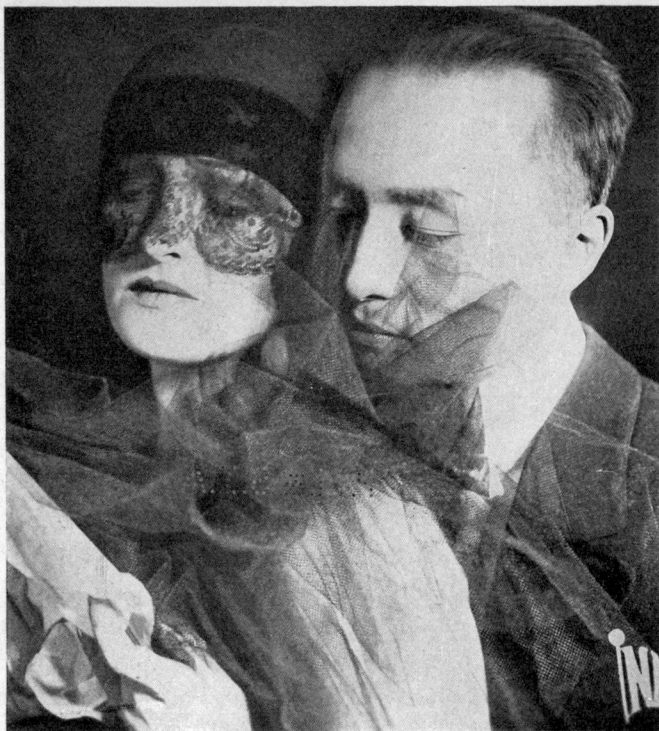

Aus dem Nationalfilm: „ZALAMORT"

Porträtaufnahme mit Darstellung von Fakturenwirkungen. (Faktur = Art und Erscheinung des Herstellungsprozesses).

92

Faktur was thus "the manner and appearance, the sensitive perceptible manifestation, (the exposure) of the working process that shows itself in any material treatment."[45] The word "exposure"—*Einwirkung*, later translated as "effect" in the English editions—relates to its photographic origins. Here we find the material transference to which we referred at the very beginning of this paper; from exposure to light (as in the case of the silver-gelatin emulsion in photography), to the exposure of the working process, the material had to perform as the recording device of its own manufacture. Matter for the artist was what plastic film was for the photographer: the very medium onto which life itself—and by extension, the social contract—could be imprinted. Indeed, the aesthetic component permeated Moholy-Nagy's narrative; in 1926 he published an article in the Austrian magazine *Vivos Voco* in which he defended photography as a new form of representation, which in its mastery over the *Fakturlose*, became the source of "luminous effects."[46] Ironically, the phenomenological effect that appeared in *The New Vision* lost its photographic genealogy yet preceded the aesthetic, experiential character that the term would acquire in the 1930s. If in the previous decade the epidermal character of *Faktur* had revealed the fashioning of materials to Moholy-Nagy, then to Albers its social and ideological connotations remained irrelevant. Although Albers may have formulated a precise definition earlier, the various editions of Moholy-Nagy's book did influence him in his transition to Black Mountain College in the mid-1930s. It was not until 1938, with the publication of the catalogue that accompanied the first exhibition of the Bauhaus at the Museum of Modern Art in New York, that we encounter, albeit in a footnote, Albers's precise definition of the three different terms:

Pep Avilés

Faktur, Photography, and the Image of Labor

77

Fig.8. Advertising design for the journal of the Left Front of the Arts, *LEF*, Alexander Rodchenko, 1923.

Fig.9. School of Design in Chicago, *Summer Sessions*, Chicago and Somonauk, June–August 1941.

"Structure" refers to those qualities of surface which reveal how the raw material grows or is formed ... "Facture" refers to those qualities of surface which reveal how the raw material has been treated technically ... "Texture" is a general term which refers to both "structure" and "facture," but only if both are present. For instance, the "texture" of polished wood reveals both the "structure" (grain) and the "facture" (polishing).[47]

Remarkably, to Albers in 1938 texture was a possible synthesis of facture and structure, a combination of mechanical treatments and the natural properties of materials regardless of the socio-economic context of the mode of production.[48] In Moholy-Nagy's narrative, however, texture, an offspring of photography, became not just another formal quality of materials but also a reminder. If divested of its ideological burdens, even Walter Gropius could defend texture as a kind of ornament for modern architecture along these lines after arriving in the United States. As he stated in 1938, "A true modern architect" introduces "refined industrial processes of surface treatment into his compositions" and "emphasizes the contrast of their component parts with different materials and textures," indicating in turn "the probable direction of further development towards ornamentation."[49] Stemming from the grammar of modern design, a new ornament based on "contrasts" generated by "industrial processes" had finally been prescribed. *Vision in Motion* merely concluded the intellectual journey from the ideologically threatening *Faktura* to the phenomenological and harmless texture.

Influenced by the Soviet avant-garde, Moholy-Nagy shared the taste, interests, and—more importantly—cultural references of his Russian comperes, as the 1923 advertisement of the magazine of the Left Front for the Arts (*LEF*) shows. [fig.8] But he did not share their ultimate political aspirations; he was willing to detach the political component of the term *Faktura*—the construction of a communist state—from the ideological value ascribed to it by Russian Constructivism. However, he viewed politics not as the functional expression of an ideological system but rather as a form of "realizing ideas for the benefit of the community."[50] During his post-Bauhaus period, Moholy-Nagy developed a systematic phenomenological grammar for materials that was rooted in the logic of Soviet Constructivism. But in the views of the Constructivists, and to a lesser extent in that of Moholy-Nagy— apart from their political discrepancies and formal similarities— the term *Faktura* entailed a practice but also a place, a *locus*, in which

ideology and artistic expression finally met.[fig.9] To Moholy-Nagy, this ideology was seemingly channeled through the struggle and incorporation of photography as a technology of production in the working process. Although traces of this significant baggage can be found in Moholy-Nagy's theoretical construction, his proposals did not suggest the political articulation of the state as did Constructivist theory in the Soviet Union of the early 1920s. Moholy-Nagy's organicism was not ideological but social, more attentive to the aesthetic experience that arose more from the management of labor power than from the political form it took within the state.[fig.10] As such, it was geared towards what Anson Rabinbach labeled "transcendental materialism": the biological, technical, and cosmic unity that industry had promised in the modern era.[51] As the bio-technical synthesis embracing production and perception, texture was not the surrogate for ornament that Moholy-Nagy had announced, but rather a form (among others) that ornament could take in modern industrial societies where the means of production had radically been altered. Once it had metamorphosed, the concept of *Faktura* could join the social contract that modern architecture had claimed during the multiple episodes in which its teleological and mechanical understanding of history had been disclosed.

1 I'm using the term "tact" since it possesses social connotations that the term "touch" lacks. As I argue in this article, the tactility of modern industrial production relates to a social and aesthetic contract.

2 For instance, an early example of the new role the sense of touch will play in twentieth-century culture was provided by Marinetti's 1921 *Manifesto of Tactilism*, which had advocated for the use of tactile boards in the education of the entire post-World War I generation. To the Italian artist, theorist, and provocateur, the emphasis on tact—which, in contrast to sight and speech, he deemed significantly a "mediocre conductor of thought"—did not mean a return to primitivism in a mechanical era, but an erotic form of communication that offered an alternative to the abused traditional plastic arts. Interestingly, the word "texture" did not appear a single time in Marinetti's "invention" of Tactilism. Filippo Marinetti introduced this argument at the Théâtre de l'Œuvre in Paris on January 11, 1921. See *Marinetti: Selected Writings*, ed. R. W. Flint, trans. Arthur A. Cappotelli, (New York: Farrar, Straus and Giroux, 1972). The "invention" of Tactilism, claims Marinetti, happened while he was standing nude on the coast at Antignano, next to a street named for Amerigo Vespucci, discoverer of South America. Marinetti published the article in the

Hungarian avant-garde magazine MA.
Filippo Marinetti, "A Taktilizmus," MA 6:7
(1921): 91–92.

3   László Moholy-Nagy, *Vision in Motion*
(Chicago: Paul Theobald, 1947), 44. Moholy-
Nagy had already introduced the identification
between texture and ornament at a symposium
organized by Paul Zucker at the Cooper Union
three years earlier. See Paul Zucker, ed., *New
Architecture and City Planning* (New York: Philosophical Library, 1944), 675–687.

4   Scholarship in the last decades has
underscored the intricate relationship between
gender, fashion, objects, and ornaments, complicating the role ornament has played in
modern architecture.

5   Walter Gropius, "Education of Architects and Designers," *Scope of Total Architecture*
(New York: Collier Books, 1962), 53. Originally
published as "Training the Architect," *Twice a
Year* 2 (1939). Marcel Breuer, "Must Architecture Be Sterile?" transcript of a speech given at
the Architectural League, New York, 1950,
Smithsonian Archives of American Art, box 7,
reel 5718, frame 977.

6   Moholy-Nagy, *Vision in Motion*, 42.

7   Moholy-Nagy arrived to Chicago in 1937
to found the New Bauhaus in Chicago. After
the first year, the Association of Arts and Industries, the industrial trustees that initially supported the project, abandoned it. Following a
moment of uncertainty, Moholy-Nagy reopened
the school in 1939 as the Chicago School of
Design. In 1944, the school took as its final
name the Chicago Institute of Design, affiliated
with the Illinois Institute of Technology. See
Sibyl Moholy-Nagy, *Moholy-Nagy: Experiment in
Totality* (Cambridge, MA: MIT Press, 1950).

8   "Texture" (26) was, after "relationship"
(32), "emotional" (31), "expression" (31), and
"structure" (28) the fifth most indexed word in
the book, way more frequent than classic Modernist catchwords such as "space" (16) and
"time" (6).

9   Previously, Moholy-Nagy had already
staged the new social, biological, and cultural
contract generated by the irruption of new
apparatuses of reproduction in his earlier work
following the influence of scientists such as
Raoul Francé. *Vision in Motion* instead was an
attempt to ideologically situate material production in the emerging US postwar design

context. Oliver A. I. Botar describes a network
of scientists and philosophers diminishing the
relevance of positivism, mechanism, and materialism to favor forces at work that were neither
physical nor chemical. This group of thinkers
includes, among others, Henri Bergson, William
James, George Simmel, Ludwig Klaes, Ernst
Mach, and Patrick Geddes. Botar identifies this
movement as a trans-geographical *Weltan-
schauung* grounded in philosophies of life tran-
scending the incompleteness of materialism.
Oliver Árpád István Botar, "Prolegomena to the
Study of Biomorphic Modernism, Biocentrism,
László Moholy-Nagy's New Vision, and Erno
Kállai's Bioromantik," PHD dissertation, Uni-
versity of Toronto, 1998. See also Oliver A. I.
Botar and Hattula Moholy-Nagy, eds., *Hun-
garian Studies Review, Special Volume: Proceedings of
the Conference "László Moholy-Nagy: Translating
Utopia into Action,"* 37:1–2 (2010): 47–59. Oliver
A. I. Botar, "Defining Biocentrism," in Oliver
A. I. Botar and Isabel Wünsche, eds., *Biocentrism
and Modernism* (Burlington: Ashgate Publishing
Company), 15–46. Oliver A. I. Botar, *Technical
Detours: The Early Moholy-Nagy Reconsidered*, exh.
cat. (New York: Art Gallery of the Graduate
Center, The City University of New York,
2006); Oliver A. I. Botar, *Sensing the Future:
Moholy-Nagy, Media and the Arts* (Zurich: Lars
Müller Publishers, 2014).

10   Although printed in Rome, the magazine
was founded by American writers Harold Loeb
and Alfred Kreymborg with the idea of taking
advantage of the lower European costs of production. The journal was edited in New York
and distributed within the United States.

11   The relevance of that book in postwar
architecture cannot be overlooked. Reyner
Banham, for instance, described it as the text
that "occupies the unexpected position of being
at the same time the first book entirely derived
from the Modern Movement, and also one of
the first to point the way to the next steps
forward." Reyner Banham, *Theory and Design in
the First Machine Age* (New York: Praeger Publishers, 1967), 319.

12   Walter Gropius, "Preface," *The New
Vision and Abstract of an Artist* (New York: George
Wittenborn, 1947), 5.

13   See Siegfried Kracauer, "The Mass
Ornament," *The Mass Ornament: Weimar Essays*,
ed. Thomas Y. Levin, trans. Thomas Y. Levin

*Pep
Avilés*

Faktur,
Photography,
and
the
Image
of
Labor

81

(Cambridge, MA: Harvard University Press, 1995), 75–88. Originally published in 1927 as *Das Ornament der Masse*.

14   László Moholy-Nagy, *The New Vision: From Material to Architecture* (New York: Brewer, Warren and Putnam, Inc., 1932), 35. The remarkable differences between the two editions compels me to cite them as different sources.

15   They all, particularly *Faktur*, presented their own difficulties to Daphne M. Hoffmann, the English translator of the work. The ideological and cultural nuances of the original term became lost in translation; the word's root lies in "manufacture," which in English had long ceased to refer to an object's mode of production. The same holds true for German, in which, despite the existence of a false cognate, the term emerged as a neologism in Western art circles in the 1920s. Yet the lack of precision in the translation of *Faktur* as "surface appearance" reveals another ornamental form—the projection of transient images onto existing surfaces—that was equally valid to him. The ghost-like character of ornamental shades, contrasts, and projections in some of Moholy-Nagy's photographic work announced the changing character of material textures in architecture and design.

16   Late twentieth-century scholarship brought to the fore the centrality of the term in the intellectual, theoretical and cultural development of the artistic avant-gardes. For literature on the origins and evolution of the term *Faktur* in Russian art and literature, see Margit Rowell, "Vladimir Tatlin: Form/Faktura," *October* 7 (Winter 1978): 83–108; Benjamin Buchloh, "From Faktura to Factography," *October* 30 (Autumn 1984): 82–119; Maria Gough, "Faktura. The Making of the Russian Avant-garde," RES: *Anthropology and Aesthetics* 36 (Autumn 1999): 32–59; Christina Lodder, *Russian Constructivism* (London & New Haven: Yale University Press, 1983); Isabelle Wünsche, "Organic Visions and Biological Models in Russian Avant-garde Art," Oliver Botar and Isabelle Wünsche, eds., *Biocentrism and Modernism* (Burlington; VT: Ashgate, 2011).

17   David Burliuk, "Cubism (Surface-Plane)" and "Faktura" (1912), Anna Kafetsi, ed., *Russian Avant-garde 1910–1930: The G. Costakis Collection* (Athens: The National Gallery and the

European Cultural Center of Delphi, 1995), 474–79.

18   "We find landscapes made out of multi-colored sand, dust ... When (Jean-Antoine) Watteau returned to a canvas which had been used he indifferently wiped it with oil and over-painted ... The oil dish which he constantly used was filled with filth and dust ...": in Vladimir Markov, "Texture Material," Anna Kafetsi, ed., *Russian Avant-garde 1910–1930: The G. Costakis Collection* (Athens: The National Gallery and the European Cultural Center of Delphi, 1995), 496–97.

19   Vladimir Markov, 496.

20   Quoted in Christina Lodder, *Russian Constructivism* (London & New Haven: Yale University Press, 1983), 94.

21   Aleksei Gan, "Constructivism," in Anna Kafetsi, ed., *Russian Avant-garde 1910–1930: The G. Costakis Collection* (Athens: The National Gallery and the European Cultural Center of Delphi, 1995), trans. Igor Serebriakov, 693. Originally published as *Konstruktivismi* (Tver, 1922). Recent English edition: Cristina Lodder, ed., *Aleksei Gan. Constructivism*, trans. Cristina Lodder (Barcelona, Editorial Tenov, 2013).

22   Gan, "Constructivism," 693.

23   Moholy-Nagy contacted Aleksandr Rodchenko in the mid-1920s about a publishing opportunity in the *Bauhausbücher* series.

24   Josef Albers interviewed by Irving Louis Finkelstein, New Haven, April 16, 1967, original tape recording in the Historical Sound Recordings Collection, Yale University Library, YT7-4287, tape 1, side A, track 2. I would like to thank Brenda Danilowitz, Chief Curator at the Josef & Anni Albers Foundation in New Haven, for providing the sound recording of the interview.

25   Albers's lecture was preceded by another one delivered in Prague in 1928, in which he first formulated his agenda.

26   Moholy-Nagy and his wife moved to Berlin from Dessau a year after Gropius's departure, and the definitions procured from Albers were lost in the interim. However, upon their request, Albers provided the couple with the materials a second time.

27   The events leading to the publication of Malevich's book are worth recalling: Malevich received permission to travel outside the Soviet Union in 1927. After a trip to Poland, he stayed in Berlin from March to June of the same year. On April 6, he traveled to Dessau, accompanied by Polish poet Tadeusz Peiper to meet Walter and Ise Gropius, László Moholy-Nagy, Hannes Meyer, and Nina and Wassily Kandinsky. During the meeting, reported by Peiper to a Polish magazine in Kraków, they spoke about the relation between "purely aesthetic forms" and both architecture and utilitarian objects. In a letter dated to the following day, Ise Gropius stated that plans to publish a book were made during that meeting. Soon later, Moholy-Nagy visited Malevich in Berlin, where they agreed to publish two manuscripts: "Introduction to the Theory of the Additional Element in Painting" and "Suprematism" under the title *Die gegenstandslose Welt*. Malevich, who during this trip also met Ludwig Mies van der Rohe and befriended Hugo Häring, was accused three years later of espionage. The original manuscripts were condensed by Moholy-Nagy. Although Walter Gropius also appears as an editor of the book, his contribution was more institutional than personal. For a full account of the events, see Lloyd C. Engelbrecht, *Moholy-Nagy: Mentor of Modernism*, 2 vols. (Cincinnati: Flying Trapeze Press, 2009), 291–99; Andrei Kanov, *Kazimir Malewicz, Catalogue Raisonné* (Paris: A Biro, 2002); Kazimir Malevich, *Die gegenstandslose Welt: Bauhausbücher* II (München: Albert Langen, 1927); Kazimir Malevich "I/45. An Introduction to the Theory of the Additional Element in Painting," *The World as a Non-Objectivity; Unpublished Writings, 1922–1925, Vol. III*, Troels Andersen ed., trans. Xenia Glowacki-Pruss and Edmund T. Little (Copenhagen: Borgen, 1976), 147–94; Kazimir Malevich, *The Non-Objective World*, trans. Howard Dearstyne (Chicago: Paul Theobald, 1959). Howard Dearstyne, an American, had been a student at the Bauhaus in 1926.

28 Lyonel Feininger to Julia Feininger, March 9, 1925. Quoted in Frank Whitford, ed., *The Bauhaus: Masters & Students by Themselves* (New York: The Overlook Press, 1993), 166.

29 Walter Gropius to Sibyl Moholy-Nagy, August 11, 1949, Bauhaus-Archiv Berlin.

30 The expression "ornamental abstraction" is taken from Hans M. Wingler, *The Bauhaus: Weimar, Dessau, Berlin, Chicago*, trans. Wolfgang Jabs and Basil Gilbert (Cambridge, MA: MIT Press), 284.

31 Johannes Itten, *Mein Vorkurs am Bauhaus. Gestaltungs- und Formlehre* (Ravensburg, O. Maier, 1963). English edition: *Design and Form: The Basic Course at the Bauhaus and Later*, trans. John Maass (New York: Reinhold Publishing Corporation, 1964), 45–46. See also Kai-Uwe Hemken, "Clash of the Natural and the Mechanical Human, Theo Van Doesburg versus Johannes Itten, 1922," in Philipp Oswalt, ed., *Bauhaus Conflicts, 1919–2009: Controversies and Counterparts*, (Ostfildern: Hatje Cantz Verlag, 2009), 34–49.

32 On Moholy-Nagy heading the workshop and Josef Albers having an independent studio, see Hans Maria Wingler, *The Bauhaus: Weimar, Dessau, Berlin, Chicago*, trans. Wolfgang Jabs and Basil Gilbert (Cambridge, MA: MIT Press), 291.

33 Moholy-Nagy, along with Raoul Hausmann, Hans Arp, and Ivan Puni, had previously advocated for elementary art. See "Aufruf zur elementaren Kunst," *De Stijl* IV:10, 136.

34 See Brigid Doherty, "László Moholy-Nagy: Construction in Enamel, 1923," in Barry Bergdoll, Leah Dickerman, eds., *Bauhaus 1919–1933: Workshops of Modernity* (New York: Museum of Modern Art, 2009), 130–37.

35 Rainer K. Wick, *Bauhaus Pädagogik* (Köln: DuMont, 1982), 125. See also Norbert M. Schmitz, "The Preliminary Course under László Moholy-Nagy: Sensory Competence," in Jeannine Fiedler and Peter Feierabend, eds., *Bauhaus* (Cologne: Könemann, 1999), 368–73. Schmitz traces the pedagogical commitment of Moholy-Nagy back to the Enlightenment and particularly to Friedrich Schiller's "model of an aesthetic education as the reconciliation of necessity and freedom." However, his description of the "elimination of the subjective view" in the duplication that occurs in photograms is disputable. See also Michael W. Jennings, "László Moholy-Nagy: Photograms," in Barry Bergdoll, Leah Dickerman, eds., *Bauhaus 1919–1933: Workshops of Modernity* (New York: Museum of Modern Art, 2009), 130–37.

36 Hannes Meyer will use the term *Oberflächenstruktur* to express similar qualities to those referred to by Moholy-Nagy. See Hannes Meyer, "Bauen," *Bauhaus* 2/3 (1928): 12.

37 *Arkhitektura raboty arkhitekturnogo fakul'teta Vkhutemasa* (Moscow: Vkhutemas, 1927).

38 Josef Albers, "Werklicher Formunterricht," *Bauhaus* 2/3 (1928): 3–7.

Pep Avilés

Faktur, Photography, and the Image of Labor

83

39 Josef Albers, "Creative Education," Hans Maria Wingler, ed., *The Bauhaus: Weimar, Dessau, Berlin, Chicago* (Cambridge, MA: MIT Press, 1969), 143.

40 For the intellectual, material, and discursive threads making possible the art forms emerging in the Bauhaus context, from paintings, interior designs and tapestries to the final accomplishment of architecture, specifically after the involvement of Gunta Stölzl and Anni Albers—that is, from the migration of the school to Dessau onwards—see T'ai Smith, *Bauhaus Weaving Theory: From Feminine Craft to Mode of Design* (Minneapolis: University of Minnesota Press, 2014).

41 "Wir klassifizieren die erscheinungen der werkstoff epidermis (aussenschicht) als wesentlich unterschieden in struktur, faktur, und texture. ihre verwertung geschieht mehr malend als bauend, so dass räumlichkeit, überschneidung und durchdringung als illusion auftreten. besonderes interesse an der materie ist eine erscheinung der besonders konstruktiv eingestellten epochen. so ist dieses kapitel sehr von der gotik gepflegt worden, wie es nachher vernachlässigt wurde, als fassade und raum, gerät und kleider nur in einem stoff gemacht wurden, als wände und möbel und dielen ganz mit farbe zugestrichen wurden." Josef Albers, "Werklicher Formunterricht," *Bauhaus* 2/3 (1928): 6. English translation in 1938: "We classify the appearance of the surface of a material as to structure, facture, and texture, which we differentiate carefully. These qualities of surface can be combined and graduated somewhat as colors in painting. The systematic arrangement of surface qualities in scales and series makes one sensitive to the minutest differences and the subtlest transitions in the tactile qualities of surfaces, such as hard to soft, smooth to rough, warm to cold, straight-edged to shapeless, polished to mat; also in the visual qualities of surfaces such as wide-meshed and narrow-meshed; transparent and opaque; clear and clouded." Probably translated by Ise Gropius. Josef Albers, "Concerning Fundamental Design," in Herbert Bayer, Walter Gropius, and Ise Gropius, eds., *Bauhaus 1919–1928* [1938] (Boston: Charles T. Branford Company, 1959), 116–18.

42 László Moholy-Nagy, "Unprecedented Photography," *Photography in the Modern Era: European Documents and Critical Writings,* *1913–1940*, trans. Joel Agee (New York: The Metropolitan Museum of Art, 1989), 79–82. Originally published as "Die beispiellos Fotografie," *Das Deutsche Lichtbild* (Berlin, 1927), x–xi; also published in *i10*, 1 (1927): 114–17. See also "Produktion-Reproduktion," *De Stijl* 7 (July 1922).

43 László Moholy-Nagy, "Response by László Moholy-Nagy," in Christopher Phillips, ed., *Photography in the Modern Era: European Documents and Critical Writings, 1913–1940*, trans. Harvey L. Mendelsohn (New York: The Metropolitan Museum of Art, 1989), 101. Originally published in *i10* 1: 6 (1927): 227–40.

44 László Moholy-Nagy, *Von Material zu Architektur: Bauhausbücher* 14 (Münich, Albert Langen Verlag, 1929), 33.

45 Moholy-Nagy, *Von Material zu Architektur*, 33.

46 László Moholy-Nagy, "Ismus oder Kunst," *Vivos Voco* 8/9 (August 1926): 8. The English edition translates the term as "surface-texture." See Hans Maria Wingler, ed., *The Bauhaus: Weimar, Dessau, Berlin, Chicago* (Cambridge, MA: MIT Press, 1969), 116.

47 Josef Albers, "Concerning Fundamental Design," in Herbert Bayer, Walter Gropius, and Ise Gropius, eds., *Bauhaus 1919–1928*, [1938] (Boston: Charles T. Branford Company, 1959), 118.

48 For Josef Albers's postwar approach to pedagogy, see Jeffrey Saletnik, "Pedagogic Objects: Josef Albers, Greenbergian Modernism, and the Bauhaus in America," in Jeffrey Saletnik and Robin Schuldenfrei, eds., *Bauhaus Construct: Fashioning Identity, Discourse and Modernism* (New York, Routledge, 2009), 83–102.

49 Walter Gropius, "Toward a Living Architecture: Ornament and Modern Architecture," *American Architect and Architecture* 152: 2665 (January 1938): 22.

50 László Moholy-Nagy, "Abstract of an Artist," *The New Vision* (New York: George Wittenborn, Inc., 1967), 76.

51 See Anson Rabinbach, *The Human Motor: Energy, Fatigue, and the Origins of Modernity* (Berkeley: University of California Press, 1990).

Part 1

Theories
of
Bauhaus
Materiality

Elizabeth Otto

Queer Coded Bauhaus

Pictorial representation has long been recognized for its ability to convey meaning through suggestion, symbols, and allegory; this has allowed artists and others to discretely communicate ideas to some viewers in ways that others would likely not perceive. Jonathan Katz refers to this tradition as "the art of the code," an approach mastered by many queer artists living in diverse contexts under regimes that criminalized their desires.[1]

In his instructively titled essay, "Hide/Seek," Katz points to how "the social universe of sexual desire, in painting, as in life, is so often of necessity communicated through the subtlest gestures, glances, and codes. When the desire in question is literally illegal, it is all the more fugitive, such that images of queer historical import ... have passed under our contemporary perception utterly undetected."[2] Further, this dynamic is familiar to members of subcultures "long used to employing protective camouflage, while at the same time searching for tiny signs, clues, or signals that might reveal the presence of other queer people."[3]

While the Bauhaus's leadership does not appear to have been particularly welcoming to gay and lesbian students, at least one student who we know in retrospect was queer joined the school the year that it opened, Max Peiffer Watenphul. Remembered mostly for his modernist city and landscape paintings, Peiffer Watenphul had already completed a law degree and a doctorate when he encountered an exhibition of Paul Klee's paintings and decided to come to the Bauhaus in 1919 to become an artist.[4] Peiffer Watenphul was immediately singled out as highly talented; Gropius gave him a studio of his own and permitted him to move freely among the workshops so as to have full autonomy in his experimentation without having to prove himself through the preliminary course. He remained at the school for

Fig. 1. Max Peiffer Watenphul, slit tapestry, circa 1921, white, grey, yellow, blue, black, and red toned hemp and wool (137 × 76 cm).

four semesters and stayed on in Weimar until 1923.[5] Part of his diverse production from his two Bauhaus years is a colorful slit tapestry, made sometime around 1921.[fig.1] At the Bauhaus, weaving was generally viewed as women's work. The vast majority of the workshop's members were women, and, for a period of time starting in 1920, the workshop was also called simply "the women's class."[6] Its clear female dominance caused Oskar Schlemmer to joke, "where there's wool you'll women find, weaving just to pass the time."[7] Because of this extremely strong gendered link, one could view this object as coded in terms of what we might call "medium drag," in which the artist is to some extent feminized by engaging a gendered mode of production. As in performative drag, this kind of crossing is playful and is usually perceived to be temporary. And indeed, the critical reception with respect to this tapestry is often at pains to emphasize that this was Peiffer Watenphul's one, brilliant weaving. The resulting work, with its bold color and abstraction through elementary forms, was perceived as quintessentially Bauhaus. In this case at least, the Bauhaus was quite tolerant of a man crossing into feminized territory; the tapestry was selected for reproduction in the 1923 *Staatliches Bauhaus* exhibition catalogue.[8]

When Peiffer Watenphul left Weimar in 1923, he continued to frequent Bauhaus circles and maintained strong friendships with Maria Cyrenius and Grete Willers, both Bauhaus weavers, and subsequently became close friends with Florence Henri and her partner Margarete Schall, also both *Bauhäusler*.[9] And it was largely through his photographic work, fostered within this circle and particularly through his friendship with Henri, that Peiffer Watenphul began making overtly

Elizabeth Otto

Queer Coded Bauhaus

queer photographs in the late 1920s, campy portraits of women and men dressed for debauchery or in drag. He also made at least two photographs of a beautiful male lover. Encoded in that abstract, woven tapestry of 1921, Peiffer Watenphul's singular experiment in the feminized medium of weaving, is his dawning consciousness of gender fluidity and play. This consciousness would later blossom in photographic realism that spoke clearly and without shame, in images of his friends and lovers that rewrite the code of what Bauhaus could be.

This text is drawn from *Haunted Bauhaus: Occult Spirituality, Gender Fluidity, Queer Identities, and Radical Politics*, published by MIT Press, Cambridge, Massachusetts, 2019.

1 Jonathan Katz, "The Art of the Code: Jasper Johns and Robert Rauschenberg," in *Significant Others: Creativity and Intimate Partnership*, ed. Whitney Chadwick and Isabelle de Courtivron (New York: Thames & Hudson 1993), 188–207, 251–152.
2 Jonathan Katz, "Hide/Seek: Difference and Desire in American Portraiture," in *Hide/Seek: Difference and Desire in American Portraiture*, ed. Jonathan Katz and David C. Ward (Washington, D.C.: Smithsonian Books, 2010), 14.
3 Katz, "Hide/Seek," 14.
4 On Peiffer Watenphul's paintings, see Mario-Andreas von Lüttichau, ed., *Max Peiffer Watenphul: von Weimar nach Italien* (Cologne: Dumont, 1999), esp. his painting of Gertrud Grunow, 18.
5 Ingrid Radewaldt, "Simple Form for the Necessities of Life: The Weaving Workshop at the Bauhaus in Weimar," in *Bauhaus: A Conceptual Model*, ed. Bauhaus-Archiv Berlin/Museum für Gestaltung, Stiftung Bauhaus Dessau, and Klassik Stiftung Weimar (Ostfildern: Hatje Cantz, 2009), 81–84.
6 Over the lifetime of the weaving workshop, thirteen men studied there, compared to 128 women. See Patrick Rössler and Anke Blümm, "Soft Skills and Hard Facts: A Systematic Overview of Bauhaus Women's Presence and Roles," in *Bauhaus Bodies: Gender, Sexuality, and Body Culture in Modernism's Legendary Art School*, ed. Elizabeth Otto and Patrick Rössler (New York: Bloomsbury Visual Arts, 2019), 3–24.

7 Oskar Schlemmer, quoted in Magdalena Droste, *Bauhaus* (Cologne: Taschen, 1990), 72.
8 *Staatliches Bauhaus Weimar, 1919–1923* (Weimar: Bauhausverlag, 1923), 136. While this is Peiffer Watenphul's one woven work, it was so well received that a copy was made of it. Only one version is now extant, and no one, including Peiffer Watenphul himself later in his life, knows which version it is. See Radewaldt, "Simple Form," 82.
9 Photography, posing, and dress up played a part in these friendships, as photographs taken over the decades document. See Grace Watenphul Pasqualucci and Alessandra Pasqualucci, *Max Peiffer Watenphul: Werkverzeichnis*, v. 2: *Zeichnungen, Emailarbeiten, Textilien, Druckgraphik, Photographie* (Cologne: Dumont, 1993), 411–420.

Persephone Allen

The Metallic Sphere as Mechanical Eye: Reflected Identities at the Bauhaus

The camera has offered us amazing possibilities, which we are only just beginning to exploit. The visual image has been expanded and even the modern lens is no longer tied to the narrow limits of our eye.[1] In 1925, László Moholy-Nagy published his manifesto for the "New Vision" as the eighth volume in the *Bauhaus-bücher* series, entitled *Painting, Photography, Film.* In this foundational theorization

Moholy-Nagy reimagined the possibilities of photography and the moving image, asserting that only these new modes of production could adequately represent the increasingly mechanized modern world. This spirited call for experiments in new media inscribed his legacy on the Bauhaus trajectory. Though no courses in photography were officially offered until 1929, by which point Moholy-Nagy had resigned from the faculty, he and his then-wife Lucia were integral in fostering students' and masters' interest in the medium. An intimate and captivating visual record of the school's activities resulted, leaving an underexplored archive ripe for further research.[2]

Within photography produced at the Bauhaus, an enigmatic motif of smooth, highly reflective, metallic spheres appears in more than twenty surviving photographic portraits and still lifes created by multiple *Bauhäusler* and their colleagues between 1921 and 1931. Rarely studied together yet repeatedly published and reproduced in Bauhaus books and exhibitions without interrogation of their deeper significance, these images and the uniquely modern visualization they comprise demand closer attention and analysis.[3] Together they evidence *Bauhäusler* interest in the creation of altered perceptions of reality, exploratory modes of self-reflection, and new relationships to modern materials.

The shiny surfaces of the metallic spheres are most frequently explored in the photographs of two Bauhaus masters, Georg Muche (1895–1987) of the weaving workshop (1919–27) and Marianne Brandt (1893–1983) of the metal workshop (1928–29). Although both were integral figures at the school, neither emigrated. As a result, neither regained the professional success they had enjoyed at the Bauhaus nor featured prominently in early histories of the school. As both a woman and someone who remained in East Germany, Brandt was initially relegated to the peripheries by authors who stressed male *Bauhäuslers'* contributions. Due to the scholarship of Elizabeth Otto and Ulrike Müller, among others, Brandt is now recognized as one of the school's foremost designers.

By analyzing the origin and development of the metallic sphere in Muche's and Brandt's photographs alongside primary texts by Muche, Brandt, Moholy-Nagy, and others, I argue that their explorations of the sphere should be read as an extension of what Moholy-Nagy terms "the amazing possibilities" of experimentation with optics, as well as complex investigations into modernity, materiality, and individual and collective identities at the school. In particular, the spheres reflect and reveal the paradoxical nature of the school's attempt to come to terms with modernity. Brandt's and Muche's interrogations of the sphere— an object that reflects yet distorts—gain heightened significance when re-contextualized within the history of the school in Weimar Germany.

Georg Muche was the first *Bauhäusler* to take and publish a series of experimental photographs with reflective spheres. Six of these photographs survive as prints or glass negatives in European and American museum collections. The dating of these photographs varies between 1920 and 1922. All but one of the images follow the same formal structure: a closely cropped sphere reveals the warped reflection of various rooms. Half of the images feature shadowy figures on the peripheries of the reflected interiors; two feature figures prominently, and one, Muche's *Self-Portrait*, reveals the artist himself. These photographs predate by at least a year, maybe more, the arrival of László and Lucia Moholy-Nagy at the Staatliches Bauhaus Weimar in 1923 and the school's redirection towards technology. As such, they constitute revelatory documents of the school's foundational years and early iterations of the machine aesthetic that later became synonymous with Bauhaus design. They also illustrate Muche's own developing vision as an artist, his sense of mastery, and his testing of the possibilities of representation with photography and new materials.

Persephone
Allen

The
Metallic
Sphere
as
Mechanical
Eye

91

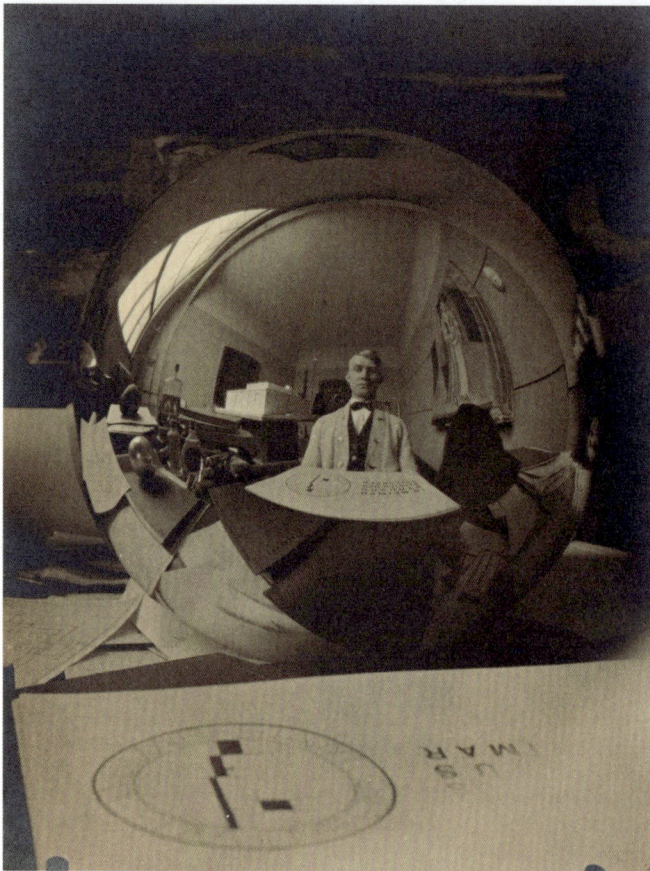

Fig. 1. Georg Muche, *Self-Portrait (Selbstporträt)*, circa 1921/22, gelatin silver print, 15.9 × 12 cm.

In Muche's *Self-Portrait*, [fig.1] the metallic sphere is centrally placed amidst a pile of papers and drawing tools in seeming disarray, angular papers sharply contrasting with the seamless perfection of the sphere.[4] Muche has positioned himself slightly off-center and leaning towards his left, underlining the sphere's potential to destabilize and distort in its reflections. He appears seated in front of his crowded desk, his hands hidden, his expression neutral and stoic as he stares directly into the sphere and meets the viewer's gaze. Framed by a large figural painting and a small plaster cast of a face on his left and tall windows on his right, the camera lens peeks over Muche's right shoulder, beyond which is a gleaming white model of the Haus Am Horn, his winning architectural design for the 1923 Bauhaus Exhibition competition. Stressing efficiency and functionality, the Haus Am Horn advanced the Bauhaus vocabulary of geometry and industrial materials.[5]

Directly in front of the sphere lies a prominently branded Bauhaus publication, identifiable by the black outline of a stylized, rectilinear face in profile inscribed within a pair of circles between which the school's name is faintly printed. The pamphlet is visible twice: in front of the sphere and reflected in the sphere's surface. Muche has arranged the pamphlet so that it faces away from him and towards the sphere, allowing the viewer to read it in the reflection. This deliberate positioning and explicit inclusion of the Bauhaus logo suggest the performative staging of this scene and Muche's claim to a position of leadership at the school. Muche investigates the studio he oversaw in a second photograph entitled *Reflection: The Weaving Workshop in the Ball* (1921), which may also be understood as a kind of self-portrait.[fig.2]

As before, *Reflection* features a single, closely cropped, metallic sphere. Barely contained within the photograph's horizontal edges, the sphere's curves exaggerate the size of the reflected room so that it, too, appears vast. Naturally lit by an expansive bank of windows, the room is sparsely furnished with relatively rudimentary weaving

Fig.2. Georg Muche, *Reflection: The Weaving Workshop in the Ball (Spiegelung: Die Webereiwerkstatt in der Kugel)*, circa 1921, gelatin silver print, 15.9 × 11.9 cm.

equipment: hand-operated, wooden looms and spinning wheels on the workshop floor with naked, unlit light bulbs above. Three or more women sit at looms, seemingly engrossed in their work, and on their left, a large dark doorway opens onto a group of people gazing at the ball from an adjacent room. Directly confronting the viewer is an operator-less camera, the dark gleam of the lens just barely visible on the surface of the large black box standing on tripod legs. Here, the lens replaces the artist's gaze. The juxtaposition of the polished, mirror-like sphere beside the unruly piles of yarn and spools of thread suggests the school's ambition to move into the mechanized future while also reflecting the reality of their use of traditional and increasingly old-fashioned methods of production.

This tension between the school's desire to harness the possibilities of industrialized production and the realities of what was achievable within their limited budget was a common theme throughout the school's fourteen-year existence, especially during the Weimar years. Muche's photographs add to this discourse in a number of ways. At this period in the school's history the gleaming sphere is an unusually clear and early visualization of interest in objects that evoke machine production. It is also uncommon to have such a cohesive body of photographic work at this early point when students and masters were only beginning to experiment with the medium.[6] Finally, as these photographs simultaneously predate the arrival of the Moholy-Nagys and assert an emerging interest in the aesthetics of technology, they call into question traditional notions of Bauhaus creativity and networks of influence.

Accepting Gropius's invitation to take over the position of weaving workshop *Formmeister,* Muche arrived at the Bauhaus in Weimar in 1919 as the youngest master aged twenty-five. He had trained as a painter at the Ažbe-Kunstschule in Munich, and then moved to Berlin, where he worked and exhibited at the Gallery Der Sturm and associated

Persephone Allen

The
Metallic
Sphere
as
Mechanical
Eye

art school. Berlin, Germany's political and cultural capital, exposed Muche to a cosmopolitan, artistic avant-garde. There, he developed his own style of colorful, abstract painting deeply influenced by Expressionist artists who, employing saturated colors, extreme angles, and distorted views, rejected realism and sought to depict the world as it was felt. In Berlin, Muche exhibited with Paul Klee and Alexander Archipenko, met members of the Novembergruppe, and formed acquaintances with Dadaists Raoul Hausmann and Hans Richter. Both Hausmann and Richter experimented with photography and would exhibit with Muche at the 1918 Galerie Dada exhibition in Zurich. In 1917, Muche briefly left Berlin to serve in the infantry during the First World War, but suffered a nervous collapse within a year of enlistment. After recuperating, he returned to his position at the Gallery Der Sturm, but left shortly after to take up his position in Weimar in 1919.

Writing decades after the disbandment of the school and a second devastating world war, Muche recalled, "the Bauhaus was a revolutionary institution ... We understood Gropius's ideas and transformed them, and we were transformed by Gropius."[7] Muche's reminiscence conveys his admiration for the Bauhaus as a site of metamorphosis and most likely, respite, after witnessing mechanized warfare firsthand. Viewed in this context, the bright sphere he photographed appears representative not only of his optimistic outlook, but also his spiritualism. Initially, Muche experimented not only with photography at the Bauhaus, but also with deepening and diversifying his spiritual interests under the tutelage of his friend and colleague, Johannes Itten.

Itten was one of Gropius's earliest and eventually most controversial appointments. He believed in educating the whole being and applied this approach to developing the *Vorkurs*, in which students received foundational training in craft and design aimed at evoking individual responses and sharpening their optic and haptic sensibilities.[8] Muche's heightened haptic sensitivity is apparent in his choice of the smooth-surfaced sphere—a clear departure from the loose, rough brushwork in his paintings. Itten also cultivated students' self-expression with esoteric methods that drew from a variety of unconventional sources, including Theosophy, Indian mysticism, Buddhism, Confucianism, and the Mazdaznan cult based on Zoroastrianism.[9] Although these methods attracted heated critiques from colleagues, Muche was a staunch follower; fellow faculty member Oskar Schlemmer described him as "Itten's second and assistant."[10] Muche also co-taught Itten's mandatory "Course on Form," according to which the sphere represented "infinite movement," and the circle, "infinite symmetry" and "peace."[11] Would these ideas and broader cultural associations of the sphere as symbolic of wholeness and unity have resonated with Muche as stabilizing elements in the chaos of postwar Germany? Goethe's *Altar of Agathé Tyché* (1777), located nearby in the garden of his Weimar residence, would have offered another notable example of a sphere imbued with apotropaic symbolism, but in stone. Muche's photographs raise the question of why he chose the mirrored sphere as the focus of his portraits. Perhaps the clarity with which it reflected the world transformed also indicated the possibility of a spiritual rebirth through art/craft—the very sentiments upon which the Bauhaus was founded.[12] The sphere as an object of spiritual transcendence and social transformation also suggests parallels with the work of Expressionist architect Bruno Taut and poet Paul Scheerbart, whose radical ideas Muche could not have failed to encounter during his employment at the Gallery Der Sturm.[13]

The variety of perspectives Muche explored in his photographs conveys his enthusiasm for experimentation. Analyzed alongside his prints, paintings, and architectural designs from the Bauhaus period, his photographs show his willingness to explore the limits of representation and his responsiveness to the Bauhaus program as it shifted from utopian to functional design. He articulated that same responsiveness in his aforementioned recollection of the transformative experience of teaching at the school. Muche arrived at the Bauhaus as an Expressionist painter. He left with an enthusiasm for architecture and industrial materials and methods demonstrated by his photographs and his designs for the Haus Am Horn and the later Steel House (1926).

Muche's developing interest in technology suggests a final facet of his interest in the sphere whose unblemished surface embodies the precision of industrial manufacture. Photography, often referred to at the time as a mechanized or automated method of artmaking, represents one aspect of his growing interest in mechanization. Muche's purchase of the weaving workshop's first Jacquard looms in 1926 is another. While only semi-mechanized technology, they significantly streamlined the weaving process, transforming handwork into machine-work. Many of his students did not yet share his enthusiasm for mechanization and their subsequent rebellion in 1926 caused his resignation from the workshop.[14] Following his departure from the Bauhaus in 1927, Muche remained in Germany and continued to teach during and after the war at various art and design schools. Though he later published *Blickpunkt: Sturm, Dada, Bauhaus, Gegenwart* (1961) as a reflection on his career, it appears to have had little impact outside of Germany, and he remained a marginalized figure in international Bauhaus histories until his death in 1987.

Muche's photographs with the spheres stretched the possibilities of photography and thus represented new ways of seeing, but, for Muche, they also represent his evolving and, at times ambivalent, relationship to the school. The sphere encapsulates the school's kaleidoscopic vision—its visual program of stripped-down geometry and its material engagement with metals, such as aluminum and chromium-plated steel, which were among the new industrial materials Bauhaus practitioners considered appropriate for "modern," dust-free design. Muche's photographs evoke the machine aesthetic that has become synonymous with the Dessau Bauhaus, but were taken at least three years before the school's move from Weimar, predating Moholy-Nagy's, Brandt's, and others' adoption of it. As such, the spheres—and the photographs—challenge traditional views of the early years of the Bauhaus as being craft-oriented and suggest a more ambiguous relationship to technology.

The Bauhaus Exhibition of 1923 marks a turning point in the school's program. As German inflation peaked, so too did the school's financial and political troubles and the friction between Gropius and Itten, leading Itten to resign. His departure marked the end of the school's first phase and signaled its reorientation towards industry proclaimed by Gropius as "art and technology – a new unity."[15] To facilitate the school's turn towards functionalism, Gropius hired Moholy-Nagy as master of the metal workshop in 1923. Following Itten's departure, Gropius promoted Moholy-Nagy to director of the *Vorkurs*. Under his leadership, the aim of the course evolved from self-expression to industrial design.

In 1925, Moholy-Nagy published two of Muche's photographs with spheres in *Painting, Photography, Film*.[16] Moholy-Nagy identified one of the spheres as a *Gartenkugel* (garden ball), and the other as a *Konvex Spiegel* (convex mirror).[17] Juxtaposing Muche's images with another photograph of flat mirrors and panes of glass, as well as with a photograph titled *Arrested Laughter in the Distorting Mirror*, Moholy-Nagy demonstrated his interest in the mirror as a photographic tool for capturing altered versions of reality. Moholy-Nagy's main argument in *Painting, Photography, Film* asserted that photography was not just a means of documenting reality, but a method of discovering reality. While many photographs in the book have short accompanying explanations identifying how they illustrate this idea, Muche's images and those immediately preceding and following do not.

Three years later, Moholy-Nagy published "Photography is Manipulation of Light" (1928), in which he announced, "the limits of photography are incalculable ... The oblivious pathfinder is technology."[18] In particular, he advised that new meaning could be uncovered by photographing objects that reflect and distort light and explicitly encouraged the use of convex mirrors. Yet neither Moholy-Nagy nor Muche appear to have written about the metallic sphere itself as an object of interest—its precise purpose and function remain ambiguous. Was it a garden gazing ball? An unusual article of interior decoration? Muche's focus on the spheres solely in photographs suggests their "thingness" is not important to him. Although Brandt's relationship to the sphere and to functionality must have been more nuanced on account of her use of spherical forms in her metalwork, she, too, appears to have largely been interested in its surface qualities. For both, it is not so much about the sphere's use or purpose as an individual object, but how the camera could capture warped reflections in its polished, curvilinear surface to offer a vision of the world not available to the naked eye—a world rapidly changing on the multiple fronts of art, technology, culture, society, and politics. Many artists believed the onslaught of such intense and varied change impacted the way people perceived the world and as such, required new forms of representation.

Marianne Brandt enrolled as a student at the Bauhaus in 1924, one year after Moholy-Nagy's appointment. Within a year the school would be forced to close and relocate to the industrial city of Dessau. Brandt initially trained as a fine artist, studying sculpture and painting at the Weimar Grand Ducal College of Art between 1911 and 1918, with a brief sojourn in Munich between 1916 and 1917. Her paintings from this period have been described as predominantly Expressionist-inflected portraits of women and women with children that "shared a general mood of suppression and melancholy."[19] Brandt exhibited her work for the first time at the Galerie Gerstenberger in her home-town of Chemnitz in 1918, but left Germany soon after she married Norwegian painter and fellow student Erik Brandt in 1919. The couple lived together in Norway and Paris, the latter of which offered Brandt a cosmopolitan milieu in which to experiment with photography and photomontage and to explore her identity as a "New Woman."[20] Brandt left her husband and returned to Weimar in 1923 intending to continue her studies in sculpture, but, upon visiting the Bauhaus Ex-hibition, chose to enroll at the design school instead. She was thirty-one years old.

Following her successful completion of the *Vorkurs* and upon Moholy-Nagy's urging, she enrolled in the prestigious metal workshop. She was one of only eleven female students admitted and would be the only one to graduate. Eager to construct a new identity for herself at the school, Brandt burned her paintings in 1926.[21] Yet for all her enthu-siasm, Brandt's initial experience was challenging—particularly in the male-dominated metal workshop. Brandt recalled: "at first I was not accepted with pleasure—there was no place for a woman in a metal workshop ... They admitted this to me later on and meanwhile expressed their displeasure by giving me all sorts of dull, dreary work."[22] Despite such frustrations, she flourished. Employing the stripped-down vocabulary of pure geometry promoted by Moholy-Nagy, Brandt reinterpreted circles, squares, and triangles to create functional, do-mestic wares that became many of the most iconic pieces of metalwork produced at the Bauhaus. Moholy-Nagy later described her as "my best and most ingenious student (90% of all Bauhaus Designs are by her)."[23] Brandt also secured the largest number of contracts with indus-trial manufacturers, and, in 1928 when Moholy-Nagy resigned, she replaced him as acting master of the metal workshop.

1928 was the same year that she began taking photographs with metallic spheres. In total, between 1928 and 1929, she took seven self-portraits and one still life, the largest number of spherical portraits taken by any individual *Bauhäusler*. [figs. 3–6] Like Muche, Brandt posi-tioned herself with spheres in a naturally-lit studio and photographed her reflection from multiple perspectives. However, she departed from his model by presenting the sphere suspended from a chain in her studio window, exaggerating its potential to warp and distort by taking photographs from various odd angles—never head-on—and by incor-porating multiple spheres of different sizes into four of her portraits.

Although both Brandt and Muche were self-taught photographers, Brandt had been experimenting with photography and self-portraiture since 1917. Moreover, as a woman and a student, her experience at the Bauhaus was markedly more challenging and her engagement with the spheres in these photographs reflects the added difficulties she faced.

Three of her photographs are taken from below a suspended sphere.[fig.4] She uses the area surrounding the sphere to add visual interest and formal contrast. In each, Brandt stares up at her reflection and balances her own presence with dark window frames or shadowy corners of the room. Brandt took another pair of photographs by standing above a mass of mirrored orbs of various sizes strewn across her studio floor.[fig.5] In these, her open-legged stance communicates confidence and capability, emphasized by the way she holds her camera with one hand, while resting the other on her hip. In yet another photograph taken with a sphere, her presentation is less direct.[fig.6] She again holds the camera in one hand, but brings it close to her face. She balances on a window ledge and crops the sphere and her upper torso, focusing more on the snowy expanse outside her window. Brandt juxtaposes the bright white of the landscape against the darkness of the interior of her studio windowsill, the shiny surface of the sphere against the matte black window frame, and the sphere's curved edges against the window's rectilinear silhouette. Her expression intent, she looks up at the sphere and appears more focused on studying her reflection than engaging the viewer. Her mouth is slightly open with a sense of expectancy, perhaps of one who is experimenting and wondering whether her hypothesis will work.

The other self-portrait and most likely the earliest one taken (although determining precise chronology is difficult) is undeniably strange.[fig.3] Brandt appears to be exploring a similar study in contrasts; she has nestled one large mirrored sphere and one smaller sphere within the folds of a striped and crinkled piece of fabric. Body obscured, her head remains visible, seemingly floating free like one of the orbs. She peers up and meets the viewer's gaze but, as before, her wide-eyed stare communicates ambivalence.

A number of Brandt's later letters survive, providing rare firsthand insights into her experiences, as well as a lens for evaluating her portraits. In her most-frequently quoted text, "Letter to the Younger Generation," Brandt recounts her male colleagues' sexism, how little

Fig. 3. Marianne Brandt, *The Studio in the Sphere / Self-Portrait in the Studio, Bauhaus Dessau (Das Atelier in der Kugel / Selbstporträt im Atelier, Bauhaus Dessau)* circa 1928/29.

Fig. 4. Marianne Brandt, *Self-Portrait with Bauhaus Material, Spheres and Corrugated Cardboard (Selbstporträt mit Bauhausstoff, Kugeln und Wellpappe)*, circa 1928.

Fig. 5. Marianne Brandt, *The Studio in the Sphere / Self-Portrait in the Studio, Bauhaus Dessau (Das Atelier in der Kugel / Selbstporträt im Atelier, Bauhaus Dessau)*, circa 1928/29.

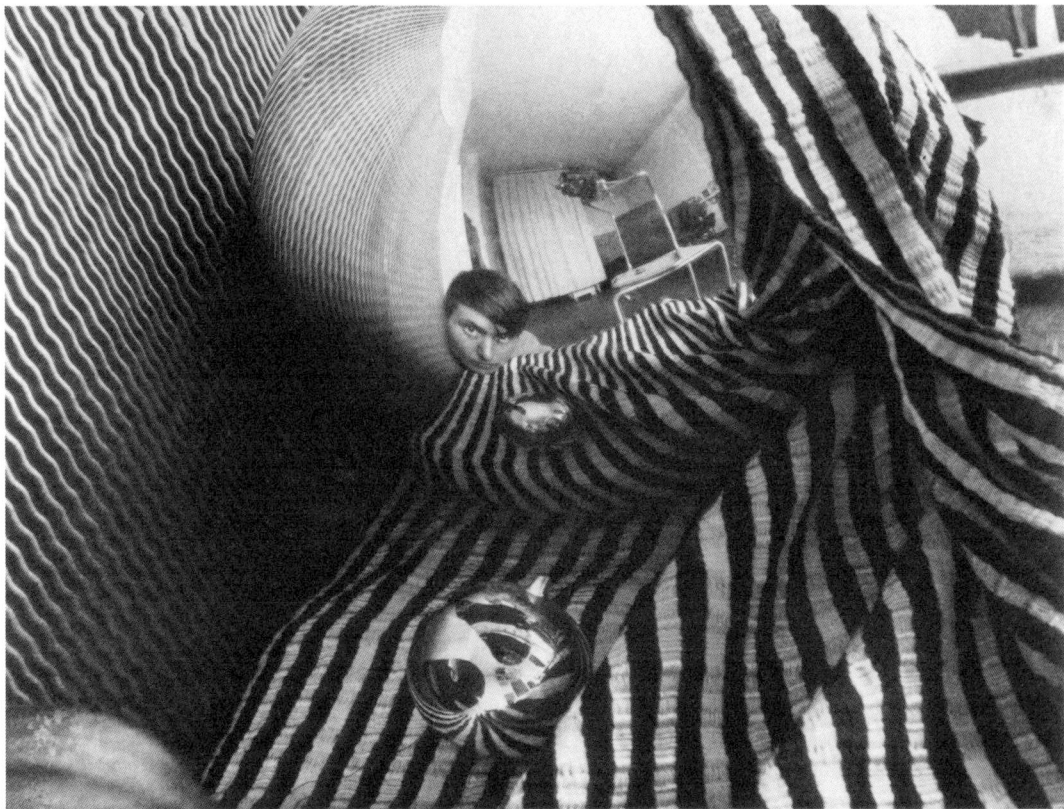

Fig.6. Marianne Brandt,
The Studio in the Sphere /
Self-Portrait in the Studio,
Bauhaus Dessau (Das Atelier
in der Kugel / Selbstporträt
im Atelier, Bauhaus Dessau),
circa 1928/29.

training time she was allowed, how quickly she was put to work, and her admiration for Gropius.[24] Apart from a brief mention of her lost opportunity to study with Walter Peterhans, she does not mention photography. As with Muche's recollections, Brandt acknowledges the school's drawbacks, but conveys an overall sense of admiration for the program. Yet, unlike Muche, Brandt communicates a lack of confidence, suggesting another explanation for the uncertain expression in her photographs.

As a specific genre, the self-portrait encompasses questions of identity, status, aesthetics, and virtuosity. These images represent simultaneously intimate and public documents of self-fashioning. Muche and Brandt also built on a long tradition of artists using mirrored reflections as a means of probing their identities in painted and photographic self-portraits. Mirrors allow artists to defamiliarize themselves and simultaneously become subjects and spectators. Historically, mirrors have symbolized *vanitas* and shrewd self-awareness.[25] During the early twentieth century, mirrors became a popular trope in modern painting and photography; especially among female photographers who employed them in constructing visions of New Womanhood.[26] Brandt was thus one of many women at the Bauhaus and across Europe and America who used both mirrors and the new technology of photography—made easier and more affordable by hand-held cameras—to interrogate her identity as a woman, an individual, and an artist/designer.[27] What is unique about Brandt's photographs is her exploitation of the sphere's convex mirrored surface to distort and disfigure her visage, thus complicating any clear statement of emancipated femininity.

Although revisionist scholarship has contributed greatly to Brandt's reinterpretation, the nature of her personality and her outlook at the school remain open questions.[28] These gaps in our understanding and the tension between interiority and performativity inherent in all self-portraits allow for multiple interpretations of her biography and her work. Brandt was a superlative designer who rose to an unprecedented degree of prominence within her field at the Bauhaus, but as Anja Baumhoff has noted, despite her success, Brandt never took the Chamber of Handicraft's apprenticeship exam, perhaps for fear of failure.[29] A rare and illuminating description of Brandt by a colleague as "in no way robust, but sensitive, moody, and at times very depressed" contrasts sharply with Brandt's own

Persephone
Allen

The
Metallic
Sphere
as
Mechanical
Eye

103

Fig. 7. Lucia Moholy, *Teapot (Model MT 49)*, 1924.

description of her time at the school.[30] Together, scholarship and first-hand accounts suggest that there was a duality to Brandt's public and private persona: the confident, capable designer/artist who challenged her male colleagues' sexism and excelled, and the individual who battled self-doubt and alienation. Elizabeth Otto argues for Brandt's agency, asserting that the various poses and perspectives Brandt adopts in these photographs show her challenging traditional preconceived notions about representation, authenticity, and, above all, who or what a modern woman could be.[31] Otto has also argued that in these photographs Brandt joins herself with metal, the material with which she flourished at the school. Brandt, like Muche, continued her work as a designer and educator after she left the Bauhaus, but she was much more isolated in Chemnitz and she struggled to eke out a living in the GDR. The complicated reception of the Bauhaus in the GDR did nothing to support her career or the recognition of her work during her lifetime. When she died in 1983, she also remained a lesser-known figure in Bauhaus histories and the broader field of design despite the success of her many designs for lamps and works in metal.[32]

Discovered and exhibited only posthumously, Brandt's photographs represent an intensely personal record of her experience at the school that, as a woman, was characterized by exclusion.[33] Brandt's experience is representative of a central paradox of the Bauhaus, that it emphasized collective production and creativity, but restricted women's involvement to all but the weaving workshop. Thus, to be a woman at the Bauhaus was to appreciate the school's utopian aims, but to never be fully allowed to participate.[34] Brandt visualizes elements of both confidence and vulnerability or insecurity in the various poses in which she obscures, magnifies, and miniaturizes herself in the sphere's reflections. Together these also suggest an awareness of how her body and her being are simultaneously in and out of place at the school.

As self-portraits, both Muche's and Brandt's photographs question their positions at the Bauhaus, yet respectively they represent each individual's very different opinion of their roles at the school and their mastery of them. While Muche's photographs with the sphere situate him as a confident artist-designer, the unusual staging of Brandt's photographs and her questioning stare express ambiguity. Muche made his photographs public and allowed them to be repro-

duced in multiple publications whereas Brandt neither exhibited nor published hers. That her images remained private suggests that she did not engage the viewer or sphere in the same way because she created the images for herself as a personal assertion of selfhood and her creative identity. Brandt's metalwork, her primary occupation at the school, the source of her greatest success, and an essential element of her identity, provides a final means of analyzing her photographs.

As an artist-designer engaged in exploring the aesthetic and practical capabilities of metal, Brandt must have been attracted to the visual and material qualities of the spheres. Their mirrored surfaces recall an aesthetic akin to many of her metal designs, which Brandt appears to have rarely photographed despite photographing herself so frequently. Brandt's most celebrated pieces are the primarily hemispherical tea and coffee services and ashtrays that she created earlier in her career in Weimar—small objects seemingly intended for domestic use. They are also handmade, executed in luxurious materials, and often finished with time-consuming, hand-hammered surfaces that root them in older silver-smithing traditions.[35]

When photographed by Lucia Moholy, however, Brandt's objects appear to correspond to the emerging industrial aesthetic.[fig.7] Moholy's now famous photographs deliberately enhanced the reflective qualities of Brandt's metalwork, and Brandt may, in turn, have been responding to those photographs with her own exploration of reflections. In particular, the careful composition of Moholy's photographs emphasized the mirror-like qualities of Brandt's metalwork—pieces arranged against blank backgrounds, but foregrounded by furnished spaces where objects and interiors could be reflected.[36] As captured by Moholy, Brandt's objects appear capable of reflecting, but distorting in a manner evocative of the spheres that Brandt photographed. Reproduced in Bauhaus books, catalogues, and advertise-

Persephone
Allen

The
Metallic
Sphere
as
Mechanical
Eye

105

ments, Moholy's photographs marketed Brandt's metalwork to outside audiences and potential patrons and were instrumental in popularizing her work; the resulting success of her products was essential to Brandt's promotion within the school.

Smooth, shiny, reflective metal was also a central visual and material characteristic of the "machine aesthetic" that became popular among European and American modernists during the 1920s. Its adoption at the Bauhaus was initially superficial, as the school was ill-equipped for industrial design.[37] It was only after the move to Dessau in 1925 that Moholy-Nagy outfitted the metal workshop with lathes, presses, and drills, and mandated that students should design functional electrical appliances and lighting accessories. Brandt demonstrated her receptiveness to technology by switching her energies from designing tablewares to designing standardized lighting fixtures. Her later smooth-surfaced, hemispherical lamps with industrial finishes bear even closer resemblance to the spheres that she photographed and strongly evoke the aesthetic of machine-milled, chromium-plated ball bearings.[38] By evoking the ball bearing, Brandt could conjure associations with advances in transportation technology, along with a sense of modern dynamism and speed—from bicycles to airplanes. Photographing herself with orbs so closely resembling ball bearings may also have been another way that Brandt declared herself a mobile, modern designer and "New Woman." Ball bearings evoke the feminine modernity of Amelia Earhart whose fashion line featured ball bearing belt buckles, Hannah Höch who incorporated their imagery into *Cut with the Kitchen Knife Dada Through the Last Weimar Beer-Belly Cultural Epoch in Germany* (1919), and Charlotte Perriand's beloved "ball-bearing" necklace. Impersonal and standardized, the "stark utilitarian beauty" of the ball bearings also appealed to and was adopted by Dadaists, Modernists, and *Neue Sachlichkeit* artists alike.[39]

Just as the ball bearing became a widely accepted icon of modernity, by the close of the 1920s, the imagery and materiality of the unadorned, mirrored sphere became a recognizable symbol of the Bauhaus. In February 1929, the Bauhaus held its famed metal party for which hundreds of metallic spheres were made as decorations. These decorations inspired Walter Funkat, Margit Kallin, and others to take photographs emulating Muche's images.[fig.8] In that same year, Moholy-Nagy reproduced one of Muche's spherical portraits for the cover of

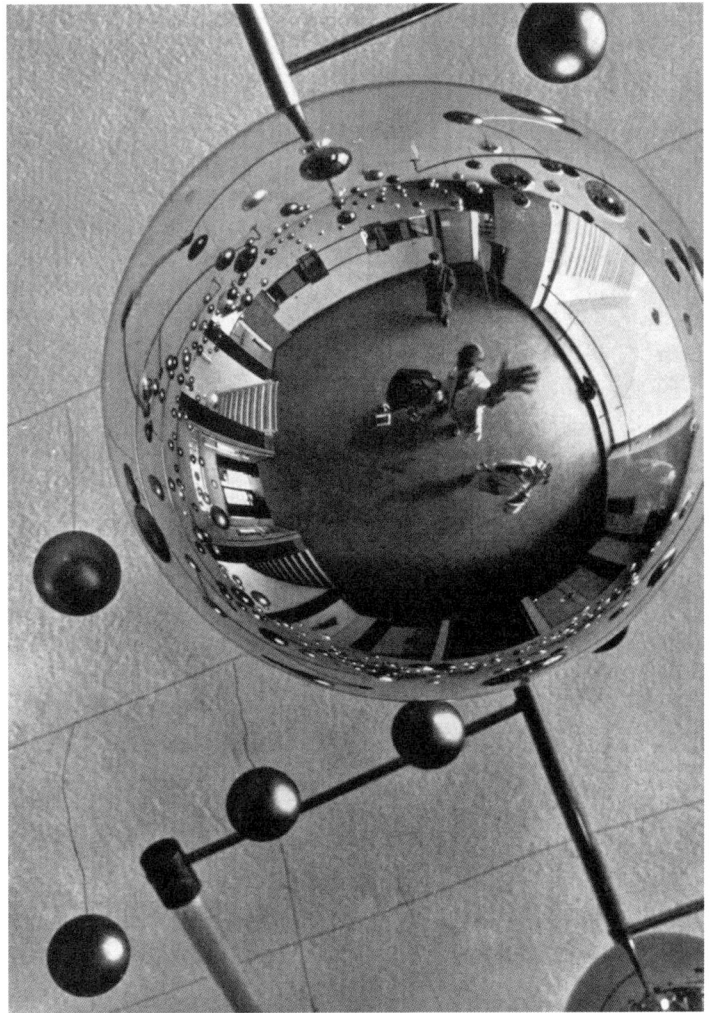

Fig. 8. Walter Funkat, *Glass Sphere / Self-Portrait in the Vestibule of the Bauhaus, Mirrored in One of the Spheres of the Metal Festival Decorations (Glaskugeln / Selbstporträt im Vestibül des Bauhauses, gespiegelt in einer der Kugeln der Festdekoration zum Metallischen Fest)*, 1929.

the *Film und Foto* brochure, presenting that image as exemplifying the most desirable characteristics of modern photography. For the cover, Moholy-Nagy cut the sphere out of its rectangular frame, quadrupled it, and arranged the cut-outs so that they appeared to jettison off in opposite directions, thus underscoring the sphere's dynamism and the possibilities of both reproducing, but also repurposing photographic images. In 1930, Joost Schmidt featured a mirrored, metallic sphere in his Bauhaus wallpaper advertisements. Schmidt's and Moholy-Nagy's deployment of the sphere in promotional and advertising materials suggests both the malleability and easy identification of the image. First employed as a means of exploring individual personas, the metallic sphere was easily commodified and eventually used to signify the school's collective identity.

As a collective, the Bauhaus was made up of individuals who were "at one time the most important ... and another time the most superfluous," but its early history often obscured the intricacies of this network.[40] By approaching Brandt, Muche, and by extension, Moholy and Moholy-Nagy through these photographs, we are better able to understand their entanglement with each other and the complex development of approaches at the school as a whole. Instead of Moholy-Nagy initiating interest in technology and the exploitation of new materials and methods at the school, Muche's photographs illustrate how part of this enthusiasm emerged earlier and from within the school. Taken years before Moholy-Nagy's arrival and later explicit recommendation for photographers' use of convex mirrors and distortions, Muche's images suggest that they mutually shaped one another's ideas about art, design, and optics. Furthermore, Moholy-Nagy's mentorship of Brandt is frequently cited, but the connection between

Moholy's and Brandt's photographs identified here demonstrates another more nuanced interchange between the two women.

Josef Albers later wrote that "the origin of art is the discrepancy between physical fact and psychic effect," and that perception is what connects the two.[41] In Muche's and Brandt's photographic interrogations of gleaming spheres we see two artists exploring this very divergence in potent, personal expressions. Both exploited the spheres' capabilities to update their practices, illustrate their shared belief in the possibilities of new materials, and animate their experiments with photography—the most modern mode of image-making. Both executed their experiments at moments of intense transformation in their personal lives, at the Bauhaus, and across German society; their portraits provide insights into their negotiations of those changes.

For Muche, the youngest master appointed shortly after the school opened in Weimar, the sphere seems to symbolize a confident, optimistic outlook, yet also represents a stage in his developing relationship to technology. By contrast, for Brandt, who arrived as an older student who worked with metal, the arrangement of multiple spheres at various angles to amplify distortions conveys ambivalence about her dual identity as an artist-designer and "New Woman" at the school. The sphere's mirror-like surface that materialized and dematerialized boundaries of gender and status could thus be used to represent the range of experiences at the school—a sense of wholeness and unity or distortion and fragmentation, exploration and constriction. For the Bauhaus as a whole, the sphere's mutability allowed it to become emblematic of the clean, streamlined aesthetic of modernity cultivated in Dessau and, eventually, a symbol of the school itself.

Representing continuity of tradition and radical departures, the sphere encapsulates and reflects many of the paradoxical aspects of production and experiences at the school, as well as the Bauhaus's relationship to modernism itself. The sphere's polished surface appears anonymous and detached as if declaring its modernity and mechanized production, but it is an ambiguous reflection—even its precise materiality and functionality remain uncertain. Being convex, it no longer produces an objective reflection, but instead reflects—and often distorts—everything, capturing the ambivalence, enthusiasm, self-doubt, and self-awareness that were aspects of each individual's complex emotional experience of the school and their collective attempt to become modern.

1 László Moholy-Nagy; translated by Janet Seligman, *Painting, Photography, Film* (Cambridge, MA: MIT Press, 1969), 7.

2 Recent research by Robin Schuldenfrei and Elizabeth Otto, among others, has revealed new insights into the Bauhaus photography of Lucia Moholy and Marianne Brandt respectively, yet many aspects of the archive and work by lesser-known *Bauhäusler* have remained understudied.

3 Bauhaus photographs with metallic spheres are reproduced without interpretation in many histories of the school. Michel Frizot mentions "many examples of the use of glass balls and distorting mirrors in French and German photography around the late 1920s," but only cites André Kertész in "The Poetics of Eye and Lens," in Mitra Abbaspour, Lee Ann Daffner, and Maria Morris Hambourg, eds., *Object: Photo. Modern Photographs: The Thomas Walther Collection 1909–1949*, An Online Project of The Museum of Modern Art (New York: MOMA, 2014), www.moma.org/interactives/objectphoto/assets/essays/Frizot.pdf, 15–16. Jeanine Fiedler refers to them as "immortal glass balls" in *Photography at the Bauhaus* (Cambridge, MA: MIT Press, 1990), 137. Britta Kaiser-Schuster simply notes that Muche began photographing spheres in 1921 and that Brandt followed in 1928 in "Brandt, Marianne," 311–314, in Delia Gaze, ed., *Dictionary of Women Artists* (Taylor & Francis, 1997). After beginning my research, I found that Anja Guttenberger devotes a chapter of her dissertation to "Sphere Photos at the Bauhaus," but provides a broader overview in "Fotografische Selbstportraits der Bauhäusler zwischen 1919 und 1933" (PHD diss., Free University of Berlin, 2011).

4 Muche's "Self-Portrait" has been variously dated: circa 1920 in the Los Angeles County Museum of Art Collection, collections.lacma.org/node/194373, and 1921–22 in The Chicago Art Institute Collection, www.artic.edu/aic/collections/artwork/70767.

5 Barry Bergdoll, "Bauhaus Multiplied," in Bergdoll and Leah Dickerman, eds., *The Bauhaus 1919–1933: Workshops for Modernity* (New York: MOMA, 2009), 45–46.

6 Lee Ann Daffner describes early photographic efforts as "disparate and unsystematic" in "Dive: A Materialist History of the Photographic Industry in Germany and the Soviet Union between the Wars," in Abbaspour, Daffner, Hambourg, eds., *Object: Photo. Modern Photographs: The Thomas Walther Collection 1909–1949* (New York: MOMA, 2014), 59.

7 Muche, "Bauhaus Epitaph," in *Bauhaus & Bauhaus People*, ed. Eckhard Neumann (New York: Van Nostrand Reinhold, 1993), 212–214.

8 Rainer K. Wick, *Teaching at the Bauhaus* (Ostfildern-Ruit: Hatje Cantz, 2000), 105.

9 Wick, *Teaching at the Bauhaus*, 120.

10 Schlemmer, "Letter to Otto Meyer-Amden from December 7, 1921," in *The Bauhaus Masters & Students by Themselves*, ed. Frank Whitford (Woodstock, NY: Overlook Press, 1993), 65.

11 Magdalena Droste, *Bauhaus, 1919–1933* (Cologne: B. Taschen Verlag, 1990), 28–31, and Wick, *Teaching at the Bauhaus*, 112–113.

12 Gropius later wrote that the school emerged out of a "mixture of profound defeat as a result of the lost war and of the breakdown of spiritual and economic life and an ardent hope that something new could be built up from these ruins." "Letter to Tomas Maldonado" (1963), in Wick, *Teaching at the Bauhaus*, 32.

13 In 1914, Herwarth Walden, owner of Gallery Der Sturm, exhibited a model of Taut's Glass Pavilion and published the first edition of Scheerbart's *Glass Architecture*. Jenny Anger, "The 'Translucent (Not: Transparent)' *Gesamtglaswerk*," in David Imhoof, Margaret Eleanor Menninger, Anthony J. Steinhoff, eds., *The Total Work of Art: Foundations, Articulations, Inspirations* (New York: Berghahn Books, 2016), 170–171.

14 Anja Baumhoff, *The Gendered World of the Bauhaus: The Politics of Power at the Weimar Republic's Premier Art Institute, 1919–1932* (Frankfurt am Main: Peter Lang, 2001), 92–93.

15 Gillian Naylor, *The Bauhaus Reassessed: Sources and Design Theory* (London: Herbert Press, 1985), 127.

16 Moholy-Nagy, *Painting, Photography, Film*, 100, 103.

17 It is not clear who assigned these titles. Therefore, the identifications might not be reliable, but "garden ball" suggests links to nineteenth-century photographic traditions.

18 Moholy-Nagy, "Fotografie ist Lichtgestaltung," *bauhaus* 2 (1928), 2–8. Transl. "Photography is Manipulation of Light," in *Photography at the Bauhaus*, ed. Fiedler, 127. In this same text, Moholy-Nagy also advised artists to "conduct practical experiments" by

Persephone Allen

The
Metallic
Sphere
as
Mechanical
Eye

109

photographing objects that reflect and distort light, and explicitly encouraged the use of convex mirrors.

19   Kaiser-Schuster, "Brandt, Marianne," 313.

20   For Otto's analysis, see "Paris–Dessau: Marianne Brandt's New Women in Photomontage and Photography, from Garçonne to Bauhaus Constructivist," in *The New Woman International: Photographic Representations from the 1870s through the 1960s*, ed. Otto with Vanessa Rocco (Ann Arbor: University of Michigan Press, 2011), 154–156.

21   Ulrike Müller, *Bauhaus Women: Art, Handicraft, Design* (Paris: Flammarion; London: Thames & Hudson, 2009), 121.

22   Brandt, "Letter to a Younger Generation" (1966), in *Bauhaus & Bauhaus People*, 106.

23   Moholy-Nagy, "Letter to Ernst Bruckmann" (June 26, 1929), Bauhaus Dessau Foundation collection.

24   Brandt, "Letter to a Younger Generation," 105–109.

25   Jonathan Miller, *On Reflection* (London: National Gallery Publications; New Haven, CT: Yale University Press, 1998), 10–11.

26   Müller, *Bauhaus Women*, 127.

27   Otto, "New Woman or Female Constructor? Marianne Brandt's Search for a Bauhaus Identity," 1–12, unpublished translation by Otto, originally published as "Neue Frau oder weibliche Konstrukteur? Marianne Brandts Suche nach einer Bauhausidentität," in Gerda Breuer and Elina Knorp, eds., *Gespiegeltes Ich: Fotografische Selbstbildnisse von Frauen in den 1920er Jahren* (Berlin: Nicolai, 2014), 116–29.

28   Baumhoff, Droste, Müller, and, in particular, Otto, have shaped Brandt's legacy.

29   Baumhoff, *The Gendered World of the Bauhaus*, 141.

30   Baumhoff, *The Gendered World of the Bauhaus*, 124.

31   Otto, "Paris–Dessau": 166.

32   Otto, "Marianne Brandt's Experimental Landscapes in Painting and Photography during the National Socialist Period," *History of Photography* 37, no. 2 (2013): 181.

33   Gropius restricted the number of female students admitted, directed most of them to enter the weaving workshop, and failed to recognize their contributions before and after the school closed. According to Freud, exclusion from the dominant paradigm in one's immediate social environment results in a sense of loss and a melancholic outlook. Sigmund Freud, "Mourning and Melancholia," 243–258, in *The Standard Edition of the Complete Psychological Works of Sigmund Freud, Volume XIV (1914–1916)*, (London: Hogarth Press, 1917).

34   Lucia Moholy described Dessau as "like a place where one has missed one's connection and has to wait for the next train." Müller, *Bauhaus Women*, 147.

35   Robin Schuldenfrei, "The Irreproducibility of the Bauhaus Object," in Jeffrey Saletnik and Schuldenfrei, eds., *Bauhaus Construct: Fashioning Identity, Discourse and Modernism* (London and New York: Routledge, 2009).

36   For more on how Moholy heightened the reflective qualities of materials, as well as the rhetorical nature of these images, see Schuldenfrei, "Images in Exile: Lucia Moholy's Bauhaus Negatives and the Construction of the Bauhaus Legacy," *History of Photography* 37, no. 2 (2013): 182–203.

37   Naylor, *The Bauhaus Reassessed*, 112.

38   Several of Brandt's post-1925 metal designs were chrome-plated, indicating that she was familiar with this technology. Junkers Aircraft Company supported the Bauhaus in Dessau and the metal workshop executed their later lamp designs "in a Junker firm." It's possible that Brandt had firsthand contact with ball bearings there. Anne-Katrin Rossberg in "Hans Przyrembel," in *New Worlds: German and Austrian Art, 1890–1940*, Price, Kort, and Topp, eds., (New Haven: Yale University Press, 2002), 571.

39   Simon Bliss, "Charlotte Perriand, Ball Bearings, and Modernist Jewelry," *Modernism/Modernity* 20, no. 2 (2013): 169.

40   Muche, "Bauhaus Epitaph," 212–214.

41   Doreen Ehrlich, *The Bauhaus* (Leicester: Magna, 1991), 104.

Part 1

Theories
of
Bauhaus
Materiality

110

Christopher T. Green

Towards a Digital Bauhaus: The Analog and the Discrete in the Glass Grids of Josef Albers

It should not be surprising that the rather overlooked works done in glass by Josef Albers throughout the 1920s have largely been discussed in terms of the canonical framing of the Bauhaus's shift from its crystalline Expressionist origins to a techno-mechanical and Constructivist aesthetic.[1] This shift pivots on the crucial moment around the Bauhaus Exhibition in 1923, the year of the departure of Johannes Itten and the arrival of László Moholy-Nagy, and is seen as the point at which Walter Gropius consciously directed the Bauhaus away from its craft-guild program to the promises of industrial and modern production.

Two portraits of Albers, one on either side of this transitional moment, seem to reinforce this narrative. The first, a 1921–22 portrait of Albers by his colleague Marcel Breuer, is a medieval caricature of the young Albers, his hair cropped into a monk's tonsure.[fig. 1][2] His sword is a craftsman's tool, and as a shield he holds an early glass work, *Gitterbild* (Grid Mounted), its modulated squares of color recognizable in a metal latticework, the imprecise handmade lines captured by Breuer's freehand etching.[fig. 2] The other, a pair of photographs by Umbo from 1928, is a much cooler, refined depiction.[fig. 3] In one image, Albers sits on Breuer's Wassily chair in a tailored suit. The artwork behind him, *Overlapping* (1927), is an example of what was his primary medium of exploration for several years following the Bauhaus move to Dessau: compositions of sandblasted flashed glass.[fig. 4] Albers would exhibit twenty such glass paintings in an exhibition of the Bauhaus masters the following year in Zurich and Basel. This commercially produced material was created by using an opaque white or transparent glass core onto which a very thin second layer,

typically of colored glass, was hand blown.[3] This second colored layer could be etched into or removed to create forms as desired. Albers used an overlay stencil, designed on gridded drafting paper, to isolate his composition which was then sent to industrial sandblasters to remove those portions and reveal the glass's white layer.[4] The stencils could be reused repeatedly, and thus could be serialized as part of the greater industrial production sought by Gropius. The sizes of the works were rarely larger than a foot or two squared, the dimensions of an easel painting, which likewise would have made them easier to market on a wider scale and more accessible than stained glass window commissions. Instead of the play of free-form lines and patterns, *Overlapping* is strictly ruled lines and rectangles, a rational repetition of the vertical rectangular format that takes up a steady rhythm of repeating horizontal elements that Albers called his "thermometer style." The move from Expressionist monk to modern rational industrial aesthete is laid bare by the camera's lens.[5]

In support of the reading of a transition from craft to machine aesthetic, Peter Nisbet wrote that *Gitterbild* in particular "is a key transitional work that seems to embody, if not prefigure, the Bauhaus's institutional shift."[6] Other scholars, such as Oliver Barker and Brenda Danilowitz, in clarifying the history of Albers's history with glass, have focused on the material nature of the medium and emphasize its symbolist and religious resonances and the immaterial affect that emerged from Albers's pre-Bauhaus training and biography. In contrast, Michael White and Achim Borchardt-Hume have argued that while it is common to imagine a shift at the Bauhaus that exchanged subjectivity, emotion, and irrationality for objectivity, sobriety, and rationality, what is often present in the work of Albers is an attempt to synthesize these opposing categories.[7]

This essay follows these latter examples to push against the reductive move from mystical expressionism to a techno-mechanical

Christopher T. Green

Towards a Digital Bauhaus

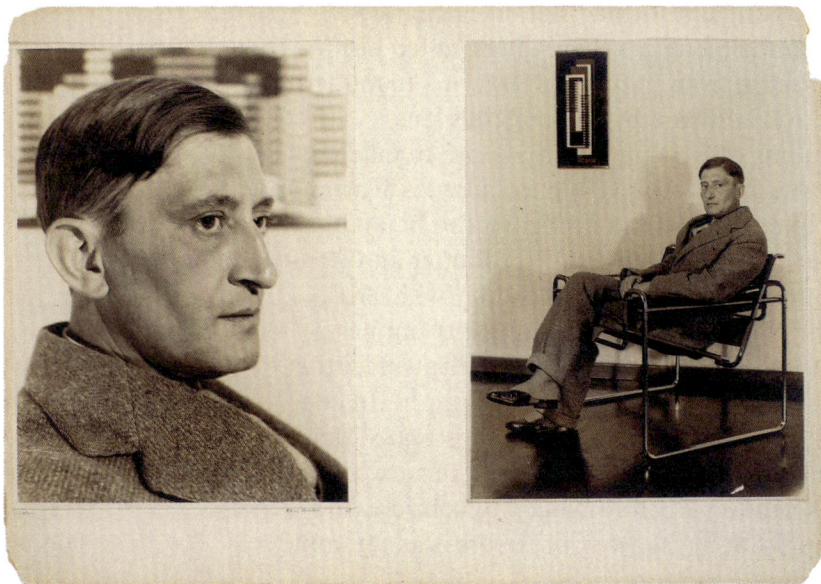

Fig.2. Josef Albers, *Gitterbild (Grid Mounted)*, circa 1921, glass, metal, and wire, 32.4 × 28.9 cm. The Josef and Anni Albers Foundation, 1976.6.21.
Fig.3. Otto Umbehr (Umbo) and Josef Albers, *J. A. / Foto Umbo 28,* 1928, gelatin silver prints mounted on cardboard, 28.3 × 41 cm. The Josef and Anni Albers Foundation, 1976.7.1106.
Fig.4. Josef Albers, *Overlapping,* 1927, sandblasted opaque flashed glass, 58.4 × 27.9 cm.

aesthetic in the glass work of Albers in the 1920s. Instead, I understand the move from the handcrafted assemblage of *Gitterbild* to the flashed glass process of *Overlapping* as the syncretization of multiple influences, desires, and pressures taking place at the most intense moments of transition at the Bauhaus. Scholars are right to point out the social, political, material, and quasi-biographical influences on Albers's quite sudden turn to the highly rationalized and delineated aesthetic of his flashed glass works. However, these works offer an opportunity to consider a broader media history of the Bauhaus. Rather than a craft-versus-industry, Expressionist-versus-geometric Constructivist opposition, I propose that the tension identified in Albers's glass works is that of the analog versus the digital, the continuous versus the discrete. This tension is the product of Albers's pursuit of what he called a "code," an order to the world that aligned with his career-long aim to pursue simple and clear forms that would make mankind more united, life more real and more essential. These forms began with the discrete and quantitative aesthetic of his glass works. Framing the work of Albers in terms of a push into a digital aesthetic mode is to position it as engaged in a politic that is often lost in the craft versus techno-industrial split of the Bauhaus. Such a framing enters this work into a future-oriented trajectory of media history and recuperates the Bauhaus from the dead end of the modern utopian project.

The digital, defined by Alexander Galloway in his 2014 book *Laruelle: Against the Digital*, does not merely refer to electronic media. Rather, Galloway shows, it is a philosophical operation of creating a basic distinction, a binary, whether zeros and ones or some other set of discrete units—fingers, letters of the alphabet, or horizontal and vertical lines. "Any digital medium will have a bed of genetically distinct elements. These elements form a homogenous substrate from which constructions are built ... The digital is new, the analog old. The digital means zeros and ones, the analog means continuous variation. The digital means discrete, the analog means integrated. The digital means the digits (the fingers and toes), the analog means proportion (ratios and correspondences)."[8] At its simplest, Galloway says, the digital is the process of distinction, "an autonomous field able to encode and simulate anything whatsoever in the universe," the dividing of one into two. It is a means of organizing the world, an essential component of philosophy, and an ever more encompassing precondition of contemporary life.

Aesthetically it is that which is made discrete, a form that is split and given a hard edge. This is in opposition to the analog and the continuous, which Galloway notes consists of "messy globs of dissimilar things," the idiosyncratic and singular of styles and shapes and relations and motifs. Deleuze's characterization of painting as "the analogical art par excellence" is related.[9] One can see a digital mode of organization in the operation that Moholy-Nagy allegedly undertook in his famous phone-paintings, where the production of the work of art was reduced to a series of distinct coordinates that were phoned in from a distance rather than the analogic painterly marks on a canvas.

Albers was working on his glass works in this context, at a time when digital means of viewing the world were dominant in the interwar period. Imminently present were the impact of the First World War's drive for technological destruction, the use of digital communication systems like the telegram and Morse code, developments in early computing, and an ever-gridded and subdivided approach to urban geography. It was in the face of such a worldview that Albers said in 1926 that he was intent on challenging his viewer's "way of seeing" to meet the demands of the speed and economy of the "stenogram and telegram and code."[10] This was to create, following Galloway's definition, a means of visually coding an increasingly digitized worldview.

Albers engaged in a coded way of seeing in his flashed glass works, despite the medium's roots in a craft and expressionist ethos. Some of his first works at the Bauhaus in 1920 were compositions of broken glass assembled in armatures of wire and metal. These *Scherbenbilder* (1920–21) were confluences of earlier lessons by Dutch glass artist John Thorn-Prikker, with whom Albers had studied at the Essen Kunstgewerbeschule, as well as the teaching of Itten, the head of the Bauhaus *Vorkurs*, who promoted strategies of collage and assemblage in material studies. With the essential play of light and transparency as an artistic means of exploration, the *Scherbenbilder* also connected with the early Bauhaus ideals, especially those of early modernist architecture as promoted by Gropius. Glass was a material embodiment of the spiritual ideal that was central to Gropius's rhetoric for the Bauhaus's founding goals: "For the longed for materials of the distant future— pure glass—we will only be ready when the spirit of the building has once again seized the entire *Volk* as it did at the time of the Gothic cathedrals."[11] Along with Lyonel Feininger's Gothic glass cathedral that illustrated the Bauhaus Manifesto, glass was an essential motif in Gropius's call for painting, sculpture, and architecture to unite in a new structure of the future.[12] The *Scherbenbilder* reflect a model of structural relationships and the artist as working not just with the materials of everyday life but with the ideal as well as the real, in order to resonate with the individual and society.[13]

Albers soon assumed the position of journeyman (*Geselle*) and later technical master (*Werkmeister*) of the glass workshop he single-handedly formed. He was joined there by Paul Klee, the workshop's form master (*Formmeister*), and executed *Gitterbild*.[14] The work synthesizes and balances competing impulses between the structural logic of the grid and the chance and insistent materiality of the handmade, and is thus seen as transitional between the subjectivism of Itten and the machine aesthetic of Moholy-Nagy after 1923. Magdalene Droste and others have said that *Gitterbild* betrays the influence of Klee, pointing to the many studies in color squares done by Klee at this time and their proximity co-teaching the workshop.[15] The painterly and analog is certainly visible in *Gitterbild*'s grid, with a lattice that is neither quite discrete nor strict in its edges. The handmade is visible in the glass and rough inlaid lattices of metal and wire, and this lattice-work of horizontal and vertical wires appears hand-woven. The modulation of colors and textures achieved by painting the glass directly creates an effect not far removed from the *Scherbenbilder*. Nonetheless the handmade and expressionistic tendencies are constrained by the order of the grid, which balances the chance of the random sequence of colors and the crudeness of the metal support.[16]

A year later, *Park* (ca. 1923) solidified the edge of the grid with iron-oxide paint that sharply delineates the grid within the metal armature. The painterly is still present where Albers has used paint on some of the glass panels to control light and tonal variations, including a scoring technique and dry-brush finish by daubing paint onto the glass with a dry bristled brush.[17] But when compared to *Gitterbild*, the more structured *Park* demonstrates the grid's shift from a much looser, expressionist play of color to a rational structure with strong architectonic forms. Appropriately, Fred Licht has described this work in terms of the tectonic, noting *Park* draws "much closer to the structural, tectonic image integrated into a larger architectural context" than the loosely woven *Gitterbild* could.[18]

Rather than Klee, Albers likely drew his grid from the more rigid example of Piet Mondrian, an oft-overlooked influence on Albers's early work. Droste and others have thoroughly discussed the influence of *De Stijl* at the early Bauhaus, particularly through the campaign of van Doesburg. *Park* resonates with Mondrian's compositions of the late 1910s in its strict delineation of the grid and balanced use of a reduced color palette, more so than prior comparisons to Klee and Itten. Mondrian's ideas arrived at the Bauhaus largely through van Doesburg, but he was praised in a way that van Doesburg never was. Oskar Schlemmer, for example, in a 1926 letter to Otto Meyer, says "Mondrian: he is really the god of the Bauhaus, and Doesburg is his prophet."[19] Albers adhered to some of Mondrian's own tenets, such as the idea that "to be concerned exclusively with relations, while creating them and seeking their equilibrium in art and in life, that is the good work of today, and that is to prepare the future."[20] And in 1925, Piet Mondrian's *Neue Gestaltung: Neoplastizismus, Nieuwe Beelding* was published in the first series of *Bauhausbücher*. The strong horizontal and vertical binary elements and black, white, and red palette of the book's cover, designed by van Doesburg, resonates with Albers's flashed glass works that he began that year.

Bernhard Siegert defines his concept of cultural techniques as those "media, symbolic operators, and drill practices ... which are located at the base of intellectual and cultural shifts."[21] It is a reconstruction of "the discourse networks in which the real, the imaginary, and the symbolic are stored, transmitted, and processed."[22] Cultural techniques are conceived of as operative chains that precede the media concepts they generate, part of an actor network that comprises technological objects as well as the operative chains they are part of and that configure or constitute them. While such media are involved in operationalizing distinctions in the real, in essence processing elemental distinctions, they do not only produce categories and delineate distinctions. Rather, they "also destabilize cultural codes, erase signs, and deterritorialize sounds and images."[23] The processing of distinctions, related to Galloway's definition, can be seen as a digital operation, yet as Siegert writes, cultural techniques assume a third position, "an interface between the real and the symbolic," always taking into account the distinctions they create and exclude.[24]

Siegert identifies the grid as one of the most fundamental cultural techniques that can merge operations of representation and

Christopher T. Green

Towards a Digital Bauhaus

119

governance in its dealing with both occupied and empty spaces. The grid functions as an imaging technology that enables us to project a three-dimensional world onto a two-dimensional plane, as well as a diagrammatic procedure that can store data to be implemented in both the real as well as the symbolic, so as to constitute a world of imagined objects. For Siegert, the representational grid is where representation and operation are merged, beginning with Alberti's 1435 treatise *De pictura* (*On Painting*), which uses grids as part of an imaging theory. Alberti's famous veil is a grid technology designed to circumscribe objects, a medium for the technical construction of paintings (as opposed to the window as the metaphor for their mathematical construction). Siegert notes that Alberti's grid is an ordered woven space in which aesthetic and diagrammatic orders exercise their power over the existence and appearance of objects, preceding the objects located therein. It is a "data space" that marked the transition from symbolically organized space to the graphically coded surface.[25] Thus when Mondrian divided the world into universal horizontal and vertical components in *Pier and Ocean* (1915), he reduced the figure-ground relationship to a similar data space of "binary opposition."[26] Mondrian digitized painting into a discrete system, moving from gridded signs to pure information. Siegert noted in *Passage des Digitalen* that "the elementary space of the sea has become the elementary space of digital media," where the continuous noise of the sea transitions to the blinking of the digital.[27] Unsurprisingly, then, he finds that in Mondrian the "motif of the sea is the starting point for a new dimension, a new conceptualization in art."[28]

Albers designed his flashed glass works with the stenciled grid, a cultural technique that leads to the annunciation of the digital. While the glass workshop was not permitted to open in Dessau, Albers pursued his glass work independently, sending his designs to commercial glass producers for fabrication. The material process of sandblasting resulted in highly distinct edges and, according to Albers, "the necessary preciseness as well as the flatness of the design elements [to] offer an unusual and particular material and form effect."[29] This precision is reflected in his use of graph paper to plan the designs within discrete gridded coordinates. The grid of *Gitterbild's* latticework becomes, in the flashed glass, the grid of drafting paper. Albers's stenciling resulted in compositions that consist of a series of horizontal and vertical binary forms with strict edges that create precise distinctions between colors and coordinates. The nuances of the hand-blown glass texture, with its handcrafted nature, are subsumed into the image of the gridded structure produced with the precision of the industrial sandblaster.

Many of Albers's glass works reference architecture, from *Tectonic Group* (1925) to *City* (1928). Scholars have suggested that the horizontal and vertical interchange of Albers's glass work may have been inspired by Gropius's new Bauhaus buildings in Dessau.[30] Two glass works made in 1927, *Interlocked* and *Façade (with Balconies),* resemble night and day views of the Dessau buildings. However, Gropius's designs were not approved until late July 1925, and the building was not inaugurated until December 1926, so Albers could only have seen the plans by the time he began to develop his new language of architectonic forms in glass in late 1925. According to Siegert, though, architecture can be understood as an additional dimension of the grid that has been "unfolded into three dimensions and repeated in vertical and horizontal directions."[31] Albers might have easily translated the three-dimensional nature of the architectural blueprint onto the sculptural two-dimensional surface of the flashed glass.

Consider the first flashed glass plates Albers made in 1925, the *Factory* series.[fig.5] As suggested by Danilowitz, these works bear a striking resemblance to the new Ullsteinhaus factory façade, under construction from 1925 to 1927.[fig.6][32] The Ullsteinhaus, designed by architect Eugen Schmohl for the Ullstein Publishing Company, was a massing of medieval-inspired masonry over a modernist frame. The *Factory* works resemble schematized versions of the Ullsteinhaus, with tall towers, regular registers of windows, and blocks of architectural mass. However, despite the striking resemblance, the façade of the Ullsteinhaus was not finished in 1925 for Albers to emulate.

Albers may have had access to the architectural drawings and plans for the Ullsteinhaus through his personal connections. Albers married Annelise "Anni" Fleischmann in May 1925, the daughter of Antonie Ullstein and the granddaughter of Leopold Ullstein, founder of the Ullstein Publishing Company. Albers coincidentally secured a commission in November 1925 to design twenty-three windows of colored and etched glass to fill the openings above the worker entrance of the Ullsteinhaus. Albers secured this commission through Gottfried Heinersdorff, an important commercial glass painter and manufacturer with whom Albers had previously worked.[33] Heinersdorff secured

Fig. 5. Josef Albers, *Factory*, circa 1925, sandblasted flashed glass with black paint, 35.9 × 45.9 cm. Yale University Art Gallery 1977.160.1. Gift of Anni Albers and the Josef Albers Foundation, Inc.

Fig. 6. Night view of the illuminated Ullsteinhaus from the southwest, 1927, in Eugen G. Schmohl, *Ein Industriebau von der Fundierung bis zur Vollendung* (Berlin: Bauwelt-Verlag, 1927).

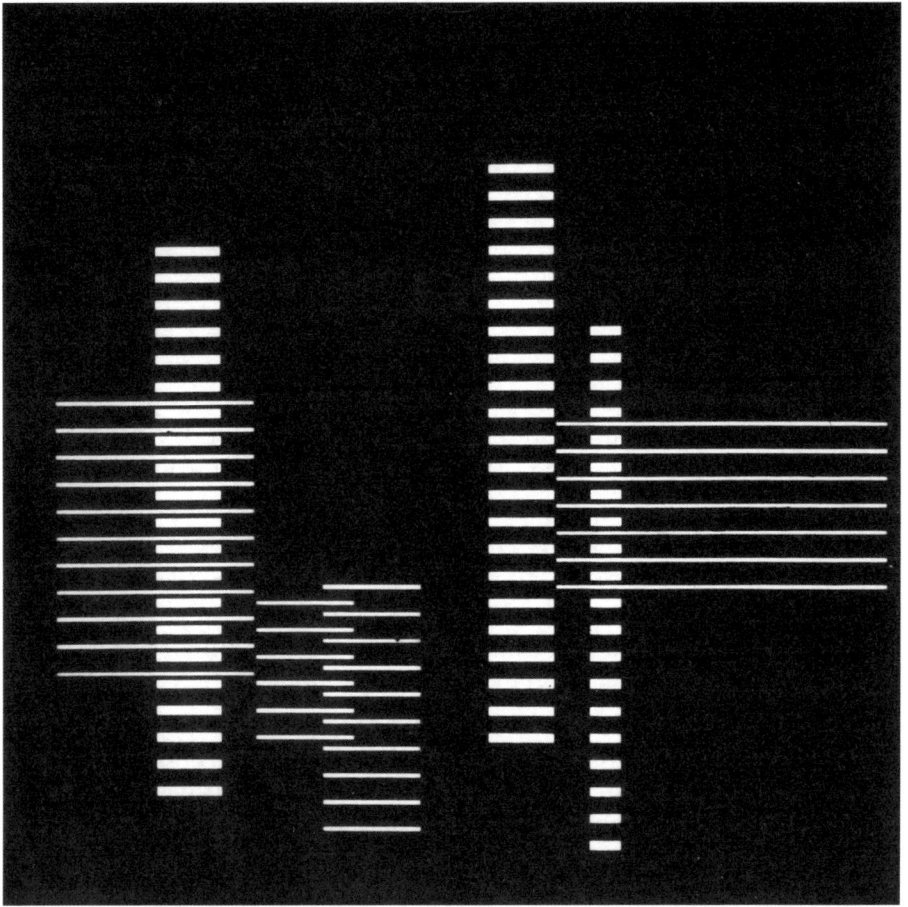

Fig. 7. Ullsteinhaus under
construction, June 20, 1926,
in Eugen G. Schmohl, *Ein Industriebau von der Fundierung
bis zur Vollendung* (Berlin:
Bauwelt-Verlag, 1927).

Fig. 8. Josef Albers, *Hoch-
bauten A* (Skyscrapers A),
circa 1929, sandblasted glass
with black paint, 34.9 × 34.9 cm.
Yale University Art Gallery
2016.64.1. Bequest of James
H. Clark, Jr., B.A. 1958.

him another window commission for the Grassi Museum in Leipzig less than a year later, recently restored after its destruction in World War II. Both the Grassi Museum and Ullsteinhaus window designs follow the vertical thrust of the high windows with towers of modular horizontal units defined against the alternating light of the window panes, precursors of his erect *Skyscrapers* series and a significant progression from the checkerboard glass windows he designed for the Otte House and the Weimar Director's Office in 1922–23. In addition to his working relationship with Heinersdorff, in 1926 Albers was commissioned to produce drawings for two Ullstein Publishing Company shops, never realized. Reproduced in a special Bauhaus issue of *Offset*, the accompanying text cites Albers's interest in the function of architectural design for both "attracting and protecting" the window shoppers.[34] The black-and-white stripes and strong right angles echo Albers's glass designs and show his further interest in the play of the architectural grid between the two- and three-dimensional.

Given the timeline of the factory's construction, Albers could only have seen the open-faced grid of the Ullsteinhaus's in-progress façade while working on *Factory*.[fig.7][35] The factory's open façade recalls early work by Mondrian based on the internal structural grids of Parisian buildings with façades removed by demolition. Mondrian's use of open architectonic structure to find a universalizing organizational principle resonates with Albers's entry into the discrete rational forms of his grid-designed glass works and the open-form architecture popular at the Bauhaus at this time. Such architectural forms would have been introduced to Albers in Weimar. The 1923 *Ausstellung Internationale Architekten* displayed the models of Mies van der Rohe's Glass Skyscraper and Gropius's Chicago Tribune Tower. The Mies and Gropius designs were likely a major influence on Albers's *Skyscrapers* series, works which might be considered the ultimate emulation of Gropius's architectonic desires.[fig.8] Siegert notes that the new materials and technologies of Bauhaus architects made it possible to construct a building from the inside out. He suggests that to Mies van der Rohe, only a skyscraper under construction was a real skyscraper, for only so long as its sides had not been closed and covered was the steel skeleton able to make the constructive idea transparent.[36] Glass façades were simply a means of making the inside out, a fact not lost on Albers when his experiments moved glass onto the wall.

The Bauhaus integration of painting and sculpture within architecture was an institutional impetus for Albers to search for the structural rather than the isolated, and he turned to glass to solve those needs. He produced works that were no longer composed of separate elements, like mosaic or stained glass, but rather were one architectonic piece.[37] The integration of these easel-sized glass pieces into the wall was essential to Albers:

> *With my wall glass paintings I have developed a new type of glass picture. By using opaque glass and only one pane for a picture I achieved the movability of a small easel painting permitting [it] to be hung on a wall, as well as to be mounted into the wall as a fixed architectural part, both indoors and outdoors.*[38]

Installed on the wall, these works would operate to, in Mies van der Rohe's terms, make the inside out. This is further reflected in Albers's later writing: "... we, therefore, do not look through it as is the case with stained glass but, because of its reflecting light, we look at it— on or in front of a wall, thus replacing a window in the opening of a wall ..."[39] The ability of these easel paintings to replace a window and to open up the wall through their reflective light is like the Mies skyscraper designs, which open up the façades of a tower through glass, or the open facades which brought Mondrian into his gridded abstractions. The installed flashed glass works would be window-like wall products, sculptural yet two-dimensional objects that fold the three-dimensional grid of architecture blueprint into the very chassis of the gridded glass to turn the skyscraper's glass facade inside-out. Albers's flashed glass works are defined by this collapse of distinctions and the operation that makes such distinctions visible in their collapse.

The interior-exterior oscillation of the gridded flashed glass works makes them interfaces rather than mere windows. Galloway explains in *The Interface Effect* that the interface is an effect, a process, or active threshold mediating between two states. The interface is the state of "being on the boundary," the moment where one significant material is understood as distinct from another significant material. And rather than functioning as a door or window, connecting things to other things, Galloway argues that the digital interface produces an autonomous zone of interaction, orthogonal to the human sensorium, concerned as much with unworkability and obfuscation as with connectivity and transparency.[40] Albers's flashed glass works can be described in terms of the interface in their creation of an effect of a digital distinction between edge and center, inside and outside, and

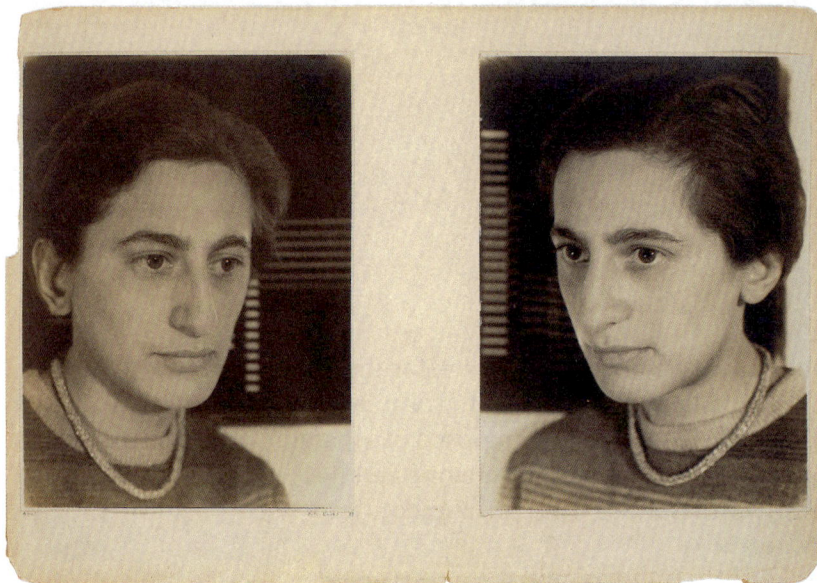

their situating on the boundary between distinct states. Such boundaries would be explored decades later when Albers returned to the thermometer style for his Pan Am Building mural *Manhattan* (1963), a composition based on the earlier flashed glass work *City* (1928) and located at the building's threshold above the escalators connecting the underground and street level. Thus, Albers's use of glass was not solely based in an expressionist craft ethos or industrial production goals, but also in a third transitional position outside of the craft-technology binary. The effect of these works, the folding of window and wall and architectonic into a two-dimensional yet sculptural plane, could only have been achieved in glass and the hard-edged aesthetic distinctions of the sandblasted grids. Only in glass as an interface could such collapse and oscillation between distinctions be possible at this early twentieth-century moment. The flashed glass works project forward as early predecessors of architectural modelling on the glass computer screen, digital media par excellence.

A consideration of the digital in the Bauhaus goes further. A 1929 photo portrait of Anni Albers, also done by Umbo, features her standing in front of Josef's *Skyscrapers A*.[fig.9] The weaving being done by Anni at the moment that Josef was developing his flashed glass aesthetic suggests how intertwined the two were in developing this aesthetic. Her wall hanging works operate in the same visual registers, creating an interchange of horizontal panels in black and white that create a vertical rhythm and infuse her hanging works with an architectonic strength, a digital grid structure. Anni's works, also hung on the wall, occupied the same position as Josef's flashed glass works—curtains, perhaps, rather than windows, not translucent interfaces but nonetheless in a boundary position interacting with the architectural precinct of the wall. A photograph of an early Anni Albers wall hanging taken by Lucia Moholy depicts a clear precursor to the shared aesthetic present in his flashed glass works and her textiles, and suggests that this digital format may have emerged from both Josef's grids and Anni's weaving process.[fig.10] Siegert considers weaving to be another cultural technique, the combination of weave and weft

Fig. 9. Otto Umbehr (Umbo) and Josef Albers, *Anni / Foto Umbo 29,* 1929, gelatin silver prints mounted on cardboard, 28.3 × 41 cm. The Josef and Anni Albers Foundation, 1976.7.1105.

Fig. 10. Photograph of an Anni Albers wall hanging by Lucia Moholy, circa 1924, gelatin silver print.

a "technical repetition [that] refers to itself" in a discrete operation.[41] The title of Anni's later work *Code* (1962) recalls the code which Josef sought as a "way of seeing," and T'ai Smith has described it as "communicating nothing but its own code ... the black lines of code appear only to transmit the operations of [weaving's own methods]."[42] It is a weaving analog to the binary system present in Josef's glass.

The digital thus might bring new avenues of investigation to some Bauhaus workshops deserving of more scholarly attention, such as the weaving workshop. In 1925 Gunta Stölzl began using Jacquard looms in the Bauhaus weaving workshop to create complex designs, looms that rely on a coded mechanical process and that have been identified as "the first specialized graphics computer."[43] Stölzl was thus using the world's first "media synthesizer and manipulator," an imaging machine before digital photography and a discreet data medium before the computer, precisely at the same moment that the Alberses were beginning their inquiries into the forms that should be considered as digital. Future inquiries will consider how we might equally fit the glass works of Josef and the weavings of Anni and Stölzl into a media history that demonstrates the early twentieth-century history of a digital aesthetic.

1   On the move from Expressionism to geometric abstraction and an emphasis on mechanical production processes, see Magdalena Droste, *Bauhaus 1919–1933* (Köln: B. Taschen, 1998), 54; Frank Whitford, *Bauhaus* (London: Thames & Hudson, 1984), 116–21; and Gillian Naylor, *The Bauhaus Reassessed* (London: Herbert Press, 1985), 93–97. Challenges to the periodization of the Bauhaus into distinctly Expressionist and functionalist moments were made by Marcel Franciscono, *Walter Gropius and the Creation of the Bauhaus in Weimar* (Urbana:

University of Illinois Press, 1971); and Jeannine Fiedler and Peter Feierabend, eds., *Bauhaus* (Cologne: Könemann, 1999).
2   Achim Borchardt-Hume, *Albers and Moholy-Nagy: From the Bauhaus to the New World* (New Haven, CT: Yale University Press, 2006), 66.
3   Albers most thoroughly describes the process behind the creation of his works in flashed glass in an undated statement in the Josef Albers Papers, vol. 2, Sterling Memorial Library, Manuscripts and Archives, Yale

University, New Haven. Reproduced in *Josef Albers: Vitraux, Dessins, Gravures, Typographie, Meubles* (Paris: Éditions Hazan, and Le Cateau-Cambrésis: Musée départemental Matisse, 2008), 62.

4   A number of German manufacturers were producing flashed glass commercially at the time. Oliver Barker notes that Albers likely did not execute these sandblasted works himself, and that the flashed glass works were etched on Albers's behalf by the Berlin firm of Puhl & Wagner under the leadership of Gottfried Heinersdorff. Many of the studies for the flashed glass works include technical instructions for fabrication in the margins. Oliver Barker, "To Open Eyes: Josef Albers at the Bauhaus," in *Josef Albers: Vitraux*, 225.

5   Sarah Hermanson Meister has recently suggested the connection between Albers's glass works and his late-1920s photography. Sarah Hermanson Meister, "Josef Albers: An Open Mind for the Newer and Nearer," in *One and One Is Four: The Bauhaus Photocollages of Josef Albers* (New York: The Museum of Modern Art, 2016), 16–17.

6   Peter Nisbet, "Josef Albers Lattice Picture. 1921," in Bergdoll, Barry, and Leah Dickerman, *Bauhaus 1919–1933: Workshops for Modernity* (New York: Museum of Modern Art, 2009), 92.

7   Michael White, "Mechano-Facture: Dada/Constructivism and the Bauhaus," in Achim Borchardt-Hume, *Albers and Moholy-Nagy: From the Bauhaus to the New World* (New Haven, CT: Yale University Press, 2006), 79.

8   Alexander Galloway, *Laruelle: Against the Digital* (Minneapolis: University of Minneapolis Press, 2014), xix–xxviii.

9   Gilles Deleuze, *Francis Bacon: Logique de la sensation* (Paris: Éditions de la différence, 1981), 95.

10   Josef Albers, "Zur Ökonomie der Schriftform," *Offset: Buch- und Werbekunst*, no. 10 (1926), reproduced in Gerd Fleischmann, *Bauhaus: Drucksachen, Typographie, Reklame* (Stuttgart: Oktagon, 1995), 23.

11   Walter Gropius, "Neues Bauen," *Der Holzbau*, supplement to *Deutsche Bauzeitung*, 1920/2, 5, translated and cited in Wolfgang Pehnt, "Gropius the Romantic," *The Art Bulletin* 53, no. 3 (September 1971): 386.

12   Brenda Danilowitz, "From Symbolism to Modernism: The Evolution of Josef Albers's Architectural Glass Works," in *Josef Albers: Vitraux*, 171. Bruno Taut's famous Glass House at the 1914 German Werkbund exhibition in Cologne was inspirational for the glass symbolism of the Bauhaus Manifesto. Prikker's work was also included in the ornament room of Taut's Glass House.

13   In a tragic sense, Albers's work with glass would come full circle to his earliest experiments with the fragments of the *Scherbenbilder*, as many of his later glass works were reduced to shattered pieces when destroyed by bombings during World War II or broken after being shipped from Germany to the US. The ideal whole constructed from individual shards in the early Bauhaus would thus be reduced to the fragment as a byproduct of the trauma of conflict and exile.

14   This work is also identified as *Lattice Painting* and *Grid Mounted*, which Albers wrote on the back of the handmade frame in the 1950s (since removed). See Nicholas Fox Weber, "The Artist as Alchemist," *Josef Albers: A Retrospective* (New York: Solomon R. Guggenheim Foundation, 1988), 49, fn. 10.

15   Droste, *Bauhaus*, 86.

16   Nisbet, "Josef Albers Lattice Picture," 92.

17   Barker, "To Open Eyes," 18.

18   Fred Licht, "Albers: Glass, Color, and Light," in *Josef Albers: Glass, Color, Light* (New York: The Solomon R. Guggenheim Foundation, 1994), 19.

19   Oskar Schlemmer, Letter to Otto Meyer, January 3, 1926, in *The Letters and Diaries of Oskar Schlemmer*, Tut Schlemmer, ed. (Middletown, CT: Wesleyan University Press, 1972), 188–89.

20   Quoted in Michel Seuphor, *Piet Mondrian: Life and Work*, (New York: Harry N. Abrams, Inc., 1957), 168.

21   Bernhard Siegert, "Cultural Techniques, or the End of the Intellectual Postwar Era in German Media Theory," *Theory, Culture & Society* 30, no. 6 (November 2013): 50.

22   Siegert, "Cultural Techniques," 52.

23   Bernhard Siegert, *Cultural Techniques: Grids, Filters, Doors, and other Articulations of the Real* (New York: Fordham University Press, 2015), 11–15.

24   Siegert, "Cultural Techniques," 62.

25   Siegert, *Cultural Techniques*, 99–100.

26   Yves-Alain Bois, *Painting as Model* (Cambridge, MA: MIT Press, 1990), 104.

27   Bernhard Siegert, *Passage des Digitalen. Zeichenpraktiken der neuzeitlichen Wissenschaften 1500–1900* (Berlin: Brinkmann & Bose, 2003), 3–10.

28   Geoffrey Winthorp-Young and Bernhard Siegert, "Material World," *Artforum* (Summer 2015), 333.

29   Josef Albers, undated statement in the Josef Albers Papers, vol. 2, Sterling Memorial Library, Manuscripts and Archives, Yale University, New Haven. Reproduced in *Josef Albers: Vitraux*, 62.

30   Barker, "To Open Eyes," 19.

31   Siegert, *Cultural Techniques*, 115.

32   Danilowitz, "From Symbolism to Modernism," 176.

33   Danilowitz suggests the commission was achieved solely through Heinersdorff, who had criticized Albers's glass work in Weimar. The windows designed by Albers were fabricated in 1926–27 by Heinersdorff's firm, Puhl & Wagner. Danilowitz, "From Symbolism to Modernism," 174, 214. On Heinersdorff and German glass producers, see Maria-Katharina Schulz, *Glasmalerei der klassischen Moderne in Deutschland* (Frankfurt am Main: P. Lang, 1987); and Helmut Geisert and Elisabeth Moortgat, *Wände aus farbigem Glas: Das Archiv der Vereinigten Werkstätten für Mosaik und Glasmalerei Puhl & Wagner, Gottfried Heinersdorff* (Berlin: Berlinische Galerie, 1989).

34   *Offset: Buch und Werbekunst*, vol. 7, special Bauhaus issue (Leipzig 1926). Reproduced in Fox Weber, "The Artist as Alchemist," 27.

35   Eugen G. Schmohl, *Ein Industriebau von der Fundierung bis zur Vollendung* (Berlin: Bauwelt-Verlag, 1927).

36   Ludwig Mies van der Rohe, "Hochhausprojekt für Bahnhof Friedrichstrasse in Berlin (1922)" in *Frühlicht 1920–1922: Eine Folge für die Verwirklichung des neuen Baugedankens*, ed. Bruno Taut (Berlin, Frankfurt am Main, and Vienna: Ullstein, 1963), 213; Siegert, *Cultural Techniques*, 117.

37   Licht, "Albers: Glass, Color, and Light," 19.

38   Josef Albers, undated statement in the Josef Albers Papers, vol. 2, Sterling Memorial Library, Manuscripts and Archives, Yale University, New Haven. Reproduced in *Josef Albers: Vitraux*, 62.

39   Josef Albers, "Jahresbericht," *Zürcher Kunstgesellschaft*, 1960. Reproduced in *Josef Albers: Vitraux*, 84.

40   Alexander Galloway, *The Interface Effect* (Cambridge, UK: Polity, 2012).

41   Siegert, *Cultural Techniques*, 61.

42   T'ai Smith, *Bauhaus Weaving Theory: From Feminine Craft to Mode of Design* (Minneapolis: University of Minnesota Press, 2014), 148.

43   Lev Manovich, *Language of New Media* (Cambridge, MA: MIT Press, 2002), 26.

*Christopher
T. Green*

Towards
a
Digital
Bauhaus

Robin Schuldenfrei

Reinscribing Mies's Materiality

Fig.1. Ludwig Mies van der Rohe, interior renovation of the Director's House (architect: Walter Gropius), Dessau, 1931. Dining room. Photograph by Walter Peterhans.
Fig.2. Walter and Ise Gropius in the living room of the Director's House, 1927. Photograph by Lucia Moholy.

Ludwig Mies van der Rohe, upon taking over the Director's House in Dessau as the third and last director of the Bauhaus, renovated it by stripping it bare of its former materials and inserting a minimum of furnishings. [fig.1]1 His interior, like his directorship, was very different from that of the house's architect and Bauhaus founder, Walter Gropius, who moved in with his new wife, Ise, in 1926, and set up a modern but comfortable interior replete with domestic objects and furniture designed by the Bauhaus: a tea corner with hot and cold running water, volumes of books, and even an interior cactus garden. [fig.2]2 Upon Gropius's resignation, architect Hannes Meyer took over the school as its second director in April 1928 and occupied the house with his wife and two children. While no photographs of the interior during Meyer's time have emerged to date, his pared-down asceticism is exemplified by the stripped-down interiors, especially the dormitories, of the ADGB Trade Union School in Bernau (1928–30), which he was designing with Hans Wittwer in the same period. Moreover, his 1926 Co-op Zimmer project—an interior intended for the modern nomad containing merely a bed, a folding chair, a shelf of edible provisions, and a phonograph—portends his own peripatetic trajectory upon leaving the Bauhaus, moving first to the Soviet Union and then to Mexico. In his refurbishment of the Director's House, Mies encased the interior in floor-to-ceiling drapes and natural floor matting, completing the living room with a pair of both his deep-set leather and chrome Barcelona and Tugendhat chairs, grouped around a glass-topped Tugendhat coffee table; the dining room was similarly sparsely furnished, with four cantilever chairs around a chromed-leg dining table. The recent past, with its domestic detritus of the previous two directors—and

their metaphorical Bauhaus dust—was swept away in favor of a present of sheening immediacy, bringing the spaces' materiality to the fore. Mies similarly sought to remove the politicized recent history of the school he had inherited from Meyer, expelling students he deemed problematic and centralizing the place of architecture within the school. In the span of his short, three-year tenure as director (1930–33), he brought order and a seriousness of purpose to the Bauhaus and began to train architects in great numbers for the first time in the school's history.[3] Although Gropius, as the founder of the Bauhaus, had always envisioned a central role for architecture at the school, in its earliest iteration in Weimar he had mainly been concerned with uniting the arts with craft production, and then in 1923 changed course with the slogan "art and technology—a new unity," converting the school into a series of laboratories that were to create prototypes of modern products for industry. While the legacy of the Bauhaus includes the dissemination of a modern architectural style globally— white façades, glass curtain walls, and flat roofs—it was only with the arrival of Hannes Meyer in 1927 that the school began to teach architecture as part of a formalized program. Under Mies, architecture was approached through a coherent and deep investigation of the design process, architecture's objects and materials. The study of history, however, had little place in Mies's curriculum, as studio practice and step-by-step learning with increasing degrees of task complexity became the method by which Mies, and his faculty, taught.

A consideration of the architectural work that Mies created just prior to his directorship is germane to understanding both his entire Weimar Republic-era oeuvre and the last period of the Bauhaus. The examination of this work—a nexus of architectural spaces and the materials comprising them, which become a means of connecting dwellers to ideas of modern habitation—will contribute to a deeper and more nuanced reading of his output. Mies's professed allegiances to the ideologies of modern architecture—to its avowed beliefs in technology, rationalism, functionalism, the mass production of housing, and ideas of replication—will be called into question. This chapter will argue that by fostering opportunities by which subjects could attach to objects in a meaningful, subjective manner, Mies put human-centered activity and a heightening of experience at the center of his design. With his seemingly empty spaces, smooth surfaces, rarified objects, and materials, he enabled subjectivity via the materiality of his modern architecture.

Ideas associated with the work of Mies tend to be all-encompassing, even totalizing. This is something that Mies himself never sought to contradict, but the legacy circling around Mies tends to be situated within a particular kind of historicity (reflective of our own billowing dust—as historians, artists, and architects) and the longer duration of the historiography of the modern movement in architecture. Present in speeches, manifestos, and exhibition publications, the discourses of functionalism within architecture came to a crescendo in the 1920s and early 1930s, before settling in for the longue durée of promoting rationalism in architectural history and theory thereafter. In looking anew at Mies's materiality, this essay seeks to draw attention to Mies's choice of materials, namely the peculiarity of his use of some of the most ostentatious materials available—onyx, antique green marble, and travertine, as well as the rarefied surfaces resulting from the use of nickel plating, chromium, and colored glass.

Finally, this essay will layer the human subject back into a reading of Mies's architecture and examine how he sought meaning not only in the materials deployed, but specifically as the means of connecting his dwellers to his spaces, therein heightening awareness of the subject in a direct relationship to the object. Using Mies's own writing, his work, and his teaching, it will argue that materials and interior objects become the points of connection, in spaces that were not abstract or cold, or unattuned to the needs of clients. Rather, materiality provided the very mode of reinscribing architecture with meaning, in an abrupt break with what Mies himself called "cold functionalism," of coming to know architecture again, through some of its most basic elements: steps and walls, frames and openings.

The materials of Mies's modern architecture stand apart from those of his peers; they are striking, whether in their stark, unadorned plainness (white linoleum), or via their technical virtuosity, or in their visual allure through the showcasing of new materials (chromium plating), in their return to and showcasing of previously concealed materials (exposed steel beams), or traditional materials newly deployed for modernism (flat planes of travertine, marble, and onyx, as well as macassar ebony, palisander, rosewood, and zebra veneers). It was not only the rigorous solidity in Mies's selection and placement of materials, but also the way in which he contrasted their presence with immateriality and the ephemeral qualities of yet other materials— from spare, blank walls, to the transparency or semi-transparency of

*Robin
Schuldenfrei*

Reinscribing
Mies's
Materiality

133

Fig. 3a. Mies, Villa Tugendhat, Brno, Czech Republic,
1928–30. Entrance façade.
Fig. 3b. Mies, Villa Tugendhat, Brno, 1928–30. Rear
façade.

varieties of glass, to the arresting voids created by his sinkable windows. In his sketches, Mies specified the direction of the wood and marble grains so that the slabs could be laid in such a way that they would explicitly contrast with the travertine and flat glass walls.[4]

Mies's domestic projects and the exhibition houses he designed in collaboration with his partner Lilly Reich engendered a new kind of experience and relationship between subjects and objects, achieved through modernism's rich materiality—whether natural or man-made, or constituting surface or form. This chapter will look to the Villa Tugendhat (1928–30) for Grete and Fritz Tugendhat and their young family in Brno, an industrial city on the eastern border of the Czech Republic. This house, made of concrete over a steel skeleton that allowed for large, open interior expanses, expressed through its materiality Mies's merging of modern form with materialized surface.[fig.3, 4] Similarly, a manifest instance of the shifting subjectivity of material form and surface in Mies's work is to be found in the materials and planes of the German Pavilion, more commonly known as the Barcelona Pavilion, Germany's contribution to the 1929 International Exposition in Barcelona, Spain.[fig.5] [5] Its interconnecting planes of stone and the cruciform supporting columns together create a loose enclosure, yet the resulting space can as easily be read as a profligate display of surfaces. The pair of villas that Mies designed in Krefeld for the Lange and Esters families will likewise be read for the multiple meanings of Mies's expressive choice of material, surface, and form. Whether for a large-scale family villa or the showcasing of modern dwelling ideals through exhibition houses for the general public, Mies, it will be shown, expressed his ideas about modern housing through his individual materials—giving careful attention to their substance and their surfaces alike.

These materials were also statements of modern elegance and luxury, rather than mass production, industry, or technology—competing concepts that captivated his peers and the period discourse alike. Materials were reappropriated by Mies with an intensified focus, and differently coded so that the luxury they represented was repositioned to emphasize materiality, surface luminosity, and refined technology. The idea of luxurious materials was neither new to architecture nor to the bourgeois interior; however, Mies utilized these materials to deploy luxury within the visual and theoretical paradigm of modernism.[6] It is without question that this had always been the case with regard

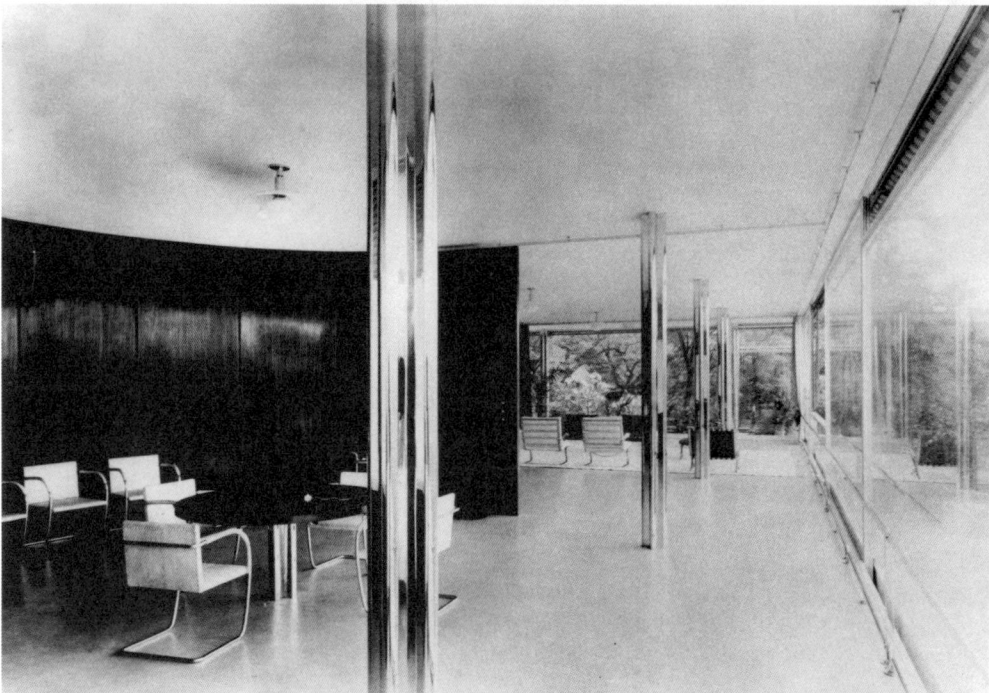

Fig. 4a. Mies, Villa Tugendhat at night, Brno, 1928–30.
Rear façade.

Fig. 4b. Mies, Villa Tugendhat, main living floor, Brno,
1928–30. View from the dining
area to the living area and
conservatory.

Fig. 5. Mies, German
Pavilion, Barcelona, Spain,
1928–29. View of the interior.

Fig. 6. Mies, Villa Tugendhat,
daughter Hanna's room,
Brno, 1928–30. Interior in
zebrawood veneer.

to an elite clientele and their architectural representations, from Louis xiv's hall of mirrors at Versailles to Karl Friedrich Schinkel's pavilion at Schloss Charlottenburg. Invoking and calling attention to the materiality of modernism, from the glass curtain wall to the intricately veined onyx slab, from the shimmering cruciform column to the white solidity of a travertine floor, from mobile, sinkable windows to his stable, heavy furnishings, Mies's material choices were meaningful in their luxurious expression of modern materiality itself. In addition to traditional meanings, the materials used in the modern period reflected new tasks for architecture and the ways in which dwelling subjects, in turn, might relate to architecture.

Mies's architecture of the 1920s and 1930s merged modern form with surface in a way that flaunted a conspicuous, potent materiality. His use of ostentatious natural materials celebrated raw details of that natural world: the marble and onyx slabs were carefully selected for their large, dramatic veins; travertine for its craggy texture; the zebra-wood or macassar veneers for their seemingly magnified wood grains.[fig.5, 6] Bold pigskin Barcelona chairs and shaggy sheepskin rugs did not try to disguise their animal origins. In contrast to the prevalent rayon of the period, with its preternatural smoothness and its slippery draping qualities, Mies and Reich's heavy, dark silks displayed the large slubs characteristic of unrefined, natural silk fibers. But even so, nature was held at bay; Mies exhibited an extravagant mastery over nature, used for maximum effect. His emphasis on natural materials was telling, as if designed to counter the superficiality of the ever more prevalent and present industrial production propagandized by—if not forming the actual substance of—modern architecture.

In the same interiors, this overstated materiality was in contrast with the dematerialized effect of other substances. At the Villa Tugendhat, and elsewhere, the shiny surface of the nickel- or chrome-plated cruciform column, through its reflection and refraction of the interior shapes, colors, and materials, deflected or absorbed the interior rather than competing with it.[fig.7] Expected and manageable borders, such as window frames, become shimmering metal chimera, while windows were folded back entirely, disappearing into themselves, or withdrawing altogether by descending into the house's depths.[fig.4] Devoid of personal artifacts and offering only smooth, flat surfaces, these interiors offered no crevices for entrapping dust, only a richly gleaming present.

In this period, vast new fortunes were being made, not only by factory owners and those directly connected to industry; an affluent managerial class and successful creative class, among others, was emerging. These new groups desired to be housed in dwellings representative of their status and wealth, which was reflected in Mies's choice of materials, illustrating one way in which objects—and their surfaces—could be aligned with subjects.[7] The complicated relationship of modern architecture to concepts of materiality, technology, and bourgeois dwelling come together in Mies's designs for Hermann Lange and Josef Esters, two industrialists for whom he built large houses (1927–30) on adjacent plots in the city of Krefeld.[fig.8]

In the Krefeld villas, extravagant baseboards, wooden wall partitions, metal frames, travertine sills and wooden paneling concealing radiators, all insistently called attention to their constitutional materiality, while also serving to delineate an unambiguous, materialized border.[fig.9] There are shifting valences of materiality at play between the solids and frames within the two Krefeld houses. Oak pocket doors between the dining room and the children's playroom of the Esters house, for example, can be slid closed, transforming a frame into a visual solid. Similarly, the four-panel wooden structure in the Lange House's dining room gives the impression of a solid wall, but it is not solid; it was demountable, allowing the dining room to be combined with the large central hall during social events.[8] Doorways are framed in walnut and oak, not precisely lined up as in an enfilade with a single vanishing point, but staggered slightly with frames visible to the left or right.[fig.10] This placement emphasizes the wood of the baseboards and door frames while offering a view across several thresholds, connecting and visually opening up these spaces.[9]

Robin Schuldenfrei

Reinscribing Mies's Materiality

139

Fig.8. Mies, Lange House, Krefeld, 1927–30.

Fig.9. Mies, Lange House, Krefeld, 1927–30. Open plan and descending window. Window frames and radiator covering in walnut, with travertine windowsills.

Fig. 10. Mies, Esters House, Krefeld, 1927–30. View from dining room into children's playroom, through to women's sitting room.

Via his use of materials, Mies's architecture suggests that what gives the impression of solidity can turn out to be mere surface, and what appears as only surface can be substantial. The finely pointed purple-red exterior brick, installed by skilled masons with utmost care, displays boldly variegated colors that appear stolidly solid. And yet the external walls are not as substantial as they appear; rather, these bricks are surface decoration, set as cladding over larger, low-grade, rough bricks.[10] The widely veined macassar wood of the front doors calls attention to each door's being a wooden front door; the otherwise everyday character of a common wooden front door is amplified here in the oversized wood grains, a radical representation of its materiality.[fig. 11] Yet it is not evidence of the solidity it projects; it is just a thin veneer, a surface materiality.

The technical complexity behind both houses' open spaces is revealed in their intricate and exacting structural engineering. The Lange House required 88 pages of structural calculations; 124 pages were required for the Esters House, which also had 350 steel beams.[11] Necessitating careful planning and structural calculations, bookshelves and smaller glass cupboards were not simply attached to the masonry, as is common, but rather set deeply into the walls themselves, rendering them effectively immobile, a stable component of the house's materiality. The Esters's casement windows were framed and hinged at 180 degrees so that they folded all the way over onto themselves when open, thereby nearly disappearing.[12] The Lange House had motorized, sinkable windows which lowered the glass to the basement for a complete opening to the garden in both the study and the living room, pre-dating those of the Villa Tugendhat.[fig. 9] The elegance of this technical luxury was in stark contrast to the very basic hand-cranked wheel by Walter Gropius that simultaneously swung open groups of six small windows at the Dessau Bauhaus building. Mies subsumed a more industrial technology in favor of elegant individual solutions.

Mies created interiors that were radical in appearance, luxurious in materiality, but accommodating of those bourgeois activities

Robin Schuldenfrei

Reinscribing Mies's Materiality

141

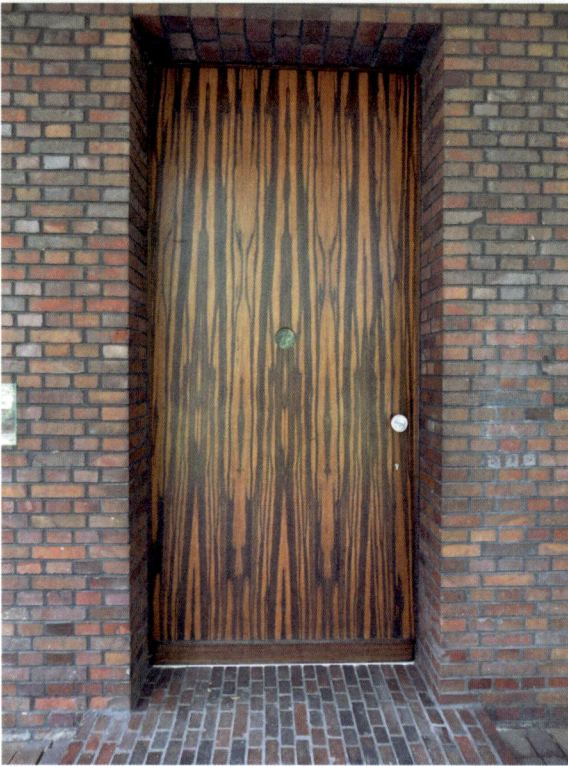

Fig. 11. Mies, Lange House, front door, Krefeld, 1927–30.

normally encouraged by—and reflected in—these traditional upper-class spaces. The materiality of these spaces took into consideration potential subjects and individual subjectivity; these houses were modern, but allowed for the individual activities of their bourgeois owners, as was evidenced by Mies's inclusion of sitting rooms, winter gardens, and studies.

While the open plan is perhaps the defining characteristic of Mies's work during this period, in other commissions, such as the German Pavilion in Barcelona, it is his placement of material objects in space that call attention to the infiniteness of surrounding space—highlighting and counteracting the space by punctuating it with columns and freestanding walls, as well as framing it at intervals and giving it intermittent borders.[fig.5] As Mies himself remembered about the Barcelona Pavilion: "One evening as I was working late on the building I made a sketch of a freestanding wall, and I got a shock. I knew it was a new principle."[13] The freestanding slab walls, cruciform columns, even metal window frames, stand out and project toward the viewer, contributing to their own infiniteness while emphasizing form and materiality.[fig.12] Mies stressed the material surfaces rather than structure or the enclosed space. The expressive effects of materiality are intensified through the employment of unconventional, luxurious materials, and are further heightened by the open surrounding space that allows them to be set apart.

In Barcelona, the interconnecting planes of stone and regular supporting columns together form a loose enclosure, yet the resulting configuration can as easily be read as a profligate display of surfaces. This is especially intensified by the reflections in the varied glass (gray, green, white, translucent), metal, and water, and by the expertly selected stone specimens (green marble, onyx, travertine), whose decorative qualities were heightened by extravagant patterning and dramatic book-matching. Visitors were enthralled. Archival documents show that the materials of the Barcelona Pavilion prompted so many inquiries from the public that the ministerial director asked Mies to provide information regarding the source of the marble, travertine,

Fig. 12a. Mies, German
Pavilion, Barcelona, 1928–29.
Photograph by Berliner Bild-
Bericht.

Fig. 12b. Mies, German
Pavilion, Barcelona, 1928–29,
crayon and pencil on
illustration board. Interior
perspective.

and other substances.[14] Mies connected material objects with experiencing subjects; materiality engendered subjectivity.

The highly reflective cruciform columns, used in Barcelona, at the Villa Tugendhat, and elsewhere, reflect, refract, and also distort both the subjects and their surrounding interior spaces.[fig. 5, 7] The interior appears to be in continual motion and flux—a destabilized yet dynamic interior always experienced subjectively—changing as the viewer moves through the space and as elements in the interior are reflected in its contents. There is an indeterminacy to these columns, as objects. They can be viewed as fixed, punctuating the open space. Or, conversely, as they reflect the unfolding space around them, nearly dissolving, they might be seen as dematerialized objects. They read less as structure than as status-shifting materialized/dematerialized objects.

Materiality, rather than structure, as the organizing aspect of the interior, is also key in smaller commissions, such as Mies and Reich's Glass Room, which had white milk glass, mouse gray, and olive-green glass partitions.[fig. 13] Due to the materials' varying levels of opacity, visitors could glimpse through to other spaces, while elsewhere only the contents of the room itself and its visitors were reflected back. The glass, set in frames, draws attention to the metal as a framing device and the room's modular organization. Here, as K. Michael Hays has noted, "the particular quality of each material is registered as a kind of absolute; thus space itself becomes a function of the specificities of the materials."[15] The human subject is not only situated by Mies's materiality (rather than structure), but also interacts with the materials, depending on their respective qualities: reflective, semi-opaque, or transparent. The experience of the space is variable—a status-shifting materiality which connects, but also destabilizes, the subject.

Although they were woefully inadequate to addressing the housing crisis underway in 1931 Berlin, the demonstration houses for *The Dwelling in Our Time* at the Berlin Building Exhibition form, perhaps, the apotheosis of Mies and Reich's ideas about dwelling as they connected to materiality.[16] In Reich's famous all-white bedroom displayed at the exhibition, a luxurious deep-piled white carpet, a white suede chair, an all-white bed, and tubular steel and glass furniture put rich materials in conversation with each other as much as the conjured dweller. Likewise, Mies's contribution, a *House for a Childless Couple*, suggests domestic use by seemingly staging a material dialogue

between imagined modern subjects and their objects. Philip Johnson's 1931 review captures the resulting experience: "The interior of this house shows the simple device Mies uses to achieve his effects—the contrast of chrome steel posts against the plain white plaster or richly grained woods, blue silk hangings and the leather upholstered chrome chairs on a dark brown carpet ... There are no windows, only glass walls. The materials themselves and the contrasts give elegance and beauty."[17]

Perhaps the most extreme example of the fluctuating, subjective effects of materiality, rather than structure, as defining space can be found in Mies and Reich's use of textiles. The pair had established the rich structure-giving possibilities of textiles in their design of the opulent Velvet and Silk café, installed at the 1927 Women's Fashion Exhibition in Berlin. The enclosing space was formed by encircling, draped velvet and silk fabric, which fulfilled a pseudo-structural function, forming curtain "walls" of gold, silver, lemon-yellow, and black silk and orange, red, and black velvet.[18] The overall resulting effect was a subjective architectural experience in which nothing was fixed—it was a fluid materiality that entirely constituted and defined the space.

The drapes of the Tugendhat functioned in a similar manner. A black Shantung silk curtain was hung in front of the winter garden, a black velvet curtain was placed beside it, a silver-gray Shantung silk was hung along the main glass wall, and a white velvet curtain was placed between the library and the entrance area.[19] These, in concert with internal curtains running on tracts, created nighttime interior enclosures, resulting in an intimate feeling of contained space, *Raumgefühl*, while simultaneously enveloping the dweller, literally and

Robin Schuldenfrei

Reinscribing Mies's Materiality

145

figuratively, in fluid material luxury.[fig. 14] In his renovation of the Director's House in Dessau, Mies repeated this treatment, installing floor-to-ceiling drapes in front of the windows, doors, and as a means of separating the open-plan living room from the dining room.[fig. 1]

Breaking with earlier bourgeoisie dwellings, open plans allowed for, and encouraged, subjects to meander at their own will, rather than follow a prescribed room sequence. At the Villa Tugendhat especially, it is the material objects which act as the organizing elements within the space; open-ended as they seem, they define and divide the living room from the dining room, the library, and the study.[fig. 4, 14] It is around these objects—fixed entities in stone, metal, and wood—that the subjects must navigate and organize themselves, and against which the activities of daily life took place, such as dining, familial interaction, play, and solitary reading.

Fritz Tugendhat's photographs of family members at close range in front of the glass and alluring macassar and onyx walls situate them as places where their daily lives unfolded.[20] These images of life in the Villa Tugendhat demonstrate the material experience of it that becomes the house's content. Each material seemingly participates in—or forms a backdrop to—the subjective actions of the dwellers. It is against these set objects—objects that are rare, auratic—that the subjectivity of Mies's architecture is made manifest.

The result is a space of varying conditions affording an ever-changing experience, as augmented by the time of day, weather, and seasonal conditions. Unlike earlier comparable representational interiors, in which certain tasks were assigned to specific rooms and utilized at distinct periods of the day—breakfast room, dining room,

Fig. 14. Mies, Villa Tugendhat, Brno, 1928–30.

ladies' parlor—the open plan affords a heightened awareness of the
changing space as a whole, as measured against its interior objects and
the activities of its inhabitants.

Surfaces, in this period, came under scrutiny. Beyond the expen-
diture needed to acquire, refine, and install the materials of modernism, even seemingly common materials such as metal and glass were
costly to maintain and keep clean. This was noted by critics as well
as lamented by modernism's proponents. Czech architectural critic
Karel Teige aptly, if polemically, enumerated the labor behind the dust-
free surfaces of modern architecture, stating, "the modern rich ... do
not mind spending large sums on construction and maintenance,
squandering money on the need to heat superfluous glass halls, and
paying their servants to polish, clean, and mop the glass and chrome
that so fascinate the modern snob architect and his clients."[21] In
the bourgeois room of the 1880s, dust had permeated the interior, as
Walter Benjamin writes: "The étuis, dust covers, sheaths with which
the bourgeois household ... encased its utensils were so many measures taken to capture and preserve traces."[22] Benjamin observed
the owner's traces as inscribed everywhere, a last attempt to "express"
one's personality.[23] But in modernism, in what Benjamin termed
"adjustable, movable glass-covered dwellings," the glass, "a cold and
sober material," a hard, smooth surface onto which nothing could be
fixed, resulted in rooms in which dwellers could no longer leave
traces.[24] A related lament at the time was the perceived coldness in
modern architecture's move towards rationality, specifically through
cold, technical materials. As Benjamin noted, "Warmth is ebbing
from things. Objects of daily use gently but insistently repel us."[25]
And the sociologist Georg Simmel had already noted with disquiet
in 1900: "Modern man is surrounded by nothing but impersonal
objects ... Cultural objects increasingly evolve into an interconnected
enclosed world that has increasingly fewer points at which the subjective soul can interpose. Objects and people have become separated
from one another."[26] Critics worried that in these new interiors
it was impossible to form habits, leave traces, or even possess objects,
contributing to the anomie of modernity.

Throughout 1927 and into 1928, Mies experienced a shift in outlook in terms of tying the encountering subject to the architectural. In
precisely the same period as he was designing the Barcelona Pavilion
and the Villa Tugendhat, his most canonical works in terms of material

*Robin
Schuldenfrei*

Reinscribing
Mies's
Materiality

147

virtuosity, he was writing in his terse, laconic manner about his search for a way to connect the form-giving process of his architecture to the dwelling's subjects in an authentic and profound manner, articulating a manifest interconnectivity between life and form. It began at the Weissenhof exhibition with his published statement: "The problem of rationalization and typification is only part of the problem ... the struggle for new housing is only an element of the larger struggle for new forms of living."[27] In his diary of 1928, Mies would write a telegraphic, condensed version: "New demands: Connections with real life. New man. Form relationship to surroundings. Not rejection but mastery."[28] Another entry is especially revealing: "We want to give meaning again to things. Who still feels anything of a wall, an opening? ... We want to give sense again to things ... Steps, spaces. One has lost the meaning of this language, one feels nothing anymore."[29] In 1928, Mies posited that "the central problem of our time—the intensification of life" needed to be showcased, in order to "bring about a revolution of our thinking."[30] In the same year, he wrote, "building art (*Baukunst*) ... is in reality only understandable as a *life process*, it is an expression of man's ability to assert himself and master his surroundings."[31] He made direct connections between an intensity and authenticity in form, and ideas of intensity and authenticity in internal life. Mies writes, "only a vital inside has a vital outside. Only life intensity has form intensity. ... Authentic form presupposes authentic life. ... We value not the result but the starting point of the form-giving process. ... Life is what matters. In its entire fullness, in its spiritual and concrete interconnection."[32]

To Mies, architecture will have meaning only if its forms and materials connect to life, that is, if humans are able to feel something meaningful for their surroundings. This runs distinctly counter to a dominant trend in modern architecture in the period, in which architects strove for the objective (*sachlich*) rationalism of standardized, mass-produced solutions that supplied the maximum number of dwelling units, with scaled-down interiors designed for a minimal existence (*Existenzminimum*). Ludwig Hilberseimer's 1924 High-rise City (*Hochhausstadt*) project for Berlin and designs published throughout his 1927 book, *Großstadtarchitektur*, exemplify this trend. Mies, taking a very different turn, began to use unexpected materials in modern housing —onyx, travertine, highly polished metals—that engendered a subjective response. Moreover, to Mies, it is the elements that make up architecture, its components, that act as the points of connection between people and their surroundings. He sought to evoke feeling for—and thus give meaning again to—the constitutive parts of which architecture is formed: walls, openings, steps, columns.

Luxurious, rarefied materials especially served this consequential goal. Mies's interiors of this period might be read not as an ostentatious display of social status, as was often charged, but rather as a means of proffering a complex sensory experience, a heightened awareness of objects, and a cognizance of the subjective conditions of space, specifically as a mode by which to reestablish meaning in architecture for its subjects. In order "to give sense again to things," Mies carefully selected his stone specimen himself and was explicit, with Reich, in the specification of other materials. As Grete Tugendhat recalled, "Mies clarified to us the importance of the use of noble (*edel*) material, especially in modern building."[33] But Mies also differentiated between the representative potential of the materials and their perceived value. He stated, "there is a hierarchy of things," and one must "assume a position that relates to them. To the hierarchy of objects corresponds a hierarchy of levels of perception on which the perceiver stands and on which he must stand if he wants to relate to the object. There is an awareness attitude assigned to each object ... [differentiated with] respect to their intrinsic nature ... [and] also according to the type and rank of their dignity."[34]

In this context, Mies uses luxury materials to reinscribe meaning into modern space, by connecting the experiencing subject to haptic materiality and optical dematerialization. Rarefied materials provided points of tactile and visual connection between a given room and its potential inhabitants, such as the deep pile of the sheepskin rug and the cherry-red leather of the Brno chair in Grete Tugendhat's bedroom or the zebrawood veneer of daughter Hanna's room.[fig.6] The Tugendhat onyx wall especially presented this opportunity. Not load-bearing, it was thus freed from performing any architectural function beyond loosely dividing up the space, and could serve as a material object onto which to attach meaning. In addition to its rich materiality, it was highly polished, and thus its reflective qualities meant that it was continually changing, acting as a central point of magnetism. Grete Tugendhat recalled that as the setting sun illuminated this semi-translucent wall, light would penetrate it, causing it to glow red on the reverse side.[35]

Robin Schuldenfrei

Reinscribing Mies's Materiality

149

Mies used the materiality of rare or new materials to heighten awareness, for the subject: the ever-changing interior and exterior conditions. By 1933 Mies could write with conviction: "Now it becomes clear again what a wall is, what an opening, what is floor and what ceiling."[36] Wall, window, and void alike were reinscribed with meaning, via their materiality and their connection to the subject.

These convictions regarding form, materiality, and the subject strongly influenced Mies's Bauhaus teaching and tenure as director. Upon taking over the directorship in August 1930, he revised the curriculum, re-orientating the school towards architecture. He created the Department of Architecture and Interior Design, which aggregated architecture, interior design, and the furniture, metalwork, and wall-painting workshops.[37] Along with Mies, Ludwig Hilberseimer taught architecture, other experts gave instruction in technical aspects, and from 1932, Lilly Reich supervised the interior design department and the weaving workshop. All three continued teaching at the Bauhaus in Berlin after it was forced to close in Dessau in October 1932.

Mies assigned his students the same tasks that he was working on in his private practice—mainly domestic projects—translating an emphasis on materials and the subjective response to them into pedagogical exercises. A typical straightforward assignment was to design a small house with a courtyard on a flat site—a simple shell that allowed students to focus on the formation of interior space, its objects, and materials. Student drawings show a careful presentation of the proposed building materials, including brick walls, carefully articulated paving stones for outdoor patios, meticulously delineated wood grains for interior walls and bookcases, and richly veined stone (see, for example, the Bauhaus student work of Eduard Ludwig, Howard Dearstyne, or Günter Conrad).[fig. 15][38] Students could follow Mies's work on the contemporaneous, small, one-story courtyard house for Karl and Martha Lemke (1932–33), a modest commission that included window walls on two sides facing the garden. The house evinced a rich materiality, beginning with the façade, whose hand-made quality—rather than a machine's precision—was due to Mies's use of a clinker brick, a rough and uneven second-class clay brick. Once inside, visitors were greeted by a macassar ebony wall and oak herringbone parquet flooring in the main rooms.[39] For his advanced pupils, Mies ran his Bauhaus studio as a master class in which he would sit with them on a one-to-one basis, sketching over their

drawings and designs-in-progress, even keeping documentary photographs of the best work.[40] No detail was too small to escape his attention—Mies was known to draw in vines and other elements.[41] Seemingly unproblematic for all participants involved, there was a fluidity between Mies's well-known interior materials and forms—rich wood and stone walls, cruciform columns, and Mies-designed furniture—and students' delineation of them in their work, as well as a larger connection between his buildings and student variations of them. As Mies would sum up his methods of teaching, developed at the Bauhaus, on the occasion of taking up his position as director of the Department of Architecture at the Illinois Institute of Technology in Chicago in 1938: "each material has its specific characteristics which we must understand if we want to use it. ... We must remember that everything depends on how we use a material, not on the material itself. ... Each material is only what we make it."[42] He continued: "we shall emphasize the organic principal of order as a means of achieving the successful relationship of the parts to each other and to the whole. And here we shall take our stand. ... We must have order, allocating to each thing its proper place and giving to each thing its due according to its nature."[43] This educational and architectural philosophy very much linked back to the deployment and control of materiality and his desire, as architect, "to give sense again to things" via columns and spaces, walls and floors, and through their materials.

From the expansive Villa Tugendhat to the diminutive Lemke House, from his renovation of the Director's House in Dessau to his instruction in the Bauhaus master classes, Mies's late German practice can be understood as singularly material. In an age in which the predominant architectural interest was in notions of the technological reproducibility of architecture, Mies can be understood as imbuing

Robin
Schuldenfrei

Reinscribing
Mies's
Materiality

151

his works with meaning, for the subject, through auratic materiality. In Mies's interiors, a dependence on process and refinement resulted in specific spatial effects and visual outcomes; the sanding, polishing, veneering, burnishing, plating, or chroming of materials allowed for interiors which reflected or refracted back to the viewer. His materiality also created spaces which permitted a subjectivity of experience —the freedom for the autonomous modern subject to dwell within. Materiality, or its absence as dematerialization, allowed for a new— and direct—engagement with modernism for these early twentieth-century denizens. Far from the criticism of cold distance or emptiness that some critics leveled at his work, Mies's materiality served as smooth points of connectivity between modern architecture's objects and its dwelling subjects, heightening subjective experience in modernism and reinscribing meaning therein.

1   A longer version of this essay is published within chapters 5 and 6 of *Luxury and Modernism: Architecture and the Object in Germany 1900–1933* (Princeton, NJ: Princeton University Press, 2018). My thinking on Mies's materials has been very much influenced by the discussions in Detlef Mertins's sustained body of work on Mies. See especially Mertins, *Mies* (London: Phaidon, 2014); Mertins, ed., *The Presence of Mies* (New York: Princeton Architectural Press, 1994); Mertins, *Modernity Unbound: Other Histories of Architectural Modernity* (London: Architectural Association, 2011). In the vast literature on Mies, in-depth and sustained discussions of Mies's materiality are less prevalent than would be expected, and are mainly directly connected to discussions of individual buildings; see Terence Riley and Barry Bergdoll, eds., *Mies in Berlin* (New York: Museum of Modern Art, 2001); Wolf Tegethoff, *Mies van der Rohe: The Villas and Country Houses*, trans. Russell M. Stockman (Cambridge, MA: MIT Press, 1985); Ignasi de Solá-Morales Rubió, "Mies van der Rohe and Minimalism," in *The Presence of Mies*, 151; Daniela Hammer-Tugendhat, Ivo Hammer, and Wolf Tegethoff, eds., *Villa Tugendhat: Ludwig Mies van der Rohe* (Basel: Birkhäuser, 2015). See also key arguments in Neil Levine, "'The Significance of Facts': Mies's Collages Up Close and Personal," *Assemblage* 37 (December 1998): 70–101; Levine, "The Reemergence of

Representation out of Abstraction in Mies van der Rohe," in *Modern Architecture: Representation and Reality* (New Haven, CT: Yale University Press, 2009), 213–42; Martino Stierli: "Mies Montage," *AA Files* 61 (2010): 54–73; Fritz Neumeyer, *The Artless Word: Mies van der Rohe on the Building Art*, trans. Mark Jarzombek (Cambridge, MA: MIT Press, 1991); Massimo Cacciari, "Mies's Classics," *RES: Anthropology and Aesthetics*, no. 16 (Autumn, 1988): 9–16.
2   On the role of the Dessau Masters' Houses as showpieces for the Bauhaus's ideas and output under Gropius, see Robin Schuldenfrei, "The Irreproducibility of the Bauhaus Object" in *Bauhaus Construct: Fashioning Identity, Discourse, and Modernism*, ed. Jeffrey Saletnik and Robin Schuldenfrei (London: Routledge/Taylor & Francis, 2009), 37–60, especially 45–47.
3   On August 8, 1930, Mies officially succeeded Meyer. The Bauhaus was closed in Dessau on October 1, 1932, re-opening in Berlin on October 18, 1932. Its final closure occurred on April 11, 1933.
4   Sergius Ruegenberg, interview by Ludwig Glaeser, Berlin, September 8, 1972, corrected typescript in German, p. 20, Ludwig Mies van der Rohe Archive, Museum of Modern Art, New York (hereinafter Mies Archive, MOMA).
5   On the German Pavilion, see Tegethoff, *Villas and Country Houses*, 66–89; Josep Quetglas, *Fear of Glass: Mies's Pavilion in Barcelona* (Basel:

Birkhäuser, 2001); George Dodds, *Building Desire: On the Barcelona Pavilion* (London: Routledge, 2005); Dietrich Neumann, "The Barcelona Pavilion," in William H. Robinson, Jordi Falgàs and Carmen Belen Lord, *Barcelona and Modernity: Picasso, Gaudí, Miró, Dalí* (New Haven, CT: Yale University Press, 2006), 390–399; Claire Zimmerman, "German Pavilion," in *Mies in Berlin*, 236–41; Neumann, "Der Barcelona Pavillon," in *Mythos Bauhaus*, ed. Anja Baumhoff and Magdalena Droste (Berlin: Reimer, 2009), 232–43; and Mertins, *Mies*, 138–67.

6   For a concise discussion of the industrialization of artistic tradition and the ways in which the middle class produced and consumed luxury, see chapter 2, "The Industry of Tradition," especially pp. 125–126 in Mitchell Schwarzer, *German Architectural Theory and the Search for Modern Identity* (Cambridge: Cambridge University Press, 1995), 88–127.

7   This extended to Mies himself. As his daughter pointed out, "Mies lived luxuriously." Georgia van der Rohe, *La donna è mobile: Mein bedingungsloses Leben* (Berlin: Aufbau-Verlag, 2001), 53–54. The living room of Mies's own Berlin apartment was furnished with Barcelona chairs, a rosewood veneer dining table, four chairs with white parchment seats, and a sideboard. According to Ludwig Glaeser, the rosewood veneer chairs in Mies's own apartment were originally intended for the Tugendhat Villa. Glaeser, *Ludwig Mies van der Rohe: Furniture and Furniture Drawings from the Design Collection and the Mies van der Rohe Archive* (New York: Museum of Modern Art, 1977), 13.

8   Christiane Lange, *Ludwig Mies van der Rohe: Architecture for the Silk Industry*, trans. Michael Wolfson (Berlin: Nicolai, 2011), 104.

9   Kent Kleinman and Leslie Van Duzer, *Mies van der Rohe: The Krefeld Villas* (New York: Princeton Architectural Press, 1995), 116.

10   Kleinman and Van Duzer, *Mies van der Rohe*, 69–70.

11   Mies Archive, MOMA, cited by Kleinman and Van Duzer, *Mies van der Rohe*, 90.

12   Mies developed these hinged casement windows together with the firm Fenestra Crittall AG. Lange, 104.

13   Mies, interview, February 13, 1952, "6 Students Talk with Mies," *Master Builder: Student Publication of the School of Design, North Carolina State College* 2, no. 3 (Spring 1952): n. p.,

off-print in Mies van der Rohe Papers, Manuscript Division, Library of Congress, Washington, DC.

14   Ministerialdirektor Ritter to Mies, July 15, 1929, Barcelona, Mies Archive, MOMA. The materials for the Barcelona Pavilion were so costly that the marble, travertine, and chromed columns were shipped back to Germany to be resold. In October of 1929 the authorities wrote to Mies and Reich, asking if they could assist with the possible resale of the materials, and by March of 1930, as a letter to Mies indicates, they planned to send the marble back to Hamburg, the travertine was to follow two weeks later, and eventually the chromed columns, also intended for resale. The iron construction was to be sold in Barcelona, with the proceeds to be used to pay for the costs for dismantling the pavilion. Letters, Dr. von Kettler to Lilly Reich, October 29, 1929, Barcelona, Mies Archive, MOMA; Unknown author [on stationery headed: Internationale Ausstellung Barcelona 1929, Der deutsche Generalkommissar] to Mies, March 5, 1930, Barcelona, Mies Archive, MOMA.

15   K. Michael Hays, "Critical Architecture: Between Culture and Form," *Perspecta* 21 (1984): 24.

16   See also Wallis Miller, "Tangible Ideas: Architecture and the Public at the 1931 German Building Exhibition in Berlin" (PHD diss., Princeton University, 1999); "Mies van der Rohe: Casas / Houses," *2G* 48–49 (2008–2009), 148–155; Mies van der Rohe, "Programm zur Berliner Bauausstellung," *Die Form* 6, no. 7 (June 1931): 242.

17   Philip Johnson, "The Berlin Building Exposition of 1931," *T-Square* (January 1932); reprint *Oppositions* (January 1974): 88.

18   For more on this design, see Marianne Eggler, "Divide and Conquer: Ludwig Mies van der Rohe and Lilly Reich's Fabric Partitions at the Villa Tugendhat," *Studies in the Decorative Arts* 16, no. 2 (Spring–Summer 2009): 66–90.

19   Grete Tugendhat, address on the occasion of the International Conference on the Reconstruction of the Villa Tugendhat, Moravian Museum, Brno, January 17, 1969, reproduced in Hammer-Tugendhat and Wolf Tegethoff, 8.

20   For reproductions of the photographs taken by Fritz Tugendhat, see Robin Schuldenfrei, "Contra the Großstadt: Mies van der

Robin Schuldenfrei

Reinscribing Mies's Materiality

153

Rohe's Autonomy and Interiority" in *Interiors and Interiority*, ed. Ewa Lajer-Burcharth and Beate Soentgen (Berlin: De Gruyter, 2015), 279–94; Ilsebill Barta, *Wohnen in Mies van der Rohes Villa Tugendhat: Fotografiert von Fritz Tugendhat 1930-1938* (Vienna: Eigenverlag der Museen des Mobiliendepots Wien, 2002).

21   Karel Teige, *The Minimum Dwelling* (1932), trans. Eric Dluhosch (Cambridge, MA: MIT Press, 2002), 181.

22   Walter Benjamin, *The Arcades Project*, ed. Rolf Tiedemann, trans. Howard Eiland and Kevin McLaughlin (Cambridge, MA: Harvard University Press, 1999), 226.

23   Walter Benjamin, "4. Louis-Philippe, or the Interior," in *Paris, Capital of the Nineteenth Century* (1935), in *Walter Benjamin: Selected Writings, vol. 3, 1935-1938*, ed. Howard Eiland and Michael W. Jennings (Cambridge, MA: Harvard University Press, 2002), 39.

24   Walter Benjamin, "Experience and Poverty" (1933), in *Walter Benjamin: Selected Writings; vol. 2, Part 2, 1931-1934*, 733–34.

25   Walter Benjamin, "One-Way Street" (published 1928, written 1923–26), in *Walter Benjamin: Selected Writings; vol. 1, 1913-1926*, ed. Marcus Bullock (Cambridge, MA: Harvard University Press, 2004), 453–54.

26   Simmel, *The Philosophy of Money*, trans. Tom Bottomore and David Frisby (London: Routledge & Kegan Paul, 1978), 460. Cited in K. Michael Hays, *Modernism and the Posthumanist Subject: The Architecture of Hannes Meyer and Ludwig Hilberseimer* (Cambridge, MA: MIT Press, 1995), 56.

27   Mies, Foreword, *Official Catalog of the Stuttgart Werkbund Exhibition "Die Wohnung"* (Stuttgart: Deutscher Werkbund, 1927), reproduced in Neumeyer, *Artless Word*, 259.

28   Mies, diary entry, page 20, 1928, reproduced in Neumeyer, *Artless Word*, 274.

29   Mies, diary entry, page 62, 1928, reproduced in Neumeyer, *Artless Word*, 289. Here Mies is reading and taking notes from Romano Guardini's *Von heiligen Zeichen*. A slightly different translation of the quote is cited again by Neumeyer in "Barcelona Pavilion and Villa Tugendhat: Spaces of the Century," *Global Architecture* 75 (Tokyo: Edita, 1995), n.p.

30   Mies, "On the Theme: Exhibitions," *Die Form* 3, no. 4 (1928): 121, reproduced in Neumeyer, *Artless Word*, 304.

31   Emphasis original. Mies, "We Stand at the Turning Point of Time: Building Art as the Expression of Spiritual Decisions," *Innendekoration* 29, no. 6 (1928): 262, reproduced in Neumeyer, *Artless Word*, 304.

32   Mies, "On Form in Architecture," *Die Form* 2, no. 2 (1927): 59, reproduced in Neumeyer, *Artless Word*, 257.

33   Tugendhat, "On the Construction of the Villa Tugendhat," in *Villa Tugendhat*, 20.

34   Mies, "On the Meaning and Task of Criticism," meeting of the Association of Art Critics, April 1930, in *Das Kunstblatt* 14, no. 6 (1930): 178, reproduced in Neumeyer, *Artless Word*, 308–309.

35   Tugendhat, "On the Construction of the Villa Tugendhat," 20.

36   Mies, "What Would Concrete, What Would Steel Be without Mirror Glass?" Prospectus, Verein Deutscher Spiegelglas-Fabriken, March 13, 1933, not published, Manuscript in Library of Congress, reproduced in Neumeyer, *Artless Word*, 314.

37   Hans M. Wingler, *The Bauhaus* (Cambridge, MA: MIT Press, 1969), 542.

38   See reproductions of student work in Wingler, *Bauhaus*, 540–41 and Riley, "From Bauhaus to Court-House," *Mies in Berlin*, 331–35.

39   Christian Wolsdorff, Bauhaus-Archiv Berlin, cited by Wita Noack, "Of Interiors and Exteriors: Lemke House (1932–33) by Ludwig Mies van der Rohe," in *Mies and Modern Living: Interiors, Furniture, Photography*, ed. Helmut Reuter, Birgit Schulte (Berlin: Hatje Cantz, 2008), 81.

40   Riley, "From Bauhaus to Court-House," *Mies in Berlin*, 332.

41   Riley, "From Bauhaus to Court-House," 380, footnote 10.

42   Mies, Inaugural Address as Director of Architecture at Armour Institute of Technology in 1938, reprinted in Philip Johnson, *Mies van der Rohe* (New York: Museum of Modern Art, 1947; 1978 reprint), 198.

43   Mies, Inaugural Address, 199.

Part 1

Theories
of
Bauhaus
Materiality

Anna-Maria Meister

From *Musterhaus* to *Meisterhäuser*: A Trajectory of Typologies

The *Meisterhäuser* (Masters' Houses) ensemble in Dessau, built between 1925 and 1926, was not a large-scale modern settlement for anonymous modern dwellers, but a series of exclusive homes created for an intimate group of people.[fig. 1][1] After the political exodus of the Bauhaus from Weimar, the school was determined to follow the promise of an even more modern, more industrialized, more efficient Bauhaus to Dessau. The families of the masters, a close-knit group despite (or because of) all the cultural disputes in the city of Weimar, saw in their move the possibility of a new beginning—one of living together in a modern Bauhaus *Siedlung* (settlement, elsewhere referred to as "colony"). Dessau would become, declared Ise Gropius, the place where "everything would start all over again"— the site where a new, better Bauhaus could emerge.[2] She would move with Walter Gropius into the single-family home often named after him, while the other families shared the three double houses: László Moholy-Nagy lived with Lucia Moholy next to the Feiningers, Paul, Lily, and Felix Klee wall-to-wall with the Kandinskys, and Georg Muche and Elsa Muche-Franke shared a house with their neighbors Oskar and Tut Schlemmer and their three children.

Going through the typological moves of a modernist *Siedlung*, the small settlement became the hinge toward a new Bauhaus, a first glimpse through the pines of the promise of mass-produced social housing—or was it not rather a set of villas, custom-built for an elite group of inhabitants? After all, the opportunity to build both the school and a housing settlement had been one of the reasons to move to Dessau in the "dance of the German cities for the Golden Bauhaus," as Schlemmer called the Bauhaus's search for a new location

in early 1925.[3] And yet he was shocked when he first saw the finished buildings after one year of construction in September 1926.[4] He wrote to his wife, Tut: "I can picture how one day the homeless will stand around while the artists sun bathe on the roof of their villas"[5]—villas that might represent a new iteration of the *Musterhaus* (model house) in Weimar, the Haus Am Horn. Famously during the Weimar years, architecture had never really been manifested in the curriculum. Teaching in the inherited buildings for the Grand Ducal Saxon School of Applied Arts and the Grand Ducal School of Arts and Crafts by Henry van de Velde in the first four years of the school's existence, "Bauhaus architecture" remained but a string of words in the 1919 manifesto. The attempt to develop an architecture for the masses remained limited to the Haus Am Horn, built for the occasion of the Bauhaus Exhibition in 1923 by Gropius's office according to Georg Muche's design. It was meant to become a *Siedlung* for the school's community. Bauhaus student Farkas Molnár, who lived in the Haus Am Horn for one summer after the exhibition, extolled it as "model home devoid of clichés"[6]; high praise given that his own "red cube" prototype had been passed over in favor of the master's proposal.

The idea of a Bauhaus housing estate was central to Gropius's conception of the school: in 1920, he had already solicited proposals from students and teachers, founded a limited liability company, the Bauhaus Siedlung GmbH, in 1921, and drawn up plans for the proposed *Siedlung* of different housing types in an area of the city "surrounded by large single-family villas ... situated between the streets Am Horn and Besselstrasse."[7] As Berry Bergdoll writes, the project became the catalyst for "not simply a vague architectural ethos but a line of research" on housing typologies from the Bauhaus's early years

Anna-Maria Meister

From Musterhaus to Meisterhäuser

157

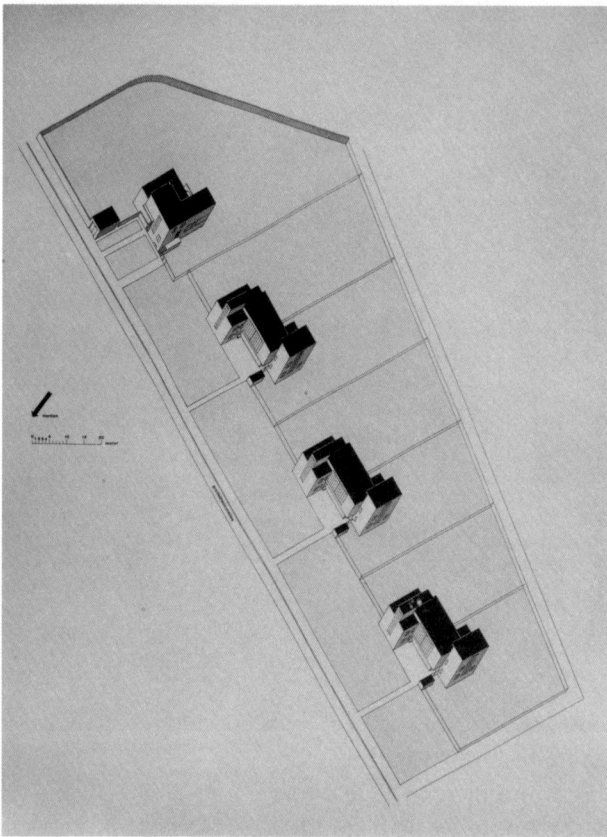

Fig. 2. Masters' Houses, Dessau, site plan, photograph of a drawing. Photograph by Technische Reproduktionsanstalt Berlin, architecture by Walter Gropius.

in Weimar.[8] The desired mass-produced serial house, however, remained a vision for the time being. The Haus Am Horn—despite demonstrating the turn of the Bauhaus from "craftmanship towards a stated desire to produce for and cooperate with capitalist industry"—remained irreproducible due to its building costs and materials.[9] Rather than a truly mass-producible house, it remained an exemplary representation—a *Gesamtkunstwerk*, reminiscent of the unfulfilled promise of Bauhaus housing.

The project lay dormant until the Bauhaus moved to Dessau, where the Masters' Houses were soon heralded as the first built Bauhaus *Siedlung*.[fig.2] The modernist *Siedlung* had the notion of repetition built in, based on the multiplication of one typological element across a site; in fact, to Gropius it formed the "distinguishing mark of a superior urban culture."[10] But the Masters' Houses foreclose any easy interpretation of repetition and repeatability, be it historical or typological. The debate around repetition in early twentieth-century architecture was heated: some dismissed it as unoriginal, uninspired and neither site- nor program-specific, while others glorified it as the arrival of mass production and serial efficiency. Over time, repetition within and of modern architecture became a different problem: now the question was no longer about mass production, but about modernism's legacy. The main turning points of these debates coincide with the decisive moments in the history of the Masters' Houses: their erection in 1926–28, the destruction of Moholy-Nagy's house and the Director's House during World War II, the latter's "replacement" with the Haus Emmer (Emmer House), and finally the most recent debate about the reconstruction (or re-conception) of the Director's House, built in 2014. And with each of those turns, Bauhaus modernism was built, erased, reconstructed, repaired, preserved, and reimagined.[fig.3]

Analyzing the Masters' Houses through the concept of repetition reveals tenuous assumptions about Bauhaus iterations as well as the preservation of its legacy. To investigate these entanglements across

Fig.3. *Bauhäusler Painting the Masters' Houses*, Dessau, 1929. Photograph by Gertrud Arndt.

time and site, I propose two categories of repetition to discuss repetition's inherent paradox of authenticity and uniqueness. Called synchronic and diachronic repetition, respectively, these categories analyze the conception of the series—the distribution of synchronic repetitions of built elements in space—and its continuous de- and reconstruction—the delayed diachronic repetition in the same space over time. Both processes emerge from the interplay between "dust" and "data": the particles of matter before and after their tentative state as "architecture," and the information necessary to organize them into that state. Repetition as a conceptual framework can provide an alternate reading of this architecture: different temporal conditions (both in the experience of a series and the time lag between a building and its reconstruction); a dependency on memory and imagination in imitation, seriality and their perception; agency in the creation and excavation of difference in form and content.

Gropius had long been testing typological efficacy in his explorations of a "new architecture" with repetition as the core practice of the envisioned serial production. During the Weimar years, the developed theorie and types remained unique "prototypes" when built, while the replication of elements and building methods rendered the Masters' Houses "finger exercises" for Gropius's large-scale Bauhaus Siedlung Dessau-Törten (1926–28), modernism's infamous manifestation of large-scale standardization.[11] One might say that the Masters' Houses link the logic of the school's beginnings on the one hand (the Director's House of the Masters' Houses was based on designs Gropius had made in 1922 for the unbuilt Bauhaus settlement in Weimar)[12] to the promise of a better, more efficient future on the other.

Anna-Maria Meister

From Musterhaus to Meisterhäuser

The repetition of housing units across a site would form, according to Gropius, a "group-organism"[13]: the *Siedlung*. Produced through an act of "synchronic repetition," the multiplication of (ostensibly) identical dwellings became a new social and economic typology. Gropius played with the Masters' Houses as the creation of a small-scale *Siedlung*, making the multiplication of plan, volume, and details essential to its conception. Gropius not only placed three seemingly "identical" double-family houses evenly spaced on the site, but he also mirrored—hence duplicated—the floor plan for one family to create the unit of the double-family house itself.[14] That the houses never were identical to begin with, but rather featured different sizes and organization depending on family size or due to production, did not lessen the rhetorical power of typological efficacy:[15]

> *Simplification through multiplication means reduction of costs ... the floor plan of one of the tow apartments is the interlocked, 90 degrees revolved mirror image of the floor plan of the other apartment. Exactly the same building parts are used, yet the elevation of both halves is different due to the mirroring.*[16]

Gropius continuously stressed the point of efficacy despite his own reservations and concerns about a potential simplification of the understanding of "New Architecture." In his book *The New Architecture of the Bauhaus*, he presents the problem of rationalization as a totalizing argument for this new architecture, and talks about the importance of two poles: the functional and the "aesthetic satisfaction of the human soul."[17] But even though Gropius poses "a new spatial vision" as the real achievement of modernism, he turns (after a brief deliberation of those main points of his new architecture) back to technology, to the opportunities of new processes, with "Rationalization" and "Standardization" being the headings of the two main chapters.

To Gropius, the issue of repetition and serialization had a moral component, bearing the possibility of "raising the social level of the population as a whole" as well as improving the (aesthetic and ethical) standards of society.[18] Stating "it is a commonplace that repetition of the same things for the same purposes exercises a settling and civilizing influence on men's mind," Gropius also assigned almost healing powers to repetition as modus operandi.[19] This moral expectation of design could be identified as a legacy of the Werkbund, which had been founded in 1907 to address the anxiety in art and design brought on by the advent of industrial production. Aspiring to remarry the two,

the Werkbund believed in the ethical value of good design and in the power of mass production as a multiplicator and disseminator.

Gropius, who had joined the Werkbund around 1910,[20] supported the move toward serial production but countered the public "fear that individuality will be crushed by the growing 'tyranny' of standardization" with cultural and social arguments; rather, serial architecture would calm the mind as a "natural" and "organic" architectural and urban tradition.[21] And yet, this line of argumentation is sandwiched by chapter names such as "Standardization" and "Rationalization," rhetoric more prevalent both in Gropius's own contemporaneous propagation of his projects.[22] To get his projects built, Gropius argued through the advantages of mass production (the production of more of the "same") and its assumed financial revenue.[23]

While the propagated mass production was more desire than reality, it offered the promise of overcoming seasonal dependencies through the "dislocation" of production in off-site factories.[24] For Gropius, the *Siedlung* as "group-organism" was a product of variations, and did not relate to the site as ground. In fact, "instead of anchoring buildings ponderously into the ground" the *New Architecture* rather "poises them lightly ... upon the face of the earth."[25] And yet, it was the site that rendered the multiplicity of serial repetition into a unique constellation. When Ise and Walter Gropius looked for a site for the Masters' Houses with Fritz Hesse, the mayor of Dessau, they came across a lot along Burgkühnauer Allee seemingly full of pine trees.[fig.4] In close proximity to the future school's location, the site was ultimately chosen for its vegetation, as Gropius had always wanted to "live in a small pine forest."[26] That the pine trees were most likely European black pines cut to look like their southern relatives remains largely unnoticed. The European black pine, a frost-resistant northern tree,

Anna-Maria Meister

From Musterhaus to Meisterhäuser

161

was employed to simulate Mediterranean pine forests already nearby in the UNESCO protected landscape of the Dessau-Wörlitz, an attempt to render the north German woods into an Italian garden.[27] The seduction of the site equally enchanted the first inhabitants Klee, Schlemmer, and Feininger. Nature and its views feature in their letters and journals as much (or more) as Gropius's architecture.[28] Klee refers to his house mostly when lauding the artist studio or the coloring of the interior. But it was the site that became an inspirational sensorium and escape, even when "the first bloom of the season [and] of course the muggy weather has arrived, as well; and thunder storms. That produced a wonderful smell, and when I stood on the balcony off the bed room it smelled more like a fairy tale and no longer like Dessau (Caprices!)."[29]

None of the masters were particularly enthusiastic about the move to Dessau, and the teaching at the school soon became a burden rather than a raison d'être. After moving in, Klee writes to Lily that "the city [of Dessau] remains so-so" and two years later calls it a "hideous one-horse town." But the promise of a house next to the other masters, set on a picturesque site, seemed to make life in Dessau bearable.[fig.5][30] Klee writes fondly and often about his immediate neighbors, the Schlemmers and the Kandinsky family, who provided a sense of home: "when I came home, it was 10 pm, and I sat down for dinner. And there came the neighbors and cared for me, stopped by and found that I had a cheerful and looked-after meal. Not to forget the music, the gramophone upstairs played a few tangos later."[31] Schlemmer as well, despite feeling slightly like an outsider, repeatedly lauds the neighborly atmosphere; at one point he even shared his house with Hannes Meyer and his family.[fig.6][32] Descriptions of the weather, the atelier and the painting done in the apartments are featured frequently, as are visitors, views, and activities. If one were to sketch those houses from the firsthand accounts of their inhabitants,

Fig.5. *Life at the Bauhaus: Wassily and Nina Kandinsky with Georg and El Muche in the Garden of the Masters' Houses in Dessau*, circa 1926–27. Photographer unknown.
Fig.6. *Life at the Bauhaus: Masters and Their Children at Schlemmer's and Muche's Double House*, circa 1927 (top left: Lou Scheper, top right: Oskar Schlemmer, first floor left: Georg Muche, right: Lucia Moholy, ground floor left: Hinnerk Scheper and daughter Britta, right: Natalie Meyer-Herkert, wife of Hannes Meyer, with daughters Claudia and Lydia). Photographer unknown.

none of them would seem the same as the other. Instead, they take on differences as bold as those between their inhabitants. As much as the hanging of paintings (Hannes Meyer reluctantly admitted to have "decorated" his house) or different furniture (when, for example, Mies removed bookshelves from the Director's House), the passing of time with its chain of people, concerts, coffees, and artistic self-doubts made each of the houses unique.[33] Their architectural "sameness" (if we want to subscribe to the term for a moment) never tried to mask those differences—rather, it provided the canvas on which these individualities played out. As architectural critic Max Osborn pointed out in 1926, "even though the halves of the twin-houses of the six masters resemble each other to a dot, it looks different everywhere. Everyone brings in his individuality. Kandinsky even brought old Russian furniture from past decades and see, it works fabulously."[34] The repetition of structures and spaces enhanced the experience of change— in fact, it was repetition which fundamentally enabled the perception of difference in the first place.

To the visitor, the repetition of the three double-houses as shown on the famous axonometric projection [fig.2] becomes the backbone of an experience of differences. When strolling through the Masters' Houses, the temporal nature of perception—the layering of the "same" perception over different moments in time—provokes the notion of difference rather than creating an impression of multiple sameness. If everything differed from one house to another walking along the Allee, the lack of reference might render everything a homogenous blur due to the impossibility of comparison. Gropius's move to enable

Anna-Maria Meister

From Musterhaus to Meisterhäuser

163

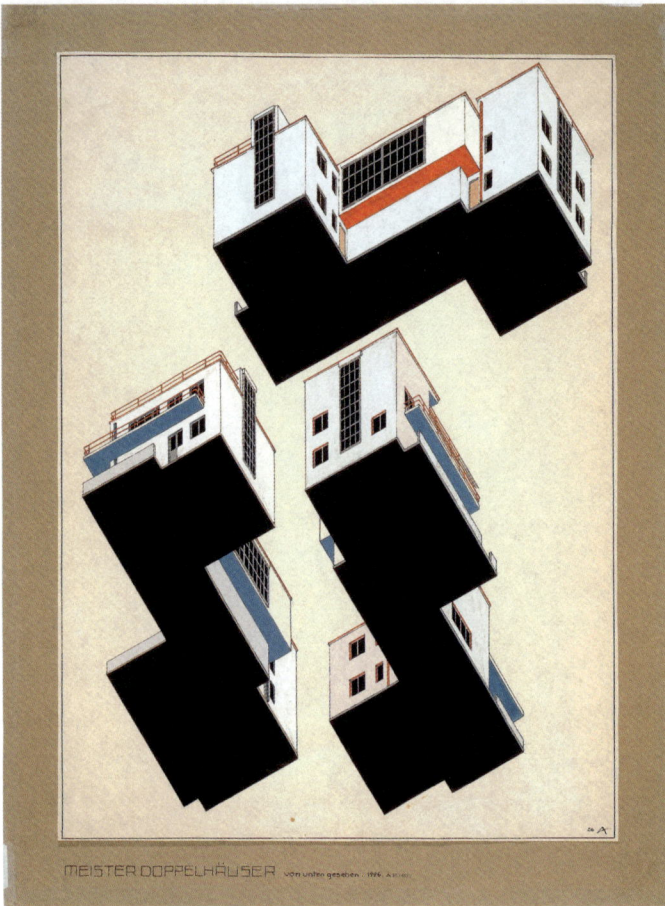

MEISTER DOPPELHÄUSER von unten gesehen. 1926. Arndt

Fig.7. *Color Scheme for the Exterior Design of the Masters' Houses (3 Double Houses)*, drawing by Alfred Arndt, 1926.

Fig.8. *The Propertied Class*, Alfred and Gertrud Arndt moving, March 1933. Photograph by Walter Kaminski.

the "almost same" experience three times could be seen as a didactic move to focus on repetition as a learning curve, teaching the visitor to grasp variations in space—and ultimately in the architecture itself. Gropius himself expected the visitor to see the difference rather than the sameness, a move that he pushed further with the different set of hues for each apartment interior: "The varying treatment of the color scheme and in the furniture in particular in the individual apartments achieves, despite the sameness of the floor plans, such a different effect that the sameness of the spaces in the different apartments will not be realized by the visitor." [fig.7] [35] While the "sameness" of the interior spatial proportions had been deliberately de-emphasized by their treatment, the similarity in color and contrast of the houses from the outside was enhanced.

The architectural repetition renders the Masters' Houses for visitor and inhabitant not into sameness—rather, the comparative process produces perceptual difference. The gardens, the colors, the location, the little details all lead to a subjectification foregrounded by the repetitive houses set in the little forest. Every house was transformed by a family into their home. Clement Greenberg's discussion of expectation and surprise could find a new interpretation here: through the repetition of the houses, surprise is ostensibly minimized as it becomes a fulfillment of the expected.[36] And yet, through that very repetition, difference itself is enhanced—creating experiential surprise: the visitor, trained by the "sameness" of the elements to expect more of the same, registers their (unexpected) differences.

The didactic demonstration of seriality by the three double houses along the Burgkühnauer Allee was highlighted by the one exception: the *Direktorenhaus*. Known also as the Director's House, Gropius's own home was the endpoint of the row of three double-family houses, an intentional stopgap, anchoring it to the Weimar

Bauhaus. It provided a necessary marker for this comparative process —the fixed point against which change can be measured. The house forms the endpoint of the short *Siedlung*. Situated on its plot closer to the street than the double houses, it closes off the houses to their surroundings with a concrete wall, the only wall proposed by Gropius for the whole complex. Due to its placement, this wall provides the backdrop for the visitor walking up the street. The changing size of the Director's House in the background (depending on the respective distance to it by each of the three repetitive houses in the foreground) provides a marker to locate the subject in one unique place within the settlement. Through the means of architecture, the Director's House defines one's position within the repetitive setup, demonstrating, reminding, and teaching the visitor that this setup was never meant to create sameness in experience, but rather to enable seeing the difference.

This measuring, or rather, providing of scale to recognize the difference in the multiplicity could only be provided by the Director's House, the individual unit, the one amongst the many. Built as the only house of the ensemble for only one master, it was also the only one that did not contain a studio. It has become an example of what will be referred to here as "diachronic repetition." Within the conceptually embedded synchronic repetition of the units in a *Siedlung* discussed above, "diachronic" repetition is a problem of history, historicity, and historical attitude: an "original" building is destroyed, and its replica or re-conception after partial or total, intentional or circumstantial destruction "repeats" its architecture in the same place, yet at a different time. One could argue that the used term is problematic, since it presupposes the feasibility of repetition, assuming "sameness" to be possible at a later time. But just as I have argued that multiple instances of the "same" architecture at the same time are not possible (and are neither the goal of repetition as concept here),

Anna-Maria Meister

From Musterhaus to Meisterhäuser

165

I would apply a similar logic in this context: not only is the "same" never possible again, but it can never be the aim of "diachronic repetition" to begin with.

In the case of the Masters' Houses, we encounter those problems of destruction, reconstruction, and manipulation several times, be they personally or politically motivated. Families moved out, others moved in, redecorating rooms, scuffing corners, changing colors.[fig.8] Party politics would not steer clear of respective aesthetic modulations either. All houses were altered during World War II by order of the NSDAP (Nationalist Socialist German Workers' Party) to make them less "*wesensfremd*" (foreign)[37]—alterations that were "removed" only in the late 1990s when the ensemble acquired UNESCO World Heritage status.[38] During the same years, the interior colors of some of the double houses were painstakingly determined and restored in efforts to recreate the modernist appearance of the *Siedlung*. But beyond adaptation, removal, and restoration, total destruction had also hit the ensemble when the Director's House and the Moholy-Nagy House were bombed in 1945. The different layers of damage and repair bring up questions of reconstruction, or rather "reconstructability," which were discussed covering all positions, from those calling a literal reconstruction "distorting history" to defenders of the "real Gropius" arguing the need to rebuild.[39] Statements of the commissioning authorities and the architects of the reconstruction of the Director's House illustrate this dilemma further. The former announced that "the City Council has passed the reconstruction [of the Director's House and the Moholy-Nagy House] and commissioned the Berlin architectural office Bruno Fioretto Marquez with the task. At the end of the restoration the ensemble will be again experienceable in its original form."[40] The latter positioned themselves against preservationists, claiming, "this project is in no way to be understood as reconstruction, but as an interpretation of the original house."[41] And yet, the debate about repeatability focused on the Director's House, the exception in the series. The interior of the Feininger House, a slightly different case, was "restored" in the late 1990s to its "original move-in" status of 1926.[42]

To trace these historic interpretations and erasures, the father of reconstruction theory, Alois Riegl, might offer tools for evaluation.[43] What he calls "historical value" would apply to both the ensemble and to the individual houses—the former as an urbanistically significant

structure of modern architecture, the latter as demonstrations of the architecture of the Bauhaus. But they could also be of "historical value" as materializations of shifting political value systems expressed through aesthetic measures. In the case of the Feininger House, the inside color scheme and furniture was refurbished to its "original" status of conception (in 1926, prior to Feininger's family moving in)—rather than to the lived-in status with the changes made (as it was after their moving out in 1932).[44] This strategy follows Riegl's "newness value," which assumes an original state that needed to be recreated. The only Riegelian value that was never called upon was "age value": the accumulated changes occurring over time, intentional or collateral, documented within the architecture. The state in which the houses were "found" at different times never became the one to be preserved: the houses were judged time and again as either "unfinished" or "altered" and in need of correction. They remained suspended between the "not yet" and the "not anymore."

Such deliberations were not limited to the Masters' Houses themselves: a foreign body, a contaminant, had entered this site of repeated destruction and reconstruction. In 1956, three years after Stalin's death, the so-called Emmer House, a "generic GDR house," had been built on the foundations of the destroyed Director's House.[fig. 9] The pitched-roof one family home "unwillingly demonstrated" the "conservative Modernism" of its time, both in form and architectural language;[45] furthermore, it could have been taken as a marker for the treatment of Modernist heritage in the early years of the GDR. At the same time, the Emmer House not only used some of the debris material from 1926, but adopted the spatial organization of the rooms of the former Director's House almost completely—making it inseparable from its predecessor.[46] When the Bauhaus heritage in the GDR gained new appreciation in the mid-1970s, marked by the restoration of the school building in Dessau to its "original state" in 1976 (for the

50th anniversary of the move to Dessau as part of the Bauhaus heritage), the question of reconstruction took on momentum. The same treatment—restoration—had been recommended for the Director's House back in 1962 after a site visit.[47] As mentioned above, the Masters' Houses ensemble has been on the UNESCO World Heritage list since 1996—the Emmer House had no such protection and was demolished in 2010, giving way for the reconstruction of the Director's House. In Gropius versus Emmer, the "genius" beat the vernacular once again. The Bauhaus ensemble ranked higher on the scale of preserved original—despite the substantial changes under the guidelines of the very protection by UNESCO; projected architectural intention trumped historic reality. Reconstruction became a tool for posterior improvement and reinterpretation of architectural heritage, replacing the "real present" with the "better past," ostensibly recreating an "authentic experience" of Gropius's conception.[48] Alas, over the decades, the concept of an "original state" became increasingly untenable, and both the Director's House and the Moholy-Nagy House remained absent from the *Siedlung*. Their treatment, however, was not the same: their respective reconstruction carried a different promise—and baggage.

The Director's House (the individual) gives names to reconstruction proposals and competitions hotly debated in the media, whereas the recreation of the destroyed parts of the three Masters' Houses (as part of a series) produced neither strong objectors nor passionate defendants. Gropius himself already enforced this asymmetry in his book *Bauhausbauten Dessau*: the vast majority of illustrations in the chapter about the Masters' Houses are taken from and inside his own home; the other three semi-detached houses are sparsely depicted and usually not distinguished by their inhabitants.[49] Gropius's presence as designer and inhabitant made his own house worthy of reconstruction (or the debate of such) over the polarizing presence of the Emmer House, the ugly duckling sitting on a site it presumably has no right to.

And yet there might be another, much simpler, and for the purpose of this chapter more intriguing argument explaining the lack of discourse or interest in its reconstruction: "What a [destroyed] semi-detached [house] used to look like is readable through the other [same] houses," claims one user commenting on a blog entry—hence rendering the reconstruction of the Moholy-Nagy House as part of six "same" semi-detached houses plainly unnecessary.[50] And when

Philipp Oswalt in 2010, then director of the Bauhaus-Stiftung Dessau, describes the reconstruction proposed by the Berlin office Bruno Fioretti Marquez, the Moholy-Nagy House receives but a posterior side note: the "architects have described their approach mainly with the Director's House, but will treat the Moholy-Nagy House accordingly."[51] Repetition here is seen as a multiplication of the same, making the repetition of this monument historically redundant. This might fall in line with an extreme interpretation of the Riegelian historical value: only if a building is representative of its time and if it is deemed "irreplaceable" does it earn historical value.[52] This trope of "irreplaceability" would then, so the above-quoted argument, apply to the Director's House as the one unique exception, but not necessarily to the Moholy-Nagy House, since it is just one instance of a multiplicity. And yet, as argued above, this multiplication through repetition does not create a sequence of sameness; rather, every iteration is necessary as part of the whole. Such a take would support reconstruction, since only then could differences be experienced, and only then could the *Siedlung* work as the "group-organism" mentioned earlier that Gropius had strived to create.[53]

The Director's House, not part of the series, posed a different problem, since its reconstruction required a literal choice of value: to exist, it needed an already-occupied space—its twenty-first-century creation depended on the destruction of the contaminant. The site of the former Moholy-Nagy House, on the other hand, was empty: ostensibly nothing stood in the way of its reconstruction. Yet, if one were to hold the empty site as the vestiges of an event, the absence of the house could comprise as much as a historical monument as the house itself. What if the bombed, missing half of the Moholy-Nagy House were as spatially present as the Emmer House occupying the foundation of the Director's House? George Bataille described architecture as the displacement of space—the substation of empty space through built matter, the reversal of which would mean that the destruction of architecture does not leave behind a vacuum, but creates space.[54]

Such an approach would consequently lead to a conflict between the intentions and effects of synchronic repetition and the problems of diachronic repetition. It poses the question whether one prefers to reconstruct the creation of difference through the experience of repetition, or to preserve the (seemingly empty) space left behind as a signifier and physical remains of the events that created it. If one concedes that it is impossible to replicate the intention of a past time, one would have to go with the latter. To maintain such a position would eventually lead to paralysis, a persistent placeholder, raising the question: How much time should pass before building something new on such preserved spaces? At the same time, however, the very politics that produced this "empty" space and its historical significance in the first place—namely, pragmatic destruction rather than preservation— would consequently end in renewed (potentially architectural) use of the space. In short, the competing architectural values read against the foil of diverging temporal durations of the Masters' Houses (both past and present) produced a Gordian knot, pulled tighter and tighter with each revolution of the construction-destruction wheel.

Repetition and its discontent

The layers of repetition in Dessau keep building. The experience of encountering three "same" houses when walking along the site might already be called a layering of specific experiences foregrounded by architectural similarities. Their simultaneous physical presence pre-scribes a trajectory for the visitor, spreading the actual perception of each one of them out over time, contrasting each iteration of a house or a room with the memory of the one that was visited before. On the other hand, the experience of a "new" Directors' House, taking the same physical place as its predecessor, is a reconstruction after the fact, relating to the memory of its other, earlier iteration in a more detached way. Here, memory is contained as transported medium, as photograph, plan, and writing, and hence persists continuously in this realm of representation, of interpretation, readings, and of translation. It seems therefore necessary to distinguish between two different termi-nologies in this realm: on the one hand, there is the family of terms like iteration, multiplication and seriality; on the other, we find the duplicate and its relatives such as imitation, copy, reproduction and replication. Whereas the former describes conceptually embedded notions of sameness at the same time, the latter depends on the exist-ence of the "original" (either temporally defined as "the first," or stylis-tically as "the best") and its successive, usually lesser-valued attempts to create the appearance of the "same." Repetition and difference are not only inseparable, they are co-dependent, as Deleuze's claims, as repetition is not an antagonist to difference, but its aid; further-more, "repetition is a necessary and justified conduct *only* in relation to that which cannot be replaced. Repetition as a conduct and as a point of view concerns non-exchangeable and non-substitutable singularities."[55]

But how to repeat "that which cannot be replaced" over time? In their repetitive conception, the "original" might have never existed, since every copy was already authentic. Historically different states could be deemed worthy of preservation, depending on political and aesthetic points of view; and yet the marketing of the ensemble operated under the premise of a reconstruction of the "original" 1926 experience. The desire that prompts attempts at diachronic repetition is often rooted in that which has been lost, that which seems to demand, or deserve, replacement. Such desire seeks to manifest itself in architecture as a signifier for the underlying collective moral judge-ments of the better past—that which needs to be preserved, or rather, created. For the reconstruction of the Director's House, the temporal gap between the original and the reconstruction was made visible through a design proposal featuring the "blurriness" of memory, as Bruno Fioretti Marquez stated:

> Not the documentation of a historical condition has priority in this task, it is not about an academic obligation towards the history of architecture. Here it is a matter of subtlety, of something more cunning; it is about a commemoration, it is about memories. ... memories live of a lack of definition, of imprecisions. We have to work with those blurrings and imprecisions to find the right tone for this challenge.[56]

What was not blurred, however, was the "better past": the 1926 status of the *Siedlung* was declared the desirable one, the lost one, the one that needed to be repeated. The discussion on the Masters' Houses is in its core about the question of repeatability, a problem that might find its answer by finding difference through repetition all along. Both synchronic and diachronic repetition touch upon the problem of type; and both problematize the concept of the "original versus the copy," the latter (ever since Benjamin's "Work of Art" essay) running the risk of becoming nothing more than aura-less duplication.[57] Difference through repetition is not merely a posterior angle for an interpretation, but a twofold operation deeply entangled with the modernist *Siedlung*: the creation of unique, distinct spaces through the composition of repetitive parts was already embedded in the concept of the Masters' Houses by Gropius himself. Especially in an ensemble built by a movement claiming to be timeless, questions of reconstruction and

Anna-Maria Meister

From *Musterhaus* to *Meisterhäuser*

171

preservation expose architecture's fragility: the decay of the built structure over time prompted repairs and reconstructions—delayed acts of "repeating" that which vanished. If we were to assess a valid position in the reconstruction of the Director's House, the conclusion by architectural historian Andreas Schwarting might seem convincing: an ensemble showing a unique layering of different episodes of German (architectural) history might embody more historical value than a reconstructed, "repaired" Bauhaus *Siedlung* of the Masters' Houses.[58] Yet this line of argument finds its catch in the same hitch used to make this point: Schwarting claims that especially the Modernists themselves would never go back in history to rebuild a house from 80 years ago, hence today's architects, supposedly, should not make that attempt either. Consequently, however, freezing the situation in its 2006 setup might be just as retrospective as the position criticized: after all, it would leave no space to produce new, future layers—the dust of life.

In the case of the Director's House, any proposed reconstruction would, according to Schwarting, bear less historical authenticity than the 2006 situation with Haus Emmer and the empty lot of the Moholy-Nagy House, as it would show ensemble's historical breaks and ruptures.[59] Schwarting poses, therefore, the built reconstruction by Bruno Fioretti Marquez necessarily as a non-house, as an upsized model. The architects of the new Director's House, however, hoped to escape this double bind by using the model quality as design directive.[fig. 10, 11] Taking forms, measures and shapes from Gropius's infamous plaster models, they scaled up the aesthetic of the small toward a constructive realization in the large. One might argue that the architects tried to introduce the notion of abstraction, scale and imagination into the Riegelian value system—where detail is not provided, the mind has to fill it in; where facts are not known, the imagination provides alternatives. The consequent visual abstraction through an ostensible lack of detail derived from the zooming up of a small model was made visible in the finished house: the architects produced the evocative illusion of abstraction, a visual relationship to the model. The office likens its "blurry reconstruction" of the Director's House (as well as the Moholy-Nagy House) to Thomas Demand's photographs of models.[60] And yet—they built houses. As buildings, those necessarily demanded the hyper-resolution prescribed by contemporary technical standards, production processes and drawing

Fig. 10. Director's House, garden façade, photograph of the plaster model. Photograph by Lucia Moholy.

Fig. 11. Double family house, garden façade, photograph of the plaster model. Photographer unknown.

Fig. 12. Photograph by Armin Linke of a construction detail by Bruno Fioretti Marquez, 2014.

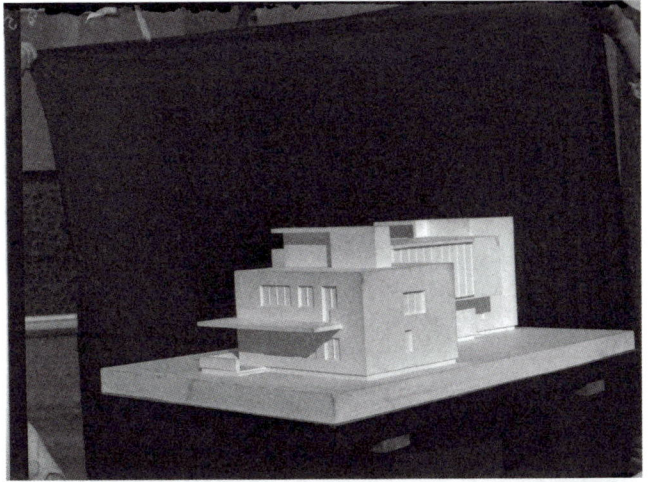

software. The blurriness that had promised an escape from the "wrong" kinds of false authenticities had become a high-resolution project, an explosion of data points to guarantee a watertight roof and drainage systems; the seamlessly flush windows require screws, bolts, joints and seams; and the exposed concrete surface intense planning of the constructing process was to obliterate all traces of human-scale production.[fig. 12] The new instances of the two houses are customized special constructions—the only standardized parts remain the white air exhaust louvre in the basement, the fire exit signs, and the accessibility ramps. One can easily imagine the contrast between a pile of plotted plans and 3-D models used to design as well as build this last iteration of the Gropius House and the straightforward, sparse floor plans and sections of the 1920s.

The promise of repetition—be it as historical reconstruction or as mass-produced object—has long been one of reliability and stability. And yet, as we have seen, in the history of the Masters' Houses it was anything but that: equally bound to the human community of the masters, which had had its beginnings in Weimar long before the large Bauhaus settlements became built reality, repetition became the tool toward change, even fragility. The everyday life of the inhabitants, the moments on the terrace together with the neighbors, those were the qualities that rendered this *Siedlung* into Bauhaus architecture—a quality that still lingered from the Weimar beginnings. But in the most recent debate, those inhabitants and the changes they made to their houses were slated as equally dangerous to the Bauhaus legacy as the political impositions and changes during the NSDAP regime, or the bomb impacts during World War II. When the competition for the "repair" of the *Siedlung* was decided, the winning project focused on the exterior image of the *Siedlung*, retrofitting seemingly missing pieces in the overall setting. Gropius's (assumed) vision of the settlement defined the reconstruction. And not only was the status of 1926 chosen,

Part 1

Theories
of
Bauhaus
Materiality

174

Fig. 13. El Muche and Nina Kandinsky in the garden of the Masters' Houses, circa 1926–27. Photograph attributed to Hugo Erfurth.

prior to the masters' moving in, but the status even before that: the moment to be resurrected was that of the model—a manifestation of the untouched imaginary of Gropius's genius.

Each reconstruction is motivated by a longing for something lost. It seems that for the Masters' Houses, this longing was not one for historical correction, maybe not even for Bauhaus architecture, but for the reconstruction of a recognizable, reliable project prior to its human contamination. And in the onslaught of data points shaping the exposed concrete with the perfectly inserted glass panes, that very longing was rendered into an object. The dust of the *Siedlung*'s human history was wiped off and cleaned up. The life of the inhabitants, the political and aesthetic frictions and transitions, the appropriations, changes, and destructions: they all were cleared away.[fig. 13] Negating the existing layers of trials and errors, political tragedy and neighborly laughter, peeling paint, and the intoxicating smell of the first bloom of the season, the new houses became more of the same: a repetition of assumed values packaged in familiar aesthetics. The fragility of experimentation, the tentative quality of historical interpretation made space for a Bauhaus as the ultimate monument.

1   The project was not financed like later mass-housing projects, since the city of Dessau did not want to be accused of spending money reserved for housing estates on the villas of the masters. See Christine Kutschke, "Bauhausbauten der Dessauer Zeit. Ein Beitrag zu ihrer Dokumentation und Wertung" (diss., Hochschule für Architektur und Bauwesen Weimar, 1981), 31–32.

2   Ise Gropius wrote in a diary entry on April 12, 1926: "in Dessau soll alles von vorne anfangen." Quoted in Boris Friedewald, "Drei Leben im Direktorenhaus," in *Neue Meisterhäuser in Dessau, 1925–2014: Debatten. Positionen. Kontexte*, ed. Wolfgang Thöner, Edition Bauhaus 46 (Leipzig: Spector Books, 2017), 69.

3   Oskar Schlemmer, *Oskar Schlemmer: Briefe und Tagebücher* (Stuttgart: Hatje, 1977), 168.

4   Kutschke, "Bauhausbauten der Dessauer Zeit," 19–20.

5   Schlemmer, *Oskar Schlemmer*, 188.

6   Originally published as Farkas Molnár, "Élet a Bauhausban," in *Periszkop* (June–July 1925), trans. John Bátki in Timothy Benson, ed.,

Between Worlds: A Sourcebook of Central European Avantgarde 1910–1930 (Cambridge, MA: MIT Press, 2002), 463–464.

7   Molnár, 463–464.

8   Barry Bergdoll and Museum of Modern Art (New York), "Bauhaus Multiplied: Paradoxes of Architecture and Design in and after the Bauhaus," in *Bauhaus 1919–1933: Workshops for Modernity*, ed. Leah Dickerman and Barry Bergdoll (New York: Museum of Modern Art, 2009), 46.

9   Robin Schuldenfrei, "Capital Dwelling: The Bauhaus's Haus Am Horn," in *Architecture and Capitalism: 1845 to the Present*, ed. Peggy Deamer (London: Routledge, 2014), 71–95.

10   Walter Gropius, *The New Architecture and the Bauhaus* (Boston: C. T. Branford, 1955), 38.

11   Polish architect Helena Syrkus said in the 1970s: "We wanted social housing and in between we did finger exercises with villas for the affluent bourgeoisie." Quoted in Kutschke, "Bauhausbauten der Dessauer Zeit," 38.

12   Wolfgang Thöner, "Modellwohnhäuser und Künstlerkolonie: Zum Entwurf und Bau der Meisterhäuser," in Thöner, *Neue Meisterhäuser in Dessau*, 41.

13   Gropius, *The New Architecture and the Bauhaus*, 4.

14   Gropius argues for repetition of elements in his introduction to the school in Karl Nierendorf and Staatliche Bauhaus Weimar, eds., *Staatliches Bauhaus, Weimar, 1919–1923* (Weimar, Munich: Bauhausverlag, 1923), 1–18.

15   See Kutschke, "Bauhausbauten der Dessauer Zeit. Ein Beitrag zu ihrer Dokumentation und Wertung" (1981); Thöner, "Modellwohnhäuser und Künstlerkolonie: Zum Entwurf und Bau der Masters' Houses" (2017), 43.

16   Original German text: "Vereinfachung durch Multiplizierung bedeutet Verbilligung ... Der Grundriß der einen der beiden Wohnungen ist das verschränkte, um 90 Grad gedrehte Spiegelbild des Grundrisses der anderen. Genau die gleichen Bauteile sind verwendet, die Ansicht beider Hälften aber durch die Verschränkung verschieden." See Walter Gropius, *Bauhausbauten Dessau*.

17   Walter Gropius, *The New Architecture and the Bauhaus* (Boston: C. T. Branford, 1955), 1–2 and table of contents.

18   For the discussion about Gropius's vision for the Bauhaus, see *Ulm: Zeitschrift der Hochschule für Gestaltung*, issue 8/9 (September 1963). For Maldonado's article "Ist das Bauhaus aktuell?" and reactions to issue 8/9 by Gropius, Maldonado, and Banham about the influence and the moral and ethical project of the Bauhaus see issue 10/11 (May 1964). The influence of the Werkbund on the Bauhaus in turn is widely acknowledged by contemporaries and historians. Nikolaus Pevsner describes the indebtedness to the Werkbund as well, quoting Gropius, *Staatliches Bauhaus Weimar*, 8, in Nikolaus Pevsner, *Wegbereiter moderner Formgebung: von Morris bis Gropius* (Reinbek bei Hamburg: Rowohlt, 1957), 220, en. 101.

19   Gropius, *The New Architecture and the Bauhaus*, 3.

20   See Julius Posener, "Zwischen Kunst und Industrie: Der Deutsche Werkbund" in Lucius Burckhardt, *Der Werkbund in Deutschland, Österreich und der Schweiz: Form ohne Ornament* (Stuttgart: Deutsche Verlags-Anstalt, 1978), 14.

21   See Gropius, *The New Architecture and the Bauhaus*, 4.

22   See chapter sections "Standardization" and "Rationalization" in Gropius, *The New Architecture and the Bauhaus*, 30 and 38.

23   "The repetition of standardized parts, and the use of identical materials in different buildings, will have the same sort of coordinating and sobering effect on the aspect of our towns as uniformity of type in modern attire has in social life." See Gropius, *The New Architecture and the Bauhaus*, 4.

24   See the description of the *Siedlung* Törten (built after the Masters' Houses) and its lack of efficiency in Hans Maria Wingler, *Das Bauhaus, 1919–1933: Weimar Dessau, Berlin und die Nachfolge in Chicago seit 1937*, 2nd ed. (Bramsche: Gebr. Rasch, 1968), 397; see article from May 1929, Walter Gropius *Werkverzeichnis* w v41, Bauhaus-Archiv Berlin.

25   See Gropius, *The New Architecture and the Bauhaus*, 42.

26   The street was later called Stresemannallee, now Ebertallee. See Reginald R. Isaacs, *Walter Gropius: Der Mensch und sein Werk* (Berlin: Mann, 1983), 361.

27   Hansjörg Küster and Ansgar Hoppe, *Das Gartenreich Dessau-Wörlitz: Landschaft und Geschichte* (C. H. Beck, 2010), 126.

28   See Oskar Schlemmer, *Oskar Schlemmer: Briefe und Tagebücher* (Stuttgart: Hatje, 1977) and Paul Klee, *Briefe an die Familie*, ed. Felix Klee (Köln: DuMont, 1979).

29   Translations by the author unless otherwise noted. See Paul Klee's letter to Lily, April 26, 1930: "... erste Baumblüte ... Natürlich ist auch schon Schwüle zur Stelle und Gewitter. Das gab zwar einen wunderbaren Geruch, und als ich neulich auf dem Schlafzimmerbalkon stand, duftete es mehr wie im Märchen und gar nicht nach Dessau (Capricen!)." See Paul Klee, *Briefe an die Familie*, 1116.

30   See Klee, *Briefe an die Familie*, and letter by Lyonel Feininger to his wife Julia, Weimar, February 20, 1925 in Hans Maria Wingler, *Das Bauhaus 1919–1933, Weimar, Dessau, Berlin und die Nachfolge in Chicago seit 1937*, 3rd ed. (Bramsche 1975), 108.

31   See letter to Lily, July 2, 1927: "Als ich nach Hause kam, war es 10 Uhr, und ich setzte mich zum Abendessen. Und da kümmerten sich die Nachbarn um mich und guckten herein und fanden, dass ich ein fröhliches und wohlgepflegtes Abendessen hatte. Die Musik nicht zu vergessen, spielte nachher das Grammophon oben ein paar Tangos" in Klee, *Briefe an die Familie*, 1047.

32   See Schlemmer, *Oskar Schlemmer: Briefe und Tagebücher* and Klee, *Briefe an die Familie*. After initial comments on the architecture in 1926, the year of completion, the masters comment in the following years mostly on the dysfunctionality of heating and the beautiful ateliers.

33   Boris Friedewald, "Drei Leben im Direktorenhaus," in *Neue Meisterhäuser in Dessau*, 69–96.

34   Max Osborn, "Das Leben am Bauhaus," in *Vossische Zeitung*, December 4, 1926. Translation by the author.

35   Walter Gropius, *Bauhausbauten Dessau: Bauhausbücher 12* (Munich, 1930), 140. Arndt's color scheme was probably carried out after all. See *Bauhaus Dessau 1926: Mappe 48*, Bauhaus-Archiv Berlin, containing offset prints of the planned color scheme by muralist Alfred Arndt, dated 1925.

36   Clement Greenberg, *Homemade Esthetics: Observations on Art and Taste* (Oxford University Press, Inc., 1999), 31–32.

37   The resolution from February 1939 ordering the treatment is quoted in Gilbert Lupfen and Paul Siegel, "'Bauen bedeutet gestalten von Lebensvorgängen': Die Meisterhäuser in Dessau," in *Architektur und Kunst: Das Meisterhaus Kandinsky-Klee in Dessau*, ed. Norbert Michels (Leipzig: E. A. Seemann, 2002).

38   Andreas Schwarting, "Das Haus als Palimpsest: Anmerkungen zu Haus Emmer in Dessau," in *Neue Meisterhäuser in Dessau, 1925–2014*, ed. Wolfgang Thöner, 181–92, www.monumente-online.de/de/ausgaben/2012/5/idee-oder-substanz.php

39   Philipp Oswalt, then director of the Stiftung Bauhaus-Dessau, is quoted stating that to attempt a verbatim reconstruction would be a "distortion of history [Geschichtsverfälschung]" in "Geschichtsfälschung? Rekonstruktion der Bauhaus Meisterhäuser, Dessau" accessed January 2, 2011, deconarch.wordpress.com/2008/03/14/geschichtsfalschung-rekonstruktion-der-bauhaus-meisterhauser-dessau/.

40   Original German text: "Der Stadtrat hatte den Wiederaufbau beschlossen und im Frühjahr 2010 das Berliner Architekturbüro Bruno Fioretti und Marquez dafür beauftragt. Am Ende der Sanierung soll das Ensemble wieder in seiner ursprünglichen Form erlebbar sein." See press report by the dpa (German Press Agency) from July 7, 2011.

41   Original German text: "Das Projekt ist in keiner Weise als Rekonstruktion zu verstehen, sondern stellt eine Interpretation des ursprünglichen Hauses dar." See "Pläne für Dessauer Meisterhaus vorgestellt / Präzision durch Unschärfe – Architektur und Architekten – News / Meldungen / Nachrichten – BauNetz.de," June 15, 2010, accessed December 4, 2011, www.baunetz.de/meldungen/Meldungen-Plaene_fuer_Dessauer_Meisterhaus_vorgestellt_1094849.html.

42   See Walter Prigge, "Alles Fassade? Der Streit um die Rekonstruktion der Meisterhäuser," in *Bauhausstreit: 1919–2009*, ed. Philipp Oswalt (Ostfildern: Hatje Cantz Verlag, 2009), 289–290; Hans Maria Wingler's introduction to the reprint of Walter Gropius, *Bauhausbauten Dessau* (Mainz: Kupferberg, 1974), where he describes the alterations ordered by the NSDAP during World War II.

43   For the different values assigned to the preservation debate, see Alois Riegl, *Der moderne Denkmalkultus: Sein Wesen und seine Entstehung* (Vienna: W. Braumüller, 1903).

44   The dpa announcement "Farben wie 1926: Das Feininger-Meisterhaus erstrahlt in neuem Glanz" from April 1, 2011 was widely published. Accessed November 29, 2018, www.n-tv.de/reise/Feininger-Meisterhaus-erstrahlt-article2992976.html. The wording of "erstrahlt in neuem Glanz" in reference to the reconstruction of the *Meisterhäuser* was used time and again, for example 11 years earlier referring to the *Meisterhaus* inhabited by Kandinsky and Klee in Bernhard Schulz's article "Das Doppelwohnhaus von Wassily Kandinsky und Paul Klee erstrahlt in neuem Glanz" in *Der Tagesspiegel* (6 February 2000): www.tagesspiegel.de/kultur/das-doppelwohnhaus-von-wassily-kandinsky-und-paul-klee-erstrahlt-in-neuem-glanz/121428.html.

45   Walter Prigge, "Alles Fassade?" 291–92.

46   Andreas Schwarting, "Aura und Reproduktion: Anmerkungen zum Haus Gropius in Dessau," in *Konstruktionen urbaner Identität. Zitat und Rekonstruktion in Architektur und Städtebau der Gegenwart*, Bruno Klein and Paul Sigel, eds.

(Berlin, 2006) (Nachdenken über Denkmal-
pflege: Denkmale nach unserem Bild? Zu
Theorie und Kritik von Rekonstruktion,
Bauhaus Dessau, 31 March 2007), 1–9.

47 Norbert Korrek and Christiane Wolf,
*Das internationale Bauhaus-Kolloquium in Weimar
1976 bis 2016: Ein Beitrag zur Bauhaus-Rezeption
Dokumentation, Ausstellungsteil, Prolog* (Weimar:
Bauhaus-Universität Weimar, 2016), 22–23. See
essay in this volume: "The Long Path to the
Restoration of the Bauhaus Dessau (1951–1976),
pp. 350.

48 The return to a lost, yet "real," past has,
I would argue, a long-standing legacy in modern
German architecture culture. Beyond nostalgic
Sehnsucht, the quest for a reconstruction of an
(often imaginary) prewar status is more than an
aesthetic desire: it is a political desire to recreate
a past that never was while eradicating the
uncomfortable immediate past or present.

49 Gropius, *Bauhausbauten Dessau: Bauhausbücher 12*, 84–151.

50 See "Geschichtsfälschung? Rekonstruktion der Bauhaus Meisterhäuser, Dessau."

51 "Berliner bauen Meisterhäuser in Dessau
auf / Unscharfe Erinnerung – Architektur und
Architekten – News / Meldungen / Nachrichten – BauNetz.de," April 1, 2010, accessed
December 4, 2011, www.baunetz.de/meldungen/
Meldungen-Berliner_bauen_Meisterhaeuser_
in_Dessau_auf_1006927.html.

52 Alois Riegl, *Der moderne Denkmalkultus:
Sein Wesen und seine Entstehung* (Vienna:
W. Braumüller, 1903).

53 Gropius, *The New Architecture and the
Bauhaus*, 4.

54 See Georges Bataille, "The Obelisk,"
in *Visions of Excess: Selected Writings, 1927–1939*
(University of Minnesota Press, 1985), 213–222;
Denis Hollier, *Against Architecture: The Writings
of Georges Bataille* (Cambridge, MA: MIT Press,
1992), 109–110.

55 From the Introduction to Gilles Deleuze,
Difference and Repetition (New York: Columbia
University Press, 1994), 1.

56 Original German Text: "In dieser
Aufgabe steht nicht die Dokumentation eines
historischen Zustands im Vordergrund, es geht
nicht um eine wissenschaftliche Pflicht
gegenüber der Geschichte der Architektur. Es
geht hier um etwas Subtiles, um etwas Hinter-
listigeres; es geht um ein Gedächtnis, es geht

um Erinnerungen. ... Erinnerungen leben von
Unschärfen, Ungenauigkeiten. Wir müssen mit
diesen Unschärfen und Ungenauigkeiten arbeiten, um den richtigen Tonfall für diese Aufgabe
zu finden." See "Pläne für Dessauer Meisterhaus vorgestellt / Präzision durch Unschärfe –
Architektur und Architekten – News /
Meldungen / Nachrichten – BauNetz.de."

57 Benjamin uses terms such as replica,
reproduction, repercussion (but not repetition),
circling around the central term of "authenticity." See "The Work of Art in the Age of Its
Technological Reproducibility" in Walter
Benjamin, *The Work of Art in the Age of Its Technological Reproducibility, and Other Writings on Media*
(Cambridge, MA: Belknap Press of Harvard
University Press, 2008).

58 Schwarting, "Aura und Reproduktion,"
62–63.

59 Schwarting, "Aura und Reproduktion,"
62–63.

60 See "Pläne für Dessauer Meisterhaus
vorgestellt / Präzision durch Unschärfe –
Architektur und Architekten – News /
Meldungen / Nachrichten – BauNetz.de."

Jörg Paulus

Reverse Typographic Impressions: Archived and Archiving Affordance between Bauhaus Lines

Paper—an important material in the Bauhaus practice and its medial proliferation[1]— unfolds its agency in many different modi of perceptibility, which can be reactivated in various ways. The act of leafing through old issues of a journal such as the *Wissenschaftliche Zeitschrift der Hochschule für Architektur und Bauwesen Weimar*

(*Scientific Journal of the College of Architecture and Civil Engineering*), on which the following considerations are based, has already been an act of cultural-technically pro-leaf-erating previous acts of leafing.[2] The novella *Gentry by Entailment* by Prussian Romantic Ludwig Achim von Arnim, published in autumn 1819 in the *Taschenbuch zum geselligen Vergnügen auf das Jahr 1820* in Leipzig and Vienna, also opens with a famous literary act of leafing,[3] in which the perception of the phenomenon of time is dissolved into the sequence of images in an imaginary almanac: *We were just now leafing through an old almanac, whose copperplate prints reflect many follies of its time. Can it be that that age already lies, like an age of fable, so far behind us! How richly realized the world was in those days, before the general Revolution, which took its name from France, reduced all forms of rubble; and how uniformly paltry it has now grown! Centuries seem to have passed since then, and only with an effort do we recall that our early years belonged to that same time. From the very depth of these eccentricities, which Chodowiecki's master-hand has preserved for us, we can appreciate the peak of intellectual clarity then attained; that clarity can, in fact, most easily be measured against the silhouettes of those who stood in the way of its light: giant shadows cast before it on the earth. What classifications and gradations, manifest not merely in the externals of society! Then again, every individual was a world in himself, in his appearance,*

in his dress; and every man made on earth his own arrangements,
so to speak, for eternity.[4]

The key term in this paper- and image-induced retrospective is "forms,"
in which the trias of the first three sentences culminates before the
clause apodictically ends the option of a dialectical effectuation of the
trias after the semicolon: the present is "uniform and poor" and bereft
of all forming potentiality. Just like in Plato's Allegory of the Cave,
only unstable "shadowy silhouettes" light the way towards a historical
anamnesis of the collective mode of existence of "height" and the
realization of the "oddities," which can only be seen from this height
and stand on the thresholds between phenomenal and intellectual
reality. The medial representation of these shadow formations emerges
from the "masterful touch" of the copper engraver Daniel Chodowiecki
and transmits itself in the medial act, the gesture of leafing. This act
in turn refers the leafer back to the "somber series" of the present—
a present, the effect of which itself is then located in an architectural
dispositive, the gentry house, within the story: initially situated in an
estate ruled by the pre-revolutionary right of succession, it ultimately
is converted into a factory, the symbol of the new times.[5]

Even if, 200 years later, leafing as a form of fleeting inspection
has been largely replaced by scrolling on a screen, the older of the two
cultural techniques also retains its unique quality of evidence, which
is connected to the materiality of paper; this quality of evidence, however, can—as the suggested path goes—be connected to a performative quality of challenge inherent to the material. Such an affordance
was traditionally assigned to phenomena such as fire or doors,
and especially chairs and their antecedent analogues (tree stumps,
rocks) as their peculiarity. Recently also discussed in the field of
material text cultures, inscription materials such as clay, stone, and
paper enter the discourse of affordance research in their different
modes of existence.[6] In doing so, a concept hailing from psychology
and ethnology is also joined by archivological questions. The following
deliberations are understood as prolegomena to such an archivology
of affordance.

In 1977 in a double issue, the *Wissenschaftliche Zeitschrift* documented the first Internationales Bauhaus-Kolloquium, which had
taken place in Weimar in October 1976.[7] The resonance of an event
archived and archiving itself in such a way can be registered micro-
historiographically at a temporally and spatially mutably definable

Jörg
Paulus

Reverse
Typographic
Impressions

location.[8] An appropriate location can be a single library, but also a college, a town, a state, a country, a continent. In all cases, specific dispositive figurations of assemblages ensue. The following observations are located on the mid-level of the dimension of observation— in the environment of a middle-sized city which is home to a technical university as well as a college of arts.

In the corresponding *Regionalkatalog Braunschweig* of the Collective Libraries, we find four issues of the *Wissenschaftliche Zeitschrift*. When visited, the respective locations make very different archival-atmospheric impressions. The mode of storage is informed by this impression just as much as this mode—especially in its particularity— contributes to this distributed quality. The four locations are the Stadtbibliothek (city library) in Braunschweig (Brunswick), which is simultaneously a research and public library; the university library of the technical university; the department library of the institute for hydraulic engineering (Leichtweiß Institute); and the library of the Institut für Baustoffe, Massivbau und Brandschutz (institute for materials, solid construction, and fire safety). The modes of storage of the journals and their physical condition are just as different as the library infrastructures in which they are embedded.

The library at the Institut für Baustoffe—part of a nested building with a core from the year 1963 (architect: Gerhard Kierig)—is surrounded by testing facilities that are accessible only once the visitor has passed through a testing hall riddled with cranes, and is normally forbidden to trespassers; the library of the Leichtweiß Institute is located on the third floor of a low high-rise from 1970 (architect: Manfred Lehmbruck)—in the lobby, a (much younger) plaque remembers Ludwig Leichtweiß, titular saint of the institute, whose merits from the years 1943, 1952 and 1955 are listed just as consistently as they are framed with the date of establishment of the institute in 1937 and the end of the patron saint's teaching activities in 1958, without any further historical contextualization; in the university library of TU Braunschweig, also built in 1970 as part of the university forum ensemble (architect: Friedrich Wilhelm Kraemer), the volumes of the *Wissenschaftliche Zeitschrift* are located—accessible to the public— in the basement, on a compact shelving system on reels; only in the Stadtbibliothek, located in a wing of the Residenzschloss of 1841— reconstructed in 2007 and predominantly used as a shopping mall— is an electronic request of an issue of the journal required.

These exemplary Braunschweig copies of the *Wissenschaftliche Zeitschrift* are thus embedded in a partially revealed, partially invisible albeit overly historical-architectural dispositive of a middle-sized West German city once located on the outer limits of the East German "Zone." The variance of the modes of existence of the 1977 volume ranges from loose issues (at the Institut für Baustoffe) to annually bound volumes (at the university library and the Leichtweiß Institute), to blank space (at the city library)—though listed in OPAC (the online catalog), the journal doesn't seem to exist in reality (meaning in the repositories of the library). Without leaving traces, the volumes must have been culled at point x in time, between the establishment of the OPAC system (as the terminus post quem) and the attempt at an order in the year 2016 (as the terminus ante quem). The different forms of storage cause varying physical conditions of the journal: the glue binding of the bound volumes results in single pages coming loose; every flipping-open-again contributes to this process of decay, which has further progressed in the—obviously more frequently used—volumes of the university library than the ones at the institute of hydraulic engineering. The unbound copies at the Institut für Baustoffe are held together by the original stitched binding, through which they are affiliated with the process of production, from which the bound ones are cut off.

The condition of the ghost copies at the city library, however, has to remain speculative: their absence is literally disconnected. What remains conserved and independent of the mode of leafing through that the booklets demand from their condition of storage is the impressive typographic quality in all copies (this also holds true for the vanished copies, wherever they might be, should they still exist). The meticulous hand-setting of the texts and distribution of images following the traditional rules of the art of typesetting define the visual impression. Nonetheless, the paper material conceals another effect, which is connected to this visual impression, yet transcends it. It is a haptic effect which relies on a visual dispositive in order to make its appearance. I am talking about the impression of hot metal type letters, which have punched through the respective recto to the verso side and vice versa. In an entanglement of optical and haptic perception, this immanent imprint of the pages is only noticeable where printed text on the inverse page meets one of the many black-and-white images of the booklet. Text/text and image/image constellations,

Jörg
Paulus

Reverse
Typographic
Impressions

7 Aula

however, remain inconspicuous. This results in effects which make it possible to recognize a specific recto-verso affordance of the paper,[9] and which network themselves with architectural figurations. The alternating agency of these constellations becomes clear when we look at a series of three articles: at the beginning of the article "Das Bauhausgebäude in seiner Bedeutung für die Entwicklung der neueren Architektur" ("The Bauhaus Building in its Importance for the Development of Newer Architecture") by historian of architecture Adalbert Behr, we find a photograph with the "Ansicht des Werkstatttraktes, um 1927–1930" (view of the workshop wing), underneath which a "model" of it is pictured.[10] If we hold the page against the light at a slight oblique angle, the structure of the paper and the structure of the writing on the other side become equally clear on the pattern of the façade as well as on the model. Three layers merge into an optical unity: in the case of the photo, the mirror-inverted writings of the rear page broach the issue of aspects of the interior design of the building and thus add yet another dimension of content and space. Two additional photos (the cafeteria and student housing and balcony of the student housing unit) are devoid of traces of imprints, because the other side shows images of the foyer and a seminar room. At the end of the article, there is an image of the famous auditorium of Dessau during the time of its construction: [fig. 1][11] the doors of the hall are open and the tiers empty as during a recess, most of the tip-up seats tipped up. Yet one on the outer side of the second row as well as several others in the first row are down—as if kept free for potential guests by the invisible hand of affordance. In this, the recto-verso quality of paper fuses itself with the quality of affordance of the pictured seating of the hall. If we concentrate haptically and visually (by tilting the pages) on the carbon copy effect, the empty rows unexpectedly fill with placeholders (letters). In the case of the Dessau auditorium, the placeholders are built from inverted letters and words which form the headline on the other side of the page: "Die Tätigkeit der Gruppe Hannes Meyer in der UDSSR in den Jahren 1930 bis 1937" ("The Activities of the Hannes Meyer Group in the USSR in the years 1930 to 1937")[12]—this phrase occupies—slightly askew—the

first two rows of the recto figure. And the letter group "Gruppe," which refers to the artistic-social assemblage around the man who had to leave the Bauhaus in 1930, finds its typographical verso-location exactly in the accentuated empty place secretly offered in the second row of the image. [fig.2, 3] However, the token "UDSSR" exile of Hannes Meyer and his "group" finds its telling verso-location on the back rest of a chair in the first row.[13]

A few pages later, the relation between groups assembled by paper in such a way is again reconfigured (one is tempted to say: substantially reconfigured, if the argument on which such substance is based wasn't to be situated beyond an emphasis on categories of substantiality and marginality). On page 469, on yet another recto-page, we find three rows of portrait photos of eight men—an additional white square in the beginning graphically completes the assemblage to a system comprised of 3×3 fields and describes the pictured men as "Members of the Red Bauhaus Brigade."[14] The single images in turn are captioned with a consecutive number and the name of the person pictured: 1. Hannes Meyer, 2. René Mensch, 3. Klaus Meumann, 4. Konrad Püschel, 5. Béla Scheffler, 6. Philipp Tolziner, 7. Anton Urban, 8. Tibor Weiner. It is peculiar that—compared to the dates of the buildings in the captions—biographical data is missing, presumably for historically ideological reasons. The concise note in the text "Philipp Tolziner, Bela Scheffler and Anton Urban stayed in the Soviet Union"[15] gilds the fact that Urban and Scheffler had fallen victim to Stalinism in 1938 and 1941 respectively, while Philipp Tolziner was still living in Moscow at that time (1976) after a longer internment in a camp.[16] Meanwhile, the dates of the Gastroi projects and founding dates of the Moscow Academy of Architecture imprint themselves from the verso-page on

Jörg
Paulus

Reverse
Typographic
Impressions

185

this one (the founding year of the academy, 1934, has its recto-location in the margins of the Hannes Meyer portrait, who belonged to this academy from that very year onward). The article that follows, by architecture theorist Christian Schädlich—"The Moscow Higher Technical Workshops and the Bauhaus"[17]—in turn takes up inscriptions from Püschel's article, but also of itself, by contrasting, for example, figure 3 ("Project of an Office Tower for Moscow, student work V. Krinsky, 1923") and figure 4 ("Project of a Mobile Cinema with Library, design diploma, D. Saonegin, 1929") with inverse lines from the reverse page.[18] These emerge especially in places where otherwise black surfaces dominate. In the case of the tower, the relief of the letters inscribes itself into the grid of stories in the design draft, while in the sketch of the mobile cinema they constitute an imaginary gaze from behind a screen, on which the end titles of a film can be seen, the "content" of which refers to the conflicts about the ideological direction of the higher technical workshops at the Moscow Vkhutemas.

"The archive: if we want to know what this will have meant, we will only know in the times to come," Derrida writes.[19] In readings such as these, the future inscribes itself again into the past, at least into an intermediate past like the one threaded between the age of Bauhaus and the present through the pages of the *Wissenschaftliche Zeitschrift* in 1976. In doing so—and with reference to Foucault—the "monumental" character of the archival object emerges from its "documentary" character.[20] According to the arbitrary character of perceptions and their associative entanglements, such readings might not be suited to found historical knowledge in the sense of historical epistemes. However, they can be considered as testimonials of a "diagonal" science

Part 1

Theories
of
Bauhaus
Materiality

186

Fig.3. Detail of obverse side of fig. 1.

in the sense of Roger Caillois,[21] related to the rocky heaves in which Caillois recognized images of a less structural and rather polyvalent system of references,[22] just as polyvalent as the inscriptions of the verso-pages in the paper of the journal. That façades with line grids, human faces with sober dates, and mobile cinema sketches are inscribed from behind with screen lines is based on subjectively colored combinatorics. Which would, however, remain baseless without the images' objective character of affordance, so that in their cross-fading of epistemic bases they might most likely be ascribed to the aesthetic principle of serendipity, for which Horace Walpole coined the term.[23] Walpole's principle should also be understood as epistemically polyvalent.[24] And the idiosyncratic scientific-aesthetic cosmos of the name-giver of serendipity prefigures this polyvalence exactly in the space between architecture and writing culture.[25] The transcription of contents from verso to recto is a diagonalization in a geometrical and at least also etymologically in an architectural-typographical double meaning. This becomes evident in two-column layouts like the one of the *Wissenschaftliche Zeitschrift*: sinistral verso columns emboss themselves on dextral recto columns and vice versa. That texts are built from columns, stacks of symbols, which—in the language of printers—constitute and simultaneously inhabit a singular "text space" (*Schriftspiegel* in German, trans. "writing mirror"), once more refers to the affordance of the printing process, which reveals itself discreetly in all observations.[26] All our leafing through is, in this sense, also a form of space inspection in which we—in manifold encodings—experience historical time.

1   Compare Jenny Graser, *In der dritten Dimension. Raumkonzepte auf Papier vom Bauhaus bis zur Gegenwart*, exh. cat., Städel Museum (Frankfurt, 2017).
2   Vilém Flusser understands "leafing through" as a gesture embedded into other acts; see Vilém Flusser, *Die Schrift: Hat Schreiben Zukunft?* (Göttingen, 1987); trans. *Does Writing have a Future?* (Minnesota, 2011). In a lucid essay, Dietmar Schmidt has transferred and differentiated this understanding to the turning of the page: see Dietmar Schmidt, "Umblättern statt Lesen. Lektüren des Nichtlesens bei Thomas Bernhard," in *Medienphilologie. Konturen eines Paradigmas*, ed. Friedrich Balke and Rupert Gederer (Göttingen, 2017), 129–57; on the cultural technique of leafing through, see also Harun Maye, *Blättern/Zapping. Studien zur Kulturtechnik der Stellenlektüre seit dem 18. Jahrhundert* (Zurich: diaphanes, 2018).
3   The "leafing scene" redefines the writing scene made prominent by Rüdiger Campe, "Die Schreibszene, Schreiben," in *Paradoxien, Dissonanzen, Zusammenbrüche. Situationen offener Epistemologie*, ed. Hans Ulrich Gumbrecht and K. Ludwig Pfeiffer (Frankfurt am Main: Suhrkamp, 1991): 759–772; Ulfert Ricklefs, "Ludwig Achim von Arnim," in *Romantik. Epoche – Autoren – Werke*, ed. Wolfgang Bunzel (Darmstadt, 2010), 152–68, here: 164.

Jörg Paulus

Reverse Typographic Impressions

4 Ludwig Achim von Arnim, *Die Majorats-herren*. English translation in *Gentry by Entailment* (London: Atlas Press, 1990), 5.

5 Compare Ulrike Vedder, "Majorate. Erbrecht und Literatur im 19. Jahrhundert," in *Generation. Zur Genealogie des Konzepts: Konzepte von Genealogie*, ed. Sigrid Weigel, Ohad Parnes et al. (Munich, 2005), 91-107.

6 Compare Lisa Gitelman, *Paper Knowledge: Towards a Media History of Documents* (Durham, 2004), 3; Richard Fox, Diamantis Panagiotopoulos, and Christina Tsouparopoulou, "Affordanz," in *Materiale Textkulturen*, Lieb Ludger n.d. (Berlin, 2015), also accessible at: www.degruyter.com/downloadpdf/books/9783110371291/9783110371291.63/9783110371291.63.pdf; Cf. the affordance of paper, see Raphael Wimmer, "Affordance of Paper, Public Administration, and Toolkits: Some Anecdotes," Lecture, Bauhaus Interaction Colloquium, May 17, 2017. Also see his research group: hci.ur.de/start.

7 "50 Jahre Bauhaus Dessau," Research Colloquium in Weimar, October 27-29, 1976, in *Wissenschaftliche Zeitschrift der Hochschule für Architektur und Bauwesen Weimar*, 5/6, no. 23 (1976).

8 About the entanglement of archiving and archived events, see Jacques Derrida, *Dem Archiv verschrieben: Eine Freudsche Impression* (Berlin, 1997), translated by Eric Prenovitz as *Archive Fever: A Freudian Impression* (London, 1996).

9 Compare Helga Lutz, Andrea Hübener, and Jörg Paulus, "Das Manicule: »The Hand and Meaning ever are ally'de,«" in *Satzzeichen. Szenen der Schrift*, ed. Helga Lutz, Nils Plath, and Dietmar Schmidt (Berlin, 2017): 363-385, here: 381.

10 *Wissenschaftliche Zeitschrift* (see footnote 7): 463, compare e-pub.uni-weimar.de/opus4/frontdoor/deliver/index/docId/879/file/Adalbert_Behr.pdf.

11 *Wissenschaftliche Zeitschrift*, 467. About Bauhaus architect and photographer Erich Consemüller (1902-1957), see Wulf Herzogenrath and Stefan Kraus, eds., *Erich Consemüller: Fotografien Bauhaus Dessau* (Munich, 1989).

12 Konrad Püschel, "Die Tätigkeit der Gruppe Hannes Meyer in der UDSSR in den Jahren 1930 bis 1937," in *Wissenschaftliche Zeitschrift* (see note 7): 468-72. Compare e-pub. uni-weimar.de/opus4/frontdoor/deliver/index/docId/878/file/Pueschel.pdf.

13 A remarkable orchestral analogy to the depiction of empty seating rows can be found parallel to the publication at the beginning of the film Человек с киноаппаратом (Man with a Movie Camera) by Dziga Vertov from 1929. I thank Ines Weizman for the hint.

14 Püschel, "Die Tätigkeit der Gruppe Hannes Meyer," 469.

15 Püschel, "Die Tätigkeit der Gruppe Hannes Meyer," 471.

16 Compare a detailed account of the biographies and fates of the pictured people in Ursula Meuscheler, *Das rote Bauhaus* (Berlin, 2016).

17 Christian Schädlich, "Die Moskauer höheren künstlerisch-technischen Werkstätten und das Bauhaus," in *Wissenschaftliche Zeitschrift* (see note 7), 472-75; compare e-pub.uni-weimar.de/opus4/frontdoor/deliver/index/docId/876/file/Schaedlich.pdf.

18 Schädlich, "Die Moskauer Werkstätten," 473.

19 Derrida, *Dem Archiv verschrieben*, 27.

20 Michel Foucault, *The Archeology of Knowledge*, trans. A. M. Sheridan Smith (London, 2002).

21 Compare Irene Albers, "Reine und unreine Literatur(wissenschaft) nach Roger Caillois," in *Zeitschrift für Kulturwissenschaft* 1 (2013): 39-53, here 47.

22 Roger Caillois, *L'écriture des pierres* (Geneva, 1970).

23 The journal *Ilinx: Berliner Beiträge zur Kulturwissenschaft* is also based on the synergy of Caillois's "diagonal science" and the principle of serendipity: www.ilinx-kultur.org/uber-ilinx/.

24 Compare "Tales of Serendipity" in *Ideas. Newsletter of the European Research Council* 2017 3, 4-6.

25 Compare Norbert Miller, *Strawberry Hill: Horace Walpole und die Ästhetik der schönen Unregelmäßigkeit* (Munich, 1986).

26 *Lexikon des gesamten Buchwesens*, 2nd ed., vol. IV (Stuttgart, 1995).

Nicholas de Monchaux

Bauhaus on the Moon

In 1968, British choreographer Margaret Hasting reconstituted the costumes and choreography of Oskar Schlemmer's pioneering Bauhaus performance, the *Triadic Ballet*. Filmed in vibrant color for Bavarian state television, the performance reveals unexpected subtleties in choreography and character. Where the seminal black-and-white photographs of the ballet's original production highlight the costumes' graphic geometry, the color film instead emphasizes their color and volume. And where the original emphasizes the order and precision the costumes give to human flesh, the broadcast's close-ups instead reveal the unexpected frailty of the costumes' materials: their similarity to, versus differences from, from, the bodies they house. Soft, sagging, and even squishy.[fig. 1]

Contrast this with another dance on film. The camera frames the torso of another remarkable costume, and shows a human figure moving and rotating its joints; the Litton RX-1, a silver experimental pressure suit intended for work on the surface of the Moon. On a background of that particular blue associated less with skies and more with middle-school corridors, the lone figure moves his arms and wrists through a full range of motion, slowly and with a smile. The connections to the Triadic Ballet, however, are more than skin-deep. Behind the piercing eyes of the Litton test subject, it turns out, lie essential connections between the second film and the first: between Bauhaus dance and movement on the Moon.[fig. 2]

"Space suit"

The first connection is historical, social, and surprisingly direct. The character inside the Litton suit is not an impartial observer, but rather the suit's author, industrial designer William Elkins. Elkins

190

Fig. 1. Schlemmer Costumes in the Staatsgalerie Stuttgart, 2018. Photograph by Vera Heinemann and Anna Luise Schubert (CDA), 2018.

Fig. 2. Frames from a film showing a 5 psi pressure test of the Litton RX-1a, 1962.

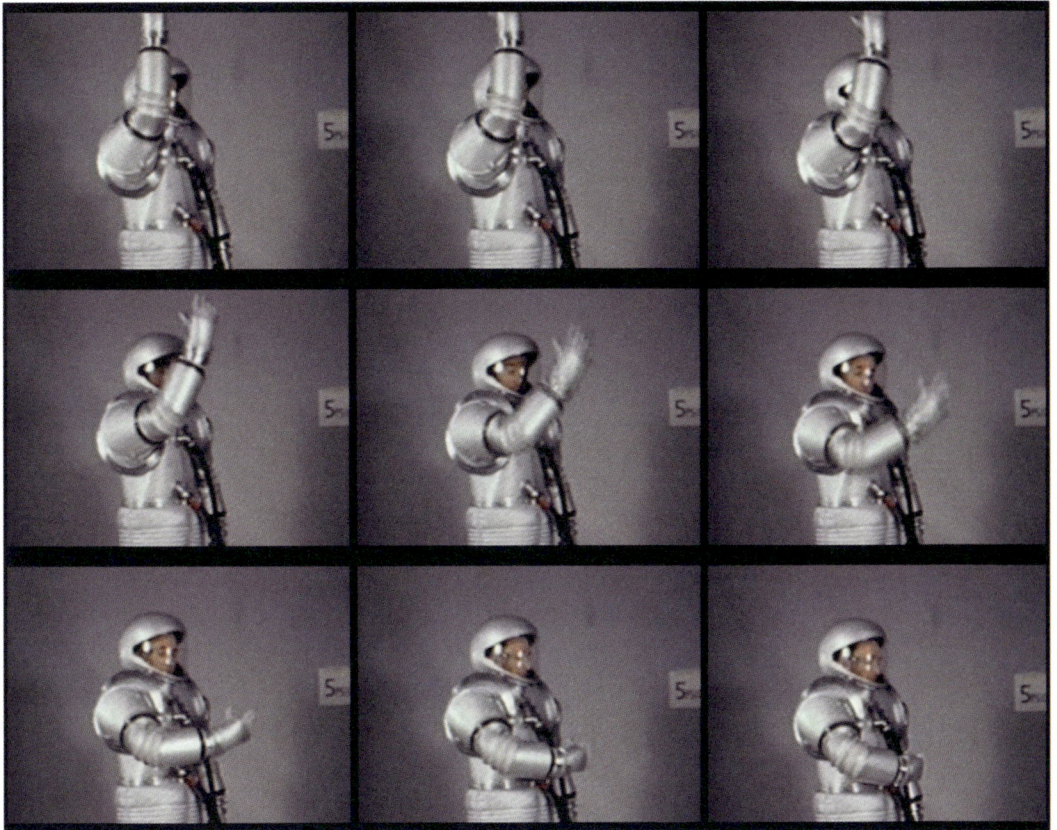

THE POPE AND HIS DOCTOR   INSIDE THE SOVIET SPY SYSTEM

LOOK

DECEMBER 10, 1957

MAN PREPARES FOR

SPACE TRAVEL

Fig.3. The Litton Mark I suit on the cover of *Look* magazine, December 10, 1957.

began his career in pressure-suit design at Beverly Hills-based Litton in 1958. Before this, however, he studied Industrial Design in Chicago on the GI Bill; and while he matriculated at the School of the Art Institute of Chicago, he was by his own telling "entranced" by a different faculty, that of the Institute of Design at the Illinois Institute of Technology—founded in Chicago as the New Bauhaus by László Moholy-Nagy. It was there in particular that Elkins was exposed—in the dark, on lantern slides—to the substance, and style, of Schlemmer's ballet, as well as the larger atmosphere of mechanized geometry that attended them, and the bodies they masked. And it was to this precedent that he, at least in part, turned when tasked with a very different kind of reduction of the body's complexity to mechanical motion.[1]

Litton's suits were originally designed for earthbound use in industrial vacuum chambers. But they quickly took pride of place in the popular imagination as heroic armor for outer space, appearing on the cover of *Look* magazine as a "space suit" just months after *Sputnik*'s launch.[fig.3] A later press release depicted Elkins' suit next to a medieval suit of armor, asking (rhetorically), "Nothing new under ye olde sun?"[fig.4] The Litton suits' popular reception was endorsed and encouraged by the nascent military-industrial space establishment. By 1962, the Litton suits had been designated by NASA Crew Systems Division chief Joe Kosmo the "RX" series—officially standing for "Rigid eXperimental," but actually reflecting his belief that they were, fundamentally, the "prescription" (Rx in the pharmaceutical sense) for how Americans would enter outer space.[2]

Under Elkins' direction, the original Litton suit design was continually developed throughout the sixties, with the aim of its use on the surface of the Moon. The silvery RX-1 [fig.5] was followed in 1962 by a more compact suit—the white fiberglass RX2. With further prototypes to follow, the RX series were tested and prepared for multiple stages of the US space program, including the planned use of Gemini hardware

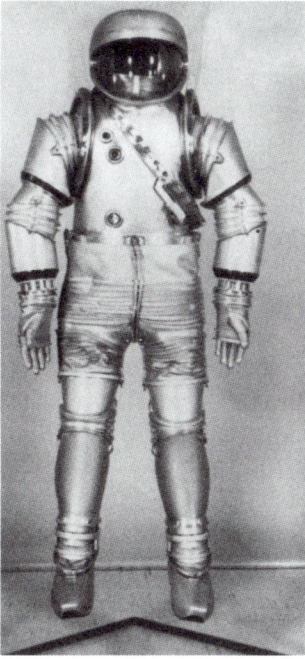

Fig. 4. NASA press release, "Nothing New under ye Olde Sun?" June 26, 1964.

Fig. 5. The RX-1 photographed on a simulated lunar landscape.

Fig. 6. Litton's RX-5 being tested on a simulated lunar surface in 1968.

Fig. 7. Harrison "Jack"
Schmitt, *Apollo 17* lunar
module pilot, uses an
adjustable sampling scoop
to retrieve lunar samples
during the second *Apollo 17*
extravehicular activity
(EVA), at Station 5 at the
Taurus-Littrow landing site,
December 12, 1972.

for military spaceflight, the Apollo flights to the Moon, and the later
"Apollo Applications Program" that resulted in the US space station
Skylab. [fig. 6] As late as the 1980s, closely related suits developed at
NASA's Ames Research Center were considered for military astronauts
as part of President Ronald Reagan's "Star Wars" initiative.[3]

"Dust, dust, dust"

As is readily apparent, however, Neil Armstrong and Edwin E. "Buzz"
Aldrin did not land on the Moon in garb with Bauhaus origins. Instead,
in fact, they were protected with soft clothing fashioned, much more
literally, from the bra straps, girdle rubber, and nylon fabric used elsewhere by its manufacturer, ILC—best known by its consumer brand
of Playtex. The reasons were manifold. They hinged as much on the
failure of a range of solutions, spanning the RX hard suits to other proposals by traditional military-industrial contractors, as on the success
of the Playtex suit. In the case of other military-industrial solutions,
these were often failures in comfort, wearability and safety; in the case
of the Litton suits, they were in both the strict requirements of weight
and storage on the suits, as well as the tendency of their failure to
be as rare as it was spectacular and total.

A final, critical factor was the doubted ability of their Teflon-
coated joints to weather the harsh and improbably effects of the highly
abrasive, corrosive lunar surface. As a 2008 report observed of manned
lunar exploration, "[t]he major issue the Apollo astronauts pointed
out was dust, dust, dust."[4]

Lunar astronauts' problems with dust derive directly from the
nature of its formation, profoundly different from the particles of our
own planetary surface. The top layer of the lunar regolith is not a
result of flows, abrasions, or organic decomposition, but is rather the
cumulative result of a billion years of small, violent, micrometeoroid
impacts. Each collision melts a portion of the lunar surface momen-
tarily into a vapor, which condenses on the cloud of small particles
thrown up inside it, encasing them in a thin, sharp shell of silica glass.
The resulting grains are tiny, irregular, adhesive, and profoundly
abrasive: "fine as flour and rough as sandpaper."[5]

The irregular sharpness of lunar dust also means that its particles
move around upon being jostled; they creep over, and even through,
layers of earthly material as they shift and scythe.[6] During the longest
moonwalks, like those of *Apollo 17*, the particles found their way

through all the eighteen outer, protective layers of the missions' soft space suits to threaten the operation of the engineered joints in their suits' arms. And after any lengthy exposure, the dust also left Apollo's iconic outerwear irrevocably blackened from shoulders to feet— which led, in turn, to an failed effort at post-flight, pre-victory-tour dry cleaning.[fig.7][7]

A single image

Writing of the *Triadic Ballet*, historian Juliet Koss observes that "the choreography leaves no doubt that the intended spectator is in fact the camera lens."[8] This is of course true of mid-century spacesuits as well. When Vice President Lyndon Johnson was charged by John F. Kennedy with conceiving a suitable US response to the remarkable effect of the launch of Yuri Gagarin on the global imagination, his advisers included not just Presidential science adviser Jerome B. Weisner, but also Frank Stanton, president of CBS. Indeed, the entire, vast apparatus of the Apollo program can be properly understood as an enormous military-industrial infrastructure for the production of a single television image: that of an American on the surface of the Moon.[9]

For all their technical limitations, the RX suits, and their heroic hardness, proved an enduringly compelling image for US space efforts to project. Throughout the decade of the space race, the RX suits continued to feature heavily in NASA publicity— as when they formed part of the enormous, concluding tableau of the US Pavilion at the 1970 Osaka World's Fair. Against a giant, halftoned image of the lunar

Fig.8. Davis, Brody with Chermayeff & Geismar: tUS pavilion, Osaka World's Fair, interior showing space exhibit and Litton RX-1 and RX-5, 1970.

Fig.9. Oskar Schlemmer's design for the congress hall in the Deutsches Museum, Munich (*Pastel für einen Wettbewerb*).

surface, the suits precluded Playtex's for pride of place: not conveying humans to space, but more purely and reliably conveying the utopian image of concert with technology that space travel, quintessentially, promises.[fig.8]

Weltpolitik and Werkbundpolitik

The connection between the Bauhaus theater of technology and the technological stagecraft of mid-century space exploration would already be fascinating as a system of comparison. Yet here a second circuit must be closed. For there is more than just a system of analogy, or even influence, between the bodies of Schlemmer's ballet and the subjects of mid-century spaceflight. For all its extensive self-presentation as a foundation of the cultural avant-garde, the Bauhaus was, like NASA, fundamentally an expression, and an artifact, of the modern nation-state— officially, even, the Staatliches Bauhaus. The school's origins can be traced directly to an argument, as early as 1907, by the government bureaucrat Hermann Muthesius, for an ambitious program of state-run education in craft and design: "Not only will it change the German apartment and the German house, but it will directly influence the character of the generation ..."[10] So equally were politics of the Deutscher Werkbund, founded at Muthesius's instigation in the same year, tied up in statecraft as well, and in particular in Germany's attempts to counter British supremacy in manufacturing and design.

Hermann Muthesius had spent the years from 1896 to 1903 as a technical attaché to the German Embassy in London, transmitting a series of influential reports not only on arts education and craft guilds, but also on railways and train design, infrastructure development, and wireless telegraphy. Eschewing the socialist politics and anti-industrial bent of major contemporary figures like John Ruskin, Muthesius instead focused on the potential for deploying design—and in particular, a *sachlich* flavor derived from, and contributing towards, industrial technology—in the service of the state's economic, political, and even military goals. This aligned with contemporaneous efforts to match the British Empire's access to exotic materials and inexpensive labor through technical achievements in German manufacturing.[11] As a result, *Weltpolitik* and *Werkbundpolitik* were continuous and interconnected in intent throughout. Yet they also obscured one another; The struggle between allies of Walter Gropius and Muthesius to

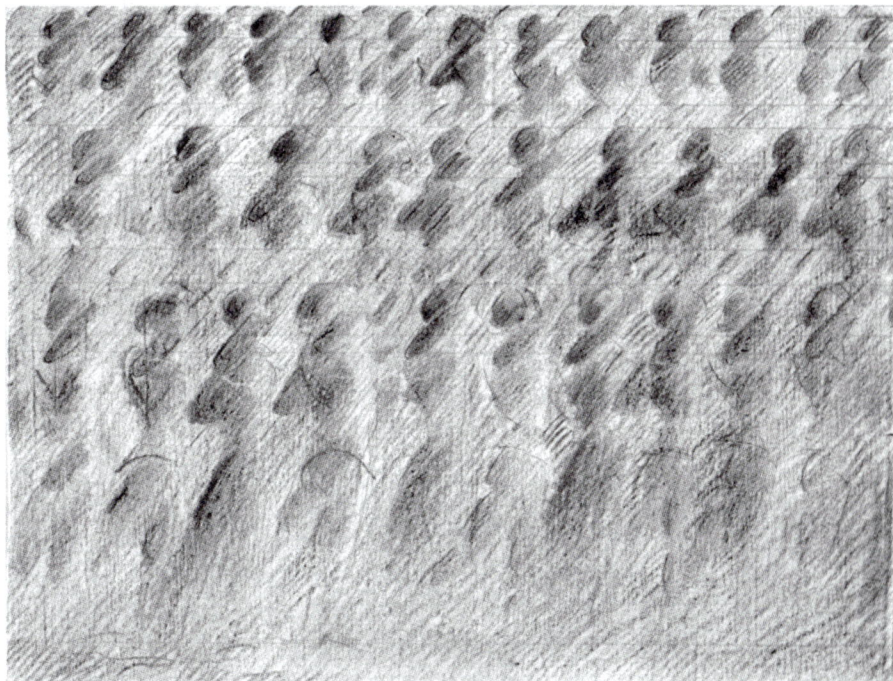

control the future of the Werkbund at the Deutscher Werkbund Congress that took place during Cologne's first Werkbund exhibition in July of 1914 was overtaken by the outbreak of more conventional warfare between Britain and Germany just days later.[12] In the end, though, it was less than a year from the completion of his World War I service in a Hussar reserve regiment that Gropius, still in state employ, would found the Staatliches Bauhaus in Weimar in 1919, ensuring his own mastery of the house, quite literally, that Muthesius built.

Stechschritte and *Bauhaustreppe*

The resulting institution succeeded remarkably in Muthesius's geopolitical aims, even as it worked assiduously to obscure its origins in them.[13] It is also against this background of continuous engagement with the goals of the German state that one should view Schlemmer's vain efforts attempts to engage with the new, post-1933 German political reality—as in the landscape of abstract bodies he sketched for an uncompleted mural for the Deutsches Museum in Munich in 1934, each mechanically abstract figure raising an arm in the Nazi salute.[fig.9] [14] It is against this background, too, that one might reexamine his far more famous *Bauhaustreppe* of the prior year and its display of geometrically abstracted figures against the grids and diagonals of the famous Bauhaus staircase.

In a remarkable essay, historian Paul Stoppard traces the painting from Germany to its purchase by Philip Johnson, ostensibly on behalf of New York's Museum of Modern Art, then through the remarkable departure of Johnson from MOMA in 1934 to attempt the founding of an American National Party along National Socialist lines. Meetings of this latter group were held in Johnson's apartment, with attendees on Barcelona chairs wearing steel-gray uniforms, and Schlemmer's *Bauhaustreppe* in the background.[15] The scene is presented by Stoppard as a study contrast between left and right, avant- and derriere-garde.

Yet what likely most excited a young Johnson about his experience of Nazi Germany—bodies, technology, and power brought in concert through design—also rendered it a set piece all too much of a piece, with no divisions between bodies and the state's bureaucratic, and militaristic whole. Johnson would not have seen the Triadic Ballet, but he would have no doubt observed a more dreadful, related dance; the *Stechschritte*—the goose step, or mechanistic "piercing step" first developed by the Prussian military but inextricably associated with dictatorships to the present day. Or as George Orwell drily observed, "One rapid but fairly sure guide to the social atmosphere of a country is the parade-step of its army."[16]

I Aim at the Stars ...

While the status of the Bauhaus' collaboration with Hitler's Germany may be a matter for contemporary debate, the corresponding status of the US space program is not. Its technology was unequivocally a direct extension of Nazi state efforts. Both the first US satellite, *Explorer 1*, and the first American astronaut, Alan Shepard, were launched on only-somewhat modified versions of the *Vergeltungswaffe* (Vengeance Weapon) 2, built by Wernher von Braun, head of rocket development first for Nazi Germany, then for the US Army, and finally NASA. The small and precarious-seeming launch infrastructure of *Explorer*'s Juno rocket and Alan Shepard's Redstone booster—a diminutive metal "firing table"—was in fact a legacy of the need to launch the V-2 quickly from temporary launch sites, including urban intersections in the Hague, so as to avoid allied attacks on fixed infrastructure.[fig. 10, 11] Operating with parts of the same team he had assembled in Peene- münde for Adolf Hitler, it was Wernher von Braun who supervised the design of the massive Saturn V rocket that launched Apollo astronauts the quarter-million miles to lunar orbit.[fig. 12]

President Eisenhower, all-too-aware of the resulting symbolism, had asked in 1958 that the first US satellite not be launched with a von Braun rocket; however, the plan had to be abandoned when a Navy- developed alternative twice failed to launch. More broadly, Eisen- hower was increasingly wary of what he was the first to call the "vast military-industrial complex," whose growing power he saw as a threat to civil society. When asked by Manhattan Project physicist and arms control-advocate Herbert York which individuals most personified this threat, Eisenhower quickly replied, "Teller," the inventor and im- presario of the hydrogen bomb, "and von Braun."[17]

In 1960, at the apex of his American renown, von Braun agreed to be both the subject and financial beneficiary of a biopic, *I Aim at the Stars*. The film was failure, both commercially and critically, and its clumsy treatment of its subject's Nazi career—including his officer's commission in the SS—marked a turning point in von Braun's image. Comedian Mort Sahl became only the first to quip that *I Aim at the Stars* should have been subtitled "*... but sometimes I hit London.*"[18]

*Nicholas
de
Monchaux*

Bauhaus
on
the
Moon

199

Yet the largest number of the V-2's victims were without a voice, and their direct subjugation was a salient distinction between the missiles of Nazi Germany and the ICBMs they became. These were the tens of thousands of slave laborers in the Dora-Mittelbau rocket factory, carved into the side of the Harz mountains just an hour north of the Bauhaus's first home in Weimar. Living in nightmarish conditions, in large part underground, more than 11,000 would not live to war's end—a number greater than all the V-2's official casualties. As the brutal details emerged later in his career, von Braun contested the idea that he had been personally exposed to, or aware of, the treatment of the Dora-Mittelbau workers—despite his not infrequent presence on the site and overall administration of their labor. Later historians have concluded, however, that he was profoundly complicit in "stoking the fires of Hell."[19]

By contrast, the enormously expensive Cold War space race can be best understood as an effort by both its combatants to undertake a competition that would demonstrate the power and precision of their nuclear technologies without genocide. The effects of this vast enterprise on the human bodies at its center were still not trivial, however. Gemini astronauts would lose several pounds of weight and suffer from dehydration and strain injuries battling the stiffness of their pressurized space suits. Operating at the far limits of their stamina a quarter-million miles from earth, the astronauts of Apollo would in later years fall victim to heart disease and other ailments at a rate much higher than the general population, victims of radiation exposure outside the Earth's protective Van Allen belts.[20]

Dust vs. data

If the human body was the singular summit of the vast, technological mountain of Apollo, then data was its vast foundation: the lifeblood of the methods of both engineering and warfare that brought it into being. The space race revolutionized the inner architecture of the computer as much as the very outer architecture of humanity's physical ambitions. From its crucible was forged our modern world.[21] Yet it is at the literal intersection of dust and data on the lunar surface that we find the ghosts of unexpected bodies as well.

Just as the literal abrasiveness of lunar dust took its toll on space suits, so did the same hazards, physical and electromagnetic, take their toll on the edifice of information that extended humanity's reach to

Nicholas de Monchaux

Bauhaus on the Moon

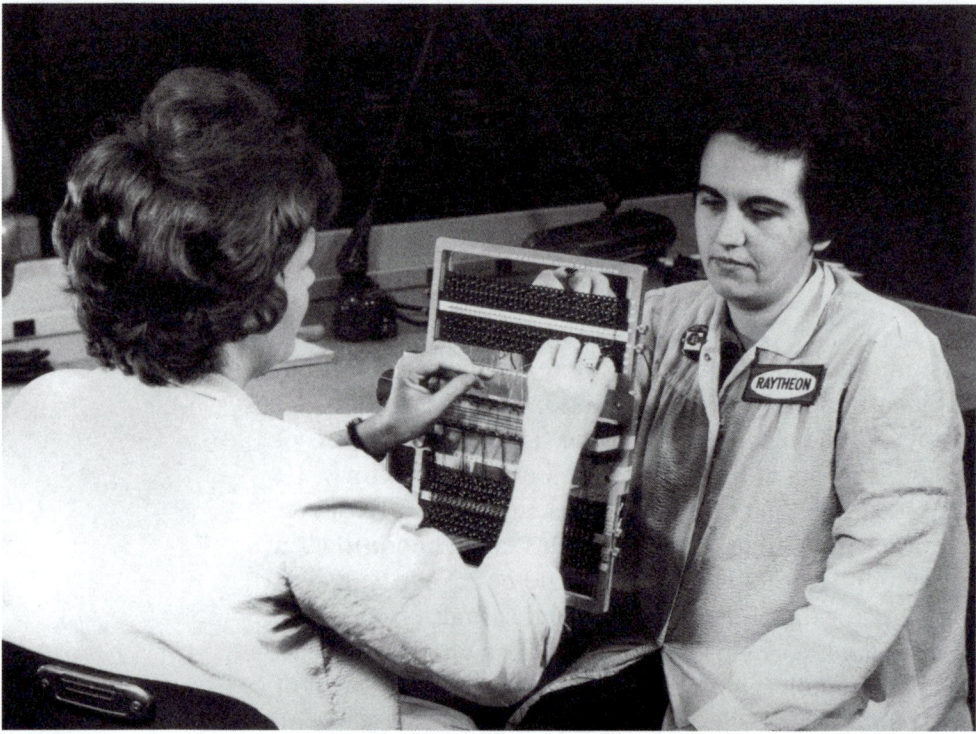

Fig. 13. Hand-weaving of rope memory wiring for Apollo guidance computer, Raytheon, Waltham, MA.

Fig. 14. Part of the Smithsonian's space suit collection in cold storage in 2004. Several Litton suits are visible at the right of the image, with Apollo lunar suits on the racks to the left. Photograph by Mark Avino.

its surface. To navigate their quarter-million-mile journey, Apollo's lunar module and command module each contained identical guidance computers to control speed, trajectory, position, and the timing of rocket burns. The Apollo Guidance Computer (AGC) was the very first, alongside all such devices today, to use multi-transistor silicon chips for its processing hardware.[22] It was soon understood, however, that the software that governed its operation, an intangible set of electronic signals, was profoundly vulnerable to the physical and electromagnetic environment of lunar, and translunar, space.

As a result, to allow the guidance computer's programs to reload their operating data reliably in the event of failure, the AGC eschewed the tapes and spinning disks that were the contemporary state-of-the-art. Instead, once a master program of operating data was created for each mission, the ones and zeroes of binary instructions were handcrafted in "ropes" of thin wire and ferromagnetic washers. A current passed through the collected strands would register each literal "bit" of magnet along its length and reliably and consistently load the spacecraft's software. To make each rope precisely, however, proved an enormous challenge.

According to an MIT manager, Raytheon "tried building the components with supervisors, industrial engineers ... [but] everything they made was scrap."[23] So, drawing from the textile mills and watchmakers around Raytheon's Waltham, Massachusetts factory, the firm hired a staff of middle-aged women (termed "LOLs," or little old ladies, by the engineers) to weave each crucial strand. Raytheon managers were so afraid the women would lose the knack of the delicate assembly work that they would pay them to sit and wait for weeks on end while each mission's software was finalized. They spent the time knitting.[fig. 13][24]

Dust to dust

The handweaving of Apollo's data-storage circuits was designed to avoid what is the way of all data, and bodies, over time. Whether "bit rot" or its older, organic cousin, the actions of entropy on digital bits and real bodies are inescapable. Against these forces, the surfaces of mechanical suits like the Litton RX suits have stood up well over time and remain able to hold a pressurized atmosphere. But suits of softer material—and in particular the A7L and A7LB suits worn on the surface of the Moon—have fared less well. Their fragility is due most

Nicholas de Monchaux

Bauhaus on the Moon

203

Fig. 15. Astronaut Edwin E. "Buzz" Aldrin on the surface of the Moon, July 21, 1969. Aldrin is looking down at the list of mission procedures sewn onto the surface of his left sleeve.

Fig. 16. The full Earth photographed by *Apollo 17* commander Eugene Cernan, December 1972. The image is usually shown, as here, upside down from its original orientation as photographed from the *Apollo 17* command module *America*.

of all to their natural core—the rubber, airtight pressure layer that is the most vital of the 21 layers of which they are made. A living material–beginning as sap from a tree—it has lost its flexibility over time, especially in the earliest suits, and become shrunken, stiff, and hard—much like any living body. Today, at the Smithsonian Institution's National Air and Space Museum, suits are mostly kept in a carefully controlled cool climate—a kind of hibernation—to minimize the damage.[fig.14] Here, too, there is a Schlemmer-space suit axis. Unlike the more mechanistic products of the Bauhaus workshops— Wassily chairs and lab-glass teapots alike—the costumes for the *Triadic Ballet* are thin, soft, and sagging. Like the Smithsonian's space suits, a multi-point program of environmental control is necessary to preserve their fabric, with attention paid not only to humidity and temperature, but also to such traditional organic pests as insects.[25] As with the cyborg visions of the early space program, the costumes' mechanical aspirations have fallen back to the way of all flesh.

When describing what most moved Hermann Muthesius in his half-decade encounter with the British architectural avant-garde of the turn of the 20th century, and most shaped his ambitions for German design education, historian John Maciuika describes the infatuation with "the design of whole environments."[26] The only match to Armstrong's photograph of Aldrin on the Moon's surface for the most reproduced photograph of Apollo (or even all time) is the image taken by astronaut Harrison "Jack" Schmitt of the full and whole earth from the command module, *America*, of *Apollo 17*.[fig.15, 16] Each image, in its own way, describes a whole environment against the void. That the delicate envelope of the Apollo space suit is akin to the thin delicacy of our own atmosphere may go without saying. In its soft, epidermal qualities, however, the Apollo space suit represented another kind of buffer: that between the crystal-hard matrix of the systems-engineering edifice supporting Apollo's chariot and that of the human beings who were its actors and subjects. Like the handwoven rope memory of the ACG, it was a circumstance in which that most archaic and superseded of Bauhaus values—craft—operated alongside, but also against, the logic of the machine.

Before the dawn of the space age, in a letter to Gunta Stölzl in 1933, Schlemmer described the relationship between the values of the new German state and his own aspirations. "I consider myself pure, and my art strong ... heroic, steely-romantic, unsentimental, hard,

sharp, clear ..."[27] Yet the truth of his, and any, body is exactly the opposite: fallible, full of feeling, soft, blunt, and mostly opaque. In different lights, in different times, the modern citizen, soldier and astronaut have been heroically conjured as ascending to a realm above such frailties, where design and technology alone hold sway. Nothing new under ye olde sun. But the wrinkles of Schlemmer's reconstructed costumes, and the unexpected softness of lunar fabric, lay bare a different truth. For all the dreams of the modern age—from Bauhaus's optimism to orbits of the Earth—the logic of our technological and political aspirations, and the logic of human bodies, remain enduringly, exasperatingly, at odds. Today, as ever, the most essential frontier for body, politics, and technology is not beyond the stars, but along the intimate intersection of their entangled, incompatible, embrace.

1   Nicholas de Monchaux, interview with William Elkins, June 2, 2009, audio recording.

2   Joe Kosmo, interview by Nicholas de Monchaux, Houston, May 1, 2006, audio recording.

3   Gary L. Harris, "The Origins and Technology of the Advanced Extravehicular Spacesuit," *American Astronautical Society History Series* 24 (San Diego: Univelt, 2001), 186–87.

4   Soil Science Society of America, "NASA's Dirty Secret: Moon Dust," *ScienceDaily*, accessed March 18, 2018, www.sciencedaily.com/releases/2008/09/080924191552.htm. Permalink: web.archive.org/web/20180318230142/https://www.sciencedaily.com/releases/2008/09/080924191552.htm.

5   Soil Science Society of America, "Moon Dust."

6   After a day of handling Apollo space suits as an archival researcher at the Smithsonian Institution in 2005–2006, even using cotton archival gloves, your author would be regularly astonished to find his fingertips peppered with microscopic grains of the Moon's surface.

7   Nicholas de Monchaux, interview with Amanda Young, Smithsonian Institution, National Air and Space Museum, January 15, 2006, tape recording.

8   Juliet Koss, "Bauhaus Theater of Human Dolls," *The Art Bulletin* 85, no. 4 (December 2003): 724–45.

9   See McDougall, Walter A. *The Heavens and the Earth: A Political History of the Space Age* (Baltimore: Johns Hopkins University Press, 1997).

10   Hermann Muthesius, "The Significance of the Applied Arts," lecture at the opening of the Berlin Commercial College, quoted in John V. Maciuika, *Before the Bauhaus: Architecture, Politics, and the German State, 1890–1920* (Cambridge: Cambridge University Press, 2005), 163.

11   Ironically, it was the poisons discovered through the harsh organic chemistry of commercial dyes that led directly to German innovations in gas warfare against Britain and its allies in World War I. See Nicholas de Monchaux, "Aerosol," in Jona Lueddeckens and Greg Bergner, eds., *Sprayed: Works from 1929–2015*, exh. cat. (London: Gagosian Gallery, 2015), 180–97.

12   John V. Maciuika, "Werkbundpolitik and Weltpolitik: The German State's Interest in Global Commerce and 'Good Design,' 1912–1914," *German Politics & Society* 23, no. 1 (74) (2005), 102–27.

13   For a full treatment of this history, see John V. Maciuika, *Before the Bauhaus: Architecture, Politics, and the German State, 1890–1920*, cited above.

14   Juliet Koss, "Bauhaus Theater of Human Dolls."

15   John-Paul Stonard, "Oskar Schlemmer's 'Bauhaustreppe', 1932: parts I & II," *The*

Burlington Magazine 151, no. 1276, and 152, no. 1290 (Burlington Magazine Publications Ltd.: July 2009 and September 2010), 456–64 and 595–602.

16   George Orwell, *The Lion and the Unicorn: Socialism and the English Genius* (London: Seeker & Warburg, 1941).

17   Michael J. Neufeld, *Von Braun: Dreamer of Space, Engineer of War* (New York: A. A. Knopf, 2007), 353.

18   Neufeld, *von Braun*, 353.

19   Neufeld, *von Braun*, 162.

20   M. D. Delp et al., "Apollo Lunar Astronauts Show Higher Cardiovascular Disease Mortality: Possible Deep Space Radiation Effects on the Vascular Endothelium," *Sci. Rep.* 6, 29901; doi: 10.1038/srep29901 (2016).

21   Two examples: the custom priority-based operating system developed by IBM for NASA's mission-control mainframes, the Houston Automated Spooling Priority program, or HASP, became the preferred operating system for all IBM mainframes into the 1970s. See Paul Cerruzi, *A History of Modern Computing* (Cambridge, MA: MIT Press, 2001), 124. The three-dimensional real-time simulation environment developed by General Electric for the Apollo Lunar Module Simulator in 1964 was used as early as 1966 to make the first real-time three-dimensional simulation of Earth-bound architecture, by Peter Kamnitzer of UCLA. See Nicholas de Monchaux, *Spacesuit: Fashioning Apollo* (Cambridge, MA: MIT Press, 2011), 300.

22   For a remarkable history of this artifact, see David Mindell, *Digital Apollo: Human and Machine in Spaceflight* (Cambridge, MA: MIT Press, 2008).

23   Jack Poundstone and Ed Blondin, Apollo Guidance Computer Conference 3 group interview, November 30, 2001, Dibner Institute of Science and Technology, History of Recent Science and Technology Program, accessed March 3, 2018, resolver.caltech.edu/CaltechAUTHORS:BUChrst06.

24   Poundstone and Blondin, interview.

25   Description of preservation measures undertaken for the costumes of Oskar Schlemmer's *Triadic Ballet*, Staatsgalerie Stuttgart, September 2018, correspondence with Ines Weizman. (Thanks to Katja van Wetten, restaurateur at Staatsgalerie Stuttgart.)

26   Maciuika, 82.

27   Letter from Schlemmer to Gunta Stölzl, June 16, 1933, quoted in Nerdinger, "Modernisierung, Bauhaus, Nationalsozialismus," in Winfried Nerdinger, ed., *Bauhaus-Moderne im Nationalsozialismus: Zwischen Anbiederung und Verfolgung* (Munich: Prestel, 1993), 19.

Nicholas
de
Monchaux

Bauhaus
on
the
Moon

Part 2

Hospital, Library, Drafting Rooms, Absent Silence: The Bauhaus in Weimar

Zeynep Çelik Alexander

1919: The Turning Point at Which History Failed to Turn

In 1922, the now-forgotten British historian G. M. Trevelyan used an intriguing phrase to describe the events of 1848—that is, that feverish moment of revolutionary action which, despite having failed to bear fruit, left indelible marks around the world. This pivotal moment in the nineteenth century, he wrote, was "the turning point at which modern history failed to turn."[1] The phrase, as uncharacteristic as it might be for a historian known as an avid advocate for Whiggish politics, nonetheless demonstrates the dilemma experienced by those who labor in the historical sciences. What changes at those moments when everything is supposed to change? What remains the same? How can one define historical change, after all?

What I would like to do in this essay is to subject the year 1919, the year of the founding of the Bauhaus, to a similar kind of thought experiment. The Bauhaus is almost always presented as the site of groundbreaking artistic reinvention, reconstruction, and revolution, but what if, following Trevelyan's provocation, the double meaning of the term 'revolution' were applied to the Bauhaus? That is, what if the so-called Bauhaus revolution were understood simultaneously as an abrupt change and a return to a previous state? Would it then be possible to conceptualize the Bauhaus as a break in the history of aesthetic modernity on the one hand and a continuation of nineteenth-century ways and traditions on the other? Might this dilemma help historians de-ontologize the Bauhaus and problematize the novelty that is unconditionally associated with it? In an attempt to answer these questions, let me turn to August 1918, when Johannes Itten, who was in Vienna teaching a version of what would become the first iteration of the preliminary course at the Bauhaus, wrote the following in his diary:

Fig. 1. Morning exercise on the roof of the Johannes Itten Schule in Berlin, 1930. Johannes Itten, *Werke und Schriften* (Zurich: Orell Füssli, 1972), 36, fig. 22.

On the course: Beginners must make exact, photographically correct drawings (in black-and-white as well as in color) from nature in order to train their ability to observe sharply and precisely. I want to train eyes, hands, and the memory. In other words, what is seen must be memorized [Auswendiglernen]. *I train first the physical body, hand, arm, shoulder, and the senses. That is the training of the externally given human. Gradually follows the training of understanding* [Verstand]. *Clear, simple, thoughtful observation of the sensually perceivable* [Beobachten des sinnlich Wahrnehmbaren]. *When this training reaches a certain state, the body will be unleashed to an increased extent. Chaotic exercises. The recognition of the self* [Erkennen des Ich]. *Two worlds: the self and the nonself, an important awareness. The outer and the inner, below and above. The goal is the pure and complete unleashing and representation of the self to the greatest extent possible. The recognition that nothing inward that is not outward leads to the pure training of inwardness. In contrast to the training of the outwardness ... Understanding* [Verstand] *always remains as the safeguard below.*[2]

Despite its philosophical hyperbole, this brief journal entry is worth examining at length, because Itten appears to be pursuing two seemingly irreconcilable epistemological goals at once here. First, like many of his reform-minded contemporaries, Itten is committed to a pedagogical model in which the training of the body takes precedence over the training of the mind, and the Enlightenment ideal of understanding (*Verstand*) is not the driving cognitive force but merely the "safeguard below." Following the example of his mentor Adolf Hölzel, who urged his students at the Stuttgart Academy to produce 1,000 pen strokes every day to harden their muscles, Itten would ask his students to permeate their entire bodies with feeling until they became fully cognizant of the expressive capabilities of their bodies.[3] This was most evident in the breathing, humming, and drawing exercises that he asked his students to undertake at the Bauhaus and elsewhere.[fig.1] In 1921, Paul Klee would describe Itten's preliminary course in his letters humorously as follows:

Zeynep
Çelik
Alexander

1919:
The
Turning
Point

211

After walking to and fro several times, Itten approaches the easel with a drawing board and scribbling pad. He picks up a piece of charcoal, his body tenses up as if becoming charged with energy, and then suddenly goes into action—once, twice. One sees the form of two forceful lines, vertical and parallel on the top sheet of the pad; the students are asked to repeat this. The master checks their work, asks some of them to demonstrate it individually, corrects their posture. He then, beating time, orders them to do it rhythmically, and then has them carry out the same exercise standing up. What is intended seems to be a kind of body massage, to train the body machine to function sensitively. Similarly, new elementary forms such as ⬚ and others are demonstrated and copied ⬚ and ⬚ with several explanations of the why and wherefore and the mode of expression. He then talks about the wind, and asks some of the students to stand up and express their feelings in the guise of wind and storm. Then he sets the task: Represent the storm. He allows them ten minutes to do it in, then inspects the results. This is followed by critical assessment. Thereafter work continues. One sheet after another is torn off, flutters to the ground. Some students work with such élan that they use up several sheets at a time. In the end they all become a little tired, and he sets his Basic Course students the same task as homework for further practice.[4]

Note how *words* are replaced by *forms* in this short passage. I have elsewhere called this kind of thinking "kinaesthetic knowing," a non-propositional, non-linguistic mode of knowledge assumed to be achieved through the movements of the body.[5] The notion that there might be an alternative way of reasoning that could not be confined to the abstract operations of the mind had existed in various forms before, but the idea took on new urgency and a different saliency in the middle of the nineteenth century in German-speaking lands.[6] Especially influential in this history was the distinction made by the formidable German physicist and physiologist Hermann von Helmholtz, who deployed two common German verbs to distinguish between *Wissen*—propositional, discursive, and conceptual knowledge that was conventionally understood to be the ideal of rigorous science—and *Kennen*, nondiscursive, nonconceptual knowledge obtained by experiential acquaintance.[7] Furthermore, Helmholtz surmised, *Kennen* had the potential to be as rigorous as *Wissen* one day.[8] Reformer after reformer in the last decades of the nineteenth century attempted to realize the potential that Helmholtz had ascribed to *Kennen*: it was during this period that school curricula were revised, following the

Fig. 2. Drawing exercises for children of varying ages. J. Liberty Tadd, *New Methods in Education: Art, Real Manual Training, Nature Study* (Springfield, MA, and New York: Orange Judd, 1899), 73. Reprinted in Rudolf Schulze, *Aus der Werkstatt der experimentellen Psychologie und Pädagogik* (Leipzig: R. Voigtländer, 1909).

Free Hand Work for Very Young Children

early nineteenth-century examples of Pestalozzi, so that children were taught something called *Formenlehre*; picture books gained new prominence; and a mid-century method called stigmography was revived, a method that operated with the assumption that young students were better off learning to read and write *forms* before *words*.[fig.2][9] (Itten, it is worth remembering here, started his career teaching primary school in a Swiss village in 1908.) It was also at this time that the first educational programs at German museums were established with faith in the power of image over text, and university students, who, professors worried, were no longer trained in the intricacies of the Classical tradition, were instructed with the slide lecture.[10]

More relevant here, just as these new pedagogical techniques put pressure on the nineteenth-century ideal of *Bildung*, a new kind of art school emerged and started to challenge the Beaux-Arts tradition that had been dominant in Europe and beyond at least since the end of the eighteenth century. This history has been almost entirely forgotten, but the pages of contemporaneous journals are full of advertisements for this new kind of school, of which the Bauhaus was definitely not the first and arguably the last example.[11] Among the largest and the most influential was the Debschitz School, founded by artists Hermann Obrist and Wilhelm von Debschitz in Munich in 1902.[fig.3][12] Unlike academic methods of drawing, predicated on the principles of copying and imitating, the new drawing technique developed at the Debschitz School drew upon the involuntary movements of the human body. Here, as at other comparable schools, the curriculum was not divided into painting, sculpture, and architecture, but was rather consolidated under a first-year preliminary course whose purpose was to train students in form, line, color, and space—that is to say, in "design" (*Gestaltung*).[13] Inherent in this new "design" pedagogy, which borrowed

*Zeynep
Çelik
Alexander*

1919:
The
Turning
Point

Fig.3. Women in the metal workshop of the Debschitz School, circa 1905.

Fig.4. Diagram of an oat husk with eight different effects. Wilhelm von Debschitz, "Eine Methode des Kunstunterrichts," *Dekorative Kunst* 7 (1904): 213.

Fig.5. Hans Kessler, Tensions and pulses of the basic colors and forms, from Wassily Kandinsky's course "Abstract Elements of Form," 1931–32.

heavily from the discipline of experimental psychology that was developing simultaneously at universities in German-speaking lands, was the assumption that each form, line, or color could be correlated exactly to a feeling because the body responded to stimuli in predictable ways. Wilhelm von Debschitz used a diagram, for example, to demonstrate to his students how the emotional effect of a line could be manipulated by making small changes to it.[fig.4] If *Bildung* hoped to train a particular kind of subject—male, bourgeois, and Protestant—whose inwardness was to be focused and attention honed through a close reading of Classicism, this kind of exercise aspired to cultivate a different kind of subject whose capacity for feeling and expression would be sharpened through an increased receptiveness to form, color, and line.[14]

Itten was not the only one who demonstrated faith in kinaesthetic knowing at the Bauhaus. One might even argue that despite all the disagreements among its numerous figures and despite the contrast between the early and the late Bauhaus, kinaesthetic knowing remained a common denominator at the school—even after this alternative epistemological principle had been discredited elsewhere. As Peter Galison has demonstrated in his account of Rudolf Carnap's visits to the school in the late 1920s, while the philosopher may have found many similarities between logical empiricism and Bauhaus thinking, he was taken aback by the tendency that he observed at the school to assign emotional value to forms, lines, and colors.[15] *Bauhäusler*—not only the students of Itten, Moholy-Nagy, and Albers, who taught the preliminary course, but also those of Kandinsky and Klee, who, for most of the history of the school, followed this course with lectures on theory of form—implicitly accepted that there existed a relationship of correspondence between physical stimulus and psychological sensation. A version of Kandinsky's questionnaire, which asked students to correlate primary forms to primary colors, demonstrates this assumption clearly: marginal notes indicate that the triangle should be matched with yellow and the circle with blue, because these form and color combinations correspond to pulse counts of 135 versus 50 and the musical tempos of presto versus grave, respectively.[fig.5] Even Gropius, ordinarily oblivious to such psychological language, would argue in 1923 that "red triggers feelings different from blue or yellow; round forms different from pointed or jagged."[16]

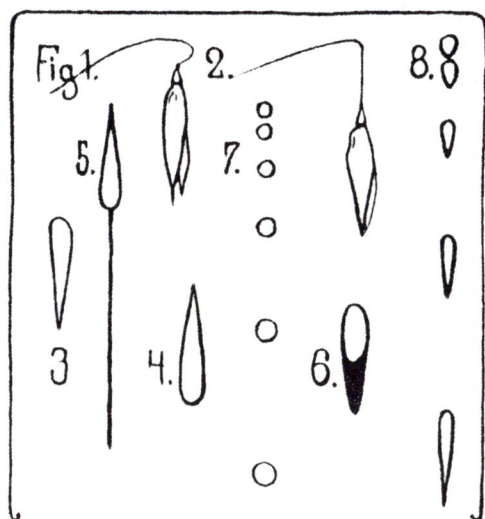

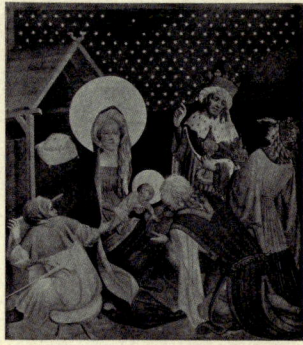

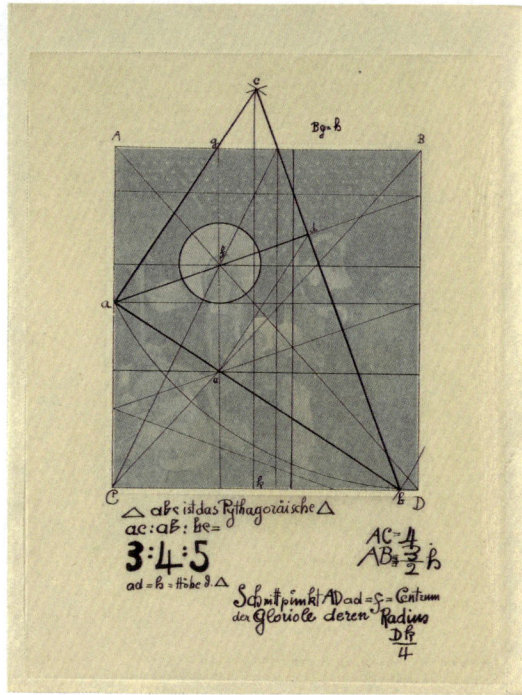

The story, however, is more complicated than it may appear at first. The work of *Bauhäusler* does not only manifest the epistemological tendency that I have called "kinaesthetic knowing"—a kind of knowledge realized through hands rather than through the mind and through image and form rather than text and word. Itten, to return to his quote at the beginning of this essay, evokes in the same breath all those techniques that one would associate with the tradition of *Bildung* and with academic training in the arts: photographically correct drawings, memorization, and, above all, the training of inwardness through a rigorous disciplining of one's attention. Is it not reasonable, then, to suspect that the pedagogy developed at the Bauhaus might have been looking backward as much as it was looking forward?

Itten, it turns out, had no qualms about adopting and adjusting practices of academic training. He regularly combined these with Eastern mysticism to carry out experiments on himself to hone his attentive capabilities: according to his diaries, he would observe an object carefully for five minutes, reproduce it from memory the following day, and, finally, compare the drawing to the original object. "Schooling of observation, attention, power of imagination, concentration, in short, of memory. I must have my students draw more from memory."[17] At the Bauhaus, after making his students spend half an hour every morning for a week drawing a potted fern, he made them reproduce the fern from memory at the end of the week.[18] In other cases, he adopted academic techniques even more openly. Among the assignments that Itten regularly used in class, for example, was the analysis of old masters' paintings: using a sciopticon and black-and-white lantern slides, he would project a painting on the wall, turn off the projector, and ask his students to examine the painting's proportions, formal arrangement, and so on from memory.[fig.6] [19]

Fig. 6. Formal analysis by Johannes Itten in which he used vellum (right) to reveal the proportions of an artwork under study (left). Bruno Adler, ed., *Utopia: Dokumente der Wirklichkeit* (Weimar: Utopia Verlag, 1921).

Fig. 7. Exercise assigned by Kandinsky in his theory of form course. Top and bottom left: Johannes Jacobus van der Linden, 1930–31.

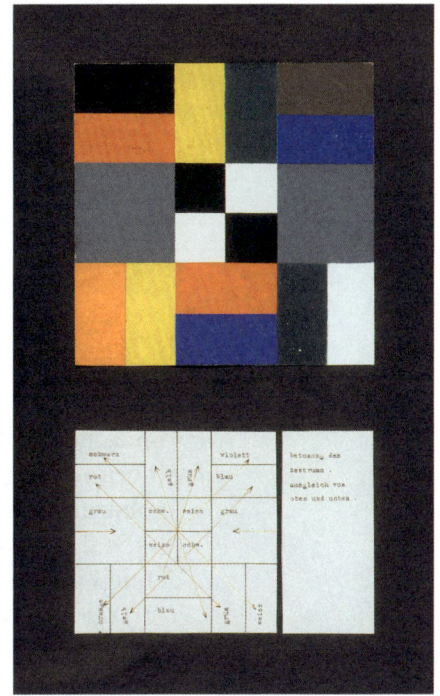

It is important to note here that Itten was not promoting copying or imitating an external model (such as a drawing, a sculpture, or an architectural fragment) as in the academic tradition. Nor was he advocating a technique whereby the student would freely express the urges of inner feeling. Instead, Itten adapted the principles of the nineteenth-century ideal of *Bildung* to formulate a pedagogical method whereby inner feeling was heeded only to be trained rigorously and the self was unleashed only to be refocused through attentive concentration. To use the object-subject dichotomy that Itten himself evoked consistently, this was a pedagogical program that entailed the training of subjective feeling with objective rigor.

In other words, kinaesthetic knowing was placed at the Bauhaus within the nineteenth-century framework of *Bildung*. Despite their differences, for example, Bauhaus masters shared the common goal of subjecting bodily sensations to strict protocols so that they could reliably serve as the building blocks of legitimate knowledge. The students were confronted with such protocols throughout their training. In one assignment that Kandinsky used repeatedly in his courses, for example, he instructed his students to use a "ground plane—30 × 30 cm, 9 colors—3 primary colors, 3 secondary colors, 3 black white gray—18 small fields 5 × 10 cm—emphasize the center, balance above and below, black and white accents—gray—mediation."[fig.7][20] Anticipating the nine-square-grid problem that would be a mainstay of architectural education in North America in the postwar period, this exercise gave students not a clean slate upon which they could express themselves with unrestricted freedom, but rather a set of strict limitations that forced them to contemplate a severely limited number of formal possibilities. After all, how many 5 × 10 cm rectangles could fit into a 30 × 30 cm square? The procedure to be followed was clear: consider all the iterations possible within the given set of limitations, test the effect of each composition upon yourself, and finally make a judgment about the best possible

Zeynep Çelik Alexander

1919:
The
Turning
Point

217

Fig. 8. Contrast-study props used by Kandinsky during lectures and accompanying student lecture notes, 1925–33.

Fig. 9. Max Bill lecturing at the Hochschule für Gestaltung in Ulm with a teaching tool of the kind used by Kandinsky at the Bauhaus to experiment with after-images, 1956. Photograph by Hans G. Conrad.

Fig. 10. Student notes from Paul Klee's theory of color course at the Bauhaus, undated. Unknown student, Bauhaus student work, 1919–33 collection.

composition. The pedagogical goal here was not to discover a correct solution, but rather to make sure that the student meticulously followed the protocols each time. Evoking techniques developed within experimental psychology, design was thus defined as a process whereby haphazard self-observation (*Selbstbeobachtung*) was converted to methodical introspection (*innere Wahrnehmung*) with the help of rigorously defined procedures.

Yet just as in the experimental psychology laboratory, the boundary between introspection and social performance was a blurry one at the Bauhaus. The process of examining one's inner experience methodically was, in fact, almost always realized in public. Just as schoolteachers employing methods of stigmography in secondary-school drawing classes performed the formalist exercise in front of a classroom full of children, Bauhaus masters combined lecturing with in-class demonstrations and exercises that frequently involved props. The student Ursula Schuh recalled that Kandinsky "brought a large number of differently colored rectangles, squares, discs, and triangles in various colors with him; he [held] these up in front of us in different combinations in order to test and develop our powers of vision." [fig. 8] 21 After leaving the Bauhaus, Max Bill at the Hochschule für Gestaltung in Ulm and Josef Albers at Black Mountain College and at Yale would continue the practice of performing in the classroom using similar teaching aids. [fig. 9]

Klee developed a different but no less rigorous set of methods for training introspection. If Kandinsky's self-contained assignments dictated the step-by-step set of operations to be performed, Klee deployed an equally rigorous method of automatism with the goal of producing series. He used mathematical formulas and geometric constructions meticulously carried out with a straightedge and a compass to produce formal iterations automatically. Both his own lecture notes and his students' notes from his courses on form and color abound with instances of a technique whereby grids of color were changed— mirrored, turned clockwise or counterclockwise, inverted horizontally or vertically, or entirely transformed—with the aid of matrices of numbers. [fig. 10] Formal variations were produced in each instance, not arbitrarily but according to a painstakingly worked-out set of rules (which might anachronistically be called "algorithms"). It followed that the grid in Klee's work was not a form intended as an end in itself but rather an *instrument* that guided the disciplined manipulation of

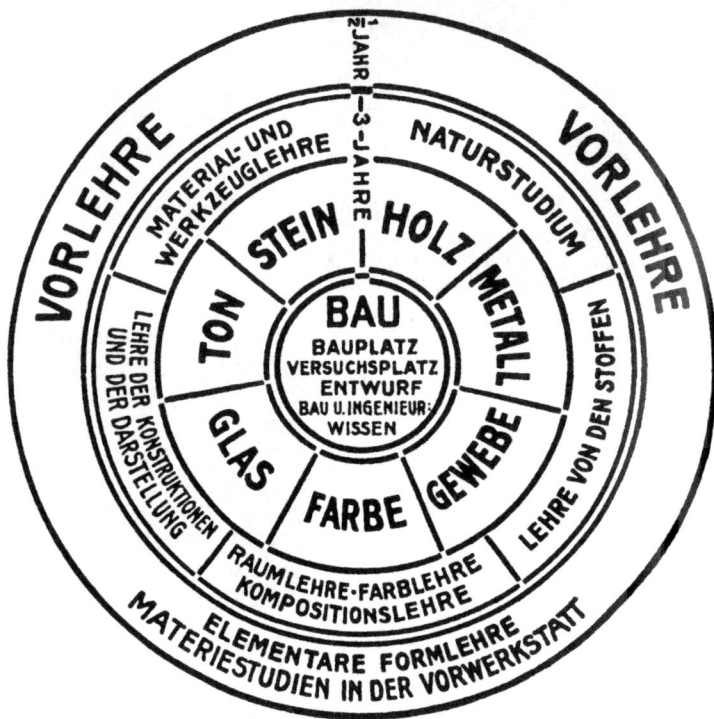

Fig. 11. Bauhaus curricular diagram, 1922. Walter Gropius from Walter Gropius, *Idee und Aufbau des Staatlichen Bauhauses Weimar* (Munich: Bauhausverlag, 1923).

other forms. In 1928, as Meyer's "constructivist" tendencies were taking over the school's pedagogical program, Klee wrote a passionate vindication of "intuition," but privileging intuition, he added, did not mean giving unlimited free rein to inner expression. Rather, echoing Helmholtz, Klee wrote of art as "accurate research":

Art too possesses sufficient room for accurate research [exakte Forschung], *and the gates leading to it have been open for some time. What had already been done for music by the end of the eighteenth century remains at least in its infancy in the pictorial field. Mathematics and physics provide a lever in the form of rules to be followed [or] broken. They compel us ... to be concerned first of all with operations* [Funktionen] *and to disregard finished form. Algebraic, geometric, and mechanical tasks are educational steps directed toward the essential and the functional, in contrast to the impressional* [Impressiven]. *One learns to look behind the façade, to grasp the roots of things. ... Learns to organize movement through logical relations. Learns logic. Learns organism. ... Passion only deep inside. Inwardness* [Innerlichkeit].[22]

Klee's words can be considered an answer to the question that Gropius would pose two decades later in *Scope of Total Architecture*: Can there be a "science of design?"[23] Contrary to the critiques of functionalism that would follow, this was not a science unconditionally committed to the natural sciences, but rather a new science of experience that only borrowed its standards of rigorousness from them. It is important to note, in light of Klee's insistence on systematic intuition, that while the production of formal iterations was made possible through a kind of automatism—whether by means of a recipe, a mathematical formula, or a geometrical pattern mattered little—the decision about the final form was ultimately expected to be made with the faculty of judgment [*Urteil*], that faculty so revered by the Enlightenment, the faculty that distinguished the human from animals and machines.

In this light, the grandiose statements made by Bauhaus masters about creating a new subject should be taken at face value. In 1937,

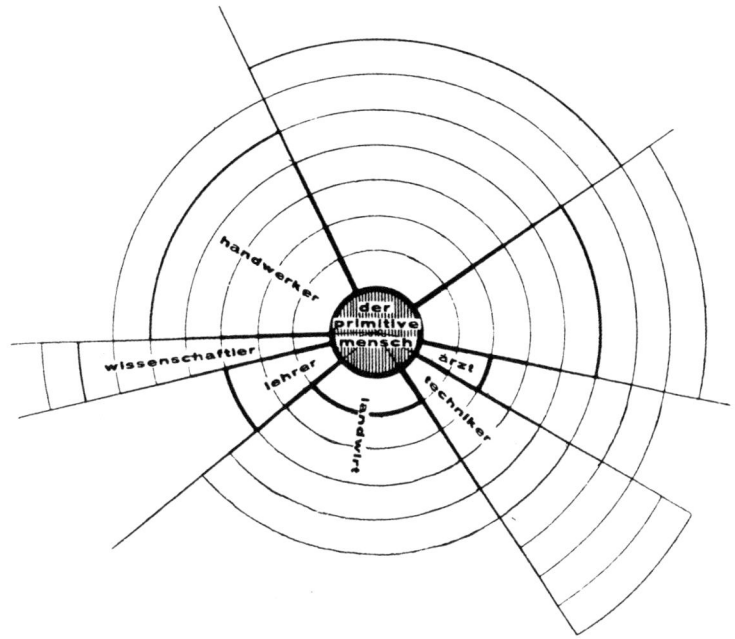

when Gropius revisited his bull's-eye curricular diagram from a decade and a half earlier, he posited design education as the guarantor of a "unity" threatened by specialized knowledge.[fig. 11] Bauhaus pedagogy, if offered at every level of the education system as he proposed, would grow "concentrically, like the annular rings of a tree, embracing the whole from the beginning and, at the same time, gradually deepening and extending it."[24] The curricular diagram, then, can also be read as a diagram of selfhood. Evoking the same concentric form, Moholy-Nagy likewise argued in 1929 that modern man—or what he called *der sektorhafte Mensch*—had been segmented by specialization.[fig. 12][25] It fell to the Bauhaus to develop an education that would make man "whole" again, by making sure that this man grew organically from the primitivism at the core of his existence.

Needless to say, such ranting against specialization imposed by the capitalist division of labor was not exactly novel at the beginning of the twentieth century. But that is exactly my point: these concentric models of selfhood drawn up at the Bauhaus were, in fact, not that different from that proposed by Humboldt, whose idea of *Bildung* aspired to shape the self as a will-centered stronghold that resisted the onslaught of external sensations, or by Johann Gottlieb Fichte, who posited an introspective, contemplative, and uniquely German inward-ness as the absolute Subject.[26] Nor was it dissimilar to the model of selfhood proposed almost century later by the psychologist Wilhelm Wundt who, reviving an ideal of *Bildung* from the turn of the nine-teenth century, imagined the self as a "whole circle of effects" held in place by attention and the process of apperception:

> Out of the multitude of actions performed by an individual, it is the inner acts, the acts of apperception that stand out as more original and immediate than the rest. ... Hence the final stage of this development consists in the individual's discovery that his own innermost being is pure apperception; that is, an inner voluntary activity distinct from the rest of conscious content. The ego feels itself to be the same at every moment of its life,

Zeynep
Çelik
Alexander

1919:
The
Turning
Point

221

because it conceives the activity of apperception as perfectly constant, homo-
geneous in its nature, and coherent in time. ... In proportion as the will
frees itself from [constraining forces of external nature], we approach the
realization of that ideal of personal existence where the whole inner life
of man appears as his own creation; where for good or evil he regards
himself as the originator of his own thoughts and emotions, and of all the
outward consequences that may flow from them. ... This unity of feeling,
thought and will, in which the will appears as the active power that
sustains the other elements, is the individual personality.[27]

Bauhäusler's adamantly centric model of selfhood for the 'new man,'
then, was unexpectedly retrograde, closer in spirit to the nineteenth
century than one would assume. Even while adopting the epistemological project of kinaesthetic knowing, the pedagogical techniques
developed within modern design education aspired to rehabilitate the
withering ideal of *Bildung*—except with *Kennen* rather than *Wissen*.
Once its anachronism is recognized, Bauhaus pedagogy takes on new
meaning. So does Gropius's insistence on the centrality of space (*Raum*)
and architecture (or, more correctly, *Bau*) in the Bauhaus enterprise.
When Gropius argued that the concept of space would be central
to every aspect of the curriculum and would serve as the medium that
united the separate workshops of the school, then, he was not simply
putting architecture, the field in which he himself had been trained,
before others. *Bau* and *Raum* (which most would recognize as the
"essence" of architecture by the early twentieth century thanks to
theorists like August Schmarsow) had much broader epistemological
significance here.[28] As Gropius put it in his lecture notes from 1921,
artistic work was merely the means through which one built oneself
(*uns selbst aufbauen*).[29] In this sense, *Bau* in the school's name signified
more than architecture. "Academies make a grave mistake by ne-
glecting the formation of the human being," wrote Schlemmer in a
letter in 1921. "Bauhaus is 'building' something quite different from
what was planned—human beings."[30]

What kind of a rupture was the Bauhaus in the history of aesthetic
modernism, then? How *new* were the "new man" and the "new
woman" of the Bauhaus? How stable were these categories, which
have been ossified into ontological categories in scholarship? In light
of the history outlined here, it becomes possible to argue that the
model of selfhood to which the Bauhaus aspired departed asymptoti-
cally from the two models available at the turn of the twentieth

century. This subject was not to conform to the idealist model devised by the likes of Humboldt and Fichte, to name two of the most important theorists of the *Bildung* tradition. Nor was it to resemble a model of selfhood that could readily make and remake itself in light of this new aesthetics. If there was a new subject at the Bauhaus, it was one that attempted a precarious balance between the apparent stability of the former and the vaunted fickleness of the latter. Seen from this perspective, 1919 might have been just another turning point at which history simply failed to turn.

1   George Macaulay Trevelyan, *British History in the Nineteenth Century*, fourth edition (London: Longman, Green, and Co., 1923), 292.
2   Diary entry from August 1918, in *Johannes Itten: Werke und Schriften*, ed. Willy Rotzler (Zurich: Orell Füssli, 1972), 60.
3   For Hölzel's drawing exercises, see Adolf Hölzel, "Die Schule des Künstlers," *Der Pelikan* 11 (1921): 7–8.
4   Paul Klee, *Briefe an die Familie, 1899–1940*, ed. Felix Klee (Cologne: DuMont, 1979). Also cited by Itten, *Design and Form*, 12.
5   Zeynep Çelik Alexander, *Kinaesthetic Knowing: Aesthetics, Epistemology, Modern Design* (Chicago and London: University of Chicago Press, 2017).
6   I am thinking here of the alternative modes of reasoning explored by Pamela Smith, *The Body of the Artisan: Art and Experience in the Scientific Revolution* (Chicago: University of Chicago Press, 2004); Matthew C. Hunter, *Wicked Intelligence: Visual Art and the Science of Experiment in Restoration London* (Chicago: University of Chicago Press, 2013); Otto Sibum, "Working Experiments: A History of Gestural Knowledge," *Cambridge Review* 116.2325 (May 1995): 25–37.
7   See Hermann von Helmholtz, "Die neueren Fortschritte in der Theorie des Sehens" [1868], in Helmholtz, *Populäre Wissenschaftliche Vorträge* (Braunschweig: Friedrich Viewig, 1871), trans. as "The Recent Progress of the Theory of Vision," in *Science and Culture: Popular and Philosophical Essays*, ed. David Cahan (Chicago: University of Chicago Press, 1995), 127–203 and Hermann von Helmholtz, *Ueber das Verhältnis der Naturwissenschaften zur Gesammtheit der Wissen-*

schaft. Rede zum Geburtsfeste des höchstseligen Grossherzogs Karl Friedrich von Baden und zur akademischen Preisvertheilung am 22. November 1862 (Heidelberg: Georg Mohr, 1862), 16, translated as "On the Relation of Natural Science to Science in General," in Cahan, *Science and Culture*, 85.
8   But he never specified how. Helmholtz, "Die neueren Fortschritte in der Theorie des Sehens," 92–93, and "The Recent Progress of the Theory of Vision," 198–99.
9   The pedagogue Carl Goetze used Helmholtz's distinction between *Wissen* and *Kennen* in Goetze, "Zeichnen und Formen," in *Kunsterziehung. Ergebnisse und Anregungen des Kunsterziehungstages in Dresden am 28. und 29. September 1901* (Leipzig: R. Voigtländer, 1902), 145–46, and Goetze, "Zeichnen und Formen," in *Kunsterziehung. Ergebnisse und Anregungen der Kunsterziehungstage in Dresden, Weimar und Hamburg*, introd. Ludwig Pallat (Leipzig: R. Voigtländer, 1929), 37–38. An example of *Formenlehre* can be found in Adolf Stuhlmann, *Zeichenunterricht und Formenlehre in der Elementarclasse* (Hamburg: F. H. Nestler & Melle, 1870). Stigmography was developed by Franz Carl Hillardt, *Stigmographie. Das Schreiben und Zeichnen nach Punkten. Eine neue Methode* (Kohlmarkt: Mueller, 1846).
10   See, for example, the Hamburger Kunsthalle and Alfred Lichtwark, who published the conversations that he carried out with children in the presence of the artworks in the museum: Alfred Lichtwark, *Drei Programme* (Berlin: Cassirer, 1902). On the essay on the virtues of the slide lecture, the following text by German art historian Hermann Grimm is illuminating: Hermann Grimm, "Die Umgestaltung der

Zeynep
Çelik
Alexander

1919:
The
Turning
Point

Universitätsvorlesungen über neuere Kunstgeschichte durch die Anwendung des Skioptikons" [1892–93], in Grimm, *Beiträge zur deutschen Culturgeschichte* (Berlin: Wilhelm Herz, 1897), 276–395.

11 For a brief history of these schools, see Hans Maria Wingler, ed., *Kunstschulreform 1900–1933* (Berlin: Gebr. Mann, 1977).

12 The Debschitz School has not attracted much scholarly attention. For the most comprehensive history of the school, see the thesis by Dagmar Rinker, "Die Lehr- und Versuchsateliers für angewandte und freie Kunst, Debschitz-Schule, München 1902–1914," master's thesis, University of Munich, 1993. Other recent accounts of the school are Helga Schmoll gen. Eisenwerth, "Die Münchner Debschitz-Schule," in *Kunstschulreform, 1900–1933*, ed. Hans M. Wingler (Berlin: Gebr. Mann, 1977): 66–82; Beate Ziegert, "The Debschitz School, Munich: 1902–1914," *Design Issues* 3.1 (Spring 1986): 28–42; Beate Ziegert, "The Debschitz School Munich: 1902–1904," master's thesis, Syracuse University, 1985; and Norbert Götz, "Die Debschitz-Schule Hohenzollernstraße 21," in *Schwabing. Kunst und Leben um 1900*, ed. Helmut Bauer and Elisabeth Tworek (Munich: Münchner Stadtmuseum, 1998), 236–55. See also Çelik Alexander, *Kinaesthetic Knowing*, 131–166.

13 Wilhelm von Debschitz, "Eine Methode des Kunstunterrichts," *Dekorative Kunst* 7 (March 1904): 209–27, and "Lehren und Lernen in der bildenden Kunst," *Süddeutsche Monatshefte* (March 1907): 266–79.

14 It should be mentioned here that this alternative subjectivity was seen to be particularly suited to women, who frequented these "design" schools. At this moment in history, women's access to conventional art academies was limited. Whereas the École des Beaux-Arts had begun accepting women in 1897, allowing them to compete for the Prix de Rome in 1903, state-run institutions of higher learning largely remained inaccessible to German women until the end of World War I. According to historian Edith Krull, the Munich academy accepted women at an annual rate of one to five students between 1813 and 1840, but these students were considered honorary members and dilettantes. Edith Krull, *Women in Art*, trans. Lux Feininger (London: Edition Leipzig, 1986), 13.

15 Peter Galison, "Aufbau/Bauhaus: Logical Positivism and Architectural Modernism," *Critical Inquiry* 16.4 (Summer 1990), 736.

16 Walter Gropius, "Idee und Aufbau des Staatlichen Bauhauses," *Staatliches Bauhaus in Weimar 1919–1923* (Weimar and Munich: Bauhausverlag, 1923), 14.

17 Notebook, July 9–19, 1918, Flirsch, in *Johannes Itten Tagebücher Stuttgart 1913–1916, Wien 1916–1919*, ed. Eva Badura-Triska (Vienna: Löcker, 1990), 302.

18 Itten, "The Foundation Course at the Bauhaus," 115.

19 Johannes Itten, *Design and Form: The Basic Course at the Bauhaus* (New York: Reinhold, 1964), 9. Schlemmer described Itten's technique as follows: "He shows photographs and the students are supposed to draw various essential elements, usually the movement, the main contour, a curve ... Next he displays the weeping Mary Magdalen from the Grünewald Altar; the students struggle to extract some essential feature from this complicated picture. Itten glances at their efforts and then bursts out: if they had any artistic sensitivity, they would not attempt to draw this, the noblest portrayal of weeping, a symbol of the tears of the world; they would sit silent, themselves dissolved in tears. Thus he speaks, then departs, slamming the door!" Oskar Schlemmer to Otto Meyer, May 16, 1921, in *The Letters and Diaries of Oskar Schlemmer*, 105–06. A similar account can be found in Felix Klee, "Mein Erinnerungen an das Bauhaus Weimar," in *Bauhaus und Bauhäusler. Erinnerungen und Bekenntnisse*, ed. Eckhard Neumann (Cologne: DuMont, [1971] 1985), 81.

20 "Assignment for 12 November 1926," Getty Research Institute, Wassily Kandinsky files, box 10, folder 84. Also see the letter from Wera Meyer-Waldeck to Otti Berger, July 27, 1927, BAB, Otti Berger, folder 16, cited in *Vassily Kandinsky: The Pragmatic Professor at the Bauhaus, 1922–1933—The Everyday Reality of Teaching under Three Directors*, ed. Magdalena Droste (Berlin: Bauhaus-Archiv, 2014), 112.

21 Ursula Schuh, "Im Klassenzimmer Kandinskys," in Neumann, *Bauhaus und Bauhäusler*, 240–41.

22 Paul Klee, "Exakte Versuche im Bereich der Kunst," *bauhaus* 2, nos. 2/3 (1928). I am using, with modifications, the translation in Wingler, *The Bauhaus*, 148. Especially important

here is the word *Funktion*, which I translate
as "operation" to avoid the confusion with the
misleading term "function" in design history.

23   Gropius, *Scope of Total Architecture*, 30.

24   Gropius, "Education toward Creative
Design," 30.

25   László Moholy-Nagy, *Von Material zur
Architektur, Bauhausbücher 14* (Munich: Albert
Langen, 1929), 10–11.

26   See, for example, Wilhelm von Humboldt, "Letter LXIII, October 1826," in *Letters of
William von Humboldt to a Female Friend*, vol. 1,
trans. Catherine M. A. Couper (London: John
Chapman, 1849), 245, and J. G. Fichte, "Foundations of the Entire Science of Knowledge"
[1794], in Fichte, *The Science of Knowledge*, ed.
and trans. Peter Heath and John Lachs (Cambridge and New York: Cambridge University
Press, 1982), 100.

27   Wilhelm Wundt, "Das Ich und die
Persönlichkeit," in Wundt, *Ethik. Eine Unter-
suchung der Thatsachen und Gesetze des sittlichen
Lebens* (Stuttgart: Ferdinand Enke, [1886] 1892),
447–48, and "The Ego and the Personality," in
Wundt, *The Principles of Morality and the Depart-
ments of the Moral Life*, trans. M. F. Washburn
(London: Swan Sonnenschein; New York:
Macmillan, 1901), 20–21. A similar idea can be
found around the same time in Georg Simmel,
"Der Begriff und die Tragödie der Kultur,"
in Simmel, *Philosophische Kultur. Gesammelte
Essais* (Leipzig: 1911), 248.

28   August Schmarsow, *Das Wesen der archi-
tektonischen Schöpfung* (Leipzig: Karl W. Hierse-
mann, 1894).

29   Transcription of Walter Gropius,
"Raumkunde," Bauhaus-Archiv Berlin, GS 20,
Mappe 21, 1.

30   Oskar Schlemmer to Otto Meyer, letter
dated February 3, 1921, in *The Letters and Diaries
of Oskar Schlemmer*, 98.

*Zeynep
Çelik
Alexander*

1919:
The
Turning
Point

Joyce Tsai

Epochal Trace: László Moholy-Nagy, Drawing, and the Task of the Artist

László Moholy-Nagy (1895–1946) included a self-portrait and landscape he made when he was in his early twenties as figures for his autobiographical text "Abstract of an Artist," written at the end of his life and published posthumously in a revised edition of *The New Vision* from 1947.[1] Of his early work he wrote that, "The young painter passes beyond dilettantism, mere subconscious doodling and somnambulistic repetition of examples when he begins to discover problems for himself and then tries to solve them."[2] Looking back at these pictures, Moholy recounted how his emulation of van Gogh's drawings led him to identify and articulate his first "problem." How can lines arrayed upon a page convey the qualities of three-dimensional space? The exploration of this basic problem lent consistency to his first sketches. In reviewing his early work over two decades later, Moholy saw an effort that "went beyond the analytical intention." The marks he laid down on the page articulated rhythmic networks, "showing not so much objects as [his] excitement about them."[3]

The self-portrait and landscape selected to illustrate these ideas in the essay roughly coincide with when the Bauhaus in Weimar was established in 1919. [fig.1, 2] But Moholy had not yet arrived on the artistic scene, nor had he joined the renowned school. He was in Budapest that year, barely twenty-four, and was still exploring what it meant to him to be an artist. Despite his youth, he had already served in the military and was also a veteran of the First World War.

There are few traces of Moholy's time in the military, but there is a formal portrait of him in full Austro-Hungarian uniform. [fig.3] It was undoubtedly taken at a studio that specialized in producing

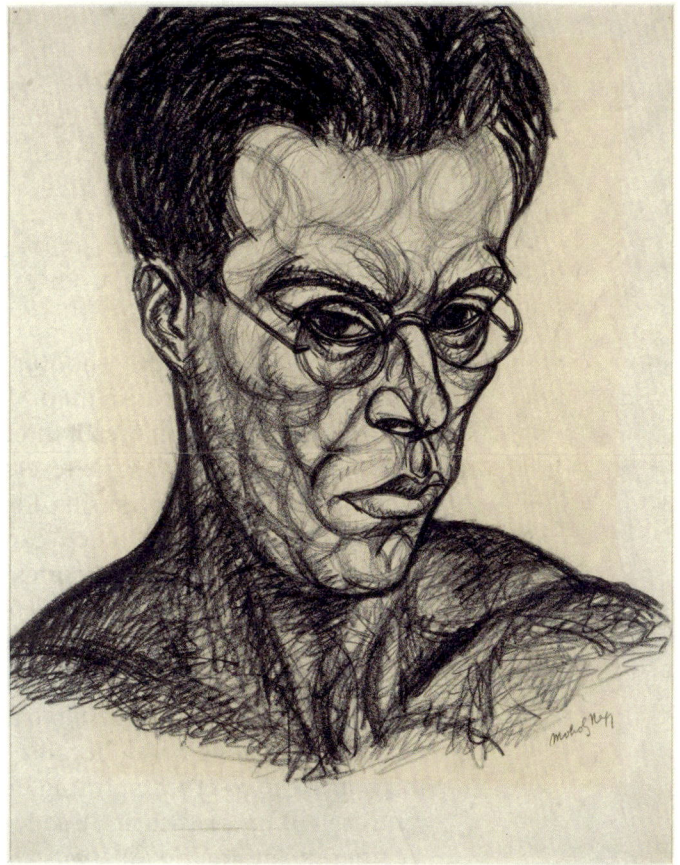

Fig. 1. László Moholy-Nagy,
Self-Portrait, n. d.
Fig. 2. László Moholy-Nagy,
Landscape, 1917, published in
*The New Vision and Abstract
of an Artist*, 4th revised edition
(New York, 1947), 68.
Fig. 3. Unknown photogra-
pher, László Moholy-Nagy in
military uniform, circa 1915–18.

memorabilia for families who were sending their sons off to war.[4] In family papers, there is a map Moholy drew, probably from 1917. The sheet describes an area in modern-day Ukraine near the Carpathians where he fought. On the reverse, he recorded numbers in a table, constituting the data necessary for the calculation of the trajectory of his unit's artillery piece, a field howitzer that weighed several tons and had to be dragged up a mountainside to be aimed in order to maximize damage to the enemy.[5] There are few other official documents of his time in the war, but that is hardly surprising. The map and the tables he made were neither works of art nor souvenirs; they would have been turned in to his superiors to advance the aims of his unit. Moholy was wounded in 1917 and, because of his injuries, spent the rest of the war in the reserves, splitting his time between training troops and returning to his studies in Budapest. He was initially preparing for a career in law, but by 1918, was already describing his profession as that of a painter.[6]

In the spring of 1919, as the Hungarian Soviet Republic was declared, Moholy joined with other artists and intellectuals to bolster and contribute to the revolution. Like many of his contemporaries, his experience in battle strengthened his resolve to ensure that the Great War not be repeated. The art he made and the rhetoric he espoused hewed closely to the revolutionary, avant-garde milieu he joined. In those years, he adopted a style informed by the Hungarian Activists, which itself drew upon German Expressionism.[7] These features are legible in the early drawings he published to accompany "Abstract"; we might say that they were made under the influence of Hungarian Activism and Expressionism.

What Moholy saw in these early drawings, however, was more than influence. At the time he drafted "Abstract" and examined the work of his youth, he had already survived multiple cataclysms. The first half of the twentieth century brought two world wars, global political and economic crises, widespread persecution, displacement, and genocide. He found himself at the dawn of the atomic age, witness to the power of the nuclear bomb as he underwent radiation therapy for his leukemia. Looking back, he identified in his lines ambitions that went far beyond mimetic description or adherence to a style, even if avant-garde. For example, the landscape he published in "Abstract" from the late 1910s offers a view obstructed by barbed wire. [fig.2] It occludes our ability to interpret the scene beyond and renders the distances

x

Fig.4. László Moholy-Nagy,
Self-Portrait [in the hospital],
1945.

*im
Hospital*

*m=n
dec 1/45*

and features of the topography
opaque. When we adopt Moholy's own
perspective on these drawings, we
begin to discern the lines as conduits
for the energies coursing through a web
of wires; they give visual form to the
tangle of nerves that engulfed the
soldier in the trenches. Likewise, his
self-portrait from around the same
time does not merely trace out his own
likeness, but conveys what he described
as "excitement" in each mark. [fig.1]
Moholy's hand presses the oil stick
deeply into the sheet, leaving behind frenetic strokes that struggle to
cohere. The varied densities and tangible pressures of each inscription
will the features of his face and muscular shoulders into being.

We rarely associate Moholy with self-portraiture, nor with expressionist figuration, yet he reconsidered these works at the end of his
life.[8] He even produced another self-portrait dated 1945, drawn in the
hospital. [fig.4] Looking at himself in the mirror, his hand holds a sharp
pencil that skims the surface of his sheet. The graphite tip traces the
terrain of his face with light broken marks, as if telegraphing the contours
of his face, relaying the hollows of his eyes, the wrinkles of his skin,
and the twisted frame of his wire-rimmed glasses. The precise hatch-
ings in this self-portrait are found in other works he made from this
period as well, especially in his abstract *Space Modulators*—Plexiglas hybrid painting/sculptures that relied on delicate scratches spread across
the glossy plastic surface to aid the adhesion of oil paint to the new
industrial material.[9] Despite the change in touch evident in the two
self-portraits, Moholy's face and the work of his hand is recognizable
in both. They differ not in style, but in sensibility. But of course, between
the late 1910s and mid-1940s, the world changed, and Moholy as well.

Moholy drew his later self-portrait around when he finished
"Abstract" as well as his last book, *Vision in Motion*. Moholy died in
November 1946, just a little more than a year after the war ended,
when little clarity about the past and future had yet been formulated.
Published in 1947, *Vision in Motion* provides a striking description of
the task of the artist that resonates with the work he was producing
and upon which he reflected. In its opening pages, Moholy discusses

*Joyce
Tsai*

Epochal
Trace

229

the "formative ideological function" that the artist must perform. As the Second World War showed, the artist must "take sides and proclaim his stand." However, what Moholy promotes is not an art of propaganda but an alertness to how "the work of the artist corresponds to the creative problems in other fields, complementing them in the structure of civilization of that particular period."[10]

> Through his sensitivity the artist becomes the seismograph of events and movements pertaining to the future. He interprets the yet hazy path of coming developments by grasping the dynamics of the present and by freeing himself from the momentary motivations and transitory influences but without evaluating their trends. He is interested only in the recording and communicating of his vision. This is what materializes in his art.[11]

In such a description, we imagine the artist as a particularly refined instrument attuned to the currents that reverberate through a particular epoch, the needle through which the felt and heard rumblings of an era come to be transmitted in graphic form, zigzagging over time across a page.

When he wrote these lines, he was closing in on a decade in Chicago as a teacher, designer, and administrator initially at the short-lived New Bauhaus, and then later at the School of Design, which was eventually renamed as the Institute of Design. He was lucky to escape the conflagration of war in Europe but grappled with its horrors. We might read *Vision in Motion* as an extended manifesto that asks the artist and teacher to contribute to creating the conditions that might foster a viable future for humankind. The actions to be taken are not singular but collective, not personal but distributed. The formulation he proposes of the artist as seismograph asks what it might mean for an artist to offer his hand to the needs of his age and not his own volition. In this evocative simile, Moholy conceived of his own hand as an instrument in service to his epoch, which would inscribe and describe a future he would not live to see. Curiously, aspects of this formulation resonate with his experience as a soldier.

In 1915, Moholy enlisted in the Austro-Hungarian military. He was just twenty. His family raised the funds to buy his horse, a prerequisite for him to join the officer class. He began as a cadet and achieved the rank of second lieutenant in the reserves by the end of the First World War. Moholy served as an artillery reconnaissance officer (*Aufklärer*). After his medical discharge from the front, he became an instructor in the reserves.[12]

We know that the First World War demanded that its soldiers master complex, technical ways of seeing, but it also required officers capable of leading and teaching their men to perform their duties and fulfill their assigned missions. The officers were given teaching manuals, which were not written for originality, but for clarity. Take, for example, *Artillerieunterricht. 10.0 cm M. 14 Feldhaubitze*, which was produced for the kind of field howitzer Moholy's unit would have used. It offered technical specifications for the weapon in question. But the publications also underscored the importance of the officer to train (*ausbilden*) his men to internalize the workings of their weapon to serve the ends of war. The mission is clear from the first sentence in the preface:

> *Die Kenntnis des Geschützes und seines Gebrauches ist die Grundlage für seine zweckmäßige Verwendung. Der praktische Kriegszweck allein ist für die Ausbildung maßgebend.*[13] [*Familiarity with the weapon and its operation are the basis for its proper use. The practical aim of war is all that matters in training.*]

Individual manuals had to be produced for each gun in the Austro-Hungarian military—different models and calibers of howitzer had distinct specifications and parts—but they all open with the sentence above.

Publications like *Artillerieunterricht* began with a general description of the specific model of gun (*Materialbeschreibung*). Those produced before the First World War included drawn schematic diagrams; those printed during the war included photographs of the parts. The second section addressed how the piece would be serviced (*bedienen*) or prepared for use. The third addressed maintenance, the fourth the skills required to implement orders and make use of multiple means of communication, including telephony, Morse code, and semaphore. The fifth section concerned the care of horses—no small matter when the movement of guns from the railway network to their place in the field relied upon these beasts of burden and the unit's men. For modern warfare to function, every soldier's body had to become the conduit through which the sights and sounds of the battlefield would be transformed into usable data for his superiors.[14]

The preface of *Artillerieunterricht* distinguishes the roles of the officer and his men. The task of the officer was to lead and to teach. The officer had to translate the complexity of the machine and the dangers of their mission to his men in ways that would compel them to the field:

Joyce
Tsai

Epochal
Trace

Der Lehrer muß bedenken, daß er nur dann für den Dienst Vorzügliches leistet, wenn er der ihm anvertrauten Mannschaft—bei verhältnismäßig raschen Erfolgen—Eifer, Lebhaftigkeit, frohe Laune sowie den festen Willen einzuflößen weiß, für den Dienst und für die Ehre ihrer Waffe das Höchste zu leisten.[15] [The instructor must bear in mind that he is serving with excellence only when he is able to instill in the men entrusted to him—with relatively rapid success—enthusiasm, vivaciousness, cheerfulness, and the resoluteness to achieve all they can for the service and for the honor of their weapon.]

The officer had to be equal parts technical expert and master of mood—the success of the unit hinged upon the ability of the officer synthesize the contributions of individual men to forge a cohesive unit in the service of their weapon. In the context of the Austro-Hungarian military, the officer had to be a translator of languages, technologies, and cultures alike. *Artillerieunterricht* continues:

Eine so ausgebildete Truppe wird aber dann auch imstande sein, im Kampfe den Jahrhunderte alten, auf vielen Schlachtfeldern errungenen Ruhm der k. u. k. Artillerie zu erhalten und zu vermehren.[16] [A unit thus trained will, in combat, also be capable of maintaining and augmenting the centuries-old glory of the imperial and royal artillery achieved on numerous battlefields.]

The idea that the officer should do all that is in his power to secure the reputation of the artillery of the k. u. k.—Imperial Austria and Royal Hungary—for generations to come might strike us as absurd. Moholy saw the madness of the enterprise even as a soldier and relayed his sentiments even then in letters and poems. Yet the language found in *Artillerieunterricht* reverberates in unexpected ways in Moholy's art and thought up into his final works. As we will see, he absorbed the lessons he had to convey to his subordinates and later transmitted aspects of its values and strategies in some of his most important theoretical writings and art. But he relayed those lessons in ways shaped by the specificity of his own commitments.

In 1922, Moholy published "Produktion-Reproduktion" in *de Stijl*.[17] There he articulated the core principles of his philosophy of technology. In it he argued that the most advanced technologies of his age—for example, the gramophone, photograph, and film—were all invented to capture existing visual and aural relationships. That is to say, the gramophone was invented to replay existing sounds that photography and film most often used to follow the conventions of naturalized seeing. These technologies held out the promise of revolutionary change, but fell short of actually transforming our perception because they merely reproduced existing perceptual patterns. For technologies to become productive, Moholy contended, they had to be used in new ways.[18]

Moholy's definition of production and productivity initially had little to do with the economic connotations most closely associated with each term. Instead, productivity had to do specifically with the extent to which human senses could be advanced.

> *Der Aufbau des Menschen ist die Synthese aller seiner Funktionsapparate,*
> *d. h. daß der Mensch in seiner Periode dann der vollkommenste ist, wenn*
> *die ihn ausmachenden Funktionsapparate—die Zellen ebenso wie die*
> *kompliziertesten Organe—bis zur Grenze ihrer Leistungsfähigkeit bewußt*
> *bzw. ausgebildet sind.*[19] *[The constitution of man is the synthesis of all of*
> *his functional mechanisms, i. e., man in a given epoch becomes most perfect*
> *if his constituent functional mechanisms—the cells as much as the most*
> *complicated organs—are trained to the limits of their ability to perform.]*

These lines bear the traces of Moholy's military experience. In the most obvious sense, the formulation appears to impose a mechanistic model of man—this might be read as the imposition of his martial training in civilian life. After all, in the science of war, we find a consistent preoccupation with maximizing performance, with pushing soldiers, to use Moholy's language, "bis zur Grenze ihrer Leistungsfähigkeit." But there is a crucial difference. Moholy might have adopted a language that seemed to turn man into parts that could be refined and honed, but he did so to acknowledge the transformative power of technology he witnessed firsthand on the battlefield. Human beings must be trained (*ausgebildet*) to push their ability to perform (*Leistungsfähigkeit*) to their limits, not to conform to the requirements of war, but to enhance human life. Such training would best be served by art. He writes,

> *Die Kunst bewirkt diese Ausbildung—und das ist eine ihrer wichtigsten*
> *Aufgaben, da von der Vollkommenheit des Aufnahmeorgans der ganze*
> *Wirkungskomplex abhängt—in dem sie zwischen den bekannten und den*
> *noch unbekannten optischen, akustischen und anderen funktionellen*
> *Erscheinungen weitgehendste neue Beziehungen herzustellen versucht und*
> *deren Aufnahme von den Funktionsapparaten erzwingt.*[20] *[Art performs*
> *such a training—and this is one of its most important tasks, since the whole*
> *complex of effects depends on the degree of perfection of the receptive*
> *organs—by trying to force the functional mechanisms to receive the most*

Joyce Tsai

Epochal Trace

233

far-reaching new relationships it creates between the familiar and the as yet unknown optical, acoustical and other functional phenomena.] Here he argues that art would accelerate the progress of humankind precisely because it is capable of generating new stimuli. By exposing man's functional mechanisms to new sensory stimuli, he claimed, we would train them to inhabit the new conditions of a modern world. As we will see, the strategies he would demand to make art and machines serve human needs require the intervention of the human hand to reveal the possibilities of existing and future technologies. The paradigm he establishes places the human being at the center as its aim, which runs fundamentally counter to *Artillerieunterricht*, which takes "praktischen Kriegszweck allein" (war being all that matters) as the ultimate goal of training.

In "Produktion-Reproduktion," he offers a series of questions, something like a rubric, to guide an inquiry as to how a technology, tool, or medium might be made productive.

Wozu dient dieser Apparat (Mittel)? [What does this apparatus (medium) serve?] Was ist das Wesen seiner Funktion? [What is the essence of its function?] Sind wir fähig und hat es einen Wert, den Apparat so zu erweitern, daß er auch der Produktion dienstbar wird? [Are we able and is it valuable to extend the apparatus's use so that it becomes serviceable to production?] [21]

One example he gave of how existing technologies could be made productive involved nothing more than a scratch inscribed "ohne mechanische Außenwirkung durch den Menschen selbst" [without external mechanical intervention through human agency itself] on a gramophone disc. The scratch introduces a new sound generated entirely without the use of a new instrument nor orchestra that nonetheless transforms music performance and composition through the introduction of "neue, noch nicht existierende Töne und Tonbeziehungen" [new, as yet non-existent sounds and tonal relationships].[22] A single scratch, introduced by human hand, he emphasizes, makes the gramophone player's needle skip, transforming the gramophone disc into something that does not merely record or replay existing sounds, but instead allows us to encounter new ways of making sound creation, and thus hearing, that expands our expectations of that machine and its impact upon our own bodies. That little scratch reveals at once how that technology operates, what it was built for, and how it could come to achieve new future aims.

"Produktion-Reproduktion" made an impact as soon as it was published. Moholy's show at the Gallery Der Sturm in Berlin began exhibiting around the same time. In part on the basis of his work in industrial-looking sculpture and the strength of the essay, Walter Gropius hired Moholy to join the Bauhaus in 1923. His appointment was part of Gropius's strategic plan to reorient the Bauhaus towards the unification of art and technology and away from its Expressionist origins. For a school seeking to define its relationship with industry and technology, the title of Moholy's essay held a particular appeal. Finding new ways of becoming productive was absolutely crucial to the publicly funded art school that faced mounting political and fiscal challenges to its continued existence.[23]

During his years at the Bauhaus, Moholy solidified his reputation as an ardent advocate for the integration of art and technology, all the more so when he showed *Enamel Constructions* at the Gallery Der Sturm in Berlin in 1924.[fig.5] In a gallery of abstract paintings on panel, canvas, and paper, he showed manufactured porcelain enamel on steel paintings, produced at a sign factory in Thüringen, the state that supported the Bauhaus in Weimar. Moholy advertised this public-private partnership. In a text explaining the show, he argued that the future of art and of painting did not lie in making precious originals, but in creating forms that instill modern modes of seeing and making—forms so clear and precise that they might even be communicated by telephone.[24] In these same years, he declared painting a thing of the past.[25]

Moholy's show of the *Enamel Constructions* was sensational. A few of his leftist critics saw them as proof of how the West was appropriating the language of Constructivism without its political substance. Conservative critics railed against his provocation as evidence of the Bauhaus commitment to liquidate the great German cultural traditions Weimar represented in pursuit of the latest fads.

Joyce Tsai

Epochal Trace

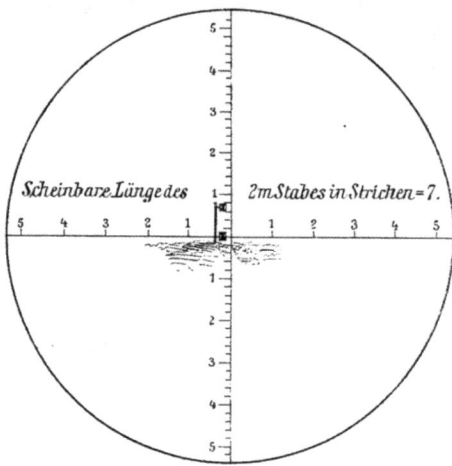

Fig.6. *Artillerieunterricht. 10.0 cm M. 14 Feldhaubitze. Zu Abt. 7 Nr 35355 vom Jahre 1916. – Normalverordnungsblatt für das k. u. k. Heer, 37. Stück von 1916* (Vienna, 1916), 105.

A few of his ardent advocates saw his aim— Adolf Behne understood the project as a proof of concept for art made for a mass public.[26]

But Moholy sought to do more than merely give the masses access to art. These works also demonstrate the key claims of "Produktion-Reproduktion." If the text queries how any means (*Mittel*)—that is to say technology, tool, or medium—might be made productive, then the question can also be posed with respect to artistic media in which Moholy worked. If painting and its highest achievement has conventionally been determined by its originality or virtuosity, Moholy asks what else might be achieved. As he showed *Enamel Constructions* in the mid-1920s, he also argued in *Malerei, Photographie, Film*, completed in 1924 and published in 1925, that new materials should be explored to make paintings available to every household, allowing for the creation of what he called domestic pinacotheca.[27] His aim was not to cultivate a broader audience of newly minted art lovers or collectors, but instead to offer everyone modern paintings as perceptual training tools. Paintings on new materials could be held in one's hands, manipulated, placed on tables, hung on walls, viewed upside down, etc. Put differently, factory-made paintings would not be made for delectation.

The fact that *Enamel Constructions* includes two crosses as part of their composition clues us in to the intent. Seen in light of his experience as a reconnaissance officer in the Austro-Hungarian artillery, the design elements begin to resemble the crosshairs of the scopes he would have used in his work in the military. [fig.6] Crosses help viewers aim in paintings and scopes alike. The target that should come into focus for them in war and peace, for Moholy as a military trainer and artist-educator, could not have been more different despite the similarity of tack. In war, Moholy learned that the human body could be remade to see through the lens of the machine and could serve its ends by subjugating the human being to its weapons. In peace, he sought to transform that lesson to reverse the relationship: human beings must manipulate the machine for it to serve human ends. The scratch unlocks the potential of technology to serve human needs. At the end of his career, Moholy applied the lessons he'd learned early on to confront a new reality.

This essay opened with an examination of Moholy's late writings and of his retrospective assessment of his early self-portraits, which also attends to the ways he read the meaning of his marks, and of his military training. At the end of his life, I wish to suggest, Moholy treated himself as a medium. In that moment, he subjected himself to the same questions he posed of other media in "Produktion-Reproduktion." How might the artist become productive? How might he become an instrument capable of serving humankind? The artist as seismograph offers one answer.

1   László Moholy-Nagy, "Abstract of an Artist," in László Moholy-Nagy, *The New Vision* (New York, 1947), 68. The author wishes to express her thanks to Kimberly Datchuk for her comments. This essay is dedicated to Zeke DeVane.
2   Moholy-Nagy, "Abstract of an Artist," 68.
3   Moholy-Nagy, "Abstract of an Artist," 68.
4   Lloyd Engelbrecht has meticulously reconstructed Moholy's life and work, offering extensive documentation on his activities, in his book *Mentor to Modernism*. Lloyd Engelbrecht, *Mentor to Modernism* (Cincinnati, 2009), 32–62.
5   Levante Nagy, "The Beginning of the Multi-Faceted Career of László Moholy-Nagy," in *László Moholy-Nagy: From Budapest to Berlin*, ed. Belinda Chapp (Newark, Delaware, 1995), 22–25.
6   "Personalblatt," September 29, 1918, Sibyl Moholy-Nagy Papers, Archives of American Art, Washington, DC.
7   Oliver Botar, *Technical Detours* (New York, 2006), 55.
8   For an account of Moholy's figurative drawings, see Krisztina Passuth, "The Postcards and Figurative Drawings of László Moholy-Nagy in an International Context," in *László Moholy-Nagy: From Budapest to Berlin*, ed. Belinda Chapp (Newark, Delaware, 1995), 59–69.
9   See *The Paintings of Moholy-Nagy: The Shape of Things to Come*, ed. Joyce Tsai (Santa Barbara, 2015).
10   László Moholy-Nagy, *Vision in Motion* (Chicago, 1947), 29.
11   László Moholy-Nagy, *Vision in Motion*, 30.
12   Engelbrecht, 32–62. Elsewhere I have examined the relationship between technologized seeing and its impact on interwar abstraction in Moholy's work. Joyce Tsai, "Reconfiguration of the Eye: László Moholy-Nagy," in *Nothing but the Clouds Unchanged: Artists and the First World War*, ed. Gordon Hughes and Philipp Blom (Los Angeles, 2014), 156–63; Joyce Tsai,

"Lines of Sight," *Artforum* (November 2015): 272–77; Joyce Tsai, *László Moholy-Nagy: Painting after Photography* (Oakland, 2018).
13   *Artillerieunterricht. 10.0 cm M. 14 Feldhaubitze. Zu Abt. 7 Nr 35355 vom Jahre 1916. – Normalverordnungsblatt für das k. u. k. Heer, 37. Stück von 1916* (Vienna, 1916), 4. Excerpts translated for this essay by Michael Pilewski.
14   Tsai, "Lines of Sight," 277.
15   *Artillerieunterricht*, 4.
16   *Artillerieunterricht*, 4.
17   László Moholy-Nagy, "Produktion-Reproduktion," *de Stijl* 5, no. 7 (July 1922): 98–101.
18   László Moholy-Nagy, "Produktion-Reproduktion," 98–101.
19   László Moholy-Nagy, "Produktion-Reproduktion," 98–99. This essay is reprinted again in modified form in his book *Malerei, Photographie, Film* (1925/27).
20   László Moholy-Nagy, "Produktion-Reproduktion," 99.
21   László Moholy-Nagy, "Produktion-Reproduktion," 99.
22   László Moholy-Nagy, "Produktion-Reproduktion," 99.
23   For documents that detail the acute challenges that the Bauhaus in Weimar faced on multiple fronts, see *Die Meisterratsprotokolle des Staatlichen Bauhauses Weimar 1919–1925*, ed. Ute Ackermann and Volker Wahl (Weimar, 2001).
24   Moholy-Nagy, "Emaille im Februar 1924," 1. Translation from Doherty, "Constructions in Enamel: 1923," 130.
25   László Moholy-Nagy, *Malerei, Photographie, Film* (Munich: Albert Langen Verlag, 1925), 37.
26   For the conservative position, see "Kommentar," *Das Kunstblatt* (March 1924): 96. For a sympathetic review, see Adolf Behne, "Snob und Anti-Snob," in *Die Weltbühne* 20 (1924), 235–36.
27   Moholy-Nagy, *Malerei, Photographie, Film*, 19.

Joyce Tsai

Epochal Trace

Norbert Korrek

"Reserve Hospital No. 11 Art School": The Bauhaus in the Period of Transition from World War I to the Weimar Republic

There was no celebratory opening of the State Bauhaus in Weimar in 1919. The story of its founding has already been mapped out by Volker Wahl in a seminal study issued in 2008 to mark the ninetieth anniversary of the institution.[1] A year later, he and his colleagues at the Thuringian Central State Archive in Weimar (Thüringisches Hauptstaatsarchiv Weimar) published what was at the time the most extensive selection of key documents recording how the Weimar Bauhaus evolved as an institution in an edition that included critical analysis of the source material.[2] This essay sets out to examine in more detail the spatial constraints that pertained in the studio building of the former Grand Ducal Saxon College of Fine Arts and in the workshop building of the Grand Ducal Vocational Arts School at the time when the State Bauhaus in Weimar began operations. For up until September 1919, numerous studios and workshops were used as the "Reserve Hospital No. 11 Art School" and were not made available to the Bauhaus until the winter semester 1919/20.[fig. 1, 2]

April 1, 1919 is the date usually given for the founding of the Bauhaus. Volker Wahl has pointed to the historical inaccuracy of this. It was not until April 12 that privy state councilor Alfred Heinemann, as representative of the office of Hofmarschall (in charge of economic affairs)—an institution that was in the process of being phased out—informed the administration of the Grand Ducal Saxon College of Fine Arts that the application they had lodged on March 20 to "change the name" of the school to State Bauhaus had been granted. One day prior to this, the directorship of the College of Fine Arts, along with the Vocational Arts School, which had been closed since

1915, had been transferred to architect Walter Gropius by the Hofmar-schall's office "with the approval of the provisional government of Saxe-Weimar-Eisenach," effective retroactively from April 1.[3]

In April 1915, Henry van de Velde, who had been discharged as director, had suggested Gropius as his potential successor, along with August Endell and Herrmann Obrist, who would later become director of the State Bauhaus. Because the Belgian van de Velde had been placed under house arrest after the outbreak of World War I, the director of the College of Fine Arts, Fritz Mackensen, took the initiative. He initially favored Endell, with whom he had initiated contact in January 1915. However, when the preliminary negotiations with Endell dragged on without showing much promise, in November 1915 he turned his attention to Gropius,[4] who thereupon led from the front, proposing "suggestions for founding an academy as an artistic advisory center for industry, craft, and trades."[5]

Mackensen's plans went beyond what Gropius suggested. After van de Velde had been dismissed at the start of the war, Mackensen endeavored to set up a "department for architecture and crafts" in addition to the studios for visual artists. To ensure the continued existence of the art college, he wanted to secure the Belgian's legacy.[6] The Grand Ducal State Ministry was ready, in late November, to negotiate with Gropius to discuss "his possible assumption of the directorship" of this department.[7] After Gropius had personally presented himself to the grand duke on December 8, 1916, the matter was not pursued any further during the war. In March 1917, Mackensen abandoned his efforts having resigned himself to the situation.[8]

At the end of World War I, Gropius made himself known again to one of the senior court officials, Oberhofmarschall Baron von Fritsch.[9] At the prompting of the newly appointed general director of the National Theater, Ernst Hardt, at the end of January 1919 he renewed his interest in moving to Weimar and becoming van de Velde's succes-sor. He reiterated the goal of his teaching work, stating that "the indi-vidual 'arts' should be redeemed from their segregated isolation and reconnected at their core under the auspices of a great architecture."[10]

In mid-February 1919, Gropius introduced himself and his concept to the teachers and students at the College of Fine Arts. Since Mackensen had now left the college, the directorship of the institution was offered to him. Gropius recognized the great opportunity this presented and set out "stringent conditions." Beside the merger of

Norbert Korrek

"Reserve Hospital No. 11 Art School"

239

the College of Fine Arts and Vocational Arts School, his main demand was to implement a "program" that would include "major innovations."[11] Moreover, in late February, Gropius went to Weimar and conducted successful negotiations with the state commissioner of the provisional government, August Baudert.[12] He submitted his financial projections for the as yet nameless institution for the fiscal year 1919/20, to which the Hofmarschall's office could only agree. Thereupon, at Gropius's suggestion and on behalf of the teaching staff, the painter and acting director of the College of Fine Arts, Max Thedy, applied for the new name Bauhaus, which Fritsch had described to Gropius as "undesirable."[13]

After the name had been confirmed by the provisional government on March 25, 1919, the Hofmarschall could do no more than delay the founding of the State Bauhaus in Weimar.[14] On March 31, Gropius wrote a triumphant letter to his mother:

The Weimar matter is now perfect and complete ... I have the directorship of v. d. Velde's Vocational Arts School and the College of Fine Arts and want to incorporate a new architecture department and then turn it into a new integrated institute with the name 'State Bauhaus in Weimar.'[15]

However, the physical situation in spatial terms, in particular, was not really "perfect," as only some of the rooms were available immediately after the founding of the Bauhaus. Since November 1914, a good number of studios in the art school building had been in permanent use as dormitories and treatment rooms for wounded soldiers. In addition, the Weimar garrison command also maintained homes for soldiers and wounded servicemen in the form of a *Soldatenheim für Verwundete* and a *Kriegerheim* in the workshop building. This made the necessary restructuring of the College of Fine Arts and the intended reorganization of the workshops of the Vocational Arts School much more difficult. The reassignment of the spaces from the military administration to the newly founded State Bauhaus developed into a slow and arduous process.

Immediately after the outbreak of World War I, Minister of State Karl Rothe informed the command of the 94th (5th Thuringian) Infantry Regiment "Grand Duke of Saxony"[16] that in accordance with "the supreme decree of His Royal Highness the Grand Duke," Wilhelm Ernst of Saxe-Weimar-Eisenach would put the rooms of the College of Fine Arts in Weimar at the disposal of the military administration of the 11th Army Corps in Kassel.[17] Since the State Ministry saw the

Fig.3. Reserve Hospital No. 11, Grand Ducal Saxon College of Fine Arts Weimar, top floor. Postcard, uncanceled. Photograph by Heinrich Koch, Weimar.

Fig.4. Reserve Hospital No. 11, Grand Ducal Saxon College of Fine Arts Weimar, top floor. Postcard, canceled as military mail on July 23, 1915. Photograph by Heinrich Koch, Weimar.

existence of the art school as being in jeopardy, the following day the order of the grand duke was specified such that in the first instance the "lecture rooms" would be considered for military usage. All the professors' second-floor studios were thus excepted from the decree along with some of the classrooms on the top floor. These continued to be "given over to private use."[18]

After the grand duke's order was made public, in August 1914 the 4th Company of the 94th Infantry Regiment began setting up a "main room and office" in the art school building.[19] For this purpose, two rooms were cleared: these were located "on the ground floor to the left of the entrance to the college"[20] on Belvederer Allee. Since kitchens were also to be installed to "serve the hospital," the Weimarfarbe company[21] was given notice to vacate one of the first-floor rooms used for commercial purposes.[22] The room was made available "with the utmost alacrity." Since production in Oberweimar had temporarily ceased, the company executives offered to also put "the hydroelectric capacity of around 15 horsepower that was thus freed up" at the disposal of the military administration.[23]

Up to mid-September 1914, the command of the 9th Army Corps in Kassel had not yet made the fundamental decision as to whether a hospital should actually be set up in the college. When Mackensen, its director, was drafted as company commander of a reserve regiment directly after the start of the war,[24] Thedy and college syndic Berthold Paul Förster urged the medical superintendent of all the reserve hospitals in Weimar, Medical Officer Dr. Arnim Knopf,[25] to "determine precisely at this juncture" which rooms would be needed for the hospital so that the remaining rooms could be used for the winter semester, which was due to commence on October 19.[26]

Once the decision had been taken to establish a hospital in the art school, on October 10, 1914, the following spaces were handed over to the reserve hospital by ministerial head of department Ernst Wuttig:[27] six studio rooms on the first floor of the art school building[28] and four on the top floor.[29] It was specified that the main entrance on Kunstschulstraße (now Geschwister-Scholl-Straße) and the main stairway should be used exclusively by the hospital.[30] The only way into the college was via the entrance on Belvederer Allee and the small side staircase by the courtyard. As of November 28, 1914, Reserve Hospital No. 11 Art School was occupied on a permanent basis. [fig.3, 4]

Norbert Korrek

"Reserve Hospital No. 11 Art School"

Fig. 5, 6. Home for soldiers
at the former Grand Ducal
Vocational Arts School
Weimar, circa 1916.

Prior to the start of winter semester 1914/15, the college administration
felt obliged to reassign the remaining classrooms. As a result, the
teaching of the classical drawing class and Walther Klemm's nature
academy were now held on the first floor of the Preller building. The
nature classes run by Mackensen and Gari Melcher used the private
studio of Ludwig von Hofmann on the top floor (now the Oberlichtsaal). Von Hofmann was already preparing for his move to the Dresden
Academy of Fine Arts and had thus made his studio available. Thedy
organized his nature class in the private studio of Theodor Hagen,
who had been given Mackensen's studio. Robert Weise's nature class
used the old master student studio on the second floor.

Immediately after the "liquidation of the Vocational Arts School,"[31]
the chair of the Heim für verwundete Krieger, Frau von Buchwaldt,
applied to install a home for the wounded in the rooms of the school,[32]
whereupon four rooms were made available to her at no cost for the
"local company of the sick and wounded" as well as the "large room
which had hitherto been used by Professor van de Velde."[33] Use of the
garden in front of the Vocational Art School was permitted. In early
February 1916, the colonel and longest-serving member of the garrison
command in Weimar, Baron von Dalwigk, followed this example.
For the establishment of a "soldiers' home" in which the "servicemen
are offered a comfortable home" and "where they are to read, write,
play, and enjoy alcohol-free drinks,"[34] the former lecture hall and
rooms from the weaving and ceramics workshops were made available,
which even led to a kiln being demolished. [fig. 5, 6]

Despite these complicated restrictions on the space available
for teaching, classes at the College of Fine Arts could be maintained.
It was only in late 1916 that the situation began to further deteriorate,
when the college administration was "confidentially" informed by
Knopf of the War Ministry's demand for an additional "450 stations
for the sick and wounded from border zones" to be prepared in
Weimar.[35] Owing to the "very good attendance," no further rooms
were to be forthcoming, so the college promptly moved into the last
available rooms of the old Vocational Arts School with its own
students.[36]

It was not until October 1918 that the reserve hospital was actually
expanded, with the addition of more than a hundred beds. The college
administration was obliged to consent to the urgent requests coming
from the hospital commission. All the studios on the top floor of the

Krieger=Heim
Weimar

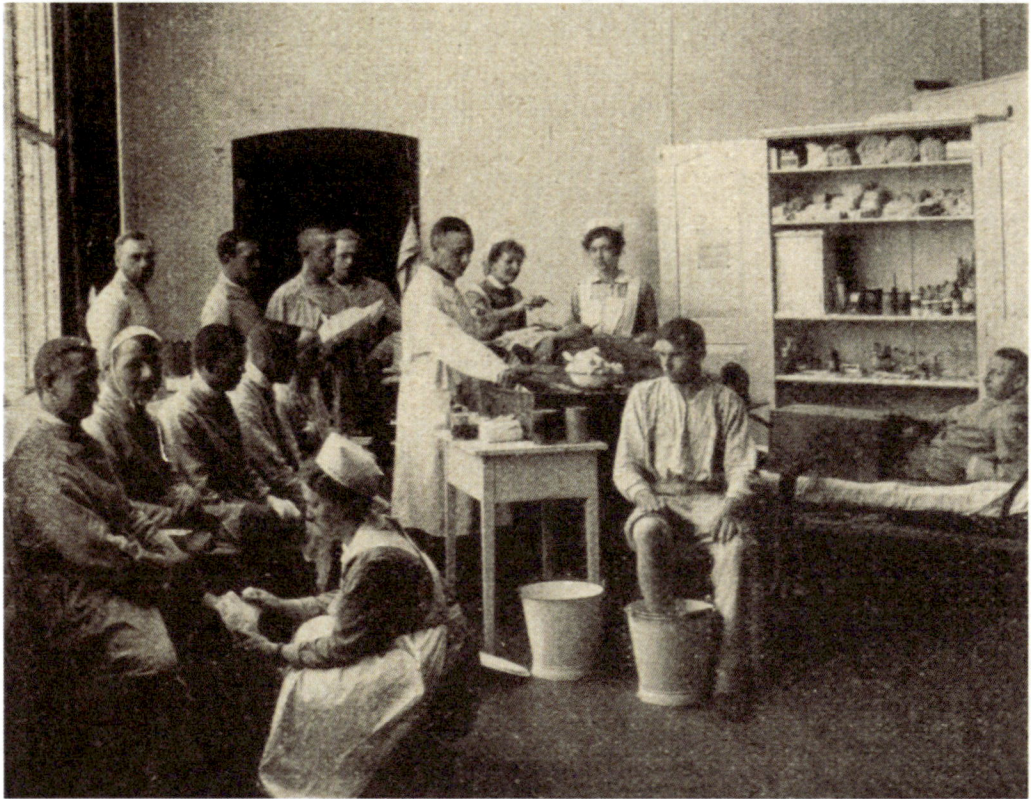

Fig.7. "The lobby of the Grand Ducal Arts School in Weimar as entertainment room of the military hospital accommodated there," contemporary caption, photo after 1916. Auguste Rodin's sculpture "Eve," which stood in the lobby of the College of Fine Arts since 1912, is missing in the picture. Director Fritz Mackensen had the bronze casting, which he himself had acquired, removed in 1916 as a work of "our abuser."

Fig.8. "A studio of the Grand Ducal College of Art in Weimar as an operating and bandaging room of the military hospital now accommodated there," contemporary caption, photo circa 1918/1919

college and all the rooms in the former workshop building at the Vocational Arts School were put at the disposal of Reserve Hospital No. 11.

Once Gropius had decided to "assume the position of director of the College of Fine Arts," he began to prepare his move to Weimar, which included relocating his architecture office. After Mackensen resigned on October 1, 1918, Thedy ran the college on an interim basis. As acting director, he applied to the provisional government to hand over to Gropius as his designated successor the spaces that van de Velde had previously "used for the same purpose" by April 1, 1919. He described this as an "absolute necessity," because otherwise it would be impossible for Gropius to take over the directorship. At this time, van de Velde's old studio was being used as a linen depot by the reserve hospital. Thedy also asked for the college building to be cleared by May 1, so that sufficient studio space would be "available for the reorganization of the school that was to be carried out." [37]

Thedy could only place his hopes in the understanding of the garrison command: it had been necessary for him to extend the usage agreement with the hospital administration on December 24, 1918, and this could not be revoked by the State Bauhaus as legal successor to the College of Fine Arts. The garrison command therefore saw no need to make rooms in the two Weimar barracks available and even announced further deliveries of linen to the former Vocational Arts School from the disbanded departments of other reserve hospitals in Weimar. Thedy was consoled with the information that "the supplies of linen [were registered] to the War Ministry" and it was therefore only a matter of time before "the stocks were released for bulk sale." It would only be possible after this to comply with the wishes of the Bauhaus. Even the clearing of the studios of the old College of Fine Arts by May 1, 1919 could only be "promised prospectively," as follow-up operations needed to be performed on many of the "war disabled" who had already been discharged. Since the doctors in the Sophienhaus and the city hospital could not take on these operations, "the art school department had recently been turned into a surgical ward," one that the hospital could not do without. [fig. 7, 8] [38]

Thereupon, Gropius called his move to Weimar into question. In order to be able to fulfill the obligations he had to his clients and staff at his architecture office, he emphatically demanded "van de Velde's studios" in the old Vocational Arts School. He did not agree with the evasive reply from the reserve hospital and was also

Norbert Korrek

"Reserve Hospital No. 11 Art School"

247

Fig.9. Letter from Walter
Gropius to the legal adviser
of the Grand Ducal College
of Art, Paul Kämmer,
March 31, 1919 (obverse).

unhappy with the solution to the question of where he would live.
He wanted the "villa"[39] of the former director of the College of
Fine Arts, Mackensen, to be reserved for him and refused to accept
the apartment that August Lehrmann, head of municipal planning,
had offered him for rent. Gropius "definitely"[40] wanted to live in
a house with a garden. [fig.9, 10]

Thedy then made another appeal to the provisional government.
He explained that it was "completely out of the question" to be
without the studios for an unspecified period, as "the college was on
the point of being reorganized" and new staff appointments were
imminent, for whom workrooms needed to be set up. The Bauhaus
would also be "extremely well attended," with numbers almost
reaching what would have been achieved in peacetime. He pointed out
that "students who had been in the field for over four years would have
a legitimate claim to the possibilities of work and education." Firstly,
though, the rooms used as the linen depot would need to be cleared
by April 25 "for the director appointed on April 1." Gropius's delayed
move from Berlin to Weimar would "substantially impair" his professional activities. To expedite the vacation of the space, Thedy requested
that there be no "further occupation" of the reserve hospital—rather,
rooms that had become free should be handed back. In this way,
he set out to arrive at a situation whereby the Bauhaus could use "the
whole building from the beginning of September 1919."[41]

Paul Kämmer, who had been secretary of the State Bauhaus since
April 12, 1919, took over the ongoing negotiations. He received confirmation from senior hospital inspector Elzer that van de Velde's old
studio would be cleared and the linen depot "relocated to some
first-floor rooms in the university building." Moreover, "the college
hospital ... was shortly to be vacated."[42] A contract concluded by the
Hofmarschall's office on April 16 indicates how contradictory the
information was and how difficult the process of taking over the rooms
turned out to be. In it, the use of the rooms in the old Vocational Arts
School, which had been occupied by the gendarmerie since February 3,
was fixed retrospectively. [43] Gropius, as director, was also obliged to
countersign the contract.

Once the process of clearing out the reserve hospital had begun
in May 1919, Gropius applied for compensation for "wear and tear
on the building" to enable him to start the necessary repair work.
Because the College of Fine Arts had been "handed over without

den 31. März 1919.

11

Lieber Herr Kämmer !

Einliegenden Brief an die Fremdenpaßstelle
Weimar bitte ich Sie, umgehend weiterzubefördern. Es handelt
sich um offizielle Zureiseerlaubnis für mich und meine Frau.

Ferner bitte ich Sie, mir sogleich ein von Herrn Professor
Thedy unterschriebenes Schreiben etwa folgenden Inhalts zu über-
senden, damit ich für mich und meine Frau, die ich in nächster
Zeit erwarte, Fahrkarten nach Weimar bekomme:

"Wir bestätigen Herrn Architekten Walter Gropius, daß er
zum Direktor der Hochschule für bildende Kunst in Weimar
berufen worden ist und bitten, ihm zum Zweck der Uebersie-
delung nach Weimar für ihn und seine Gemahlin Reiseerlaub-
nis ausstellen zu wollen."

Es tut mir sehr leid, daß ich Sie gestern in Berlin
verfehlt habe. Es ist Ihnen fälschlich vom Portier bestellt worden, daß ich in Weimar sei; ich war in Hagen i/ Westf.

Ihren Brief vom 27. d.M. bestätige ich dankend. Die Stif-
tungsfrage läuft nun wohl in richtiger Bahn.

Mit der Antwort des Reservelazaretts kann ich mich nicht
einverstanden erklären. Es müssen unbedingt Schritte getan werden,
um die Van de Veldeschen Ateliers für mich freizubekommen. Ich
kann nicht übersiedeln, ehe ich nicht ein regelrechtes Atelier
mit mehreren Räumen beziehen kann, denn ich habe ja noch ander-

249

weitige Verpflichtungen gegen meine Bauherren. Es müßte nun zu-
nächst festgestellt werden, um was für einen Vertrag vom 24/12.18
der seitens der Hochschule unkündbar sein soll, es sich handelt.
Ich bitte, sich mit dem Hofmarschallamt in Verbindung zu setzen,
daß auf die darüber zu befindenden Stellen Druck ausgeübt wird.
Sobald ich wieder persönlich nach Weimar komme, werde ich auch
selbst dahinterhaken.

Von besonderer Wichtigkeit, lieber Herr Kämmer, ist mir
meine Wohnungsfrage. Ich bitte Sie, sogleich Herrn Stadtbaurat
Lehrmann im Stadtbauamt anzutelephonieren. Er ist vermöge der
Bestimmungen durchaus in der Lage, die Villa Mackensen für mich
zu reservieren, scheint aber aus Schwäche nicht dazu schreiten
zu wollen. Die Etagenwohnung, die er mir angeboten hat, will ich
nicht mieten, ich möchte entschieden in einem kleinen Haus mit
Garten wohnen. Könnten Sie sich nicht in Oberweimar erkundigen,
ob dort etwas zu haben ist? Auch von Herrn Westberg und Frau
v. Bredow (Dr. Wedekind), die mir sogleich Bescheid schicken
wollten, habe ich noch keine Antwort.

Ebenso dringend ist die 3-4 Zimmerwohnung meines Bürochefs
Herrn Meyer. Das Stadtbauamt hat auf meine Anmeldung noch nicht
reagiert.

Ist wohl das allgemeine Schreiben, um das ich gebeten habe,
an das Hofmarschallamt, die Regierung und das Stadtbauamt abgegan-
gen? Wir müssen möglichst schnell unsere Ansprüche geltend machen
da ja die weiteren Neuberufungen vor der Tür stehen.

Verzeihen Sie, daß ich Sie mit diesen Wohnungsfragen belä-
stige, ich weiß mir aber im Moment nicht anders zu helfen, da ich
hier noch so viel zu tun habe, daß ich im Augenblick nicht nach
dort kommen kann. Einstweilen meinen herzlichsten Dank für Ihre

1 Prospekt   Ihr ergebener Gropius-

250

Fig. 10. Letter from Walter Gropius to the legal adviser of the Grand Ducal College of Art, Paul Kämmer, March 31, 1919 (reverse).

contract" to the military administration, no notes had been taken to record the structural condition of the building in 1914. However, the rooms *must have been* in "immaculate condition," because the college building had only been completed in late 1913. Gropius's argument was that after the abdication of the grand duke, "who would most certainly have taken on the restoration of the college," the Bauhaus had no funding to remedy the "damage caused by the hospital." He described this as "a moral obligation on the part of the hospital administration," affirming that the repair costs should come out of the hospital funds even after the grand duke had abdicated.[44]

The State Bauhaus eventually received a lump sum of 10,000 Reichsmarks in compensation. Through the summer of 1919, renovation and repair work was carried out, including the installation of a Bauhaus canteen in the "glass dome" of animal painter Adolf Brendel. For this, Gropius took over some of the kitchen facilities of the reserve hospital[45] and added a kitchen annex to the old studio building.

Considering the bleak conditions in the studio and workshop rooms and the now limited possibilities for teaching, the first annual exhibition of Bauhaus student works in July 1919 appears in a new light. Gropius had identified and criticized the "most tremendous disjointedness" in the works on display. Despite the "gloomy economic prospects," he wanted to secure financing for the Bauhaus until the fall in order to "create a base" on which the *Bauhäusler* "will feel comfortable."[46] His optimistic idea was doomed to failure early on. The Weimar Bauhaus would not achieve institutional stability as a necessary basis for implementing a program of educational reforms until its move to Dessau.

1 Volker Wahl, "Wie Walter Gropius nach Weimar kam: Zur Gründungsgeschichte des Staatlichen Bauhauses in Weimar 1919," *Die große Stadt: Das kulturhistorische Archiv von Weimar-Jena* 1, no. 3 (2008): 167–211.
2 Volker Wahl, *Das Staatliche Bauhaus in Weimar: Dokumente zur Geschichte des Instituts 1919–1926* (Cologne, 2009).
3 Wahl.
4 To present the two candidates to the grand duke, Mackensen prepared an exhibition of craft and architectural works by Endell and Gropius. Gropius suggested showing the study and living room at the Cologne Werkbund exhibition of 1914, as well as the Mendel residence in Berlin. Endell's work was to be illustrated by the racetrack in Berlin-Mariendorf and the Moll residence in Breslau. See Landesarchiv Thüringen – Hauptstaatsarchiv Weimar (hereafter LATH–HSTAW), Großherzoglich Sächsische Hochschule für bildende Kunst 50.
5 Karl-Heinz Hüter, *Das Bauhaus in Weimar: Studie zur gesellschaftspolitischen Geschichte einer deutschen Kunstschule* (Berlin, 1976), 201–03 (document 1).

6 "Allow me to express the hope that—in the interest of our work—we might attempt in future to build a bridge forged in mutual trust between our two natures, which may ultimately be opposed to one another." Henry van de Velde, letter to Mackensen, March 19, 1914, LATH-HSTAW, Großherzoglich Sächsische Hochschule für bildende Kunst 29, sheet 314.

7 Mackensen, letter to Gropius, November 22, 1916, LATH-HSTAW, Großherzoglich Sächsi sche Hochschule für bildende Kunst 97, sheet 7.

8 Mackensen, letter to the Department of Internal and External Affairs, March 24, 1917, LATH-HSTAW, Großherzoglich Sächsische Hochschule für bildende Kunst 50, sheet 21.

9 Gropius, letter to Oberhofmarschall Baron von Fritsch, January 31, 1919, in Hans M. Wingler, *Das Bauhaus: Weimar Dessau Berlin 1919–1933 und die Nachfolge in Chicago seit 1937*, 5th ed. (Cologne, 2005), 32–33.

10 Hüter, *Das Bauhaus in Weimar* (see note 5), 204–05 (document 4).

11 Reginald R. Isaacs, *Walter Gropius: Der Mensch und sein Werk*, vol. 1 (Berlin, 1985), 204.

12 See Wahl, *Das Staatliche Bauhaus in Weimar* (see note 2), Erläuterungen zu den Dokumenten (Notes on the Documents), 261.

13 Hüter, *Das Bauhaus in Weimar* (see note 5), 205 (document 5).

14 See Isaacs, *Walter Gropius* (see note 11), 207.

15 Gropius, letter to his mother, Berlin, March 31, 1919, cited in Isaacs, 207.

16 This regiment was the 5th Infantry Regiment of the province of Thuringia and the 94th of the German Reich. At the same time, it was a contingent of the Grand Duchy of Saxony.

17 State Ministry, letter to the Ministerial Department of the Interior, August 5, 1924, LATH-HSTAW, Großherzoglich Sächsische Hochschule für bildende Kunst 47, sheet 1.

18 State Ministry, letter to the Royal Command of the Infantry Regiment in Weimar, August 6, 1914, LATH-HSTAW, Großherzoglich Sächsische Hochschule für bildende Kunst 47, sheet 3.

19 Jordan (presumably Dr. Michael Jordan, born January 17, 1867, member of the medical column and column physician), letter to the College of Fine Arts, August 21, 1914, LATH-HSTAW, Großherzoglich Sächsische Hochschule für bildende Kunst 47, sheet 7.

20 See LATH-HSTAW, Großherzoglich Sächsische Hochschule für bildende Kunst 47, sheet 5 reverse.

21 Weimarfarbe GmbH was founded in 1917. It marketed the so-called Weimar paint, a tempera-style product that painter Felix Hasse had developed in the laboratory of the Weimar art school—later painter and author Adolf von den Velden (1853–1932) had temporarily taken over his responsibility for the production. Cited in Peter Stapf, *Der Maler Max Thedy (1858–1924): Leben und Werk* (Cologne, 2014), 200, esp. notes 33 and 34.

22 College of Fine Arts, letter to Weimarfarbe GmbH, August 13, 1914, LATH-HSTAW, Großherzoglich Sächsische Hochschule für bildende Kunst 47, sheet 4.

23 Weimarfarbe GmbH, letter to the College of Fine Arts, August 15, 1914, LATH-HSTAW, Großherzoglich Sächsische Hochschule für bildende Kunst 47, sheet 5.

24 "On Sunday my reserve regiment, where I am assigned as company commander, is being deployed in the field." Mackensen, letter to Hermann Bruchlos, secretary of the college, August 7, 1914, LATH-HSTAW, Großherzoglich Sächsische Hochschule für bildende Kunst 29, sheet 371.

25 Dr. Armin Knopf was employed—between 1913 and 1915 at any rate—as a teacher of plastic anatomy at the College of Fine Arts.

26 Knopf, letter to the College of Fine Arts, September 13, 1914, LATH-HSTAW, Großherzoglich Sächsische Hochschule für bildende Kunst 47.

27 Wuttig was a member of the management committee of the Vocational Arts School. At the session convened on January 28, 1915, he questioned Henry van de Velde about the future development of the school, although this matter was not addressed any further in the meeting itself. Cited in Volker Wahl, *Henry van de Velde in Weimar: Dokumente und Berichte zur Förderung von Kunsthandwerk und Industrie (1902 bis 1915)* (Cologne, 2007), 464.

28 Today these rooms are numbered 002, 003, 018, 019, 020, 021.

29 Today these rooms are numbered 203, 204, 205, 206.

30 See LATH-HSTAW, Großherzoglich Sächsische Hochschule für bildende Kunst 47, sheet 16.

31 Secretary Kammer, letter to Mackensen, October 15, 1915, LATH–HSTAW, Großherzoglich Sächsische Hochschule für bildende Kunst 29, sheet 466.

32 Transcript from September 2, 1915, LATH–HSTAW, Großherzoglich Sächsische Hochschule für bildende Kunst 51, sheet 1.

33 Count von Finckenstein, letter to the College of Fine Arts, October 20, 1915, LATH–HSTAW, Großherzoglich Sächsische Hochschule für bildende Kunst 51, sheet 6.

34 Dalwigk, letter to the College of Fine Arts, February 16, 1916, LATH–HSTAW, Großherzoglich Sächsische Hochschule für bildende Kunst 51, sheet 11.

35 Königliches Reservelazarett Weimar (Royal Reserve Hospital), confidential letter to the College of Fine Arts, December 20, 1916, LATH–HSTAW, Großherzoglich Sächsische Hochschule für bildende Kunst 47, sheet 42.

36 See LATH–HSTAW, Großherzoglich Sächsische Hochschule für bildende Kunst 47, sheet 43.

37 Thedy (acting director of the College of Fine Arts), letter to the provisional government in Weimar, March 21, 1919, LATH–HSTAW, Großherzoglich Sächsische Hochschule für bildende Kunst 47, sheet 90.

38 Oberstabsarzt (senior medical officer) Reserve Hospital, letter to the administration of the College of Fine Arts, March 25, 1919, LATH–HSTAW, Großherzoglich Sächsische Hochschule für bildende Kunst 47, sheet 91.

39 Painter Fritz Mackensen lived in the urban villa at Lindenberg 11.

40 Gropius, letter to Paul Kämmer, March 31, 1919, LATH–HSTAW, Staatliches Bauhaus Weimar 75, sheet 11.

41 Thedy, letter to the Reserve Hospital, April 2, 1919, copy dated April 3 to the provisional government, LATH–HSTAW, Großherzoglich Sächsische Hochschule für bildende Kunst 47, sheets 92–93.

42 Kämmer, letter to Gropius, April 17, 1919, LATH–HSTAW, Staatliches Bauhaus Weimar 75, sheet 21.

43 Hofmarschallamt Fritsch, letter to the administration of the College of Fine Arts with a copy of the conditions, April 16, 1919, LATH–HSTAW, Großherzoglich Sächsische Hochschule für bildende Kunst 47, sheets 92–93.

44 Gropius, letter to the hospital administration, May 10, 1919, LATH–HSTAW, Großherzoglich Sächsische Hochschule für bildende Kunst 47, sheet 97.

45 Gropius, letter to the hospital administration, May 23, 1919, LATH–HSTAW, Großherzoglich Sächsische Hochschule für bildende Kunst 47, sheet 103.

46 Hüter, Das Bauhaus in Weimar (see note 5), 210–11 (document 11).

Norbert Korrek

"Reserve Hospital No. 11 Art School"

Anna Bokov

Vkhutemas and the Bauhaus: On Common Origins and "Creation with Fire"[1]

In his canonical 1936 chart mapping the development of modern art, the founding director of New York's Museum of Modern Art, Alfred H. Barr, Jr., prominently placed Constructivism and Suprematism just below Cubism. [fig. 1] The two art movements of the Russian avant-garde were considered Cubism's more prominent outcomes, along with Futurism, Orphism, (Abstract) Dadaism, Purism, De Stijl, and Neoplasticism—all of which drew upon what Barr called the "machine esthetic." The Bauhaus was positioned as a product of the aforementioned movements along with (Abstract) Expressionism, powered by the "machine esthetic." Notwithstanding the prominent role assigned to Constructivism and Suprematism, Barr chose to omit a contemporary of the Bauhaus—a Moscow-based institution that, arguably, played a central role in articulating both the theoretical programs and the practical outcomes of the two avant-garde movements.[fig.2][2] Established by Lenin's government as a "specialized educational institution for advanced artistic and technical training," the Higher Art and Technical Studios, collectively known as Vkhutemas [Вхутемас],[3] were created to "prepare highly qualified artist-practitioners for the modern industry."[4]

From its foundation in the fall of 1920, this interdisciplinary school offered free education and accepted students from underprivileged backgrounds, regardless of their artistic talent or academic standing, including of course, in line with the new socialist directives, women.[fig.3] While similar, according to Barr, to the Bauhaus in its "communistic spirit," Vkhutemas, with an enrollment of more than 2,000 students, was an unprecedented modern undertaking.[5] Both a school and a design laboratory, where training, experimentation, and

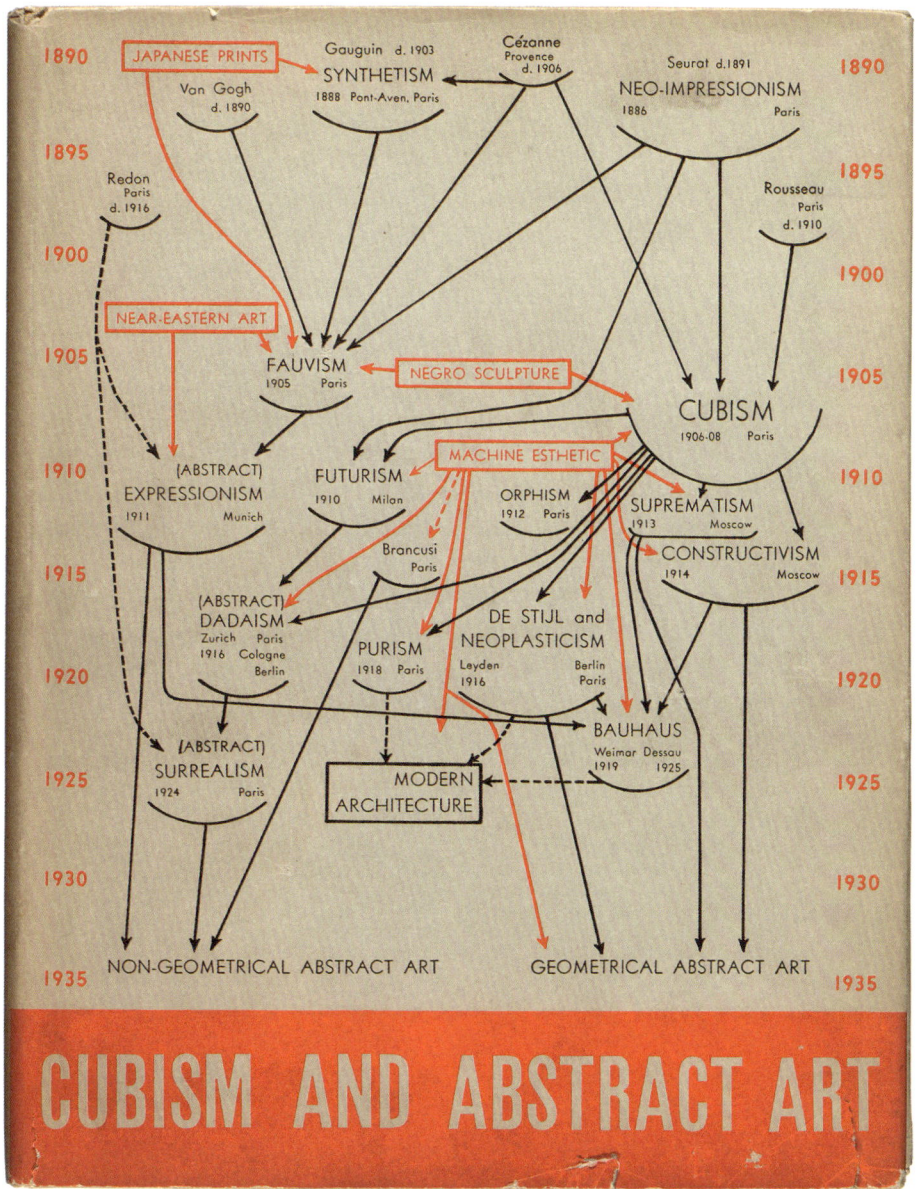

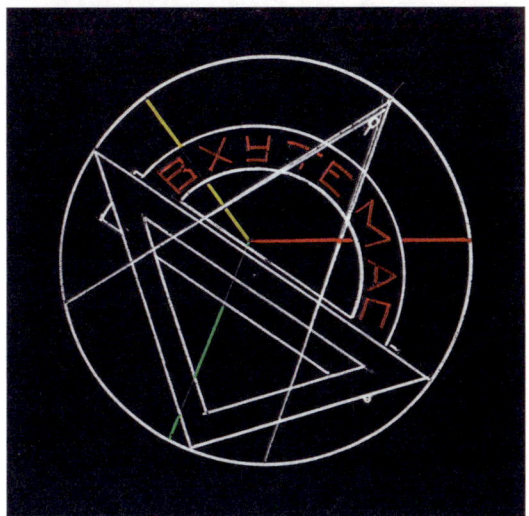

Fig. 1. Alfred H. Barr Jr. Dust jacket of *Cubism and Abstract Art*, featuring the diagram of evolution of modern art by Barr. New York: The Museum of Modern Art, 1936.
Fig. 2. Vkhutemas emblem designed by Alexander Vesnin, Moscow, 1922.

Fig. 3. Students in costumes designed by Varvara Stepanova. Academy of Social Education, Moscow, 1924.

Fig. 4. Student members of the communist cell at Vkhutemas, Moscow, 1920s.

Fig. 5. Students at a demonstration, Vkhutemas, Moscow, 1920s.

production happened side by side, Vkhutemas introduced a new
model of education: a type of an educational "condenser," to borrow
a term from Constructivist architects.[6] The school itself functioned
like a commune: a place for collective study, labor, and life.[fig.4] Its
faculty and students were not seeking to develop personal creative
agendas; rather, they were charged with the mandate of implementing
a new state doctrine aimed at developing a new "artistic culture" and
building a "communist future."[fig.5] Vkhutemas was a platform for
the institutionalization of the avant-garde—an educational experiment of unprecedented scale and complexity that distilled radical
experiments in art, architecture, and design into a systematized
pedagogy. Major progressive artists and cultural luminaries embraced
the revolution. Many sought to participate in the new regime in an
official capacity, and as educators at Vkhutemas saw it as an opportunity to disseminate their design philosophy on a mass scale.

    As a dynamic young scholar of modern art, Barr was evidently
well aware of the central role the Soviet school played at the time.
In fact, he reportedly visited Vkhutemas three times during his two-
month stay in Moscow in the winter of 1927–28 and must have had the
opportunity to carefully examine the school.[7] Nearly a decade later
for his 1936 show "Cubism and Abstract Art," Barr chose to exhibit
the work of Russian artists, including Vladimir Tatlin, Alexander
Rodchenko, and El Lissitzky—all professors at Vkhutemas.[8] Yet Barr
did not frame these works as projects produced by Vkhutemas faculty
and thus affiliated with the school. In fact, there was no mention of
Vkhutemas at all. Posters by Herbert Bayer advertising exhibitions
about Hans Poelzig, Wassily Kandinsky, an arts and crafts exhibition in
Leipzig, and a poster for the lecture series at the Bauhaus in Dessau,
as well as pages takes from the magazine *Sovremennaya Arkhitektura*
(Contemporary Architecture) were shown next to panels presenting

Anna
Bokov

Vkhutemas
and
the
Bauhaus

257

works by the Bauhaus faculty, Walter Gropius, and Oscar Schlemmer.
Labeled as German Bauhaus, it included Gropius's and Adolf Meyer's
Sommerfeld House, the recently constructed *Meisterhäuser* in Dessau
and the figurines of Schlemmer's ballets, and curiously also included
a photograph of El Lissitzky's *Abstract Cabinet* that he had exhibited at
the Sprengel Museum in 1927.[9] Though Lissitzky visited the Bauhaus
a number of times in the early 1920s and also lectured there in 1928,
he was not a part of the faculty. Meanwhile, he taught at Vkhutemas
from 1925 until 1930 and headed a woodworking department there.
Wassily Kandinsky, the only faculty member who taught at both
schools, and who turned 60 that year, was featured above his namesake chair in a poster designed by Bayer. [fig.6 a, b] One cannot omit
Kazimir Malevich's publication in the *Bauhausbücher* series *Gegenstandslose Kunst* introduced by Gropius and Moholy-Nagy. On the whole,
the 1936 New York exhibition reflecting back at late 1928 was a testament to the active "traffic" of artists between Germany and Soviet
Russia, Bauhaus and Vkhutemas.

East-West dialogue

Despite their eventual differences, the Bauhaus and Vkhutemas were
fundamentally aligned at the time of their conception. Both sought
to develop "a new art for the new life"—a visual language capable of
addressing the needs of industrial mass society by bringing the art and
technology of production (or craft) together. The key issue in the histories of both Vkhutemas and the Bauhaus is the question of the
emergence of the very idea of a new school of spatial arts. The most
common view is that the idea of such a school could have arisen independently in Russia and in Germany, since its founders "breathed the
same air" and shared similar left-wing beliefs. Both aimed to build an
educational model that would democratize art education and would
be open to everyone "according to their abilities" by establishing
workshops or studios [*masterskie*] and forming "a working community."[10] The question of whether this striking alignment was a coincidence based on shared historical circumstances or the result of a
more direct transfer of ideas through its protagonists and media, where
the impetus was coming from one of the parties, which during the
period under review found itself in the leadership role, remains open.

 While historically the leading position of the Bauhaus has been
undeniable, today there are reasons to believe that the idea of a new

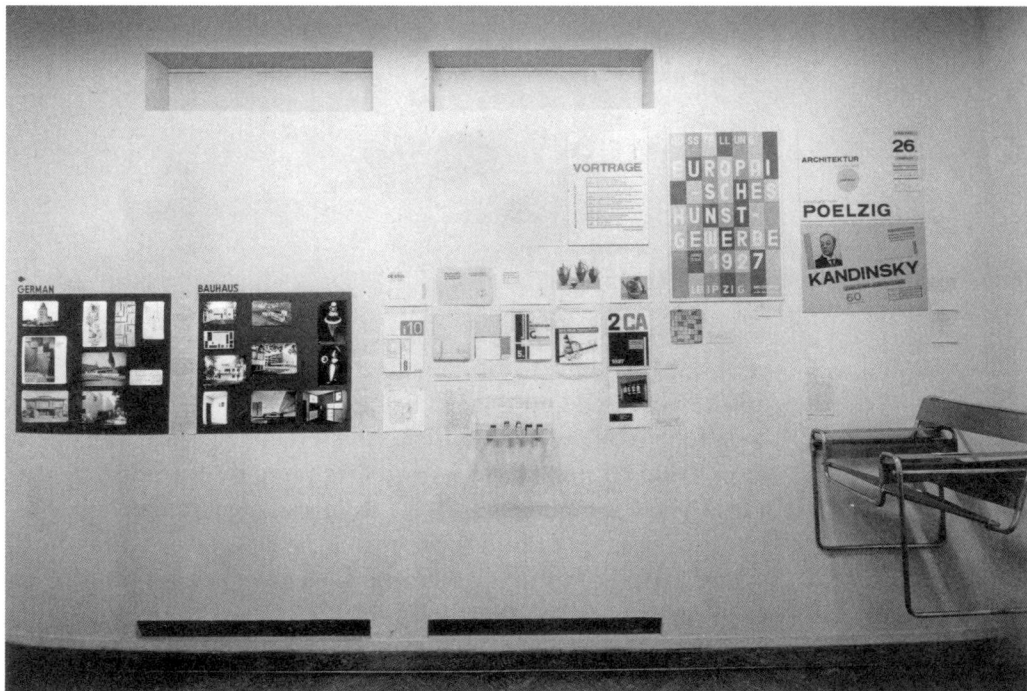

school, subsequently implemented by the Bauhaus, arose in Soviet Russia, which was on the forefront of social and cultural transformations, fueled by political shifts to the left. The active dialogue between key cultural figures of Russia and Germany is supported by a number of historical documents and by direct and indirect evidence.[11] Both groups of sources essentially confirm the assumption that during a short period of time—1918 to 1919—a group of left-leaning Russian artists, including Kandinsky, Tatlin, and others, supported by the Bolshevik government and aware of their leading role, developed a radical program for the creation of the new art and the new school. But perhaps the most remarkable thing is that this leadership not only was not disputed, but was clearly recognized by the founders of the Bauhaus. Among those who enthusiastically responded to this revolutionary "call" was Walter Gropius.

World War I had dire consequences for both countries—which went from being on the opposite sides of the battlefield to being tentative allies after the Treaty of Brest-Litovsk. As both countries underwent leftist revolutions—Russia in October 1917 and Germany in November 1918—this alliance naturally extended from the political sphere to the cultural one, supported by progressively minded luminaries in both countries. The changes in Russia had a statewide impact and occurred on a much greater scale than in Germany. Immediately after the revolution, the Bolshevik government started the reorganization of all spheres of culture and education in an effort led by Anatoly Lunacharsky, the head of the People's Commissariat of Education [Narkompros].[12] An integral part of Narkompros was the Department of Visual Arts, known as IZO [*Otdel izobrazitelnykh iskusstv*], established in Petrograd in January 1918.[13] This department, headed by the most progressive "futurist" artists of the time, was responsible, according to its founding member Kandinsky, for creating a "new artistic culture"—one in which artists should take a "direct and active part in all spheres of artistic life."[14] The so-called "Art Program" developed by IZO called for: "[t]he elimination of the classifying distinctions between sculptor and plasterer, painter and sign painter; the elevation of crafts to an art, ... the fertilization of the crafts by the artist innovator."[15] Striking here are the similarities to Gropius's founding manifesto for the Bauhaus, unveiled in April 1919, which famously called on architects, sculptors, and painters to "return to the crafts," proclaiming that there is "no essential difference between the artist and the craftsman" and urging the creation of "a new guild of crafts-men without the class distinctions that raise an arrogant barrier between craftsman and artist!"[16]

Although communication between Russia and Germany was challenging at the time, an intensive cultural exchange was established starting in late 1918 between the members of IZO and leftist German organizations, such as the Workers' Council for the Arts [*Arbeitsrat für Kunst*], of which Walter Gropius was chairman at the time, as well as the November Group and the West-Ost Group.[17] Kandinsky, who played a key role as a member of IZO's steering committee from its establishment, writes: "During the early days ... even a more significant problem was raised, that of extending the sphere of the artists['] activity ... beyond the borders of the Russian Republic and uniting not merely Russian but also foreign artists to attain these goals."[18]

Gropius personally was most likely familiar with the Moscow "Art Program" through painter Ludwig Bähr, a close associate of Kandinsky, who was delegated a mission by IZO Narkompros in December 1918—four months before the founding of the Bauhaus—to disseminate Soviet art materials to leftist German organizations. Bähr was an artist and a former German officer who had been attached to the German diplomatic mission in Moscow after the Treaty.[19] Here is how Kandinsky describes this official initiative:

> ... [T]he Bureau charged the artist [Ludwig Bähr] (along with several other artistic missions of international scope), to convey an appeal to German artists' organizations of a similar mind to [the] Department. This appeal consisted of a comradely greeting and a call to internationally unite in the creation of a new artistic culture.[20]

A wider network of German artists received the details of the radical institutional reorganization of the arts in Russia through *Das Kunstblatt*. The issue published in March 1919 featured a report containing the Lunacharsky commissariat's "Art Program"—a month before Gropius issued *The Bauhaus Manifesto and Program*.[21] The possibility that the programs Bähr distributed influenced Gropius's manifesto is supported by the evidence of communication between IZO and the Workers' Art Council.[22] On January 26, 1919, Gropius, Bruno Taut, and Max Pech-stein, representing the Workers' Art Council and the November Group, sent a reply to the Moscow "greeting" in which they enthusiastically supported the endeavors of IZO: "We greet with warmest sympathy the efforts of the Moscow Collegium for Art. We are prepared to work

Anna Bokov

Vkhutemas and the Bauhaus

261

Fig. 7. "An Approximate
Distribution of the Art
Movements in Painting for
Candidates Nominated at
Free State Workshops,"
Svomas, Moscow, 1918.

in unity with the Collegium, and with all artists of all as yet unaligned
nations."[23] The bilateral dialogue between German and Russian artists
was as energetic as ever at this historical moment. Kandinsky quotes
another letter, this time by the West-Ost Group, from March 3, 1919:

> The West-Ost Group of radical artists in Baden replies with greetings
> to the appeal by Russian artists to their German comrades, celebrating
> the all-embracing victory of the new, sincere spirit. It rejoices in the orga-
> nization and the success of consistently pursued leftist politics.[24]

Kandinsky attributed the exalted tone of the letter of the German
artists to the "impossibility of putting their ideas into practice"—in
contrast to the "freedom" that the Russian artists enjoyed. West-Ost
members concluded by asking "the Moscow Collegium" for further
information about its "progress that would serve as authoritative
confirmation of our own activities."[25] It is clear from these accounts
that the exchange between Russia and Germany during 1918–20 was
taking place in the most intense manner—as both sides inspired and
supported one another's cultural initiatives and educational projects.
It is possible to contend that massive shifts in art education in Soviet
Russia just after the revolution played a formative role in the conception of the Bauhaus while, in turn, the idea of the Bauhaus as a
synthetic school was central for the establishment of Vkhutemas.

Free state art studios

An essential mechanism for implementing the "new culture" in Russia
was a massive educational reform initiated in February 1918, which
reorganized, among other things, the entire system of higher art
education.[26] One of the first steps of the reform was the dissolution of
the existing art institutions—art academies and applied arts schools—
and the creation in their place of two Free State Art Studios or Workshops [masterskie], known as First and Second Svomas, in September
1918.[27] The term "studios "or "workshops," used in the context of
higher education, intended to communicate the importance of crafts
and industrial production as a foundation of artistic practice—an
idea fundamental to the Bauhaus as well. However, unlike the Grand
Ducal Vocational Arts School under Henry van de Velde preceding the
Weimar Bauhaus, which had already established workshops and artists'
studios to prepare works in conjunction with industry, Svomas "workshops" went beyond that and were set up as experimental laboratories
hosting different artistic directions, from Realism to Suprematism.

Svomas was founded on the principles of student governance and complete artistic freedom, which at times escalated to complete anarchy. Its mission was to make artistic training accessible to "anyone willing to dedicate themselves to art."[28] It was free to everyone and open to the previously underprivileged social groups. Entrance exams were abolished and the curriculum had no defined structure. In the Free Studios, "every student was given the opportunity to develop their own individuality in any direction of their choice."[29]

At Svomas, professors were nominated and then elected by the student committees in a truly democratic manner. They then went through an elaborate election process involving both faculty and students. An important agenda of this art-education reform was to introduce "the representatives of all the new trends" of the avant-garde as part of the new structure of the Free Studios. The composition of the faculty reflected the emergent field of modern art—Suprematism, Cubism, and Futurism. Professors would propose their candidacy and students would freely cast their vote. A document titled "An Approximate Distribution of the Art Movements in Painting for Candidates Nominated at Free State Workshops" from fall 1918 shows how important the goal was of developing an equal representation of the different movements that were emerging at the time.[fig. 7][30] Svomas faculty candidates were divided into six groups, including:

I. Realism-Naturalism
II. Impressionism
III. Neo-Impressionism
IV. Cubism
V. Suprematism
VI. Futurism. [31]

Anna
Bokov

Vkhutemas
and
the
Bauhaus

Fig.8a, b. Free State Art Studios (Svomas) student records, academic year 1918–19. Kandinsky Studio sign-up list. Svomas, Moscow, 1918.

Fig.9. Paul Klee and Wassily Kandinsky, Dessau, 1927. Photograph by Nina Kandinsky.

The first Svomas elections occurred in September 1918, with faculty comprising such artists as Kandinsky, Tatlin, and Malevich. The sign-up "list of student-apprentices of the 2nd Free State Studios for the 1918–19 academic year" reveals that Kandinsky, for example, originally only got four students. However, subsequent documents reveal that Kandinsky taught at Svomas for the entire two years (from fall 1918 to spring 1920). His studio counted 50 students the first year and 38 the following. Ten of these students studied with him for two years. [fig. 8 a, b] [32]

It became clear after the first academic year that although radical in principle, Free Studios lacked any cohesiveness or "synthetic unity," something Kandinsky lamented. [33] On the other hand, a new "Weimar Academy," i. e. the Bauhaus, pursued that unity not merely mechanically, as in "our art schools," but "organically." Both the Workers' Art Council and the November Group were composed of "not simply painters, or sculptors, or artists"; rather, "members of all three professions participate in the general organization." [34] Likewise, at the newly formed Bauhaus, according to Kandinsky, "every student is obliged to study all three arts." [35] Clearly, that model was better suited for systematically developing the "new artistic culture." After two years, the chaotic Free Studios were consolidated into the Higher Art and Technical Studios, or Vkhutemas—this time following the lead of the Bauhaus, and conceived as a unitary inter-disciplinary institution, not least through the efforts of Kandinsky and his circle.

Kandinsky also implemented a version of the synthetic model in the research organizations he founded. In December 1919 he established the so-called Council of Masters in Moscow, which was promptly renamed the Institute of Artistic Culture (Inkhuk) in March 1920. [36] Inkhuk members played a key role in developing the foundational ideas of Vkhutemas—in particular, a system of preliminary courses—initially under the guidance of Kandinsky, and clearly inspired by the developments in Weimar. By November 1920, however, the dynamic within Inkhuk had shifted. Kandinsky's "Monumental Art Program" with its ideas of synthesis and analysis of "elements of art" was considered overly individualistic or "subjective" by the younger artists, led by Rodchenko, who instead advocated for an "objective" approach and set up a "Group of Objective Analysis." Kandinsky was forced to leave Inkhuk. In late 1921, along with his wife, Nina, he left for

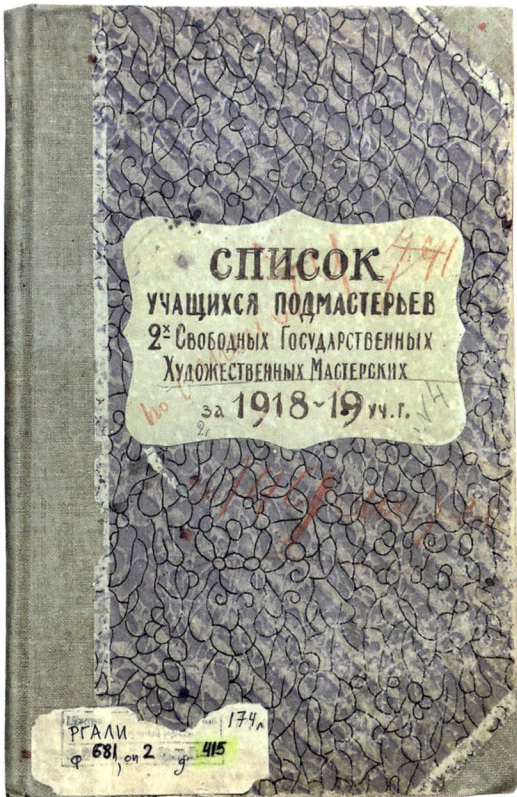

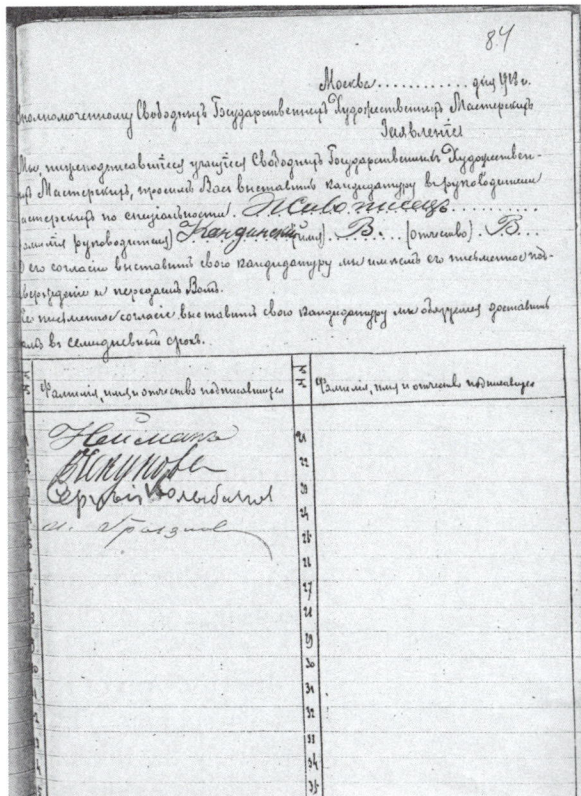

Germany on an official mission—to establish a branch of the Russian Academy of Artistic Sciences (RAKHN) in Berlin. A few months later they moved to Weimar, where Kandinsky was given a teaching appointment at the Bauhaus in the summer of 1922. He taught until the school's closure in 1933, making his the longest tenure at the Bauhaus.[37] The mission from Moscow seems to have been annulled without further ado, or at the latest in 1928, when he received German citizenship and lost his allegiance to Russia.[fig.9]

Instruction of the masses

Although supported by the local governments of Weimar and Dessau, respectively, the Bauhaus never enjoyed the high-profile union of official policy on the state level and educational agenda of its Soviet counterpart. Moreover, although it, too, embraced diverse candidates "of all levels," it charged a tuition fee and attempted to earn revenue, especially from the sale of its industrial design products. Vkhutemas, in contrast, was free to everyone.[38] Moreover, members of formerly disenfranchised classes were encouraged to apply; in fact, there was a quota for students of formerly more advantageous wealthy backgrounds. Some of the students received a form of subsidy through housing and food stamps, while others had to work part-time and even full-time in order to survive.

While Gropius initially aimed only to "return to the crafts," he promptly recast the Bauhaus workshops as "essentially laboratories in which prototypes of products suitable for mass production and typical of our time are carefully developed and constantly improved," echoing the initial call to train specialists for "modern industry" at the Soviet institution.[39] Vkhutemas further articulated its mission, in turn reminiscent of that of the Bauhaus, by aiming to train "a new type of specialist, who not only can manage production and conduct research based on the most recent conquests of science and technology but also has the ability to be the organizer and leader of the creative initiative of the masses."[40] The student body at Vkhutemas was about ten to twenty times larger than that of the Bauhaus. In 1924–25, for example, Vkhutemas had 1,445 students. That same year the Bauhaus counted 127.[41] The size of Vkhutemas, on the one hand, as well as its agenda of modernization, on the other, posed a very different set of challenges and created a need for a standardized pedagogical approach across disciplines.

While outwardly silent on the matter of Vkhutemas, Barr privately acknowledged the school. He even went so far as to provide a comparison of Vkhutemas and the Bauhaus in his diary, something he would not have done had he felt that Vkhutemas was not a noteworthy institution at the time. The question of the "chief differences between the two" is perhaps best summarized by his dialogue with artist David Sterenberg, the head of IZO and a professor at Vkhutemas. According to Barr, Sterenberg stated that "the Bauhaus aimed to develop an individual, whereas the Moscow workshops focused on developing the masses."[42] Sterenberg's comment, dismissed by Barr and others as "superficial and doctrinaire," nonetheless had far-reaching implications. Indeed, the difference between Vkhutemas and the Bauhaus was not a mere matter of enrollment. Predicated on a radically different approach to design education, the Soviet model was socially and ideologically distinct. If the Bauhaus, especially in its Weimar phase, was about educating an "artist-craftsman" who was first and foremost an individual, Vkhutemas was established in order to fulfill an ambitious political mandate of educating the working-class society. It was not simply a school, but an instrument for reconceptualizing and reorganizing an entire rationale of life on a statewide level and on a mass scale.

Preliminary Course

The exchange between art, architecture, and the production departments at Vkhutemas was facilitated by a system of foundational training, which was developed by a group of artists and architects—members of the Inkhuk. Founded the same year as Vkhutemas, the Institute of Artistic Culture was conceived by its first director, Wassily Kandinsky, as a research organization for developing the scientific basis for visual, spatial, and temporal arts. This "new system of training and education" became mandatory for all students, irrespective of their subsequent specialization, starting in 1923. Originally meant to last two years, it aimed "to give students the core knowledge and skills of artistic craftsmanship, which were shared by all branches of the fine arts and served as the basis for a new synthetic art."[43] The establishment of the Core Division was a powerful strategic step towards defining Vkhutemas as an institution, consolidating its avant-garde leadership, and directing its overall educational vector.[44]

At both Vkhutemas and the Bauhaus, training progressed from basic and broad to specialized. According to Gropius's famous curriculum diagram of 1922, the Preliminary Course [*Vorkurs*] took one semester and included "the elementary study of form and the study of materials." **[fig. 10a, b]** Upon completing it, Bauhaus students gradually proceeded towards their specialization, taking five types of classes in the process: the Study of Nature, the Study of Space, the Study of Construction and Representation, the Study of Materials and Tools, and Color and Composition. The culmination of the Bauhaus preliminary and intermediate training—at the center of the diagram—was *Bau*, translated as "building" or "construction." The idea of the basic training—the great equalizer—originates in the idea of artistic synthesis, which Gropius calls the "merging of all the arts under the umbrella of great architecture." In his letter responding to the "Art Program" of the Russian artists, quoted by Kandinsky, Gropius elaborates on his educational program for the Bauhaus:

> The proposed curriculum also follows from this thought. Realizing that it is impossible to learn (to be taught) art, we consider it necessary to give all artists of visual arts (architects, artisans, artists, sculptors) the same basic training: each of them should be trained in some craft in the educational workshops that should be arranged by the state. The theoretical end of art education should be a special architectural faculty—at universities that would unite all the sciences related to art. A person striving for higher knowledge will find here spiritual foundations for understanding art as the cause of the entire nation ...[45]

At Vkhutemas, in turn, the focus of the Preliminary Course lay in the search for universal formal principles across all disciplines and in the examination of abstract elements of art. The school's foundational curriculum was developed by several faculty—all of whom at one point were members of the Working Group of Objective Analysis at Inkhuk. The Group, led by Rodchenko, included Varvara Stepanova, Lyubov Popova and Alexander Vesnin, Boris Korolev, Alexey Babichev, Anton Lavinsky, Vladimir Krinsky, Nikolay Dokuchaev, and Nikolay Ladovsky. Their goal was to identify and analyze the fundamental elements common to all visual and plastic arts. The research resulted in the general concept for the curriculum—that of a "quartet" of four thematic units [*kontsenters*]—"Graphics" [*grafika*], "Color" [*tsvet*], "Volume" [*ob'em*], and "Space" [*prostranstvo*].**[fig. 11]**

The course "Space" offered one of the earliest alternatives to

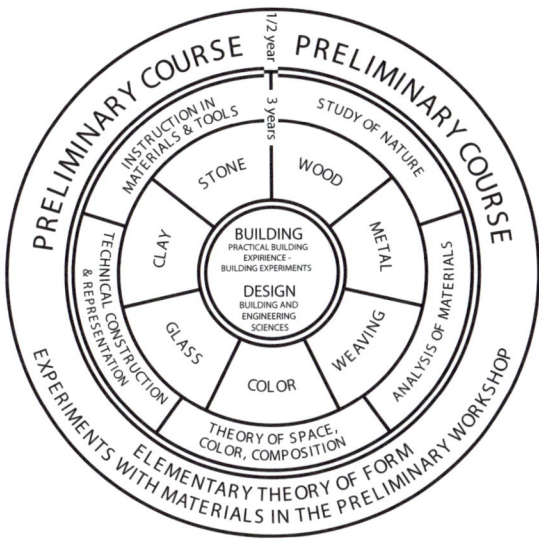

BAUHAUS
Teaching program diagram, Gropius W., 1922

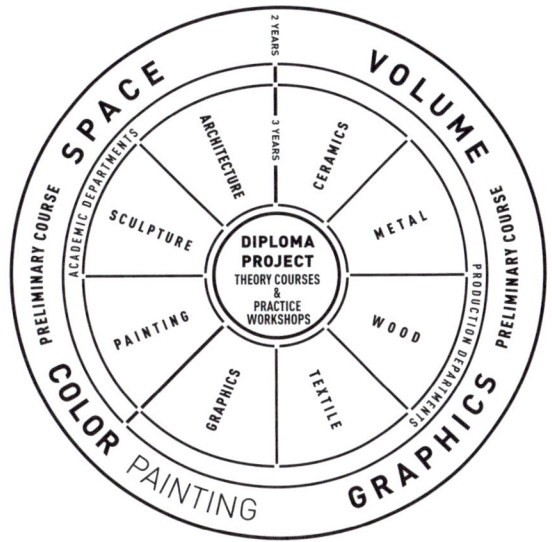

VKhUTEMAS
Teaching Program Diagram, 1923

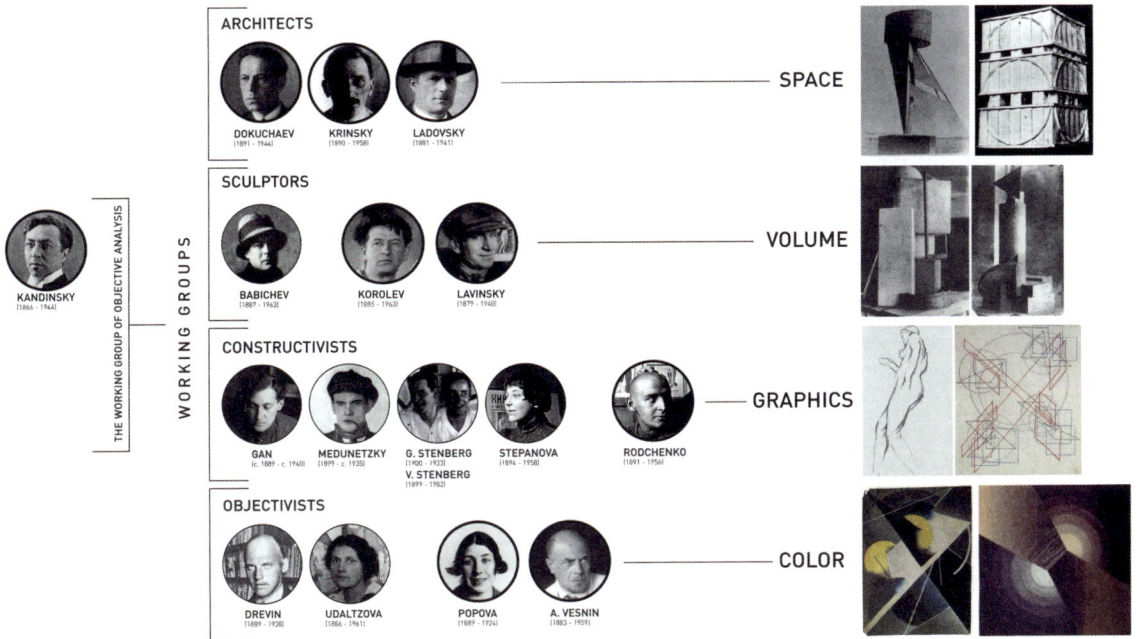

ARCHITECTS

DOKUCHAEV [1891 - 1944]
KRINSKY [1890 - 1950]
LADOVSKY [1881 - 1941]

—— SPACE

SCULPTORS

BABICHEV [1887 - 1963]
KOROLEV [1885 - 1963]
LAVINSKY [1879 - 1940]

—— VOLUME

CONSTRUCTIVISTS

GAN [c. 1889 - c. 1940]
MEDUNETZKY [1899 - c. 1935]
G. STENBERG [1900 - 1933]
V. STENBERG [1899 - 1982]
STEPANOVA [1894 - 1958]
RODCHENKO [1891 - 1956]

—— GRAPHICS

OBJECTIVISTS

DREVIN [1889 - 1938]
UDALTZOVA [1886 - 1961]
POPOVA [1889 - 1924]
A. VESNIN [1883 - 1959]

—— COLOR

KANDINSKY [1866 - 1944]

THE WORKING GROUP OF OBJECTIVE ANALYSIS

WORKING GROUPS

INKhUK (Institute of Artistic Culture) 1920 - 1924

VKhUTEMAS (Higher Artistic and Technical Studios) 1920 - 1930

269

two traditional forms of architectural training: the classical academic atelier and the system of apprenticeship at the side of a master. Originally developed for architects, "Space" became mandatory for all Vkhutemas students, regardless of their future specialization. Studio instruction—the key practice of mass education—was structured through standardized assignments. Step-by-step algorithmic operations were designed to guide the students through a set of formal exercises, starting with the most basic tasks. Students were asked, for example, to express the form of a rectangular prism of certain proportions, to counteract a mechanical force, acting on an inverted cone, or to articulate space within a cube, thereby engaging both their creative intuition and analytical skills.[fig.12]

The original core "quartet," however, was short-lived. By the end of its first academic year, 1923, some of the disciplines had already been modified, augmented or replaced by traditional academic equivalents. The course "Color," for example, was split into two: more traditional "oil painting on canvas" and an "auxiliary" discipline of color studies.[46] By 1927 the core became a one-year program, while the *Vorkurs* at the Bauhaus was run as two semesters. Despite these changes, the Core Division, like the *Vorkurs*, became a "unifying structure" of the entire school and all in all its most significant pedagogical achievement. Lunacharsky, who visited the Vkhutemas exhibition held in 1928, observed:

> *Essentially this preparatory course, where young people study elements of all artistic disciplines (painting, sculpture, graphics) in the form of separate disciplines (line, color, space, volume, and so on), turned out to be a firm result of our search, which began with the onset of the Revolution. And that result is strong. ... Now it is clear that this innovation has taken root and has become a solid foundation for future accomplishments of our artistic pedagogy.*[47]

Fig. 12. Exhibition of student work, course "Space," Vkhutemas, ca. 1927.
Fig. 13. *VKhuTeIn, Vysshiy Khudozhestvenno-Tekhnicheskiy Institut,* Moscow, 1929. Front cover of pamphlet.

After passing the Core curriculum, students would proceed to their respective specialization. Like the Bauhaus, Vkhutemas was a school offering a comprehensive education in art, architecture, and design. Its original eight departments— five so-called production departments, consisting of Graphics [*Poligrafia*], Textiles, Ceramics, Wood-, and Metalworking, and three formerly fine art departments comprising Architecture, Painting, and Sculpture—were constantly being readjusted throughout the decade. This account varies throughout the existence of Vkhutemas. Barr, for example, lists "painting, sculpture, architecture, color and various processes, typography, graphic arts, furniture designing, advertising posters, and culture of materials [*Materialien-Kultur*]."[48] Upon completing their diploma projects, Vkhutemas graduates earned the title of "engineer-artist" or "artist-technologist," indicating specialization in a certain industry, such as woodworking or ceramics, or a profession such as architecture.[fig. 13] While formally the departments were equal in terms of academic status, in reality the composite interdisciplinary structure remained somewhat disjointed. The original Vkhutemas mission, initially outlined by Inkhuk, was to integrate the production departments and the "pure half," an undertaking in which the core curriculum played an instrumental role.[49] However, once the cross-disciplinary foundational training was complete, the majority of students still preferred the more prestigious "purist" disciplines such as painting and architecture.

Architecture versus *Bau*

Both Vkhutemas and the Bauhaus "brought together ... all the disciplines of practical art" by offering instruction in fields such as woodworking, metalworking, textiles, graphics, as well as painting ("Color" at the Bauhaus), ceramics ("Clay" at the Bauhaus), and sculpture ("Stone" at the Bauhaus). While industrially developed Germany was already invested in mass production, economically devastated Russia

Anna Bokov

Vkhutemas and the Bauhaus

271

was desperate to urbanize and to take drastic measures to solve its housing shortage. As such, while the theme of architecture was implicit at the Bauhaus, it was central at Vkhutemas. At Vkhutemas, architecture was envisioned on an institutional level, as an independent department, along with the arts and production departments. It was an equal player within other fields of study and, from the outset, offered a comprehensive academic program that ran from the first year through the diploma.

At the Bauhaus, all the disciplines—"sculpture, painting, handicrafts, and the crafts"—were regarded as "inseparable components" of "a new architecture" that came together in "the unified work of art: the great structure."[50] Conceived by Gropius not as an autonomous discipline, but as the sum total of all the disciplines taught at the school, *Bau* was the final project, a synthesis of every form of visual and spatial art and industrial design. Ultimately, both schools were structured around the idea of "total design": artists claiming the right to create the entire world, "from the face of the city to the coins and the postage stamps."[51] While this approach aimed at serving the "new social order," the artistic doctrine was not subservient to it. The new artistic language was not socially determined; rather, it itself constituted the new (aesthetic) order—the new (physical) world—giving an unprecedented agency to those who were generating it.

The Program for the Work Council for Art, developed by Gropius, Taut, and others in Berlin was based on the following slogan:

Art and the people must become a unity. Art should not be a delight of the few, but should become happiness and life for the masses. ... Connecting the arts under the umbrella of architecture is our goal. From now on, only the artist, as the exponent of popular sentiment, is responsible for the visible attire of the new state. He must give form to everything: from the face of the city to the coins and the postage stamps.[52]

This idea echoed the program put forward by Narkompros and further elaborated upon by Kandinsky as a "Monumental Art Program" at the Institute of Artistic Culture. Kandinsky proposed a "monumental" art form that combined diverse fields such as music, painting, dance, and sculpture into a synthetic whole. Kandinsky's notion of synthesis was not subordinate to the discipline of architecture and differed radically from the idea of its "hegemony," which was advocated for at the Bauhaus by Gropius and at Vkhutemas by its dean at the time, Pavel Novitsky. Kandinsky points out this difference in a short article on "architecture as synthetic art" which he published in 1920. In it, he quotes a letter from Gropius sent via artist Ludwig Bähr, "who left for Germany from Moscow in December 1918, and as is known, laid the first stones to the fraternal union of German and Russian artists." In the material that Bähr managed to send to Russia there were, according to Kandinsky, "some comments relating to the actual architecture that are of outstanding interest," in particular a letter by Gropius, who writes: [53]

> Today, I again read and thought about the program of Russian artists with great interest; beautiful thoughts are expressed in it; you yourself can see on the basis of the materials transferred to you by Bruno Taut that they essentially coincide with our aspirations, except for one moment, not fully revealed in the Russian program and which seems to us especially significant: "the merging of all the arts under the umbrella of great architecture." We would ask that the idea be conveyed to Russian artists. Art should rid itself of the stamp of salon design, once again freeing itself from the isolation that it has been in until now. The painting and the statue again, as in the past great eras, require an architectural frame; they again become an integral part of a building. [54]

"The ultimate aim of all visual arts," as Gropius proclaims in the Bauhaus Manifesto, "is the complete building!" While the Bauhaus curriculum reflected this idea by combining art courses with industrial ones and practice with theory, its ultimate achievement lay in the act of building. This was manifest in several specific structures—both imaginary and built—throughout the Bauhaus's existence. Originally envisioned as a "crystal symbol of a new faith" in a woodcut by Lyonel Feininger, this concept evolved into a landmark of functional architecture—the school itself—designed by Gropius in Dessau. With its large expanses of glass, the Dessau building embodied the modern ideal of light and technology through material (or "literal") transparency.[fig.14]

Despite the fact that Gropius's own architectural practice thrived side by side with his running of the school—often relying on student labor—the official architectural program at the Bauhaus was initiated by Gropius's successor, Swiss architect Hannes Meyer, and was not set up until 1928. At Vkhutemas, by contrast, the discipline of architecture was an equal component, if not the main one, within the overall curriculum.[55]

Furthermore, at Vkhutemas, architecture was being transformed from an elitist practice into a task of and for the masses: "the mother

БАУХАУЗ
АРХИТЕКТОР ВАЛЬТЕР ГРОПИУС

of all arts," gradually assuming a cross-disciplinary, synthesizing role. By the second half of the 1920s, architecture emerged as the dominant discipline, taking the traditional place of the fine arts, namely, painting and sculpture, as is clear from Lunacharsky's commentary on its projects:

In my opinion, the crown of Vkhutein is its architecture department. There is a huge charge of some practical, unbiased, accurate, coherent dream that can really enter into the chord of our socialist construction. Young people often have overly broad aspirations. They are already dreaming about the city, what it will be in 50 years; but how they dream—with practical inventiveness unprecedented until now, with accurate scientific calculations! [56]

From the mid-1920s onward, "in the era of emerging grandiose monumental construction," the Vkhutemas Architecture Department became the dominant unifying discipline within the institution.[57] Design education was framed as part of the larger project of industrialization and as a bridge from mass pedagogy to mass standardized construction [*massovoe stroitelstvo*], the primary mode of operation for Soviet architecture and planning starting with the First Five-Year Plan. Architecture was no longer seen as an artistic discipline; rather, it was being recast as a scientific one at the service of rapid statewide industrialization. In his opening remarks to *Arkhitektura Vkhutemas,* the school's dean Novitsky affirmed the discipline's absolute power as the chief "art of the [era of] proletarian dictatorship."[58] "All other visual arts should serve it or die," he writes. "[Architecture] will change the face of the Earth, reconstruct the everyday [*byt*], reorganize and transform our social life and work." [fig. 15] [59]

Contested legacy

Unlike the Bauhaus, Vkhutemas was not a homogenous school; rather, it was a pluralist platform for different competing factions. The composite of images shown in its publication from 1929, ranging

Fig. 15. *Arkhitektura Vkhu- temas,* Moscow, 1927. Front cover of pamphlet, design by El Lissitzky.

from functional design (the "chair for the masses") to socialist realism (academic painting), appears anachronistic. Even Osip Brik, one of the founding figures of Vkhutemas, seemed to have contempt for the school. He felt that the school was "disconnected from both ideolog- ical and practical tasks of the emerging proletarian culture." "The production departments are empty," he writes, "but to make up for this, various individual studios of painting and sculpture are being opened by second- and third-rank easel artists."[60] And yet, it is this heterogeneity of Vkhutemas, which was born out of the heated polemic of different camps and schools of thought— the Beaux-Arts and the avant-garde, the Constructivists and the Rationalists—that constituted the uniqueness of this educational condenser.

In addition to politics and ideological shifts, there were other reasons behind Vkhutemas's limited historiographic reach. Through- out the decade of its existence the school ostensibly lacked a cohesive identity. It not only brought together different camps within the Russian avant-garde but also maintained a strong conservative

Anna
Bokov

Vkhutemas
and
the
Bauhaus

275

Fig. 16a, b. *VKhuTeIn,*
Vysshiy Khudozhestvenno-
Tekhnicheskiy Institut,
Moscow, 1929. Examples of
works from the Wood- and
Metalworking Department
(a). Examples of works from
the Painting Department (b).

academic presence. This heterogeneous composition was a source of
much contention within the school, as well as a likely cause of
confusion from the "outside." Even those who visited it, such as MOMA
director Barr or Bauhaus master Hinnerk Scheper, who, together with
his wife Lou (Louise Berkenkamp)—a Bauhaus alumna—stayed in
Moscow from 1930 to 1932 to collaborate on the color scheme for the
Building Institute Malyarstroi (Wall Painting Institute), were confused
by the presence of both traditionalist and "futurist" strongholds.[61]
In an "open letter" to Vkhutein, they write:

> *You cannot paint academic nudes and at the same time construct a chair*
> *for the masses ... You are studying academic painting, but academic*
> *painting is dead—throw away its corpse. In this stifled atmosphere, nothing*
> *new can be born—wipe it off with the dust of the atelier![62]*

Yet, I would argue, it was that plurality and multiplicity of positions—
the ability to "construct a chair for the masses" *and* "to paint academic
nudes" that was integral to the nature of the school. [fig. 16 a, b] Although
Vkhutemas counted the most progressive leftist artists and architects
among its faculty—with more than ten times the number of students,
it also had more than ten times the faculty of the Bauhaus, who represented diverse positions. The fact that Vkhutemas was not a conceptually unified institution, but rather a large-scale polycentric amalga-
mation, might have contributed to the challenges in understanding the
school and to Barr's decision to exclude it from his chart. [fig. 17]

There were other reasons for Barr's conspicuous omission. While
the early 1920s witnessed an incredible optimism in terms of cultural
exchange between Soviet Russia and the West, by the end of the decade
the political climate has changed completely. Hostile international
relations and ideological divergence were having a decisive impact on
the historiography of Vkhutemas, which was seen as a product of
the communist regime, rather than a cradle of modernism. Western
art historians, including Siegfried Giedion, Nikolaus Pevsner, and
Barr, painted Vkhutemas as an instrument of Soviet propaganda and
viewed it as an ideological threat.[63] The biggest attack, however, was
carried out by the Stalinist authorities, which shut down the school
in the spring of 1930 and denounced its legacy as "formalist" and
"Trotskyist."[64]

Similar to the Bauhaus, whose faculty and students were suddenly
pressured to hide their artistic and ideological views with the arrival of
the Hitler regime, Vkhutemas affiliates had to embrace the new vision

Факультет
ПО ОБРАБОТКЕ
ДЕРЕВА
и
МЕТАЛЛА

Земляницын. „Складной стул".
Дипломная работа по деревообра-
боточному отделению. Рукова.
проф. Лисицкий и проф. Чернышев.

Л. Галактионов. „Стол разборный
приспособленный для массового
транспортирования". Дипломная
работа по металлообрабатываю-
щему отделению. Рукова. проф.
Родченко и доц. Милославский.

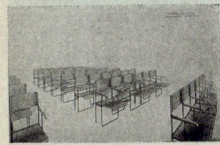

Л. Галактионов. „Кино - студия".
Дипломная работа по металло-
обрабат. отделению. Рукова. проф.
Родченко и доц. Милославский.

ЖИВОПИСНЫЙ
факультет

Мальцев. Фреска „Нальчицане".
IV курс. Монументального отделе-
ния. Мастерская Кузнецова.

Тавадзе. Дипломная работа по
станковому отделению.

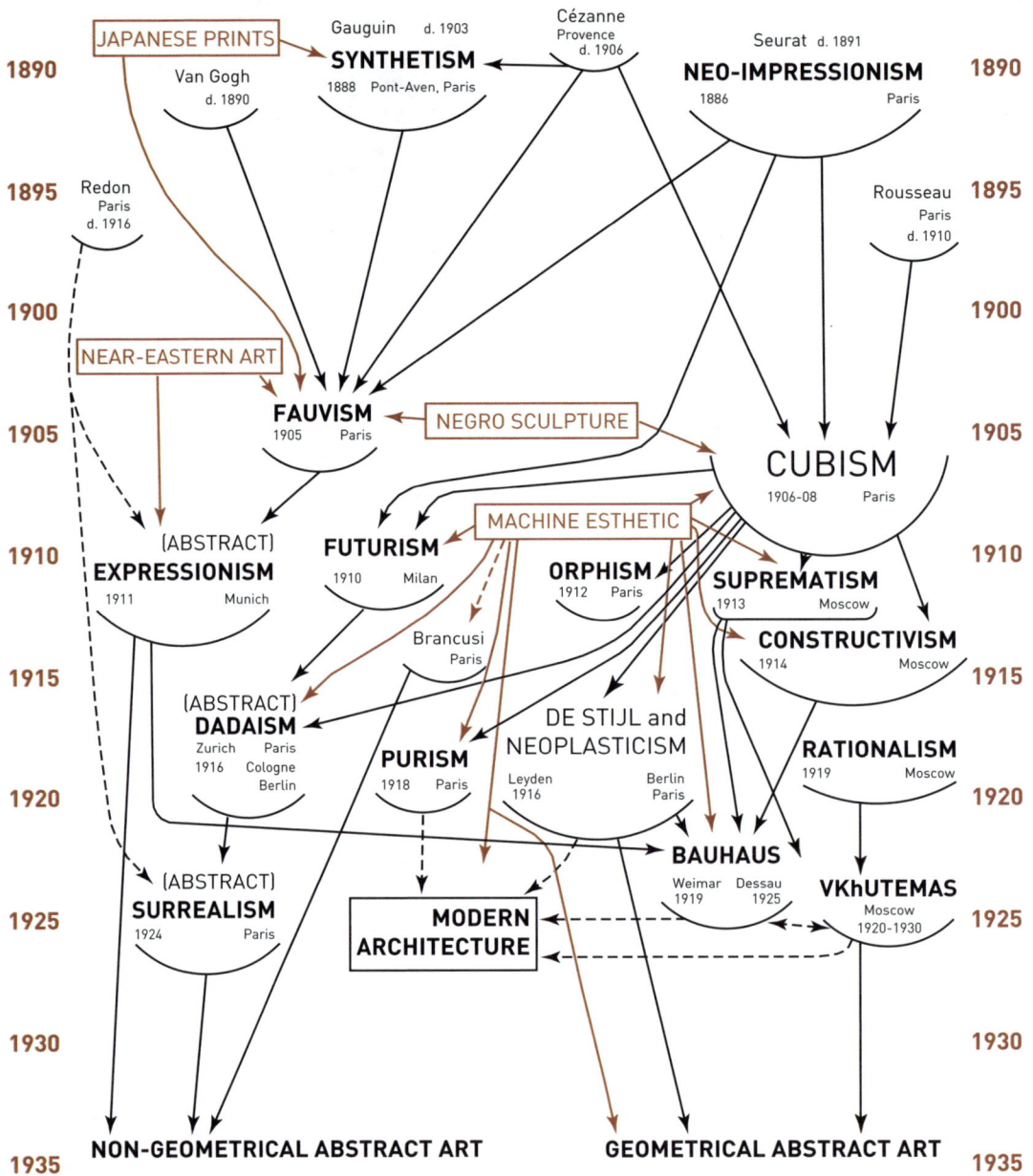

1890

JAPANESE PRINTS

Gauguin d. 1903
SYNTHETISM
1888   Pont-Aven, Paris

Van Gogh
d. 1890

Cézanne
Provence
d. 1906

Seurat d. 1891
NEO-IMPRESSIONISM
1886   Paris

1890

1895

Redon
Paris
d. 1916

Rousseau
Paris
d. 1910

1895

1900

NEAR-EASTERN ART

1900

1905

FAUVISM
1905   Paris

NEGRO SCULPTURE

CUBISM
1906-08   Paris

1905

1910

(ABSTRACT)
EXPRESSIONISM
1911   Munich

FUTURISM
1910   Milan

MACHINE ESTHETIC

ORPHISM
1912   Paris

SUPREMATISM
1913   Moscow

1910

Brancusi
Paris

CONSTRUCTIVISM
1914   Moscow

1915

(ABSTRACT)
DADAISM
Zurich   Paris
1916   Cologne
            Berlin

DE STIJL and
NEOPLASTICISM

1915

PURISM
1918   Paris

Leyden
1916

Berlin
Paris

RATIONALISM
1919   Moscow

1920

1920

1925

(ABSTRACT)
SURREALISM
1924   Paris

**MODERN
ARCHITECTURE**

BAUHAUS
Weimar Dessau
1919   1925

VKhUTEMAS
Moscow
1920-1930

1925

1930

1930

1935

NON-GEOMETRICAL ABSTRACT ART

GEOMETRICAL ABSTRACT ART

1935

278

Fig. 17. Re-inserting
Vkhutemas into Alfred H.
Barr's diagram. Diagram by
the author.

of socialism and the resultant aesthetic paradigm. Many *Bauhäusler* in Germany had to face persecution and exile, but those who could leave in time with their friends and families were able to give their Bauhaus experience and ideas a second life abroad, most famously in the United States. In contrast, their Vkhutemas colleagues were ompletely cut off from the rest of the world and forced into silence for decades.[65] Vkhutemas's vast visual institutional archives (of models, drawings, objects, and prototypes) were for the most part destroyed, and access to the school's documents remained limited. As such, this avant-garde condenser remained in nearly complete oblivion from the 1930s until its slow rediscovery both in Russia and abroad, in particular in East Germany, beginning in the late 1960s.[66]

1 This quote is from the inscription of a book copy autographed by Wassily Kandinsky. Wassily Kandinsky, *Tekst khudozhnika. Artist's Text: 25 Reproductions of Paintings 1902–1917.* Moscow: Izdatelstvo Otdela izobrazitelnykh iskusstv Narodnogo Komissariata po Prosvesh-cheniyu, 1918. The page with the portrait has an inscription from the artist: "Ognem tvori ot Kandinsky. 19. I. 1919 N.K. i pr. Moskva." (Created with (by) fire by Kandinsky. 19. I. 1919 N.K. and others. Moscow.) The copy is listed by the Auction House Litfond (Auction number 20, Rare books, manuscripts, photos and graphics, 2016).

2 Alfred H. Barr, Jr., *Cubism and Abstract Art* (New York: Museum of Modern Art, 1936).

3 Vkhutemas (Russian: Вхутемас) is an acronym of Высшие художественно-технические мастерские *(Vysshiye Khudozhestvenno-Tekhniches-kiye Masterskiye)*, translated as Higher Art and Technical Studios. In 1927, Vkhutemas was renamed Vkhutein (Russian: Вхутеин), an acronym of Высший художественно-технический институт *(Vysshiy Khudozhestvenno-Tekhnicheskiy Institut)*, translated as Higher Art and Technical Institute.

4 Vladimir Lenin, *"Dekret Sovnarkoma ob obrazovanii Vkhutemasa"* [Sovnarkom Decree on the Establishment of Vkhutemas] (December 19, 1920), in *Complete Works of V. I. Lenin*, vol. 52 (Moscow: Izdatelstvo Politicheskoy Literatury, 1967), 17. Author's translation.

5 The term is used by Alfred H. Barr, Jr. in his "Russian Diary, 1927–1928." *Defining Modern Art: Selected Writings of Alfred H. Barr, Jr.,* ed. Irving Sandler and Amy Newman (New York, 1986), 125.

6 First mentioned in print in the "Rezolut-ziya po dokladam ideologicheskoy sektsii osa, prinyataya na pervoy konferentsii Obschestva Sovremennykh Arkhitektorov v Moskve 25 aprelya 1928 goda" ["The Resolution on the Reports of the Ideological Section of the osa, adopted at the First Conference of the Society of Contemporary Architects in Moscow on April 25, 1928"], in *Sovremennaya Arkhitektura* [Contemporary Architecture] 3, ed. Gan Alexey, Moisey Ginzburg (Moscow, 1928): 78. Author's translation.

7 Sybil Gordon Kantor, *Alfred H. Barr, Jr. and the Intellectual Origins of the Museum of Modern Art* (Cambridge/London: MIT Press, 2002), 177. At the time of Barr's Moscow visit, Vkhutemas was headed by its third dean, Pavel Novitsky.

8 Kandinsky had been affiliated with Vkhutemas in two major ways: he had taught at the school's precursor, the Free State Art Studios (Svomas/sgkhm), from 1918 to 1920 andhad headed the Institute of Artistic Culture (Inkhuk), a research arm of Vkhutemas, from 1920 to 1921.

9 Sybil Gordon Kantor writes that Barr was actually introduced to El Lissitzky by Walter Gropius. See *Alfred H. Barr, Jr. and the Intellectual Origins of the Museum of Modern Art* (Cambridge/London: MIT Press, 2002), 181.

*Anna
Bokov*

Vkhutemas
and
the
Bauhaus

279

10 Walter Gropius, "Programme of the Staatliches Bauhaus in Weimar" (1919) in: *Programs and Manifestoes on 20th-Century Architecture*, ed. Ulrich Conrads (Cambridge: MIT Press, 1971), 50.

11 See Rainer K. Wick, *Teaching at the Bauhaus* (Hatje Cantz, 2000), 62.

12 Narkompros is an acronym of *Narodnyy komissariat prosveshcheniya*, or People's Commissariat for Education (or Enlightenment). Narkompros was a cultural organization founded in Soviet Russia in November 1917, replacing the former Ministry of Culture, directed by Anatoly Lunacharsky.

13 IZO is an acronym of *Otdel izobrazitelnykh iskusstv*, or Department of Visual Arts. IZO was headed by artist David Sterenberg. Its steering committee included Vladimir Tatlin (chairman and deputy of IZO), Wassily Kandinsky, Kazimir Malevich, Natan Altman, Boris Korolev, Vladimir Mayakovsky, Osip Brik, and others. See Anatoly Lunacharsky, "Ob otdele izobrazitel'nykh iskusstv" [About the Department of Visual Arts], manuscript (1920), in *Novyy Mir* 9 (1966): 236–39. Author's translation.

14 Wassily Kandinsky, "Shagi otdela izobrazitel'nykh iskusstv v mezhdunarodnoy khudozhestvennoy politike" ["Steps taken by the Department of Fine Arts in the Realm of International Art Politics"], *Khudozhestvennaya Zhizn'*, 1920. Translated in *Kandinsky: Complete Writings on Art*, ed. Kenneth C. Lindsay and Peter Vergo (Da Capo Press, 1994), 448–49.

15 Anatoly Lunacharsky, "Art Program" (1918) was published in *Das Kunstblatt* 3 (March 1919): 91–93. Quoted in Rainer K. Wick, *Teaching at the Bauhaus* (Hatje Cantz, 2000), 62.

16 Walter Gropius, "Programme of the Staatliches Bauhaus in Weimar" (Bauhaus, April 1919), in *Programs and Manifestoes on 20th-Century Architecture*, ed. Ulrich Conrads (Cambridge: MIT Press, 1970).

17 The Arbeitsrat für Kunst ("Workers' Council for Art" or "Art Soviet") was a Berlin-based organization that united architects, painters, sculptors and art critics, active 1918–21. The Council worked closely with the Novembergruppe (November Group) and the Deutscher Werkbund. The November Group merged with the Workers' Art Council in 1918. The Baden-based group of radical artists known as "West–Ost" included Walter Becker, Georg

Scholz, Vladimir Zabotin, Egon Itta, Rudolf Schlichter, Oscar Fisher, and Eugen Sepevitz.

18 Wassily Kandinsky, "Shagi Otdela izobrazitel'nykh iskusstv v mezhdunarodnoy khudozhestvennoy politike" ["Steps Taken by the Department of Fine Arts in the Realm of International Art Politics"], *Khudozhestvennaya Zhizn'* (1920). Translated in *Kandinsky: Complete Writings on Art*, ed. Kenneth C. Lindsay and Peter Vergo (New York: Da Capo Press, 1994), 448–49.

19 Joan Weinstein, *The End of Expressionism: Art and the November Revolution in Germany, 1918–1919*. (Chicago/London: University of Chicago Press, 1990), 68. Kandinsky and Bähr knew each other in Munich, where Bähr, who was a lawyer, allegedly helped Kandinsky with his separation from Gabriele Münter.

20 *Kandinsky: Complete Writings on Art*, ed. Kenneth C. Lindsay and Peter Vergo (New York, 1994), 448.

21 Weinstein, 69.

22 This point was argued by one of the major Bauhaus historians, Rainer K. Wick. See Rainer K. Wick, *Teaching at the Bauhaus* (Hatje Cantz, 2000), 62.

23 *Kandinsky: Complete Writings on Art*, 450.

24 *Kandinsky: Complete Writings on Art*, 449.

25 *Kandinsky: Complete Writings on Art*, 450.

26 The Soviet educational reform instituted by Narkompros made higher education free and accessible to all, privileging those of proletarian and low-income background and abolishing pre-revolutionary quotas for minorities.

27 Svomas was also known as SGKHM (an acronym of *Svobodnye gosudarstvennye khudozhestvennye masterskiye*). Free State Art Studios were founded in several Russian cities. The Moscow Svomas was founded in 1918, replacing the Stroganov Art School (First Svomas) and the Moscow School of Painting, Sculpture, and Architecture (Second Svomas). In 1920, the two sets of Free State Art Studios were combined and reformed into Vkhutemas.

28 Svomas announcement, Moscow, 1918. Collection of the Museum of MARKHI. Courtesy of Larisa Ivanova-Veen. Author's translation.

29 Svomas announcement.

30 "Primernoye opredeleniye khudozhestvennykh techeniy zhivopisi v kandidaturakh, vystavlyayemykh v svobodnykh gosudarstvennykh masterskikh" ["An Approximate Distribution of the Art Movements in Painting for Candidates Nominated at Free State Workshops"], Moscow, 1918. Collection of the Museum of MARKHI. Courtesy of Larisa Ivanova-Veen. Author's translation.

31 "Primernoye opredeleniye."

32 Based on Svomas student records, academic years 1918–20. Collection of the Museum of MARKHI. Courtesy of Larisa Ivanova-Veen.

33 *Kandinsky: Complete Writings on Art*, 451.

34 *Kandinsky: Complete Writings on Art*, 451.

35 *Kandinsky: Complete Writings on Art*, 451.

36 Inkhuk, an acronym of *Institut Khudozhestvennoy Kultury*, is translated as Institute of Artistic Culture. The Moscow Institute of Artistic Culture was founded in the spring of 1920 as a division of IZO Narkompros. Inkhuk was defined as "an institution for the development of the science of art, exploring the essential elements of individual art, and art in general" (Inkhuk Charter, May 1920).

37 Selim O. Khan-Magomedov, *Inkhuk i ranniy konstruktivizm* [Inkhuk and Early Constructivism] (Moscow, 1994).

38 Vkhutemas's budget was distributed through Narkompros.

39 Walter Gropius, "Principles of Bauhaus Production" (1926). Translated in Ulrich Conrads, *Programs and Manifestoes on 20th-Century Architecture* (MIT Press, 1971), 96.

40 The text on the front of a diploma from MVGKHTI (Moscow Higher State Art and Technical Institute), Architecture Department, in 1930. Author's translation.

41 Khan-Magomedov, *Vkhutemas*, vol. 1 (Moscow, 1995).

42 Alfred H. Barr, Jr., "Russian Diary, 1927–1928," in *Defining Modern Art: Selected Writings of Alfred H. Barr, Jr.*, ed. Irving Sandler and Amy Newman (New York, 1986), 125.

43 *Vkhutein: Vysshee Khudozhestvenno Tekhnicheskiy Institut v Moskve* [Vkhutein: Higher Art and Technical Institute in Moscow] (Moscow: Vkhutein, 1929). Author's translation.

44 Selim Khan-Magomedov, *Vkhutemas*, vol. 1 (Moscow, 1995). *Osnovnoe Otdelenie* is translated here as Core Division.

45 Walter Gropius, letter to the Russian artists, sent via Ludwig Bähr in 1919. The letter is quoted in Wassily Kandinsky, "Arkhitektura kak sinteticheskoye iskusstvo (iz pisem i programm germanskikh khudozhnikov)"

["Architecture as Synthetic Art (from Letters and Programs of German Artists)"], *Khudozhestvennaya zhizn'* [Art Life] 4/5 (May–October 1920: 23–24. Author's translation.

46 *Vkhutein*, 1929. Author's translation.

47 Anatoly Lunacharsky, *Izvestiya* 122 (May 27, 1928). Quoted in Vitaly Lavrov, "Proyektirovaniye rabochego poselka u izmaylovskogo shosse" [Designing a Workers' Settlement at Izmailovskoe Shosse], *Stroitelstvo Moskvy* 8 (1928). Author's translation.

48 Alfred H. Barr, Jr., "Russian Diary," in *Defining Modern Art: Selected Writings of Alfred H. Barr, Jr.*, ed. Irving Sandler and Amy Newman (Harry N. Abrams, Inc.: New York, 1986), 125.

49 Osip Brik, *October* 134 (2010): 89.

50 Osip Brik, *October* 134 (2010): 89.

51 Walter Gropius, Bruno Taut et al., "Program for the Work Council for Art" (March 1919). Quoted in Gropius's letter to Russian artists. Published by Wassily Kandinsky in his article "Arkhitektura kak sinteticheskoye iskusstvo (iz pisem i programm germanskikh khudozhnikov)" ["Architecture as Synthetic Art (from Letters and Programs of German Artists)"], *Khudozhestvennaya zhizn'* [Art Life] 4/5 (May–October 1920): 23–24, in *Izbrannyye trudy po teorii iskusstva v 2 tomakh* [Selected works on the theory of art in two volumes] (Moscow, 2001). Author's translation.

52 Walter Gropius et al., "Program for the Work Council for Art."

53 Walter Gropius et al., "Program for the Work Council for Art."

54 Walter Gropius, letter to the Russian artists, quoted in Wassily Kandinsky, "Arkhitektura kak sinteticheskoye iskusstvo (iz pisem i programm germanskikh khudozhnikov)" ["Architecture as synthetic art (from letters and programs of German artists)"], *Khudozhestvennaya zhizn'* [Art Life] 4/5 (May–October 1920): 23–24. Author's translation.

55 Paradoxically, the pinnacle of Gropius's career was the Bauhaus building in Dessau. His later works in the US—the Pan Am building, Baghdad University, and Harvard dormitories, designed by TAC, were rather generic. The last director of the Bauhaus, Mies van der Rohe, became the leader in the profession.

56 Anatoly Lunacharsky, *Izvestia* 122 (May 27, 1928). Quoted in Vitaly Lavrov, "Iz poslednikh rabot arkhitekturnogo fakul'teta

Vkhuteina" ["From the Last Works of the Architectural Faculty at Vkhutein"], *Stroitelstvo Moskvy* 10 (1928). Author's translation.

57 Pavel Novitsky, "On the Architectural Construction of the Epoch," *Arkhitektura Vkhutemas (Arkhitektura.* Raboty arkhitekturnogo fakul'teta *Vkhutemasa, 1920–1927),* Moscow, 1927. Author's translation.

58 Pavel Novitsky, "On the Architectural Construction of the Epoch," *Arkhitektura Vkhutemas,* 1927. Author's translation.

59 Pavel Novitsky, "On the Architectural Construction of the Epoch," *Arkhitektura Vkhutemas,* 1927. Author's translation.

60 Osip Brik, "The Breakdown of Vkhutemas: Report on the Condition of the Higher Artistic and Technical Workshops," *LEF* 4, 1924.

61 Hinnerk Scheper and his wife, Lou Scheper-Berkenkamp, were invited to come to Moscow from July 1929 until August 1930 (and thereafter from June to September 1931). Sheper was asked to set up an "Advisory Center for Color in Architecture" at Malyarstroy in his capacity as a specialist for color design. The Schepers returned to Dessau in 1931.

62 Hinnerk and Lou Scheper, "Offener Brief an die Schüler des VCHUTEIN" (Open Letter to Vkhutein Students). Originally published in *Moskauer Rundschau* 4 (1930). In *Bauhaus v Moskve* [Bauhaus in Moscow], ed. T. Efrussi, L. Ivanova-Veen, and A. Ilycheva (Moscow: MARKHI, 2012), 3. Author's translation.

63 The undertones of the "Red scare" were ever-present in the 1930s and lasted until the fall of the Soviet Union in the early 1990s.

64 The term "formalist" was intended to describe the arbitrariness and lack of relevance to the "proletariat's needs." The term "Trotskyist" referred to denounced politician Leon Trotsky, the former leader of the communist party, who by 1930 was forced into exile by Stalin's government.

65 Vkhutemas's pedagogical practices—in particular, fragments of its core courses—were revived in a number of higher art institutions in the Soviet Union in the 1960s and continue to play a formative role in design education.

66 The visual records of student work available today were compiled mainly from personal archives by several scholars, starting in the Khrushchev era. Among the art historians responsible for preserving the heritage of Vkhutemas are Selim Khan-Magomedov (1928–2011), Vigdaria Khazanova (1924–2004), Larisa Ivanova-Veen, Alexander Lavrentiev, and others. They gathered and systematized the remnants of the school's materials by documenting the private archives of former teachers, students, and their families. Since then, institutions including the Museum of the History of Moscow Architectural School at MARKHI (Moscow Architectural Institute), also known as Museum of MARKHI, and the State Shchusev Museum of Architecture (MUAR) have been collecting Vkhutemas materials. Parallel efforts were made starting in the late 1960s at the HAB in Weimar, where faculty and students were trained in Russian and could use an institutional network of the Eastern bloc. See Christian Schädlich, "Die Moskauer Höheren künstlerisch-technischen Werkstätten und das Bauhaus," in *Wissenschaftliche Zeitschrift* 23 (1976): 472–75.

Frank Simon-Ritz

Fate of the Books: The Library at the Weimar Bauhaus

The founding in April 1919 of the Staatliches Bauhaus in Weimar—with Walter Gropius appointed as the school's first director—involved a merger of the Grand Ducal Saxon College of Fine Arts, which had been in existence since 1860, and the former Grand Ducal Vocational Arts School, which had operated from 1907 to 1915.[1] The library was also one of the areas in which the legal process by which the Bauhaus succeeded its institutional predecessor played an important role. Most notably, the College of Fine Arts, which had been founded as an art school in 1860, had a considerable holding of books and magazines: we have a detailed knowledge of this by virtue of a handwritten index that was created in 1895 and that continued up to 1916.[2] According to this document, the collection contained some 1,175 titles corresponding to approximately 2,375 single volumes. In the index, the books are organized into twenty-eight subject groups, which equates to the simplest form of classification. The individual books in each subject group were numbered consecutively with Roman numerals. This meant that each work had a unique call number.

The book holdings at the art school, or rather art college, were more geared to classical models. There were large reference works and dictionaries and encyclopedias such as Brockhaus (from 1901 onward) and general historical works by von Ranke, Burckhardt, von Raumer, Macaulay, and Buckle. General art history was represented by such works as Georg Kaspar Nagler's *Neues allgemeines Künstler-Lexicon* (1835–52), the German edition of Vasari's *Lives* (*Leben der ausgezeich-netsten Maler, Bildhauer und Baumeister*, 1832–79), and numerous artist's monographs, exhibition catalogues, catalogues raisonnées, and survey works on art history. The magazine holdings included such titles as

284

Gazette des beaux-arts (from 1862 on) and *International Art* (from 1896 onward), which corroborate the idea that people in Weimar were looking beyond the country's borders. Periodicals such as *Die Kunst für alle* (from 1886 on) and *Der Kunstwart* (from 1887 onward) formed part of the repertoire that an art college might be expected to encompass at that time.

The collection at the Vocational Arts School, in the period when it was headed by Henry van de Velde, was, relatively speaking, more modern. Here one could find texts by John Ruskin and van de Velde himself, while acknowledgment was also given to modernist movements, in the form, for instance, of the graphic design journal *Gebrauchsgraphik*. One discernible focus was on bookbinding and book art: this was surely connected with van de Velde's own activities in these areas, which consequently led to the establishment of both a bindery (1908) and a printshop (1909) at the school.[3] The library holdings here included textbooks on typeface, cover design, and printing. There were ongoing subscriptions to such journals *Archiv für Buchgewerbe* (1908–13). This stock of literature was available to the Bauhaus from the beginning. It was approached in a pragmatic way, as is borne out by the fact that the system developed at the College of Fine Arts was continued, along with the call numbers assigned on this basis.

In the documents recording the history of the Weimar Bauhaus, there are various clear indications to suggest that the library was not organized in the optimal way, starting with the fact that no one was working there full-time. Closely connected to this was the limited accessibility of the collections of books and journals. Moreover, the arrangement and cataloguing of the books left a great deal to be desired, especially from the students' point of view. This emerges from a letter written by Gropius to the "representatives of the student body," dated May 18, 1920, which reads,

> *For some time now, the intention has been to reorganize the library at the State Bauhaus in line with changing circumstances, so that the books that are currently most important and most in demand are set apart and the kinds of chaotic situations that the students keep causing in the library are prevented by means of better organization.*[4]

Gropius also asked for "2–3 students to register to assist in the reorganization process." His plea seems to have been heeded: this is corroborated by a letter Gropius received from a student, Rudolf Franz Hartogh, dated December 7, 1924, informing him that Hartogh

Frank
Simon-Ritz

Fate
of
the
Books

285

had "almost completely organized" the books so that they were now "easy to manage." In light of this, he formally asked Gropius to "discharge him from his administrative duties in the library."[5]

The reading room was initially housed in the "Ittenraum," next door to the secretariat of the director. In addition, there must also have been bookstacks from which books and journals could be ordered using a call slip. The library was managed part-time by an administrative secretary, Lotte Hirschfeld. The opening times of the reading room were Monday to Saturday from 10 am to 1 pm. From Mondays to Fridays, it was also open from 2 to 5 pm. This added up to thirty-three hours a week. However, loans and returns were only possible Monday through Thursday from 3 to 5 pm.

The secession of the more conservative-minded College of Fine Arts from the Bauhaus in April 1921—just two years after the founding of the Bauhaus—led to some revealing disputes about the library. The regional government determined that the library, which was to remain under the direction of the Bauhaus, should be used jointly by both institutions. Subsequently, the students from the newly founded College of Fine Arts, in particular, frequently complained about the meager opening hours and the poor accessibility of the books and journals. The complaints culminated in a letter from the college to the Thuringian ministry of education, dated November 15, 1922, requesting that the management of the joint library be put in the hands of the college.[6]

Quite understandably, the students wrote a letter to the college administration, dated April 16, 1924, regarding the overall stock of books and journals, stating that the library essentially consisted of works and treatises on old art and everything that pertains to this context. Their position was a polemical one: "It is our opinion that there is no justification for transferring the management of the library to an institute that has a hostile attitude to a majority of the works."[7]

The inward flow of books in the period between 1919 and 1925 can largely be reconstructed based on the fact that even in the Bauhaus period the staff in charge of the library marked new acquisitions— and also, in some exceptional cases, books from the holdings of the predecessor institutions—with the particular Bauhaus inventory stamp in use at the time. For this purpose, the two famous signets of the Weimar Bauhaus were employed, the one designed by Karl Peter Röhl (up to 1922) and the other by Oskar Schlemmer. Even if it does not involve a huge number of titles, these say something about the Weimar Bau- haus—its interests, methodology, and the way it networked with other people and institutions from cultural and academic realms. In addition to this, individual books tell stories that continue beyond the year 1925.

The allocation of the 146 documented titles to the subject groups in the classification system makes certain focuses clear. History of art and architectural history are well represented. In Group III (General Art History), records show that twenty-two books were added to the library holdings during the Bauhaus period. These twenty-two titles are distributed between call numbers III 162 and III 206—which means that in this sequence a further twenty-two books are missing. Group VI (History of Architecture) presents a similar picture. Here the college's index up to 1916 accounts for only twenty-two books; in the Bauhaus period—based on the call numbers—twenty-seven new titles were acquired, seventeen of which are still extant today.

Cultural history (Group XV) also played an important role. This group goes up to call number XV 50. If, in this case, one compares the new acquisitions from the years 1919 to 1925 with the inventory at the College of Fine Arts, which was maintained up until 1916, it quickly becomes clear that here things were completely the other way around. The older index lists thirty-four titles, none of which were transferred to the holdings of the Bauhaus library. Of the fifty books from the group that had been reorganized in the Bauhaus, twenty are still extant today.

The *Kulturen der Erde* series published in quick succession in 1922/23 by Folkwang Verlag is well represented. Twenty-two volumes had appeared by the end of 1923, of which at least nine were certainly acquired during the Bauhaus period and are still part of the Bauhaus library to this day. The spectrum of subjects covered ranged from the Incan Empire in Peru through the "Works of the Proto-Germanic Peoples" and sacred rituals in Africa to the indigenous peoples of North America. The agenda of this series of publications allows us to draw conclusions about the interests of the Weimar *Bauhäusler*.[8] The editor, Ernst Fuhrmann, set out to produce a "rough picture of what man has been able to achieve on earth." Thus, in conceptual terms, the series explicitly opposed the "intellectual Darwinism" that, with regard to the history of culture, holds the conviction that, "looking backward in time, there would naturally be an ever-greater dependence on the qualities of the apes."[9]

The holdings at the Bauhaus library also clearly show what positions were taken in the contemporary discourse on art and cultural politics immediately after World War I. What is initially striking is that the important publications of the Workers' Council for Art, which had been founded in Berlin in the winter of 1918/19 and chaired by Gropius as of December 1918, are included in the collection. Not only this, but the contemporary discourse on art-pedagogical reform movements was reflected in the library's stock of books.

Besides the books focusing on cultural history and politics, there are also titles with a more technical orientation covering crafts and materials science. These included the *Handbuch der Glasmalerei*, which must have been of considerable interest to the glass-painting workshop, and Tina Frauberger's tatting manual, the *Handbuch der Schiffchenspitze*, which would surely have acted as a textbook and illustrative material for the weaving workshop. From the point of view of graphic design, of particular interest here are the publications on official government graphics (*Amtliche Graphik*, 1918), railway advertisements (*Eisenbahnreklame*, 1922), and printed advertising material (*Werbedrucke*, 1914). Such publications would have served directly as visual material for the work in the printing workshop.

Overall, the stock of books gives the impression of belonging to a working research library. One part was directly geared to practice and served as source material and a set of guidelines for the Bauhaus workshops. But it is also true that many other works were acquired with a particular regard for the illustrations they contained. Here, too, it was a matter of broadening horizons and deriving specific stimuli from these illustrations.

In the original records covering the period at the Weimar Bauhaus, there are various references to the library of one kind or another. Thus, in a letter to Otto Meyer dated March 2, 1921, Oskar Schlemmer wrote, "Picasso. I have borrowed from the Bauhaus library a new book on him."[10] Since this work cannot be readily verified in the published inventory,[11] other evidence was needed to identify this work. In the letter quoted here, there are even more specific references to the Picasso book. In one place Schlemmer writes, "The author of the book quotes a philosopher who says, 'Man spends the first third of his life among the dead, the second third among the living, and the third third with himself." This quotation could be used to conduct a search in what is now the Weimar university library for old holdings that

The
Bauhaus
in
Weimar

288

were not directly assigned to the Bauhaus library and track down a
work from the year in question, where it can be established with a
degree of probability bordering on certitude that the title (and the
particular copy of the book) was the one Schlemmer had in his hands
in 1921. This is a work with the title *Picasso* by Maurice Raynal, published by Delphin Verlag in Munich, after the search for a publisher in
France had evidently been fruitless.[12]

As with the books, it is also apparent from the journals that
current trends were followed with some interest. The library holdings
have at least preserved the only published German-language edition of
Wendingen, which was conceived as a trilingual magazine.[fig. 1] Contemporary concepts of modernism were also followed in *Die Freude:
Blätter einer neuen Gesinnung* and in *Frühlicht* [fig. 2], the periodical edited
by Bruno Taut, which was initially published as a supplement in *Stadt-
baukunst alter und neuer Zeit.*[fig. 3]

Dealing with the current editions of ongoing journal subscriptions constitutes a particular problem in the Bauhaus library. Here the
biggest gaps can be found in the relevant groups in the library index.
The index maintained until 1916 lists twenty-nine titles in Group XXI
(art periodicals). The call numbers in the Bauhaus library run through
to XXI 56. However, between XXI 29 and XXI 56, we can now verify only
four journals in the holdings of today's university library.

In their meeting on May 26, 1923, the master of form and the
master of works at the Bauhaus also discussed the problems in dealing
with the art journals. The minutes of the meeting record that the art
journals could not be lent out. Complaints had been received that the
journals were not being handled with the proper respect. Individual
issues had disappeared altogether, or illustrations had been torn out.
For instance, the magazine *De Stijl* had lost almost all of its pictures.
In response, it was announced "that anyone caught tearing out a
picture would be liable for the loss of all the missing illustrations."[13]

In light of this, it is perfectly understandable if, in his letter dated
December 7, 1924, the reason that Hartogh gave to Gropius for asking
to be relieved of his duties supervising the library was that he could
no longer bear the responsibility "in particular, for the ill-treatment of
the magazines."

Naturally, the Bauhaus's own journalistic activities were also
included in the library holdings. This applies, for example, to the
collection "Pressestimmen (Auszüge) für das Staatliche Bauhaus

*Frank
Simon-Ritz*

Fate
of
the
Books

289

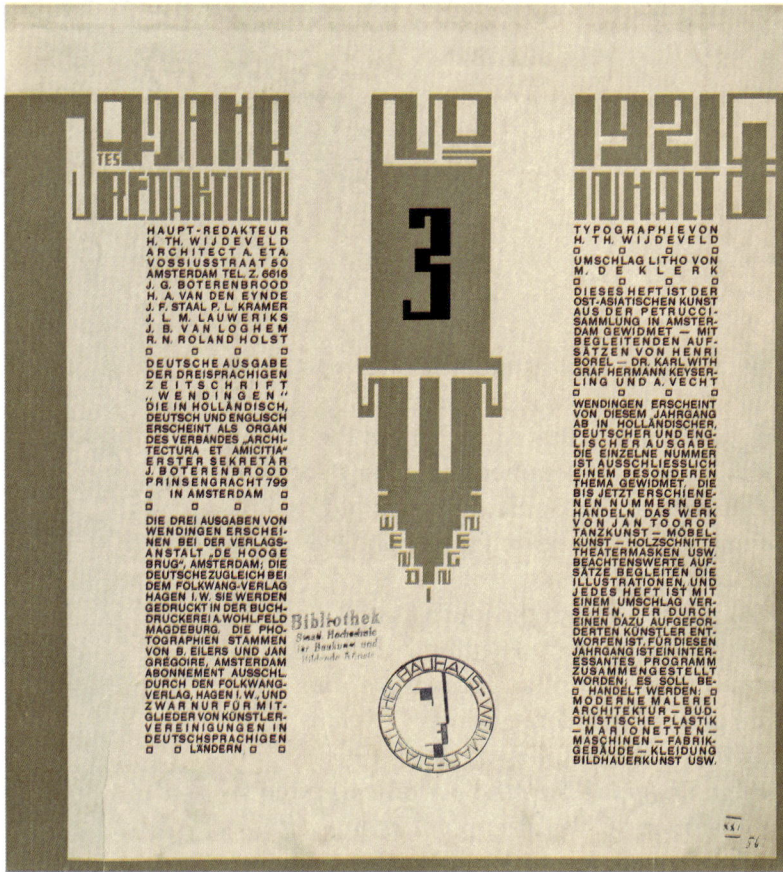

10 JAHR — DES REDAKTION — 1921 — INHALT

3

HAUPT-REDAKTEUR
H. TH. WIJDEVELD
ARCHITECT A. ETA
VOSSIUSSTRAAT 50
AMSTERDAM TEL. Z. 6616
J. G. BOTERENBROOD
H. A. VAN DEN EYNDE
J. F. STAAL P. L. KRAMER
J. L. M. LAUWERIKS
J. B. VAN LOGHEM
R. N. ROLAND HOLST

DEUTSCHE AUSGABE
DER DREISPRACHIGEN
ZEITSCHRIFT
"WENDINGEN"
DIE IN HOLLÄNDISCH,
DEUTSCH UND ENGLISCH
ERSCHEINT ALS ORGAN
DES VERBANDES "ARCHI-
TECTURA ET AMICITIA"
ERSTER SEKRETÄR
J. BOTERENBROOD
PRINSENGRACHT 799
IN AMSTERDAM

DIE DREI AUSGABEN VON
WENDINGEN ERSCHEI-
NEN BEI DER VERLAGS-
ANSTALT "DE HOOGE
BRUG", AMSTERDAM; DIE
DEUTSCHE ZUGLEICH BEI
DEM FOLKWANG-VERLAG
HAGEN I.W. SIE WERDEN
GEDRUCKT IN DER BUCH-
DRUCKEREI A. WOHLFELD
MAGDEBURG. DIE PHO-
TOGRAPHIEN STAMMEN
VON B. EILERS UND JAN
GREGOIRE, AMSTERDAM
ABONNEMENT AUSSCHL.
DURCH DEN FOLKWANG-
VERLAG, HAGEN I. W. UND
ZWAR NUR FÜR MIT-
GLIEDER VON KÜNSTLER-
VEREINIGUNGEN IN
DEUTSCHSPRACHIGEN
LÄNDERN

TYPOGRAPHIE VON
H. TH. WIJDEVELD
UMSCHLAG LITHO VON
M. DE KLERK
DIESES HEFT IST DER
OST-ASIATISCHEN KUNST
AUS DER PETRUCCI-
SAMMLUNG IN AMSTER-
DAM GEWIDMET — MIT
BEGLEITENDEN AUF-
SÄTZEN VON HENRI
BOREL — DR. KARL WITH
GRAF HERMANN KEYSER-
LING UND A. VECHT

WENDINGEN ERSCHEINT
VON DIESEM JAHRGANG
AB IN HOLLÄNDISCHER,
DEUTSCHER UND ENG-
LISCHER AUSGABE.
DIE EINZELNE NUMMER
IST AUSSCHLIESSLICH
EINEM BESONDEREN
THEMA GEWIDMET. DIE
BIS JETZT ERSCHIE-
NENEN NUMMERN BE-
HANDELN DAS WERK
VON JAN TOOROP
TANZKUNST — MÖBEL-
KUNST — HOLZSCHNITTE
THEATERMASKEN USW.
BEACHTENSWERTE AUF-
SÄTZE BEGLEITEN DIE
ILLUSTRATIONEN, UND
JEDES HEFT IST MIT
EINEM UMSCHLAG VER-
SEHEN, DER DAZU VON
EINEN DAZU AUFGEFOR-
DERTEN KÜNSTLER ENT-
WORFEN IST. FÜR DIESEN
JAHRGANG IST EIN INTER-
ESSANTES PROGRAMM
ZUSAMMENGESTELLT
WORDEN. ES SOLL BE-
HANDELT WERDEN:
MODERNE MALEREI
ARCHITEKTUR — BUD-
DHISTISCHE PLASTIK —
MARIONETTEN —
MASCHINEN — FABRIK-
GEBÄUDE — KLEIDUNG —
BILDHAUERKUNST USW.

Bibliothek
Staatl. Hochschule
für Bauhaus und
bildende Künste

WINTER 1921/22

FRÜHLICHT

HERAUSGEBER
BRUNO TAUT
KARL PETERS VERLAG IN MAGDEBURG

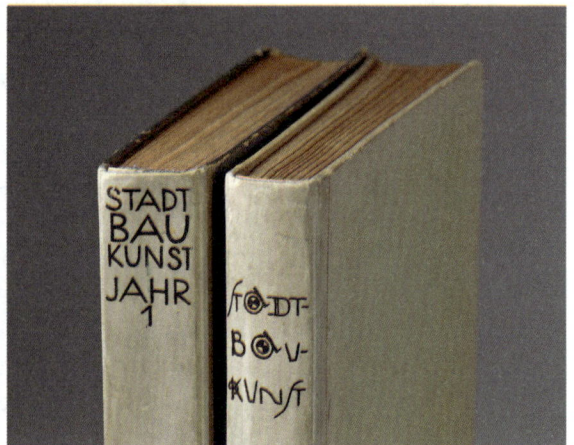

STADT
BAU
KUNST
JAHR
1

STADT-
BAU-
KUNST

Weimar" (Press comments [excerpts] for the State Bauhaus Weimar) from the fateful year 1924—the creative drive of the Bauhaus can clearly be seen in the cover and typographic design. The publication *Staatliches Bauhaus 1919–1923* also appeared in the Bauhaus's Weimar period. This documentation of the Bauhaus Exhibition of 1923 had been produced in the same year in the Bauhaus publishing house, which had premises in Weimar and Munich but did not survive the economic crisis of 1924.[14] Although other journalistic activities on the part of the Bauhaus had their origins in the Weimar period, they could, in the end, only be realized in Dessau. This was particularly true of the *Bauhausbücher* series, which was published by Langen Verlag from 1925 onward, under the creative direction of László Moholy-Nagy.[15] The first titles were produced over a period of one and a half years. The principal objective of this series was to present, explain, and defend the work that was carried out at the Bauhaus. The first eight volumes came out in October 1925—i.e., six months after the Bauhaus moved from Weimar to Dessau. All the same, original editions of at least the first (Gropius, *Internationale Architektur*) and seventh volume (*Neue Arbeiten der Bauhaus-Werkstätten*) can still be found in the holdings of the Weimar university library.

One of the special features of the Bauhaus library holdings in today's university library is that specific volumes clearly point to the bindery at the Bauhaus.[16] One particularly distinctive example of the experimental nature of the work the bindery did in the Bauhaus workshop is the 1919 book *Die Stadtkrone*, edited by Bruno Taut. The half-bound cover has certain design peculiarities that enable us to attribute it to Anny Wottitz:[17] a three-part paper covering (black, gray, and parchment), with the parchment strips enchased. A further accent is provided by the handwritten title in the form of a parchment label inscribed with colored inks.

Individual books that have been preserved in the Bauhaus library tell revealing stories, not only about the Bauhaus's Weimar years but also about their subsequent impact. One example here is the book *Utopia: Dokumente der Wirklichkeit*, published by Utopia Verlag in Weimar in 1921.[fig. 4] [18] The book was edited and published by art and literary historian Bruno Adler, who also taught art history at the Bauhaus. This book can be regarded as a "manifesto," so to speak, of the new publishing house. The book itself is divided into two parts. In the first part, Adler, in his role as editor, compiled religious and spiritual texts

Frank Simon-Ritz

Fate
of
the
Books

291

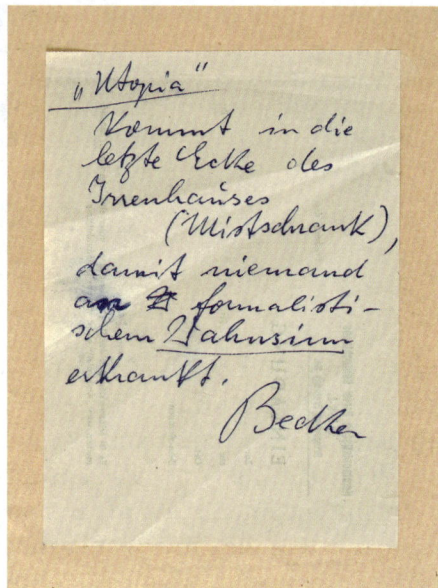

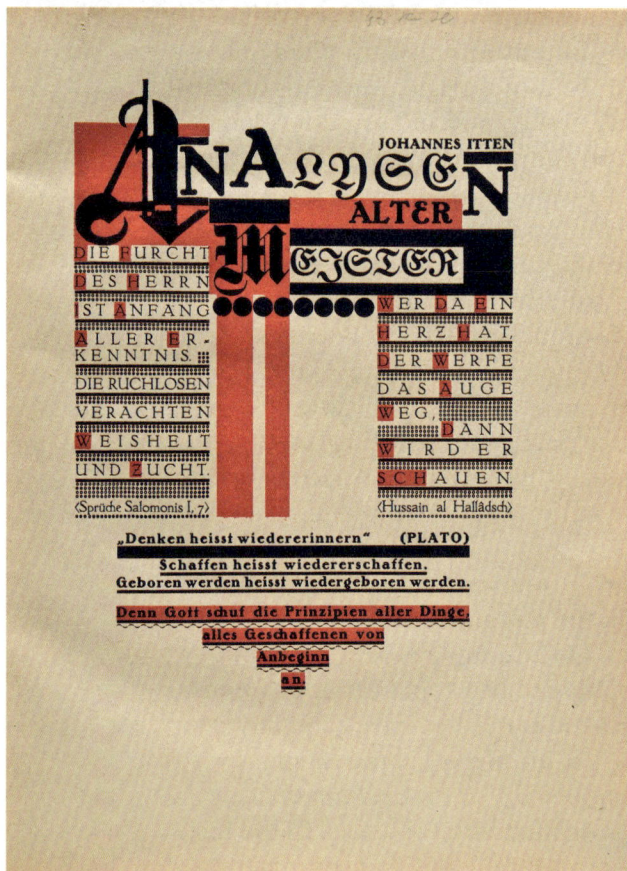

ranging from the Rigveda to Nicholas of Cusa. The second "install-ment," which can basically be seen as an independent publication, is reserved for Johannes Itten's "Analysen alter Meister" (Analyses of Old Masters)[19]—it also has a different graphic design, right down to the typeface that is used.[fig.5] The title page of this section alone indicates that what is aimed at here is not so much an intellectual textual analysis, but rather a typographic pictorial transcription. In essence, they are discrete graphic artworks in printed form commenting on the old masterpieces. Itten's "analyses" can thus be seen as paradigmatic of his design ideas and pedagogic program.

Because there was no library running full-time at the Weimar academies of art and architecture,[20] the old inventory of what is now the university library actually belonged over the years to the library of the chair for "Art Appreciation and Descriptive Geometry" (later "Theory and History of Architecture"). It was probably on his own initiative that Alfred Becker, a lecturer at the time, carried out a selective audit and appraisal of the holdings in the early 1950s based on shifting ideological conditions. On the back of the half-title of *Utopia*, he pasted a handwritten note, which brings out with unusual clarity how categorically people distanced themselves from the Bauhaus in the early GDR—in the context of the formalism debate that began in 1948: "it goes in the furthest corner of the madhouse (in the junk cabinet) to stop anyone coming down with formalistic insanity." [fig.6] This verdict proves that—after a brief "interregnum" under Hermann Henselmann from 1946 to 1949— the time was not yet ripe to build upon the innovative artistic approaches of the years between 1919 and 1925. As a result, the Department of Fine Arts, which was initially re-established after World War II, was closed in 1951.[20]

1   On the history of the founding of the Weimar Bauhaus, see Volker Wahl, "Auf dem Weg zur Bauhaus-Gründung von 1919," in *Aber wir sind! Wir wollen! Und wir schaffen! Von der Großherzoglichen Kunstschule zur Bauhaus-Univer-sität Weimar, 1860–2010*, vol. 1, ed. Frank Simon-Ritz, Klaus-Jürgen Winkler, and Gerd Zimmer-mann (Weimar, 2010), 147–63. See also the extensive collection of materials in Volker Wahl, ed., *Das Staatliche Bauhaus in Weimar: Dokumente zur Geschichte des Instituts* (Cologne, 2009).

2   Thüringisches Hauptstaatsarchiv Weimar (hereafter: THSTAW), Großherzoglich Sächsische Hochschule für bildende Kunst (Grand Ducal Saxon College of Fine Arts), no. 123.
3   See Frank Sellinat and Frank Simon-Ritz, "Henry van de Velde als Buch- und Bibliotheksgestalter in Weimar: Ein Beitrag zum Jubiläumsjahr 2013," *Imprimatur: Ein Jahrbuch für Bücherfreunde*, n. s., 23 (2013): 305–22.

Frank Simon-Ritz

Fate of the Books

4   Walter Gropius, letter to the representatives of the student body, dated May 18, 1920, THHSTAW, Staatliches Bauhaus Weimar, no. 91, sheet 1.

5   THHSTAW, Staatliches Bauhaus Weimar, no. 91, sheet 12. Gropius's reply of April 5, 1924, in which he appreciates Hartogh's work in systematizing the library, is published in his *Rudolf Franz Hartogh: 1889–1960* (Fischerhude, 1991), 23. On Hartogh, see also Cornelia Schertler, *Rudolf Franz Hartogh (1889–1960): Norddeutscher Maler und Grafiker; Monographie und Werkverzeichnis* ([Fischerhude], 2010).

6   THHSTAW, Staatliches Bauhaus Weimar, no. 91, sheet 5.

7   THHSTAW, Staatliches Bauhaus Weimar, no. 148, sheet 3a–4v.

8   See Justus H. Ulbricht, "'Bauhaus-Aufgabe: Registratur alles Besten der Vergangenheit': Zur weltanschaulichen 'Architektonik' der Bauhaus-Bibliothek," in *Die Bauhaus-Bibliothek: Versuch einer Rekonstruktion*, ed. Michael Siebenbrodt and Frank Simon-Ritz (Weimar, 2009), 51–103.

9   Ernst Fuhrmann, *Peru*, Kulturen der Erde 2 (Hagen, 1922), 7. Cited in Rainer Stamm, *Der Folkwang Verlag: Auf dem Weg zu einem imaginären Museum* (Frankfurt am Main, 1999), 83.

10   Oskar Schlemmer, *The Letters and Diaries of Oskar Schlemmer*, ed. Tut Schlemmer (Evanston, IL, 1990), 102.

11   Sylvelin Rudolf, Jana Schröder, and Frank Simon-Ritz, "Die Bibliothek des Staatlichen Bauhauses in Weimar. Ein annotiertes Verzeichnis," in Siebenbrodt and Simon-Ritz, *Die Bauhaus-Bibliothek* (see note 8), 128–69.

12   Maurice Raynal, *Picasso*, translated from the French manuscript with 8 copperplates and 95 illustrations of etchings, drawings, sculptures, and paintings (Munich, 1921). The quote used by Schlemmer can be found on p. 36.

13   Volker Wahl, ed., *Die Meisterratsprotokolle des Staatlichen Bauhauses Weimar 1919–1925* (Weimar, 2001), 311.

14   See Frank Simon-Ritz, "'Ein gut fundiertes und aussichtsreiches Unternehmen': Vom Scheitern des Bauhausverlags," *Imprimatur: Ein Jahrbuch für Bücherfreunde*, n. s., 25 (2017): 295–310.

15   See Ute Brüning, "Bauhausbücher: Grafische Synthese – synthetische Grafik," in *bauhauskommunikation: Innovative Strategien im Umgang mit Medien, interner und externer Öffentlichkeit*, ed. Patrick Rössler (Berlin, 2009), 281–96.

16   On the bindery at the Bauhaus, see Klaus-Jürgen Winkler, ed., *Bauhaus-Alben*, vol. 3, *Weberei, Wandmalerei, Glasmalerei, Buchbinderei, Steinbildhauerei* (Weimar, 2008), 176–[195].

17   On Anny Wottitz, see Nina Wiedemeyer, "Zwischen van de Velde und Bauhaus," in *Zwischen van de Velde und Bauhaus: Otto Dorfner und ein wichtiges Kapitel der Einbandkunst*, ed. Mechthild Lobisch (Halle, 1999), 82–162.

18   On Utopia Verlag, see Renate Müller-Krumbach, "Mitwirkung im Widerspruch: Der Utopia-Verlag und das Staatliche Bauhaus in Weimar," *Marginalien* 177 (2005): 32–44.

19   See Rainer K. Wick, "Kunst als mystische Schau: Johannes Ittens Beitrag zu Bruno Adlers Almanach 'Utopia' 1921," in *Esoterik am Bauhaus*, ed. Christoph Wagner (Regensburg, 2009), 175–92.

20   See Johannes Schild, "Hochschule und Bibliothek für Architektur und Bauwesen: 40 Jahre Bibliotheksarbeit an traditionsreicher Weimarer Hochschule," *Zentralblatt für Bibliothekswesen* 101 (1987): 15–22.

21   See Anne Hoormann, "Von der Weimar-Idee zur Formalismusdebatte," in Simon-Ritz, Winkler, and Zimmermann, *Aber wir sind!* (see note 1), vol. 2: 39–59.

Peter Bernhard

The "Second Faculty" at the Weimar Bauhaus, with a Sidelong Glance at Dessau

In March 1920, a Bauhaus leaflet announced "an ongoing series of evening lectures," which were to vividly set forth "the inner necessity of art today" and "its importance for culture and the individual."[1] The leaflet dubbed the speakers "the most notable artists and scholars"[2] from both Germany and abroad; the venue was to be the Oberlichtsaal at the Bauhaus, which had been laboriously renovated for the purpose.[3] The Bauhaus program published the previous year had promised "individual talks of general interest from all areas of art and science," thus enabling the Bauhaus to offer an "education based in scientific theory" alongside the training it provided in crafts, painting, and drawing.[4] Viewed from this perspective, the guest speakers could be regarded as the "second faculty" of the avant-garde school. Their importance to the overall program can be gauged by the fact that Gropius stood by this setup even when the financial situation was at its gloomiest,[5] and his successors Hannes Meyer and Ludwig Mies van der Rohe carried it on despite having very different focuses in terms of content. Thus in the fourteen years of the Bauhaus's existence there were at least 190 guest events, with around fifty of them taking place in Weimar and three in Berlin.[6] Although the list of speakers certainly comprises various "networks of the modern,"[7] overall we see here a broad spectrum of different conceptual tendencies from the artistic and cultural, sociopolitical, and scientific worlds of the interwar period, of which the Bauhaus acted as a focal point. The lecture program thus sheds light on the intellectual contexts in which the avant-garde school was located. The fact that its official launch came in this period, at the very moment when a massive denigratory press campaign had to be fended off, also shows that what

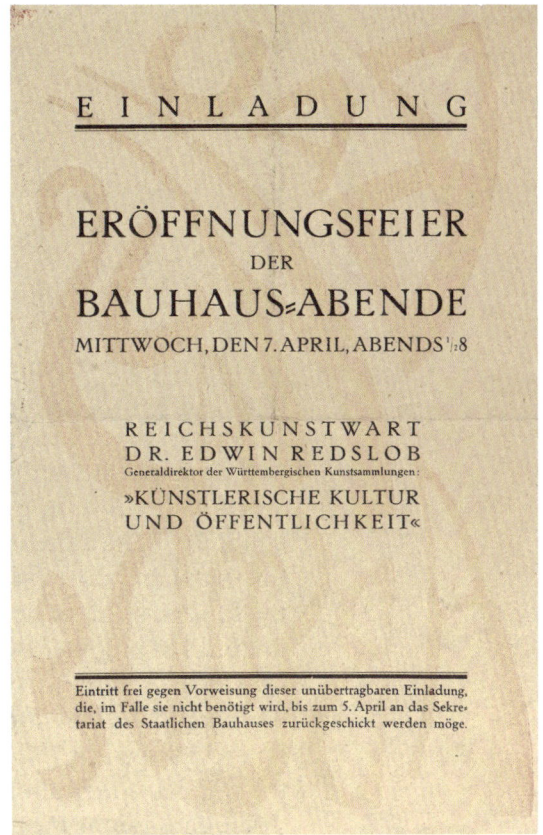

EINLADUNG

ERÖFFNUNGSFEIER
DER
BAUHAUS=ABENDE
MITTWOCH, DEN 7. APRIL, ABENDS ½8

REICHSKUNSTWART
DR. EDWIN REDSLOB
Generaldirektor der Württembergischen Kunstsammlungen:
»KÜNSTLERISCHE KULTUR
UND ÖFFENTLICHKEIT«

Eintritt frei gegen Vorweisung dieser unübertragbaren Einladung,
die, im Falle sie nicht benötigt wird, bis zum 5. April an das Sekretariat des Staatlichen Bauhauses zurückgeschickt werden möge.

are now called the Bauhaus evenings had a supplementary purpose, as a public-relations move, which is why a select group of city dignitaries were invited as well.[8] In light of this situation, persuading Edwin Redslob— newly appointed as national commissioner of the arts—to give a talk on the relationship between art and public opinion at the start of the series represented a major coup.[fig. 1] [9]

Gropius also highlighted the significance of the Bauhaus evenings as part of the school's advertising strategy in the dispute he had with Johannes Itten about the direction they should take, emphasizing the point in a circular to the Bauhaus masters: "The basis on which our work is built cannot be broad enough; today it has rather the opposite tendency of being too narrow. This is confirmed by the stories we hear of parallel experiments in Russia, where music, literature, and science are integrated as all coming from a single source. Another reason that a broad basis seems so important is that a single complex established in its own right on new principles may too easily fall prey to being stifled."[10] Accordingly, the Bauhaus director saw the people who were invited not only as kindred spirits but also as allies involved in the struggle against conservative, reactionary forces. Against this backdrop, the representatives of other progressive institutions were an obvious choice as speakers. These included Gustav Wyneken, the founder of the Freie Schulgemeinde Wickersdorf, a rural private school based on democratic self-determination by teachers and pupils that seemed to be an ideal preparation for training at the Bauhaus with its adjunct workshops and the high value it put on art classes (in fact, the Bauhaus masters sent their children to Wickersdorf, and Wickersdorf alumni went on to the Bauhaus).[11] Hedwig von Rohden and Louise Langgaard also came: in their women's community, Loheland, a school for physical education, agriculture, and crafts founded near Fulda in early 1919, they likewise saw artisanal activity as part of a holistic education[12]—Gropius was so convinced by their approach that he wanted to appoint a teacher for Loheland gymnastics at the Bauhaus.[13] Another contributor was Hermann Keyserling, whose criticisms of academic philosophy deployed arguments that were similar to those

Peter
Bernhard

The
"Second
Faculty"
at
the
Weimar
Bauhaus

297

with which the Bauhaus rejected the traditional art academies—
as an alternative, he founded his School of Wisdom in Darmstadt in
November 1920.[14] Finally there was Heinrich Vogeler, whose Barken-
hoff property situated in the Worpswede artists' colony became, after
World War I, a work-oriented commune organized in democratic
councils.[15] The adherents of anthroposophy can also be assigned to
this group of reformist schools and communities, which represented
the general spirit of optimism in the young Weimar Republic. It was
not until September 1920 that they finally created a center in Dornach
near Basel when the so-called Goetheanum was completed—a
building that aspired to "an integrative total work of art [through a]
synergy of the arts"[16] and thus seemed to fulfill the demand set out in
the Bauhaus program for the "reintegration of all the art and craft
disciplines—sculpture, painting, applied arts, and handicrafts—into
a new architecture."[17] However, although Gropius approached Rudolf
Steiner at an early stage, he received no reply to his request.[18]

The list of speakers also contains indications of expansion plans
for the Bauhaus that failed to materialize.[19] While Gropius actually
managed to implement his decision to introduce a movement class
following the Loheland performances (in the end not by employing
one of the women from the Loheland community itself, but instead
engaging music teacher Gertrud Grunow as external faculty),[20]
Carl Koch's film screenings[21] are in themselves a reminder of the
unsuccessful attempt to establish an "Experimental Center for Cinematic Art" at the Bauhaus.[22] And there would certainly not have been
so many music evenings at the Bauhaus—about a third of all the
events held there—if the efforts to recruit Arnold Schönberg or Josef
Matthias Hauer to Weimar had met with success.[23] Together with the
dance and poetry events and recitations, the musical performances
were meant to convey rhythm as a formative interdisciplinary
principle. All in all, guided by the idea of the total work of art, the
broad-based lecture program presented an outstanding opportunity
to comprehensively delineate general design tools such as contrast,
proportion, and balance.

Beyond that, some of the guest lectures also offer insight into
what was going on inside the Bauhaus. Thus, the invitations issued by
Itten and his circle[24] (namely, to Otto Rauth,[25] Anna Höllering,[26]
Emmy Heim,[27] Helge Lindberg,[28] and possibly to Adolf Hölzel as
well;[29] there were also plans to invite Hauer[30] and Ferdinand Ebner[31])

provide an outline of his vision of the Bauhaus, which ultimately proved incompatible with Gropius's. The Bauhaus director's change of heart in this regard is probably already apparent in the canceled lecture by Johannes Schlaf.[32] The writer, who believed that "he was a reincarnation of Tycho Brahe," had been running courses in both astronomy and astrology since the 1910s.[33] He prepared horoscopes for some of the Bauhäusler. There is no record of whether he also did one for Gropius, though it is perfectly possible, given that in 1919 the architect was still dreaming of an "architectural circle" in which books on astrology would also be read together.[34] But then in spring 1921 Gropius, after some hesitation, called off the Bauhaus lecture that Schlaf had agreed to give on his obscure geocentric theory—officially on financial grounds.[35]

Finally, the guest lectures also give more detailed information about certain Bauhaus students, often via the posters they made to announce the events. For instance, Karl Peter Röhl's sense of solidarity is expressed in the fact that, on the poster for the lecture by Redslob, he terms the students "Bauhaus sisters and brothers."[36] He also revives the star manikin he had designed for the Bauhaus signet,[37] perhaps with the idea of a corporate image in mind. By the same token, Friedl Dicker's familiarity with Else Lasker-Schüler's artistic perception is shown in her depiction of the latter's personal development in the poetry she wrote interwoven with Oriental elements.[fig.2, 3] [38] However, Dicker may also have revealed a tendency to jealousy when on the poster for the twelfth Bauhaus evening she "tore a crude diagonal slash" through the name of one of the invitees, Emmy Heim.[fig.4] [39]

In Dessau, the lecture program was continued along with the custom of using prestigious spaces outside the school for special events. In Weimar this was typically the "Erholung" building, a bar and restaurant with adjoining concert hall and ballroom that had originally belonged to the Erholungsgesellschaft (a bourgeois social club) and can still be found on Goetheplatz, virtually unchanged [fig.5]; in Dessau there was the Messelhaus, the former mansion of Baroness Cohn-Oppenheim designed by architect Alfred Messel [fig.6], which had been owned by the city since 1922. (It was later demolished, having suffered severe damage in an air raid in 1945.) Under the directorship of Hannes Meyer, the curriculum was by and large systematized and put on a scientific footing. In the course of this, the guest lectures

Peter
Bernhard

The
"Second
Faculty"
at
the
Weimar
Bauhaus

299

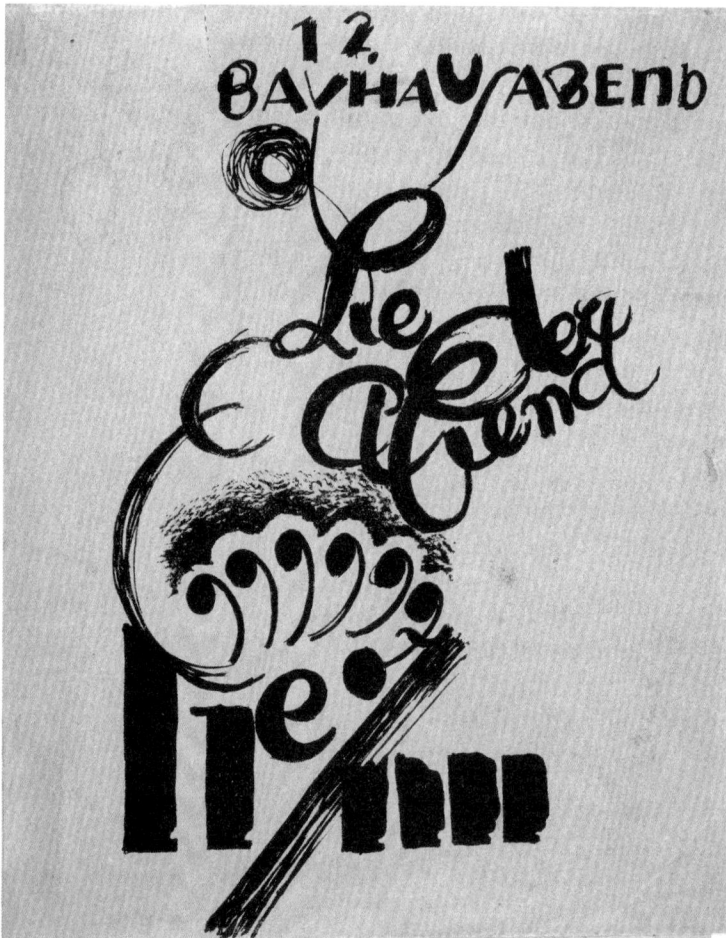

Fig. 2. Else Lasker-Schüler, *Selbstbildnis im Sternenmantel*, 1913, ink (quill and brush), chalk on paper, mounted on cardboard.

Fig. 3. Friedl Dicker, poster for the "Bauhaus evening" by Else Lasker-Schüler on April 14, 1920.

Fig. 4. Friedl Dicker, program for the "Bauhaus evening" by Emmy Heim on December 17, 1920.

Fig. 5. Erholungsgesellschaft building, circa 1895.
Fig. 6. Messelhaus in Dessau, circa 1910.
Fig. 7. Hannes Meyer, brochure *junge menschen kommt ans bauhaus!* 1929.

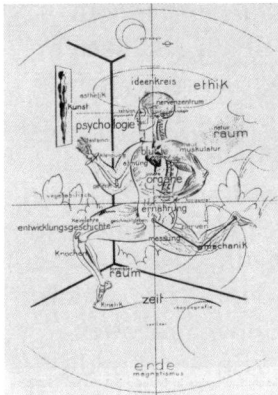

were for the first time given a fixed place in the syllabus, subdivided into eighteen (!) specialist fields and split between the two disciplines of art and science: on the art side, there were (1) Philosophy, (2) Psychology, (3) Film and Theater, (4) Music, (5) Painting and Sculpture, (6) Art History, and (7) Literature, and on the science side, (1) Advertising Theory, (2) Hygiene, (3) Anatomy, (4) Spatial Acoustics, (5) Color Theory, (6) Light Technology, (7) Physics and Chemistry, (8) Scientific Management, (9) Psychomechanics, (10) Biology, and (11) Sociology.[40] The integration of the guest lectures into the curriculum can be seen even more clearly in the prospectus devised by Meyer in 1929, *junge menschen kommt ans bauhaus* (young people, come to the bauhaus).[41] There the lecture program from summer 1928 to summer 1929 is summarized under the heading "der mensch als einheit" (the human being as a unified entity—of "mind/soul" or alternatively "body/soul"), framed by two images that illustrate this motto: [fig.7] on the one hand, a photograph of two students playing soccer in front of the Bauhaus school building, with a strong focus on the physical, giving symbolic expression to the unity of body and mind experienced there;[42] on the other, the "schematic overview"[43] that Oskar Schlemmer had added to the text announcing the new specialist field "Man" that had been introduced under his direction. He explained the specialty as follows: "a vital part of the 'new life' that is to be presented as the most modern sense of the world and of life is man's knowledge as a *cosmic being*. the conditions of his existence, his relationships to the natural and man-made environment, his mechanism and organism, his material, spiritual, and intellectual appearance—in short, man as a physical and spiritual being is both essential and relevant as an area of study."[44] Based on this, the sketch shows the profile of a person going at full speed, with X-rays seemingly shining through him so that the individual bones, organs, muscles, blood vessels, and nerve pathways can be seen. Captions appear in various places: these either emphasize the details portrayed by labeling them or point to overarching thematic areas such as nutrition, graphology, and body measurement. The running figure is surrounded by two shapes that are merely suggested in the drawing: a cube, which is identified as "formal space," and a circle whose upper and lower borders point to natural influences with the words "Astrology" and "Earth/Magnetism." Between these poles, other terms are invoked that have a bearing on the human realm, such as time, ethics, and art.

This image thus records the thematic areas covered by the list of guest lectures or connected with the professions of the speakers.

The new direction of the Bauhaus prompted by Mies van der Rohe's appointment as director seems to be evident in the guest lectures insofar as representatives of the so-called Conservative Revolution such as Hans Freyer (author of *Revolution von rechts*) and Felix Krueger (a member of the Militant League for German Culture) appeared there under his aegis.[45] However, this superficial impression is incorrect inasmuch as Meyer had already started collaborating with Krueger's Institute of Psychology at Leipzig University, and despite its "antithetical ... world view,"[46] he was still planning, shortly before his abrupt dismissal, to develop it further. Thus the guest lectures by Krueger's colleagues in the first six months of Mies's directorship had already been set up by Meyer (Meyer had also scheduled a talk with Krueger himself, although it was then postponed for some months).[47] The fact that Meyer also invited representatives of logical empiricism, who were opposed to the Leipzig school on grounds of both content and political persuasion—and here, too, Mies inherited a prearranged series of lectures (with Philipp Frank of the Vienna Circle)—shows that the Bauhaus virtually forced a collision between different points of view.[48] The guest lectures also served to further this end.

1 "Bauhaus evenings" invitation, Bauhaus-Archiv Berlin, inv. no. 11268.

2 "Bauhaus evenings" invitation.

3 The hall retained a large heating stove (see Thüringisches Hauptstaatsarchiv Weimar, Staatliches Bauhaus Weimar, no. 95, sheet 35) and had recently had electricity installed (Thüringisches Hauptstaatsarchiv Weimar, no. 27, sheet 14). The ornamental painting had been carried out by Johannes Itten with some of the students he had brought with him from Vienna (among them Franz Skala, Carl Auböck, and Alfred Lipovec): "The rounded end walls of the large communal hall were colorfully decorated with centered color circles, moving from the white of the innermost circle to dark blue via gradually darkening shades of yellow. The other walls glowed dark purple." Wulf Herzogenrath and Stefan Kraus, eds., *Bauhaus-Utopien: Arbeiten auf Papier* (Stuttgart, 1988), 171; see Volker Wahl, ed., *Die Meisterratsprotokolle des Staatlichen Bau-*

hauses Weimar: 1919 bis 1925 (Weimar, 2001), 423.

4 Walter Gropius, "Manifest und Programm des Staatlichen Bauhauses Weimar," in *Das Staatliche Bauhaus in Weimar: Dokumente zur Geschichte des Instituts 1919–1926*, ed. Volker Wahl (Cologne, 2009), 97–100, here: 99.

5 At the meeting of the council of masters on September 20, 1920, Gropius was obliged to announce a deficit of around 1,200 marks for the Bauhaus evenings: see Wahl, *Die Meisterrats-protokolle* (see note 3). The closed Bauhaus evenings were free for members of the school; people invited from outside of the school could purchase tickets in various price categories. In winter 1921 this system was replaced by admission through voluntary donation: see Wahl, 108–09. For more contextual background and details of the inauguration and organization of the Bauhaus evenings in Weimar, see Peter Bernhard, introduction in *bauhausvorträge: Gastredner am Weimarer Bauhaus 1919–1925*, ed. Peter Bernhard, *Neue Bauhausbücher, Neue Zählung*, vol. 4 (Berlin, 2017), 13–23.

6 Because no complete list has survived and the events were not open to the public, it is difficult to determine the nature of the individual lectures. On the current state of research on this subject, see Bernhard.

7 For analysis of this term, see Jan Broch, Markus Rassiller, Daniel Scholl, eds., *Netzwerke der Moderne: Erkundungen und Strategien* (Würzburg, 2007).

8 Former Bauhaus student Toni Schrammen proudly wrote to her mother in October 1920: "On Sunday, we were invited to [Hedwig] Rücker's house. Yesterday to the Bauhaus evening. A huge honor, don't you think?" Letter dated October 27, 1920, Bauhaus-Archiv Berlin, Toni Schrammen documents, folder 4.

9 Redslob's talk has not been preserved verbatim, but there are contemporary accounts of it from people who attended the lecture. See Volker Wahl, "Ein Weimaraner für das Staatliche Bauhaus Weimar: Edwin Redslob," in Bernhard, *bauhausvorträge* (see note 5), 81–94.

10 Walter Gropius's explanation on February 3, 1922, of the basic conceptual and practical questions facing the Bauhaus, in Wahl, *Das Staatliche Bauhaus in Weimar* (see note 4), 157–61, here: 157. Gropius had already written to Adolf Behne in this vein on June 2, 1920: "The thing is, we now have no possibility of pursuing partial reform; rather we must tackle the entirety of life: housing, parenting, gymnastics, and many other areas." Cited in Winfried Nerdinger, *Walter Gropius* (Berlin, 1985), 58. When he talks of "parallel experiments in Russia," he is referring to Vkhutemas in Moscow. See Barbara Kreis, "Modell Moskau? Vchutemas, die Höheren Künstlerisch-Technischen Werkstätten," in *bauhaus global: Gesammelte Beiträge der Konferenz bauhaus global vom 21. bis 26. September 2009*, ed. Bauhaus-Archiv Berlin, *Neue Bauhausbücher, Neue Zählung*, vol. 3 (Berlin, 2010), 123–32.

11 See Peter Bernhard, "Die Freie Schulgemeinde Wickersdorf und das Staatliche Bauhaus Weimar," in Bernhard, *bauhausvorträge* (see note 5), 59–65.

12 See Ute Ackermann, "Abend ausverkauft: Reklame unnötig," in Bernhard, *bauhausvorträge*, 49–57.

13 See Ute Ackermann, "'In Freiheit dressiert': Magdalene Trenkel und die Klassische Gymnastik am Weimarer Bauhaus," in Bernhard, 25–36.

14 See Peter Bernhard, "Schule der Weisheit und Bauhaus," in *bauhausvorträge*, 75–80. Gropius would certainly have fit in well in this context as the architect of the Academy of Philosophy in Erlangen. See Christian Thiel, "Carnap und die wissenschaftliche Philosophie auf der Erlanger Tagung 1923," in *Wien – Berlin – Prag. Der Aufstieg der wissenschaftlichen Philosophie*, ed. Rudolf Haller and Friedrich Stadler (Vienna, 1993), 175–88.

15 See Riccardo Bavaj, "'Aufbau von unten her': Heinrich Vogelers Lebens-Revolution," in Bernhard, *bauhausvorträge*, 209–15.

16 Hagen Biesantz, "Das erste Goetheanum," in *Das Goetheanum. Der Bauimpuls Rudolf Steiners* by Hagen Biesantz and Arne Klingborg (Dornach, 1978), 24. See Willy Rotzler, "Das Goetheanum in Dornach als Beispiel der Integration der Künste," in *Rudolf Steiner in Kunst und Architektur*, ed. Walter Kugler and Simon Baur (Cologne, 2007), 291–98.

17 Gropius, "Manifest und Programm" (see note 4), 97.

18 When Itten suggested Steiner as a speaker at the meeting of the council of masters on October 9, 1920, Gropius reported that Steiner had not answered the request he had sent him on the subject. See Wahl, *Die Meisterratsprotokolle* (see note 3), 103.

19 Although there were also guest lectures on architecture, they cannot be seen as compensation for the lack of a building department, which for a long time was conspicuous by its absence. Instead, the school made do with giving teaching contracts to staff from the Baugewerkenschule, the building-trades school in Weimar. See Klaus-Jürgen Winkler, *Die Architektur am Bauhaus in Weimar* (Berlin, 1993). A comprehensive study of the different teaching contracts awarded at the Bauhaus has yet to be conducted. For more on the Dessau period, see Lutz Schöbe, "'Schulungsmomente in der Richtung zum Wesentlichen': Bemerkungen zum außerkünstlerischen Unterricht am Bauhaus," in *Dessauer Kalender* (2011), 40–59.

20 See Cornelius Steckner, "Die Musikpädagogin Gertrud Grunow als Meisterin der Formlehre am Weimarer Bauhaus: Designtheorie und produktive Wahrnehmungsgestalt," in *Das frühe Bauhaus und Johannes Itten*, ed. Rolf

Bothe, Peter Hahn, and Hans Christoph von Tavel (Ostfildern-Ruit, 1994), 200–14.

21 See Jeanpaul Goergen, "Über das Film-programm im Rahmen der Bauhaus-Woche 1923 in Weimar," in: Bernhard, *bauhausvorträge* (see note 5), 283–98. In the Dessau period, there were still a few guest lectures on film theory. See Hannes Meyer, letter to National Commissioner of the Arts Edwin Redslob dated August 20, 1930, in *Hannes Meyer: 1889–1954; Architekt, Urbanist, Lehrer*, ed. Magdalena Droste and Werner Kleinerüschkamp (Berlin, 1989), 176–78.

22 See Thomas Tode, "Schule des Sehens: Über einige interdisziplinäre Aspekte des Films am Bauhaus," in "bauhaus & film," ed. Thomas Tode, *Maske und Kothurn: Internationale Beiträge zur Theater-, Film- und Medienwissenschaft* 57, nos. 1–2 (June 2011), 17–46.

23 When the time came to appoint a new director of the Weimar music school, Gropius had brought Schönberg into the discussion back in 1919—see Walter Gropius, letter to Ernst Hardt dated April 14, 1919, in Wahl, *Das Staatliche Bauhaus in Weimar* (see note 4), 87–88—and then again in 1923, this time with the support of Kandinsky (while Gropius's ex-wife Alma Mahler formed a successful cabal in opposition). See Oliver Hilmes, *Witwe im Wahn: Das Leben der Alma Mahler-Werfel* (Munich, 2004), 201–03, and Wolfram Huschke, *Zukunft Musik: Eine Geschichte der Hochschule für Musik Franz Liszt in Weimar* (Cologne, 2006), 156–57. The plan to bring Hauer to Weimar, either directly to the Bauhaus or to a new music school cooperating with the Bauhaus, was initially pursued by Itten but then abandoned—for reasons that are not entirely clear. See Dieter Bogner, "Eine Musikschule für Weimar?" in Bothe et al., *Das frühe Bauhaus und Johannes Itten* (see note 20), 364–73.

24 Besides the students that Itten had brought with him, Erwin Ratz and Bruno Adler—both also originally from Vienna—should also be included in this group, as should Georg Muche, who, as a devotee of Mazdaznan, was regarded for a time as "Itten's second." See Oskar Schlemmer, letter to Otto Meyer-Amden dated December 7, 1921, in *Oskar Schlemmer: Idealist der Form; Briefe, Tagebücher, Schriften*, ed. Andreas Hüneke (Leipzig, 1989), 82.

25 See Ulrich Linse, "Der spurenlose Mazdaznan-Vortrag von Otto Rauth," in

Bernhard, *bauhausvorträge* (see note 5), 217–32.

26 See Peter Stasny, "Anna Höllering: Potenziale des Performativen für die Erziehungsarbeit am Bauhaus?" in Bernhard, 141–55.

27 See Ute Ackermann, "Wien in Weimar: Emmy Heims Liederabend," in Bernhard, 179–86.

28 See Martha Ganter, "Die Musikvorträge am Weimarer Bauhaus," in Bernhard, 317–62.

29 See Ulrich Röthke, "Adolf Hölzel und das Bauhaus," in Bernhard, 243–54.

30 See Bogner, "Eine Musikschule für Weimar?" (see note 23); however, Gropius also suggested having Hauer perform as part of the Bauhaus Exhibition of 1923. See Wahl, *Die Meisterratsprotokolle* (see note 3), 235.

31 See Ferdinand Ebner, *Schriften*, vol. 3, *Briefe*, ed. Franz Seyr (Munich, 1965), 273.

32 See Peter Bernhard, "'Unser Freund und Meister': Johannes Schlaf und das Bauhaus," in *bauhausvorträge* (see note 5), 201–08.

33 Erika von Watzdorf-Bachoff, *Im Wandel und in der Verwandlung der Zeit: Ein Leben von 1878 bis 1963*, ed. Reinhard Doerries (Stuttgart, 1997), 273.

34 See Annemarie Jaeggi, "Ein geheimnisvolles Mysterium: Bauhütten-Romantik und Freimaurerei am frühen Bauhaus," in *Das Bauhaus und die Esoterik: Johannes Itten – Wassily Kandinsky – Paul Klee*, ed. Christoph Wagner (Bielefeld, 2005), 36–45.

35 Schlaf, who lived in Weimar, nevertheless stayed connected to the Bauhaus, and after the masters of form left the city with some of the students in April 1925, his house retained a certain importance as a center for those who remained. On the institutional situation after the Bauhaus move from Weimar, see Frank Boblenz, "Das 'doppelte' Bauhaus: Zur Geschichte des Staatlichen Bauhauses Weimar von 1925–1926," *Weimar-Jena: Die große Stadt* 9, no. 4 (2016): 314–42.

36 See Bernhard, *bauhausvorträge* (see note 5, frontispiece and 88).

37 Bernhard.

38 See Meike Feßmann, *Spielfiguren: Die Ich-Figurationen Else Lasker-Schülers als Spiel mit der Autorrolle; Ein Beitrag zur Poetologie des modernen Autors* (Stuttgart, 1992). Related drawings by Lasker-Schüler that were already published at the time included *König Abigail III. der oberste Priester empfängt sein Volk*, in Else Lasker-Schüler, *Der Prinz von Theben. Ein Geschichtenbuch* (Leipzig, 1914), frontispiece—also reproduced in Ricarda Dick, ed., *Else Lasker-Schüler. Die Bilder* (Berlin, 2010), 268; and *Selbstbildniß des Prinzen von Theben im Kriegshut*, in *Saturn: Eine Monatsschrift* 3, no. 4 (1913): 113—also reproduced in Dick, 264. On the motivic development of Lasker-Schüler's alter ego, Jussuf, see "Else Lasker-Schüler als Künstlerin," in Dick, 117–58, here: 126–32.

39 Elena Makarova, *Friedl Dicker-Brandeis: Ein Leben für Kunst und Lehre* (Vienna/Munich, 2000), 19 (although Makarova is evidently unaware that the poster comes from Dicker). At the time Dicker was involved in a love affair with Franz Singer, who married Heim the following year: Singer and Heim had a child together in April 1921.

40 A schematic plan of the syllabus is reproduced in, for example, Magdalena Droste, *bauhaus 1919–1933* (Cologne, 1990), 168–69. The curriculum from November 1925 contains only the following note—with almost identical wording to the Bauhaus program—under the rubric "supplementary subject areas": "lectures from the areas of science and art." Jeannine Fiedler and Peter Feierabend, eds., *Bauhaus* (Cologne, 1999), 185, and Droste, 136. The first curriculum produced under the directorship of Mies van der Rohe adopted only a third of the eighteen guest lecture fields in Meyer's plan: namely, "lectures on psychology/psychomechanics/business and economics/color theory/art history/sociology (Droste, 208)—these subjects were not only addressed in individual lectures but were also covered in courses held by adjunct faculty during the semester.

41 See the brochure *junge menschen kommt ans bauhaus*, Bauhaus-Archiv Berlin, inv. no. 12635.

42 Attempts had already been made in Weimar to introduce a gymnastics course. See Ackermann, "In Freiheit dressiert" (see note 13). But it was not until 1927 that "gymnastics or dance" appeared in the semester syllabus with an optional two to four hours per week in the first semester. See Droste, *bauhaus 1919–1933* (see note 40), 136. Under Meyer, sports finally became a subject offered in all semesters. See the syllabus plan in Droste.

43 Oskar Schlemmer, "unterrichtsgebiete," *bauhaus* 2/3, no. 2 (1928): 22–23, here: 22.

44 Schlemmer. "Cosmic being" was a term used by Schlemmer to refer to the work *Vom Wesen des Menschen* by Ricarda Huch, which was dealt with in his course. In it, man is presented as a "trinity" of nature, soul, and mind, mimicking the macrocosm. Based on this threefold division, Schlemmer subdivided his course into sections on natural science, psychology, and philosophy. See Oskar Schlemmer, *Der Mensch* (Mainz, 1969), 30–31 (this work addresses a selection of lecture notes taken during Schlemmer's classes that have been preserved and published by Heimo Kuchling in collaboration with Schlemmer's wife, Tut; they are organized in a somewhat unfortunate way, as Schlemmer's basic concept tends to be obscured), and Ricarda Huch, *Natur und Geist als die Wurzeln des Lebens und der Kunst* (Munich, 1914), reissued under the title *Vom Wesen des Menschen* (Leipzig, 1922).

45 This thesis has been consistently advocated in the literature. See Peter Bernhard, "Neopositivismus und Neues Bauen: Zur einer 'inneren Verwandtschaft,'" in *Architektur und Philosophie: Grundlagen, Standpunkte, Perspektiven*, ed. Jörg Gleiter and Ludger Schwarte (Bielefeld, 2015), 162–75, 267–75 and last in Anne Siegetsleitner, *Ethik und Moral im Wiener Kreis. Zur Geschichte eines engagierten Humanismus* (Vienna/Cologne/Weimar, 2014), 123.

46 Hannes Meyer, letter to Karlfried Graf Dürckheim dated August 24, 1930, in Meyer, *Bauen und Gesellschaft: Schriften, Briefe, Projekte* (Dresden, 1980), 75–76, here: 75.

47 See Droste and Kleinerüschkamp, *Hannes Meyer* (see note 21), Peter Bernhard, "The Leipzig School in Dessau," in *Bauhaus Saxony*, ed. Olaf Thromann (Stuttgart, 2019), 368–70, Peter Bernhard, "Die Leipziger Schule in Dessau," in Olaf Thormann, ed., *Bauhaus Sachsen* (Stuttgart, 2019), 365–67.

48 "There were the most acrimonious discussions," reports Tut Schlemmer, "but they were always sustained by a sense of responsibility for the whole." Tut Schlemmer, "... vom lebendigen Bauhaus und seiner Bühne," in *Bauhaus und Bauhäusler: Erinnerungen und Bekenntnisse*, ed. Eckhard Neumann, rev. ed. (Cologne, 1995), 224–32, here: 226–27); from a student perspective, Kurt Kranz later recalled, "I sometimes wondered about the sense of all the upheaval ... It was a process of opening up to the world of international affairs. There was no desire for provincial tranquility at the Bauhaus." Kurt Kranz, "Pädagogik am Bauhaus und danach," in Neumann, 339–55, here: 343.

Zsófia Kelm

The Influence of the Bauhaus on the State Academy of Crafts and Architecture (1926–30) in Weimar

the successor institution to the school in weimar was not popular with us at the dessau bauhaus. we had the impression that the people who were left there were the ones who did not identify with gropius. in retrospect, one knows more—for example, that neufert and van eesteren were working there, and there was nothing negative about that! i'm not so familiar with the bauhaus in weimar, but wingler's accounts invariably suffer from one-sided information coming from gropius.[1]

The story of the institution that succeeded the State Bauhaus, the State Academy of Crafts and Architecture (1926–30) in Weimar, run by Otto Bartning, was overlooked for a long time, and its portrayal and reception in the media at the time seem biased and one-sided. And although it can "even perhaps [be called] one of the key reform-oriented sites representing the modernist conception of architecture within the federal educational landscape of the Weimar Republic"[2] and created numerous buildings executed as assignments in the school's construction workshop, this architectural legacy likewise received only limited attention, historically speaking, and is now for the most part forgotten and in a state of decay. Yet these buildings, which include the Musikheim in Frankfurt an der Oder, constitute an important part of the architectural history of modernism and are testimony to a school that for the first time—concurrently with the Dessau Bauhaus—included practical building in its curriculum and thus made a considerable contribution to the renewal of architecture training in the Weimar Republic. Nevertheless, it was no easy task for the academy under Bartning to find its own form, operating as it did in the shadow of the Bauhaus, which was characterized early on by a well-established system of public relations with an extremely broad network.[3] Over time, evident parallels with the Bauhaus program and the wholesale takeover of many of the instructors from the *Bauhäusler* circle gave the school a reputation as a "Bauhaus spin-off"[4] and it was even called the "other Bauhaus,"[5] which contributed to the somewhat negative connotations associated with being a mere "emulator." This disdainful misconstruction of the State Academy can certainly be examined critically from a modern-day perspective.

"Consciously following Gropius's ideas, Bartning created something new, not a unique entity but rather a type of school that might serve as a model for all the smaller institutes that still bear the unfortunate legacy of the old-style schools of arts and crafts."[6] When, in 1930, Justus Bier wrote an article in the magazine *Die Form* with the title "The Dissolution of the State Academy in Weimar,"[7] in which he lists the outstanding accomplishments of Bartning in his four-year term as director of the academy, the praise did not last long. Bier revised his arguments a few months later, and his amended article now portrayed Bartning's institution as an extremely expensive successor to the Bauhaus, which, in Bier's view, merited a great deal less admiration than the Bauhaus.[8] Reviews like this were fatal for the historiographical reappraisal and appreciation of the State Academy. In a sense, pronouncements like this and the Nazi incursion, which brought the Bartning era to an abrupt end in 1930, overshadow or preempt the historical account of the academy and, with it, its reformist educational ideas.[9] Fifty years later, the academy was still not the subject of any scholarly scrutiny. Thus, in 1980, in his "Lectures on the History of the New Architecture," Julius Posener had this to say about Bartning and his role as director of the academy:

> Between 1926 and 1930 he was director of the Weimar Academy of Architecture, Fine Arts, and Crafts—I assume that this is the school founded by Henry van de Velde and the remnant, so to speak, of this school, which continued in Weimar after the Bauhaus moved to Dessau: the other Bauhaus, one might say. [10]

Posener's use of the soubriquet "the other Bauhaus"—which ultimately went down in history as the new name of the academy per se and became the title of the only detailed research conducted on the school in 1996—was indicative of his failure to really get to grips with Bartning's school.[11] Moreover, by erroneously calling the institution the State Academy of Architecture, Fine Arts, and Crafts, as the school was called in the Nazi period under Paul Schultze-Naumburg, he also shows how unimportant this chapter appeared to him in "his" architectural history of the twentieth century.[12]

However, in terms of its genesis, its objectives, its form, and its architectural legacy, it is clear that the academy was not—and much less wanted to be—some nondescript offshoot of the Bauhaus. Rather, it followed its own ideas, which Bartning developed and refined over a period of years in his numerous writings and publications. Thus it is no coincidence that, at the International Congress on the Training of Engineers in Darmstadt in 1947, Otto Bartning and Ernst Neufert spoke about the academy, which focuses on architects, engineers, and builders and debates the function of construction.[13] For it was practical building projects that Bartning saw as the key to successful architecture training, which he was able to put into practice with the founding of his school in 1926.

> For the craftsman, we want to develop a sense of the machinery that can manufacture standardized products; for the technician, we want to develop a sense of the hand that feels and grips, drawing inspiration from the material it touches; for the craftsman and the technician, we want to awaken a sense of how their work interconnects in the architecture they create; and for the builder, we want to empower his great endeavor: craftsmanship and machine production, single piece and serial manufacture combine to create the most human of achievements, the built structure.[14]

Although Bartning's words on the opening of his academy in 1926 were redolent of Walter Gropius and his manifesto for the State Bauhaus in Weimar, which opened by extolling the building as "the ultimate goal of all creative activity,"[15] the former plays a key role in the creation of new reformist educational ideas in modernist architecture (and its development). For he was one of those figures who were instrumental in powering the development of architecture in the twentieth century and helped shape this process through a broad range of activities. He himself took up the study of architecture in 1902 at the Königliche Technische Hochschule in Berlin-Charlottenburg and soon came to the realization that the new buildings of his time were "stillborn children."[16] He ultimately broke off his studies in 1906/07 after another winter semester at the Großherzogliche Badische Technische Hochschule Fridericiana zu Karlsruhe. Although there were sporadic signs of reformist tendencies at the universities, as espoused by Bartning's professor in Karlsruhe, Max Laeuger, who subsequently facilitated

Bartning's acceptance into the German Werkbund, all the major reformist measures came from outside the technical universities. Added to this, there was a general mood of optimism after World War I. When Germany was proclaimed a republic, associations like the November Group and the Workers' Council for Art were formed, the latter initially headed by Bruno Taut, who eventually handed over the reins to Gropius. Many notable architects, painters, sculptors, and writers signed their names to the council's slogan: "Art and people must form a unity. Art should no longer be the pleasure of a few but should bring joy and sustenance to the masses. The goal is the union of the arts under the wings of a great architecture."[17]

How serious the demands were for new building alternatives, for the resuscitation of the museums, and for a new kind of schooling in architecture, sculpture, painting, and crafts can be seen in the efforts made in the following years, which ultimately provided the cornerstone for the founding of the Bauhaus and later for the establishment of the Weimar academy. This merging of the arts can be clearly seen in the Musikheim—which would be realized in 1928 as one of the academy's projects under Bartning—inasmuch as architects, craftsmen, and music educators were able to work together to create a harmonious whole. Toward the end of 1918 and in early 1919, Bartning, as part of the Workers' Council, was preoccupied with a "syllabus for architecture and fine arts based on craft," addressing the matter in the first sessions of the teaching committee of the Workers' Council for Art in the German Werkbund. His colleagues included not only people like Taut and Emil Pottner but also Gropius.[18] In his talk at the International Congress on the Training of Engineers in Darmstadt in 1947, Bartning outlined the Bauhaus idea in embryonic form:

> In the winter of 1918/19 I sat together with Gropius in Berlin and, on the basis of the journeyman and master craftsman system of training, we prepared the teaching plan, a revolutionary one for the time, for an association of free arts, craft, and architecture, that is to say, the basic plan of the 'Bauhaus.' And so, when Gropius went to Dessau in 1925, I founded the Academy of Crafts and Architecture on the Weimar premises and staffed it with a group of progressive masters of art, craft, technology, and science.[19]

Although Bartning was certainly a driving force in the Workers' Council, it was only decades later that he commented on his seemingly central role in the emergence of the Bauhaus idea and was extremely well-disposed toward Gropius at the time when the latter was running

Zsófia
Kelm

The
Influence
of
the
Bauhaus

311

the Bauhaus in Weimar.[20] Gropius also maintained a correspondence with Bartning, writing to him years later from the United States: "Dear Bartning, I take my hat off to you for your BDA [Association of German Architects] speech! Only a true president goes the whole hog like that. Yours, Gropius."[21] In the following years, when Gropius was busy setting up the Bauhaus in Weimar, Bartning continued to take part in the public debate on the training of architects. Thus, in 1919/20, he published his proposals for a "syllabus for craftsmen, architects, and fine artists"[22]—the program that was developed jointly with the Workers' Council's special committee for teaching and that served Gropius as a template on which to base his implementation of the Bauhaus—dating the document December 18, 1918, the veracity of which is now generally questioned.[23] There can be no doubt that the collaboration in the Worker's Council was fruitful for both Gropius and Bartning, yet one should not forget that in January 1916, on the recommendation of van de Velde, Gropius had already applied to become his successor as director of the school of arts and crafts and had made proposals for founding an academy as an artistic advisory center for industry, craft, and trades.[24] The Bauhaus program can thus be seen as a mix of ideas from the Werkbund and the Workers' Council rather than a finished concept developed by Bartning. Moreover, Bartning's focus at the time was on practical building, more specifically on the importance and influence of building as part of the training itself. In 1919/20 he delineated his core ideas on the subject in a text entitled "Practical Proposal for Teaching Architects,"[25] explaining that the building in its entirety is itself teaching material for theory and practice. His 1924 article "The Training of Architects," written shortly before the Weimar Bauhaus was wound up, once again detailed the advantages of an education that combined the best features of the university, the building trades school, the workshop, and the construction site.[26]

> If a gradual process of development, effected by the building trades school, the construction site, the university, and the master studio—starting, in other words, from the fundamentals and progressing through crafts and science—is structured, as outlined above, by means of the simplest possible examination regulations, the master builder as supervisor must be given free rein to shape the process incrementally from beginning to end.[27]

In the same year, the idea for an architecture department was put forward at the Bauhaus: it was to work together with the existing workshops and tackle the housing problems of the day, so that the focus would be on construction, as stated in the program right at the start.[28] As detailed and substantial as the concept might appear, there was no longer any intention to realize it in Weimar. There is no record of whether Bartning knew of these plans. But when, on the recommendation of Heinrich Tessenow, he was offered the chance to found a successor institution in Weimar, he had a well-prepared program to hand.[29]

The transition from Bauhaus to Academy would turn out to be a long one. The closing of the Bauhaus was the prelude to a difficult relationship between Gropius and the Thuringian government, and although he published an announcement—together with several Bauhaus masters—on December 26, 1924, declaring the Bauhaus dissolved as of April 1, 1925, exactly six years after its opening, the official inauguration of the academy under Otto Bartning did not take place until one year later on April 19, 1926.[30] Because he was already in discussion with the Thuringian administration in January 1925 about the possibility of succeeding Gropius, Bartning was able to prepare himself thoroughly for his new function.[31] Along with the fact that the State Academy of Fine Arts (1921–30), which was still partially linked to the Bauhaus during Gropius's time in charge, was no longer part of the new academy, there was also no guarantee that the existing workshops could be continued: this brought the idea of a building studio more into focus—a working structure outside of the training facilities available to an art and architecture school. In a letter to Bartning, Gropius had spoken of a "completely new structure"[32] that would be necessary for him in Weimar; accordingly, Bartning was able to draw on some of the former *Bauhäusler* in his new institute. Yet, in spite of all the pressures on him, Bartning was at pains to find a fair solution for the transition period and for the remaining staff members.[33] The work he undertook to rebuild the school between February 1 and December 31, 1925, was compensated with a sum of 6,000 Reichsmarks.[34] The fact that the work did not commence immediately is indicated by a letter from Bartning to the Thuringian Minister of Education and Justice dated September 16, 1926.[35] Bartning also envisaged minor modifications to the school building, but this work did not receive official blessing.[36]

Despite certain parallels with the Bauhaus, Bartning's school differed fundamentally in type from its precursor. The ideas that Bartning wrote in the years prior to this in articles, speeches, and

Zsófia
Kelm

The
Influence
of
the
Bauhaus

313

programs on the subject of a new form of architecture training took
shape in the process of setting up the academy. The focus was purely
on the schooling of architects and was closest to the core concept
developed in 1918, which envisaged a training conducted in teaching
workshops for prospective craftsmen, architects, and fine artists. The
academy was not geared to beginners, but rather to students who had
taken a preliminary examination at a technical university or had
graduated from an accredited building trades school. The construction
department constituted the heart of the academy and consisted of a
theoretical basic study program and an Active Building Studio. Having
broken off his university studies, Bartning had acquired his own
knowledge of building through a process of "learning by doing," and
he was at pains to implement his ideas of the connection between
theory and practice. Thus Oskar Schlemmer writes,

> In Weimar itself the real father of the Bauhaus idea is being appointed—
> the architect from Berlin—and he will, people say, begin in reverse: with
> the actual building from which everything else is to proceed, provided that
> the Thuringian government gives him the opportunity he needs.[37]

Bartning's lively publishing activities, his commitments to various
institutions, and his private architecture office in Berlin prevented him
from undertaking the practical teaching himself. His ideas of a
building architect, who understood the structure with his own hands,
aligned with those of Neufert, who at that time was still working for
Gropius. After apprenticing as a bricklayer, carpenter, formworker,
and concreter, Neufert had completed a two-year training at the
Weimar building trades school under Paul Klopfer. In 1919 he had
been one of the first students at the Bauhaus under Gropius and had
even worked in Gropius's architecture practice.[38] His decision to
exchange his involvement with Gropius for a professorship was a
major loss to Gropius. In a letter to Gropius in 1926, Bartning writes,

> I sincerely regret that Neufert's departure affects you so severely. But I
> repeat that only N's clearly stated intention to enter another field of work
> that is suited to him resolved me to enter into negotiations with him and
> to engage him before he ended up leaving for America or going into
> industry ... in other words, there was no 'poaching with exalted promises.'
> Because of the relationship between us, it is important for me to make
> this declaration.[39]

Neufert turned out to be a driving force at the academy. He headed its
nucleus, the Active Building Studio, the part of the construction

department that included a theoretical foundation course along with an active building program. Different lectures were intended to sensitize students to the various aspects of building and equip them with a solid set of basics. Only the last two semesters were devoted to practical work. The academy as a whole had a strong focus on practice, as Neufert corroborates:

> Here the students worked together with a growing sense of personal responsibility for the actual building tasks. They were trained in this way for work in a building studio organized according to modern methodology ... They discovered the difference between 'knowledge' and 'proficiency.'[40]

Like Gropius before him, Bartning opened up his architecture office for students to assist, thus increasing the school's productivity at the same time. In conjunction with the school's workshops, which were run as production operations, a number of buildings and institutional structures were erected in the academy's lifetime: these were illustrated in the academy's annual prospectus and gave the school a name as an important "architecture office" and "production site."

The commission to build the Musikheim, or rather Musiklandheim, as it was called, can be classed as one such "office project," carried out in conjunction with the Weimar academy. Bartning's personal network was responsible for helping secure the commission awarded to him and his State Academy in Weimar to build a training center for music teachers in Frankfurt an der Oder.[41] The 1920s were marked by major reforms of the school system. The Prussian minister of culture at the time, Carl Heinrich Becker, was committed to promoting art and music education. As a means to implement his idea, he saw the need for a Musikheim and tasked the music educator and subsequent head of the institution Georg Götsch with creating a center for music educational programs in Frankfurt (Oder). Götsch's diary entries between 1924 and 1927 trace the germination of this idea, which would come to fruition, not in Berlin but in eastern Brandenburg.[42] At the time, the city was in an optimistic mood, and after the border adjustments that accompanied the creation of the new province of Posen–West Prussia, it became an economic and cultural center.[43] Brandenburg played an important role in the modernist period, as many architectural masterpieces were built there after 1919: these include Peter Behren's AEG workers' housing in Hennigsdorf (1919) and Hannes Meyer's Trade Union School in Bernau (1930). Modernism took Frankfurt by storm, occupying the city at breakneck

Zsófia Kelm

The
Influence
of
the
Bauhaus

315

speed. In 1911, the Neo-Renaissance style still prevailed.[44] Less than two decades later, the Musikheim was built, followed a year later by a "Pedagogical Academy" designed by architect Hans Petersen and erected in close proximity. The latter was part of an extensive network of such academies, which gradually sprang up throughout Prussia as a "poster child of the paradigm shift in educational policy":[45] this was based on the initiative of Culture Minister Carl H. Becker, who outlined his vision in the text "The Pedagogical Academy in the Development of Our National Education System."[46] Although the plan was for the Musikheim to also serve as a further education center for teachers and laypeople, it was not, as is often claimed, part of the network of Pedagogical Academies.

The property that was selected for the purpose, located in the western part of the city of Frankfurt, was originally meant to become part of the Paulinenhof housing estate, designed by Martin Kießling. In formal terms, the estate was geared to romantic images of the village and small town and was to be extended in a second construction phase to include the plot that now contains the Musikheim.[47] Instead, Bartning and his students designed a building whose modernist plainness and clear lines contrasted with Kießling's development, although its red facing bricks and pitched roof drew on regional traditions.[fig. 1] [48] In comparison to other buildings at the academy created under the directorship of Ernst Neufert, such as the student residence and Abbeanum faculty building in Jena, which were characterized by uniform ribbon windows and a flat roof, the Musikheim seemed at first glance to reject the pure style of the New Objectivity. Considered by critics of the day to be reminiscent of a basilica or monastic complex,[49] it is a building whose form draws on the tradition of the *Volkshochschulheim*, a residential school for adult education typically located in rural areas. Consciously conceived as a "pedagogic island," it was, in a sense, a place of detachment from everyday life.[50] Years later, Bartning would stress this in a personal letter to Carl H. Becker, writing that "lesson and space, teaching style and structural form, community and home are twinned in their very essence."[51] The form of the structure thus completely complies with its function and follows a principle of complexity that is mirrored in his other buildings. The building thus looks different from every angle. It is characterized for one thing by its coherence, which is evident most notably in the entrance area facing onto the street. However, looking at the multi-unit plan, the hall presents itself to the viewer as the focal point and a connecting element for the wings, creating a link to the inner gardens.[fig.2] The importance in this project of the connection between building and nature is evident in the development plan by Cornelis van Eesteren, who at the time ran urban planning courses at the academy in Weimar. Designed for the area around the Musikheim reproduced in the 1929 school yearbook, it included provision for an adjustment to the existing development plan to enlarge the green zone within the sight lines of the Musikheim and thus create the impression of an undeveloped environment.[52] However, this plan was never realized. Nevertheless, the complex articulation of the building made it possible to maximize the integration of the garden area, which was designed with an orchard to the north and a pond to the south.[fig.3] Thus, the main space becomes a kind of passage flooded with light, surrounded on both sides by nature with its form determined to the greatest possible extent by its function:

> The great hall has a longitudinal tension that develops between the stage and the room with the ascending seating tiers. At the same time, it has the light passing through it obliquely, and it is by this transverse passage that the dancers process from one part of the garden to the other. And finally, for the round and square contra-dances it has a central tension, whereby the stage on one side and the stepped gallery on the other hold the central space between them. The requirements for movement have defined the form of the main hall—it is the spatial design of the processions, the contra-dances and the music leading these dances.[53]

The garden design therefore played an important role in the overall concept of the Musikheim: it can thus be grouped as part of a series of buildings in the Neues Bauen movement that follow the same idea.[54] At about the same time, Neufert was grappling with garden design in the process of planning his house in Gelmeroda.[55] Clear lines, a two-sided glazed façade and an open roof structure give the space an impressive lightness, supported by the lighting created by Wilhelm Wagenfeld, which seems to float in the air.[fig.4] The Musikheim thus lays claim to the rhythm of its form in the act of walking through it and becomes a spatiotemporal construct. Elements like stairs and passages attain added significance and are subsumed into a rhythmic whole. It is tempting to think of Le Corbusier's promenade architecture, of a path through the built space that is oriented toward the viewer, a kind of "internal circulation" of the architecture.[56] In addition to the great

Zsófia Kelm

Zsófia Kelm

The Influence of the Bauhaus

317

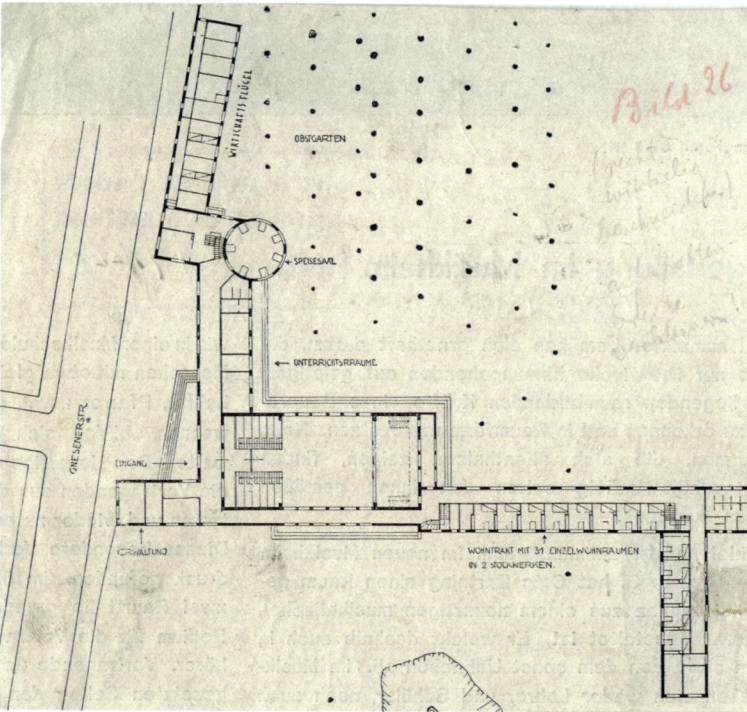

Fig. 1. Musikheim, Frankfurt (Oder), exterior view, street side.

Fig. 2. Otto Bartning, floor plan of the Musikheim.

Fig. 3. Exterior view, garden side.

Fig. 4. Musikheim, Frankfurt (Oder), 1929, interior view, main hall.

Fig. 5. Musikheim, Frankfurt (Oder), 1929, interior decor, fireplace room.

hall, the tower with refectory interrupts the uniformity of the cell-like spaces and takes up two motifs that would influence Bartning's later work.[57]

Yet it is not only the architectural form that contributes to the character of the complex. Under Bartning and the State Academy in Weimar, the furnishing of the spaces was fully included in the commission of the Musikheim and allowed the academy workshops to fit out the interiors. The furniture thus came from the carpentry workshop run by Erich Dieckmann, the lights from Wilhelm Wagenfeld, head of the metal workshop, and the materials from the weaving workshop.[fig.5] The color scheme was implemented by Ludwig Hirschfeld-Mack. This collaboration of the workshops with the active building studios made it possible to harmonize the details to a high degree. Moreover, the interior design was undoubtedly good advertising for the workshop products, which were marketed by the "sales force" of the State Academy.[58]

We can surmise that—in contrast to the student residence and Abbeanum in Jena, built under the direction of Neufert—the academy's Active Building Studio had little actual involvement in developing the structural concept, which was drawn up in close collaboration with the music educator Götsch. Although academic project work indicates that the students were grappling with the structural concept, it is unclear whether they accompanied Bartning on site to contribute to the construction phase: "Apart from some general lectures, Bartning did not offer any regular classes in Weimar; instead, he carried on living in Berlin and, when he came to Weimar, he was completely swamped with administrative work."[59] Moreover, Bartning had an ongoing preoccupation with the power of music to create space that preceded the design of this building. This is reflected in his church buildings as well as in his Wylerberg House near Cleves, built between 1921 and 1924, which is described by Ernst Pollak as a "boldly constructed symphony,"[60] in which every space is reminiscent of a musical work. Despite its pitched roof and facing bricks, the Musik-heim's modernity is captivating; this manifests, above all, in the construction of the main chamber. Here, the room is dominated by its large windows with clear lines and a sense of spaciousness, which is only apparent when you enter the facility and thus represents a contrast to the Dessau Bauhaus, whose prominent glass façade dominates the building.

When National Socialism descended on Germany, putting a sudden end to the academy under Bartning in 1930,[61] it also led to the seizure of this building and the co-opting of the Musikheim, possibly because it had a hint of Domestic Revivalism (*Heimatstil*), which may have been reflected in the brick architecture and the pitched roof. Although its director, Georg Götsch, clung to his educational vision, he came under increasing political pressure. His connections abroad and his friendly relationship with the senior government official did enable him to continue running the school, but in 1941 he was obliged to join the Nazi Party in return. In 1939, for the tenth anniversary of the Musikheim, the college's initial goals gave way to a heavily politicized musical training promoting "German national traditions."[62] The Musikheim closed in 1941.

In 1945 the Musikheim was occupied by Soviet troops and was used as a hospital after the war.[63] From 1946 on, it acted as a substitute venue for the Kleist Theater in Frankfurt, which resulted in extensive structural modifications. Bartning's carefully considered concept received little recognition in the GDR era and fell victim to the government's severe plans to create more space at any price. Although the building did not suffer any great damage in the war, in the following two decades it was converted in several stages to enlarge the site and thus make it more profitable.[64]

The first major phase of alterations in 1954 affected the auditorium: the windows of the main hall that had once been so important for the spatial ambience were darkened and reduced in size on the northern aspect; Wagenfeld's lights were removed, and a part of the space was extended to create a gigantic stage area.[fig.6] Although the dimensions of the stage completely overwhelmed the main hall, its artistic design was matched to the existing fabric of the building.[65] The more active the theater became, the less suitable the building seemed for its everyday use. The Musikheim was given another major structural overhaul in the mid-1960s. In 1963, when the building of a new theater for the city was postponed, the State Planning Commission, the Ministry of Culture, and the district council together with the city of Frankfurt (Oder) decided to reconstruct the Kleist Theater. This decision involved a program of major repairs to the auditorium, a further extension to the backstage area, and the erection of a new functional building with a café and snack room, a foyer, a cloakroom facility, a rehearsal stage for the theater, a ballet rehearsal room,

Zsófia
Kelm

The
Influence
of
the
Bauhaus

321

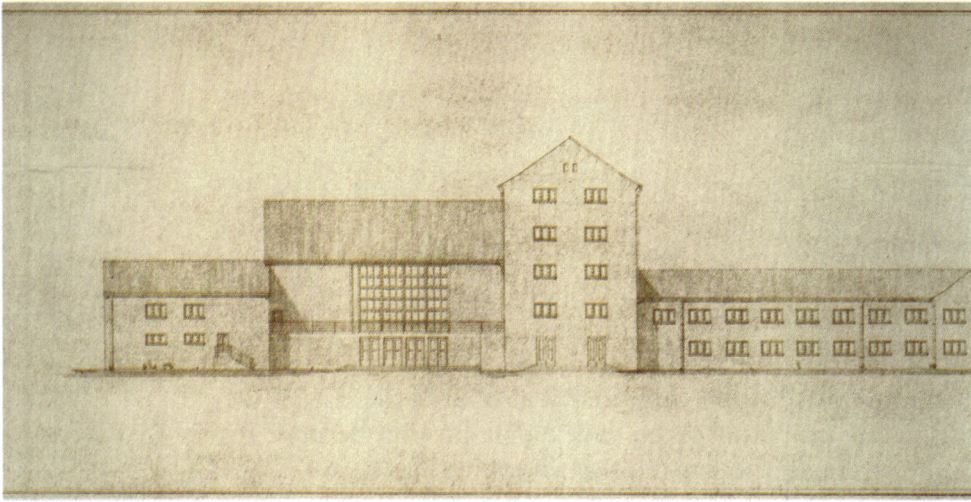

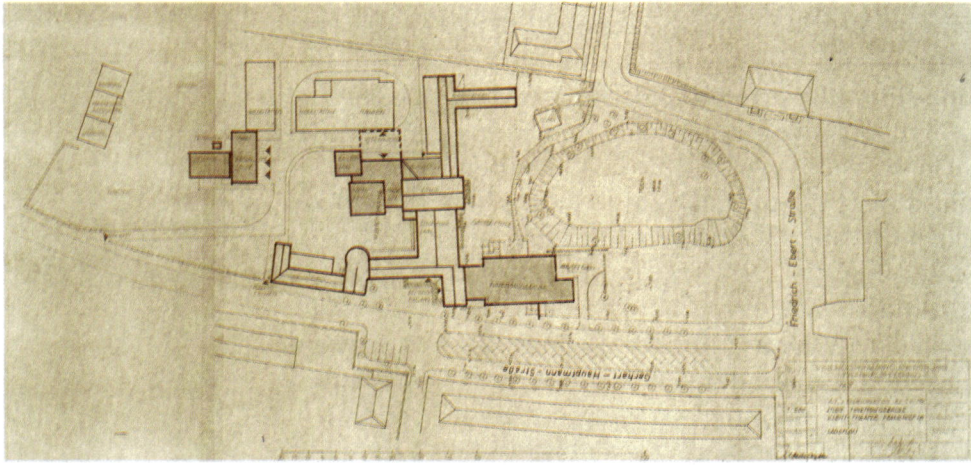

Fig. 6. Kleist-Theater Frankfurt (Oder), renovation 1954, south facade (detail).

Fig. 7. Kleist-Theater Frankfurt (Oder), study for a functional building, site plan, 1964.

Fig. 8. Musikheim, Frankfurt (Oder), 2018, exterior view, street side with glass-fronted café annex from the 1960s. Photograph: Jens Stöbe (CDA).

Fig. 9. Musikheim, Frankfurt (Oder), 2018, exterior view, street entrance. Photograph: Jens Stöbe (CDA)

Fig. 10. Musikheim, Frankfurt (Oder), 2018. Photograph: Jens Stöbe (CDA)

Fig. 11a. Musikheim, Frankfurt (Oder), 1929, main hall entrance.

Fig. 11b. Musikheim, Frankfurt (Oder), 2018, main hall entrance. Photograph: Jens Stöbe (CDA).

and the reconstruction of technical installations such as the stage lighting and rigging system. These plans were intended to turn the former Musikheim into "a wellspring of verve and vitality."[66] The addition of a functional building with a café completely changed the southern aspect of the complex.[fig.7, 8] This involved the choice not only of a totally different building style and new materials but also of a construction method that made use of prefabricated components. Nevertheless, people spoke of a "functional completion of the whole facility in accordance with the latest understanding of design, function, and structural engineering."[67] The creation of a foyer and the enlargement of the stage area did away with the original architectural idea of the main hall altogether. The functional building that had previously been erected in the garden area and the street that had been incorporated as an entrance to the individual areas transformed the site into a series of buildings with different design qualities.[fig.9] Although the existing fabric was not torn down, in formal terms it was given a thorough "pruning" by the numerous alterations. Now, fifty years on, architect Hans Albeshausen, who was partly responsible for the modifications in the GDR period, rejects the changes he helped carry out; he is in favor of undoing them and returning the Musikheim to its original form.[fig.10][68]

Today, the Musikheim, which once combined the harmony of its parts into a mellifluous whole, has fallen into decay, although here and there one can still get a sense of how it once was.[fig.11a, b] Since September 13, 2002, it has been on the list of heritage buildings in Land Brandenburg and for at least as long on the list of buildings for sale, put on the market by its owner, the cash-strapped city of Frankfurt (Oder). With its prospects so far bleak, the building, which has long since fallen silent as a venue and, above all, as a piece of musical architecture, is advertised as "the Bauhaus-Ensemble Musikheim"—with a total area of 12,500 square meters, free of commission, and with price available on application.[fig.11] The use of the Bauhaus "label" is an attempt to reassert the architectural importance of the Musikheim and put it on a footing with the Bauhaus buildings that now enjoy a significant degree of protection by virtue of their heritage status, including the distinction of being honored by UNESCO. Yet their past has certain parallels. It was only in 1976 that the Bauhaus legacy in Dessau was rediscovered by the GDR. While the scholarly analysis of modernism in architecture is now mostly confined to well-known players, we are seeing the disappearance of important works that bear witness to the building activity of the time.

The State Academy under Otto Bartning did not enjoy widespread recognition as an institution that educated its students concurrently with the Bauhaus in Dessau. Besides Walter Gropius's flamboyant personality, the main reason for this was the effective public relations work carried out by the Bauhaus. At the time, more than 1,500 articles on the Bauhaus appeared in different media outlets, which repeatedly put the school in the spotlight. On top of this, there were the Bauhaus journals, magazines, and special editions, which fed into a process of self-marketing.[69] Although the State Academy tried to advertise its program in prominent media, it did not have a proper promotional mechanism in place. Nevertheless, many structures were built under Bartning in his time at the academy. These not only provide information about an era that has faded from memory but also add another piece to our overall picture of modernism.

1   Max Bill, letter to Helmut Lerch, November 4, 1981, Otto Bartning Archiv Darmstadt, call no. 2008V06708.
2   Gernot Weckherlin, "'… die herrliche Atmosphäre eines bauenden Ateliers …': Die Staatliche Hochschule für Handwerk und Baukunst und das 'aktive Bauatelier' von 1926–1930," in *Aber wir sind! Wir wollen! Und wir schaffen! Von der Großherzoglichen Kunstschule zur Bauhaus-Universität Weimar, 1860–2010*, ed. Frank Simon-Ritz, Klaus-Jürgen Winkler, and Gerd Zimmermann (Weimar, 2010), 281–304, here: 281.
3   On the Bauhaus's public relations work, see Patrick Rössler, ed., *The Bauhaus and Public Relations: Communication in a Permanent State of Crisis* (New York, 2014).
4   Adalbert Behr, "Die Bauhochschule Weimar 1926–1930," *Wissenschaftliche Zeitschrift der Hochschule für Architektur und Bauwesen Weimar* 26, nos. 4/5 (1979): 382.
5   Julius Posener, "Vorlesungen zur Geschichte der Neuen Architektur II," *Arch+* 53 (1980): 72.
6   Justus Bier, "Zur Auflösung der Staatlichen Bauhochschule in Weimar," *Die Form* 5, no. 10 (May 15, 1930): 270–71.
7   Bier, "Zur Auflösung," 269–74.

8   Justus Bier, "Bauhaus und Bauhochschule," *Die Form* 5, nos. 19/20 (October 15, 1930): 536.
9   On the political debate that led to the dissolution of the academy, see Klaus-Jürgen Winkler, "Die Staatliche Hochschule für Handwerk und Baukunst und die politische Debatte," in Simon-Ritz, Winkler, and Zimmermann, *Aber wir sind!* (see note 2), 245–64.
10   Posener, "Vorlesungen" (see note 5), 72.
11   It was not until 1996 that the academy was accurately portrayed through the exhibition and publication entitled *Das andere Bauhaus: Otto Bartning und die Staatliche Bauhochschule Weimar 1926–1930*. In it, the director of the school, its program, and its staff were presented in detailed portraits: Dörte Nicolaison, ed., *Das andere Bauhaus: Otto Bartning und die Staatliche Bauhochschule Weimar 1926–1930*, exh. cat., Bauhaus-Archiv / Museum für Gestaltung (Berlin, 1996).
12   Not to be confused with the Weimar Academy of Fine Arts, which existed parallel to the Bauhaus and Otto Bartning's academy.
13   The International Congress in Darmstadt took place at the instigation of Ernst Neufert, who in 1946 was made professor at the Technische Hochschule Darmstadt after years

working in Nazi Germany. The congress offered engineers and architects the opportunity—for the first time since World War II—to discuss the future of architectural training in an international context. The diversity of different positions, the international flair introduced by speakers from a wide variety of countries and all the occupied zones in Germany, and the readiness of participants to enter into lively discussion (there were over seventy-five contributions registered) represented a new mood of optimism in a generation of architects and engineers who had not the slightest interest in processing the Nazi period and thus passed over it without comment. See Ernst Neufert, ed., *Der Architekt im Zerreisspunkt: Vorträge, Berichte und Diskussionsbeiträge der Sektion Architektur auf dem Internationalen Kongress für Ingenieursausbildung in Darmstadt 1947* (Darmstadt, 1948); "Eröffnung des Internationalen Ingenieurkongresses: Feierlicher Auftakt, Organisatorisches, Interview, die ersten Vorträge," *Darmstädter Echo*, August 2, 1947, 8ff.

14 Otto Bartning, in Achim Preiss and Klaus-Jürgen Winkler, eds., *Weimarer Konzepte: Die Kunst- und Bauhochschule 1860–1995* (Weimar, 1996), 173.

15 Walter Gropius, "manifesto," in *Programm des Staatlichen Bauhauses in Weimar* (Weimar, April 1919).

16 Otto Bartning, in Werner Durth, Wolfgang Pehnt, and Sandra Wagner-Conzelmann, eds., *Otto Bartning: Architekt einer sozialen Moderne* (Darmstadt, 2016), 16.

17 Rose-Carol Washton Long, ed., *German Expressionism: Documents from the End of the Wilhelmine Empire to the Rise of National Socialism* (Berkeley, 1995), 193. The pamphlet of the Workers' Council for Art was printed in several editions, and in April 1919 thousands of copies were sent to artists and public figures as well as to newspapers and magazines. The German original is cited in Akademie der Künste, ed., *Arbeitsrat für Kunst Berlin 1918–1921: Ausstellung mit Dokumentation*, Akademie-Katalog 129 (Berlin, 1980), 88–89.

18 Dörte Nicolaison, *Otto Bartning und die Staatliche Bauhochschule in Weimar 1926–1930* (Berlin, 1996), 17.

19 Otto Bartning, "Die Einheit des Menschen," in *Der Architekt im Zerreisspunkt: Vorträge, Berichte und Diskussionsbeiträge der Sektion*

Architektur auf dem Internationalen Kongress für Ingenieurausbildung in Darmstadt 1947, ed. Ernst Neufert (Darmstadt, 1948), 28.

20 Bartning's support for Gropius and his work can be gleaned from an exchange of letters between the two in January 1920, along with Gropius's grateful reply. THHSTAW, Staatliches Bauhaus Weimar, no. 6, sheets 1–3.

21 Gropius, letter to Bartning, dated September 16, 1957, reproduced in Jürgen Bredow and Helmut Lerch, *Materialien zum Werk des Architekten Otto Bartning* (Darmstadt, 1983), 35.

22 Otto Bartning, "Vorschläge zu einem Lehrplan für Handwerker, Architekten und bildende Künstler," *Mitteilungen des Deutschen Werkbundes* 2 (1919/20): 42–47.

23 Dörte Nicolaison assumes that Bartning's date was selected retrospectively to highlight his authorship of the idea of an innovative syllabus prior to the foundation date of the Bauhaus. Nicolaison, *Otto Bartning und die Staatliche Bauhochschule in Weimar* (see note 18), 17.

24 Preiß and Winkler, *Weimarer Konzepte* (see note 14), 123.

25 Otto Bartning, "Praktischer Vorschlag zur Lehre des Architekten," *Mitteilungen des Deutschen Werkbundes* 5 (1919/20): 148–56.

26 Otto Bartning, "Ausbildung des Architekten," *Der Neubau* 6, no. 1 (1924): 2–4.

27 Bartning, 4.

28 THHSTAW, Staatliches Bauhaus, no. 77, Gründung der Architekturabteilung [Founding of the Architecture Department], April 2, 1924.

29 On the recommendation of Heinrich Tessenow, Undersecretary Dr. Ortloff contacted Bartning on behalf of the Ministry of Education in January 1925. See Nicolaison, *Otto Bartning und die Staatliche Bauhochschule in Weimar* (see note 18), 29.

30 Press release in the *Allgemeine Thüringische Landeszeitung Deutschland* in Weimar from December 28, 1924, in Volker Wahl, ed., *Das Staatliche Bauhaus in Weimar: Dokumente zur Geschichte des Instituts 1919–1926* (Cologne, 2009), 736. A special thank-you to Norbert Korrek for directing me to this source.

31 Nicolaison, *Otto Bartning und die Staatliche Bauhochschule in Weimar* (see note 18), 29.

32 Walter Gropius, cited in Nicolaison, 30.

33 We may gather from the files of the workshop staff that—in the case of Mr. Zaubitzer (printing), for example—Bartning offered him an additional month's pay after the end of his service at the State Bauhaus, should he be unable to find new employment right away. THHSTAW, Staatliches Bauhaus, no. 114, sheet 299, March 4, 1926.

34 See THHSTAW, Personalakten aus dem Bereich Volksbildung [Personnel files from the education section], call no. 1027, sheet 46, November 5, 1925.

35 Because the general subjects and field trips could not be offered in full in the first summer semester, Bartning insisted on a reduction in the tuition fees. See THHSTAW, call no. C1474, sheet 29, September 16, 1926.

36 Prior to the opening, syndic Paul Kämmer from the State Academy of Crafts and Architecture requested the necessary funding for structural alterations to the college building. See THHSTAW, Staatliche Hochschule für Handwerk und Baukunst Weimar, no. 22/23, sheet 59, March 23, 1926.

37 Oskar Schlemmer, cited in Durth, Pehnt, and Wagner-Conzelmann, *Otto Bartning* (see note 16), 53.

38 See Ines Weizman, "The Exception to the Norm: Buildings and Skeletons in the Archive of Ernst Neufert," in *Quote*, Perspecta 49, ed. A. J. P. Artemel, Russell LeStourgeon, and Violette de la Selle (Cambridge, MA, 2016), 134–46.

39 Otto Bartning, in Wahl, *Das Staatliche Bauhaus in Weimar* (see note 30), 768–69.

40 Ernst Neufert, "Ausbildung der schöpferischen Fähigkeiten bei Architekten," in *Der Architekt im Zerreisspunkt*, 85–86.

41 It was thanks to the friendship and cordial relations between Georg Götsch, the then culture minister Carl Heinrich Becker, and Otto Bartning that the commission was not advertised and went directly to Bartning and his academy in Weimar.

42 Erich Bitterhof, *Das Musikheim Frankfurt/ Oder 1929–1941: Beiträge der Jugendbewegung zur preußischen Kulturpolitik, Lehrerfortbildung und Erwachsenenbildung* (Ludwigstein, 1980), 39–44.

43 Ralf-Rüdiger Targiel, *Frankfurt (Oder)* (Erfurt, 2012), 90.

44 Rolf Lautenschläger, "Als Brandenburg revolutionär war," *taz*, April 28, 2011, accessed January 19, 2018, www.taz.de/!5121806/.

45 Mark Escherich, *Städtische Selbstbilder und bauliche Repräsentation: Architektur und Städtebau*

in *Erfurt 1918–1933*, Erfurter Studien zur Kunst- und Baugeschichte 5 (Berlin, 2010), 177–78.

46 C. H. Becker, *Die Pädagogische Akademie im Aufbau unseres nationalen Bildungswesens* (Leipzig, 1926).

47 Sybille Gramlich, Andreas Bernhard, Andreas Cante, and Irmelin Küttner, *Denkmaltopographie Bundesrepublik Deutschland: Denkmale in Brandenburg, Vol. 3; Stadt Frankfurt (Oder)* (Worms, 2002), 312.

48 Christof Baier, "Überlieferung und bewusste Kunst: Traditionsbezug und Sachlichkeit im Werk von Otto Bartning," *Kritische Berichte* 2 (2007): 62–74.

49 Wolfram Lotz, "Das Musikheim Frankfurt an der Oder," *Die Form: Zeitschrift für gestaltende Arbeit* 4 (1929): 507–14.

50 Josef Olbrich, *Geschichte der Erwachsenenbildung in Deutschland* (Opladen, 2001), 173.

51 Otto Bartning, letter to Carl Becker, Berlin, October 28, 1932, Geheimes Staatsarchiv PK, VI HA NL Becker, C.H., no. 6244, sheet 8.

52 Otto Bartning, *Bauhochschule Weimar 1929* (Weimar, 1929), 24.

53 Otto Bartning, "Musik und Raum," in *Spannweite: Aus Schriften und Reden ausgewählt und eingeleitet von Alfred Siemon* (Bramsche bei Osnabrück, 1958), 90–95, here: 92.

54 A notable example here is Hannes Meyer's Trade Union School in Bernau (1928–1930). See also Michael Siebenbrodt, "Zwischen Tradition und Moderne – Haus Neufert in Gelmeroda 1929," in Nicolaison, *Das andere Bauhaus* (see note 11), 75–80.

55 See Weizman, "The Exception to the Norm" (see note 38), 142.

56 Turit Fröbe, "Weg und Bewegung in der Architektur Le Corbusiers," *Gebaute Räume: Zur kulturellen Formung von Architektur und Stadt* 9, no. 1 (November 2004), accessed December 16, 2016, www.cloud-cuckoo.net/openarchive/wolke /deu/Themen/041/Froebe/froebe.htm.

57 The circular shape is found in the form of polygonal altar spaces in the emergency church program along with the use of wood and the exposed roof structure.

58 Although the Musikheim was built extremely economically, with the overall costs running to only 300,000 Reichsmarks, the finished building, in spite of the emphatic connection between music and architecture, exhibited certain shortcomings, which made the actual

Zsófia Kelm

The Influence of the Bauhaus

artistic work problematic. According to reports by course participants, there were no exits in the stage area, which was too low, and some rooms were not suited to playing music on account of their size. See Kurt Sydow, in Erich Bitterhof, *Das Musikheim Frankfurt/Oder 1929–1941: Beiträge der Jugendbewegung zur preußischen Kulturpolitik, Lehrerfortbildung und Erwachsenenbildung* (Ludwigstein, 1980), 92–93.

59   Ernst Neufert, "Ausbildung der schöpferischen Fähigkeiten bei Architekten," *Zentralblatt für Industriebau* 1, no. 3 (1970): 98.

60   Ernst Pollak, *Der Baumeister Otto Bartning* (Bonn, 1926), 31–32.

61   On November 10, 1930, the school re-opened as the State Academy of Architecture, Fine Arts, and Crafts, operated by Schultze-Naumburg under the auspices of the Nazi Party.

62   Report on the tenth anniversary of the Musikheim, November 18/19, 1939, in Bitterhof, *Das Musikheim Frankfurt/Oder* (see note 58), 86–87.

63   Brandenburgisches Landeshauptarchiv, Aktenzeichen Rep. 601, no. 7627.

64   A preliminary report on the conversion of the theatre dated July 12, 1954, mentions cracks on the building as structural damage. Brandenburgisches Landeshauptarchiv, Aktenzeichen R. 601, no. 3699, sheet 7.

65   Brandenburgisches Landeshauptarchiv, Aktenzeichen R. 601, no. 3699, sheet 18.

66   "Eine[r] Quelle neuer Lebensfreude," Brandenburgisches Landeshauptarchiv, Aktenzeichen R. 601, no. 7627.

67   "Eine[r] Quelle neuer Lebensfreude," Brandenburgisches Landeshauptarchiv, Aktenzeichen R. 601, no. 7627.

68   Hartmut Kelm and Katja Gehring, "Am Tag des offenen Tores wurde dem Gelände des ehemaligen Kleist-Theaters mit viel Engagement wieder Leben eingehaucht," *Der Oderlandspiegel*, July 22, 2016, www.der-oderlandspiegel.de/news/artikel/am-tag-des-offenen-tores-wurde-dem-gelaende-des-ehemaligen-kleist-theaters-mit-viel-engagement-wiede.html.

69   Patrick Rössler, ed., *The Bauhaus and Public Relations: Communication in a Permanent State of Crisis* (New York, 2014), 159–84.

Part 2

The
Bauhaus
in
Weimar

Ines Weizman (editorial)

The Legacy of the Bauhaus in East Germany: Debates at the University of Architecture and Civil Engineering (Hochschule für Architektur und Bauwesen, HAB) in Weimar

In the immediate postwar era, after failed attempts to revive the Bauhaus school both in Weimar and in Dessau, even research on Bauhaus history was largely unthinkable in the architecture schools of East Germany, as it could not be suitably rationalized within the pedagogical dogmatism of the Stalinist and post-Stalinist regimes, and also because the lines of historical continuity lead out of the school to the US or other so-called "capitalist" or "non-socialist" countries. The following section aims to sketch out some of the complexities of the legacy of the Bauhaus in East Germany as it slowly, and under much difficulty, emerged as a field of research at the University of Architecture and Civil Engineering (Hochschule für Architektur und Bauwesen, HAB) in Weimar.

In the late 1950s, discussions concerning the reappraisal of Bauhaus history slowly emerged at the HAB Weimar when the school prepared for the centenary of the university. The university's history had to involve the story of the foundation of theGrand Ducal Art School in 1860 and the new Grand Ducal Vocational Arts School that Henry van de Velde directed between 1908 until its closure in 1915. And, of course, it also had to include the history of the Staatliches Bauhaus in Weimar (1919–25), which could not be told without its successor institutions, the State Academy of Crafts and Architecture under Social Democratic director Otto Bartning (1926–30) and the State Academy of Architecture, Fine Arts, and Crafts in Weimar under National Socialist director Paul Schultze-Naumburg (1930–45). Unable to loosen the ideological straitjacket of the regime, these complex histories of the school could not be addressed, and in consequence of this, state and university officials decided to cancel the celebration of the hundred-year anniversary of the university. Karl-Heinz Hüter, a researcher at the department of architectural history and theory, was initially tasked with conducting research for a memorial publication for that 100th anniversary of the school. He eventually published the first comprehensive book about the Bauhaus in Weimar (*Das Bauhaus in Weimar*, The Bauhaus in Weimar) which was immediately censored from publication in 1964 after it was discovered that Hüter had initiated unauthorized correspondence with Walter Gropius in the United States. This section includes an excerpt of the letters exchanged and an interview transcript in which Hüter reflects on the political constraints on his research which eventually ended his academic career.

The Bauhaus building in Dessau, originally designed by Walter Gropius in 1926, had barely survived the war, given that Dessau was bombed as an industrial center. By the 1970s, it was a wreck and needed urgent repair. Professors of history and design, among them Konrad Püschel, a former *Bauhäusler*, and Karl-Heinz Hüter, along with students from the Weimar school, first undertook a survey of the building, recorded all original elements that remained, and later helped restore it. This was the first step in bringing the school back into history.

The first Bauhaus colloquium (then still called "Wissenschaftliches Kolloquium," Academic Colloquium) was held in October 1976 in Weimar, a few months before the reopening ceremony of the Bauhaus building in Dessau on December 4, to celebrate the restoration of the derelict Bauhaus building in Dessau and discuss the legacy of the school. The conference, which was staged every three or four years thereafter, is in some ways both an outcome of and a contributor to the process through which the Bauhaus became accepted as a heritage. The invitation of international guests to Weimar marked not only the relative openness of the start of the meltdown years of the Soviet Bloc, but also an important shift in the reception of Bauhaus history. Each of the meetings in Weimar brought together scholars, theorists, artists, architects, and former *Bauhäusler* from both the East and the West. Given the political climate, presentations necessarily tested the limits of political speech and laid the foundation for an imagined, and indeed fragmented, collection constrained by geopolitical and ideological divisions. Constrained by the different ideological positions, the discussion offered divergent readings of the school in a

*Ines
Weizman*

The
Legacy
of
the
Bauhaus

331

conference room that became one of the heated, if now tamed, arenas for Cold War encounters. It was only when the Iron Curtain was fully drawn aside that a set of historical black boxes, locked up in state and private archives, was opened, allowing for new light to be shed on the period and the ideological coloring of the divergent stories.

After 1989, the concerns about the history of the Bauhaus, which had covered some political criticism and debates, acquired a different meaning. It was even questioned whether the conference should be continued at all. The decision taken by Gerd Zimmermann, who in 1992 had become both a professor of history and the theory of architecture as well as the director of the school, to continue the colloquium series was predicated on the idea that the discussion must change. He titled the 1992 colloquium *Architektur und Macht*—architecture and power—and engaged in a quite timely way with the possibility of— for the first time—openly speaking about architecture in the context of politics, free of the ideological limitations and the posturing of the Cold War. The 1992 colloquium pointed to a new engagement with architecture as a medium and instrument of politics.

When I became director of the Bauhaus Institute of History and Theory of Architecture and Planning, I also decided to continue the tradition of the colloquia and to plan the 2016 event both as an opportunity to reflect on new methods of Bauhaus historiography and the history of the conference itself. Precisely forty years after its inauguration in Weimar, and just prior to the 100th anniversary of the Bauhaus, the XIII. International Bauhaus-Kolloquium titled *Dust and Data* defined the conference as a historiographical institution—a barometer within a changing political and cultural landscape.

On its occasion, together with Norbert Korrek and Christiane Wolf, I curated an exhibition on the history of the Bauhaus colloquia at the HAB Weimar. In its first part, the exhibition documented the discussions surrounding the legacy of the Bauhaus at the HAB in the 1960s and 1970s. It included a section on the networking between the Bauhaus Dessau and the HAB, and reconstructed the practical and academic contribution made by the architecture department in the renovation of the Bauhaus building in Dessau, which is also included in an edited version in this section.[1]

The second part of the exhibition, a collaboration between the curators and students at the Bauhaus-Universität Weimar and the Centre for Documentary Architecture (CDA)[2], reviewed the history of the International Bauhaus-Kolloquium from 1976 to 2016. In 2019, as part of the XIV. International Bauhaus-Kolloquium, together with graphic designer Moritz Ebeling, I developed this exhibition, which contained statistics, photographs, and film interviews, as a website and an online database.[3] Excerpts of this exhibition and a selection of interviews with organizers, speakers, and guests from East and West are reproduced in this section of the book. The interviews illustrate the difficult minefield in which Bauhaus history was caught until 1989 on both sides of the ideological divide and contrast not only the different historiographical approaches of the East and West, but also the ideological transformation of the Soviet Bloc itself. The colloquium had been a place where speakers used the then officially endorsed reception of the Bauhaus in order to explore the expanding limits of what could be said under a slowly melting authoritarian regime; after 1989, speakers and guests continued to progress in terms of presenting knowledge regarding the whereabouts of objects and protagonists of the Bauhaus, or regarding archiving and conservation initiatives, as well as questions about the history and theory of architecture and its connection to politics. It is in this way that the conference in Weimar, as an institution of academic reflection and assembly, has contributed to the reappraisal of Bauhaus history and has also set the stage for recognizing and studying the hundred years of Bauhaus history.

1   Norbert Korrek and Christiane Wolf, *Das Internationale Bauhaus-Kolloquium in Weimar 1976 bis 2016: Ein Beitrag zur Bauhaus-Rezeption; Dokumentation, Ausstellungsteil, Prolog* (Weimar: Verlag der Bauhaus-Universität Weimar, 2016).
2   The Centre for Documentary Architecture (CDA), founded and directed by Ines Weizman, is an interdisciplinary project that explores architecture's materiality and is undertaken in relation to archives, drawings, photography, and literature, mobilized by digital research techniques and film. Its projects include, but are not limited to, publications, exhibitions, installations, films, new media projects, and public programs. Website: www.documentary-architecture.org
3   Special thanks to all interview partners. Sadly, Professor Grazioli passed away in 2018. The publication of the interview was kindly permitted by his family. Special thanks also to Norbert Korrek, who for years has been in charge of organizing the Bauhaus-Kolloquium under Professor Schädlich and in collaboration with professors of the Chair of Theory and History of Modern Architecture at the Bauhaus-Universität Weimar until 2013 and has hence accumulated an enormous knowledge and archive of the history of the university and the colloquia. Special thanks also to Christiane Wolf and the staff at the Archiv der Moderne at the Bauhaus-Universität Weimar, which has supported the research and has kindly permitted the reproduction of archival images.

Website "Das Internationale Bauhaus-Kolloquium in Weimar 1976–2019. Ein Beitrag zur Wiederaneignung des Bauhauses": www.bauhaus-kolloquium.de/archiv/

Ines Weizman

The Legacy of the Bauhaus

Kathrin Siebert

Party Politics and Architecture: The Schmidt-Basel Episode at the HAB Weimar in 1958

On September 29, 1958, Swiss architect and theoretician Hans Schmidt (1893–1972) was officially appointed by the government of the German Democratic Republic (GDR) as a "professor, with lecture-ship, in the theory of archi-tecture and standardization and the basics of building construction" in the architec-ture faculty at the University of Architecture and Civil Engineering (Hochschule für Architektur und Bau-wesen, HAB) in Weimar. Schmidt's estate in the gta archives at Swiss Federal Institute of Technology (Eidgenössische Technische Hochschule, ETH) Zurich includes the typed docu-ment that was issued at the time, bearing the seal of the Department of Higher Education and the signature and embossed stamp of State Secretary Dr. Wilhelm Girnus.[1] However, Schmidt's extensive papers contain no references to an applica-tion or to an appointment process nor any supporting document to show that Schmidt ever taught in Weimar. This raises questions that are now—sixty years after this authenticated appointment—all but im-possible to check based on the document in the archive and the memories of his colleagues at the time; yet they prompt us to paint a portrait of the Swiss maverick and to cast a critical eye on the power structures and mode of thinking at the HAB in the late 1950s. Ultimately, it was these factors that determined the difficult reception of the history of the Bauhaus in the postwar GDR.

Schmidt already had an eventful life behind him when he moved to East Berlin in January 1956 to take up a position as chief architect of the Institute for Standardization in the Ministry of Construction, where he was charged with advancing the industrialization of building in the GDR. In the second half of the 1920s, Schmidt had emerged as the leading figure in the *Neues Bauen* movement in Switzerland, having cut his teeth in Rotterdam familiarizing himself with rational building methods. Concurrently with the Bauhaus in Weimar and Dessau, Schmidt started experimenting with industrial production in construction in the 1920s, when he built some of the most important modernist houses in Switzerland. For example, in 1927 he collaborated with Basel architect Paul Artaria on the construction of a generously proportioned single-family house for the Colnaghi-Abt family in Riehen near Basel and used available industrial products for the purpose, including steel and pumice concrete slabs.[2] This prototype steel-frame house, the first of its kind in Switzerland, is still regarded as an "incunabulum" of *Neues Bauen*. The modular regularity of the steel-frame structure and standardized floor plans were important parameters for him in the design process.

In the course of opening the Weissenhof Estate in Stuttgart, Schmidt and Artaria had designed the layout and furnishings for a three-bedroom apartment in Mies van der Rohe's apartment building; in August 1927, Schmidt not only visited Ernst May's New Frankfurt housing but also went to the Bauhaus in Dessau, where Hannes Meyer, who also hailed from Basel, had been appointed head of the architecture department that April. An exchange of letters that took place between Schmidt and Meyer has not been preserved. References to contact between them can sometimes be found in letters to third parties. It can be verified that Schmidt kept in contact with Hans Wittwer, a contemporary of his from Basel who was Meyer's office partner and who also taught at the Bauhaus in the same period. Together with Meyer, he designed the ADGB Trade Union School in Bernau. From this period through to the 1950s, Schmidt also maintained cordial relations with German architect Hans Volger, a friend of Wittwer's who was ten years their junior. In a letter from Wittwer to his fiancée in Basel, mention is made of a period Schmidt spent in Dessau in December 1927.[3]

In 1927 Schmidt wrote a report on the Dessau Bauhaus for the *Sonntagsblatt der Basler Nachrichten*.[4] One year later, as part of his application for a professorship at ETH Zurich, he developed ideas for an alternative architecture school in Switzerland that had similarities to the Bauhaus.[5] By this time, Schmidt had also established himself as an acerbic architecture critic. In 1924, together with Mart Stam and Emil Roth, he founded the avant-garde magazine *ABC: Beiträge zum Bauen*.[6]

As co-founder and an active member of CIAM, Schmidt had personal contact with the principal modernist architects, including Walter Gropius. In 1930, Schmidt moved to Moscow as an advisor to the People's Commissariat for Heavy Industries; there he drew up plans for the first socialist cities in the Soviet Union. As a member of the "May Brigade," he developed proposals for Magnitogorsk, the Soviets' model planned city.[7] In 1932, under May's aegis and together with his colleagues Werner Hebebrand and the *Bauhäusler* Gustav Hassenpflug, Schmidt submitted an entry for the invited competition for Greater Moscow, although their proposal was not honored with an award under the newly modified design directives.[8] In 1934 Schmidt took on the sole responsibility for planning the city of Orsk in the Urals.[9] Schmidt engaged some German architects from Meyer's Rotfront Brigade to work on the project, among them Philipp Tolziner and Konrad Püschel, who had both studied at the Bauhaus in Dessau.[10] While Tolziner remained in the Soviet Union until his death in 1996, Püschel returned to Germany in 1937 and after the war became a lecturer and subsequently professor at the HAB Weimar. Püschel appears to have entirely missed the episode of Schmidt, as he returned to Weimar only in 1960, after having worked as city planner and architect for the reconstruction of the North Korean cities of Hamhung and Hungnam from 1955 to 1959. The connections between Schmidt, the Bauhaus, and the HAB were varied and narrow.

Schmidt returned to his home country from the Soviet Union in 1937. During the war, besides doing military service, he also built a hospital extension for the city of Basel and, from 1943 on, became heavily involved in political activities, first for the outlawed Communist Party of Switzerland (KPS) and subsequently for the newly founded Swiss Labor Party (PdA).[11] After the war, he successfully built various housing estates for building cooperatives: these are illustrative of the gap in formal terms between his ideas and those of the Neues Bauen movement.[12] In 1946, Schmidt was retained by the Polish government as a consultant for the first Warsaw reconstruction plans. This contract came about through his Polish friends Helena and Szymon Syrkus and his Swiss mentor Hans Bernoulli.[13] Schmidt's political activities and his connections and repeated extended journeys on the other side of the Iron Curtain made his work as a freelance architect increasingly difficult in Switzerland, where in the 1940s and 1950s the state expressly prohibited collaborations with communists. Schmidt encountered hostility and, like Meyer, who returned to Switzerland from Mexico in 1949, he became more and more marginalized both socially and economically.

The call to the GDR in 1956 was a welcome way out of this growing sense of isolation. Schmidt wanted to pass along his ideas and experience. Throughout his life he expressed his ideas on paper, critiquing and reflecting on events in contemporary architecture. Even after he left the GDR in 1969 and went back to Switzerland, he took a position on the question of architecture training.[14] Given his ambitions, there is nothing odd about the fact that Schmidt actually held a professorship. In 1928 he had applied to ETH Zurich for the position of professor of design but had been rejected on ideological grounds. In summer semester 1930, Schmidt taught at the trade school in Basel. He may also have taught at the Bauhaus, although the personal documents in his estate give no information on the subject. References to this teaching stint can be found in the work of Püschel, who noted in the letter of condolence he wrote in response to Schmidt's death in 1972: "Hans Schmidt was my teacher at the Bauhaus Dessau. Greatly appreciated and loved by us young *Bauhäusler*, he guided us with patience and care, introducing us to new basic concepts in architecture and urban design."[15] In the Bauhaus annals, Schmidt is listed under the heading "Other Instructors," although no other information is given.[16] In Moscow, Schmidt was again hoping for a teaching post. He had his course materials sent from Basel, as Meyer was to make "proposals for university training."[17] As an avowed communist, a teaching post in Switzerland had become impossible for him in the tense period during and after the war.

In a letter to his sister, Margarethe, dated November 1, 1958, several weeks after his appointment, Schmidt gave the following report:

> I have now been appointed professor at the University of Architecture and Civil Engineering in Weimar. We will be staying in Berlin, however, where I have to fulfill my main task of managing the Institute for the History and Theory of Architecture. Like the Institute for Standardization, where I worked until May of this year, this institute is part of the German Building Academy. My professorship is linked with a teaching position: however—for the time being at least—I have not done any lecturing.[18]

He seemed at this point in time not to have had any concrete sense of what his job in Weimar would entail. Schmidt's files also contain a

Kathrin
Siebert

Party
Politics
and
Architecture

337

Fig.1: Hans Schmidt, Schillerstrasse in Weimar, sketchbook, July 10, 1956.

Fig.2: Hans Schmidt, Rathaus in Weimar, sketchbook, July 10, 1956.

manuscript for a lecture entitled "Partisanship in Art and Architecture" (Die Parteilichkeit in der Kunst und in der Architektur), which he held at the HAB Weimar in December 1958.[19]

At the All-Union Building Conference in Moscow in November 1954, Nikita Khrushchev—who had taken over Stalin's official functions after the latter's death in March 1953—proclaimed a new policy direction in architecture and construction. He called for the immediate renunciation of the rigidified conception of architecture inherent to the classical and national building traditions and announced the immediate introduction of industrial building methods to quickly and efficiently overcome the shortcomings in the construction sector and the problem posed by the acute shortage of housing. The new architectural direction adopted in the socialist countries after this speech also paved the way for the slow rehabilitation of the pioneers of industrial building, and thus also of the Bauhaus.

Following the Moscow Conference, the First Building Conference of the GDR took place in April 1955. Standardization and industrialization now became the new doctrine for construction in the GDR as well. By the time Khrushchev held his secret speech on Stalin's crimes at the 20th Congress of the Communist Party in February 1956, Schmidt had already relocated to East Berlin to take up his position at the Institute for Standardization. His sketches of the time testify to his travels as well as his interest in urban planning and standardization. [fig.1–4]

Schmidt had a clear idea of how industrial building should be implemented. In the 1920s he had determined that standardized planning was key to the process of efficient production.[20] His idea was based on a systematic concept, which required a fundamental rethinking of architecture and the design process. The consequence of this would be not the free design of individual components, but rather designs using predetermined components within a prescribed frame. The debates about the theories of industrial building and socialist architecture were conducted in June 1959 at the Theoretical Conference at Schmidt's institute in Berlin, to which he had invited around sixty participants representing the realms of theory and practice.

From October 1958 to June 1959, in parallel to the episode in Weimar in 1958 and the preparations for the Theoretical Conference, Schmidt collaborated closely with Bruno Flierl, who was 34 years his junior colleague at the time, on a contribution to the most prestigious ideas competition of its day, "The socialist redesign of the center of

Part 2

The
Bauhaus
in
Weimar

Weimar
Schillerstraße
10.7.56

5,0   10,00   6,0

Weimar Rathaus
10.7.56

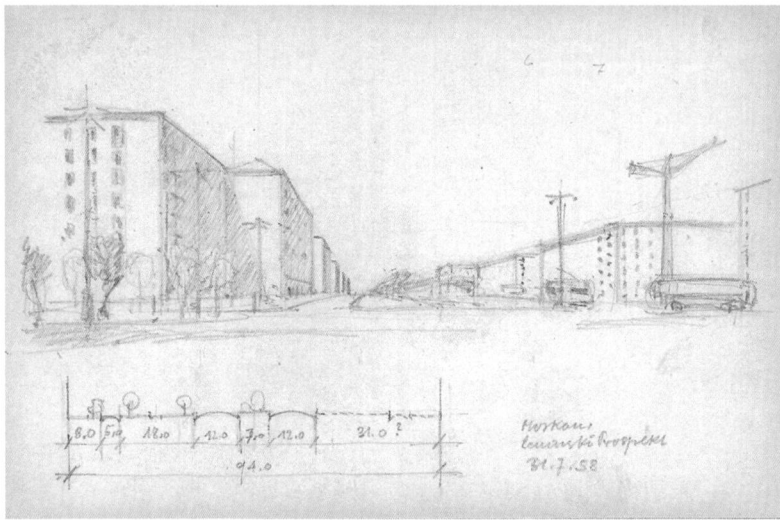

Berlin, the capital of the GDR."[21] The proposal elaborated under the direction of Schmidt and Flierl was focused on a rigorous and radical application of industrial building and was more or less hushed up in the ensuing discussions. The leadership of the GDR was still looking for appropriate architectural models that not only distanced themselves from Western architecture—which was also conducting new experiments in industrial housing construction at the time—but that were also a departure from the planning directives coming out of Moscow.

In retrospect, Flierl could not remember Schmidt working in Weimar in addition to his activities in Berlin.[22] He also stated that Schmidt had not made efforts to secure a professorship, but was quite content with the research work he was doing at the Building Academy. Moreover, Christian Schädlich (who did his doctorate at the HAB in 1957 and was subsequently engaged there, from 1967 to 1987, as a professor in the history and theory of architecture) and Anita Bach (who was then a teaching assistant to Otto Englberger, professor of housing and community facilities design, and subsequently herself professor of interior design at the HAB from 1969 to 1992) both remembered Schmidt as a personality. However, they each affirmed, independently of one another, that they had never seen Schmidt at the HAB, and certainly not in the role of professor.[23] By contrast, Schmidt's daughter mentioned that her father would have liked to have a professorship during his stay in the GDR but that he had not been wanted at the university.[24]

On July 29, 1957, director Franz Latus and Party secretary Emil Schmidt from the Institute of Standardization wrote an "assessment of chief architect Hans Schmidt, Dip. Eng." and sent it to the department of universities and technical colleges at the Ministry of Construction.[25] It is not clear who commissioned this assessment. Schmidt—who is not to be confused with Hans Schmidt—and Latus both agreed "that the great abilities of their colleague Schmidt would be harnessed in the most efficacious way if, besides his work at our institute, he were to take on a professorship at the University of Architecture and Civil Engineering in Weimar."[26] A confidential letter from the Ministry

Fig.4: Hans Schmidt, Reichstagsruine und Hansaviertel in Berlin, sketchbook, August 29, 1958.

of Construction to the president of the HAB, dated August 28, 1957, and pertaining to "an adjunct teaching position for Mr. Hans Schmidt, Dip. Eng.," makes reference to a face-to-face meeting that had taken place beforehand.[27] Hans Schmidt had not been present at this discussion. There is no indication of whether he was even aware of the process that was in play. A résumé included in the personnel file is dated July 16, 1957, although it is not signed by him personally.[28]

On November 5, 1957, together with Benny Heumann, who was working in the building department of the Central Committee (Zentralkomitee, ZK) of the SED, Hans Schmidt traveled to Weimar—apparently clueless of what was going on—in order to moderate a discussion at the HAB on the future of socialist education.[29] In light of the critical political situation in the aftermath of the death of Stalin, it seemed necessary to clarify the political orientation at the universities. A few days previously, the two had been on a similar mission to the University of Technology (Technische Universität, TU) in Dresden, which Schmidt commented on in detail in his notebook.[30] In it, he noted that Heumann, a member of the ZK, was to offer ideological instruction to comrades, while Schmidt was responsible for communicating the architectural issues.[31] The thematic focus was on the question of socialist education as well as on the socialist housing complex and the ideological face of architecture. In addition to this, current political issues were discussed in Dresden, such as the Interbau in West Berlin [fig.4] "as a political problem" and the increasing exodus to the West of those "who did not believe in the future of the GDR."[32] Schmidt made no mention of a discussion of the pending professorship in Weimar.

Some ideological U-turns had also been performed in Weimar between 1945 and 1958. In the period between 1946 and 1949, Hermann Henselmann, as newly appointed director and professor of the Academy of Architecture and Fine Arts (Hochschule für Baukunst und Bildende Künste), attempted to build upon the Bauhaus legacy of the 1920s.[33] Henselmann therefore engaged former Bauhau students and architects of the *Neues Bauen* movement, such as Gustav Hassenpflug.

Kathrin Siebert

Party Politics and Architecture

341

The teaching staff also included architects whose thinking followed the so-called Stuttgart School, which had influenced the college during World War II when it was under the directorship of Nazi propagandist Paul Schultze-Naumburg. Among their ranks were such instructors as Heinrich Rettig and subsequently Emil Schmidt, who in 1958 was still the dean of the faculty of architecture. Thus, in the first years after the war, a traditionalist architectural approach was cultivated alongside modern attitudes.[34] Thereafter, Henselmann left for Berlin, and, in conjunction with the second university reform in 1951/52, aforementioned architect Otto Englberger took over as director of the school. The classics were now a compulsory area of study. The teaching was adapted to the prevailing ideological doctrine, which bore the stamp of Stalinism. In 1954, the school was renamed the University of Architecture and Civil Engineering (HAB). Englberger became president and remained in office until the summer semester of 1957.

That Schmidt's appointment to the HAB Weimar came at the directive of the ministry was understandable in light of the political changes, but in Weimar it led to internal turmoil, as it seemed as if Schmidt had been sent to see to the implementation of a new policy. This paternalism was unwelcome. On November 9, 1957, after a process of "in-depth discussion," the architecture faculty council under the directorship of the dean, Professor Emil Schmidt, concluded the following:

> The Faculty Council considers the method by which Mr. Hans Schmidt, Dip. Eng., was put forward for the post to be unacademic and that it goes over the head of the university's democratic institutions. The Council does not believe that this does justice to Mr. Schmidt's great merits, of which there can be no doubt. In consequence of this, the Council sees no reason to comply with what has been proposed, especially as no suitable vacancy is currently available.[35]

This was communicated to the university senate on November 12. The situation was then discussed once again in the senate meeting on November 13.[36] After further "in-depth discussion," the decision was now taken by newly incumbent president Gustav Batereau to endorse the award of a teaching position and professorship with part-time lectureship.[37] In other words, after the faculty council had rejected the proposed appointment, it was then approved in the senate. This constituted a clear affront, but there was nothing more that could be done to prevent it.

The next stage of the process called for expert opinions, and these were submitted in December.[38] We can ultimately glean from the cover letter accompanying the assessment by Hans Collein that State Secretary Gerhard Kosel had responsibility within the ministry "for filing the motion for the appointment of Mr. Hans Schmidt, Dip. Eng."[39] It was Kosel, too, who had invited Schmidt to come to the GDR. The two knew each other from their time together in Moscow. Kosel had only returned to the GDR in 1954 and had been given the task of implementing industrial building.[40] The appointments procedure in Weimar continued on its course in December 1957, protracted for some time by the unclear circumstances surrounding Schmidt's party membership. In the subsequent correspondence, which is also filed with Schmidt's personnel records, the reluctance on the part of the HAB to accept this decision is repeatedly made clear: "In the case of the appointment of Mr. Schmidt-Basel, Dip. Eng., we must rely on the recommendation of the Ministry of Construction."[41] From then on, in order to avoid confusion, Schmidt was known in Weimar as Schmidt-Basel, as the incumbent dean of the architecture faculty was also called Schmidt. We have no clear record of when Hans Schmidt was informed and at what point he became involved in this process. At the end of September, he received his letter of appointment, effective retroactively from September 1.

The minutes of the faculty council meeting of January 16, 1959 once again clearly show that the appointment was forced through by the ministry in Berlin against the will of the faculty and that in actual fact the two sides—both Schmidt and the architecture faculty—were "somewhat piqued" by the process.[42] We can also surmise that Kosel, acting from Berlin, had a significant hand in things and that the HAB ultimately succumbed in order to avoid difficulties with the ministry. According to the minutes, the HAB used the latitude that it had—adding the peculiar attribute "part-time" (*nebenamtlich*) and justifying Schmidt's rejection on the basis that no vacancy was available—to make a stand against Berlin.

As the minutes show, it was Schmidt's expectation that he would be required to give guest lectures, at least now and then, "to warrant his title," whereupon he was confronted fairly bluntly with the unwelcome course of action taken by Berlin and informed that as a result he need not feel obligated to the HAB. According to the minutes, Professor Weidhaas, who shortly thereafter taught a course with the

Kathrin Siebert

Party Politics and Architecture

343

cumbersome title "Theory of Socialist Architecture and Socialist Urban Development," would give up three ninety-minute lecture periods and transfer them to Schmidt. The final minute states that, if Schmidt should actually accede to his post in Weimar, "a certain degree of caution should be exercised to prevent a similar situation from transpiring such as had taken place at the colloquium with the students in the student club."[43]

The minutes log internal and external details and disagreements put together with a clarity that can seldom be found in surviving records documenting GDR history. The minutes not only attest to the conflicted relationship between the HAB Weimar and the Ministry of Construction in Berlin but also document in exceptional fashion the fairly open criticism that was leveled at the directives issued by a higher-ranking institution in Berlin.

One month prior to this, on December 17, 1958, a minor event had taken place in the student club in Weimar with the newly appointed "Prof. Schmidt-Basel"; it was not widely publicized and was all but overlooked. For Schmidt, however, it had far-reaching consequences. Schmidt was invited to give his opinion on the question of partisanship, an explosive topic at the time.[44] Schmidt's talk, which is preserved as a fifteen-page manuscript, concentrated on the question of whether there was such a thing as capitalist or socialist art or architecture and what might distinguish their basic principles and forms of expression. Schmidt interpreted partisanship to mean the "taking of sides in the conflict between capitalism and socialism." Schmidt argued that, in art, partisanship did indeed exist and that there was thus also a socialist and a capitalist form of art. However, he went on to observe that architecture and art could not be equated because "art is not an object of material production." The discussion should, in his opinion, be less concerned with the nature of architecture and focus rather on the application of new materials and modes of construction and on the functional and economic aspects of building: "The artistic side must be subordinated to structural engineering." Here Schmidt directly invoked a personal "talk" he had had with Khrushchev at the Congress of the International Union of Architects in July 1958 in Moscow. The distinction between "buildings of ideational significance," with a claim to art, and "merely utilitarian buildings" that were not classed as architecture should be overcome once and for all. Schmidt stated that a socialist architecture differed from its capitalist counterpart in its ideational content and in comprehensive industrialization, but avoided using the term "partisanship" here. He endeavored to keep the discussion of architecture apart from the ideological discussion of art, which Schmidt associated with the notion of partisanship.

Schmidt's way of thinking was diametrically opposed to the line of argument that was still quite usual at the time, which was informed by a Stalinist model. It caused a scandal. In a two-page "memo" dated December 20, 1958, which is preserved in Schmidt's personnel records, Mr. Elschner, assistant lecturer at the department of Marxism and Leninism at the HAB, advises that "should Comrade Prof. Schmidt-Basel be deployed again for lectures and colloquia," it would be absolutely essential to hold an up-front discussion with the "Comrade Professors and the Faculty of Architecture," the purpose of which would be "not to potentially stifle any contrary opinion but rather to recognize the limits of what can be offered to students without thoroughly confounding them."[45]

Arguments based on Stalin's art ideology were used up until the early 1960s, even in official contexts. Kurt Magritz, in particular, in his function as acting editor-in-chief of *Deutsche Architektur*, defended this position vehemently. Just a few months before Schmidt's arrival in Weimar, he used a prominently placed article in his magazine— entitled "The Principle of Open Partisanship and Architecture"— to argue that architecture is art and advocated an "open and conscious partisanship to advance the cause of socialism."[46] Six months after the incident in Weimar, Siegfried Tschierschky, professor of fine art at the HAB, also had his say in *Deutsche Architektur*. As vice-dean of the architecture faculty, he had followed events at first hand. In his article, published in June 1959—exactly one year after Magritz's article appeared—he argued in favor of partisanship in architecture: "Unlike applied art, architecture can and should be a partisan statement with significant social impact."[47]

The principle of partisanship is a proposition introduced by Lenin in his early writings "Party Organization and Party Literature" (1905) and *Materialism and Empirio-Criticism* (1908), according to which an objective and unbiased observation and interpretation of reality is impossible. According to Lenin, within the context of a Marxist interpretation of history and the world, a position must always be taken that is strictly in the interests of the working class. In the Soviet Union, and later in the GDR, this principle was understood to mean that the

Kathrin
Siebert

Party
Politics
and
Architecture

345

party should always be given the power of interpretation to determine what was to be regarded as true. However, Marx himself thought that any form of direct doctrinal partiality was unacceptable. He advocated scientific objectivity. Moral valuation and political leanings have no place in theory, according to Marx, but rather constitute an aspect of the subject addressed. Partisanship is thus unnecessary, because the more seriously the theory takes the facts, the more inevitably will it confront the fact that the existing relations of production and their superstructure are historically impermanent.[48]

Schmidt's opinion coincided with the thinking of a number of other intellectuals. In 1956, for example, historian Jürgen Kuczynski questioned whether science or the party had primacy.[49] Kuczynski presented himself as a champion of orthodox Marxism. He explicitly advocated the primacy of science and thus took a clear stand in opposition to the established thinking based on Lenin's ideas.[50] Schmidt, too, advocated a neutral position in the Marxist sense and thus turned against the increasingly rigid ideas in circulation at the time postulating partisanship in architecture, which were geared solely to the party line. His view of partisanship did not run afoul of Marxist thinking, but it did contradict Leninist notions, which were the basis for the party's official position at the time.

The Schmidt-Basel episode at the HAB Weimar points to the difficulty facing the historian in reconstructing a conflict that we can be certain was handled differently in different circles and was in part treated as an internal confidential matter and in part aired publicly. It also highlights how hard it is to evaluate the stories of people and courses of action in an account of history that is ideologically determined, distorted by a dictatorial or totalitarian system, and imbued with double connotations.[51]

Schmidt reacted with personal intellectual obstinacy to the issue of partisanship. Presumably he completely understood the unequivocal words addressed to him in Weimar after his appointment at the turn of the year in 1958/59, as recorded in the minutes. Schmidt was forced to recognize that the progressive thinking in relation to the rationalization of building processes that he had developed back in the 1920s when grappling with the positions held by Gropius and Meyer did not as yet have any place in the contemporary approach of the former Bauhaus. From that point on, he held lectures and seminars at the university in Dresden and not in Weimar. It was not until ten years later that he returned to the place where these events had unfolded to give two lectures at an institute of further education at the HAB.[52]

In the 1950s, Schmidt had been faced with what amounted to closed ranks in Weimar; however, in the 1970s the situation changed fundamentally when the group of people in question retired. The HAB opened itself up to more critical positions. Referring to this period, Anita Bach called the HAB in retrospect an "island of bliss."[53] After 1976, the International Bauhaus-Kolloquien, in particular, made it possible to engage in an open process of international exchange of a kind that allowed hosting a network of former Bauhaus members and friends and that was otherwise not practiced or experienced anywhere in the GDR with this degree of regularity. Hans Schmidt did not live to see this phase. In 1969 he returned to Switzerland and died there in the summer of 1972.

1 The document is held at ETH Zurich. September 29, 1958, gta archives, ETH Zurich, 61-4-3-3.

2 Ursula Suter, "Haus Colnaghi-Abt," in *Hans Schmidt 1893–1972: Architekt in Basel, Moskau, Berlin-Ost* (Zurich, 1993), here: 160–63.

3 Hans Wittwer to Jula Rieder, December 6, 1927, gta archives, ETH Zurich, 35-K-6-8.

4 Hans Schmidt, "Das Bauhaus in Dessau und seine Aufgabe," *Sonntagsblatt der Basler Nachrichten*, September 11, 1927.

5 Hans Schmidt, "Akademische oder praktische Architektenausbildung?," TS, 4 pages, March 20, 1928, gta archives, ETH Zurich, 61-T-59.

6 ABC: *Beiträge zum Bauen*, ed. Emil Roth, Hans Schmidt, and Mart Stam, 2 series, 6 issues, published at irregular intervals between 1924 and 1928.

7 Thomas Flierl, ed., *Standardstädte: Ernst May in der Sowjetunion 1930–1933; Texte und Dokumente* (Berlin, 2012).

8 The estate of Werner Hebebrand includes a copy of the plan, on which Schmidt's name is also noted as one of the authors. Akademie der Künste Berlin, Archiv Werner Hebebrand. See also: Hans Schmidt, "Diskussion um Rußland: Der Sowjetpalast; An den Internationalen Kongreß für Neues Bauen; Generalsekretariat," *Die Neue Stadt* 6, no. 7: p. 146.

9 Ursula Suter, "Stadtplanung Orsk," in *Hans Schmidt 1893–1972* (see note 2), here: 208–12. See Konrad Püschel, "Die erste Aufbauperiode der sozialistischen Stadt Orsk," *Wissenschaftliche Zeitschrift der HAB Weimar* 14, no. 5 (1967): 451–58.

10 Winfried Nerdinger, "Philipp Tolziner: Lebenswege eines Münchner Bauhäuslers," in "Kunststadt München? Unterbrochene Lebenswege," *Münchner Beiträge zur jüdischen Geschichte und Kultur* 6, no. 2 (2012): 55–61.

11 Ursula Suter, "Infektionskrankenhaus des Bürgerspitals (1939–1946)," in *Hans Schmidt 1893–1972* (see note 2), here: 228–29.

12 Ursula Suter, "Siedlung Haslerrain (1945–1947) und Siedlung 'Im Höfli' (1946–1954)," in *Hans Schmidt 1893–1972* (see note 2), here: 252–53 and 257–62.

13 The Syrkuses also supported Schmidt in a follow-up project in Warsaw: the renovation of a classicist palace for the Swiss Legation that Schmidt carried out between 1947 and 1949.

14 Hans Schmidt, opinion on the propositions relating to architecture training, gta archives, ETH Zurich, 61-T-448. Published under the title "Hans Schmidt BSA/SIA, Basel," *Werk* 10 (1970): 690–91.

15 Konrad Püschel, letter to Lilly Schmidt, July 11, 1972, MS, 1 page, gta archives, ETH Zurich, 61-K-1972-07-11.

16 Folke F. Dietzsch, "Die Studierenden am Bauhaus: Eine analytische Betrachtung zur Struktur der Studentenschaft, zur Ausbildung und zum Leben der Studierenden am Bauhaus sowie zu ihrem späteren Wirken," diss. (Weimar, 1990). Ursula Muscheler, who described Schmidt as a guest instructor at the Bauhaus, probably also refers to this dissertation by Dietzsch. See Ursula Muscheler, *Das rote Bauhaus: Eine Geschichte von Hoffnung und Scheitern* (Berlin, 2016), here: 21.

17 In a letter dated October 5, 1930, Hans Schmidt asked his brother Georg in Basel to send his teaching materials to Moscow, as Meyer was supposed to make suggestions there for tertiary education. See Hans Schmidt to his brother Georg, October 5, 1930, MS, 1 page, gta archives, ETH Zurich, 61-K-1930-10-05.

18 Hans Schmidt to his sister Margarethe, November 1, 1958, gta archives, ETH Zurich, 61-K-1958-11-01.

19 Hans Schmidt, "Die Parteilichkeit in der Kunst und in der Architektur," lecture, MS, 15 pages, HAB Weimar, December 17, 1958, gta archives, ETH Zurich, 61-T-304.

20 See Hans Schmidt, "Die Beziehungen der Typisierung zur Architektur," in *Die Typenprojektierung im zweiten Fünfjahrplan: Reden gehalten anläßlich der Gründungsfeier des Instituts für Typung beim Ministerium für Aufbau, 19. Juni 1956* (East Berlin, 1956), 16–20, and *Deutsche Architektur* 12 (1956): 575–76. See also Hans Schmidt, "Keine Furcht vor Monotonie!" *Deutsche Architektur* 8 (1956): 389; "Architektur und Typenprojektierung," *Deutsche Architektur* 2 (1957): 87–89; "Vor der Schwelle des sozialistischen Städtebaus," *Deutsche Architektur* 9 (1957): 481–82.

21 Ideas competition, jury report, Berlin, August 17, 1959, gta archives, ETH Zurich, 61-0191.

22 Bruno Flierl, conversation with the author, Weimar, October 25, 2016.

23 Anita Bach, conversation with the author, Prerow, May 12, 2016; and Christian Schädlich, conversation with the author, Weimar, July 19, 2016.

24 Madleen Lamm-Schmidt, conversation with the author, Vienna, December 11, 2014.

25 A copy of this letter can be found in Schmidt's personal files in the university archives in Weimar. See Franz Latus, Institute of Standardization, letter to the Department of Universities and Technical Colleges at the Ministry of Construction, assessment of chief architect

Hans Schmidt, Dip. Eng., July 29, 1957, TS 1 page, Archiv der Moderne, Bauhaus Universität, 11-02-075.

26 Latus, letter, July 29, 1957 (see note 30).

27 Kant (first name unknown), head of the Department of Universities and Technical Colleges at the Ministry of Construction, letter to Otto Englberger, president of the HAB, August 28, 1957, TS, 1 page, Archiv der Moderne, Bauhaus Universität, 11-02-075.

28 Hans Schmidt, résumé, July 16, 1957, TS, 4 pages, Archiv der Moderne, Bauhaus Universität, 11-02-075.

29 Hans Schmidt, notebook, entry dated November 5, 1957, gta archives, ETH Zurich, 61-3-19.

30 Hans Schmidt, notebook, entry dated November 5, 1957.

31 Hans Schmidt, "Vom Gesicht der sozialistischen Architektur," MS, 2 pages, November 1957, gta archives, ETH Zurich, 61-T-268. Published under the title "Vor der Schwelle des sozialistischen Städtebaus," *Deutsche Architektur* 9 (1957): 481–82.

32 Hans Schmidt, notebook, entry dated November 3, 1957, gta archives, ETH Zurich, 61-3-19.

33 See Klaus Jürgen Winkler, ed., *Neubeginn: Die Weimarer Bauhochschule nach dem Zweiten Weltkrieg und Hermann Henselmann* (Weimar, 2005). See Norbert Korrek, "Neubeginn," in *Städtebau-Debatten in der DDR: Verborgene Reformdiskurse*, ed. Christoph Bernhardt, Thomas Flierl, and Max Welch Guerra (Berlin, 2012), 19–41.

34 See Klaus-Jürgen Winkler, "Der Aspekt der Architekturtheorie in der Weimarer Architektenausbildung: Die ersten drei Jahrzehnte; Vom Bauhaus bis zum Beginn der 1950er-Jahre," in *Wirklichkeitsexperimente: Architekturtheorie und praktische Ästhetik; Festschrift zum 60. Geburtstag von Gerd Zimmermann*, ed. Jörg H. Gleiter, Norbert Korrek, and Sandra Schramke (Weimar, 2006), 185–220, esp. 205–216.

35 Minutes of the meeting of the architecture faculty council, November 9, 1957, TS, 4 pages, Archiv der Moderne, Bauhaus Universität, 1957-11-9-I-12-007_FRA.

36 Minutes of the senate meeting, November 13, 1957, TS, 12 pages, Archiv der Moderne, Bauhaus Universität, 1957-11-13-I-07-057_Senat.

37   Minutes of the senate meeting, November 13, 1957.

38   Kurt Liebknecht, assessment, December 3, 1957, TS, 2 pages; Hans Karthaus, expert opinion, December 4, 1957, TS, 2 pages; Hans Collein, assessment, December 2, 1957, TS, 1 page, all from the Archiv der Moderne, Bauhaus Universität, 1957-11-13-I-07-057.

39   Letter dated December 11, 1957, TS, 1 page, Archiv der Moderne, Bauhaus Universität, 11-02-075.

40   Christine Hannemann, "Der 'system builder' Gerhard Kosel," in *Die Platte: Industrialisierter Wohnungsbau in der DDR* (Braunschweig, 1996), here: 68–74, esp. 71.

41   Letter from the university trade union committee to the cadre committee, January 23, 1958, TS, 1 page, Archiv der Moderne, Bauhaus Universität, 11-02-075.

42   Minutes of the architecture faculty council meeting, January 16, 1958, TS, 18 pages, Archiv der Moderne, Bauhaus-Universität Weimar, 1958-01-16-I-02-953_FRA.

43   Minutes of the architecture faculty council meeting, January 16, 1958.

44   Hans Schmidt, "Die Parteilichkeit in der Kunst und in der Architektur," lecture, MS, 15 pages, HAB Weimar, December 17, 1958, gta archives 61-T-304.

45   Memo, Department for the Foundation Course in Social Sciences (Marxism/Leninism), TS, 2 pages, December 20, 1958, Archiv der Moderne, Bauhaus-Universität Weimar, 11-02-075.

46   Kurt Magritz, "Das Prinzip der offenen Parteilichkeit und die Architektur," *Deutsche Architektur* 7 (1958): 357–58.

47   Siegfried Tschierschky, "Es geht um die Parteilichkeit in der Architektur," *Deutsche Architektur* 6 (1959): 343–44.

48   Karl Marx, *Das Kapital: Kritik der politischen Ökonomie*, vol. 1 (Berlin, 1968), 21. See Michael Quante and David Schweikard, eds., *Marx Handbuch: Leben–Werk–Wirkung* (Stuttgart, 2016), here: 289–90.

49   Jürgen Kuczynski, "Parteilichkeit und Objektivität in Geschichte und Geschichtsschreibung," *Zeitschrift für Geschichtswissenschaft* 4 (1956): 873–88.

50   Helmut Rumpler, "Parteilichkeit und Objektivität als Theorieproblem der DDR-Historie," in *Objektivität und Parteilichkeit in der Geschichtswissenschaft*, ed. Reinhart Koselleck, Wolfgang J. Mommsen, and Jörn Rüsen (Munich, 1977), here: 228–62, esp. 239.

51   Ines Weizman, "Als die Architekten die Revolution verließen: Regimekritiker und Dissidenz in der DDR und Osteuropa vor 1989," in *Vergessene Schulen: Architekturlehre zwischen Reform und Revolte um 1968*, ed. Nina Gribat, Philip Misselwitz, and Matthias Görlich (Leipzig, 2017), 291–306; see also Ines Weizman, "Mobilizing Dissent: The Possible Architecture of the Governed," in *The SAGE Handbook of Architectural Theory*, ed. Greig Crysler, Stephen Cairns, and Hilde Heynen (London, 2012), 107–20.

52   See Hans Schmidt, "Die Umgestaltung der Stadt," training seminar, MS, 17 pages, Weimar, November 7 and 14, 1968, gta archives, ETH Zurich, 61-T-433. See Hans Schmidt, "Brauchen wir eine Ästhetik der Architektur?," training seminar, MS, 11 pages, Weimar, June 22, 1969, gta archives, ETH Zurich, 61-T-438.

53   Anita Bach, conversation with the author, Prerow, May 12, 2016.

Norbert Korrek
Christiane Wolf

The Long Path to the Restoration of the Bauhaus Dessau (1951–76)[1]

The reception of the Bauhaus and its history in the GDR was as intense as it was contradictory, and at the Weimar academy it even generated a sometimes grotesque conflict of political and academic interests. The architect Hermann Henselmann's desire to reconnect with the Bauhaus tradition in Weimar in the years following World War II was initially a matter of political expediency, following the general trend in Germany of espousing educational traditions that predated the National Socialists' seizure of power.[2] In Weimar, the continuity of these traditions had been broken for longer than in other parts of the country, starting as early as 1930, when Paul Schultze-Naumburg was appointed director of the State Academy of Architecture, Fine Arts and Crafts, and was escorted into office by a Nazi squad bearing the swastika.[3] In spite of the academy counting five former *Bauhäusler*—Gustav Hassenpflug, Hanns Hoffmann-Lederer, Peter Keler, Emanuel Lindner, and Rudolf Ortner—among its staff after reopening in 1946, by 1951 at the latest the Bauhaus had been sidelined ideologically as a result of the debate on formalism.

Karl-Heinz Hüter, the founder of Bauhaus research in the GDR, spoke in 1990 of "the severity with which the state institutions attempted to prevent a fact-based historical evaluation of the achievements of this school and working community." The following notes and documents present some of the key moments in the slow and difficult reappraisal of Bauhaus history at the HAB Weimar which, when it was assigned a central role in the scientific assessment of the Bauhaus, also reflected the larger cultural and political context of the GDR.

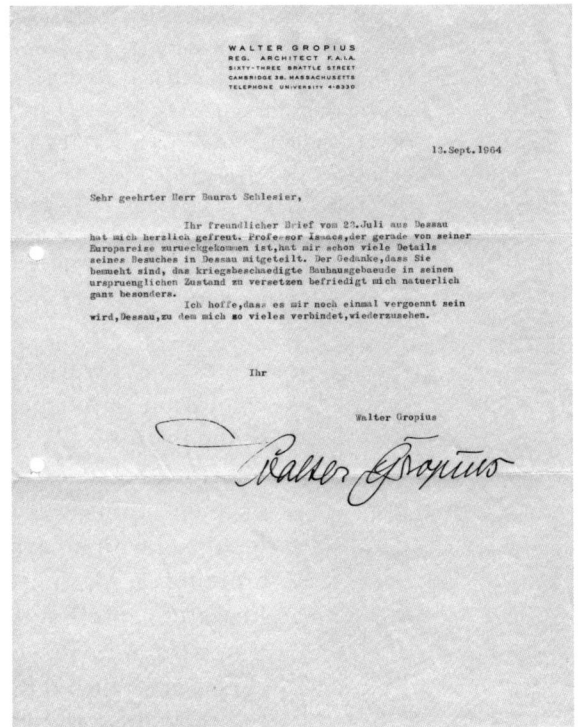

Cancellation of the 100th anniversary of the university

1   In preparation for the 100th anniversary of the university in 1960, the senate decided, in 1957, to form a committee tasked with publishing, "in more depth and more comprehensively than ever before," a "historical assessment of the development" of the university in Weimar and to present it to the public in a "lavish exhibition." Responsibility was given to Konrad Werner Schulze (Chair of Architectural History). His assistant, Karl-Heinz Hüter, whose survey of the university's history had just appeared in print, was put in charge of determining the content. Peter Keler, a former Bauhaus student, was responsible for the design.

2   It took a year for the committee to take shape. Hüter put forward his idea of the university's history as a "complete overview" including all the stages of development from 1860 to 1960. His presentation included a discussion of the State Bauhaus and the schools under the direction of Paul Schultze-Naumburg. His attempt to collaborate with art historian Hans Maria Wingler on the work of the Bauhaus in Weimar came to nothing.

3   In 1957, in preparation for the first book laying out the basics of the Bauhaus, Wingler visited the sites in Weimar where the Bauhaus had been active and documented them in photographs.

4   The 100th anniversary came to grief because of ideological reservations about some of the phases in the university's development. In May 1959, the senate followed the advice of the university's SED party leadership and canceled the centenary on the pretext that presenting an overall view of the university's development from a "Marxist perspective" was no longer possible. The Bauhaus and the schools under Paul Schultze-Naumburg were referred to as being "exceptionally problematic."

5   Following the cancellation of the university's centenary celebrations, the Staatliche Kunstsammlungen Weimar paid tribute to the founding of the Grand Ducal Art School in 1860 with an

Norbert
Korrek
Christiane
Wolf

The
Long
Path
to
the
Restoration

351

exhibition of works from the Weimar school of painters. In the exhibition catalogue, director Walther Scheidig gave an overview of the institution's development up until 1960.

6 Shortly after the cancellation of the centenary event, a week of celebrations took place to mark the GDR's tenth anniversary. It started with an exhibition in the newly opened auditorium building on Marienstraße. Entitled "Examples of the Teaching, Research, and Practice of the University," the exhibition illustrated the ways in which the demands of the 3rd Building Conference were realized in the education of students.

7 For the course catalogue of 1956/57, Hüter wrote a version of the university's history that remains valid to this day. Although the political environment was deteriorating at the time, it gave a "cautiously positive assessment of the Bauhaus." Hüter's later publications made him the driving force behind Bauhaus research in the GDR.

Pragmatic rapprochement and scientific research

8 After the cancellation of the 100th anniversary, the senate decided, with the approval of the State Secretariat for Higher Education, to form a Committee for the Study of the Bauhaus. Schulze once again took on the leadership role. In addition to his assistants, Karl-Heinz Hüter and Christian Schädlich, Keler and another former Bauhaus student, Konrad Püschel, were also appointed as members.

9 At the invitation of the city of Dessau, a visit to the Bauhaus buildings took place on May 12, 1961. Along with the Törten housing estate, the employment office, the Masters' Houses, and the Kornhaus, there was a particular interest in the nascent process of "preserving the value of the vocational schools" that had been located in Walter Gropius's former Bauhaus building since 1946.

10 After a further visit to the Bauhaus buildings in Dessau by a group that included Ludwig Deiters, the general curator of the GDR's Institute for Monument Preservation, the Institute for Urban Development and Architecture of the Deutsche Bauakademie proposed to declare the Bauhaus building in Dessau a

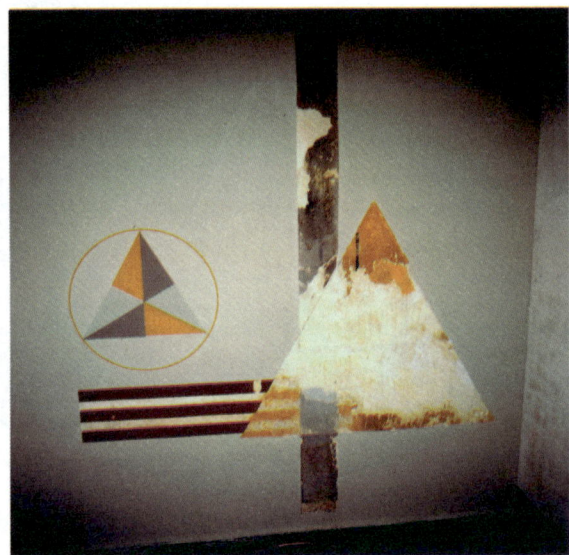

Fig. 6. Impressions of students contributing their labor, June 1976.

Fig. 7. Bauhaus Dessau during reconstruction, shop building and skyway (bridge), summer 1976. Photograph by Christian Borchert.

Fig. 8a–c. Werner Claus had begun to uncover Herbert Beyer's murals in side stairway in the van de Velde building in Weimar.

historic monument, "in accordance with its progressive significance for the development of German and international architecture." For this purpose, a "restoration of the original state of the ensemble in its outer form, details, and floor plans" was considered necessary. The reconstruction of Walter Gropius's house, which had been destroyed in the war, was also recommended.

11 Another outcome of the site visit was the establishment of a working group. Their first "Bauhaus briefing" on December 21, 1962, which was led by Kurt Junghanns, also included Püschel, as well as Karl-Heinz Hüter and Christian Schädlich, representing the HAB Weimar.

12 In the summer of 1964, five third-year architecture students prepared a two-volume survey of the Bauhaus building as part of their practical training, under the guidance of former Bauhaus student Konrad Püschel and the city architect of Dessau, Karlheinz Schlesier. Schlesier, who held a non-degree research assistantship at the HAB at that time, had actively supported the idea of a restoration since 1962. In light of the "reconstruction work necessitated by the war and its aftermath and the long-neglected upkeep of the building" (Püschel, 1964), the city council decided to restore the "Bauhaus to its original state." Keler agreed to contribute to the color design.

13 In July 1964, Reginald R. Isaacs, a student of Gropius and professor at Harvard University, stayed in Dessau and Weimar to study for his monograph on Gropius. Through him, Gropius learned about the plan to "return the war-damaged Bauhaus buildings to their original condition." He also expressed his wish to "see Dessau once again." (Gropius, 1964)

14 The idea of inviting Gropius was supported by the Association of German Architects, as well as by Schlesier. In 1964, Isaacs confirmed to him that Gropius was open to the idea and would likely accept "an invitation to the reopening and fortieth anniversary of the Dessau Bauhaus."

15 Starting in October 1964, the HAB pursued the goal of inviting Gropius to Weimar. Later, the planned invitation was associated with the idea of bestowing the title of honorary senator upon him. Issacs, who was also in Weimar in July 1964, studying for his monograph on Gropius, again acted as intermediary. Because the Ministry of Higher and Technical Education had asked that

Norbert Korrek Christiane Wolf

The Long Path to the Restoration

355

"no action be taken in this matter," Keler noted with weary resignation in late 1965 that the "whole question of the 'Bauhaus' ... at a core level" was still not clarified. Gropius never received an official invitation.

16 In the summer of 1968, the senate considered it necessary to acknowledge the fiftieth anniversary of the founding of the Bauhaus; because otherwise, the national and international experts and the architecture students in Weimar would not understand why the "university, as the successor institution, takes no notice of its own tradition." Adalbert Behr, research assistant in the department of theory and history of architecture, was responsible for the academic and organizational aspects of preparing for the anniversary.

17 Behr compiled a 200-page comprehensive timeline for the planned Bauhaus exhibition with the Kunstsammlungen. Although the manuscript was not published, it did form an important basis for further research on the Bauhaus in the coming years.

18 The extensive exhibition and event program "50 Years of Bauhaus," which also included a three-week planning seminar for young architects and a scholarly colloquium for basic artistic training, was never realized. The international success of the anniversary exhibition, opened in Stuttgart by Gropius in the summer of 1968, surely played a key role in this. Once again it was left to the Kunstsammlungen to commemorate the founding of the Weimar Bauhaus with an exhibition of items from its workshops.

The Bauhaus as a socialist legacy

19 After Behr left for the Deutsche Bauakademie in September 1970, Bauhaus research at the Department of Architectural History stopped. It was not until the the family of Bernd Grönwald moved into the Bauhaus's experimental Haus Am Horn that research was given new momentum. On September 26, 1973, fifty years after its construction, an exhibition on the house's history and original form was displayed in its main room. For a long time, this exhibition was the only museum site of the Bauhaus in Weimar, and it encouraged Georg Muche to make a donation to the Kunstsammlungen's existing Bauhaus collection.

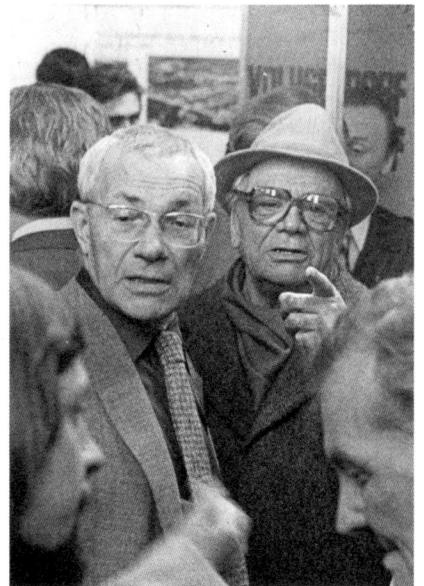

20 On October 15, 1974, Muche visited the Haus Am Horn. There followed numerous encounters with former Bauhaus members and researchers from East Germany and abroad, and soon a national and international network was formed. Prompted by these contacts, students from the HAB carried out targeted surveys of people who had been involved with the Bauhaus during its existence.

21 During the following years, Grönwald became the lead source of inspiration for the reception of the Bauhaus in the GDR. In the fall of 1974, after a series of internal discussions and consultations that were not recorded in detail, he was "tasked by the party with the care of the Bauhaus legacy." On February 12, 1975, he sent information about "the Bauhaus legacy" to the scientific department of the Central Committee of the SED. This would have far-reaching consequences.

22 In his letters to the Central Committee in February 1975, Grönwald referred to a cultural and political statement made by committee member Kurt Hager, who was a key participant in determining the direction of the GDR's cultural and educational policy and who, in 1972, had demanded that closer attention be paid to the "research of the country's historical, cultural, and artistic heritage." Without going into the political barriers impeding Bauhaus research in the GDR in the 1950s and 1960s, Grönwald criticized the present lack of "any historical materialistic evaluation of the development of the Bauhaus." The Bauhaus had been "unilaterally appropriated by the enemy."

23 Grönwald's letter had far-reaching consequences. The ministry transferred the scientific responsibility for Bauhaus research in the GDR to the university in Weimar. Further work on the history of the Bauhaus, the maintenance of its physical heritage, and preparations for the fiftieth anniversary of the inauguration of the Bauhaus building in Dessau (which was to be honored with a scholarly colloquium, an exhibition on fifty years of the Dessau Bauhaus, and publications in the trade press) were then discussed with several state institutions.

24 In a letter to the Central Committee of the SED, Grönwald also criticized the delayed publication of Hüter's book about the "sociopolitical contextualization of the Weimar Bauhaus," which had existed in manuscript form since 1967.

25 Christine Kutschke and Michael Siebenbrodt, students at the Faculty of Architecture, developed documents for the reconstruction of the Bauhaus building during their practical training in the fall of 1975. Part of the job included designing the color scheme for the former "festive level" of the Bauhaus (vestibule, auditorium, stage, and canteen). Studies of the building carried out for restoration purposes and interviews with former Bauhaus students helped determine the color palette that had actually been used by Hinnerk Scheper.

26 In their diploma theses in the spring of 1976, Kutschke and Siebenbrodt explored the possible uses of the Bauhaus buildings in Dessau. They conducted a study on the conversion of one of the Masters' Houses into a Bauhaus museum and the possible use of the Bauhaus building by the Hochschule für Industrielle Formgestaltung Halle, Burg Giebichenstein, whose move to Dessau was being discussed at the time.

27 In the period between June 21 and July 17, 1976, fifty-one students of the Faculty of Architecture completed their internships or summer programs at the VEB Bau Dessau, a paid working vacation program organized by the Free German Youth (FDJ). This company carried out the bulk of the reconstruction work on the Bauhaus building. Students were employed at various contruction sites. It had been contractually agreed that each student would work at least one week at the Bauhaus building.

28 On April 7, 1976, the secretariat of the Central Committee of the SED decided to "prepare for and implement the fiftieth anniversary of the opening of the Bauhaus in Dessau." Finally, the Bauhaus in Dessau was politically recognized as a "humanistic and progressive cultural achievement," part of the "heritage of the German people" and part of the "national socialist culture of the GDR." This decision rehabilitated the most successful design school in Germany, which had been blighted by the negative political verdict imposed by Walter Ulbricht, in the context of the formalism debate, at the 3rd Party Congress of the SED in 1950.

29 Klaus-Jürgen Winkler had been brought into the department of theory and history of architecture specially to oversee preparations for the Bauhaus anniversary in Dessau and Weimar in 1976. His numerous publications over the following decades

Norbert Korrek Christiane Wolf

The Long Path to the Restoration

359

Fig. 14a–d. Impressions of
the opening of the exhibition
on the history of the Bauhaus
in Dessau curated by
Klaus-Jürgen Winkler.

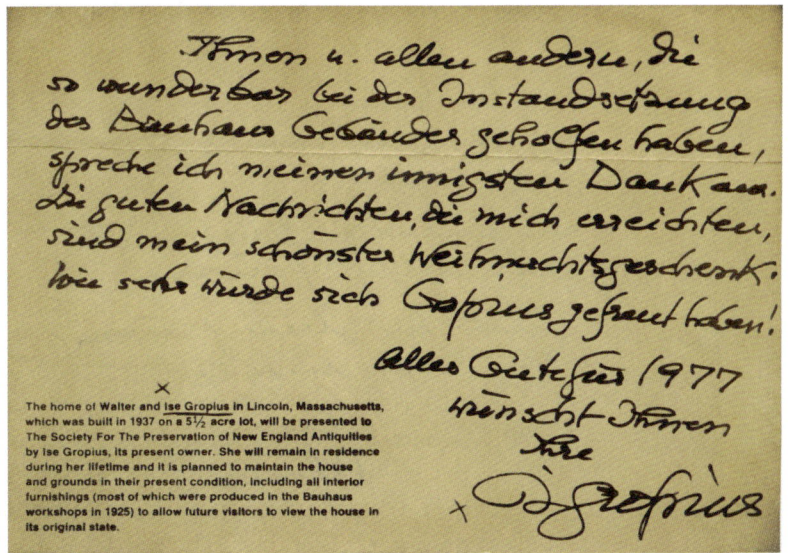

The home of Walter and Ise Gropius in Lincoln, Massachusetts, which was built in 1937 on a 5½ acre lot, will be presented to The Society For The Preservation of New England Antiquities by Ise Gropius, its present owner. She will remain in residence during her lifetime and it is planned to maintain the house and grounds in their present condition, including all interior furnishings (most of which were produced in the Bauhaus workshops in 1925) to allow future visitors to view the house in its original state.

Fig. 15. Letter by Ise Gropius thanking all "who so wonderfully assisted in the restoration of the Bauhaus," late 1976.

Fig. 16. From left to right: Christian Schädlich, Bernd Grönwald, and Konrad Püschel on the day of the reopening of the Dessau Bauhaus building, December 4, 1976.

contributed to the changing reception of the Bauhaus in the GDR, liberating it from its shadowy, taboo existence.

30   A decision of the Central Committee of the SED on April 7, 1976, tasked the university in Weimar with mounting a scholarly colloquium. At the first Bauhaus- Kolloquium, fifteen former Bauhaus members took part. The participants dealt with the history of the Bauhaus, above all with the Dessau era and the preservation of its legacy in the GDR.

31   The colloquium was accompanied by an exhibition on the work of the second Bauhaus director, Hannes Meyer, material for which had been entrusted to curator Klaus-Jürgen Winkler by Léna Meyer-Bergner, Meyer's wife and a *Bauhäusler* herself.

32   On December 4, 1976, the fiftieth anniversary of the opening of the Bauhaus Dessau was celebrated in the auditorium of the reconstructed Bauhaus building, with a ceremonial event staged by the GDR Council of Ministers. Vice-chancellor Karl Albert Fuchs, party secretary Bernd Grönwald, Christian Schädlich, and Konrad Püschel were invited from the university in Weimar. Photographs, which were not taken at the actual ceremony, also show Christina Kutschke and Michael Siebenbrodt. Whether Klaus-Jürgen Winkler was present remains unclear.

33   After the ceremony, an exhibition titled *The Progressive Legacy of the Bauhaus* opened, the historical part of which was conceived by Klaus-Jürgen Winkler. He was supported by Christine Kutschke and Michael Siebenbrodt, who, in January and February 1976, analyzed the spatial and creative integration of the exhibition into the Bauhaus building as part of their student research projects. Also on display were workshop pieces from the Weimar Kunstsammlungen and architectural models of Bauhaus buildings, which were constructed in the model workshop of the Weimar HAB according to Winkler's instructions.

34   By the time the Bauhaus-Kolloquium began in Weimar, a permanent working group for Bauhaus research had already been founded. Under the leadership of Christian Schädlich, thirty researchers were to "focus on planning and coordinating the scientific work on the history of the Bauhaus and address questions relating to the preservation of the Bauhaus legacy." The state also tasked the university in Weimar with coordinating and spearheading Bauhaus research in the GDR.

1 This article is an excerpt, and a revised English translation for this volume, of the publication: Norbert Korrek and Christiane Wolf, *Das internationale Bauhaus-Kolloquium in Weimar 1976 bis 2016: Ein Beitrag zur Bauhaus-Rezeption; Dokumentation, Ausstellungsteil, Prolog* (Weimar: Verlag der Bauhaus-Universität Weimar, 2016).

2 Norbert Korrek, "Zur Bauhaus-Rezeption an der Weimarer Hochschule von 1945–1979," in *Aber wir sind! Wir wollen! Und wir schaffen! Von der Großherzoglichen Kunstschule zur Bauhaus Universität Weimar 1860–2010, Vol. II*, ed. Frank Simon-Ritz, Klaus Jürgen Winkler, and Gerd Zimmermann (Weimar: Verlag der Bauhaus-Universität Weimar, 2012) 177–227.

3 Norbert Korrek, "*Vom Heimatschutz-Appell zum baukünstlerischen Vermächtnis. Die Architekturlehre an der Weimarer Hochschule unter Paul Schultze-Naumburg*," in *Kulturreformer. Rassenideologe. Hochschuldirektor. Der lange Schatten des Paul Schultze-Naumburg*, ed. Hans-Rudolf Meier, Daniela Spiegel, arthistoricum.net, 125–140.

Norbert Korrek Christiane Wolf

The Long Path to the Restoration

The International Bauhaus-Kolloquium in Weimar (1976–2019)

Transcripts of Filmed Interviews
Edited by Ines Weizman

Hilde Barz-Malfatti

What motivated you to participate at the International Bauhaus-Kolloquium?

It was Professor Alfred Grazioli, whose assistant I was at the HdK in then West Berlin, who encouraged me to participate in the International Bauhaus-Kolloquium in Weimar in 1986. I was attracted by the range of topics that were presented there. The lectures ranged from subjects on urban planning to the history of architecture, but also on historic preservation. I remember a passionate lecture by Hermann Wirth, who later became a professor for historic preservation at the HAB and a colleague of mine. He was amazingly ardent whenever he talked about preservation. He actively fought for the preservation of historic buildings that East German authorities had scheduled for removal, either to make space for their urban planning schemes or simply because they could not afford to maintain them. In the 1980s, I was deeply impressed by his openness to both the past and the future. In my notes, I even placed an exclamation point, emphasizing his lecture. Apart from that, during these conferences a lot of approaches concerning architectural theory and, of course, on the history of the Bauhaus and the *Neues Bauen* movement were presented. Lore Kramer and Jonas Geist from West Berlin talked about Ernst May, about *Laubenganghäuser*, and about housing typologies. The most amazing thing I remember was that I could meet former *Bauhäusler* such as Hubert Hoffmann and Selman Selmanagić. Also, I met Margarete Schütte-Lihotzky, the well-known architect who developed the Frankfurt Kitchen, as well as Max Bill, who founded the HfG Ulm.

What role do you think politics played during these conferences?

The politics of the GDR certainly played a role; you could feel it everywhere. It was not particularly clear to us how openly we could discuss issues. Some of the lectures were very loyal to the Party, and as guests we politely listened to them. We knew that political catchphrases had to frame the conference and that everybody had to accept that. Other lectures were absolutely great and particularly stimulating in their diversity and daringness. From a political point of view, I thought it was wonderful to see that such a mixture of audience and lecturers was even possible. There were a lot of guests from the Eastern Bloc, from Cuba, but also a lot of people from the United States, from Italy, from France, and from Switzerland. It was exciting to meet people from both East and West. This excited us, because during that time of the Iron Curtain we did not have any contact with socialist countries. Knowing that East Germans could not travel to the West, the fact of being able to meet one another in Weimar was absolutely great. The Bauhaus-Kolloquium was a special event in the international academic calendar. It is hard to describe how difficult it was to conceive of such an international colloquium in the cultural climate of the time, in which so many bureaucratic hurdles had to be tackled. The result was truly magnificent.

Did you keep any of the documents of the colloquia?

All the participants of the Bauhaus-Kolloquium were handed these beautiful black folders. They were wonderfully prepared. We would walk around the city, holding these folders, which helped of course to identify us as participants of the colloquium. I was walking through the pedestrian zone with my colleague, along Schillerstraße, where we met Olaf Weber. And he said: "Ah, you've come from the Bauhaus-Kolloquium!" And we started talking, and he said: "Would you like to come over for a cup of coffee? I live close by." So he made us a cup of coffee and we had a really nice talk, and we would later also stay in contact. It was the summer of 1989. The atmosphere of 1989 was a bit different to that of 1986. It was more relaxed. Our colleagues from East Germany were now talking much more openly about politics. It sometimes made me think: "Oh, is this possible and are they allowed to say that here?" One could feel that something was on the brink of a transformation. Obviously, none of us thought that suddenly the Wall would collapse and the political shift would happen.

Hilde Barz-Malfatti studied architecture at the Technische Hochschule Darmstadt and opened her own practice in Berlin in 1985. From 1985 to 1990, she was a research assistant to Alfred Grazioli at the Hochschule der Künste Berlin (HdK), and from 1990 to 1992 a lecturer at the HdK. In 1994 she was appointed professor at the Bauhaus-Universität Weimar. In this position she was vice-dean at the Department of Architecture and Urbanism and a member of several committees and juries in urban planning until her retirement in 2019. From 2000 to 2006, she held an office partnership with the architecture practice of Karl-Heinz Schmitz to design the study center of the Anna Amalia Library in Weimar, for which they received several prizes and awards. [Interview conducted by Lena Laine, May 18, 2016, Weimar]

Alfred Grazioli

In 1976, you were already involved in the first International Bauhaus-Kolloquium. How did this come about?

That was fairly simple. I was a friend of Selman Selmanagić, who had been invited, of course, as a former student at the Bauhaus. He said I had to come as well and probably arranged for me to get an invitation for myself and some other people, too. I took Ludwig Leo with me—the architect—and also Nick Roericht—one of the oldest graduates of the Ulm School of Design, an industrial designer—and also two assistants. Getting a visa was not a problem, since we had gotten the invitation from Professor Christian Schädlich. Schädlich and his wife were, as we sensed it, the organizers of the whole thing, and we ourselves were in contact with Bernd Grönwald.

From West Berlin we drove to Dessau, where we had a guided tour of all the Bauhaus buildings, especially the masters' houses and the main building. This was organized by Bernd Grönwald. He looked like someone receiving hotel guests on the Mediterranean, wearing white clothes: it was odd, but very sincere. Christian Schädlich was more in the background at first. In Weimar, at the start of the colloquium, there were welcoming speeches—endless speeches. I still remember how the director or the president of the university in Weimar was a structural engineer, how he only spoke about the Party, about Party programs, how the nth Party Conference decided that this many residential buildings were to be completed by a certain date. So that was the reception, and after that various interesting events started.

Do you remember any of the presentations from the conference?

Yes, Christian Schädlich held a brilliant lecture about Gropius, as another opening speech. Schädlich was—how should I say it?—an expert. I also vividly remember meeting Georg Muche. He participated in a panel debate and didn't really say anything professional. Instead he railed against the politics of the United States, talking about a movie actor who was governing the US at that time, meaning Ronald Reagan. I still have this image in my head. My lecture was, not officially but unofficially, about West Berlin housing, which was received with much criticism. I noticed how people from the East were very happy with someone talking critically about the West. I mean, they really absorbed every criticism of the West.

Did you get in contact with students at the HAB Weimar?

The students were real quick-change artists. They had to manage the reception. They handed out programs. During lunch, they were serving the food. During the evening, there was a concert and the students sang in the choir—but they were always the same ones! So everything was really well-orchestrated, and everybody was very friendly on the surface.

Then I met a student at the urinal and he started to clamor about the GDR and its single-minded political economy and all these rascalities that did not leave any room for imagination in architecture. Another man, a young architect who had just graduated, was also completely frustrated. He said that for two years now, as a qualified architect, he'd been designing transformer buildings—small power utilities. The same thing over and over again, because it's run by the structural engineers. The other one, for months, had to draw plate segments for the façades and was complaining that the architecture was mostly contrived by the engineers. It was about construction and not about living. So in the restrooms there were peculiar and probably more truthful conversations. I think the problem in Weimar was not the education: the students were exhibiting their work as well during the colloquia and it was of good quality and imagination, I remember. No, the problem was the professional practice in the East, which in no way complied with what was promised at the universities. That is why most of the people who studied, so I was told, wanted to stay at the universities, as researchers or historians, just to avoid the disillusions in the realities of architectural practice.

Alfred Grazioli (1940–2018), born in Basel, studied architecture at the HfG Ulm and the École d'Architecture de l'Université de Genève (EAUG). In 1972, he was appointed a professor of design and urban planning at the Universität der Künste in Berlin. He ran an architecture practice with Wieka Muthesius and later also with Adolf Krischanitz. [Interview conducted by Lena Laine, June 21, 2016, Berlin]

Bruno Flierl

What was so special about Weimar in the 1970s and 1980s?
Weimar was always on a different turf than Berlin, in a positive way. I have stayed loyal to Weimar, not just because I had good colleagues, like Olaf Weber or Gerd Zimmermann, who worked with me in Berlin at the Bauakademie, but I also enjoyed lecturing in Weimar. When I became a pensioner after a stroke and could travel around the world, including to the West, to conduct analysis into the development of high-rise buildings all over the world, I was always giving my lectures in the Kasseturm, the Weimar student club. It was always crowded. Everyone sat on the floor; I was the only one standing. But the professors of the HAB did not come, so that they did not need to react or even report on my political transgressions. **367**

How did the international students influence the architectural discourse in Weimar? Where they speaking more openly politically?

In the 1970s and 1980s, there were so many young people studying at the HAB in Weimar who had arrived from countries that had just gained their independence and could take up scholarships offered to them in the GDR, which had friendly relations with those countries. But there were also students whose parents or who themselves were being persecuted in their homeland. Some of them were ardent Marxists supporting international solidarity, but as refugees in the GDR, they had the discipline not to speak against the GDR. It was in many ways their way of showing their respect to a country that welcomed them and offered them education. But secret discussions were held, and that was possible in Weimar more so than in Berlin. They came to Weimar, a place far from Berlin, "behind the seven mountains with the seven dwarfs," so this did not really attract any-one's attention in Berlin. Then came students from Chile, a very important group because they had ideas about modern architecture. Most of them came for the World Youth Congress in 1973 and then some remained, because just as the decorations for these games were taken down, the coup by Pinochet happened. These people were all an enormous addition to the international thinking of the young genera-tion in the GDR. When the first Bauhaus-Kolloquium took place in 1976, these events had just happened, and it offered to be a place for true internationalization. I think some scholars and bureaucrats in the GDR, in addition to Grönwald, must have risked the experiment so that the students and contacts would reach a new international level.

At that time in the Soviet Union, the stubborn policy of Brezhnev was already collapsing as a result of the actions of his successors. Then came Gorbachev, and when I spoke very critically about the GDR's cultural policies in 1986, at the 4th Bauhaus-Kolloquium, Gorbachev was already demanding a new form of socialism. Of course the international students in Weimar also expected that teachers and professors would address these political efforts, which was obviously not so easy. That is why the Bauhaus-Kolloquien became so attractive, because they were the place where the threshold of what could be said would be tested.

Did the Bauhaus-Kolloquien have an influence on building practice in the GDR?

Barely, I think. As scholars we never had a direct influence on practice, because everything was controlled and the planning directives were under state socialism. What mattered in the 1980s was to achieve the yearly plans via the construction of prefabricated buildings and to make sure that everyone had an apartment by 1990. That was the political goal. And in the end, they had it, while the rest of the historic cities had almost collapsed as they were so dilapidated and nobody could afford to renovate them. There was no energy left to really plan a city, because everyone was focusing so narrowly on one single task in the planned economy. An impact could have been made through progressive, collective consultation and democratization, in the sense that all those who had something critical to say about socialism, or about a better version of socialism, would have become active. Some of this was discussed in Weimar, but I am not sure it really had an impact.

Do you remember speakers at the colloquium who challenged what could be said about politics in the framework of architectural history or theory?

Yes, I remember one Bauhaus-Kolloquium, to which Grönwald had invited Claude Schnaidt, the Swiss theorist who lived in Paris. Grönwald and Schnaidt had a special personal relation. In his presentation, Schnaidt—a rather short guy—arrives and says in his Swiss German accent: "Today I'm not going to talk about architecture, although I'm a professor in that field, but I am going to talk about peace. It has certainly not been secured." And then Schnaidt, a member of the French Communist Party, gave a speech about the threat to worldwide peace as a condition, and argued that securing peace should be the motive and reason to build. Fantastic. Speaking a French-communist language, not a GDR-communist language; no platitudes; no statements about Party resolutions; just the opinion of a creative human, who, for humanity and for himself as an architect, needed peace, and who simply wanted to share his thoughts. He ended claiming that everyone in the country had to figure out how to do this on his or her own. He gave no specifications about how it was to be done; he simply exposed the problems of a serious topic. That was part of the Bauhaus-Kolloquium! Of course, that surprised those who, at the Bauhaus-Kolloquium, or in the GDR generally, were used to hearing explanations of what we had already achieved so far.

What were the new challenges facing the Bauhaus-Kolloquium after 1989?

After German unification, it appeared that the Bauhaus-Kolloquium in 1989 had been the last one. It was hard to find a new beginning. The history of the Bauhaus that had once offered the framework for a unique discourse was suddenly of no effect in the new political landscape. Bernd Grönwald, seriously ill for years and greatly disappointed about the future of his own social and architectural ideas—and especially of his personal role in developing architecture and society in present-day Germany—took his own life in 1991. But luckily Gerd Zimmermann decided to continue the tradition of the Bauhaus-Kolloquien, and I am glad it is being continued.

Bruno Flierl studied architecture at the Hochschule für bildende Künste Berlin from 1948 until 1951 and at the Weimar HAB as a visiting student until 1953. From 1952 to 1979, he worked as a research assistant at the GDR Bauakademie in Berlin. From 1962 to 1964, he was the editor-in-chief of Deutsche Architektur. From 1980 to 1984 he was a lecturer at Humboldt University in Berlin. After retiring, he continued to work as an architecture critic and published numerous works about the complications in urban planning arising from the process of uniting East and West Berlin since 1990. [Interview conducted by Lena Laine and Wolfram Höhne, November 27, 2016, Berlin]

Peter Hahn

You participated in several Bauhaus-Kolloquien. Do you still remember the first one?

Yes, that was in 1976. For the first time, it was possible for West Germans to be invited to such a conference in East Germany. To me it was foremost a matter of curiosity to go and visit Weimar. Several groups of foreigners were invited, from socialist countries but also from the West. I can clearly remember how they welcomed the Soviet delegates with great respect. It was very clear that Big Brother was present, making sure that nothing got out of hand, and that everything was in line with Party ideology. But they also treated us very cordially and politely and respected us as experts in the understanding of the Bauhaus.

I recall how impressed I was to meet Georg Muche, who was now living in Lindau am Bodensee and that he was treated as a state guest in the GDR. He was shown around by important people and was well taken care of. This had to do with the fact that Muche—whom I knew very well—stood as an artist above all political contradictions. He wanted to create an equidistance between the two German states. He didn't want to have anything to do with the Federal Republic of Germany, other than being a citizen. But he didn't want to exclude the GDR, and that was important to the politicians and to those who played a role in the first East-West contact on a cultural level, namely, Christian Schädlich and Bernd Grönwald. Grönwald seemed to be the one with the political contacts. As far as I could tell, he did an excellent job.

What kind of discussions with colleagues, scholars, or students do you remember?

I tried to participate in all the International Bauhaus-Kolloquien. The very first one was still a bit odd, as at Western universities we were used to a lecture being discussed immediately and students perhaps interrupting, but here in Weimar there was not the slightest bit of discussion afterwards. They would say, "We're not having any discussion now." Only in the evenings at the so-called Kasseturm, the student club, was there actually a chance for discussion. But that didn't correspond with Western university customs at all. The point was to have clarifying discussions, to allow further questions, to allow criticism—but criticism was obviously just not wanted. I went to the Kasseturm and I met happy, beer-drinking students there and we had nice conversations; but a scientifically oriented discussion is something I never experienced. Maybe it was happening somewhere else. I don't know.

How would you describe the different meanings of "Bauhaus heritage" in both parts of divided Germany?

The term "Bauhaus heritage" is a very typical East German term. We wouldn't have called it that in West Germany, but it doesn't really matter. Of course, there were attempts to further the reception of the Bauhaus, but after the war there were so many other concerns, in West Germany and under the occupation of the Western Allies as well. Hans Maria Wingler was one of the first people to have started in the late 1950s to piece together some of the history of the Bauhaus. Only a few years after the war, he started writing a book about the Bauhaus and was in close contact with Gropius and the other Bauhaus masters, most of whom were still alive back then. Wingler collected a huge amount of material. So the beginning of the Bauhaus archives wasn't really a collection of materials, but rather a scientific account of what the Bauhaus aimed for and achieved. So much came together because of Gropius's endorsement and with the great willingness of the living former Bauhaus students to make their work available. From that material and these renewed contacts, the idea came about very quickly not of a museum, but of an archive about the Bauhaus. Wingler was a highly respected journalist on art objects at the time. He specialized in Oskar Kokoschka, but he managed to put together the foundations of the Bauhaus archive. Otherwise, there was no initiative to set up such a collection within the museum sector, which says a lot.

Of course, there were also university initiatives that dealt with the Bauhaus, or which at least partially dealt with the Bauhaus. The best-known example is the Ulm School of Design, but also there, under the directorship of Max Bill, nobody thought to establish an archive. So both in the West and in the East, there was simply no broad acceptance of the Bauhaus nor any reception of the Bauhaus. That came only in subsequent years, little by little—and the Bauhaus Archive, first in Darmstadt and then in Berlin, was an important institution that carried it forward.

Still, in the GDR it was somewhat different. Much of the Bauhaus collection in Weimar was preserved in a museum, where it was walled in to be protected against robbery during the Nazi period. Later, during the GDR regime, it was protected there by simply not being shown. I think it is to the credit of Schädlich and Grönwald that they created a certain openness step by step. Bauhaus research in East Germany had already existed before that, but it was largely silenced. As you know, in the early 1960s, the most important book about the Bauhaus in Weimar was the one by Karl-Heinz Hüter.

Peter Hahn attended the Freie Universität Berlin, completing his doctorate in 1969 in the philosophical and social sciences. From 1971 to 1984, Hahn was a research assistant in Darmstadt and later in Berlin. From 1985 to 2002, he was director of the Bauhaus-Archiv Berlin. In 2004, Hahn was awarded the 1st class Order of Merit from the Federal Republic of Germany for his achievements as director of the Bauhaus-Archiv Berlin. [Interview conducted by Adrienne Michels, January 22, 2016, Berlin]

Christian Schädlich

Professor Schädlich, you were actually trained as an architect. How did you get involved with architectural history and theory, and how did you get involved with the task of organizing the colloquia in Weimar?

Yes, that is true: I was trained as an architect. I was lucky because I had the chance to realize my graduation project right after the exams. That was certainly unusual, but back in my school years in the 1930s and 1940s I'd wanted to study history, especially the history of Saxony. I dreamt of becoming an archivar to be able to study. In the early 1950s, I became interested in the history of architecture. I became an assistant at the HAB and began my dissertation on the history of classical architectural history from Vitruvius to Alberti and Palladio and their importance for contemporary practice and architectural theory. I worked in a small team with the later Professors Anita and Joachim Bach. In 1954 I was appointed assistant to the chair of theory and history of architecture and was very open to all sorts of subjects. One day we received the task from the director (*Rektor*) of the school to write a brief outline of the history of the university for our course catalogue and staff index, which was published every year. So we divided up the tasks. I had two other colleagues. One was Günter Steiger, an art historian, who soon returned to the University of Jena. The other was Karl-Heinz Hüter, an art historian and archaeologist who studied the Bauhaus. I was researching the successor institute to the Bauhaus in Weimar under Otto Bartning. And that's how I got to know the Bauhaus. We looked through the collection of the State Archive, which had still mountains of unordered files and documents. At that time, I didn't go much further with the Bauhaus research; the next time was perhaps five or six years later. That was mainly Karl-Heinz Hüter's domain. He also did archival research with his students, and collected material, which ultimately led to the development of his book. Hüter was busy researching van de Velde at that time, and was one of the first to write a dissertation about him. He prepared an exhibition titled "100 Years of van de Velde," for which he collected a lot of material and objects, among them his writing desk, which is now in the museum here in Weimar.

A new opportunity to work on the Bauhaus arose in the 1960s. And a new assistant, an art historian who had studied at Humboldt University, Adalbert Behr, joined our team and then also started to research the Bauhaus. I actually gave him this task, but naturally through this my knowledge was also enriched. I collected material, held public lectures in the "Klub der Intelligenz," as it was called back then, ultimately to do a kind of public advertisement for the Bauhaus. But there were still a few problems with it. As you probably know, the celebration of the 100-year anniversary of the university was canceled at short notice. To me, that was totally incomprehensible. In 1964, I was again tasked by a new director (*Rektor*) to write a summary of the university's history until the reopening after the war; the other part he did by himself. So, I eventually dealt with the Bauhaus, and the students and employees were glad that finally the Bauhaus was mentioned and appreciated by the university leadership.

How did the idea for a conference about Bauhaus research come about?

In the early 1970s, there was a change in the perception of modern architectural heritage and its preservation, and this also led to a different openness towards Bauhaus history. Yes, and then it began! We could finally devote ourselves to the Bauhaus. The fact that Bauhaus heritage received recognition in the GDR had its origins at our university, because it was Bernd Grönwald, then the secretary of the university's Party leadership, who wrote a letter to the office of the Central Committee, to the Department of Sciences, in which he raised awareness of the fact that the Bauhaus building in Dessau was in a terrible condition and that, from a historical-materialistic point of view, in a philosophical sense, the entire history of the Bauhaus, which had been negated or disparaged in bourgeois historiography, had to be written. He especially pointed out that the Bauhaus also had a communist student cell and that the whole relation of the Bauhaus to the workers' movement was still a desideratum of research. And this letter had consequences! Together with Bernd Grönwald and Konrad Püschel, we began to meet regularly once or twice a week to decide how we could address what was outlined in that letter. Together with the Bauakademie in Berlin, where Adalbert Behr and Hüter had now gone, we began to plan how we could celebrate the 50th anniversary of the Bauhaus in Dessau, which eventually led to the renovation of the Bauhaus building in Dessau but also to publications and exhibitions and the International Bauhaus-Kolloqium in Weimar. However, it really remained Grönwald's initiative that the Bauhaus eventually became recognized in the GDR as a subject worth studying, and within this framework I also undertook the organization of the colloquia. But carrying out the colloquia and those festivities, was also a collaborative effort in every respect. I sincerely wish to thank all the colleagues who worked together and perhaps still remember that time, because I couldn't have made it without them, right?

Christian Schädlich was a professor of history and theory of architecture at the HAB from 1967 to 1989. He did an apprenticeship as a bricklayer from 1947 to 1952, after which he began his studies in architecture under Hermann Henselmann at the newly established Staatliche Hochschule für Baukunst und bildende Künste in Weimar. He graduated from the HAB Weimar in 1957 after completing his doctoral dissertation and was appointed as a lecturer. His 1967 postdoctoral thesis (*Habilitation*), "Das Eisen in der Architektur des 19. Jahrhunderts," was published. [Interview conducted by Adrienne Michels, December 2, 2015, Weimar]

Wolfgang Thöner

How did you discover the history of the Bauhaus as a subject of research?

Since my childhood in the 1960s, I've known this building here in Dessau, even if it was of course not in great shape then. My grandfather, who was a bookbinder near Dessau, always provided me with literature. He used to have a lot of *Bauhäusler* as customers for their portfolios or other works produced in his workshop. He even kept some of the correspondence he'd had with *Bauhäusler*, and among them also the head of construction of the masters' houses. When I studied art history at Humboldt University, I also tried to follow my interest in Bauhaus history. After my studies, I was employed by the newly founded WKZ (Wissenschaftlich-Kulturelles Zentrum Bauhaus Dessau) under the directorship of Rolf Kuhn as an academic assistant tasked to deliver lectures, but also later in charge of exhibitions and work on cataloguing the estates of architects and artists that had become part of the collection. This center was financed by the city of Dessau, but the academic supervision was undertaken mainly by the HAB Weimar, so I was always close to discussions in Weimar, and also participated in the Bauhaus-Kolloquien.

There were intentions immediately after the war to revive the Bauhaus. How did these plans fail, and why was there no discussion of the Bauhaus until the early 1960s?

Interestingly, these ideas to revive the Bauhaus were discussed both in Weimar and in Dessau, because initially in the Soviet occupied zone, the Bauhaus appeared untouched by National Socialism and it seemed possible to reconnect to this institution. Both in Weimar and in Dessau there were former *Bauhäusler* who had become architects, city planners, or artists who reconnected after the war and seriously discussed the possibility of reopening the school. Together, Hubert Hoffmann, in 1945 city architect of Dessau, and Mayor Fritz Hesse, who had been the mayor who'd brought the Bauhaus to Dessau in 1926, developed detailed plans to revive the Bauhaus. But when a new mayor from the Socialist Unity Party (SED) was elected in 1947, he adopted the Soviet doctrine of socialist realism, and the idea to revive the Bauhaus died.

In Weimar it was Hermann Henselmann, who did not study at the Bauhaus, but who in 1945 was put in charge of founding a new architecture and art school and was determined to reconnect it to the Bauhaus. But here as well, the establishment of the GDR in 1949 under the influence of Soviet policies, along with Henselmann's departure for projects in Berlin, laid these plans to rest. What could be sensed in the cultural politics was clearly expressed, when in 1951, on the occasion of a Party congress of the SED, Walter Ulbricht delivered a speech in which he openly attacked formalism, not only in architecture and urban planning, but also in visual arts and theater. He particularly mentioned the Bauhaus as a negative example that he described as imperialistic and cosmopolitan. He literally described it as the enemy of the people. Only after Stalin's death in 1953 and Khrushchev's famous speech in 1956 did the era of socialist realism end. And then, quietly and cautiously, there was a return to the principles of modernism in the GDR.

How would you describe the influence of former Bauhäusler on the way the Bauhaus was received in the East and the West?

If we look only at the difference between West Germany and East Germany, of course, in West Germany the discussion wasn't state-controlled and it was possible to have a critical stance and to discuss the pros and cons in public. In West Germany, there were *Bauhäusler* at many universities and art colleges and architecture schools, and of course, Max Bill founded the HfG Ulm, at which specific reflection about the Bauhaus was possible. In East Germany, too, there were schools in which the *Bauhäusler* had some effect. Selman Selmanagić in Berlin-Weißensee had an essential impact on urban planning, design, and architecture in the GDR, under totally different conditions and with different possibilities.

It was not until the mid-1970s, with reopening of the Bauhaus building in Dessau, the International Bauhaus-Kolloqium, and later the establishment of the WKZ, that a connection with the Bauhaus and between *Bauhäusler* from East and West was made possible again. There are beautiful photos, where you can see them. There was Richard Paulick next to Max Bill, next to Franz Ehrlich, next to Marianne Brandt, and many others.

Wolfgang Thöner studied art education and German philology at Humboldt University in Berlin. Since 1986, he has worked at the Wissenschaftlich-Kulturelles Zentrum (WKZ), then Bauhaus Foundation Dessau, as a curator and researcher. In these roles, he has realized numerous exhibitions on the history of the Bauhaus. In 2009, he became the director of collections at the Bauhaus Foundation Dessau. He is also the editor and author of numerous books, essays, papers, and lectures. [Interview conducted by Adrienne Michels, January 15, 2016, Dessau]

Karl-Heinz Hüter

After training as an archaeologist with expertise on ancient Greece, what got you involved with research on the Bauhaus?

That is true: I have been trained as an archaeologist. My thesis was on the representation of space in Greek art, exemplified in its architecture. But when I arrived in Weimar, I was more drawn to topics that related to this place and about which there was still a lot of ignorance and obscurity. Strangely, not even Henry van de Velde was very highly regarded, as his work did not fit the cultural policies and ideologies of the leadership; and of course, the Bauhaus did not fit at all. And that is why I chose these topics, to write a monograph of Henry van de Velde and about the political history of the Bauhaus in Weimar. Van de Velde became the topic of my dissertation; later, I wrote the book about the Bauhaus.

In 1960, the HAB Weimar had planned to celebrate the 100th anniversary of the university, which coincided almost exactly with the 40th anniversary of the Bauhaus. You were tasked with organizing these jubilees, but then the celebrations were canceled. Did you ever find out why?

Well, I think I was assigned to this task to prepare the jubilee because it was known that I was studying this material relating to van de Velde and the Bauhaus. Letters, documents, and papers were kept in the State Archive in Weimar then. It must be said that it appeared as though they had just been thrown in there. Most of these delicate papers and documents were, by the early 1960s, just lying there in a pile, covered by dust. Some had already yellowed and had stains. With three students helping me, I started to carefully review the material and, obviously, evaluate it at the same time, to take notes and so on. I was also able to use some materials from the Bauhaus Archive in Darmstadt. At some point, I had accumulated a real treasure trove of documents, and it was this collection that allowed me to understand the challenging topic of the political history of the Bauhaus in Weimar.

Yes, the celebrations for the important jubilee were canceled in 1958, I think. The background to this was still the discussion about formalism: national traditions and everything that took place in the non-Schinkel era, maybe even after Schinkel, or before, was rejected and regarded as formalistic. Even back then, it was hard for me to understand the reasons for that, and today even more so, obviously.

Did you still continue your research on the Bauhaus after the jubilee was canceled?

Yes, I continued. In fact, I did everything that I had in mind. I dealt first with the Bauhaus, and then later also with the history of modern architecture between 1900 and 1930. I wrote the book *Das Bauhaus in*

Dr. Karl-Heinz Hüter   Berlin, den 26.1.1968
B e r l i n DDR
Rummelsburger Straße 88

        Herrn Prof. Walter Gropius

        46 Brattle Street
        Cambridge, Mass 02138 USA

        Sehr geehrter Herr Professor Gropius !

        Ich bin sehr froh über Ihre Bereitschaft, mir mit Material
        für meine zukünftigen Publikationsvorhaben zu helfen und
        die Arbeit über die politische Geschichte des Bauhauses
        Weimar durchzusehen.

        Die Korrekturfahnen kamen gerade an. Da es dem Verlag eilig
        ist (drei Wochen), schicke ich sie mit getrennter Post sofort
        ab. Dem Paket lege ich mein Buch über van de Velde bei, das
        ich Ihnen überreichen möchte.

        Die politische Geschichte ist eine Quellenarbeit, im wesent-
        lichen nach Materialien im Staatsarchiv Weimar und im Bauhaus-
        archiv Darmstadt. Im ersten Teil behandle ich chronologisch
        die Ereignisse, im zweiten nach bestimmten Fragestellungen
        wichtige Probleme. und zwar nüchtern wie sie mir aus dem
        Material entgegentraten, ohne die Absicht zu schonen oder zu
        verurteilen. Eine kritische Durchsicht auf Grund Ihres besse-
        ren Wissens kann vielleicht noch vorhandene Irrtümer korri-
        gieren. Ich würde Ihnen dankbar sein, wenn Sie mir Ihre Be-
        merkungen, Einwände usw. schrieben, vielleicht unter Markierung
        der entsprechenden Textstellen durch eine Ziffer, oder auch
        (ohne Erklärungen) durch entsprechende Vermerke (Fragezeichen
        usw.).

        Meine Wünsche hinsichtlich Fotos und Auskünfte über Bauten
        sind sehr vielfältig. Es handelt sich nämlich um zwei Vorhaben,
        und zwar erstens um eine über längere Zeit laufende Quellen-
        arbeit über die Architektur des Bauhauskreises, zweitens um
        eine Monographie über Ihr Werk, die in einer als populär-
        wissenschaftlich bezeichnete Reihe "Architektenmonographien",

Fig. 1. Letter from Karl-Heinz
Hüter to Walter Gropius,
January 26, 1968 (front)

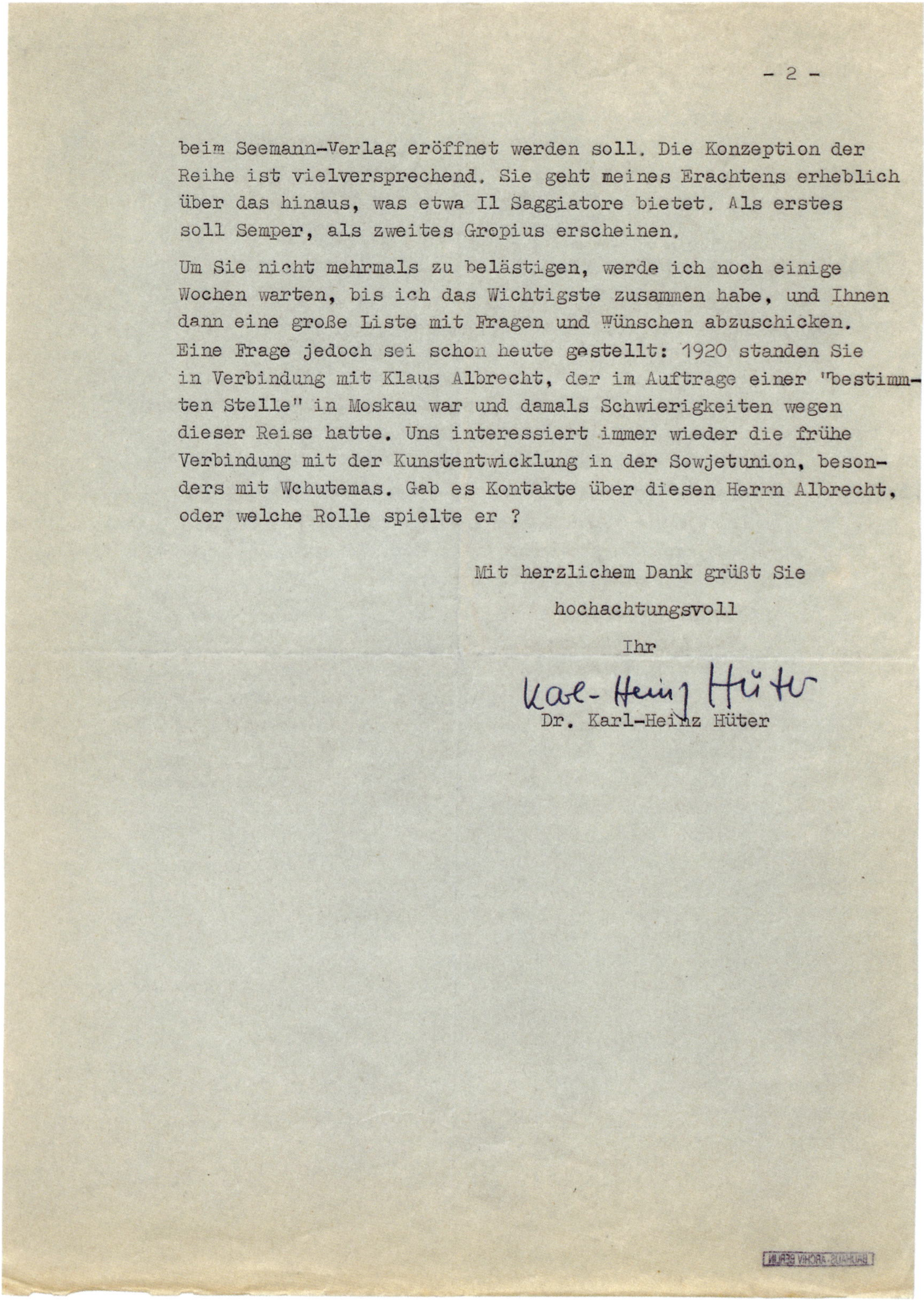

beim Seemann-Verlag eröffnet werden soll. Die Konzeption der
Reihe ist vielversprechend. Sie geht meines Erachtens erheblich
über das hinaus, was etwa Il Saggiatore bietet. Als erstes
soll Semper, als zweites Gropius erscheinen.

Um Sie nicht mehrmals zu belästigen, werde ich noch einige
Wochen warten, bis ich das Wichtigste zusammen habe, und Ihnen
dann eine große Liste mit Fragen und Wünschen abzuschicken.
Eine Frage jedoch sei schon heute gestellt: 1920 standen Sie
in Verbindung mit Klaus Albrecht, der im Auftrage einer "bestimm-
ten Stelle" in Moskau war und damals Schwierigkeiten wegen
dieser Reise hatte. Uns interessiert immer wieder die frühe
Verbindung mit der Kunstentwicklung in der Sowjetunion, besonders mit Wchutemas. Gab es Kontakte über diesen Herrn Albrecht,
oder welche Rolle spielte er ?

Mit herzlichem Dank grüßt Sie

hochachtungsvoll

Ihr

Dr. Karl-Heinz Hüter

Fig.2. Letter from Karl-Heinz Hüter to Walter Gropius, January 26, 1968 (reverse)

February 8, 1968

Dr. Karl-Heinz Hüter
Rummelsburger Strasse 88
Berlin, D D R

Dear Dr. Hüter:

You can hardly imagine what a strong impression your manuscript has made on me.
It is the most complete, scholarly writing on the Weimar years of the Bauhaus which
has ever been made, and I am amazed about your many sources which even had
slipped out of my own memory. The highly complicated, involved process of the
Bauhaus development has never been traced as well to the basic facts, politically
or philosophically, as you have managed to do.

Although I have, as you rightly state, never been politically active, I know for sure
that this very fact has made it possible to bring the Bauhaus as far as I did. Otherwise
it would have been swept away already in its beginning. I am quite convinced that
totality of approach theoretically includes everything, but a man doing a job must
know where his limitations are and where he can give his best contribution. I
deliberately kept to my own field. You may see this also from a letter which I wrote
in the year 1938 to the Banker Simon in Paris. My attitude was necessary to keep the
ship going. I am convinced that by this very fact I made the most out of my contribution with the basic limitation given to every individual.

In your really very good build-up of the book, I miss only one point which I think
should be principally stressed. I think it was the first time that in the Bauhaus an
objective method of teaching was developed, against the usual imitative approach of
the student who imitates the way of his teacher. We tried to build up the beginning of
a science of design by collecting objective technical and psychological facts. These
we considered to be the necessary tools for the student to build up himself. The usual
imitative method educates assistants, but not independent men. This consciously-
developed approach perhaps is best expressed in my book "Architektur" under the heading
"Gibt es eine Wissenschaft der Gestaltung?". I refer also to the enclosed letter to the
Editor of the "Journal of The American Institute of Architects", 1962.

You seem to be pretty well aware that a lot of steps I did in the beginning were made
for expediency. For instance, I was told by Mackensen that no workshops should be
reinstated, so I had to write Document 1 in 1916, hoping that I would be able later on
to build up workshops, which I did (see your page 44, third and fourth paragraphs).

Fig. 3. Letter from Walter
Gropius to Karl-Heinz Hüter,
February 8, 1968 (front, page
1 of 3)

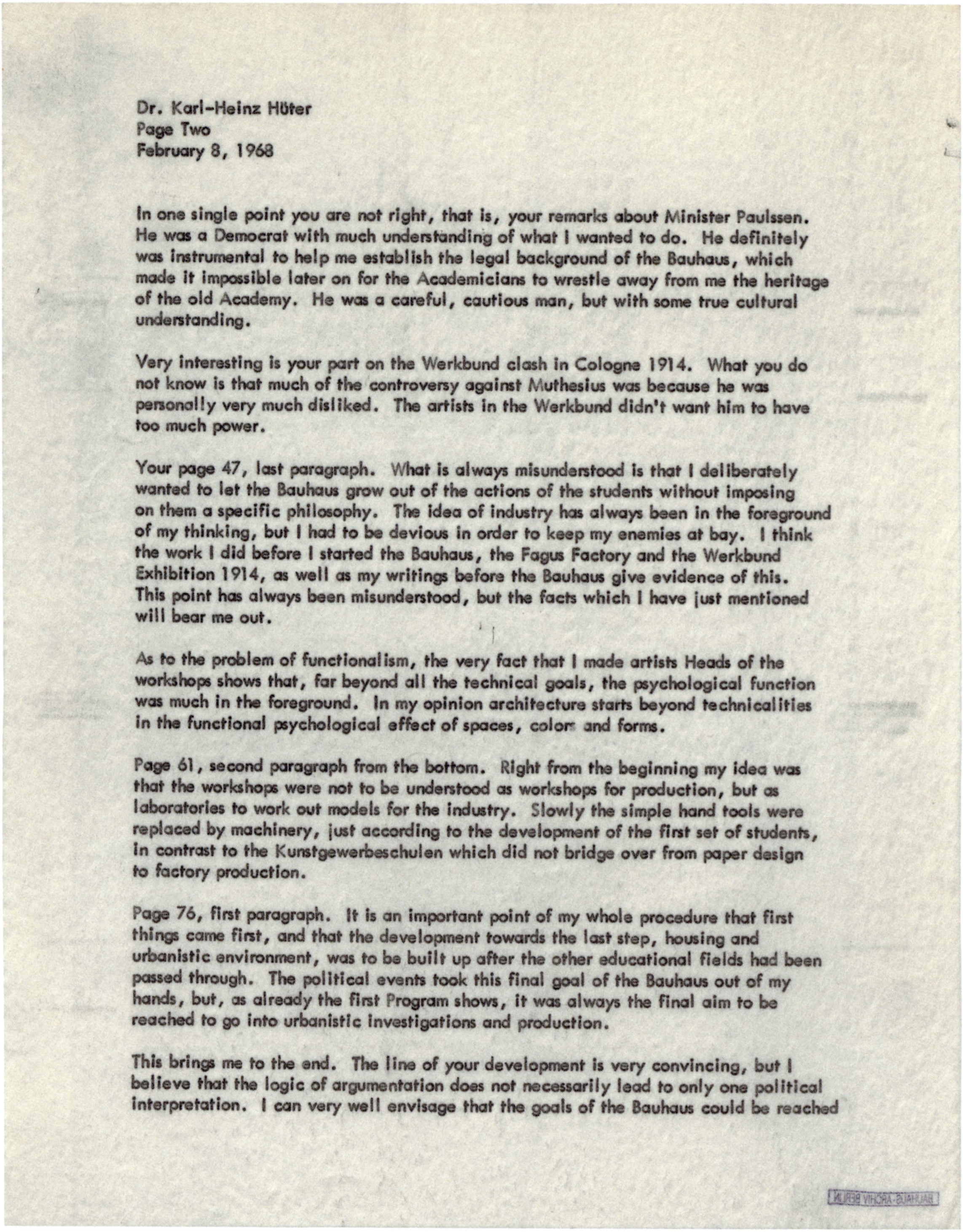

In one single point you are not right, that is, your remarks about Minister Paulssen. He was a Democrat with much understanding of what I wanted to do. He definitely was instrumental to help me establish the legal background of the Bauhaus, which made it impossible later on for the Academicians to wrestle away from me the heritage of the old Academy. He was a careful, cautious man, but with some true cultural understanding.

Very interesting is your part on the Werkbund clash in Cologne 1914. What you do not know is that much of the controversy against Muthesius was because he was personally very much disliked. The artists in the Werkbund didn't want him to have too much power.

Your page 47, last paragraph. What is always misunderstood is that I deliberately wanted to let the Bauhaus grow out of the actions of the students without imposing on them a specific philosophy. The idea of industry has always been in the foreground of my thinking, but I had to be devious in order to keep my enemies at bay. I think the work I did before I started the Bauhaus, the Fagus Factory and the Werkbund Exhibition 1914, as well as my writings before the Bauhaus give evidence of this. This point has always been misunderstood, but the facts which I have just mentioned will bear me out.

As to the problem of functionalism, the very fact that I made artists Heads of the workshops shows that, far beyond all the technical goals, the psychological function was much in the foreground. In my opinion architecture starts beyond technicalities in the functional psychological effect of spaces, colors and forms.

Page 61, second paragraph from the bottom. Right from the beginning my idea was that the workshops were not to be understood as workshops for production, but as laboratories to work out models for the industry. Slowly the simple hand tools were replaced by machinery, just according to the development of the first set of students, in contrast to the Kunstgewerbeschulen which did not bridge over from paper design to factory production.

Page 76, first paragraph. It is an important point of my whole procedure that first things came first, and that the development towards the last step, housing and urbanistic environment, was to be built up after the other educational fields had been passed through. The political events took this final goal of the Bauhaus out of my hands, but, as already the first Program shows, it was always the final aim to be reached to go into urbanistic investigations and production.

This brings me to the end. The line of your development is very convincing, but I believe that the logic of argumentation does not necessarily lead to only one political interpretation. I can very well envisage that the goals of the Bauhaus could be reached

Fig. 4. Letter from Walter Gropius to Karl-Heinz Hüter, February 8, 1968 (reverse, page 2 of 3)

Weimar. It wasn't a monolithic block that sat on top of everything else, but it showed that there were always individuals who had influence at a certain time, or who prevented certain things, and that there were always ways to get things through. I completed the manuscript in 1966, and in 1968 I sent the proofs to Walter Gropius at Harvard. Gropius's reply was very positive. He read it very carefully and wrote back with some answers to my questions. We corresponded well about this. But because the book had not yet been approved by GDR Party officials for publishing, the fact that I had contacted Gropius did not go over well and they did not allow the book to be published. It was not until 1972 that the book was released for printing, and in 1976 it was finally published, ten years after I had completed the manuscript.

What do you think changed the officials' opionion about your book in 1972?

The most important thing in 1972 was, of course, the replacement of Walter Ulbricht, who had had an aversion to the Bauhaus. I still don't know exactly why this was, but in the crucial Weimar years of the Bauhaus, he was secretary of the KPD (Communist Party of Germany) district of "Greater Thuringia"—this is what it was called back then—and he was partly based in Jena. Maybe during this time, he attended one of those Dadaist things that the Bauhaus used to arrange. I was told a story about a theater play by the "Bauhaus Stage," and that there was only one person there who had to console people with the comment that if a play starts, it's normal, but if it doesn't start, it isn't—and then he disappeared! Things like that were getting around and influencing opinions for quite a while.

Do you remember the International Bauhaus-Kolloquium that also began in 1976?

Yes. They were always interesting, at least while I was there. You met people who were involved back then. For example, I think of Mrs. Itten. We sat for a long time at the Tempelherrenhaus and we missed the beginning of the new lecture panel up there in the auditorium, because it was a very interesting conversation with someone who had been around Itten and could talk about that time. She got to know him very late, but she learned a lot from him about the early years.

Karl-Heinz Hüter studied classical archaeology in Jena, graduating in 1952. From 1952 until early 1963, he worked as a research assistant at the HAB Weimar at the Chair of Architectural Theory and History. In 1962, he completed his doctoral thesis about Henry van de Velde at Humboldt University in Berlin. From 1963 to 1978, he worked as a researcher at the GDR Bauakademie in Berlin. In 1966, he defended the manuscript for his book, *Das Bauhaus in Weimar*, which was then printed by Henschel publishing house. Hüter sent the page proof for the publication, along with his book on van de Velde, officially through the office of the president of the Bauakademie, Professor Werner Heynisch, to Walter Gropius in the United States. Only the letter with which Gropius replied in February 1968 was discovered by the censorship office. **[fig. 1–4]** For his "unauthorized" contact with an American, Hüter received disciplinary punishment and was threatened to be laid off. The publication of the book was put on hold. In 1972 the Bauakademie re-treated from any rights to Hüter's Bau-haus book and handed it over to him for his personal use. Eventually it was printed unchanged by the Akademie Verlag in 1976 in its first edition. In 1976 Hüter was awarded the Bauhausmedaille of the Bauakademie for his contribution to re-search about Bauhaus history. Despite the recognition of his book, he left the Bauakademie in 1978 and worked as a freelance architectural historian and journalist, which, in the GDR, represented an existential challenge. In 1996, he was awarded the Fritz-Schumacher-Preis für Baugeschichte der Alfred Toepfer Stiftung an der Technischen Universität Hannover for his efforts in the dissemi-nation of historical knowledge about architecture. [Interview conducted by David Keogh, December 11, 2015, Königs Wusterhausen-Wernsdorf]

Marco De Michelis

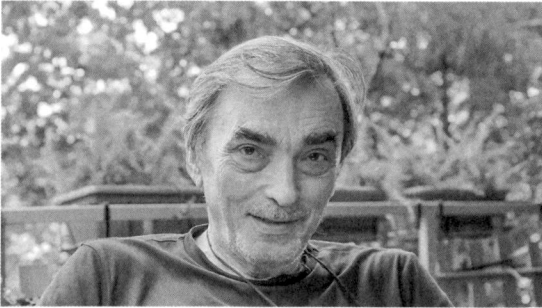

How did you get involved with the International Bauhaus-Kolloquien?

In 1971 or 1972, there was an excursion or-ganized by my university, the Istituto Univer-sitario di Architettura di Venezia, to the GDR. To us it was a legendary excursion, because the whole group consisted of archi-tects who would later found the Tendenza movement in Italy. They were important people: Aldo Rossi, Carlo Aymonino, Gianugo Polesello, Luciano Semerani, and all their assistants. Rossi and Aymonino had already been to the GDR. Rossi had partici-pated in the famous World Youth Congress in East Berlin in 1951. The trip was organized by the Thomas Mann Center, which tried to establish cultural rela-tions between the GDR and Italy at a time when Italy did not yet have any diplomatic relations with the GDR. We traveled to Berlin, and from Berlin to Weimar and back via Leipzig and Halle. It was a very inter-esting week, and I planned to return.

What interested you at the time about the GDR and its architectural discourse?

People at my university were greatly interested in the GDR. We talked a lot about standardization, industrialization, about typology and historic preservation. You could say that the theory of Aldo Rossi was basically in line with the concepts and aims of GDR architecture. In 1975, about half a year before the first Bauhaus-Kolloquium, two repre-sentatives of the university in Weimar suddenly appeared in Venice. One of them was Walter Pasinato. He was Italian, the son of a commu-nist worker in Italy, who'd received a scholarship to study in Weimar. The other one was Konrad Püschel, a former Bauhaus student who in the 1950s had worked on the postwar reconstruction of North Korea. I don't know why he was privileged to receive permission to travel at that time, but they came with the intention of inviting Manfredo Tafuri to the first Bauhaus-Kolloquium. Tafuri and his colleagues approached me and said, "I am not going. You should go with Francesco Dal Co." Both of us were 31 years old, and together we went to Weimar. We did not speak at the colloquium. We were just there as guests.

The first Bauhaus-Kolloquium in 1976 was very interesting, because the last few former Bauhaus students were there: Max Bill and Georg Muche, and Lena Meyer-Bergner, the wife of Hannes Meyer, were there as well. Claude Schnaidt, who had published the first monographic book about Hannes Meyer, gave a lecture. Edmund Goldzamt had come over from Poland. I saw this colloquium as the beginning of a friendship that became more and more important to me.

Was it possible to debate differently in Weimar than at Western universities and institutions, and did your arguments and critiques find any resonance in Weimar?

Some of the Western Europeans who came to the Bauhaus-Kolloquien were friends of mine: Jean-Louis Cohen, for example—he came to the 1983 event. Franco Stella, the architect who is now in charge of rebuilding the Berlin Castle, was there, and West Berliners as well, like Jonas Geist, for example. I was always arguing with them, because in Weimar they pretended to be the "super friends of the GDR," saying freedom is totally unimportant and civil liberty is superfluous while they were obviously benefiting from those liberties in West Berlin. I spoke once about the Bauhaus. It was a strange lecture because it was very complicated. Very Tafuri, very Adorno, very Benjamin. So my impression of the GDR was that the people listened, but they did not really understand anything and just smiled. They did not want to understand, or they were not able to understand. They were smiling approvingly in silence. In East Germany, I learned to speak a language that was foreign to the people from the start. But students came up to me and said, "It's so refreshing to hear you speak! You speak another language!"

Most of the colloquia also included a trip to the Bauhaus building in Dessau. Do you still remember them?

Yes, we went to Dessau during the second Bauhaus-Kolloquium, where they had organized another reunion with all the old Bauhaus students. It was very amusing when they tried as a group to remember the colors of the original Bauhaus building. "What do you think? Was it this green?" "No, a little more gray!" "No, a little more green!" "No, you have no idea!" It was pure affection and perhaps a bit of nostalgia, which I felt was almost more important than the scientific exactness of reconstruction.

Bernd Grönwald played a key role in the reception of the Bauhaus in the GDR and the international reputation of the Bauhaus-Kolloquien. How did you meet him?

Let's say the majority of the GDR scholars were always kind and cautious. Not Bernd Grönwald. Grönwald was always someone who was courageous and idiosyncratic. He came to Weimar as a young professor and moved immediately into the Haus Am Horn. He **383** renovated the house with his bare hands with the help of his wife. He felt that the political philosophy of the Bauhaus was completely wrong during the GDR regime, and he basically conjured the Bauhaus-Kolloquien from a hat, protected them, supported them.

At the last Bauhaus-Kolloquium before the upheaval, in June 1989, I presented a paper on the Luxemburg-Liebknecht Monument by Mies van der Rohe. The scene that ensued belongs to my most precious memories. During a lunchtime meeting of twelve people who were sitting around a table, Grönwald told us that by the end of the year the GDR would no longer exist. All of us said: "Are you crazy?" He said: "Not at all. We don't have money or oil. We cannot heat our apartments. We will have to close the factories." It was strange, because while the official propaganda was triumphant in preparation for the 40th anniversary of the GDR in October 1989, the most important representative of GDR architecture was convinced that the crisis was unsolvable and the fate would be that the GDR would no longer exist. And he was right. ... So, really, for an Italian, experiencing the GDR at that moment was a highly intellectual experience.

How important were the colloquia to international research on the Bauhaus?

The colloquia were important to Bauhaus research. I remember that when Christian Schädlich gave a paper on the relations between the Soviet Union and the Bauhaus and the Vkhutemas school, it was a revelation, because we did not know anything about that back then. Simone Hain gave a paper on the relations between Karel Teige, the Czech avant-garde, and the Bauhaus. Scholars in the GDR had the ability to do research in the socialist countries, and in that the Bauhaus-Kolloquien were able to really be original. Over the years in which these conferences in Weimar took place, it was interesting to witness how the Bauhaus slowly evolved from being a bourgeois and negative example of formalism, to being one of the most important protagonists of the political culture and debate in the GDR.

Were you aware of the manuscript of Karl-Heinz Hüter's book on the Bauhaus?

This was the absurdity of rule and freedom in the GDR. Hüter was excluded because he had committed a capital crime: he had discussed his dissertation with an enemy foreigner (Walter Gropius), which was prohibited. Bernd Grönwald had given me Hüter's book as a present. What Hüter had written was clear as day. His book: everyone read it, but it was censored from publishing and you were not able to discuss it, not even the fact that his book was prohibited. When I asked about him, I was told that there was no reason to talk about Hüter. That's it! Problem solved.

Hüter was categorically excluded from having an academic career. In his book there is nothing politically incorrect. But it was too early under the political circumstances. It is one of the most important historical contributions to the rediscovery of the Bauhaus after the war. Let's not forget: the Bauhaus was not so well-known back then, not even in the West. The Bauhaus Exhibition in New York in 1938 did not mention the name of Hannes Meyer, and it left out that of Johannes Itten. It was the story, more a self-portrait, of Walter Gropius. In the late 1970s, Bauhaus research was really just at its beginning. Hüter's book offered completely unknown facts. After that, there were Magdalena Droste and the wonderful contributions by the Bauhaus-Archiv in West Berlin, but for the Weimar years, Hüter's book was crucial.

Marco De Michelis studied architecture at the Istituto di Architettura di Venezia, completing his doctorate in 1969. Next, he worked as an assistant to Manfredo Tafuri, until becoming a professor of architectural history at the IUAV in Venice in 1980, and later dean of the Faculty of Art and Design. He researched and published about Heinrich Tessenow, the Bauhaus, the history and theory of modernism in architecture and design, and Soviet architecture of the 1920s and 1930s. From 1989 to 1991, he was editor-in-chief of the architecture and design magazine *Ottagono*. From 1997 to 2003, he was the Gropius professor at the Bauhaus-Universität Weimar and was also involved in the conception of the Medium Architecture Colloquium in 2003. [Interview conducted by Lena Laine, June 27, 2016, Milan]

Michael Siebenbrodt

Thank you for coming to the Haus Am Horn and for giving us this interview today. Before we talk about the International Bauhaus-Kolloquium, can you tell us a bit about your memories of that time?
I am also happy that we are able to meet here for the interview. Interestingly, in 1974 I was also part of a comparable study project at the HAB Weimar, in which every year since 1973 about 15 to 20 students conducted interviews with former *Bauhäusler* who would be available to talk to. We had a questionnaire with 20 to 25 questions which we usually collected in written form, but we also conducted interviews in person. While you come here today with cameras, sound recording and film lighting, forty years ago we were happy if we could find a recorder; but even if you'd found a recorder, the next thing you had to find were tapes. After each interview, we had to transcribe the recording and then delete it so that the tape could be reused. So no audio files remain of those conversations. I don't know the whereabouts of those enquiring, but as far as I know this was the first large-scale interview series of Bauhaus protagonists back then.

Do you still remember teachers who were former students at the Bauhaus?
After the war, with the opening of the Staatliche Hochschule für Baukunst und bildende Künste in Weimar in 1946, there were Gustav Hassenpflug, Hanns Hoffmann-Lederer, Emanuel Lindner, Rudolf Ortner, and Peter Keler who were employed to teach there and **385**

who were former *Bauhäusler*. I remember Peter Keler, the designer
of the Bauhaus cradle, who was already a professor emeritus when
I started my studies here in Weimar. He taught a *Vorkurs* in the school
right after the war and was later in charge of exhibition design. He was
probably one of the most important former *Bauhäusler* who taught in
Weimar in the 1960s. And of course, Konrad Püschel was still teaching
when I started my architecture studies in Weimar in the early 1970s.
I became a student assistant at the chair of Professor Schädlich, who
introduced me to two important things. One was the Bauhaus Library,
which still existed then and which was also an important source for
our research about the Bauhaus.

   Now, over 40 years later, I've published a book about this library
with Frank Simon-Ritz, the director of the university library today.
Sometimes some projects need a long breath. And the other thing was
a historical collection of black-and-white photographs which—as we
found out later—included some that had been used in the *Vorkurs*
taught by Johannes Itten.

How would you describe the role the HAB played in the recognition of the
Bauhaus in the GDR and potentially internationally as well?

   Yes, I would say internationally as well. It is important to look back
to the 1960s in Weimar, when a number of researchers turned their
attention to the topic of the Bauhaus after it was completely taboo
in the 1950s. In the field of research, it was Karl-Heinz Hüter and
Adalbert Behr, with their research about Henry van de Velde that
logically lead to further research on the history of the Bauhaus. Before
I could get to know them, they had already left for the GDR Bauakademie in Berlin.

   While they were in Weimar, Konrad Püschel had, in 1964,
conducted a detailed site measurement of the Bauhaus buildings in
Dessau with a large group of students. That was a pioneering effort
in the field of conservation. It was indeed unique. Imagine: in the
mid-1960s nobody in the whole world—not in Paris with Le Corbusier,
nor in Moscow with the avant-garde buildings of the Soviet avant-
garde—had dealt with these buildings in a deeper way, with scholarly
interest and with proper preservationist techniques and methods.
On the contrary: at that time, modernist buildings were still being
demolished for the most part. And so it's remarkable that the impulse
started in Weimar. Nearly everything that had to do with Bauhaus
research, with maintaining Bauhaus heritage, started in Weimar.

   The survey consisted of two volumes, in which every room, every
detail, every original door, every original door handle, every lamp
that was completely or partly in good condition, is documented.
It was a milestone in the historical conservation of classical modernism worldwide.

How would you describe the different approaches to studying the history of the Bauhaus in divided postwar Germany before 1976, when the Bauhaus-Kolloquium opened its doors to an international audience?

In 1946, when the museum in Weimar—the Staatliche Kunstsammlung zu Weimar, Staatsgalerie des Landes Thüringen—reopened after the war, it presented an exhibition of its Bauhaus collection, at least parts of it which remained continuously on display without interruption throughout the 1950s and into the 1970s. The museum standard was of course not comparable to today's standards, but the two or three rooms existed to be seen by visitors. Undeniably, the work of Hans Maria Wingler, which led to the foundation of the Verein Bauhaus-Archive e. V. in Darmstadt in 1960, was a milestone for the reception of the Bauhaus in the West. But his collection and his comprehensive book of 1962 also gave impulses for changes in the cultural politics of the GDR. In 1966, Walter Scheidig, the director of the Staatliche Kunstsammlungen zu Weimar, who had held that position since 1933, published the book *Bauhaus Weimar: Crafts of the Weimar Bauhaus, 1919–1924*, a catalogue of the first authorized Bauhaus collection that he seemed to have kept in his collection somehow in fairness. The collection went on an international exhibition tour in 1967. That same year, in the Georgium castle in Dessau, another Bauhaus exhibition opened. And in 1968, my colleague Wulf Herzogenrath, then curator at the Württembergischer Kunstverein Stuttgart, edited the catalogue "50 Jahre Bauhaus" for the first major exhibition on the international influence of the Bauhaus which traveled the word from Stuttgart. It is interesting that the first international Bauhaus exhibition from the East in 1967 is followed by an international exhibition in the West. I think these exhibitions gave impulses on the respective sides that encouraged a friendly rivalry.

From the 1960s until the end of the GDR, there were about twenty Bauhaus exhibitions, some with record numbers of visitors, because some exhibitions came from the West, sometimes in exchange for exhibitions coming from the East. There were publications and monographic exhibitions about Xanti Schawinski and Max Bill, and these led to new working contacts between curators and researchers in East and West. Max Bill donated a sculpture to the Dessau Bauhaus collection, but the Weimar Bauhaus collection was also trying to grow in the 1980s and until 1992, when I took over the directorship of the Kunstsammlungen zu Weimar.

How did you get involved with the International Bauhaus-Kolloquium?

From 1976 to 1985, I was teaching at the chair of theory and history of architecture, but I also taught freehand drawing to add muscle training to the exercises of thought. I had two tasks that were directly related to my own research on Bauhaus history. One was to develop, in collaboration with the chair of preservation, conservation studies for the Bauhaus buildings in Dessau which brought me into close cooperation with the city of Dessau, its city architects, and its planning offices. **387**

My second task was to help in the organization of the International Bauhaus-Kolloquium in 1979 and 1983. At some point, the first task took over and I was delegated by the HAB to work in Dessau and later became an assistant at the Bauakademie der DDR, Dessau branch. From the intersection between Weimar and the Bauakademie eventually grew the idea for an academic-cultural Bauhaus center in Dessau (Wissenschaftlich-Kulturelles Zentrum, WKZ), which in the 1980s put on several Bauhaus events, including the Bauhaus-Bühne and Bauhaus-Parties, which were to resonate with their origins in the 1920s.

Michael Siebenbrodt received his artistic education from 1958 to 1970 at both the Martin-Luther-Universität in Halle and the Hochschule für industrielle Formgestaltung at Halle's Burg Giebichenstein. From 1972 to 1976, he studied architecture at the HAB Weimar, where he then worked as a research assistant in the Department of the History and Theory of Architecture until 1985. As a student, Siebenbrodt participated in the interviews of former *Bauhäusler*, and as part of his graduation thesis, co-written with Christine Engel-mann (formerly Christine Kutschke), he conducted detailed research on the preservation of the Bauhaus building in Dessau. From 1988 to 1992, he held a leading position at the culture department in the city of Weimar. In 1992 he became the acting director of the Kunstsammlungen zu Weimar; and in 1993 he became curator of the Bauhaus collections at the Kunstsammlungen zu Weimar (later named Klassik Stiftung Weimar) [Interview conducted by Annika Eheim, December 9, 2015, Weimar].

Karin Wilhelm

You participated in several Bauhaus-Kolloquien. Do you still remember those held before 1989?
I always found it a very special experience to stay at one of the most beautiful hotels, at the Elephant, or when I could see Goethe's garden house, and we always had a very intense and well-organized program—although I have to admit that there always remained a certain distance between Easterners and Westerners. You did not really yet know where everyone stood and how you had to assess each other. Even in personal conversations, you tried to avoid certain topics, or you would be very careful about what you said. So everyone was treading carefully.

Did the Bauhaus-Kolloquien in Weimar find any response in discussions on architectural history and theory in the Federal Republic?
Oh, yes. They certainly found a strong response here in the Federal Republic—because, after all, what they offered was an explicitly political position with a clearly specified sociopolitical impetus. You have to consider that in the Federal Republic, leftist positions that might have been related to the Bauhaus were not actually much talked about. Younger people like myself were particularly intrigued by

questions about the kind of movements that happened within the Bauhaus, its proletarian cultures or its political connections in an international context. In the West, these had been completely brushed aside or, rather, one did not remember them anymore. And in the GDR, or rather precisely in response to the colloquia in Weimar, very specific research focused on those interests. We found it absolutely relevant and observed the discussions with great curiosity.

Do you remember any more critical discussions or debates during the Bauhaus-Kolloquien?

I remember the colloquium in 1992, titled "Architecture and Power," to which Gerd Zimmermann had invited Charles Jencks. He captivated the audience, but to "Adornites" like me the memorable thing was the consumerist aspect of his postmodernist agenda: "Everything is so nice and colorful here." Nina Hagen would later sing; it was not really my cup of tea. In comparison, the Bauhaus could suddenly offer quality and above all also diversity, which now we were able to rediscover with access to archives and materials. Now after 1989, when all this seemed possible, I was worried that the pluralist approach would relativize the political history of the Bauhaus that we were now able to reconstruct.

Particularly in the discussion moderated by Heinrich Klotz, who had organized an exhibition at the Museum of Architecture in Frankfurt called *Modernism and Postmodernism*, I sensed some ideological distortions. Postmodernism introduced the idea of disposing of the sociopsychological impetus of modernism. I realized that something was being sealed off when one did not want to have anything to do with modernism anymore. In the East German context, it must have been completely different. There the possibility of reactivating ornamentation, decoration, and certain aesthetic models was also met with a very understandable wish for a liberation of the imagination in design and artistic creation.

When the Iron Curtain fell, we also had to lift the curtain that was in front of our heads, our eyes, and our thoughts. It was a unique historic situation, and I'm also noticing now how these emotions resurface.

Karin Wilhelm studied sociology, psychology, and art history at the Universities of Heidelberg, Munich and Berlin. In 1991, Wilhelm was appointed to be a professor of art and architectural history at the Department of Architecture at the Graz University of Technology. In 2001, she moved to the Braunschweig University of Technology, where she was a professor of history and theory of architecture and the city. Her publications include *Walter Gropius – Industriearchitekt* (Wiesbaden: Vieweg Verlag, DAM, 1983), *Portrait Frei Otto: Architekten heute* (Berlin, 1985), *Kunst als Revolte* (Anabas-Verlag Gießen, 1996), und *Neue Städte für einen neuen Staat – die städtebauliche Erfindung des modernen Israel und der Wiederaufbau in der BRD: Eine Annäherung* (ed. with Kerstin Gust; Bielefeld: transcript-Verlag, 2013). [Interview conducted by Lena Laine, May 22, 2016, Berlin]

Charles Jencks

During the Bauhaus-Kolloquium in 1992, you opened the conference with a lecture on postmodernism and your contempt of the politics of Prince Charles in Britain. But you also used the title of the conference, "Architecture and Power," to speak about some of the lesser-known collaborations of modernism with the Nazi regime. Did your work on postmodernism, which you largely discussed in Western architectural circles, receive a new historical perspective when you presented it in Weimar?
My paper was titled "Modernists, Prince Charles, the Nazis and Ethics." I was not really speaking on postmodernism; I was speaking on Prince Charles and the modernists—how they polarized each other because of their extreme paranoia. At the time, most of my work was about the postmodern position on pluralism. Together with people like Leon Krier, we wanted to have an equal say in architecture. In Britain at the time, the profession, schools of architecture, and the RIBA—the Royal Institute of British Architecture—were run more or less by modernists, and they wouldn't allow a pluralist position. Prince Charles did realize that, too. It wasn't a level playing field, as they say; it was already skewed in favor of modernism. And modernism as I found it with Gropius was actually very reactionary: it wasn't moving; it was corrosive. I think in Weimar at the time they had not heard of such connections before, or they had different ideological interpretations and questions of this history. In fact, I am sure it was not a subject you could study so easily at the time, neither in the East nor in the West. I remember the feeling in the audience was electric when I was speaking.

When the Iron Curtain was lifted, a new political and cultural plurality emerged with global effects. How did you see the role of architecture in these landslide developments when the political front lines were about to be reconfigured?
In the postmodern position of pluralism, of course, it's very hard to defend pluralism if both sides are shouting and killing each other—it's impossible, actually, because you have to have a proper discourse on all sides if any of the minorities are to survive, and we know that dogmatists drive out minorities. By people living under the Soviet system, modernism was seen quite understandably as the mass-produced, top-down, imposed, minimalist solution, which was repressing the locals, which was repressing art, free thinking—repressing everything. And so postmodernism was stronger in a way, I would argue, in those countries. Certainly in Poland, where I went many times, I was impressed by the many ways they could hide their dissidence from the state. I think the political collapse in Eastern Europe had the potential of a new kind of freedom, a new kind of discourse, that could affect politics and culture not only in the East, but also in the West.

To what extent do you think the political transformation allowed for new possibilities in researching the history of modernism and the Bauhaus?

In Weimar, I was moved to see the place of the early Bauhaus, to see what I knew from reading. I love that early Bauhaus spirit before it became heavy with ideology. So speaking in Germany on the Bauhaus in 1992 was very interesting. I came to Weimar with my student Elaine S. Hochmann, who was speaking about Mies van der Rohe and the Third Reich. The audience was excited, upset, divided and angry with me and her, but at the same time interested—but certainly confused to hear about Mies and his collaboration with the Nazis. I also remember a talk by Magdalena Droste from the Bauhaus-Archiv Berlin, who spoke about Bauhaus design during National Socialism. So one could sense that this history was about to be addressed anew with the collapse of the Wall. I think postmodernism made history possible to think about again. With the announcement of the death of modernism, it liberated all of us who thought that modernism was eternal. It allowed modernism to be debated.

Charles Jencks studied English literature at Harvard University and architecture at the Harvard Graduate School of Design. He completed his doctoral thesis in architectural history at University College London in 1970. His publications include *Le Corbusier and the Tragic View of Architecture* (Cambridge, MA: Harvard University Press, 1974), *The Language of Post-Modern Architecture* (New York: Rizzoli, 1988), *Critical Modernism* (London: John Wiley, 2007), and *The Story of Post-Modernism: Five Decades of the Ironic, Iconic and Critical in Architecture* (London: John Wiley, 2011). [Interview conducted by Lena Laine, David Keogh and Ines Weizman, July 8, 2016, London]

Chup Friemert

You participated in all the Bauhaus-Kolloquien between 1976 and 1989. Do you remember how the conference developed over that period?

The first one was very impressive, because Georg Muche was there—this unbelievably tall man, a giant, two meters tall or so, with an incredibly deep voice and an enormously strong presence—and there were all the other *Bauhäusler* as well. People met each other officially at the congress, but then I was also invited to the Haus Am Horn, the house that was now inhabited by the family of Bernd Grönwald. These get-togethers had another quality that was very charming. The house became its own center. I remember Marco De Michelis, Jean-Louis Cohen and Claude Schnaidt who were invited. I remember that Muche then saw the house he'd designed for the first time since leaving Weimar. When the Grönwalds had lived there as a family of five, they'd added a room. Muche liked that idea, because it was part of his concept that this should be possible.

*What role did Bernd Grönwald play in Weimar, and what did he contribute to
the legacy of the Bauhaus in the GDR?*

Bernd Grönwald had an important role in the rediscovery and appropriation of the Bauhaus as heritage in East Germany. He acted on political levels to make these colloquia possible. Somehow he had managed to get carte blanche for his ideas from the Bauakademie and the state officials. He pulled strings so that others could actually develop the theoretical and organizational structure of Bauhaus research in Weimar. I never had the impression that he was a careerist. He was very invested in his ideas. In fact, he believed so firmly in socialism that I was indeed irritated by it. Bernd Grönwald was not a very eloquent speaker, but he was a very honest and precise person. When the GDR collapsed, it was clear that this would lead to conflicts for him. Unfortunately, he took his own life, because he didn't see a way forward. That was very sad—a real tragedy. I remember after 1989, I met Grönwald in Switzerland at Max Bill's house with Claude Schnaidt. He was tormented by that moment of transition and couldn't be calmed down. At the Bauakademie and in Weimar, especially in the late '80s, he had planned to introduce new ideas and suddenly, right when he thought he could do something, the tools were taken out of his hands. It was a tragedy.

*How did the political environment in the 1970s and 1980s impact
the Bauhaus-Kolloquien?*

We need to remember that these colloquia were taking place during the Cold War, when tensions were very high. There was the issue of stationing American missiles in West Germany and generally of rearmament in East and West. Tension would ease up a little, and then it would rise again. The political atmosphere did not impact the colloquia directly, but I remember it strongly as the context in which I was planning my presentation to the colloquium and my travel to Weimar and the GDR. It was not self-evident that a person would cross this border to attend a conference in Weimar. During these conferences in Weimar, we thought a lot about what we could contribute to ease the tension. One of the questions that Western theorists on the left and theorists in the socialist countries discussed in the late 1970s was the meaning of progress. What would progress mean in relation to architecture? Is there such a thing as being progressive and advanced in architecture? How do you recognize it? Do you recognize it by its form? Its purpose? By its ownership structure?

I remember Claude Schnaidt's paper, when he argued that everybody should think about what he or she can do to secure peace by means of architecture. It impressed us at the time to think about architecture potentially having such an impact or such importance. It meant introducing politics into architecture. That is why I did not like the postmodernist trend, because in my view it depoliticized the architectural community. All those who dealt with Bauhaus history knew what politicization of a field of study was.

It might be hard to reconstruct this today, or even to communicate it appropriately, but during these Bauhaus-Kolloquien, things were said in a covert way. Bauhaus history in some ways covered up what could be said about politics. To some people, presenting more radical positions during the conference in Weimar, in front of an international audience, also offered a level of protection. Participants at the conference were very aware of the political environment and you could trust that every word of dissent, covert or not, could be heard.

Chup Friemert studied at the Staatliche Akademie der Bildenden Künste Stuttgart and the Freie Universität Berlin, graduating from the Staatliche Hochschule für Bildende Künste Braunschweig. He completed his doctoral studies at the University of Bremen in 1977. In 1984, he was appointed professor of the history and theory of design at the Hochschule für Bildende Künste in Hamburg. From 1989 to 2010, he acted as co-publisher and editor of *Form und Zweck*. His numerous publications include *Produktionsästhetik im Faschismus: Das Amt "Schönheit der Arbeit" von 1933 bis 1939* (Munich: Damnitz Verlag, 1980), *Weltausstellung 1889: Der Maschinenpalast* (ed. with Susanne Weiß; Hamburg: Textem Verlag, 2009), and *Hegel: Philosophie der Kunst. Bearbeitete Mitschriften* (Hamburg: Materialverlag, 2012). [Interview conducted by Lena Laine, June 16, 2016, Süderstapel]

Olaf Weber

You attended the first Bauhaus-Kolloquium in 1976. What expectations did you have of the event?
Yes. At first I'd hoped that the conference would help to expand the ways of thinking about architecture. In the GDR, the Bauhaus could only be rehabilitated by first pointing out the parallels between GDR planning policies and the social side of the Bauhaus. Interestingly, the Bauhaus-Kolloquien also functioned as counterpoints and corrections of the Western image of the Bauhaus. There they discussed Gropius, Mies, Breuer, Kandinsky, and Klee, while for example Hannes Meyer was forgotten. In the GDR in the mid-1970s, Hannes Meyer was crowned the prince. In that sense, the colloquium was a corrective.

Shortly after the first colloquium, you wrote a letter to Bernd Grönwald.
In 1976, I had just been drafted as a soldier, at the age of 35, but I took a few days off to attend the Bauhaus-Kolloquium as an audience member. It was with those impressions that I returned to the barracks and there I wrote that letter, addressed to Bernd Grönwald, who was Party secretary at the time, and one who had significantly developed and promoted the colloquia, and who, in my opinion, played a very positive role in all this. That's why he was the right recipient. I wrote that I was pleased that the Bauhaus was positioned

further within the center of architecture and architectural theory of the GDR, and at the same time I deplored the fact that the idea of the Bauhaus was so strictly defined, that certain aspects were highlighted and others ignored. Above all, at the time, I thought that it would be especially suitable to represent the aesthetic side in its entirety; more specifically, the art that had played a very important role at the Bauhaus: Kandinsky, Klee, Schlemmer, and so on. This side of the Bauhaus had not been rehabilitated at all. I argued that through the rehabilitation of the Bauhaus, including in the fields of art and fine arts, in the GDR some changes could be made and that one could build upon that momentum. That was correct, but of course it was too much to ask, especially since we had no arts education in Weimar; there was only architectural education. So it was also right that these Bauhaus-Kolloquien at an architecture school focused on architecture and not on art. My letter had no effect, but a little later, Grönwald tapped me on the shoulder somewhere on the way to the cafeteria and said, "Yes, what you wrote was OK."

Do you remember the controversies in the years leading up to and following the political transformation of 1989, when the Bauhaus was discussed in the framework of postmodernist discourse?

As soon as the Bauhaus was rediscovered and rehabilitated in the GDR, the discussion about postmodernism started. And suddenly, the way of thinking about the Bauhaus had on the one hand to resist the old, traditional way of thinking about the Bauhaus and on the other had to defend itself against the postmodernist tendency to negate or nullify important, valuable achievements of the Bauhaus, precisely its social impetus and its constructive honesty. Postmodernism meant turning the entire history of construction and all the ethnicities of the world into a toolbox for architectural design. Well, it was the language of consumerism. The critics were mainly Western scholars like Chup Friemert from Hamburg and Claude Schnaidt from Paris, and many more, who dealt with postmodernism in the colloquium in 1989 and in 1992.

I, too, wrote about postmodernism, but in the 1980s I was once banned from publishing for a year because of an article I had published in *Architektur der DDR*. In it I had confronted decorativism, saying that prefabricated buildings were now suddenly being decorated with all kind of squiggles, were painted to produce a pseudo-plurality, and I criticized it, saying that the diversity which we of course need in architecture should much rather come from within, from a sociocultural differentiation of the life of its residents. My argument was apparently discussed at the highest levels. Here in Weimar—yes, thanks to a few people who were here—we could actually test the limits of what could be said.

You then also actively participated in the organization of the Bauhaus-Kolloquien.

When I returned to Weimar in 1980, as an aspiring professor, I happened to be on the staff organizing the Bauhaus-Kolloquien and I realized what an immense amount of work went into it. Christian Schädlich was at the center of the organization. He had managed it all with great attention to detail. And for students, the Bauhaus-Kolloquien were real highlights, too. It wasn't just something incidental, somehow, like someone just held a meeting somewhere. Instead, students had the days off. It was sort of a duty to participate in the colloquium. Many students helped out with the organization as well, and as a result it was very lively there. It was a very pleasant atmosphere, and that's why people liked to come.

Olaf Weber began his architecture studies at the HAB Weimar in 1964. In 1973 he completed his doctoral thesis. From 1973 to 1980, he worked as a research assistant at the GDR Bauakademie. In 1984, he completed his postdoctoral thesis and began working as a research assistant at the HAB Weimar. In 1992, he became head of the working group for founding a Faculty of Design and was appointed professor of aesthetics, one of only two professors from former East Germany among 18 newly appointed professors after the university was restructured after reunification. Weber retired from his position in 2009. [Interview conducted by Lena Laine and Annika Eheim, December 3, 2015, Weimar]

Michael Müller

In 1992 you participated at the first Bauhaus-Kolloquium since the reunification of Germany. Do you still remember the atmosphere then?
The atmosphere was very open. What disturbed me, though, and at another convention a year before, was the way "second-tier" academics from West Germany were—how should I say it?—behaving like imperialists. Well, it was not always the best academics who went east to occupy the vacant professorships. You could see a certain fear and worry in the East German colleagues about what might happen to them in the future, and they had to come to grips about what had just happened with the political transformation. Certainly, there were some people whom one should not necessarily have set loose on students, but when I came to Weimar then, my impression was also that the syllabus was being directed quite rigidly towards the discourse in the West. I had seen other chances with the collapse of the division between East and West Germany, and I felt a rather unpleasant cultural atmosphere that could also be sensed among the participants of the colloquium. The subjects of discussion, too, I felt had suddenly changed. I realized that, strangely, the Bauhaus-Kolloquium left aside the discussions that were taking place in East Germany at the time, and that these were being replaced by a West German discussion.

You also participated in a panel discussion with Kristiana Hartmann,
Hans G. Helms, Charles Jencks, Karin Wilhelm and Gerd Zimmermann,
with Heinrich Klotz as panel chair. Debates about postmodernism were
relatively well-known in Western discourse. What made the discussion different
in Weimar in 1992?

Yes, I remember the discussion, and I think it was not really different in Weimar from those in the West, in a sense that it would take on board a new political configuration after the reunification and a much needed conversation about the power system that had just been overcome, which relates to what we discussed before. Even worse, the discussion was highly influenced and overpowered by the panel chair, our good Heinrich Klotz, who strongly monopolized the debate and who instead of taking the role of moderating, revealed strange animosities, thinking that he had to justify himself, and often tried strike a blow. It was the old polemic about modernism versus postmodernism and their respective affinities to power.

In the course of the discussion, the social agenda of modernism in the tradition
of critical theory was pitted against the pluralist agenda of postmodernism
as a way of questioning the modernist project and its affiliations with power.
What was your stance on this?

The most fascinating question behind these two arguments was certainly that of the responsibility of architects to address the urgent social and political problems of our times. Klotz argued that architects are not sociologists, but that is of course evidence of architecture's incapacity. If you are dealing with architecture, you are dealing with society. You do not have to be a sociologist or a politican to dispute social and political processes in our society. The architect might even display better judgment than a politician. Concerning the topic of architecture and power, I believe the way of approaching it was still limited by the understanding that power could most easily be detected in architecture under a totalitarian regime. Whether it was in Fascism or Stalinism, it was architecture that communicated from miles away that there is someone in charge of suppressing others. But I think the question posed at that conference meant for us to think about other forms— less obvious forms—in which architecture is aligned with power.

A good friend of mine, Hans G. Helms, who was invited to join the panel at the beginning of the discussion, spoke about the latest horror scenarios of world domination from th US, as he always would—I already knew about this from him. In what Klotz in his later response described as "sketching a panorama of fear," Helms talked about the latest technological devices that would be able to control people, but he also spoke about American shopping malls and enormous parking lots that would be perfectly suitable for shooting down the assailing masses who would gather for a revolution because they didn't have enough money to buy anything in the malls. Back then, one was not familiar with the phenomenon of terrorism, and today we would certainly not joke about this image he was painting.

But what he meant to say was that postmodernism essentially advocated the consumable aesthetic and society's functioning by means of consumption. Undoubtedly a colorful bouquet and compared to the horrible settlements of the 1960s which seemed to have become the dead end of modernism, postmodernism was certainly something wonderful. When criticizing the virtually impoverished and unimaginative modernity, postmodernism fueled the dominance of a mass culture capable of consuming, which is highly aestheticized because it is in constant need of new editing of new surfaces, so that we are not just entertained but we also have the feeling we have to buy something new without actually needing it, right? So to assume that within this architecture power would slip away and the land of plenty would emerge: that would surely be naïve. So this conversation was a bit out of context of the previous conferences before 1989, in which I think Bauhaus history was also used as legitimization for an increasingly courageous talk about power, but I think we all realized that this opening in the East had been harshly interrupted by a Western discourse that intended to fundamentally reorient the debate.

Michael Müller studied art history, archaeology, philosophy, and sociology in Vienna, London, and Frankfurt am Main. He completed his doctoral thesis at the University of Frankfurt am Main in 1974. From 1977 to 2013, he was a professor of aesthetic and cultural science and art education at the University of Bremen, where he acted as head of the Institute for Aesthetics and Art Education. His publications include *Die Villa als Herrschaftsarchitektur* (Frankfurt am Main: Suhrkamp, 1970), *Funktionalität und Moderne* (mit Christoph Mohr, Cologne: Edition Fricke, 1984), and *Architektur und Avantgarde* (Frankfurt am Main: Syndikat, 1984). [Interview conducted by Lena Laine, May 28, 2016, Bremen]

Gerd Zimmermann

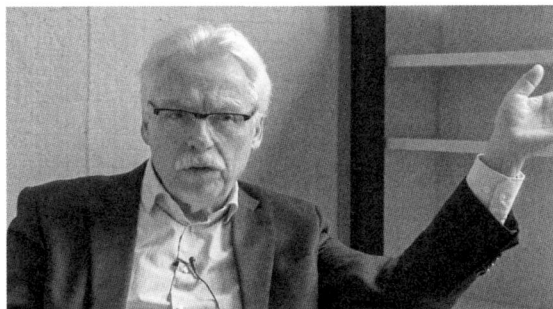

How did you get involved with the history of the Bauhaus and the Bauhaus-Kolloquien at the HAB Weimar?

In the 1980s, Olaf Weber and I were invited by Bernd Grönwald, who had just been appointed as a professor of architectural theory, to be his assistants. We agreed immediately, because we had the feeling that something new was starting there and that we would get the opportunity to work with a really interesting person. In the 1970s, Grönwald had seized the moment of slowly surfacing research and interest in the Bauhaus, and he managed to argue the legitimization of the Bauhaus on a larger scale, which led to a central role of the HAB in Bauhaus research in the GDR and the restoration of the Bauhaus building in Dessau. He argued that the Bauhaus could be legitimized by stressing it as a historical foundation of the industrialization of construction methods, which was one   397 of the main agendas of GDR planning efforts to provide housing for everybody. And, of course, in Weimar Walter Gropius had developed the building-block system as a principle of large-scale planning, and Hannes Meyer realized his vision of social housing in Dessau-Törten. Later, with an echo to the Bauhaus, Grönwald even founded the Künstlerisch-experimentelle Werkstätten at the HAB Weimar, led by Norbert Korrek, which would officially recognize the creative potential of the Bauhaus and would also connect with the international community of the Bauhaus. Grönwald used the vehicle of the Bauhaus to open the GDR to international cooperation, and with that in mind he really laid the foundation for the Bauhaus-Kolloquien. That was the personal achievement of Bernd Grönwald, assisted by a team of professors and researchers. He was the initiator and nobody else. That must be pointed out clearly.

What importance did the Haus Am Horn have during the time when Bernd Grönwald lived there with his family?

At some point, the Grönwald family needed an apartment in Weimar. The Haus Am Horn, as you already know, stood empty; nobody wanted to move in there. And so he said, "Yes, then I'll do that. The house is here, and if it can be used, I'll do that." So, he moved into this house, and understood at that moment, while residing there, what the house actually is: an icon of the avant-garde. At the same time, he opened it up for meetings and friendship with Bauhaus supporters from all over the world—especially in the old Federal Republic, in West Berlin, for example. Jonas Geist, Joachim Krause, and Claude Schnaidt, people who were big followers of the Bauhaus, often came to the GDR because for certain publications, they had to search the Prussian bequest in the archive in Merseburg, and then they came to Weimar to the Haus Am Horn. With that, a community arose, and with that a discourse, as it were, emerged, and they started to rediscover the Bauhaus. It is interesting to see how a house has inspired a community and a discourse.

After the political transformation of 1989, was it obvious that the Bauhaus-Kolloquien would be continued?

First, the GDR rediscovered the Bauhaus quite late. Too late, in a way, because the international discourse was much more advanced. Especially in the 1980s, when postmodernism was on the rise, before the Bauhaus was rediscovered, it was already caught up in a massive criticism of modernism.

The Bauhaus was virtually understood as a synonym for the whole of modernism. The GDR rediscovered the Bauhaus late, but it also tried to take immediate ownership of it and declared the Bauhaus to be a new doctrine, combined with a strong ideologically motivated rejection of all postmodern tendencies. To a certain extent, this indoctrination was similar to the rejection of the Bauhaus around 1950. While the Bauhaus had been interpreted then as "capitalist," the postmodern movement was now made the embodiment of capitalism, a way of thinking I don't like so much.

The end of the GDR, this so-called *Wende*, the "peaceful revolution," produced a completely new situation of freedom and openness. In 1992 I was appointed professor of design and architectural theory, and almost at the same time, I was elected rector of the HAB. For me, there was the question of whether to continue the International Bauhaus-Kolloquium. While we had to break with the past, Norbert Korrek — a friend and the long-time secretary of the Bauhaus-Kolloquium — and I said: We will continue with this. The first colloquium was in 1992, and I titled it "Architecture and Power." That was of course born of the current events, as it sought to ask: How does architecture represent power? In what way is architecture power? At a moment when one could see the long-term effects of modernism, and when postmodernism critiqued the "bloodless" modernism that was reduced to economic functionalism, the discussion with Charles Jencks was controversial, but it also revealed the various interpretations of the Bauhaus and the historic possibility of rethinking the history of modernism outside of the ideological divide.

I wanted to make the Bauhaus-Kolloquien now, after the fall of the Wall in a much more globalized situation, an internationally relevant colloquium about architectural theory. And I don't hesitate to say that we were successful. Although in 1976 it was also a meeting of *Bauhäusler* and Bauhaus researchers, Bernd Grönwald had already developed it with focus on theory, as you can see in the themes discussed since 1976. And in the colloquia that followed, I wanted to emphasize contemporary issues of architectural theory, the relationship between architecture and media. I am happy that the colloquium in 2016 will connect Bauhaus history with digital cultures of collecting and research and open architecture to current discourse on Big Data.

Gerd Zimmermann studied architecture at the HAB Weimar and completed his doctoral studies in architectural theory in 1974. From 1973 to 1980, he did research at the GDR Bauakademie in the fields of architectural psychology and semiotics. From 1980 onward, he was an assistant to the chair of architectural theory of Professor Bernd Grönwald. In 1992, he was appointed a professor of design and architectural theory and was also appointed to be the rector of the HAB Weimar, where he was in charge of renaming and restructuring the HAB as the Bauhaus-Universität Weimar in 1996. [Interview conducted by Annika Eheim and Lena Laine, December 10, 2015, Weimar]

Part 3

Refugees, Migrants, Returnees, Travelers: Bauhaus Architects in Exile

Thomas Flierl

Migrant with a Conflicted Sense of Home: Hannes Meyer after the Bauhaus

"as creators we fulfill the fate of the landscape"

Before taking over the newly instituted architecture class at the Dessau Bauhaus on April 1, 1927, Hannes Meyer had left Walter Gropius in no doubt as to his basic methodology: "the fundamental tendency of my teaching will be strictly geared to a functional, collectivist, constructive approach in the spirit of 'abc' and 'the new world.'"[1] ABC refers to the group of Swiss architects (Hans Schmidt, Werner Moser, Paul Artaria, and Emil Roth) inspired by El Lissitzky and Mart Stam with which Hannes Meyer and Hans Wittwer were also associated. They "became the most important architectural constructivist group outside of the USSR,"[2] editing the magazine of the same name—*ABC: Beiträge zum Bauen*—from 1924 to 1926. "the new world" was Meyer's futuristic manifesto published in *Das Werk* in July 1926. In it, he stated that the new technology liberated "our place-bound senses" and "our earthbound spirits": "Our homes are more mobile than ever. Large blocks of flats, sleeping cars, house yachts, and transatlantic liners undermine the local concept of the 'homeland.' The fatherland goes into a decline. We learn Esperanto. We become cosmopolitan."[3] Meyer's and Wittwer's designs for the Petersschule in Basel and the Palace of Nations in Geneva are representative of this period.[fig.1, 2]

Meyer subsequently modified his position at the Bauhaus. However, even in April 1928, at the time when Meyer was chosen as Bauhaus director after Gropius had suggested him as his successor, his text "building"—which used the famous formula "all things in this world are a product of the formula: (function times economy)"—took this functionalist line. Among other things, it stated that "thinking of

402

Fig. 1. Design by Hannes Meyer and Hans Wittwer for the Palace of Nations (1927).
Fig. 2. Hannes Meyer and Hans Wittwer, design for the Petersschule in Basel.

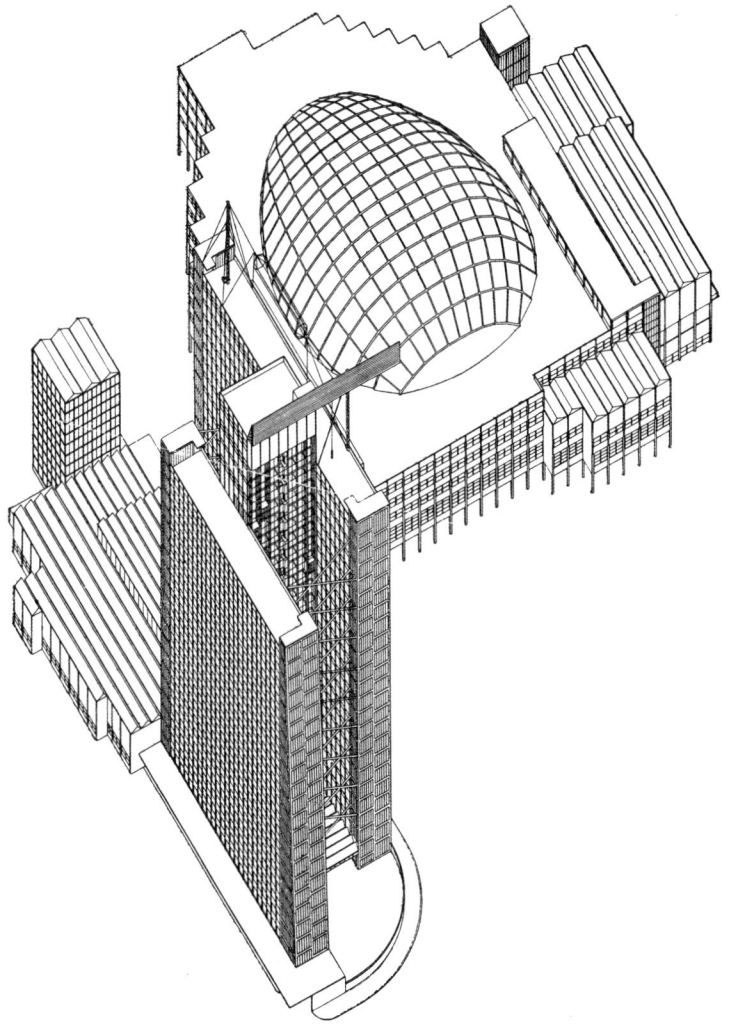

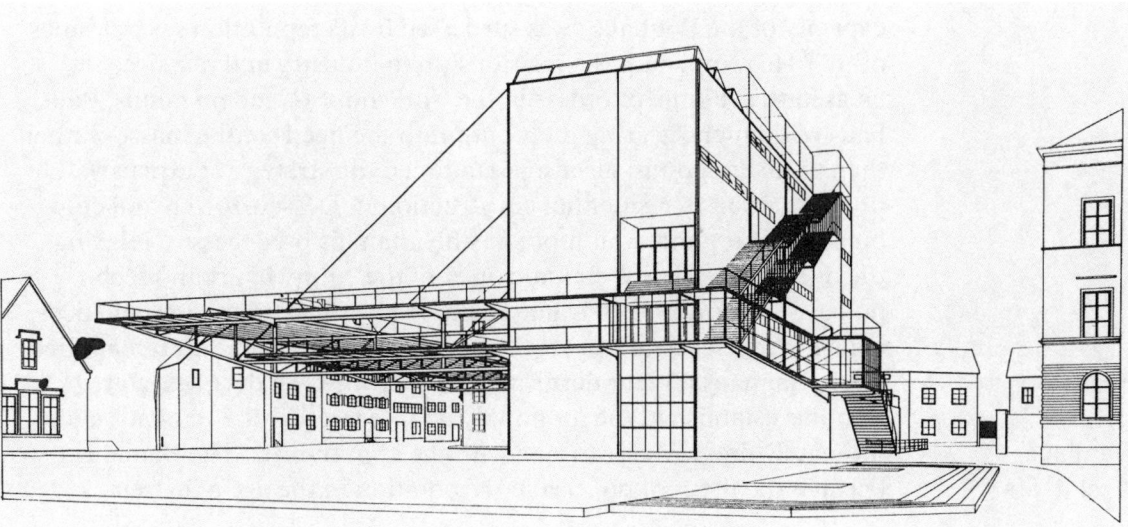

building in functional and biological terms as giving shape to the living process leads logically to pure construction: these constructive forms have no native country, they are the expression of an international trend of architectural thought."[4]

In early 1929, we can detect a significant change in Meyer's thinking. His program text "bauhaus and society" culminates in the following sentences:

> *finally all creative action is determined by the fate of the landscape which for the man with roots there is peculiar and unique, his work is personal and localized. if a floating population lacks these roots its work easily becomes stereotyped and standardized. a conscious experience of the landscape is building as determined by fate. as creators we fulfill the fate of the landscape.*[5]

The houses with balcony access in Dessau-Törten and, most notably, his ADGB Trade Union School in Bernau, which was handed over in May 1930, typify this new attitude to architecture.[fig.3 a–c] This remarkable act of recalibration on the part of Meyer, who at the time, influenced by his Swiss experience, was still thinking very much in leftist socialist and cooperative terms and was focused on harmony instead of class struggle, got completely lost in the public uproar over his summary dismissal in summer 1930. Meyer had realized that the effective capacity of the Bauhaus "was surpassed by its reputation several times over."[6] He ramped up the relationship to industry and massively increased the volume of orders in the workshops (Kandem lamps, Bauhaus wallpaper), gearing their output to the needs of the masses rather than to luxury goods. He also abandoned the strategy of expensive prefabrication in residential construction in Dessau-Törten and combined industry and craft more flexibly than his predecessor, relaxing the overly constrictive mental corset of the "unity of art and technology." The political intrigue against Meyer had grave consequences, delaying the necessary process of self-criticism, which was not applied to the Bauhaus and modernism until years or even decades later: Gropius established the monopoly on interpreting the Bauhaus and ultimately drove Meyer to side with the communists. The Bauhaus became the focus of political confrontation in the age of extremes.

Intrigues in Moscow

Meyer contacted the Soviet embassy in Berlin and moved to Moscow in October 1930 with a group of affiliated *Bauhäusler*. Having arrived

Fig.3a, b. Hannes Meyer,
Hans Wittwer, and Bauhaus
students: ADGB School in
Bernau, near Berlin, 1928–30.
Fig.3c. Hannes Meyer,
Hans Wittwer, and Bauhaus
students: ADGB School
in Bernau, near Berlin,
1928–30, axonometric drawing of the whole complex,
Sovremmenaia Arkhitektura
5/1928, 149.

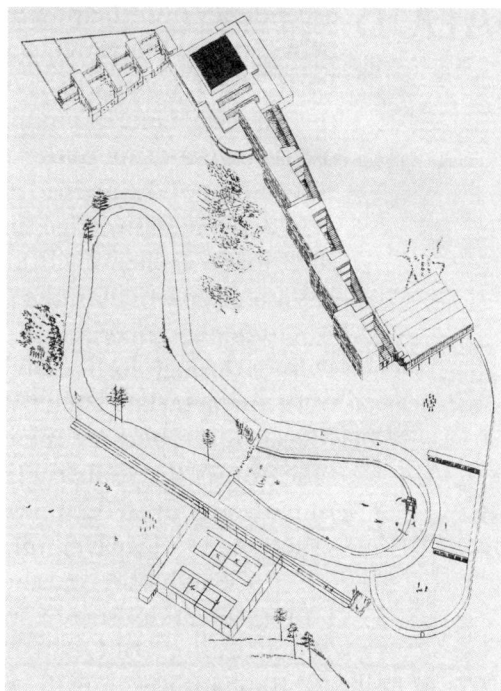

there, he joined the militant organization VOPRA, the All-Union Alliance of Associations of Proletarian Architects. In so doing, he disappointed the partners in the Soviet Union who had previously been allied with the Bauhaus, such as the Constructivists from the Organization of Contemporary Architects (OSA) under Moisei Ginzburg and the Vesnin brothers or the formalists from the Association of New Architects (ASNOVA) under Nikolay Ladovsky and El Lissitzky, who had jointly made the case for an "international front of modernist architects"[7] and cooperation with the International Congresses of Modern Architecture (CIAM). The continuity of Gropius and Meyer had always been stressed by this side; for the Soviet side, Gropius and Sigfried Giedion had been the key partners in preparing the CIAM Congress in Moscow. Ernst May and his group had started planning and building the new industrial cities in October 1930. The responsible actors in industrializing the country had entered into a strong alliance with the international movement Neues Bauen (New Building).

Architecture and urban planning played a key role in the struggle for power launched by Stalin in April 1929. It was a matter of taking them under ideological control—only in this way could he also gain ascendancy over the powerful agencies of industrialization. At the behest of VOPRA, which was affiliated with the Party, the Communist Party of the Soviet Union (CPSU) embarked on a factional struggle and put forward a line of argument that linked Stalin's disastrous theory of "the aggravation of the class struggle" with the demand for the restoration of the artistic nature of architecture: whereas the eclectics would still acknowledge this aspect of building, while summoning their forms exclusively from the past, it was disavowed by the formalists and, in particular, the Constructivists. However, such a restoration would depend precisely on developing the artistic character of architecture through formal innovations responding to the class content of the proletariat. The criticism of the Bauhaus—including under Meyer—thus became the vehicle in the Soviet Union for attacking "the ultra-leftist constructivism that wanted to transpose the architecture of capitalism (Corbusier, the Dessau Bauhaus in Germany, and others) to our [Soviet] soil"[8] (Simbircev, VOPRA).

In search of recognition, Meyer took over the role applied to him by the Stalinist side, which cast him as a witness of the general "fascistization" of Germany. He acknowledged that, even under him, the Bauhaus was only the end point of a failed development, that a

Fig.4. Front cover of the catalogue for the exhibition *Bauhaus Dessau 1928–1930*, held at the Moscow State Museum for New Art from the West in 1931.

БАУХАУЗ ДЕССАУ
1928—1930

DIE KÄMPFERIN
ORGAN DER GESAMTINTERESSEN DER ARBEITENDEN FRAUEN

werktätige Frauen
Kämpft mit uns
um Lohn u. Brot!

WÄHLT KOMMUNISTEN LISTE 4

ВОКС
ГМНЗИ
1 9 3 1

"Red Bauhaus" could exist only to the extent that it could put itself directly in the service of a communist takeover in the West or else of the "building of socialism in the Soviet Union." Instead of striving for a broad alliance against the seizure of power by the Nazis in Germany, he thus legitimized the false offensive strategy of the Comintern and Stalin's disastrous position of regarding social democracy as the real archenemy. Meyer paid a high price for the recognition bestowed on him (chair at the Architectural Institute and the only foreign participant at the briefing of architects with Stalin in the Kremlin on the future location of the Palace of the Soviets in June 1931). Meyer accepted that, in the catalogue of the Moscow exhibition *Bauhaus 1928–1930*, [fig.4] it was not his buildings but rather the German Communist Party posters designed by communist students outside of the Bauhaus in Germany that were honored as the most advanced product of the Bauhaus. His justified criticism of the Bauhaus under Gropius did not lead to an in-depth international dialogue between leftist bourgeois/socialist and Soviet/communist ideas of modernism, but rather contributed to the severing of these ties. Quite possibly, Meyer did not have an overview of the political circumstances in which he was acting—narcissistic wounds do indeed make one blind.

Meyer made efforts to get to grips with the new architectural concept that was called for. In 1931, while still in Moscow, he wrote, "architecture is no longer the art of building."[9] It was not until 1932 that his conversion seemed complete:

> I judge the rejection of art in building, advocated by some modern, capitalist architects, as one of the symptoms of the collapse of bourgeois culture … With regard to socialist architecture, we grasp 'art' as the sum of all measures demanded by the ideological organization of a building or city,

Thomas Flierl

Migrant with a Conflicted Sense of Home

407

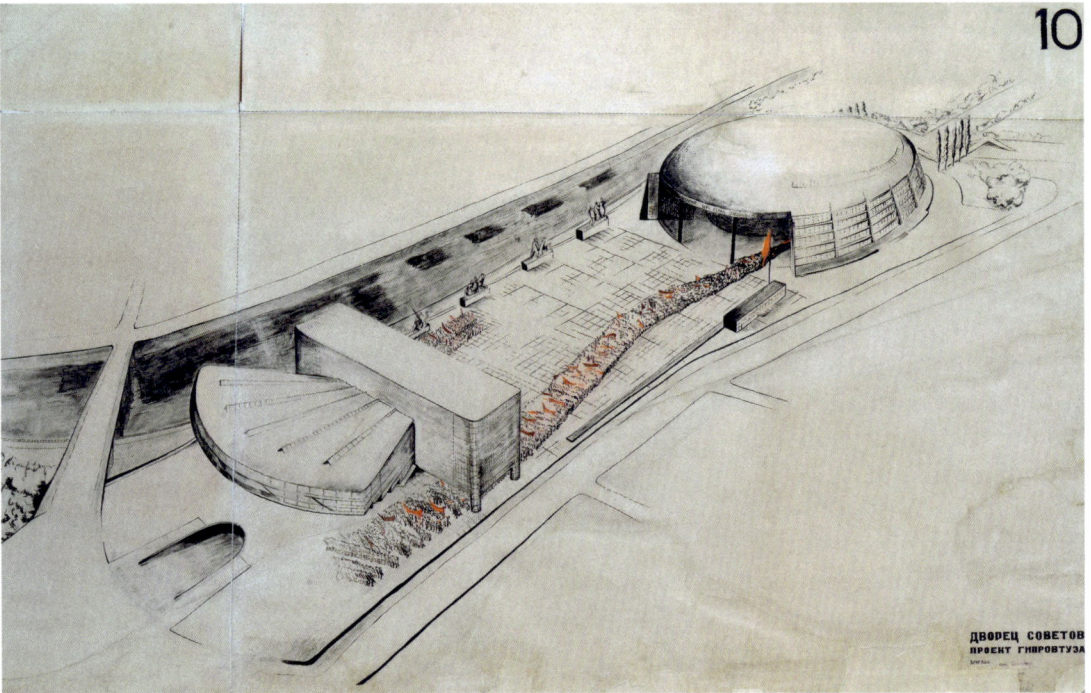

ДВОРЕЦ СОВЕТОВ
ПРОЕКТ ГИПРОВТУЗА

to become directly vivid to the proletariat. The value of this art is determined by its political content. In this proletarian architecture, the maximum experience of the mass of workers is the prime achievement, the ideology of the working class, its heroism and its revolutionary will are the inexhaustible sources of this architecture.[10]

However, this is not an empathic imitative realism but rather a special kind of psychosocial functionalism, targeting design as an organization of a mass experience. The project dating from this time is the design of the Bauhaus Brigade for the Palace of the Soviets.[fig.5]

Meyer taught at the Higher Architectural and Building Institute (VASI) in Moscow. He also worked in project and urban planning trusts and subsequently at the Academy of Architecture. In 1931, he zealously tried to thwart the preparations for the CIAM congress, and in 1932 he agitated against the convertible currency agreements of other foreign experts, notwithstanding that he had had one of his own up to that point. Removed from Ernst May's authority, he headed a special group for militarily important cities in May's "standardized city project" trust. He subsequently switched to the rival organization, the People's Commissariat for Internal Affairs (NKVD)'s planning trust, Giprogor. In 1933, Meyer applied to join the communist party but was not accepted, presumably because of the general bar on new admissions at the time.

While Meyer was very involved in political maneuvering and scheming, as an architect he remained incorruptible. In 1935, when the criticism of Constructivism and the Neues Bauen movement not only took on an ideological character but was also connected with the creative demands for the development of a "national tradition," he became embroiled in an open, and for him rather dangerous, conflict with the Soviet architectural administration.

Part 3

Bauhaus
Architects
in
Exile

408

"Communist in content, regional in form"

As a multilingual Swiss citizen who had lived amidst the country's different cultures, it was impossible for him to accept the concept of a unified Soviet culture in the multi-ethnic state that was the USSR. Acting with others, who would pay bitterly for it, he advocated the concept of an architecture that was "communist in content and regional in form"—that is, he wanted in this way to retain "the national panorama" and orient it so that the focus was on the search, specific in each case, for pre-bourgeois regional traditions, which needed to be taken up in a modern way, instead of eclectically inventing "national cultures" under the dominance of Greater Russia. He was an internationalist and a regionalist. This again brought him into proximity with the Constructivists, who had already put forward similar arguments. With reference to his design for a House of the Soviets in Dagestan, Moisei Ginzburg had reasoned as follows back in 1926: "It was clear to me that the splendid mosque belonged to the dead material of history, whereas the simple house of the poor Muslim is a starting point for his new culture."[11] When, as one of the directors of the House of Architects, Meyer had organized a talk by Mikhail Okhitovich in January 1935 entitled "The National Form of Socialist Architecture," Meyer was sharply reprimanded by the party, losing his positions in the architects' union and at the Architectural Institute. Okhitovich was arrested and murdered two years later.[12]

For a second time, Meyer had been thrust from the architecture scene. But once again, there was evidently an agency in the background to save him. In his "Entwurf für einen autobiographischen Roman" (Draft for an Autobiographical Novel, ca. 1936–39), he wrote,

> the understanding of socialist development as a struggle between the best,
> the new slogans for the popular front, and the knowledge and insight
> to work in a uniquely productive way as soviet-trained western europeans
> impel the author to go to the battle front in the west."[13]

Of course, even after the 7th World Congress of the Communist International in summer 1935, which moved away from the catastrophic theory of social fascism and paved the way, far too late, for the politics of the popular front, it was not easy to reach the "battle front in the west" as a volunteer. As Meyer himself wrote, in the last eighteen months of his time in the USSR, he had been with the leaders of the Swiss Communist Party (CP) on an almost daily basis and had received "an excellent theoretical training."[14] It is evident from this that Meyer

Thomas Flierl

Migrant
with a
Conflicted
Sense
of
Home

409

Fig.6. Hannes Meyer, home
for children in Mümliswil
1938/39.

joined the Swiss CP in Moscow in 1935. After a lecture tour in western
Europe in early 1936, he and his wife, Lena Bergner, left the Soviet
Union in summer 1936, with Meyer apparently entrusted with a special
Soviet mandate. His assignment, to set up an urban planning institute
in Spain, came to nothing, as it was thwarted by Franco's coup. He
went next to Switzerland, where he remained for three years.

In 1935/36, his mindset must have crystallized as well, as he developed an understanding of the phenomena of historicism and eclecticism in Soviet architecture as an "essential and indispensable evolutionary stage"[15]—albeit in the profound conviction "that even after the
terrible confusion evident in some Roman [Zholtovsky] or American
[Iofan] style or other, the economically regulatory forces of today's
building technology and of today's science, coupled with a new artistic
force, will turn out to be the eventual winner."[16] His teachers at that
(still obscure) school would also have conveyed to him this historical
perspective: they would probably have assumed that it was only a
matter of a temporary step backward and that their thinking was still
internationalist and based in a socialist viewpoint. It is only against the
background of this particularly political support that we can understand where Meyer found the chutzpah to write a letter—on July 29,
1937, in Geneva—to Nikolai Kolli in which he quite rightly repudiated
the latter's keynote speech directly after the 1st Congress of Soviet Architects: in the speech, Kolli had maligned the work of foreign architects and urban planners in the Soviet Union.[17]

In Switzerland, Meyer settled first in Zurich and then in Geneva,
giving lectures and acting as a courier for Swiss volunteers in the
Spanish Civil War. His other functions for the party and in the circle
around it are largely unknown, as he avoided the communist circles
in Geneva. Nevertheless, he maintained contact with leading Swiss CP
functionaries Edgar Woop and Jules Humbert-Droz, which did not
escape the attention of the police. He gave his own account of his involvement in setting up the Parti Ouvrier et Paysan (POP) in a letter
from Mexico written in 1947:

> You may not know that POP was the first unity party in Europe and was
> founded in 1937 based on a new model. Léna and I have played a practical
> part in laying the ground for it, and the crucial discussions between Léon
> Nicole, at the time leader of the Parti du Travail (leftist socialist wing),
> and our general secretary, who was living illegally at the time, took place
> in our Geneva apartment.[18]

In the almost three years that Meyer spent in Switzerland, he was able to realize only one project, the cooperative children's home in Mümliswil (1938/39).[fig.6] As Meyer himself later explained, he drew on "the local craft and architectural resources of a Jura community," channeled through "a typically Swiss synthesis of traditional building methods and standardized construction elements." Never seen front-on as a whole, the building reveals "its architectural charm to the receptive visitor as a consequence of what is experienced in the space and in the context of the landscape."[19]

Quarrels in exile

In 1939, at the invitation of the Mexican government, Meyer became the director for a while of the newly founded Institute of Town and National Planning in Mexico City, where he later also worked as a publisher and journalist. Meyer carried on his Comintern activities in Mexico as well. This is confirmed indirectly by the Swiss party newspaper *Voix Ouvrière*: in the edition of June 19, 1946, we learn that Meyer and his wife were in the best of health and living in Mexico, "where, besides his professional work, he plays a role in the Central American labor movement. It is this that brought opprobrium on his head from the newspaper *Der Bund* in summer 1942."[fig.7][20] If you look at the Bern newspaper *Der Bund*, for the date June 15, 1942, you will find the relevant article, "Mexico and the Refugee Problem."[fig.8] There we read that in Mexico:

> a communist center *has grown up, from which, it would seem, all operations in North and South America are directed. Technically speaking, the organization of this apparatus has become possible by virtue of the fact that the communist functionaries come to the country as* Spanien- kämpfer *["Spanish fighters"], even if in most cases they played no part at*

Thomas Flierl

Migrant with a Conflicted Sense of Home

Des nouvelles de Hannes Meyer

Le panneau ornant le vestibule de l'ambassade soviétique à Mexico. Il représente une fête de nuit à Moscou.

Ce panneau, qui représente une fête de nuit à Moscou, orne le vestibule de l'ambassade soviétique, à Mexico. La photographie nous en a été adressée par Hannes Meyer, architecte et urbaniste fort connu, qui séjourna de longues années en U.R.S.S. où il participa à la construction de plusieurs villes ainsi qu'à la préparation du nouveau plan d'urbanisme de Moscou. Hannes Meyer habita Genève de 1935 à 1938, date à laquelle il partit pour le Mexique où, à côté de ses travaux professionnels, il joue un rôle en vue dans le mouvement ouvrier de l'Amérique centrale. C'est ce que le journal « Le Bund » lui reprocha véhémentement au cours de l'été 1942.

Hannes Meyer est en parfaite santé ainsi que sa femme. Il s'impatiente simplement de recevoir les organes du Parti suisse du Travail, la « Voix Ouvrière », le « Vorwärts » et « Il Lavoratore ». Il fait tout spécialement saluer ses amis de Genève, de Bâle et de Zurich.

all in the civil war in Spain ... Every nationality is represented, and Switzerland has the dubious honor of providing the Comintern leader for Mexico. *We are dealing here with an architect whose* GPU [*Russian intelligence service*] *connections have been fully documented and whom the Mexican police have credited with the authorship of Trotsky's murder.*[21] This is not the place to speculate about Meyer's involvement in the murder of Leon Trotsky in August 1940. In his letters, Meyer also responded to the *Bund* article, referring to the police investigation which exonerated him of the charge of participating in the assassination. Meanwhile, he wrote nothing about his activities for the Comintern.

The author of the article in *Der Bund*, Günther Reinhardt, a journalist and private detective born in Germany and living in the United States, also worked for the FBI from 1936 to 1943. One may take a skeptical view of Reinhardt's assertions, but their plausibility is attested to both by the indirect endorsement couched in the commendatory reporting of *Voix Ouvrière* in 1946 and by the comment made by Paul Merker, head of the group of German CP exiles in Mexico, in a letter to Soviet ambassador Konstantin Umansky dated June 9, 1944, in which he reports that Meyer had earlier "masqueraded as a GPU agent in Mexico."[22] Based on this, it is perfectly credible that Meyer was working for the Comintern and/or for one of the Soviet intelligence services in Mexico.

Finally, we also have a statement made by Meyer himself, when he conceded in one letter that "in the critical years" he had been "employed" by the "big boys' firm."[23] And the "big boys" were definitely not the All-Union Society for Cultural Relations with Foreign Countries (VOKS), for which Meyer demonstrably worked as a representative in Mexico until 1943. Before and after this date, he organized a series of Soviet exhibitions in Mexico. After the war, Meyer's political work shifted, and he was primarily engaged in forming the new leftist party in Mexico, Partido Popular, led by Lombardo Toledano.

Der Bund — Bern, Montag, 15. Juni 1942, Abend-Ausgabe, 93. Jahrgang, Nr. 273

Mexiko und das Flüchtlingsproblem

Heißer Kampf um Sebastopol

In one of his letters, Meyer stated, "Today [1947] I belong more than ever to the tight-knit group of its members."[24]

In Mexico, Meyer got involved, in turn, in a serious political clash that—at the instigation of the group of exiled members of the German Communist Party (KPD)—led to him and his Italian friends Mario Montagnana and Vittorio Vidali being expelled from the Mexican Communist Party after the Comintern was disbanded in 1943. Meyer had vehemently opposed the KPD's ambition to organize itself as an independent body outside of the Mexican CP, a demand that was not granted until 1941 (after Germany's invasion of the Soviet Union). The dispute with the KPD group escalated after the arrival of Paul Merker in 1942.

If Léna and I are to be judged fairly, consideration must be given to our deep sense of belonging to Switzerland and to our friends there. It should be noted that in all my thinking I am a person of two cultures, one who takes a natural pleasure in sliding back and forth between [Swiss] French and Swiss German. As expatriate Swiss citizens, we belong to the 'fourth Switzerland,' who are expected to speak at least four languages at home ... Why do I mention all this here? Well, my friends among the 'Germans' here, of both the benign and the malicious varieties, have repeatedly tried to claim me as a fellow countryman: to start with, because they wanted to use me for their own purposes, and then, after the 'crisis of 1943,' because they wanted to bring me under the sway of their great 'Führer figure Merker.' ... Today, the word from the Merkerites is that I'm a 'German-eater,' a Germanophobe, etc. Why? Because Merker wanted to accommodate all the nations of Germany in his 'Free Germany.' Just like Hitler. And so, in his magazine and at meetings, he presented Bukovinians, Poles, Hungarians, Serbs, Czechs, Dutchmen, a Swiss woman, Austrians, etc., even the French, as members of the GERMAN NATION, which he succeeded in doing with various refugees, especially Jews, because they hoped he would give

Thomas Flierl

Migrant with a Conflicted Sense of Home

413

them support and other benefits. It's a con then when Merker babbles on about a 'German group in Mexico.' In his hunger for power, he has imitated—in caricature—the system of 'minority oppression' as a means to get power over all the foreigners here.[25]

Meyer was especially provoked by the fact that in 1942, without being asked, his name appeared as part of an appeal "in which the 'Free Germans' acknowledge with a profound sense of regret their responsibility for Hitlerism, their complicity in the Nazi war, etc., and pledge to do everything to kill Hitler."[26] Meyer also criticized the laziness of German exiles who pocketed their monthly donations from the United States rather than getting "economically involved" in Mexico. "At holiday gatherings, these men and women presented themselves as 'victims of fascism.' As a Swiss, what am I supposed to find good about that???"[27] Meyer was also critical of the "aestheticism and German chauvinism," the literary "claptrap" of the German writers-in-exile in Mexico. "Apart from our [Meyer took on the design] LIBRO NEGRO (black book opposing the NAZI TERROR) and Anna Seghers' DAS SIEBTE KREUZ, there are almost no books at all that are actively engaged."[28] Meyer's suspicions even led him to accuse Otto Katz of being the "real director of the 'German group'" and a Western agent.[29]

The party ban on Meyer was lifted only when his Italian friends returned to Europe and were accepted there again, and the Swiss party also renewed contact with him. Nevertheless, it was not until 1949 that Meyer went back to Switzerland and became a party member there again.

Return to limbo

When World War II ended, Meyer entertained the idea not simply of returning to Europe but of settling in the Soviet-occupied zone, which was where he had worked as Bauhaus director: here the shortage of skilled antifascist professionals in postwar Germany was evident and his political affiliations were known to the authorities. While still in Mexico, Meyer wrote letters to old cronies, enquiring about the possibility of reactivating the Bauhaus in Dessau. Friends in Soviet-occupied Germany sounded out the options that might present themselves "if Hannes Meyer reappeared in Europe or in Germany."[30] There were even ideas of "opening a university for applied art" with Meyer as director.[31] But the conflicts he had had in exile continued to reverberate. "It will be difficult," as *Bauhäusler* Waldemar Alder wrote to Meyer in 1947, "to move against the Mexico bunch."[32] This is not the place to describe Meyer's failed integration into the GDR. He found himself in a paradoxical position: politically, he had been rehabilitated and accepted back into the Swiss Communist Party, and high-ranking functionaries in the Socialist Unity Party (SED) had expressed an interest in him—particularly in the context of the preparations being made for a political show trial of Paul Merker[33]—yet in terms of architectural policy, the Soviet verdict was what still counted. When the East German architects traveled to Moscow in spring 1950, Ernst May, Hannes Meyer, and Walter Gropius had been declared enemies of a "new German architecture" by the president of the Soviet Academy, Arkady Mordvinov.[34] When Merker was eventually arrested in the course of the show trials of emigrants to the West, which were imbued with anti-Semitism, and Otto Katz and others were executed following a show trial in Prague, Meyer expressed a distasteful glee at the fact that "this swamp is finally being drained."[35] A narcissistic wound gives birth to monsters.

Meyer's inclusion in the architectural discussions in the early GDR also foundered on the establishment of the Building Academy, which—without any open professional discourse—was effected as an institutional transfer in accordance with the Soviet model and supported by other powers than those that were no longer bent on impeding a rapprochement with Meyer. The Soviet architecture administration had not lifted the ban on Meyer and still abused him as a puppet, reducing him to his 1928 theories. Walter Ulbricht criticized Meyer's ADGB Trade Union School in Bernau, calling it "cosmopolitan,"[36] while Hermann Henselmann detected the "reactionary character of constructivism" in Meyer's Bauhaus.[37] In 1951, East Berlin witnessed a repeat of the phantom Moscow debate of 1937.

A gulf opened up between his life in Switzerland and the architecture discussions in the GDR. When he addressed the architectural legacy in Switzerland, he was regarded as a "building reactionary"; conversely, when he involved himself with "functional design," he was seen in East Berlin as "a diehard." As a solution to this seeming dilemma, Meyer recalled the principles he had applied in developing the concept for his Freidorf housing estate near Basel. At that time, he had used "Jura-style proportions, of the kind that appear from Geneva to Basel." It was thus a question
not of reusing the Jura architectural details in the first instance but of

Thomas
Flierl

Migrant
with a
Conflicted
Sense
of
Home

adhering to some extent to the relationships between masonry-wall and window-opening that are typically applied along the French border ... In those years, I was very preoccupied with the question of regional proportional characteristics in architecture and specifically the 'Jura' style, which is very close to the Burgundian canon both in architecture and in other matters.[38]

He wrote to East Berlin about "regional expression in the proportions of architectural art," saying that he would like to contribute to journals in the GDR. Of course, this no longer had anything to do with devising a "new national architecture," but rather with his own theories from the late Bauhaus period, with Okhitovich's idea of the regional and Meyer's experiences with "tropical urban planning" in Mexico.

In 1952, he perceptively wrote to US architect Kay Kulmala that in the GDR press he "was held up as a lackey of imperialism who had been captivated by the USA." Too communist for the one, too bourgeois for the other. As Meyer put it, "that must have done Mr. Gropius a power of good!" He went on to say that he ended up "scratching his head": "Where do I really belong then?"[39]

Breakfast in Turin, lunch in Geneva, dinner in Trieste

Finally, we find in Hannes Meyer a vital southern European vision:
Switzerland is indeed a difficult country to understand and this is also the case among our friends. In the summer, there was many a night when guests would suddenly drop by our garden on their way up or down the Gotthard route ... Sometimes five or six brothers from the street would spend the night with us. — I am often in northern Italy. For some weeks Mario, the Mexican, has been working as a trade union secretary in Milan. When we saw each other, we spoke of the (internal) struggles that we went through in Mexico with people who have now become smoother in practice with you. And we laugh together with Carlos, the Spanish commander, who told us in Mexico that the three of us with our wives would get together in no more than ten years and have breakfast in Turin, lunch in Geneva, and dinner in Trieste, with no need for a passport. He saw the borders as having already fallen. An 'outcast' in Mexico under the control of Merkerism, he is now something like no. 4 in Italy and fêted by the masses.[40]

Meyer felt thoroughly at ease, culturally and politically, in northern Italy with its connections to the partisan movement and neorealism. To Karel Teige he mentioned the writers Carlo Levi, Emilio Vittorino, and his friend Montagnana as well as Gramsci (the "Italian 'Lenin'").

Of the Italian artists, I particularly like RENATO GUTTUSO, *who lives in Rome. I saw a rather large* ALBUM *of his on* FASCIST BARBARISM IN ITALY, *very nicely printed and extremely impassioned in its presentation.* GABRIELE MUCCHI, *graphic designer and architect from Milan, showed me a very realistic series of illustrations for a new book that is now coming out. There is a whole group of architects and artists working around him, in search of a new way.*[41]

The life of the Italian masses, he reported to Karola Bloch, is

really expressive, spontaneous, and humane. Our friends in Milan (the painter Gabriele Mucchi, for example) produce their work in a stimulating atmosphere and you can see the efforts they are making (particularly in painting and film) to create a connection with the masses.[42]

Against this backdrop, it is all the more regrettable that Meyer did not articulate his ideas back in 1947 in a text on the relationship between "soc. realism and sur-realism" that *Bauhäusler* Max Gebhard had approached him about—Meyer had declined, though, because "nothing by me ever gets printed!!!!!"[43]

Yet even in the Arcadia between Ticino and northern Italy, Meyer's professional expectations were not fulfilled. His attempt to show the "Red Bauhaus" or his own works at the Milan Triennale in 1947 fell afoul of the programming structures, the limited possibilities of organizing an exhibition from Mexico, and his refusal to present himself as a Swiss and come to terms with Max Bill or Alfred Roth.

I don't want to exhibit my work with the SWISS. *The Swiss are profiteers par excellence and know how to exploit every situation: in the arts, in banking, etc. etc. Guys like Bill, A. Roth, etc. have no social or economic training and no political credo ... They are eternally '*NEUTRAL,*' because they can do business with this 'neutrality.'*[44]

The idea of appointing Meyer to a university in Turin came to nothing, as did the job of building a "palace of culture" in Trieste.

Among the bitter experiences mentioned in the correspondence, often proffered as "amusing entertainment," was the hostility that Meyer had met with in the Association of Swiss Architects or after a lecture to the Basel Society of Engineers and Architects. And finally, there was "Nicole's tragicomic debacle in Geneva." Meyer's long-term political confidant Léon Nicole, the general secretary of the Swiss Labor Party (PdA), had attacked his party for its positive appraisal of Swiss neutrality, whereupon he gave up running the newspaper *Voix Ouvrière* and was expelled from the PdA in December 1952.

Thomas
Flierl

Migrant
with a
Conflicted
Sense
of
Home

417

With a realism born of hindsight, Meyer commented on this event: "After my experience in Mexico, absolutely nothing surprises me anymore, and I think it is wiser to remain steadfast and more than ever to serve the leisurely call of the architectural muse."[45]

Meyer's biography gives us a sense of how much of the architect's energies were consumed by emigration, the political struggles, and secret operations, and why he was unable to find any professional continuity in Europe after World War II. The phase of a productive—i.e., a relative—decoupling of politics and architecture, culminating in a late work was not vouchsafed to Hannes Meyer.

1   Hannes Meyer to Walter Gropius, February 16, 1927 (as a retrospective cementing of the agreement they had reached), in *Hannes Meyer, Bauen und Gesellschaft: Schriften, Briefe, Projekte*, ed. Lena Meyer-Bergner (Dresden, 1980): 44.
2   Sima Ingberman, ABC: *International Constructivist Architecture, 1922–1939* (Cambridge, MA, 1994): x f.
3   Hannes Meyer, "Die neue Welt," *Das Werk* 7 (1926): 221. Translated by D. Q. Stephenson in Hannes Meyer, *Buildings, Projects, and Writings* (Teufen, 1965). See "Hannes Meyer's 'The New World' (1926)," The Charnel-House: From Bauhaus to Beinhaus, accessed December 11, 2018, modernistarchitecture.wordpress.com/2010/10/20/hannes-meyer's-"the-new-world"-1926/.
4   Hannes Meyer, "bauen," in *Bauen und Gesellschaft* (see note 1), 47. Translated by D. Q. Stephenson in Hannes Meyer, *Buildings, Projects, and Writings* (Teufen, 1965). See "Hannes Meyer's 'building' (1928)," The Charnel-House: From Bauhaus to Beinhaus, accessed December 11, 2018, modernistarchitecture.wordpress.com/2010/10/20/hannes-meyer's-"building"-1928/.
5   Hannes Meyer, "bauhaus und gesellschaft," in *Bauen und Gesellschaft* (see note 1), 53. Translated by D. Q. Stephenson in Hannes Meyer, *Buildings, Projects, and Writings* (Teufen, 1965). See "Hannes Meyer's 'bauhaus and society' (1929)," The Charnel-House: From Bauhaus to Beinhaus, accessed December 11, 2018, modernistarchitecture.wordpress.com/2010/10/20/hannes-meyer's-"bauhaus-and-society"-1929/.
6   Hannes Meyer, "Mein Hinauswurf aus dem Bauhaus: Offener Brief an den Herrn Oberbürgermeister Hesse, Dessau," *Das Tagebuch* (August 1930): 1307.
7   See Moisei Ginzburg, "Mezhdunarodnyy front sovremennoy arkhitektury" [The International Front of Modern Architecture], *Sovremennaya architektura* 2 (1926): 41–46.
8   V. N. Simbircev, "Itogi goda" [Annual Results], *Stroitel'stvo Moskvy* 11 (1929): 2.
9   Hannes Meyer, "Über marxistische Architektur," in *Bauen und Gesellschaft* (see note 1), 92. Translated as "On Marxist Architecture" (1931). Quoted in Claude Schnaidt, "Hannes Meyer, Marxist and Modernist (1889–1954)," The Charnel-House: From Bauhaus to Beinhaus, accessed December 11, 2018, thecharnelhouse.org/2013/08/10/hannes-meyer/.
10   Hannes Meyer, "Antworten auf Fragen der Prager Architektengruppe 'Leva Fronta'" (1932), in *Bauen und Gesellschaft* (see note 1), 122–23. Quoted in Thomas Flierl, "From Recognition to Rejection: Hannes Meyer and the Reception of the Bauhaus in the Soviet Union," *bauhaus imaginista Journal*, September 4, 2018, www.bauhaus-imaginista.org/articles/1734/from-recognition-to-rejection.
11   Moisei Ginzburg, "Natsional'naya arkhitektura narodov SSSR" [National Architecture of the Peoples of the USSR], *Sovremennaya architektura* 5–6 (1926): 114.
12   See Hugh D. Hudson, "Terror in Soviet Architecture: The Murder of Mikhail Okhitovich," *Slavic Review* 51, no. 3 (Fall 1992): 448–67; Hudson, "Mikhail Okhitovich and the Terror in Architecture," in *Blueprints and Blood: The Stalinization of Soviet Architecture* (Princeton, 1993).

13 Hannes Meyer, "Entwurf für einen auto-biographischen Roman" (ca. 1936–39), Deutsche Architektur Museum (DAM), quoted in Klaus-Jürgen Winkler, *Der Architekt Hannes Meyer: Anschauungen und Werk* (Berlin, 1989), 180.

14 Hannes Meyer to Max Gebhard, February 1947, SAPMO-BARCH DY 30/70987, sheets 295–96.

15 Quoted in Winkler, *Der Architekt Hannes Meyer* (see note 13): 178–79. Talk on February 23, 1936, reproduced in *Rudé právo*, February 28, 1936.

16 Meyer to Nikolaj Kolli, July 29, 1937, DAM.

17 See Nikolai Kolli, "Zadachi sovetskoy arkhitektury: Osnovnye etapy razvitiya sovetskoy arkhitektury" (Tasks of Soviet Architecture: The Main Stages of the Development of Soviet Architecture), *Pervyy vsesoyuznyy s'yezd sovetskikh arkhitektorov* (1st All-Union Congress of Soviet Architects) (Moscow, 1937).

18 Meyer to Waldemar Alder, August 16, 1947, SAPMO-BARCH DY 30/70987, sheet 288.

19 Hannes Meyer, "Kinderheim in Mümliswil," *Das Werk* 7 (1953): 216, 213.

20 *Voix Ouvrière*, June 19, 1946: 1.

21 G. P. R. [Günther Reinhardt], "Mexiko und das Flüchtlingsproblem," *Der Bund*, June 9, 1942: 1.

22 Paul Merker to Konstantin Umansky, June 9, 1944 (copy), in SAPMO-BARCH DY 30/70988, sheets 150–62, here: sheets 157–58.

23 Meyer to Waldemar Alder, November 7, 1947, 1, SAPMO-BARCH DY 30/70987, sheet 284.

24 Meyer to Waldemar Alder, April 28, 1947, 3, SAPMO-BARCH DY 30/70987, sheet 298.

25 Meyer to Waldemar Alder, August 16, 1947, SAPMO-BARCH DY 30/70987, sheet 288.

26 Meyer to Waldemar Alder, August 16, 1947, SAPMO-BARCH DY 30/70987, sheet 288.

27 Meyer to Waldemar Alder, August 16, 1947, SAPMO-BARCH DY 30/70987, sheet 288.

28 Meyer to Waldemar Alder, September 3, 1947, SAPMO-BARCH DY 30/70987, sheet 279.

29 Meyer to Waldemar Alder, September 3, 1947, SAPMO-BARCH DY 30/70987, sheet 279, 2.

30 Georg Münter to Waldemar Alder, August 18, 1947, 2, DAM.

31 Georg Münter to Waldemar Alder, August 18, 1947, 1.

32 Waldemar Alder to Meyer, October 15, 1947, 1, DAM.

33 In the early 1950s, show trials were held in almost all of the countries of the Eastern bloc in the process of establishing the Stalinist regime. These trials involved high-ranking party and state functionaries who, owing to their exile in the West and their contact with Jewish aid organizations, were accused of collaborating with Western intelligence agencies: in many cases they were condemned to death. Paul Merker was arrested in November 1952 and sentenced to eight years in prison in 1955, before being released in January 1956. Unlike in Hungary and Czechoslovakia, there were no death sentences passed in the GDR in this context.

34 See Institut für Regionalentwicklung und Stadtplanung, ed., *Reise nach Moskau: Dokumente zur Erklärung von Motiven, Entscheidungsstrukturen und Umsetzungskonflikten für den ersten städtebaulichen Paradigmenwechsel in der DDR und zum Umfeld des Aufbaugesetzes von 1950* (Berlin, 1995).

35 Meyer to Heinrich Starck, October 13, 1950, DAM.

36 Walter Ulbricht, "Kunst und Wissenschaft im Plan: Aus der Rede des Stellvertreters des Ministerpräsidenten, gehalten am 31. Oktober vor der Volkskammer," *Aufbau* 12 (1951): 1071–76.

37 Hermann Henselmann, "Der reaktionäre Charakter des Konstruktivismus," *Neues Deutschland*, December 4, 1951.

38 Meyer to Heinrich Starck, March 14, 1952, 2, DAM.

39 Meyer to Kay Kulmala, April 24, 1952, Stiftung Bauhaus Dessau.

40 Meyer to Heinrich Starck, December 16, 1952, DAM.

41 Meyer to Karel Teige, February 23, 1950, Literárni archiv Památniku národniho písemictvi (LA PNP), Prague.

42 Meyer to Karola Bloch, May 2, 1952, 2, DAM.

43 Meyer to Waldemar Alder, September 27, 1949, 2, SAPMO-BARCH DY 30/70987, sheet 283.

44 Meyer to Gabriele Mucchi, February 20, 1947, APICE Milano.

45 Meyer to Karola Bloch, May 2, 1952, 1, DAM.

*Thomas
Flierl*

Migrant
with a
Conflicted
Sense
of
Home

Daniel Talesnik

Tibor Weiner's Architectural Design Curriculum in Chile (1946–47)

In April 1927, Walter Gropius appointed Hannes Meyer as the founding director of the architecture department at the Hochschule für Gestaltung (Bauhaus) in Dessau. Only a year later, Meyer became director of the school, a position he retained until August 1930, when the Dessau authorities expelled him, adducing his political ideas. This expulsion had more to do with the politics of part of the student body: since 1927, when Gropius was still the director, the Bauhaus Kommunistische Studenten-fraktion (Communist Student Cell) or Kostufra had been active and organ-ized activities with help from the local Communist Party. This group grew strong, and although Meyer attempted to tone them down, the city administra-tion preferred in view of upcoming local elections to get rid of him and bring in someone who could better exercise control over the students.[1] Upon his expul-sion, Meyer arranged to be hired in the Soviet Union, taking with him the so-called Red Bauhaus Brigade, a politically driven and short-lived group of seven students who were for the most part aligned with his politics and his pedagog-ical project. Some of these students, Tibor Weiner, René Mensch, Konrad Püschel, and Philipp Tolziner, were active as designers, city planners, teachers, polemicists, and/or political activists beyond their collective Soviet experience, working independently in such countries as Mexico, Chile, Hungary, Iran, and North Korea. Their experiences begin to draw a different Bauhaus migration map—different from those frequently studied of the Bauhaus migrations to Great Britain, America, and Palestine, for example. There was an itinerant continua-tion of Meyer's Bauhaus that covered "other" territories, and one aspect of this continuation happened through Meyer and some of his students' teaching activities. In this text, I will focus on the career of Tibor Weiner, particularly his teaching experience in Chile in the 1940s.

Weiner was born in Budapest in 1906. From 1924 to 1928, he studied architecture at the Franz Joseph Hungarian Royal University (since renamed the Technical University of Budapest). From March to October 1929, Weiner worked at the office of Pál Ligeti (1885–1941) and Farkas Molnár (1897–1945), who had a partnership at the time. While Ligeti was a leading Modernist theorist in Hungary, Molnár had studied at the Bauhaus Weimar from 1922 to 1925 and was later employed at the architecture office of Walter Gropius until his return to Hungary. Molnár, a skilled architect from a younger generation than Ligeti, would later become involved in the Hungarian section of the CIAM group. It is likely that Molnár played a part in Weiner's decision to study at the Bauhaus in Dessau. Hungarians were a significant foreign national group at the Bauhaus. Among the Hungarians were prominent teachers such as László Moholy-Nagy as well as students who became teachers such as Marcel Breuer, both of whom left the school with Gropius in 1928.[2] When Weiner arrived in Dessau in the winter semester of 1929, he took the *Vorkurs* with Joseph Albers, "Artistic Design" with Wassily Kandinsky, "Figure Drawing" with Joost Schmidt, and "Representational Drawing" with Fritz Kuhr. Additionally, he audited classes of Dr. Hanns Riedel and guest lecturer architect Paul Artaria. Meyer would later write of Weiner's first year at the Bauhaus: "During his first semester of studies at the Bauhaus Dessau, [Weiner] excelled due to his outstanding professional qualifications, and because of the thoroughness and diligence with which he approached the problem of building design."[3] Thanks to his pre-Bauhaus architectural studies, Weiner became an assistant to Meyer during his second semester at the Bauhaus. Following Meyer's dismissal on August 1, 1930, Weiner, along with several other foreigners, was expelled from the Bauhaus on September 9, 1930. Weiner and six other classmates followed Meyer to the Soviet Union, where he worked on several projects between 1930 and 1937. Weiner and his Bauhaus classmates first worked for Giprovtus (Construction of Higher and Technical Education Colleges Trust), a trust overseen by the Commissariat for People's Economy in Moscow. The main function of Giprovtus was to design technical schools and educational institutions. Meyer's instructions at Giprovtus were maximum standardization in all types of commissions, and the simplest possible architecture (with

Daniel Talesnik

Tibor Weiner's Architectural Design Curriculum in Chile

421

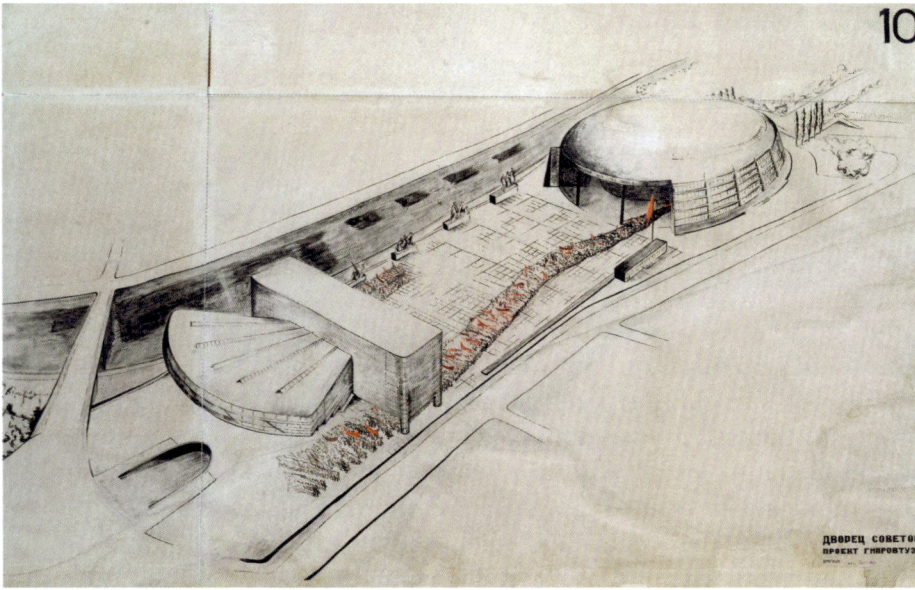

ДВОРЕЦ СОВЕТОВ
ПРОЕКТ ГИПРОВТУЗА

the most common structural systems and building materials). In trusts like this, foreign specialists worked side by side with Russian specialists, and as we know from testimonies of the period, their work experience was rather dry and at times boring.[4]

In 1931, Weiner and two Bauhaus classmates, with Meyer as a consultant, designed the Giprovtus proposal for the second Palace of the Soviets competition in Moscow.[fig.1] After Giprovtus, Weiner went to work for Vusstroiproekt (City Building Projects Trust), overseen by the same Commissariat and also in Moscow. From 1933 until 1936, Weiner and two Bauhaus classmates worked with Mart Stam (who left in 1934) and Hans Schmidt at the Urbanism Institute in the city of Orsk, in Orenburg Oblast. As was normally the case with new towns, Orsk was built to accompany an industrial operation on the banks of a river (the Ural River in this case). They worked specifically on urban planning and on the design of individual buildings. After Orsk, Weiner worked in Moscow for Metroproekta (the subway project office) where he participated in the design of Moscow's Aeroport subway station; other minor jobs would follow. The first show trials in 1936 prompted the beginning of the exodus of foreign architects. Even those who remained an extra year left the Soviet Union by November 1937 at the latest, if they could, and this was the case with Weiner. Those who stayed usually had no choice and ended in a gulag, accused of espionage.

After his time in the Soviet Union, Weiner had a stint in Paris, where he collaborated on the design of a series of sanatoria, preventoria, and health colonies in the studio of Pierre Forestier. Politically, Forestier was certainly on the left, but he does not appear to have been a member of the French Communist Party. The link between Weiner and Forestier appears to have been Margarete Schütte-Lihotzky, with whom Weiner had worked in his final period in the Soviet Union. Schütte-Lihotzky had moved to Paris earlier than Weiner and was doing some reports on architecture for tuberculosis patients (she had tuberculosis herself), something directly connected to Forestier, who

Part 3

Bauhaus
Architects
in
Exile

422

Fig. 1. Philipp Tolziner,
Antonin Urban, and Tibor
Weiner (with Hannes Meyer
as a consultant), competition
entry for the second com-
petition for the Palace of
the Soviets, 1931. Panel 10
(perspective).

was one of the foremost architectural authorities on architecture
for the treatment of tuberculosis in France at the time, and probably
the one who had commissioned those studies in the first place.
Forestier, Schütte-Lihotzky and Weiner did a school competition
together in this period. Weiner had tried to leave Europe since the
moment he'd arrived in Paris. As a matter of fact, he led a rather
desperate search for his next destination. This speaks to the urgency
of his situation in France at a time when his work papers were becoming increasingly difficult to maintain. He unsuccessfully attempted to
emigrate to Australia and later to Turkey, where he applied for a
teaching job at the Construction School in Ankara (an attempt most
likely in connection with Schütte-Lihotzky's move to Turkey during
this period).

On January 24, 1939, an earthquake shook south-central Chile
with an official death toll of around 30,000 people and severe damage
to building structures. We can suppose that the demand for architects
and building professionals for the reconstruction effort in the wake
of these dramatic events allowed Weiner to receive immigration papers.
He left Paris for Chile in August 1939, where his first job was as an
architectural draftsman for the Ministry of Development.[5] Weiner
eventually started working with local architect Ricardo Müller Hess
(1897–1943), who had designed the Chilean National Stadium in
Santiago dedicated in 1938, and who held the posts of chief architect
at the National Office of Public Works and technical consultant at the
Ministry of Education. Müller spoke German, which was an important
detail, considering Weiner arrived with no Spanish. They worked
together until Müller's death in 1943, collaborating on several competitions, most of which were related to post-earthquake reconstruction,
and designing thirty-two houses together.[6] Of the competitions Weiner
did with Müller during this period, two are well known, but only one
came to fruition: the Fire Department of Chillán. The project was
built in reinforced concrete, and its main features make full use of the
possibilities offered by this material, starting with the corner entrance
distinguished by a cylindrical volume and a bell tower with a helix
cantilevered staircase. The mushroom columns in the parking garage
for the fire trucks are the most telling functionalist feature. These
columns eliminate the need for beams, which would have prevented
tall fire engines from parking inside. The other project was the Municipal Market of Concepción, which was won but never took off. It is

*Daniel
Talesnik*

Tibor
Weiner's
Architectural
Design
Curriculum
in
Chile

423

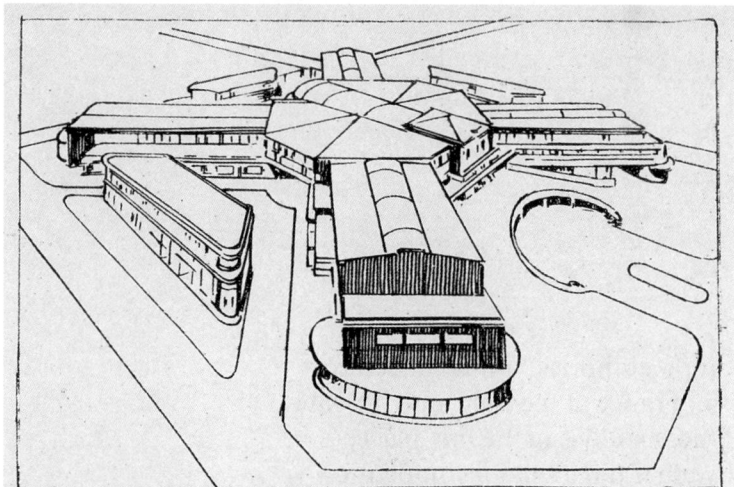

CROQUIS DEL PROYECTO del Mercado Municipal de Concepción, que dentro de poco se construirá de acuerdo con los planos de que es autor el Arquitecto señor Müller Hess.

a complex project with a central nucleus—an octagon—and four two-story wings spanning twenty-six meters each. The design principle was that each of the four wings would serve a different type of food (meats, fish, milk and animal produce, and wholesale products). The central space, where all the wings converge, was reserved for fruits and vegetables; the functionalist approach is evident in the specialization of each pavilion. [fig.2] [7]

After Müller's death, Weiner started working independently. Weiner declared in a letter that he expected this new scenario to allow him to get better deals than those reached while working with Müller. The commissions in this period were mainly houses and some small-scale buildings; Weiner usually paired up with builders as business partners. [8] A highlight from this period is a 1946 building in downtown Santiago at 536 Guayaquil Street. This six-story building is located on a curved street. The first floor is aligned with the neighboring buildings, but starting at the second floor, the façade protrudes approximately 50 cm (20 inches), creating an interesting façade composition. From a general perspective, Weiner's designs in Chile were the work of an architect who adapted to the circumstances he found. When he ran out of public commissions, based on a letter he sent Meyer, one may assume that he had no problem adjusting to real-estate speculation projects or to small private commissions. [9] This flexibility speaks to the fact that Weiner's career was at times guided by militant criteria, and at other times by doing what architects usually do, which is to take on any design job they can get to sustain themselves.

In 1946, six years into Weiner's Chilean sojourn, a group of architecture students from the University of Chile contacted him in search of someone to help them outline a new academic program. His position as an informal mentor to these students, and eventually as a teacher at the university, allowed Weiner to develop a pedagogical project that was based heavily on his Bauhaus experience. In order to unfold the details of Weiner's teaching career in Chile, and in order to highlight aspects of his pedagogy, Hannes Meyer's own teaching efforts during his years in Mexico—where he had emigrated in 1939—will be brought to the fore.

Fig.3. Tibor Weiner, diagrams that explain the program of the reform, circa 1947.

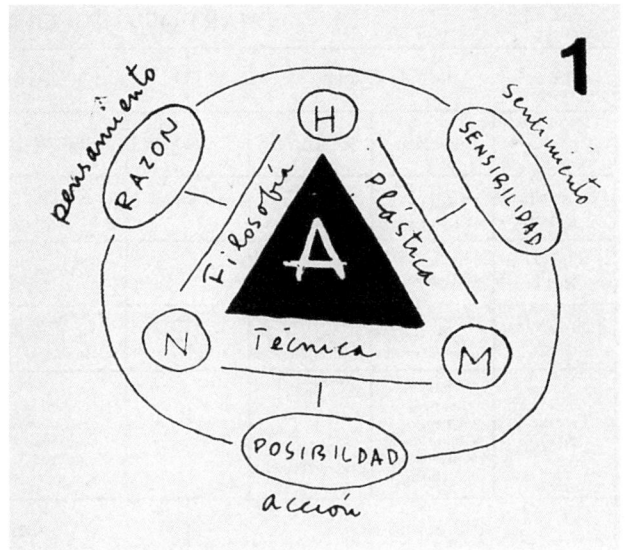

Before 1946, the University of Chile's School of Architecture had seen two reform attempts led by students in 1933 and 1939, but neither attempt was able to push for substantial changes. The students aimed at bringing their architectural education closer to Modernist principles and make it more in tune with the social reality of Chile at the time, where serialized responses to housing where needed.[10] The current study plan was based on a hybrid Beaux-Arts/technical school model, where students were still asked to draw the classical orders by copying plaster casts, while at the same time the connection with the engineering school provided solid structural and construction training.[11]

During the first few months of 1946, Weiner met the leaders of the so-called Reform Movement and began helping them shape what was to become a groundbreaking plan of architectural study in Chile. The first student leader that Weiner met was Abraham Schapira, a fifth-year student who along with his classmates Gaston Etcheverry and Hernán Behm was coordinating the revolt.[12] The students were in a hurry: the school was on strike and they needed a solid proposal to challenge the university authorities. Weiner helped these students by suggesting a curriculum that offered aspects of the "scientific approach" of Hannes Meyer's Bauhaus along with bio-functionalist methods.

The basic proposals of the reform considered architecture to be defined by a triangle between man, nature, and materials as the essential and determining aspects of any given architectural project. They developed a series of diagrams to explain their ideas: The first diagram shows that the reformers understood *material* and *nature* as categories that needed to be mediated by *technique*; *nature* and *man* as categories that needed to be mediated by *philosophy*; and *man* and *material* as categories that needed to be mediated by *plasticity*.[fig.3]

The new curriculum was divided into dialectical stages—two years of *analysis* and four years of *synthesis*—crowned by a one-year diploma.[13] The classes in the scheme were organized under four blocks: *plastic*, *technical*, *sociological*, and *philosophical*. If one looks at Meyer's last organization scheme for the Bauhaus, which he meant to implement in the winter semester of 1930–31, there are some overlaps on a subject-to-subject basis. Among others, "Hygiene,"

Daniel Talesnik

Tibor Weiner's Architectural Design Curriculum in Chile

425

	Analysis Cycle			Synthesis Cycle			Final Degree Project
	First Year	Second Year	Third Year	Fourth Year	Fifth Year	Sixth Year	
Philosophical Block	Architectural Analysis First Part	Architectural Analysis Second Part	Architectural History	Architectural History	Architectural History	Architectural History Seminar	
Sociological Block	Biology and Hygiene	Social Economy	Urbanism	Urbanism	Urbanism	Urbanism Seminar	
Philosophical Block	Composition Plastics Technical Drawing	Composition Plastics Technical Drawing	Plastics Free Hand Drawing	Plastics Free Hand Drawing	Plastics Free Hand Drawing	Plastics Free Hand Drawing	
Technical Block	Mathematics Descriptive Geometry Technical Physics and Tecnology of Materials	Infinitesimal Analysis Applications of Descriptive Geometry Theoretical Physics Topography	Applied Mechanics Construction	Applied Mechanics Construction Instalations Organization	Applied Mechanics Construction Instalations Organization	Stability and Construction Seminar Instalations Organization	
	Elemental Studio			Central Studio			
Additional Subjects Block	Languages Photography Applied Arts	Scenography	Botany	Statistics	Physical Education	Furniture	

"Sociology," and "Technology of Materials" were all part of Meyer's Bauhaus curriculum, the first two as part of the reinforcement of the curriculum provided by "scientific guest lecturers," and the third as a topic that appeared in several classes during his tenure. Many of the science and social science courses at Meyer's Bauhaus were also replicated in the Chilean curriculum.[fig.4] While some classes can be related to the Bauhaus *Vorkurs*, others can be connected to the architectural curriculum under Meyer, and there is also a set of classes that can be associated directly with the engineering tradition of the Chilean school: classes that placed an emphasis on structural concerns, given the likelihood of earthquakes in the country.

A noteworthy difference is that third- through fifth-year students had an "Architecture History" class, since Meyer's Bauhaus study plan did not offer history classes. Another break from the Bauhaus curriculum is that in the senior year the architectural studies were completed by a final degree project.[14]

In the Philosophical Block, Weiner's influence on the reform became tangible in the "Architectural and Urban Analysis" class for first- and second-year students, which he taught in 1946–47. In Weiner's own words, the class was "some sort of introduction to architecture, with historical, philosophical, and technical inputs and practical exercises that tackled the human measures. I tried to communicate a methodology that could be deployed by the students in the later stages of their studies."[15] The curriculum's core class was "Introductory Studio" in the first and second year and "Core Studio" from the third to the sixth year. "Introductory Studio" was taught together with "Architectural and Urban Analysis," which meant coordinated theoretical and practical exercises. The first- and second-year students, as well as the students in the "Core Studio" from the third through the fifth year,

Part 3

Bauhaus
Architects
in
Exile

Fig. 4. Layout of classes, University of Chile School of Architecture, circa 1946. Chart translated by Daniel Talesnik.

shared a classroom and teacher, but each cohort had separate assignments. Students signed up by teacher, and the studio had a central topic. A topic might be, for instance, "education," where third-year students designed a kindergarten, fourth-year students an elementary school, and fifth-year students a university campus.

In order to be more specific about the content of Weiner's "Architecture and Urban Analysis" class, and its connections to Meyer's Bauhaus pedagogy, it is necessary to analyze the practical exercises done by the students. The first assignments were studying independent human activities, looking at interrelations and measures. Students analyzed elements in their own household, such as the relationship between a man and a certain piece of furniture through architectural plans and diagrams. The aim was that the students would understand the relationships between activities such as resting and eating, the furniture or objects that are involved in those activities, and the overall relationship between those objects and architectural spaces in order to define the measures to be undertaken.[16]

A surviving first-year exercise by students Miguel Lawner and Ricardo Tapia focuses on circulation.[17] They created analyses of existing spaces and uses, and studied the movements of individuals within these spaces. Complexity increased until they arrived at an analysis of the movements of a family within a house. These exercises aimed at rethinking the house starting from its uses, resulting in new forms of circulation and access along with the re-dimensioning of existing spaces and the elimination of spaces without function. The first year ended with a design exercise in which students took a unit they had analyzed during the semester and completely redesigned it. In the second year, complexity increased and students faced such challenges as the design of a bathroom and a kitchen for a house, which they had to justify by providing the analytical method learned in the first year. These studies are reminiscent of Weiner's own work during his Bauhaus period, such as the self-commissioned exercise done with Philipp Tolziner in 1930 entitled "Test for Communal Residential Buildings for the Workers of a Factory in a Socialist State," in which the preliminary studies for the project were done with spatial tests and measurements in Tolziner's Dessau apartment. The studies are comparable since they started by studying functions and the associated spatial requirements in the students' own domestic life, and later used those analyses to properly dimension habitation units.[fig.5]

Daniel Talesnik

Tibor Weiner's Architectural Design Curriculum in Chile

427

In order to further explore the pedagogical approach that is being analyzed, a comparison between a 1946 exercise done for Weiner's class, a 1940 exercise done for Meyer's Mexican class, and a 1929 exercise done for Meyer's Bauhaus class can lead to deeper insights.[18] In a first-year exercise done in 1946 by Miguel Lawner for Weiner's class, there is a first board of historical analysis, a second board with a chronological analysis of activities, a third with schemes of relationships and circulation, a fourth with an analysis of weather and climate, a fifth with a seasonal analysis, and finally a sixth board with an atmospheric analysis. The best materials for a comparison are the second and third boards.[fig.6, 7] Meyer's students in Mexico did similar analyses, where in 1940–41, he taught an urban planning studio at the Planning and Urbanism Institute. The class was called "Study of the Vital Space of Workers' Families and Employees of Mexico City." The student Ricardo Rivas studied a "room for a worker in the village of Nativitas in Mexico City." His board includes analyses of the daily, weekly, and yearly activities of the worker and his family. The codification is made with hatching of different densities.[fig.8]

At the Bauhaus, Edmund Collein—a student of the Bauhaus architecture department from its inception in 1927 until Meyer's departure in 1930—did an exercise called "Study of the Periodicity of the Habitat."[19] First, there is an analysis of the seven inhabitants of the house, who have been arranged spatially in a diagram and classified by gender. The description of each inhabitant is provided underneath. There are charts of the daily activities of the inhabitants of the house that correlate with the day's hours and activities using isotypes that describe sleeping, working, and so on. There are also seasonal variations for each of these diagrams—summer and winter—and also one for Sundays. Finally, there are yearly diagrammatic analyses of the activities of each member of the house, a list of spatial requirements, and an outline of the ground floor of the house.[fig.9]

Through this comparison, we can also see that in Lawner's board done at the University of Chile, he analyzed the chronological development of the daily activities of a worker in three given circumstances: "normal work day," "sick day or day off," and "intense work day." For each of these, there is an analysis in cold and warm weather— exactly as in Collein's Bauhaus analyses.

Weiner might have been aware of the studies Meyer had conducted in Mexico. In April 1943, the Mexican magazine *Arquitectura*

Fig. 5. Philipp Tolziner and Tibor Weiner, "Community Dwelling for the Workers of a Factory in a Socialized State," circa 1930, Archiv der Moderne, Weimar. This work was not a school assignment, but it was discussed at the Bauhaus.

Fig. 6. Miguel Lawner, "Chronological Development of Activities," student work from Tibor Weiner's Architectural Analysis class at the School of Architecture of the University of Chile, 1946.

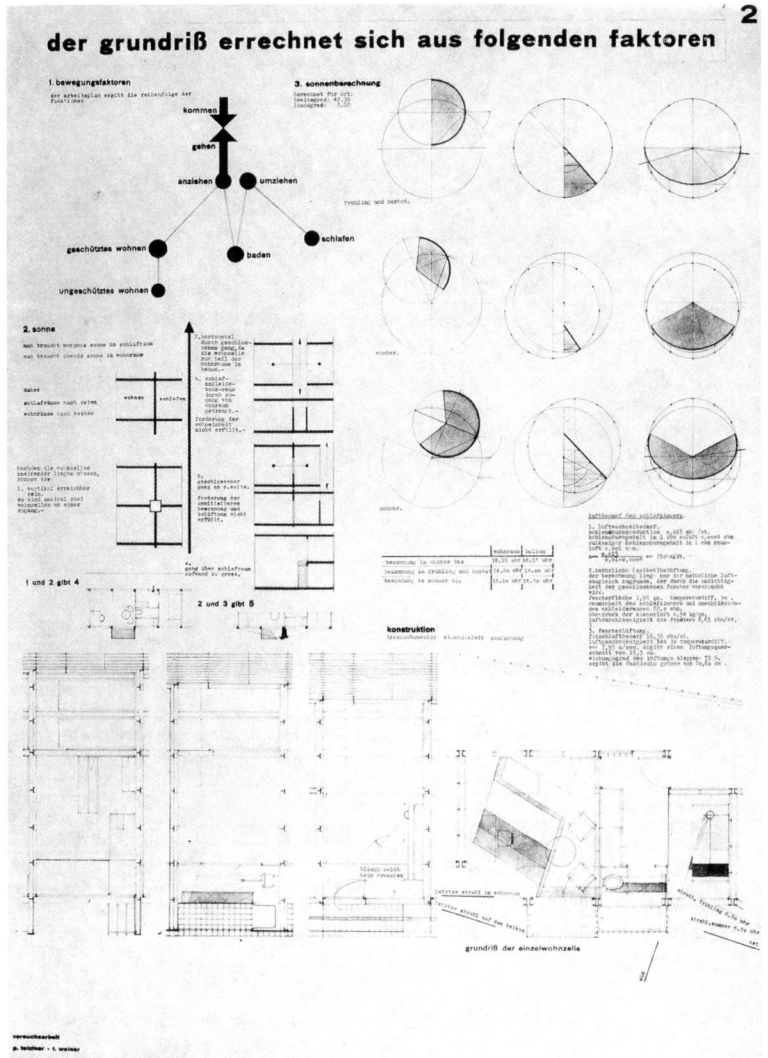

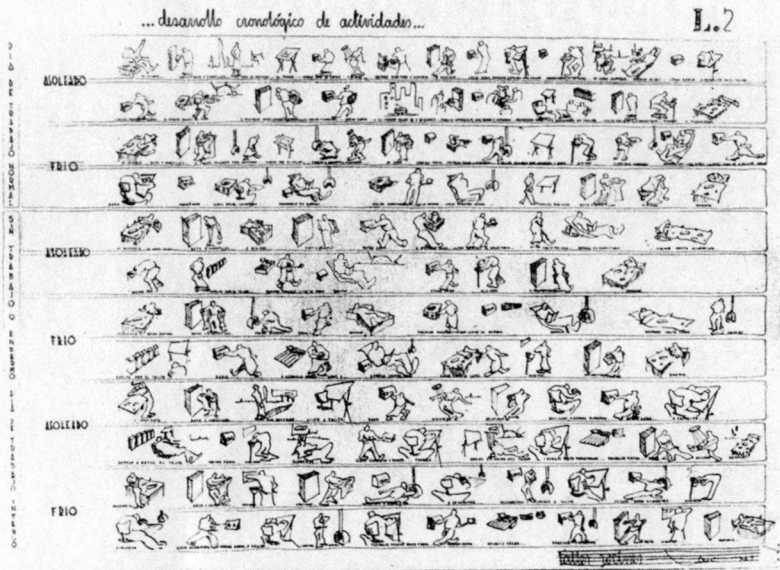

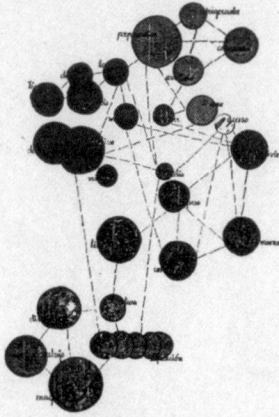
esquema de relaciones

T. WEINER

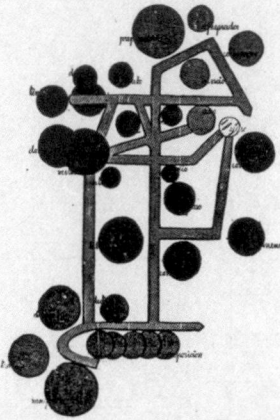
esquema de circulación

L. 3

M. LAWNER

Fig. 7. Miguel Lawner, "Scheme of Relationships and Scheme of Circulation," student work from Tibor Weiner's Architectural Analysis class at the School of Architecture of the University of Chile, 1946.

Fig. 8. Student work from Hannes Meyer's class in Mexico by Ricardo Rivas, circa 1940: "Study of the Vital Space of the Families of Workers and Employees of Mexico City," "Room for a Worker in Nativitas in Mexico DF"; from "El espacio vital de la familia," *Edificación* 32 (1940), 165–71.

Fig. 9. Edmund Collein, "Studie zur Periodizität des Lebensraum" (Study of the Periodicity of the Habitat), work from Hannes Meyer's Bauhaus class, circa 1929.

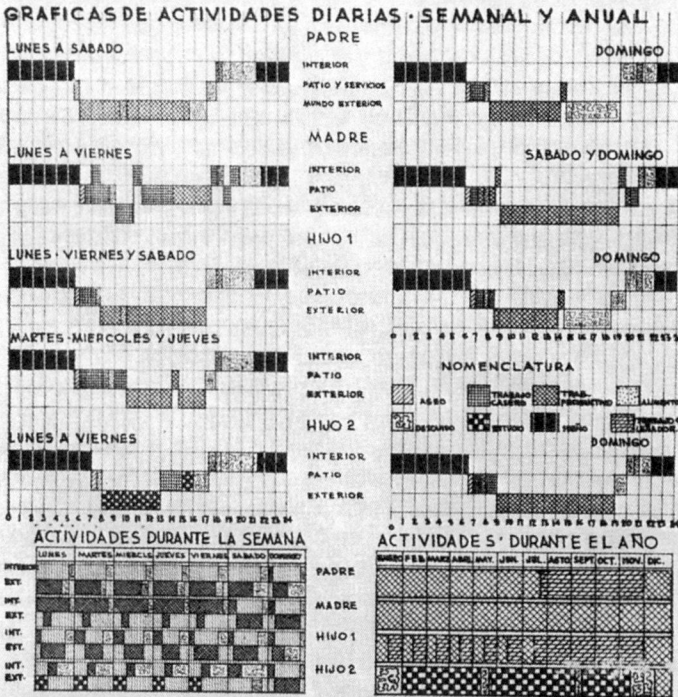

CASO No. I.— HABITACION DE JORNALERO EN EL POBLADO DE NATIVITAS, D. F.
Investigador: RICARDO RIVAS.

GRAFICAS DE ACTIVIDADES DIARIAS · SEMANAL Y ANUAL

La siesta del padre.

Interior de la cocina.

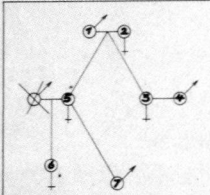

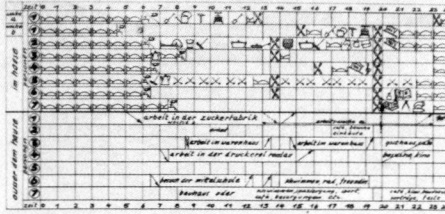

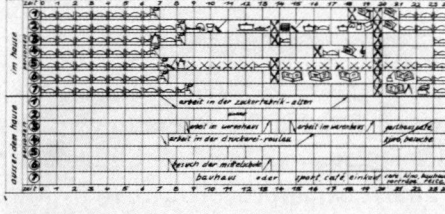

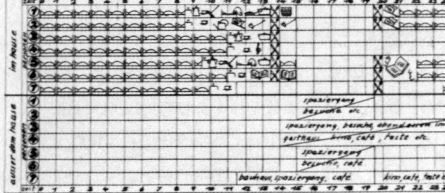

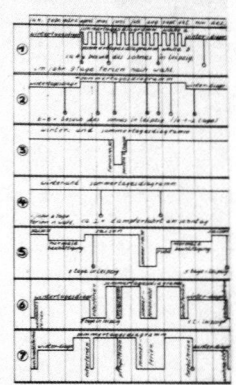

had published Meyer's "Mexico City: Fragments of an Urban Analysis." On page 106, there are two charts from 1940 done by engineer-architect Antonio Gonzalez Juárez that analyze the daily activities of a family of six for a weekday and a weekend day.[20] The charts organize each family member separately, and use different hatching to code sleep, work, rest, leisure, sports, shopping, study, commuting, eating, hygiene, and church. Weiner might have had a copy of this magazine, which was published three years before he began teaching in Chile, since Meyer had been sending him his Mexican material in the early 1940s. The analytical approach of Lawner's Chilean charts and Gonzalez Juárez's Mexican charts is similar.[21]

In brief, Lawner's Chilean exercise, Meyer's Mexican student's exercises, Collein's Bauhaus exercise, and Weiner and Tolziner's Bauhaus exercise all apply a similar graphic analysis of circulation and spatial relationships. These exercises suggest that *architectural analysis* was a research strategy and an architectural exploration tool, and as such it was Weiner's main educational legacy in Chile—and a paradigmatic example of the itinerant pedagogy of Meyer. *Architectural analysis* was a method for facing any given architectural problem.

The 1946 University of Chile reform study plan was more basic than Meyer's Bauhaus study plan, but despite the differences, it was an innovative proposal for a South American context. It brought to architectural education in Chile a structured method of analysis, a technical impulse, and a sociopolitical awareness. Although the Chilean educational project happened sixteen years after Meyer's dismissal from the Bauhaus, the signature of his pedagogy can be traced in the South American context. The graphic language was science-infused, visible in the Bauhaus-inspired diagrams and charts made by his Chilean

Daniel Talesnik

Tibor Weiner's Architectural Design Curriculum in Chile

students. Under Weiner's guidance, the design objectives of these exercises changed the way architecture was taught at the University of Chile. The 1946 reform consolidated aspects of the bio-functionalist and analytical approach favored by Meyer into the basis of a full-fledged study plan: the ideas were institutionalized. The reform study plan was in use until 1963, when most of the original advocates left the university under contested circumstances.[22] Although the architecture school did not return to pre-reform mandates, the loss of the fore-runners and teachers who had originally been students of the reform evidently took a toll on the quality of the program.

In 1946, president Gabriel González Videla had been elected as the third—and last—successive president from the Radical Party. Under his government, members of the Communist Party who had effectively helped in electing him began to be persecuted. In September 1948, "Law No. 8,987 for the Permanent Defense of Democracy," also known as the "Accursed Law," which proscribed the Chilean Communist Party, was approved. With this law, many of the members of the Communist Party were forced to go underground or into exile; some ended up in internment camps. Although Weiner was not a member of the Party in Chile, he was a member of the Alliance of Intellectuals for the Defense of Culture, an antifascist organization dominated by intellectuals of the Communist Party.[23] Weiner had lectured in 1947 on Soviet architecture at the invitation of another Communist Party-related institution, the Chilean-Soviet Institute of Culture, and wrote about Soviet architecture in Party-related publications.[24] Also, Weiner's wife worked as a journalist for the Party newspaper, and in that capacity he was directly implicated in the political life of the country. In March 1948, only six months before the approval of the "Accursed Lay," Weiner and his family hastily left Chile. Weiner was once again leaving a country due to political vicissitudes.

After leaving Chile in 1948, Weiner reconnected with the communist project when he returned to Hungary and won the competition for Sztálinváros (the first socialist city in the country) and became the chief architect of the project. The city was organized along three axes: the road to Budapest, the road connecting the city with the steel works, and the road to the railway station. Organizing the city around roads and preexisting infrastructure was characteristic of Soviet planning during the First and Second Five-Year Plans, with which Weiner had firsthand experience. Weiner summarized the objectives of the master

Fig. 10. Dunaújváros (formerly Sztálinváros), Hungary, town planning by a team led by Tibor Weiner. Modernist buildings in the former May First Street, circa 1950s.

plan of Sztálinváros as: first, a city with no "inner" or "outer" neighborhoods, adding the politically charged idea that the democratic nature of a socialist city should be manifested in the equality of its parts; second, that the city and factory should be given equal importance; and third, a city designed for public events that unite the community while also being able to provide shelter for individual and family life.[25] Besides leading the team in charge of the urban layout, Weiner also designed the Communist Party headquarters, a building that can be described as Socialist Realist and one that is totally disconnected from Weiner's pre-Hungarian designs. The plans for the city were modified many times, and as some historians have noted, the official emphasis on planning actually gave way to a relatively unplanned construction phase. Weiner eventually became the town architect and a member of the city council, and was officially connected to the city government until his death in 1965.[fig. 10]

"Itinerant modernism" is an apt term for describing the work of architects such as Weiner. Implied in the word *itinerant* is the idea that this version of modernism had no time to fully develop, only to rapidly adapt to circumstances. Architectural ideas shifted both conceptually and physically due to jumps from one location to the other. My larger research understands Hannes Meyer's Bauhaus pedagogy as the beginning of an educational approach to architecture with long-term historical ramifications. Looking into aspects of the post-Soviet careers of some Red Bauhaus Brigade members such as Weiner allows for an evaluation of the outcomes of their Bauhaus and Soviet education, and in turn it enables the appraisal of their own roles as architects and educators within a broader architectural culture. Although an analysis of the reception of Bauhaus ideas in Eastern Bloc countries surpasses the ambitions of this chapter, it is relevant to mention that during the final stage of his career, Weiner was part of another Bauhaus legacy scene. He worked and taught in a postwar Stalinist, and later post-Stalinist, context in Hungary, where the impact of Bauhaus ideas and pedagogy is more nuanced and at times less evident if compared to other stages of his career.[26]

Daniel Talesnik

Tibor Weiner's Architectural Design Curriculum in Chile

433

1 For more details about Meyer's Bauhaus expulsion, as it was understood at the time by him, see Hannes Meyer, "My Dismissal from the Bauhaus: Open Letter to Mayor Hesse," August 1930, in Claude Schnaidt, *Hannes Meyer: Buildings, Projects, and Writings* (Teufen: A. Nigli, 1965), 101–05.

2 For more information on Hungarians at the Bauhaus, see H. Sipos, Edith, and Edith H. Sipos. n.d. "Hungarian Relations with Bauhaus and their Influence in Hungary," *Periodica Polytechnica Architecture* 30 (1–4), 97–115.

3 Hannes Meyer, "Recommendation Letter for Tibor Weiner," October 6, 1930, Tibor Weiner Papers, Magyar Kereskedelmi és Vendéglátóipari Múzeum Archív, Budapest.

4 Philipp Tolziner, "Leben und Werk der Mitglieder der Bauhaus Brigade Hannes Mayers in der Sowjetunion und in anderen Ländern," (unpublished, Bauhaus-Archiv Berlin, 1995), 20–21.

5 Tibor Weiner (Santiago) to Hannes Meyer (Mexico City), January 1, 1940, Hannes Meyer Papers, Deutsches Architekturmuseum-Archiv, Frankfurt am Main.

6 Tibor Weiner (Chile) to Hannes Meyer (Mexico), February 8, 1948, Hannes Meyer Papers, Deutsches Architekturmuseum-Archiv, Frankfurt am Main.

7 These competitions in the south of Chile were organized by the Relief and Reconstruction Corporation (Corporación de Reconstrucción y Auxilio), created under a law of July 21, 1939. This development corporation was created in response to the earthquake, and its purpose was to facilitate and administer the reconstruction efforts.

8 Tibor Weiner (Chile) to Hannes Meyer (Mexico), February 8, 1948, Hannes Meyer Papers, Deutsches Architekturmuseum-Archiv, Frankfurt am Main.

9 Tibor Weiner (Chile) to Hannes Meyer (Mexico), February 8, 1948, Hannes Meyer Papers, Deutsches Architekturmuseum-Archiv, Frankfurt am Main.

10 There was already a countrywide process of modernizing institutions. Led by the motto "to govern is to produce," Juan Antonio Ríos's government was the second successive presidency of the Radical Party, a left-wing party of a social democrat persuasion. Ríos's government was marked by instability from the beginning, partly due to Chile's neutrality in the Second World War and the international and national pressures to break diplomatic relations with the countries of the Axis. Ríos's predecessor, Pedro Aguirre Cerda, who had been elected in 1938 with his motto "to govern is to educate," oversaw the enlargement of the school and university system in the country. When Ríos was elected in 1942, he did manage to continue a series of Aguirre Cerda's initiatives.

11 The University of Chile's School of Architecture, which had originated in 1849 as the School of Civil Architecture, was part of the Engineering School until 1944.

12 The other important person in the Weiner-University of Chile connection is Carlos Sandor (d. 1980), a structural engineer and Hungarian émigré who brought Weiner to the attention of Schapira.

13 It should be noted that the use of the *analysis* and *synthesis* dialectical stages in a project was characteristic of Meyer's pedagogy and work system.

14 Jorge González, Abraham Schapira, and Tibor Weiner, "Fundamento del Plan de Reforma de la Enseñanza de la Arquitectura en la Universidad de Chile," Pan-American Architecture Congress, Lima, Peru, 1947; Ana Maria Barrenechea, Hernán Behm, Osvaldo Cáceres et al. "A 53 Años de la Reforma de la Reforma de 1946" Santiago: Facultad de Arquitectura de la Universidad de Chile, 1999.

15 Tibor Weiner (Chile) to Hannes Meyer (Mexico), February 8, 1948, Hannes Meyer Papers, Deutsches Architekturmuseum-Archiv, Frankfurt am Main.

16 Tibor Weiner, "Programa del Curso de Análisis Arquitectural" (1946); Beatriz Mella, "Curso de Análisis Arquitectural, Tibor Weiner, 1946–1947," Seminar Paper, Pontificia Universidad Católica de Chile, 2004; Daniel Talesnik, "Tibor Weiner, una Re-Introducción," *De Arquitectura* 14 (2006): 64–70.

17 Years later, Ricardo Tapia became a teacher at the University of Chile's School of Architecture, and he was professionally active in association with his architect brother William, mainly designing housing projects in Santiago. During the military dictatorship, Tapia was exiled in Venezuela for several years. Miguel Lawner also became a teacher at the same architecture school. He had an architectural practice called BEL with his wife, Ana María Barrenechea, and Franciso Ehijo (both architecture school classmates), and eventually worked for the government of Salvador Allende (1970–73) as executive director of the CORMU (Urban Development Corporation). After the coup d'état in 1973, Lawner was held prisoner at several detention camps and eventually went into exile in Denmark for several years. After leaving the university in 1963, both Tapia and Lawner were founding members in 1965 of AUCA, an influential architectural magazine that was published until 1986.

18   It is important to keep in mind that the University of Chile offered a seven-year undergraduate architecture program; Meyer's Mexican program was a two-year strictly post-professional specialization in urbanism, offered to engineers, economists and architects; and Meyer's Bauhaus was a four-and-a-half-year architecture program that required students to come with practical training or previous studies (basically a pre- and post-professional hybrid).

19   Edmund Collein was not a member of the Red Bauhaus Brigade.

20   "Ejemplo de análisis del espacio de vida de una familia de empleado commercial en la ciudad de Mexico, D. F., (Puente de Alvarado), investigador: Antonio Gonzalez Juárez, ing-arq. (elaboración en el Instituto de Urbanismo y Planificación del I. P. N. en el año de 1940 bajo la dirección del Arq. Hannes Meyer)," in *Arquitectura* (April 1943): 96–109.

21   The assumption that Meyer sent Weiner a copy of the April 1934 issue of *Arquitectura* magazine is based on an undated letter from Meyer to Weiner from the period that states that Meyer sent Weiner fifty copies of *Arquitectura* magazine (two different issues, twenty-five copies of each issue) in which Meyer's Mexican work had been published, and that Weiner should keep an issue of each and sell the rest. The April 1934 issue of *Arquitectura* magazine can be found in the library of the school of architecture of the Catholic University in Santiago, which proves that copies of the periodical circulated in Chile at the time. This issue is not, however, in the library of the school of architecture of the University of Chile.

22   In 1963, a large group of teachers at the school, basically the majority of the faculty, submitted their resignation in order to pressure for changes. To their surprise, the president of the university accepted their "symbolic" resignation, discontinuing the legacy of the reform and leaving them without a public platform for action. This development brought about the exchange of the entire faculty, ending the original impulse of the Reform Movement.

23   The most prominent member of the Alianza de Intelectuales para la Defensa de la Cultura, and at one point its president, was the poet Pablo Neruda. Neruda was an active communist. He officially joined the Party in 1943. (Neruda received the Nobel Prize for Literature in 1971).

24   Tibor Weiner, "Arquitectura en la URSS," *Aurora de Chile* 25–26 (October–November 1946).

25   Tibor Weiner, quoted by Endre Prakfalvi, "Hungarian Architecture 1945–1956," in *Architecture and Planning in Hungary 1945–1956* (Budapest: Magyar Építészeti Múzeum, 1996), 7–23.

26   Of the remaining members of the Red Bauhaus Brigade, Béla Scheffler and Antonin Urban died in a Soviet gulag and there is no trace of Klaus Meumann after the 1930s, which probably means he shared the same tragic fate. After leaving the Soviet Union, René Mensch worked as an architect in Iran, Chile, and his native Switzerland, under circumstances that were very different from those of Tibor Weiner, since he had more freedom of movement. Weiner's post-Soviet career is comparable to that of Konrad Püschel in the GDR, who was a teacher in Weimar and also worked as an urban planner in North Korea in the late 1950s as head of an East German architectural task force. Comparisons could also be made with the final stage of Philipp Tolziner's architectural career in the Soviet Union: after surviving the gulag and being rehabilitated, Tolziner went back to the Moscow to the Trust where h ad been working before his imprisonment and continued to design collective housing.

Marija Drėmaitė

Bringing Bauhaus Modernism to Lithuania: Vladas Švipas's Life and Influence

Fig. 1. Vladas Švipas, color scheme for the atelier of Wassily Kandinsky, published in Gustav Adolf Platz, *Die Baukunst der neuesten Zeit* (Berlin: Propyläen Verlag, 1927).

In 1919, when the Staatliches Bauhaus was established in Weimar, the second largest city of the newly independent Republic of Lithuania—Kaunas—unexpectedly became the provisional capital of the country. Kaunas was then a small, provincial city, the center of the former Kaunas Governorate of Tsarist Russia. In 1915, during World War I, Germany had occupied the western parts of the Russian Empire, including Lithuania. In the aftermath of the war, the opportunity was taken by the Council of Lithuania to declare the independent Republic of Lithuania, with Vilnius as its capital, in 1918. However, due to the political and territorial tension in January 1919, the government was temporarily relocated to the second largest city, Kaunas. In 1920, Vilnius was annexed by Poland, so that Kaunas maintained its status as provisional capital until 1939.[1]

A desolate city during the First World War, Kaunas was not really prepared to function as the new capital in 1919. But by the mid-1930s it faced a construction boom. Kaunas became a modern, elegant European city, with thousands of new buildings finished in granite and shiny glass, a state-of-the-art water supply and sewage system, 14,000 regular radio broadcast listeners, fourteen daily newspapers (published in five languages), fourteen cinemas, an opera house, cafés, restaurants, and museums. Kaunas's population grew from 99,000 in 1931 to 154,000 in 1939. This was the fastest rate of Eastern European urban population growth recorded in the 1930s. It was equally impressive in terms of urbanization and social/individual self-awareness: every resident could see him- or herself as a participant in the great experiment to attain a fast-paced, modern lifestyle. Vladas Švipas, a young architect, the one and seemingly only student at the Bauhaus

436

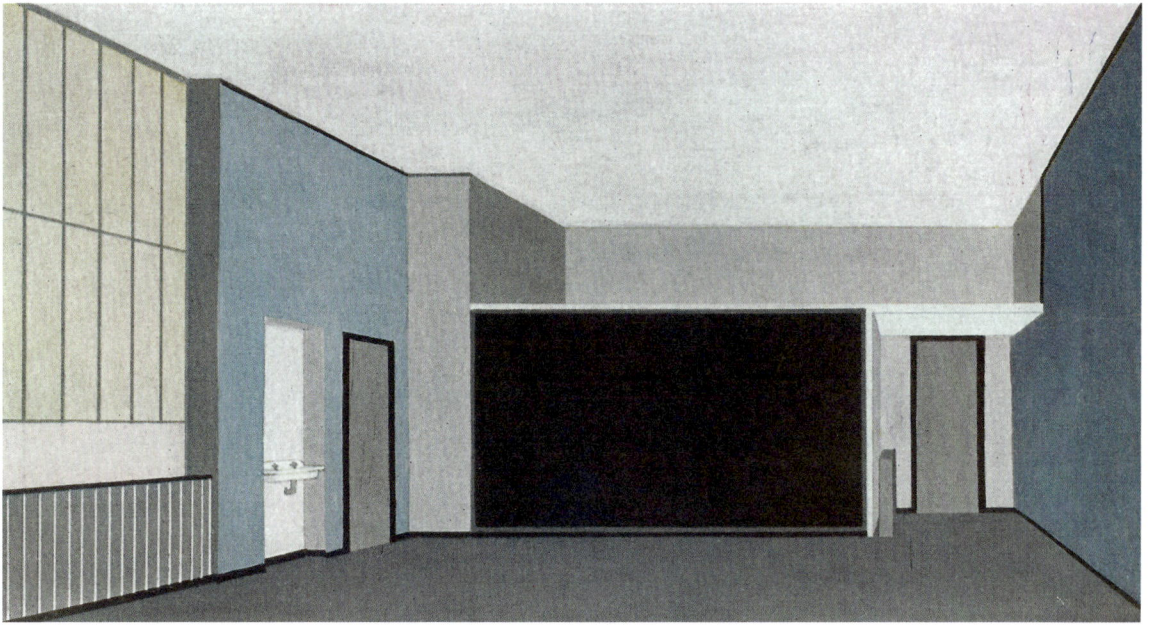

from the young Republic of Lithuania, was among them, and he played an important role in the architectural modernization of Kaunas and Lithuania as a whole.

In Kaunas, modern architecture was tasked with shaping a new national identity through novel methods of construction, design, and curricula in education.[2] However, there were very few architects in 1919. In 1795, the Grand Duchy of Lithuania lost any vestige of independent statehood and was incorporated into the Russian Empire as the Northwestern Krai. After Lithuania and Poland waged their first unsuccessful uprising against the tsar in 1831 in an effort to reestablish the Polish-Lithuanian Commonwealth, the regime in Moscow retaliated by closing Vilnius University, the last institution of higher learning on Lithuanian territory offering studies in architecture. From the mid-nineteenth century to 1918, students from former Lithuania usually obtained degrees in architecture in St. Petersburg or Riga. After the collapse of the Russian Empire and the declaration of an independent Republic of Lithuania, Kaunas began to see the arrival, or return, of many designers with various educational backgrounds.

Therefore the circle of architects working in Kaunas in the 1920s was a true melting pot of specialists with different ethnic (German, Swiss, Polish, Jewish, Russian, Lithuanian, Danish) and educational backgrounds. Most of the eighty-three specialists authorized by the State Reconstruction Committee to work in design and construction in 1924 were construction engineers, born in the 1880s or early 1890s and graduates of the Institute of Civil Engineering in St. Petersburg. The German-influenced Riga Polytechnic Institute in Livonia/Latvia (then also part of the Russian Empire) was another important center of education for Lithuania-born students, who become the driving force behind numerous national engineering societies and academic institutions in the 1920s. They established the Department of Technology at the newly opened University of Lithuania in Kaunas in 1922.

*Marija
Drėmaitė*

Bringing
Bauhaus
Modernism
to
Lithuania

437

Professor Mykolas Songaila (1874–1941), a graduate of the St. Petersburg Academy of Art with considerable teaching experience, was invited to oversee its architecture program at the Department of Construction. Songaila's methodology was based on academic tradition, and he upheld it until 1941. Architecture at the university was classified as a technical profession, and graduates obtained the diploma of construction engineering.

While the senior generation of engineers had been trained at technical schools in the Russian Empire, the new generation of Kaunas architects born between 1900 and 1910 were directed to study at Western European schools. Indeed, a Western education was part of the official national policy at the time: the Lithuanian government had approved a program for allocating stipends for foreign study as early as 1919.[3] Stipends were granted as long-term, zero-interest loans; rules required that recipients work at their designated posts for one and a half years for every financed year of study and return thirty percent of their grant.

The state stipend program appears to have been really successful and there even exists an established narrative that modernist Kaunas was actually designed by the Western European graduates who came back home and shared their knowledge. Indeed, in 1934, some 46 of 311 engineers and architects registered in Lithuania had received their degrees in Western and Central Europe.[4] Students pursuing technical professions often chose to attend schools that followed a German curriculum: the Darmstadt Technische Hochschule, the Zurich Polytechnic School, the Mecklenburg-Strelitz Polytechnic Institute, the Dresden Technische Hochschule in Saxony, and especially the Berliner Technische Hochschule in Charlottenburg. Future architects were also drawn to the Deutsche Technische Hochschule in Prague, where the quality of education was considered high but the cost of living was relatively low. Other students went to Rome, Ghent, Brussels, Paris, and elsewhere, from where they could bring modern trends back to their native city. Vladas Švipas chose to study at the Staatliches Bauhaus in Weimar.[5]

In 1919, Švipas—born on November 10, 1900 in Palėvenė, a well-to-do farm in northern Lithuania—graduated from a Gymnasium in Panevėžys, where he met his art teacher Juozas Zikaras, a Lithuanian sculptor.[6] Zikaras established a painting group at the Gymnasium, and according to Švipas got him interested in arts. In 1920 Švipas had

Fig.2. Vladas Švipas (left) during his studies in Germany (location unknown), late 1920s.

already presented two of his paintings at the first Lithuanian art show in Kaunas. It seems that his interest in studying abroad was driven primarily by his passion for painting and the desire to be part of an avant-garde art scene.

After serving in the Lithuanian military in 1920–21, Švipas's first recorded foreign visit was to Czechoslovakia and Germany in April 1922, where he fed his interest in modern painting.[7] From April 1923 to April 1924, he attended the private, anti-academic art school *Der Weg – Schule für neue Kunst*, established by Edmund Kesting in Dresden. Švipas most likely heard about the Bauhaus there, because he soon applied and received the state stipend from the Lithuanian Ministry of Finance, and began his studies in the *Vorkurs* at the Staatliches Bauhaus in Weimar in April 1924.[8] In his second year, he attended the workshop for wall painting (*Wandmalerei*). One of his works for a color scheme that he produced in the atelier of Wassily Kandinsky was published in *Die Baukunst der neuesten Zeit* in 1927.[fig.1] [9]

In May 1925 he moved to Dessau with the school, but in November 1926 he took a leave of absence to study architecture at the Städtische Ingenieurakademie Oldenburg, which was renamed the Hindenburg-Polytechnikum in 1927. When he applied to the school, "in search of deeper technical knowledge,"[10] as he later noted, Švipas was accepted directly into the fourth semester of the architecture department and also received permission from Lithuania to transfer his state stipend. He graduated with a diploma in architecture and construction engineering in April 1928 from the Hindenburg-Polytechnikum.[fig.2] [11]

Throughout his studies in Oldenburg, he maintained a close connection to the Bauhaus. During a holiday stay in summer 1927 in Pušalotas, a small town close to his home farm in Lithuania, Švipas designed and built a modernist monument to those who died in the fight for Lithuania's independence. The Constructivist concrete

Marija Drėmaitė

Bringing Bauhaus Modernism to Lithuania

439

monument was probably inspired by Gropius's 1921 Monument to the
March Heroes in Weimar.[fig.3] Švipas also published his first article
dedicated to modernist architecture in a Lithuanian cultural journal,
where he focused on the topic of modern houses and described the
Werkbund exhibition in Stuttgart.[12]

In winter 1928, Švipas continued his studies at the Hochschule für
Gestaltung (Bauhaus) in Dessau, where he was employed at the newly
established building department under the directorship of Hannes
Meyer. While apparently still taking lessons from Wassily Kandinsky
he, along with Ursula Schneider, was engaged to run the office of
Hannes Meyer and Hans Wittwer for the ADGB school (Federal School
for the German Trade Unions) in Bernau that would be constructed
in record time between 1928 and 1930.[13] In a short interview for
bauhaus journal in 1928, Švipas reflected on his time at the Bauhaus:

> *i was born just like everyone else, and arrived at the bauhaus totally
> unprepared, like a fourth grader, just like everyone else. before that i had
> been studying interminably, all over the place, and was forced to admit
> that it had all been completely wrong.*
> *how embarrassing! ...*
> *twenty-seven years old, single ...*
> *a romantic with his eyes set on the lofty heights of personal art. that was
> before the bauhaus. now i'm a recovering romantic trying to come to terms
> with reality.*
> *but can one be real enough? can one be sober enough? it doesn't matter
> how careful you are, you always end up stumbling over your own shadow.*
> *it is unfortunately true that from time immemorial humans have
> evolved—or perhaps better, convolved—in such a scrawny way. first indi-
> vidually, then collectively, but everywhere free. now however, people are
> bound hand and foot and loaded down with culture.*
> *at the bauhaus, one can and must throw this ballast overboard. here, we
> have to become free, in order to be able to soak up new histories.*
> *here, at the bauhaus, is where i committed myself to architecture, not for
> its form but for the human element. for content, rather than appearance.*

*in this respect the bauhaus dedicates as much of its education as possible
to the human, artistic, and technical aspects of the architect's design work.
i believe that the time is not far off when people will devote as much of
themselves to designing a modern lifestyle as they did in the gothic era.
unfortunately, there is still too much of yesterday clinging to all of us. that is
why the bauhaus attempts to render its young people immune to cultural
cancer. apart from that, however, we work with the same objective methods
as are employed in science and technology.*[14]

When Švipas returned to Lithuania after his studies at the Bauhaus in
late 1928, he took on a different role in order to promote modern ideas
in Lithuanian architecture. After receiving a state stipend for four
years and three months (seven semesters at the Bauhaus, and three at
Hindenburg-Polytechnikum), he had an obligation to the state service
for several years, and immediately entered service as a state employee
in January 1929, as an assistant at the Construction Department in
the Chamber of Agriculture.[15] In this function, Švipas took it upon
himself to promote the fundamental modernization of rural construction (following the land reform in 1922), drafting standardized plans
for farm infrastructures and emphasizing the need for the planned
development of rural homesteads. As head of the Construction Department beginning in 1932, he set up standardization projects and introduced new books and manuals for rural construction as part of a series
titled "Farmer's Bookshop," published in 1934–36 by the Chamber
of Agriculture. He also promoted the modernization of interiors and
amenities—for example, he proposed installing salons in new rural
houses, as well as modern guest rooms with armchairs, coffee tables,
and a bathroom.[fig.4, 4a]

Rural modernization as well as overall modernization of agricultural industry was of utmost importance to the modern state of
Lithuania, because not having other resources, it aimed at food
(butter, dairy, eggs, and meat) exports. The state funded numerous
modern dairies in villages and bacon factories in larger towns, and
encouraged modern farming. In this context, Lithuania's participation
at the international exhibition on modern village life (*Exposition
européenne de l'Habitation rurale*), organized by the United Nations in
connection with the 1937 World Expo in Paris, was very important.
Vladas Švipas was commissioned to design a model Lithuanian rural
homestead for the Lithuanian stand. For the execution of his model,
Švipas invited his Gymnasium teacher Juozas Zikaras, who was

*Marija
Drėmaitė*

Bringing
Bauhaus
Modernism
to
Lithuania

Fig.4. A view of modern Kaunas in 1937, center: Chamber of Agriculture (designed by Karolis Reisonas, 1931).

Fig.4a. Vladas Švipas as a director of the Construction Department of the Chamber of Agriculture in his office, Kaunas, Lithuania, late 1930s.

already an established national artist. The model was awarded a gold medal at the fair. The small Lithuanian stand showed projects for modern dairies and diagrams illustrating the advances in agroindustry, and was a big contrast to the Lithuanian National Pavilion at the *Exposition internationale des Arts et des Techniques appliqués à la Vie moderne*, which was dominated by religious, ethnographic and nationalist motifs[16]. Many new European states were looking for their own representative visions—a national style and uniqueness by means of which they could stand out. Even though an attempt was made to create an image of a modern Lithuania, traditional means were drawn upon to do this—with folklore and ethnographic heritage having to represent a country having a long history. However, the creators of the Lithuanian pavilion (the Ministry of Foreign Affairs and a specially organized Artistic Committee) received criticism that the focus, in effect, was on national folk art, technology was forgotten, and its accomplishments completely unrepresented.[fig.5, 6]

In parallel to his career at the Chamber of Agriculture, Švipas continued to pursue his interest in the innovations of modern urban housing. He traveled to important international events at his own expense, for example to the Stockholm Fair in July 1930, and continued writing on modern residential architecture and lifestyle.[17] Through his numerous publications, he promoted the Bauhaus ideology of rational housing, which culminated in his book about the architecture of town houses, published in Kaunas in 1933.[18] A 148-page book was richly illustrated with 100 images of modernist houses from international architectural journals and books. The book was published at Švipas's own expense, as his application for advance payment was rejected by the Chamber of Agriculture in 1931.

When discussing plots for residential construction, Švipas, like many European modernists, advocated land expropriation, "without which the urban municipal policy of rational construction and expansion is not possible."[19] Contemporary urban growth and planning were, to him, inseparable from industrialization, and he wrote about similar issues that all modernists were concerned about, such as lighting, ventilation, and hygiene issues dealt with through urban zoning. He used modern rhetoric to describe the kitchen as a laboratory, and promoted the rationalization of domestic work and housing following the aims of the National Society for Research in Building and Housing Economy (*Reichsforschungsgesellschaft für Wirtschaftlichkeit*

Marija Drėmaitė

Bringing Bauhaus Modernism to Lithuania

443

im Bau- und Wohnungswesen) that had existed between 1927 and 1931 during the Weimar Republic and that counted politician Marie-Elisabeth Lüders and architects such as Walter Gropius, Ernst May, Bruno Taut, and Martin Wagner among its members. Švipas was keen to bring their ideas about the modernization and standardization of construction practices to Lithuania. And regarding furniture, his essay also echoed some of the Bauhaus ideas: "It seems to me that we are able to produce good furniture in Lithuania, if the work were taken by serious people and attracted the artists. Our artists mistakenly believe that adaptation of their art to life is something odd. In foreign countries, people noticed long ago that producing artistic products is necessary, and sometimes even more cost-effective than creating entirely *l'art pour l'art* works. We should establish at least one journal for art in Lithuania."[20]

Švipas also supported the initiatives of his younger sister, Bronė Švipaitė (1903–2007), in household modernization. She studied at the Housekeeping Institute in Brussels (*L'école professionnelle et ménagère de Laeken*) and later taught at the Academy of Agriculture in Dotnuva, Lithuania. She published an influential book on modern house-keeping[21] (1930) funded by the Chamber of Agriculture. All 18,000 copies were distributed as a free add-on to the "Farmer's Advisor" and reached a large audience. Together with his sister, Švipas also contributed to the book for housewives with a chapter dedicated to the benefits of a modern apartment.[22]

In his own book (*Town Houses*), he also discussed the house's interior, where the very essence of modernism was defined in his words: 'Wigs, crinoline, and masks are no longer used by people. People love reality and truth, clarity and simplicity. The new architecture is brief, precise and logical."[23] In the book, Švipas published his own ten designs for a house with minimal apartments, a minimal single-family house, and specialized houses for a worker, a craftsman, a doctor, a lawyer, an engineer, [fig.7] and an artist. However, Švipas designed only several houses that were constructed. He mentioned in his record that he privately designed five single-family houses in Kaunas. One remaining design in the Kaunas Regional State Archives shows a small one-family wooden house.[24] Although well planned, it appears to be far from the ambitious modernist designs Švipas showed in his book. But Švipas's own house, that he designed in 1936, and lived with his family in 1938–44, was a really rational two storey modern

Marija Drėmaitė

Bringing Bauhaus Modernism to Lithuania

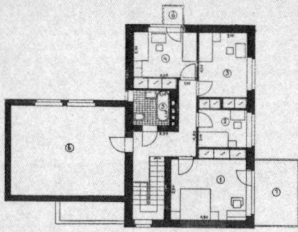

Pav. 92. Namo II-ro aukšto planas. 1), 2), 3) ir 4) — miegamieji,
5) prausykla, 6) naudotina pakraigė, 7) ir 8) balkonai. S-sieninės
spintos. Štrihuotas langas aklai uztaisytinas

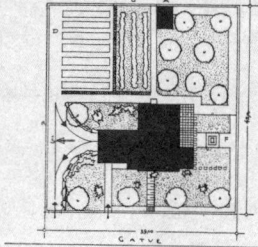

Pav. 93. Situacijos planas. F- fontanas, A- altana, U-
uogynas ir D- daržas.

142

Namas—mūrinis, dviejų aukštų, dengtas lėkštais, vienašlai-
čiais skardos stogais. Prie terasės galo prijungta pergola. Po
namo dalimi darytiname rūsyje tilptų garažas, centr. šildymo
patalpos, skalbykla ir sandėliai. II-ram aukšte numatyta ne-
aukšta be lubų patalpa (6), kaip pastogė. Žinoma, jos galima
ir nedaryti, tada priestatas būtų tik vieno aukšto.

I aukšte talpa:
1) gyvenamasis — 38,22 kv. mtr.; 2) valgomasis — 16,06
kv. mtr.; 3) serviravimo — 3,75 kv. mtr.; 4) tarnaitės kamba-
rėlis — 3,32 kv. mtr.; 5) produktų sandėliukas — 1.75 kv. mtr.;

Pav. 94. Namo perspektyvinis vaizdas.

6) virtuvė — 6,90 kv. mtr.; 7) holas su laiptais — 17,86 kv. mtr.;
8) v. klozetas — 1,56 kv. mtr.; 9) tamburas — 2,70 kv. metr.;
10) kabinetas — 7,36 kv. mtr.; 11) reikmenų sandėliukas —
6,45 kv. mtr. ir 12) braižykla — 14.85 kv. mtr..

Šalia gyvenamojo yra veranda — 9,37 kv. mtr. ir greta —
terasė — 20,45 kv. mtr..

II aukšte talpa:
1) miegamasis — 19,11 kv. mtr.; 2) mažas miegamasis —
9,61 kv. mtr.; 3) miegamasis — 13,02 kv. mtr.; 4) miegamasis

143

building, very close to the minimal single-family house design he
published in his book.[fig.8a–c]

In the late 1930s, Švipas became a leader of the large state project
dedicated to the modernization of brick construction. Although the
boom in construction in Lithuania optimistically was associated
with the construction of the modern state, building standards in the
mid-1930s still lagged behind those in the rest of Europe, and even
behind those of neighboring Latvia and Estonia. Engineers kept saying
that one of the reasons for this was a shortage of bricks. In 1937, brick
construction accounted for only six percent of all buildings (traditional
construction material was timber), although thirty-eight percent of
urban houses were made with brick. In 1937, an active "Brick Lithuania" campaign was launched in the press. By March 1939, the government had approved a plan for brick construction development, which
was actually a state development plan to promote the industry for
building materials. The plan involved increasing brick production,
establishing a local cement industry, reducing the cost of brick, establishing a state construction company, and modern urban planning
(densification). Authored by Švipas and economist Vladas Juodeika—
a graduate of Graz University, an official at the Ministry of Finance,
and later the director of the Department of Industry—the 122-page
text of the plan was under preparation for almost a year.[25] Both
authors were young professionals, typical of the new generation of
Western-educated civil servants involved in the rationalization,
planning, and management of the state economy.

The "Brick Lithuania" plan was unique and innovative in the
context of Lithuania, as it set building standards as part of a series of
economic and demographic forecasts and data research. According
to the authors, all of Lithuania's construction should be built entirely

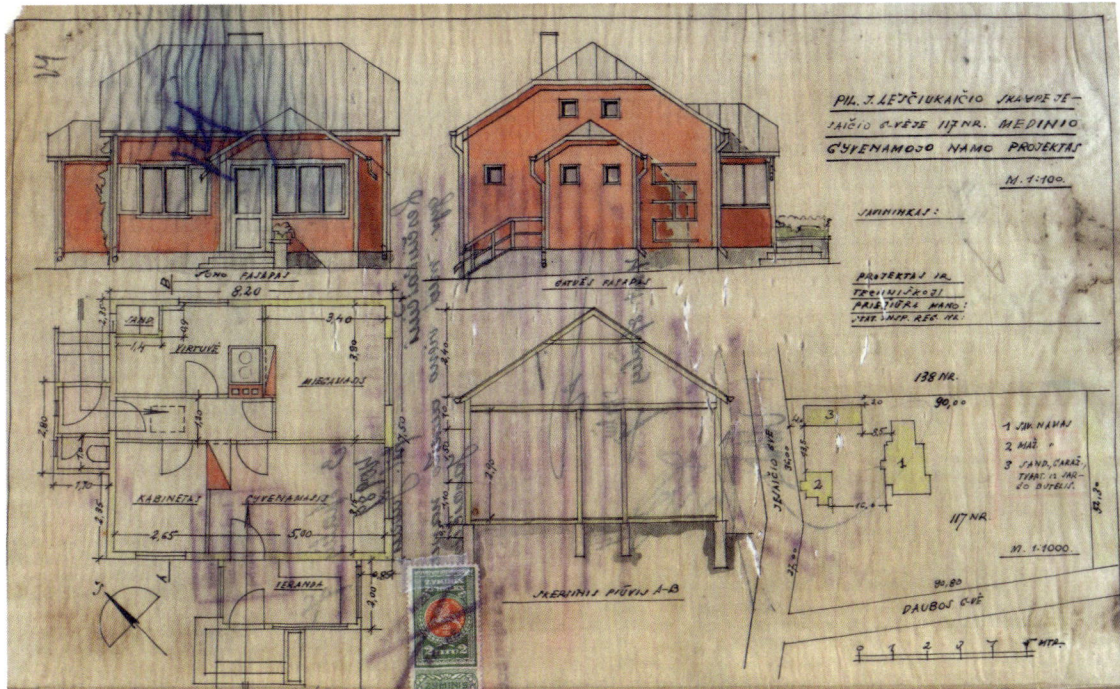

Fig. 7. Design for the model engineer's house in Vladas Švipas's book *Miesto gyvenamieji namai. Jiems statomi reikalavimai ir jų projektavimas* (Town Houses: Their Design and Requirements), published in Kaunas in 1933.
Fig. 8a. Vladas Švipas's design for a wooden house for Juozas Lesčiukaitis family in Kaunas, A. Jasaičio Street No. 4, in 1933 (the house did not survive). *Kaunas Regional State Archives*, f. 218, ap. 2, b. 2049, p. 14
Fig. 8b, c. Vladas Švipas with his family at his own house, Kaunas, 1939.

of brick by 2000–2030. This plan can be viewed as a logical result of Švipas's activities promoting the rational planning for the entire country. The press called the plan "one of the most daring and popular initiatives by government," and the prime minister in his 1939 speech wished that "in the next twenty years, Lithuania would become fully electrified and built of brick."[26]

Though Europe's new countries adopted modernism as the foundation of a new national architecture, they were faced with the dilemma of aiming to reconcile modernity with the pursuit of unique national identities.[27] By the 1930s, the architecture in Kaunas was sufficiently diverse: graduates of the University of Lithuania and some specialists trained in Italy and France adhered to a decorative, emotional style of architecture, while students graduating from German-curriculum schools were more inclined to a rational approach, taking an interest in urban planning issues. As in many European countries under authoritarian regimes, proponents of the Lithuanian national style criticized the internationalism as being incapable of expressing the national spirit. Lithuanian politicians avoided excessive intrusion into architecture, but President Antanas Smetona did feel the need to voice his doubts in 1937.

> Are we not seeing too much of a rise in so-called modernism, with our engineers taking so much from Italy and other Western countries? After all, we admire and take pride in the heritage of our Lithuanian farmhouses, crosses and chapels. Why don't our architects create something Lithuanian? We mustn't lose Lithuania's national identity in our effort to modernise.[28]

Indeed, not the political speeches, but tradition and the priorities of a new state bureaucracy played the most important role in restraining avant-garde social and architectural experiments in Kaunas. Rather than emerging as center of radical modernism, it eventually embraced an intermediate path between modernism and classical tradition. Architects did not shy away from incorporating decorative details (cornices, niches and bas-relief ornamentation); the flat roofs were rarely seen, replaced instead by a unique design of low-pitched tiled roofs with cornices. In the latter half of the 1930s, architects began to embrace a new traditionalism, featuring elements of modernized neoclassicism. As a result, Kaunas saw the gradual proliferation of the Art Deco style, which was seen as both sufficiently modern and receptive to individual stylization—with multiple examples of the Lithuanian national approach appearing in interior designs in particular.

Švipas also reflected on the issue of national style, which was constantly being debated in the Lithuanian architectural environment by the older generation of nationally driven politicians and intellectuals. Like many modernists of his generation, he aimed for an international modernism: "Lifestyle creates the basis for the forms and styles of Lithuanian cities. Phantasies and imaginary national styles are not going to take root, as they haven't anywhere else," Švipas wrote in 1933.[29] However, in the late 1930s he started to advocate the study of ethnic architectural heritage as the basis for the national architecture,[30] took part in ethnographic travels throughout Lithuania, proposed establishing an open-air folk museum, and wrote an article about the historic architecture of Lithuania.[31] This interest of Vladas Švipas developed even further in the postwar years, under the rather dramatic circumstances of the life of an émigré. In retrospect, it might be that in the premonition of leaving the country, he looked for its historical features and localities, overwriting his modernist principles of borderless internationalism.

The period of the first Soviet occupation and the Second World War was a turbulent time in Kaunas. When the Soviets occupied Lithuania in June 1940, they closed the Chamber of Agriculture and reorganized it into the Commissariat of Agriculture in August 1940. Švipas continued to work for the Construction Department, but left the office in July 1941 to work as Vice Minister of the Municipal Economy for the short-lived Lithuanian Provisional Government (June 24 to August 5, 1941), which aimed to maintain local government under Nazi occupation. When the Provisional Government was dissolved, he worked as director of the Construction Directorate in 1941–44 (now under the Nazi government), and also lectured at the Department of Architecture of Vytautas Magnus University in Kaunas from 1942 to 1944.

In July 1944, with the German front line breached and the Soviet army arriving in Lithuania, almost 60,000 Lithuanian citizens left with the German front, escaping from the threat of Soviet terror. Like many intellectuals and professional people, Švipas also left Lithuania with his family (a wife named Bronė and two daughters: Raminta, born in 1934, and Daiva, 1937) and fled in the direction of Germany. After the German capitulation, the United Nations Relief and Rehabilitation Administration (UNRRA) was appointed to take care of the mass number of refugees, accommodating them in displaced persons' (DP)

*Marija
Drėmaitė*

Bringing
Bauhaus
Modernism
to
Lithuania

V. ŠVIPAS, 25 ha ūkiui gyv. namo projektas; III premija

Inz. Archit. VLADAS ŠVIP,
laimėjęs už miesto namu
projekta II ir už kaimo nam
projekta III premijas

V. ŠVIPAS, miesto gyv. namo projektas; II premija

Fig. 9. Vladas Švipas's competition entry for the architectural competition organized by the Association of the Lithuanian Expatriate Engineers at Dillingen DP Camp, Germany, *Inžinieriaus kelias* 7 (1947).

camps. Švipas's family settled at the displaced persons' camp in Dillingen, Germany, where he worked as an administrator, but also took up design tasks.

Optimistic that with the help of the United States, the Baltic states would soon regain their independence and refugees would be able to return to their homeland, Lithuanian DPs showed an active architectural life at the DP camps. In 1944, Lithuanian refugee engineers and architects in Germany established an Association of the Lithuanian Expatriate Engineers with 345 members in 1946, and even organized architectural competitions for the reconstruction of Lithuania after the war.[32] One such architectural competition was organized in 1946, in search of the ideal future Lithuanian house, and Švipas received two prizes—a second prize for a single-family town house design, and a third prize for a single-family village house design.[fig.9] [33] So in the small town of Dillingen, close to the French border, the memories of the Bauhaus seemed far away as he now designed houses in Lithuanian vernacular style. He also published a long article on the characteristics of the future Lithuanian architecture in the Association's professional magazine, *Inžinieriaus kelias* (The Engineer's Way), in which he further developed his ideas about brick construction.[34]

But soon his Bauhaus connections became relevant again. In 1947, a new immigration law ratified in the United States allowed 30,000 Lithuanians into the country (in 1951, around 300 immigrant Lithuanian architects and engineers were counted in the US).[35] Švipas and his family arrived in New York in 1949. Correspondence between Švipas and Walter Gropius between 1948 and 1953 shows that Gropius helped his former student in finding an architectural job in the USA and obtaining the professional license.[36] Švipas stayed in Brooklyn, New York, where he found work in design offices, and later purchased a house in Queens in 1953. There is not much of a record of where in

Fig. 10. Vladas Švipas in the architectural office in New York (not specified, not dated, circa late 1950s)

particular he worked, but his encyclopedic entry says that he designed schools, hospitals, airports, and offices.[fig.10] [37] In parallel, he became a very active member of the Lithuanian émigré engineer associations in the US—in 1950, Švipas was elected a vice-chairman of the central board of the Association of American Lithuanian Engineers and Architects and read a keynote presentation on the architecture of the new era at the Association's congress in February.[38] He died in New York in 1965.

The architectural career of Vladas Švipas presents several different stages of adaptation to different political agendas and even countries, as an experience of a migrant. As an architect, writer and public intellectual in the interwar period, he eagerly participated in building a new identity for the modern Lithuanian state through modern architecture and rational planning. However, his career can be seen as a conflict between that of a free-thinking Bauhaus graduate and that of a state architect who had little chance to present his creative side. On the other hand, the opportunities that were opened to Švipas as a head of the Construction Department of the Chamber of Agriculture allowed him to draw up modernization plans for the entire country—in rural modernization and in the grand Plan for the Brick Construction Development. Therefore, his ambitions of rational planning could be fulfilled. In the late 1930s, though he remained in favor of rational planning, he began to demonstrate a certain conservatism of a civil servant with some more outspoken national sentiments, which grew even more noticeable under the nostalgic atmosphere in emigration.

Švipas's career, on which we must still find more data and insight in order to be able to portray the complex struggles he had to face, exemplifies the ambitions of a young artist and architect who had trained at one of the most avant-garde institutions, but also of one who struggled to find his ground and sphere of influence within the maelstrom of the dangerously changing sides of stylistic meaning, political allies, employers, and ideologies. His life and work certainly had a strong influence on the architecture and planning of Lithuania, but could also be described as part of the narrative about the fading paths of Bauhaus influence.

Marija
Drėmaitė

Bringing
Bauhaus
Modernism
to
Lithuania

451

The author thanks Ines Weizman for her generous help with translation and archival sources.

1   *Architecture of Optimism: The Kaunas Phenomenon, 1918–1940*, ed. M. Drėmaitė (Vilnius: Lapas, 2018), 15–20.

2   Steven Mansbach, "Modernism and Nationalist Architecture in the First Lithuanian Republic," in *Neue Staaten – neue Bilder? Visuelle Kultur im Dienst staatlicher Selbstdarstellung in Zentral- und Osteuropa seit 1918*, ed. Arnold Bartetzky, Marina Dmitrieva, and Stefan Troebst (Cologne: Böhlau Verlag, 2005), 47–55.

3   Giedrė Jankevičiūtė, *Dailė ir valstybė. Dailės gyvenimas Lietuvos Respublikoje, 1918–1940 m* (Art and the State: Artistic Life in the Republic of Lithuania from 1918 to 1940) (Kaunas: Nacionalinis M. K. Čiurlionio dailės muziejus, 2003), 178–198.

4   Inžinierių ir technikų sąrašas (List of Engineers and Technicians), *Savivaldybė* 1933, no. 6: 40–43; 1933, no. 7: 36–40.

5   Another student, Moï Ver (Moshé Raviv-Vorobeichic), who was born in 1904 in Vilnius (Lithuania, then a part of the Russian Empire) also came to the Bauhaus in Dessau to take courses with Paul Klee, Wassily Kandinsky, and Joseph Albers in 1927, before he left for Paris to study at the École de Photo Ciné. He emigrated to Palestine in 1934, and from 1950 he devoted himself to painting. He died in 1995. His first photography book, "The Ghetto Lane in Vilna" (published in 1931), documented the everyday life of the city's Jewish residents. Because Vilnius in the 1920s and 1930s was a part of Poland, Vladas Švipas is the only known person from the Republic of Lithuania to study at the Bauhaus. Correspondence with Ines Weizman. (Thanks to Ita Heinze-Greenberg, interviewed about Moï Ver and *Bauhäusler* in Palestine by the Center for Documentary Architecture, August 2018.)

6   Juozas Zikaras (1881–1944) was one of the first professional Lithuanian sculptors. He graduated from the Imperial Academy of Arts in St. Petersburg in 1916, and in 1919–1929 was an art teacher at the Panevėžys State Gymnasium. As one of the most active sculptors in Lithuania, he served as head of the sculpture studio at the School of Fine Arts in Kaunas in 1928–1944.

7   Vladas Švipas, "A letter from Prague to the Lithuanian Association of Artists," March 18, 1922. National Martynas Mažvydas Library of Lithuania, Department of Manuscripts, F7-866.

8   Vladas Švipas, personal file of the state scholarship recipient, Lithuanian Central State Archives, f. 391, ap. 9, b. 961. Regarding Švipas's studies at the Bauhaus, see also records of Bauhaus-Archiv Berlin.

9   Gustav Adolf Platz, *Die Baukunst der neuesten Zeit* (Berlin: Propyläen Verlag, 1927).

10   File of Vladas Švipas's application to the University of Lithuania, 1929, Lithuanian Central State Archives, f. 631, ap. 7, b. 7294, pp. 8–9.

11   Although no archival evidence could be found, there might also have been personal connections between Švipas and other Bauhaus students from the Oldenburg region, such as Karl Schwoon, Herman Gautel, Hin Bredendieck and Hans Martin Fricke; the latter also studied architecture at the Hindenburg-Polytechnikum in Oldenburg after his studies at the Bauhaus. Regarding these four Bauhaus students in Oldenburg, see: Gloria Köpnick and Rainer Stamm, *Zwischen Utopie und Anpassung – Das Bauhaus in Oldenburg* (Petersberg: Michael Imhof Verlag, 2019).

12   Vladas Švipas, "Architektūros reikalu" (On Architecture), *Kultūra* 7–8 (1927): 329–334.

13   See biographical files at the Bauhaus-Archiv Dessau (thanks to Sylvia Ziegner) and at the Bauhaus-Archiv Berlin (thanks to Nina Schönig).

14   "Interview mit Bauhäuslern: Vladas Švipas," *bauhaus zeitschrift für gestaltung* 4, no. 2 (1928): 20. Translation by Simon Cowper.

15   Vladas Švipas, personal file of the employee of the Construction Department at the Chamber of Agriculture, Lithuanian Central State Archives, f. 392, ap. 3, b. 1309.

16   Lithuanian exhibition at the 1937 World Expo in Paris. Three Baltic countries—Lithuania, Latvia and Estonia—built a shared Baltic Pavilion after an architectural competition, won by Estonian architect Alexander Nürnberg. Each of the three countries had a separate exhibition space in the pavilion. The Lithuanian exhibition was designed by the joint national artistic committee.

Part 3

Bauhaus
Architects
in
Exile

17   Vladas Švipas, "Menas ir technika" (Art and Technology), *Kultūra* 1928, no. 7–8: 334–337; no. 9: 394–397; Vladas Švipas, "Kultūringos gyvenimo formos" (Cultural Ways of Life), *Naujas žodis* 1929, no. 9: 6–7; Vladas Švipas, "Butas egzistencijos minimumui" (An Apartment for the Existenzminimum), *Naujas žodis* 1929, no. 20–21: 10–11.

18   Vladas Švipas, *Miesto gyvenamieji namai. Jiems statomi reikalavimai ir jų projektavimas* (Town Houses: Their Design and Requirements) (Kaunas, 1933).

19   Vladas Švipas, *Miesto gyvenamieji namai*, 17. Translation by the author.

20   Vladas Švipas, *Miesto gyvenamieji namai*, 49. Translation by the author.

21   Bronė Švipaitė, *Pažvelgęs į namus – šeimininkę pažįsi* (When You Look at a Home – You Will Know the Housewife) (Kaunas: Žemės ūkio rūmų leidinys, 1930).

22   Elena Starkienė, ed., *Namie ir svečiuose* (Home and Away) (Kaunas: Žaibas, 1938).

23   Vladas Švipas, *Miesto gyvenamieji namai*, 86.

24   Vladas Švipas design for a wooden family house for Juozas Lesčiukaitis in Kaunas, A. Jasaičio Street No. 4, in 1933 (the house did not survive). Kaunas Regional State Archives, f. 218, ap. 2, b. 2049, p. 14.

25   *Mūrinės statybos ugdymo planas* (The Plan for Brick Construction Development) (Kaunas: Ekonominių studijų draugijos leidinys, 1938).

26   "Priimtas mūrinės statybos ugdymo planas" (The Brick Lithuania Plan Was Approved), *Amatininkas* 7 (1939): 2.

27   David Crowley, "National Modernisms," in *Modernism: Designing a New World* (London: Victoria and Albert Museum), 341–360.

28   "J. E., Lietuvos Respublikos prezidentas rašo" (Commentary by His Excellency, the President of the Republic of Lithuania), *Technika ir ūkis* 1937 no. 2: 1.

29   Vladas Švipas, *Miesto gyvenamieji namai* (Kaunas, 1933), 87.

30   Vladas Švipas, "Architektūra tautos kultūroje" (The Role of Architecture in the National Culture), *Naujoji Romuva* 1937, no. 4–5: 107–108.

31   Vladas Švipas, "Lietuvių architektūros praeities bruožai" (Characteristics of Lithuanian Historic Architecture), an article for the unpublished issue of the cultural journal *Kūryba*

1944, no. 6. Manuscript, Lithuanian National Martynas Mažvydas Library, Department of Manuscripts, F. 31–527.

32   "Gyvenamųjų namų projektų konkursas, Augsburg, 1946 09 28," (Architectural Competition for a Dwelling), *Inžinieriaus kelias* 1946, no. 4: 13–14. Forty-five competition entries were submitted by about thirty authors.

33   Vladas Švipas, "Gyvenamų namų projektų konkursui pasibaigus" (After the Architectural Competition for a Dwelling), *Inžinieriaus kelias* 1947, no. 7 (January–April): 46–48; "Gyvenamų namų konkursas" (Competition for a Dwelling), *Ibid.*, 54–60.

34   Vladas Švipas, "Lietuvių architektūros ateities bruožai," *Inžinieriaus kelias*, Augsburg, 1946, no. 4: 1–4.

35   *Annual Journal of American Lithuanian Engineers and Architects of New York*, 24 June 1949 – 24 February 1951 (New York, 1951): 1.

36   Some of the letters to Walter Gropius (two letters from Švipas, three letters to him, 1953) are preserved at the Bauhaus-Archiv Berlin and at the Harvard University Library (Walter Gropius papers: six letters from Švipas, five letters to him, 1948–1951). Walter-Gropius-Archiv, GN Box no. 7, Magazines, Other Publications, Portfolio 438. See also the forthcoming publication by Marija Drėmaitė and Robertas Motuzas, "Vladas Švipas – Walter Gropius. Laiškai, 1948–1953 m. (Correspondence, 1948–1953)," *Lietuvos istorijos studijos / Studies of Lithuania's History* 43 (2019).

37   "Švipas Vladas," *Lietuvių enciklopedija* (Lithuanian Encyclopaedia), vol. 30 (Boston: Lietuvių enciklopedijos leidykla, 1964), 248–249.

38   *Amerikos lietuvių inžinierių ir architektų draugijos New Yorke metraštis* (A Yearbook of the Lithuanian Society of Architects and Engineers in New York), ed. K. Krulikas (New York, 1951).

Ines Sonder

"i have 'changed color' from job to job, and people have always believed me" Bauhäusler and architect Selman Selmanagić in Palestine (1934–38)

Selman Selmanagić (1905–86) was one of the twenty-five or so Bauhaus students and graduates who were active in the 1930s in what was then the British Mandate of Palestine.[1] The majority of them were of Jewish descent, including a few who had already lived in Palestine prior to studying at the Bauhaus.[2]

However, most of them came to the country as refugees from Germany. Selmanagić's Muslim heritage gave him a special status within this group, as his journey to Palestine was prompted neither by Nazi persecution nor by Zionist motives. Although he was not an émigré in the sense of having been hounded into exile by racist attacks, as a communist he was a political migrant, and as an architect an economic migrant, owing to the circumstances prevailing in the 1930s both in Germany and in his native Yugoslavia.

Selmanagić's time in Palestine is a pretty much uncharted facet of his richly varied life. "Study trips to Turkey, Greece, Syria, Jordan, Palestine, and Egypt" and "Many years of traveling in the countries of the Middle East" were the first concise entries in the jungle of dust and data.[3] This cast very little critical light on his personal and professional experiences as a "wanderer between worlds." And to this day there is still a lack of key information, as documented records continue to clash with unsubstantiated reports.[4] One important source is Selmanagić's letter to his Bauhaus friend Hajo Rose, sent from Jerusalem and dated October 1, 1935, in which he reports on the period after finishing his studies at the Bauhaus, his travels, and the early part of his stay in Palestine.[5] It makes clear above all that his characteristic cultural openness was decidedly controversial, even confrontational, in the heated ideological climate of the British Mandate.

The research carried out to date on the history of architecture in Israel in the 1930s has also paid little attention to Selmanagić's Palestinian work, as its primary focus has been on the life and work of Jewish architects.[6] Moreover, in the discourse on the topic of the "Bauhaus in Palestine"[7]—beyond the hype surrounding Tel Aviv as the putative "Bauhaus city"—there are still significant gaps in our knowledge: it is unclear, for example, whether and to what extent the Bauhäusler working in Palestine collaborated with one another.

Selman Selmanagić was one of six Bauhaus students from the former Kingdom of Yugoslavia.[8] Although he was officially born on April 25, 1905, in Srebrenica—at that time part of the Austro-Hungarian Empire—his actual birthplace is said to have been Istanbul.[9] He was from an aristocratic Muslim Bosnian family that had fallen on hard times. His father worked as a farmer. At the age of fourteen, he began studying carpentry at the state-run vocational school in Sarajevo (1919–23) and then completed training at the trade school in Ljubljana (1924–25), from which he graduated with a master's certificate as a carpenter and cabinetmaker. After a year of military service, he worked as a carpenter in Srebrenica until 1929. As he had heard that there were modern furniture factories in Germany, he planned to go to Berlin to enter a joinery to gain further experience. On the train to Berlin, one of his fellow travelers was a German who spoke some Serbo-Croatian. He drew Selmanagić's attention to the Bauhaus, telling him that following its move from Weimar to Dessau in 1926, its progressiveness and technical focus had given it a particular appeal to students from Germany and abroad. Equipped with a dictionary and a letter of recommendation from the Yugoslavian consulate in Berlin, he arrived at the Bauhaus in Dessau in October 1929. Initially he worked there in the carpentry workshop to earn a living for himself. Later he wrote, "During that period I learnt that it is harder to build a plain cupboard than one with ornamentation."[10] Up to that time, his carpentry designs had featured Arabic decorations and rosettes.

In winter semester 1929/30, Selmanagić started the preliminary course as part of a group of fifty-six students. The twenty-four-year-old was fascinated by Josef Albers's teaching of form through practice and by Paul Klee's elementary course. However, his modest language skills in German led to him failing the preliminary course—together with thirty-five others.[11] At the intervention of the student council, he was

Ines
Sonder

Bauhäusler
and
architect
Selman
Selmanagić
in
Palestine

455

nevertheless admitted to the second semester, initially as a guest student in the building and interior design workshop.

The student council also included members of the communist cell, which supported student sympathizers from the working class. The communist student group (Kostufra) had been founded by Béla Scheffler at the Bauhaus Dessau in the summer of 1927 and was headed by Albert Buske from 1928 until the middle of 1930.[12] Through him and his student friends Isaak Butkow and Waldemar Alder, Selmanagić was introduced to communism, the ideas of which determined his path through life from that point on.[13] He was still a member of the German Communist Party in 1930.

Swiss architect Hannes Meyer had been director of the Bauhaus since 1928: he himself was closely connected to the labor movement, and as a Marxist he supported the politicization of the school. After the departure of his predecessor Walter Gropius, the founder of the art school and its director from 1919 to 1928, Meyer had thoroughly overhauled the educational structure at the Bauhaus and introduced a programmatic shift whose keynote was "The needs of the people over the need for luxury." This rallying cry was directed against an elitist Stilarchitektur—an architecture based on historical style canons— and the idea of the new program was to develop inexpensive housing for workers on minimum wage. During his time in office, Meyer had also appointed guest instructors at the Bauhaus with left-wing leanings: these included Hermann Duncker, Otto Neurath, Karel Teige, and Georg Schmidt. The general training program was supplemented by lively lectures on a wide range of different areas of life, as Selmanagić and Hajo Rose, his comrade at the Bauhaus, later recalled.[14] On August 1, 1930, Meyer was dismissed without notice by the Dessau municipality on politically motivated grounds, amid heavy protests from the students, especially those on the left.

In winter semester 1930/31, with the school now under the directorship of Ludwig Mies van der Rohe, Selmanagić was admitted to the building and interior design department and attended the introductory design seminars offered by Ludwig Hilberseimer. The following winter, as part of Hilberseimer's urban development seminar, he was involved in a project for the Junkers estate in Dessau, which was designed for twenty thousand residents.[15] Operating under the rubric "Junkers builds for its workers," members of a socialist student collective, among them Waldemar Alder, Isaak Butkow, Wilhelm Heß,

Cornelius van der Linden, Hilde Reiss, Isaak Weinfeld, Wera Meyer-Waldeck, and Selman Selmanagić, were entrusted with specific design tasks. These included three-and four-story houses, high-rise apartment buildings, club houses and boarding houses, all-day kindergartens, a Kinderstadt (or "kids' city") with all-day kindergartens and schools, as well as theaters for stage and film. Selmanagić researched and devised an efficient street plan for traffic and transport needs and, together with Pius Pahl, designed the hospital complex and swimming pools with a restaurant.[16]

Besides being involved in various building contracts for the Bauhaus, including commissions in Czechoslovakia—for a sanatorium in the Tatras and a school—Selmanagić designed a home for the disabled and infirm and a cultural center in Zemun in 1931, both located in modern-day Belgrade.[17] He also built a house for his family in Zvornik (now part of Bosnia and Herzegovina)—it was the only project that he realized during his time at the Bauhaus. When Hilberseimer was shown the design, he called Selmanagić "Le Corbusier des Balkans."[18] In the summer semester of 1932, Mies van der Rohe's seminar produced a competition design for the state printing house in Belgrade for which he was awarded the first acquisition.[19] In August 1932, shortly before the school in Dessau closed, Selmanagić received the hundredth Bauhaus diploma, signed by Mies van der Rohe and Hilberseimer.[20]

After moving to Berlin, Selmanagić remained at the Bauhaus for a further semester.[21] He worked sporadically as a draftsman for Gropius's architectural firm and was involved in preparing plans for the CIAM conference in Athens. When the Bauhaus closed for good under pressure from the Nazis, Selmanagić initially returned to Yugoslavia for three months, where he took part in two competitions, including a design for Yugoslavia's state printing house (1933), which won fourth prize and was purchased by Yugoslavia's education ministry.[22] During this time, he received a visit from his former classmates Ernst Mittag, Albert Kahmke, and Albrecht Heubner, who were members of the communist cell at the Dessau Bauhaus. After their return to Nazi Germany, Heubner began suffering persecution at the hands of the fascists in mid-1933;[23] Mittag later emigrated to South Africa with his wife, photographer Etel Fodor-Mittag, who was also a Bauhäusler.[24]

For Selmanagić, returning to Germany was out of the question for the time being. However, the poor economic situation in his homeland meant that also there was little prospect of finding an acceptable position. He thus decided to use the competition prize money of 6,000 dinars to go to Constantinople, where he worked as a freelancer in the office of Halil Seyfi, a former student of architect Hans Poelzig, until March 1934. But since he had no real interest in this work, he made plans to travel to Afghanistan together with a German acquaintance. However, the plan was abandoned when his companion kept vacillating. "if i'd been alone," he wrote from Jerusalem to his friend Rose in 1935, "(you know me, i never seek out information, i just set off), i would now be in afghanistan, in much the same way as i once came to germany."[25] [fig. 1, 2]

In the end they decided to travel together to Cairo. From Turkey, they went by car and train via Syria and Palestine to Egypt, stopping for a few weeks in each place to explore the country.[26] Selmanagić found the contact with other cultures and architectural traditions stimulating: he was particularly fascinated by the ancient arts of Cairo. In this period, the decision took shape to settle for a time in Palestine. In a letter to Rose, he wrote,

> when i traveled through jewish territory for the first time, i thought it would be good to stay here for an extended period and to study the supposed economic boom. on the other hand, i was also interested in the jumble of different peoples, races, and religions.
> at the same time, I saw then that the country has really developed at a tremendous rate. here, as nowhere else, a very modern life is in stark contrast to very primitive ways dating back two thousand years (dwelling, craft, art). as a result, i have decided to come back and spend some time here.[27]

Since the early 1930s, the British Mandate in Palestine had experienced an unprecedented economic upswing that was particularly marked in the Jewish sector. It was triggered by the wave of migrants in the Fifth Aliyah, which brought around 250,000 German and central European Jews to Palestine at the outbreak of World War II. The emerging city of Tel Aviv, in particular, enjoyed a real construction boom in those years as the population grew significantly. Among the immigrants were many Jewish architects who had completed their training at architectural colleges and art schools in Germany and other parts of Europe. They transformed Tel Aviv into a "laboratory for architectural modernism"—an impulse that could be felt throughout the country and that helped create the legend of the "Bauhaus city"

Fig. 1. Selmanagić (left) and a traveling companion in Egypt, 1934.
Fig. 2. A ticket held by Selmanagić, April 21, 1933.
Fig. 3. Richard Kauffmann, Ambache House, Jerusalem, 1934–35, assisted by Selmanagić.

RICHARD KAUFFMANN ריכרד קאופמן
MEMBER TOWN PLANNING INSTITUTE
ARCHITECT AND TOWNPLANNER אדריכל ובונה ערים
JERUSALEM TEL. 1105 1105 .תל ירושלים
Jerusalem, 20.April 1935

Z e u g n i s s .

    Hierdurch bestaetige ich, dass Herr Diplom.Architekt
Salman Selmanagić vom 12 August 1934 bis 15 April 1935 in meinem
Architekturbuero als Architekt angestellt war.
    Herr Selmanagic hat waehrend dieser Zeit bei folgenden
Projekten mitgearbeitet:
Aufstockung Haus Granowsky, Jerusalem   Plaene   1:100
Villa Frau Dr.Strauss, Karmel Haifa   "   1:100
Haus Dr.Kruskal , Tel-Aviv. Aufstockung   1: 50
Villa Dr.Krojanker, Jerusalem   "   1:100
Aufstockung Haus Ing.Pomerantz, Jerusalem "   1:100
Haus Ing.Ambache, Jerusalem   "   1:100
Eingebaute Moebel Speisez.Schlafzimmer
Haus Dr.Waldmann, Jerusalem   Details

    Mit den Arbeiten von Herrn Architekt Selmanagić war
ich sehr zufrieden. Er verbindet eine gute kuenstlerische Begabung
in der Architektur mit besonderem Interesse und Eifer an den ihm
anvertrauten Arbeiten, und ich moechte darueber hinaus noch seine
persoenliche Zuverlaessigkeit besonders betonen.
    Herr Selmanagic verliess seine Stellung auf eigenen
Wunsch, um sich selbstaendig zu machen.
    Ich kann Herrn Selmanagic nur auf das waermste
empfehlen.

                    Dipl. Ing. Richard Kauffmann
                    Richard Kauffmann
                    Diplom Ing. Architekt

RICHARD KAUFFMANN
ARCHITECT AND TOWNPLANNER
JERUSALEM
ריכרד קאופמן
אדריכל ובונה ערים
ירושלם

Fig. 4. Richard Kauffmann,
Pomerantz House,
Jerusalem, 1932–36,
assisted by Selmanagić.
Fig. 5. Letter of reference
for Selmanagić by Richard
Kauffmann, April 20, 1936.

that took shape decades later when the "White City" of Tel Aviv was
added to the UNESCO World Heritage List in 2003.[28]

Selmanagić settled in Jerusalem. Having initially worked for
different employers, he found a position at the offices of architect and
urban planner Richard Kauffmann in August 1934. Kauffmann, a
native of Frankfurt am Main, had been brought to Jerusalem to head
the Zionist Executive's first department of urban development and
architecture in late 1920. He was given responsibility for planning
numerous agricultural community settlements—the kibbutzim and
moshavim—and the Jewish garden suburbs on the periphery of Palestinian cities.[29] After the department was dissolved in 1927, Kauffmann
ran his own office in Jerusalem, with construction contracts all over
the country. Selmanagić worked with Kauffmann for eight months
and was involved in several projects on a freelance basis, including the
upward extension of Dr. Granowsky's house in Jerusalem, the villa of
Dr. Krojanker, a house for Dr. Waldmann (with built-in furniture,
dining room, and bedroom), the upward extension to the Pomerantz
House, and the Ambache House, which was one of the biggest
buildings Kauffmann designed for a private client. Other commissions
included a villa for Dr. Strauss on Mount Carmel near Haifa and the
addition of an extra story to Dr. Kruskal's house in Tel Aviv.[30] [fig. 3–5]

In the early 1930s, Kauffmann had turned his back on the eclectic
style that was prevalent in Palestine. His buildings show a clear orientation toward the International Style with functional façades and flat
roofs, augmented by such details as roof overhangs, projecting concrete
slabs to provide shade, and small ventilation holes. These additions
were geared to efficiency and tailored to the country's climatic conditions. The façades of the buildings in Jerusalem were also typically
clad with Jerusalem stone, a practice that can be traced back to a
decree issued by the first British governor in the city, Ronald Storrs.
The use of white limestone later became a key feature of Selmanagić's
own practice in Jerusalem.

Besides photographs of the buildings he had a hand in while
working for Kauffmann, Selmanagić's estate has also preserved photos
that were taken during his stay in Palestine, showing buildings for which
we have no record of his involvement. These include Villa Aghion
in the Jerusalem district of Talbieh, which Kauffmann designed in
1935 for a wealthy Jewish couple from Egypt—it has served as the
official residence of Israel's prime minister since 1974; the Yeshurun

*Ines
Sonder*

Bauhäusler
and
architect
Selman
Selmanagić
in
Palestine

461

Synagogue, built between 1934 and 1936 by Alexander Friedman and Meir Rubin in the district of Rehaviah; and Villa Lea (Villa Abcarius), planned in 1934 by Dov and Raphael Ben Dor and later occupied by Ethiopian emperor Haile Selassie after his flight into exile. All three buildings are outstanding architectural examples of the International Style in Jerusalem, which Selmanagić presumably wanted to document for himself.

When Selmanagić stopped working with Kauffmann in April 1935, he left with a reference endorsing not only his "fine artistic talent in architecture and his particular interest and zeal in tackling the work entrusted to him" but also "his personal dependability." It further stated that Selmanagić had quit the position of his own volition in order to set up shop for himself. By his own account, however, his departure was not by choice. Kauffmann had been unaware at the beginning that Selmanagić was not a Jew, and their collaboration subsequently ended the moment he was alerted to this.[31] This episode yet again reflects the potential for ideological conflict that was an inherent part of building a "home for the Jewish people." The employment of non-Jewish workers was a general problem, starting with the Arab artisans and construction workers on Jewish building projects—who were used in the early years, in particular, because there was a shortage of skilled Jewish labor in the country—and extending to the Fellah who helped with the agricultural work in the Jewish settlements. For Kauffmann, too, the employment of a worker with a Muslim background would have posed problems for his Zionist conscience, even if he valued him as an architect. In his letter to Hajo Rose, Selmanagić wrote of the dilemma of religious and racial affiliation:

> i have been part of every race and religion (from moses to comintern).
> to be able to work for jews here, you must be jewish, and if you want to
> work for arabs, you must be mohamedan [sic]. consequently, i have
> "changed color" from job to job, and people have always believed me.
> in the process, i have seen that it depends solely on outward form—
> if i wear a red fez, i am taken for a mohamedan [sic]. if i don't wear
> it but can recite from the koran, no one believes me: they say I could
> have learned the text. and if i don't work on saturday, people think i am
> jewish. the whole thing is phoney. you know my perspective.[32]

Selmanagić's letter from Jerusalem was typed by Ricarda Schwerin—all in lower case, as had been standard practice at the Bauhaus since 1925. Ricarda (whose maiden name was Meltzer) and her husband,

Fig.6. Selman Selmanagić in Jerusalem, 1936.

Heinz Schwerin, had known Selmanagić since their time at the Bauhaus in Dessau; the couple had emigrated to Palestine three months earlier, in July 1935.[33] Heinz, a trained carpenter like Selmanagić, was a student representative and a member of the communist cell at the Bauhaus. After the Bauhaus scandal in the spring of 1932,[34] the couple were obliged to leave the school without graduating. After Heinz was imprisoned for a short period in April 1933 for illegally distributing leaflets, he could no longer be certain of his safety and well-being as a Jew and communist in Germany. Once in Jerusalem, after struggling at the start, the couple established the "Schwerin Wooden Toys" workshop.[35]

In the letter, Selmanagić also mentioned the names of other former *Bauhäusler*, whom he ran into again in Palestine: Arieh Sharon, Chanan Frenkel, Shlomo Bernstein, Shmuel Mestechkin, Bella Ullmann, Ruth Cohn (later Kaiser), Jaschek Weinfeld, Munio Weinraub, and Edgar Hecht. They were all busy and earning well. At the end of the letter, Ricarda wrote a personal note to a friend from her time in Dessau, whose photograph of "*Bauhäuslerin* Ricarda Melzer" (1930) later became famous:[36] "dear rose, i have tried to put what selman wanted to write you into generally comprehensible german. this is, however, at the expense of its originality, but it was impossible to type selman-german." [fig.6]

Reflecting on his professional situation at the time he wrote his letter, Selmanagić remarked, "i have recently been working for an arab, but the jackass has no idea about architecture and we had a row, and today, on the first [of October 1935], i quit. i'm planning to go into business for myself." [fig.7, 8]

His jobs as a self-employed architect included contracts for a joinery in Jerusalem (1935) and several private houses for Arab clients, including a villa in Gaza (1935) and a duplex for Dr. Abdallah Moghrabi (1937/38) in Jerusalem. In stylistic terms, the buildings have a clear debt to modernism, and their clarity and simplicity in the handling of proportions show how Selmanagić expanded on the ideas he had absorbed as a student of Mies van der Rohe. [fig.9, 10]

He also adapted typical regional elements of the International Style in Palestine, such as sun shields, pergolas on the flat roofs, and recessed balconies—specific features that he found already in use in

Ines
Sonder

Bauhäusler
and
architect
Selman
Selmanagić
in
Palestine

463

Fig. 7. Model for a furniture factory in Jerusalem, 1935.

Fig. 8. Design for a single-family house in Jerusalem, 1935.

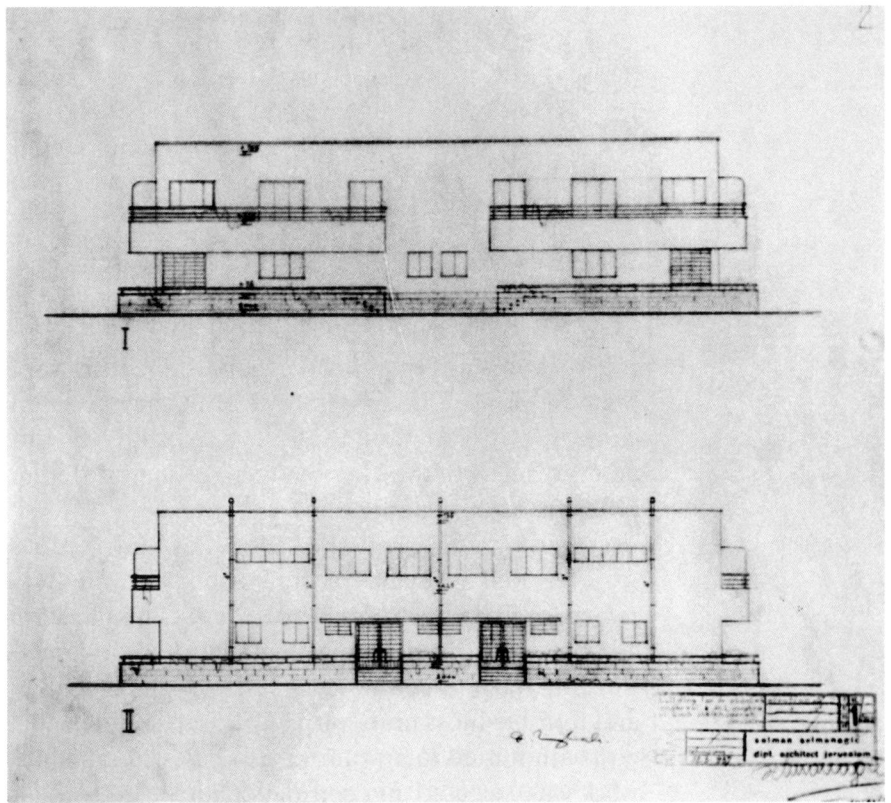

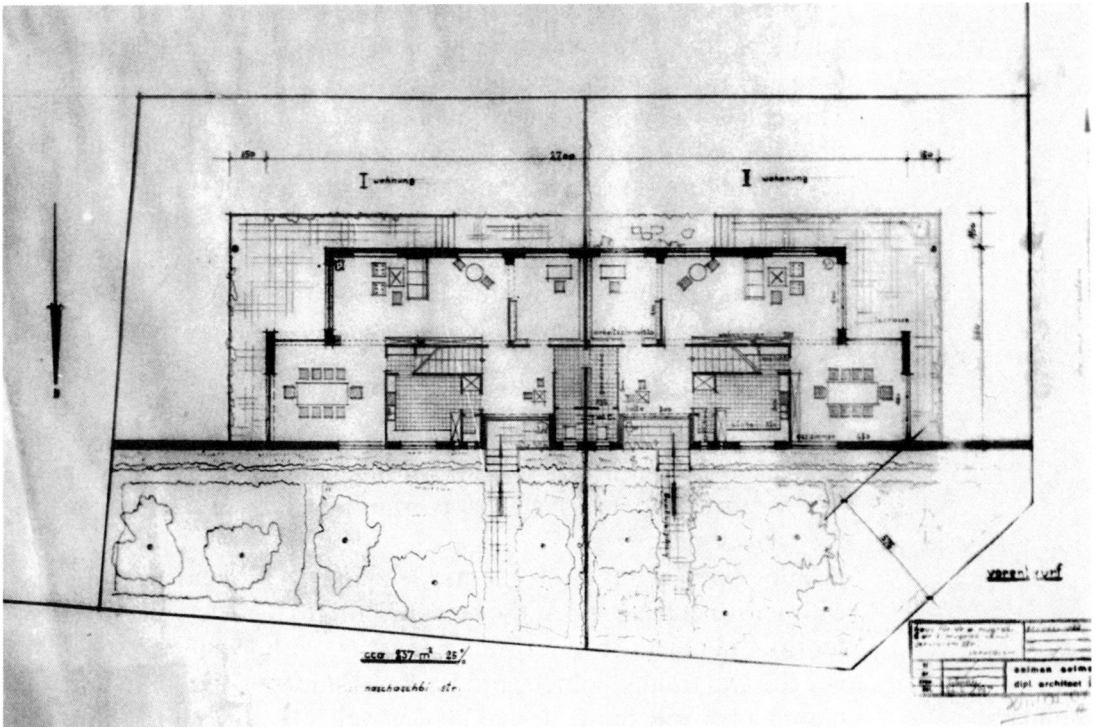

Fig. 9. Design for the duplex of Dr. Moghrabi, slanted view, 1937.

Fig. 10. Design for the duplex of Dr. Moghrabi, floor plan, 1937.

Fig. 11. Multiple-family dwelling in Jerusalem, model, 1937.

Fig. 12. Selmanagić (left) with Arab workmen in Jerusalem, 1937.

the work of Kauffmann and other architects in the country. For every building project, he sought to eke out the maximum of creativity and came up with functional solutions, modified by the particular location and the needs of the client in spite of their different ethnic and religious backgrounds.

Photographs show the "Model of Mufti's House in Jerusalem" (1937) as well as images of the finished building. There is an extant reference from the Supreme Moslem Council, Jerusalem, dated June 20, 1938, confirming that Selmanagić had designed a block for the Muslim Wakf: it contained seven completely equipped apartments and four business units with all the latest amenities. The construction costs amounted to around 12,000 Palestinian pounds. The building work was executed and completed under his sole supervision.[37] [fig. 11–14]

To put himself in a position to take on projects for Muslim municipalities, Selmanagić supposedly asked the mufti of Sarajevo for a letter of recommendation addressed to the mufti of Jerusalem. This tale is not without a certain poignancy. There can be no denying that the mufti of Jerusalem, Mohammed Amin al-Husseini, played a key role in propagating modern anti-Semitism in the Arab territories and collaborated with the Nazi regime.[38] However, Selmanagić was a communist and a fervent opponent of the Nazis, like his friends Hajo Rose and Heinz Schwerin. He had written to Rose as follows:

> and at this point i reject all theories of race and religion, because i know that it is all just a product of the general development of capitalism. i've seen just the same thing in every country i have been to. people here wanted to draw me into different racial and religious groups, and in order to live, i was obliged to play along, despite my different view on things. here i had the opportunity to study the whole sham from scratch.[39]

Besides his work for Arab clients, Selmanagić also realized projects with Jewish colleagues. At the beginning of 1937, he designed the seating for the Café Siedner in Jerusalem together with Heinz Schwerin.[40] For the two trained joiners and Bauhaus students, functional factors played a key role in the design here as well. Decades later, Selmanagić quoted Walter Gropius: "Anyone who can build a chair can also build a house."[41] He also designed the interior décor for the Café Tabor, which opened in 1935 in Ben Yehuda Street, a popular meeting place for Jewish emigrants in Jerusalem and the place to which Selmanagić had his mail sent intermittently.[42] It would seem that, in collaboration

Part 3

Bauhaus
Architects
in
Exile

466

المنوان البرقي : المجلس الاسلامي القدس

صندوق البريد : ٥١٧

التلفون : ٣٧٧ و ٣٧٨

العدد

الرقم

التاريخ

القدس الشريف

Supreme Moslem Council
Jerusalem.

June 20, 1938.

TO WHOM IT MAY CONCERN.

This is to certify that Architect Salman Salmanagich has designed and constructed for the Mosłem Wakf in Jerusalem a block containing seven complete appartments and four shops provided with all the most up-to-date accomodations, which costs about twelve thousand Palestinian Pounds.

The construction of the building was carried out and completed under his sole supervision and over 20 tenders were engaged on this building.

Architect Salman Salmanagich's work was very satisfactory.

Awkaf Officer,
Jerusalem.

with a Jewish architect, he developed suggestions for the repair of
the Wailing Wall, whose foundations he proposed strengthening by
injecting reinforced concrete.[43]

The beginning of the Arab revolt in April 1936, which culminated
in spring 1938, led to a general exacerbation of the political situation
in Palestine. Even though Selmanagić was able to keep doing projects
for Jewish and Arab clients during this period, his interest in the
cultural diversity of races and religions would have given way to the
recognition that the country was involved in an antagonistic and radicalized conflict. Back in 1935 he had written the following to Rose:

> *just as workers in germ. are being set against the jews, here jewish and
> arab workers are being pitted against each other. there is a tremendous
> hatred between the two groups, and the only people who stand to gain from
> this struggle are the bourgeoisie on both sides. i've had a clear view of this
> because i've been working on both sides of the divide.*[44]

One of the political activities that Selmanagić engaged in with other
communists living in Palestine was collecting money for the International Brigade, which was fighting for the Republicans against Franco
in the Spanish Civil War.[45] Heinz Schwerin had even considered going
to Spain, as he indicated in a letter to his friend Heinz Pol.[46] In it he
also complained that he was "without any contact with other people,
without any direct news material—just as if I were on the moon."[47]

Unlike Heinz Schwerin, Selmanagić was able to openly maintain
contact with his communist group at the Bauhaus, which included
architect Albert Buske.[48] At their request, he returned to Germany in
the early part of 1939 to join in the resistance to the Nazi regime. In
her essay in celebration of the hundredth anniversary of Selmanagić's
birth, Simone Hain writes:

> *There was nowhere where what was happening in Germany could be more
> clearly identified than in Jerusalem. Selmanagić knew about the dangers
> he was facing—he delayed his journey to Germany in 1938, vacillating
> for several weeks while he poked around in Italy. Set against the high level
> of risk, the illicit activities that he later undertook—by his own account—
> seem rather insignificant. Was it necessary for a foreign-looking man to be
> summoned specially from Jerusalem to intercept foreign transmissions in
> Germany and print leaflets? It is still unclear to this day why he was
> called. A politically motivated sense of obligation to the demands of friend-
> ship perceived as a response to party orders caused Selmanagić to take an
> extreme risk in the struggle against fascism.*[49] [fig.15]

*Ines
Sonder*

Bauhäusler
and
architect
Selman
Selmanagić
in
Palestine

469

In the early part of 1939, Selmanagić worked in Berlin, initially as a freelancer in the architecture offices of Egon Eiermann, who let him go shortly afterward on the grounds that "new instructions exclude the use of foreigners."[50] During World War II, he worked in the construction department at Universum Film AG (UFA) in Potsdam-Babelsberg, where he was involved in building and remodeling cinemas prior to 1942 and then as a set designer until 1945.[51]

One person who applied a critical eye to Selmanagić's return to Nazi Berlin—and more particularly the work he did (evidently unmolested by the Gestapo) as a communist and foreigner for the UFA, which was forced into line by Goebbels's propaganda ministry—was Jewish Serbian author and Shoah survivor Ivan Ivanji.[52] An exhibition mounted in 2009 about Bauhaus artist Franz Ehrlich[53] gave rise to his novel *Buchstaben von Feuer* (2011). It takes the form of bold literary fiction in which the author interweaves Selmanagić's biography with the twentieth-century environment of the intelligence services.[54] In his autobiographical novel *Mein schönes Leben in der Hölle*, he makes further reference to it:

> *In the course of World War II, many agents from all the important countries worked in Turkey and Palestine. Can Selman have been anything other than a double agent, only working for the Nazis pro forma, while actually staying true to the ideals of his youth and acting as a Soviet operative?* [55]

To his comrade friends, Selmanagić's allegiance was beyond question. At the end of the war, he was appointed head of the unit for cultural and recreational facilities by Hans Scharoun, the municipal building officer for the newly formed Berlin administration, which also included other members of the Berlin resistance group. In 1950 he was invited by Mart Stam to the Hochschule für angewandte Kunst—since 1969, the Weissensee Academy of Art Berlin—where he took over as director of the architecture department and remained as a professor of architecture until his retirement in 1970.[56]

Fig. 15. Selmanagić on his way back from Palestine to Germany, 1939.

Selmanagić never subsequently gave a detailed account of his years in Palestine. The "GDR's troubled relationship with Zionism and the State of Israel"[57] may provide a possible clue to the distance he took to the country and the creative period he had spent working there. He summed up the home he had adopted in one of his witty remarks, stating that "for all its Saxon efficiency and Prussian thoroughness," the country lacked "a sense of Jewish fantasy and oriental serenity"[58] —a comparison of mindsets that can be read as a form of reminiscence, recalling his years in voluntary exile in Palestine.

Selman Selmanagić died on May 7, 1986, in East Berlin. Now, decades after his death, the architect and university lecturer has been acknowledged as an "independent spirit" in his interpretation of modernism,[59] as characterized by "contradiction and self-assertion,"[60] and as a "Bauhäusler who influenced the way architecture was taught in the GDR."[61]

The editor and author would like to thank Jasemin Hundertpfund-Selmanagić for her kind permission to publish images from the family archive.

1   This essay is a revised and expanded version of the article "a communist muslim in israel," bauhaus: The Bauhaus Dessau Foundation's magazine 2 (November 2011): 36–39 (with Aida Abažić Hodžić).

2   See "routes to the promised land," bauhaus 2: 35.

3   See Kunsthochschule Berlin, ed., *Selman Selmanagić: Festgabe zum 80. Geburtstag am 25. April 1985*, Beiträge 10 (Berlin, 1985); Simone Hain, "Gegen die Diktatur des Auges: Selman Selmanagić zum 100. Geburtstag," Form + Zweck 21 (2005): 78–98.

4   Besides documents from his estate, much of the information is based on family lore.

5   See Selman Selmanagić to Hajo Rose, Jerusalem, October 1, 1935, Bauhaus-Archiv / Museum für Gestaltung Berlin, Selman Selmanagić, Folder 2, Letters.

6   See, for example, *Myra Warhaftig, Sie legten den Grundstein: Leben und Wirken deutschsprachiger jüdischer Architekten in Palästina, 1918–1948* (Tübingen, 1996).

7   On the continuing impact of the Bauhaus in Palestine/Israel, see Ita Heinze-Greenberg, "Bezalel und Bauhaus," David: *Jüdische Kulturzeitschrift* 112 (April 2017): 48–51; Gideon Ofrat, "a zionist bauhaus?," bauhaus 2 (see note 1): 30–33.

8   See Želimir Koščević, "Jugoslawische Bauhausschüler," *Wissenschaftliche Zeitschrift der Hochschule für Architektur und Bauwesen Weimar* 33, nos. 4–6 (1987): 328–30.

9   According to information supplied by his family, Selmanagić was born in Istanbul. However, most biographies surmise that his actual birthplace was Srebrenica, since his mother returned there shortly after giving birth and Selmanagić spent his childhood years there.

10   Heinz Hirdina, "Selman Selmanagić über das Bauhaus: Erinnerungen von Bauhäuslern an das Bauhaus," *form + zweck* 11, no. 3 (1979): 67–68, here: 67.

11   Insufficient knowledge of German was a problem for a great many international students at the Bauhaus.

12   See Michael Siebenbrodt, "Zur Rolle der Kommunisten und anderer fortschrittlicher Kräfte am Bauhaus," *Wissenschaftliche Zeitschrift der Hochschule für Architektur und Bauwesen Weimar* 23, nos. 5–6 (1976): 481–85.

13   See Sonja Wüsten, "Selman Selmanagić: Biographisches," in Kunsthochschule Berlin, *Selman Selmanagić* (see note 3), 6–41, here: 20.

Ines Sonder

Bauhäusler and architect Selman Selmanagić in Palestine

471

14 See Hajo Rose and Selman Selmanagić, "Erinnerungen an das Bauhaus," *Dessauer Kalender* 18 (1974): 56–58.

15 See "Das Bauhaus plant für Junkers eine 'Großsiedlung' in Dessau," Junkers, accessed November 7, 2017, www.junkers.de/junkers-und-das-bauhaus/das-bauhaus-plant-für-junkers-eine-„großsiedlung"-dessau.

16 See Klaus-Jürgen Winkler, *Baulehre und Entwerfen am Bauhaus 1919–1933* (Weimar, 2003), 119–20.

17 See "Curriculum des Studenten Selman Selmanagic," in Winkler, 158–61.

18 See Wüsten, Selman Selmanagić (see note 13), 11.

19 Reproductions of the floor plan and a perspective view can be found in Wüsten, 160–61. Originals at the Bauhaus-Universität Weimar.

20 Published in Kunsthochschule Berlin, *Selman Selmanagić* (see note 3), 20.

21 See "Bauhaus Berlin: Liste der Studierenden im Winter-Semester 1932/33," in *Bauhaus Berlin: Auflösung Dessau 1932, Schließung Berlin 1933, Bauhäusler und Drittes Reich. Eine Dokumentation*, zusammengestellt vom Bauhaus-Archiv Berlin, ed. Peter Hahn and Christian Wolsdorff (Weingarten, 1985), 294.

22 This was apparently the same design for the "state printing house in Belgrade" he had made in Mies van der Rohe's seminar. The project included thirteen drawings entitled "Space and Light." See Aida Abadžić Hodžić, *Selman Selmanagić und das Bauhaus* (Berlin, 2018), 106–07.

23 See Gerhard Franke, "Kommunistische und sozialdemokratische Bauhäusler für ein gemeinsames Ziel: Vernichtung der faschistischen Diktatur in Deutschland," *Wissenschaftliche Zeitschrift* 33, nos. 4–6 (see note 8): 325–27.

24 See Etel Mittag-Fodor, "Not an Unusual Life, for the Time and the Place – Ein Leben, nicht einmal ungewöhnlich für diese Zeit und diesen Ort," *Bauhäusler: Dokumente aus dem Bauhaus-Archiv Berlin*, vol. 3 (Berlin, 2014).

25 Selmanagić to Rose (see note 5).

26 Nothing is known about the precise route or the identity of Selmanagić's companion.

27 Selmanagić to Rose (see note 5).

28 See Ines Sonder, "Bauhaus Architecture in Israel: De-Constructing a Modernist Vernacular and the Myth of Tel Aviv's 'White City,'"

in *Handbook of Israel: Major Debates*, ed. Eliezer Ben-Rafael, Julius H. Schoeps, Yitzhak Sternberg, and Olaf Glöckner (Berlin, 2016), 87–101.

29 See Ines Sonder, *Gartenstädte für Erez Israel: Zionistische Stadtplanungsvisionen von Theodor Herzl bis Richard Kauffmann* (Hildesheim, 2005).

30 See reference from Richard Kauffmann, Jerusalem, April 20, 1935, Selmanagić family estate. Selmanagić worked for Kauffmann from August 12, 1934, to April 15, 1935. The reference is reproduced in bauhaus 2 (see note 1): 69.

31 See Abadžić Hodžić, *Selman Selmanagić* (see note 22), 392.

32 Selmanagić, letter to Rose (see note 5).

33 The address is given as c/o Mülgram, Aron St. 4, Rehavia, Jerusalem. There is no record of whether this was Selmanagić's or Schwerin's house.

34 The outward cause of the conflict between the Bauhaus management and the students was the allocation of income under license agreements from the sale of Bauhaus products. Student representatives Heinz Schwerin and Cornelius van der Linden demanded a cut in the masters' salaries and an increase in scholarship funding. The scandal erupted when a student assembly in the Bauhaus canteen was scheduled to debate the issue publicly: Mies van der Rohe forbade the meeting and had the police clear the canteen. After protests, fifteen students, among them Heinz Schwerin, were suspended by the school. Ricarda and others were banned from entering the building.

35 See Ines Sonder, "Vom Bauhaus nach Jerusalem: Die Fotografin Ricarda Schwerin (1912–1999)," in *Entfernt: Frauen des Bauhauses während der NS-Zeit; Verfolgung und Exil, Frauen und Exil* 5, ed. Inge Hansen-Schaberg, Wolfgang Thöner, and Adriane Feustel (Munich, 2012), 195–209.

36 See *Bauhaus: Fotografie aus der Sammlung der Stiftung Bauhaus Dessau*, ed. Lutz Schöbe, Stiftung Bauhaus Dessau (Dessau, 2004), 96.

37 See reference from the Supreme Moslem Council, Jerusalem, June 20, 1938, Selmanagić family estate.

38 See Klaus Gensicke, *Der Mufti von Jerusalem und die Nationalsozialisten: Eine politische Biographie Amin al-Husseinis* (Darmstadt, 2007).

39 Selmanagić, letter to Rose (see note 5).

40   Designs for a chair and a stool for the Café Siedner have been preserved in the estate of Heinz Schwerin, dated February 1, 1937. See Archiv Jutta Schwerin.

41   See Rose and Selmanagić, "Erinnerungen an das Bauhaus" (see note 14).

42   See Hannes Meyer, letter to Selman Selmanagić, September 26, 1937, Bauhaus-Archiv/Museum für Gestaltung Berlin, Selman Selmanagić, Folder 2, Letters. In the letter from Geneva, Meyer asked for Halil Seyfi's address in Istanbul.

43   Selmanagić supposedly went back to this idea when Berlin was being rebuilt after the devastation of World War II. See Simone Hain, "Berlin, schöner denn je: Stadtideen im Ostberliner Wiederaufbau," in DAM-*Jahrbuch* (Munich, 1992), 9–22.

44   Selmanagić, letter to Rose (see note 5).

45   See Wüsten, Selman Selmanagić (see note *13*), 22.

46   The journalist and author Heinz Pol (Pollack) was editor of the *Vossische Zeitung* until 1933 and wrote for the *Literarische Welt* and *Weltbühne*.

47   See Jutta Schwerin, *Ricardas Tochter: Leben zwischen Deutschland und Israel* (Leipzig, 2012), 51. In the letter cited here, he also wrote about his idea of going to Spain.

48   Other members of the group included architect Luise Seitz, painter Fritz Duda, and graphic designer Max Gebhard.

49   See Hain, "Gegen die Diktatur des Auges" (see note 3), 84.

50   Here he was involved in different projects, including a machine-tool factory in Velten, a crematorium for an undertaker named Grieneisen, and a fire extinguisher factory in Apolda. See reference from Egon Eiermann addressed to Selman Selmanagić, April 6, 1939, Bauhaus-Archiv/Museum für Gestaltung Berlin. See also "Selmanagic, Selman," Deutsche Fotothek, accessed November 7, 2017, www.deutschefotothek.de/documents/kue/70123060.

51   About his work for the UFA, see Abadžić Hodžić, *Selman Selmanagić* (see note 22), 148–158.

52   Ivan Ivanji, born in 1929 in Banat, Serbia, has worked as a writer, translator, diplomat, and journalist. In 1944 he was deported to the Auschwitz concentration camp and then to Buchenwald. After World War II he worked as, among other things, an interpreter for Yugoslav president Josip Broz Tito.

53   See Franz Ehrlich, *Ein Bauhäusler in Widerstand und Konzentrationslager*, a special exhibition mounted by the Buchenwald and Mittelbau-Dora Memorials Foundation in conjunction with the Klassik Stiftung Weimar and the Bauhaus Dessau Foundation, Neues Museum Weimar, August 2, 2009 – October 11, 2009.

54   See Ivan Ivanji, *Buchstaben von Feuer* (Vienna, 2011). His literary hypothesis was chiefly disseminated in Croatian Internet portals, including an interview with Ivan Ivanji, "Vječna u životu samo je promjena" (2011), www.vijesti.me/caffe/vjecna-u-zivotu-samo-je-promjena-4204; Ivan Ivanji, "Šmit, Šreder, Tito i Selman Selmanagić iz Srebrenice" (2014), www.vreme.com/cms/view.php?id=1188825; Muharem Bazdulj, "Neimar iz Srebrenice" (2015), www.vreme.com/cms/view.php?id=1309659. All sites accessed November 7, 2017.

55   He went on to add, "After the novel came out, I was curious as to whether Selman's heirs—there is still a Selmanagić architectural firm in Berlin to this day—would get in touch, and possibly even protest. This has not been the case." See Ivan Ivanji, *Mein schönes Leben in der Hölle* (Vienna, 2014), 237.

56   Elmar Kossel, "Widerspruch und Selbstbehauptung: Der Mies-Schüler Selman Selmanagić und die Kunsthochschule in Berlin-Weissensee," *M Mies Haus Magazin* 9 (2012): 35–37.

57   See Angelika Timm, *Hammer, Zirkel, Davidstern: Das gestörte Verhältnis der DDR zu Zionismus und Staat Israel* (Bonn, 1997).

58   Cited in Hain, "Gegen die Diktatur des Auges" (see note 3), 83.

59   See Michael Kasiske, "Auf Hochglanz getrimmt: Selmanagićs Aula an der Kunsthochschule Weißensee," *Bauwelt* 8 (2012): 2.

60   Kossel, "Widerspruch und Selbstbehauptung" (see note 56), 34.

61   See Abadžić Hodžić, *Selman Selmanagić* (see note 22), blurb.

Ines Sonder

Bauhäusler
and
architect
Selman
Selmanagić
in
Palestine

473

Veronica Bremer

The Design Centre in Sydney and its Bauhaus Origins

Fig. 1. The Design Centre, 1939. From left to right: Dahl Collings, Geoffrey Collings, and Richard Haughton James.
Fig. 2. Portrait of Richard Haughton James, 1930s.
Fig. 3. Passport issued to Geoffrey Collings by the Commonwealth of Australia on April 8, 1930. From left to right: Dahl and Geoffrey Collings.

In 1939, Australian couple Dahl (1909–88) and Geoffrey Collings (1905–2000) and British expatriate Richard Haughton James (1906–85) established the Design Centre, an industrial design studio in Sydney, Australia. Although the Design Centre existed for only one year, it was one of the earliest institutions that would promote the ideas of the Bauhaus and modern art and design in Australia. [fig.1] [1] As this essay aims to show, the Design Centre was strongly influenced by the ideas and teachings of Walter Gropius, László Moholy-Nagy, and György Kepes, whom they had met in London between 1935 and 1937.

They all had arrived in London through diverse circumstances. James, [fig.2] a native Englishman born in Sussex, had already been living and working in London for several years as an art director and designer. Gropius, the former director of the Bauhaus in Weimar and Dessau, had arrived in 1934 as a result of the right-wing political atmosphere transpiring in Germany. For the same reasons, Moholy-Nagy had left Germany and had since 1934 begun to commute from Amsterdam to England. He eventually moved to London in 1935, where he was joined by his long-term collaborator Kepes. Dahl and Geoffrey Collings [fig.3] were attracted to London as they wanted to be exposed to the European modern-art scene.

Dahl Collings (born Dulcie Wilmott in Adelaide) had received an art education from East Sydney Technical College from 1926 to 1932 and had been enrolled in various painting courses at the J. S. Watkins Art School. Born in Brisbane, Geoffrey Collings had commenced his studies at Brisbane Technical College at the young age of fourteen, attending from 1919 to 1921, and had already studied drawing, painting,

and etching in London at St. Martin's School of Art and London Central School in 1930.[2]

Upon their arrival in London in 1935, the Collingses immediately began to source work opportunities. Though they completed a variety of freelance work immediately after their arrival, no other work experience in London proved as pivotal to their artistic development and careers as working at the Simpson department store and learning first-hand from Moholy-Nagy and Kepes.

The grand retail store, conceived by Alexander Simpson to house the S Simpson Limited brand, had only just opened its doors in 1936 in central London, near Piccadilly Circus.[3] In 1934, he commissioned young British architect Joseph Emberton to design a modern department store [fig. 4] that would be exclusively devoted to catering for men; a "pioneer of new forms and masculine consumption, combining modern retail methods and modernist style."[4] In addition to its underlying modern conception, every element of the department store, from its architectural exterior and interior, furnishings, and innovate merchandise, was to exude modernity in terms of function and overall appearance. It was through a connection with graphic designer Ashley Havinden[5] that the former Bauhaus master Moholy-Nagy and his collaborator Kepes joined the Simpson team as design consultants in January 1936.[6] The team was joined by young Australian designer Dahl Collings on February 21, 1936.[7] Altogether, they were responsible for "creating a unity and personality throughout all windows, interior displays, exhibition floors, down to details of styling of merchandise and packaging."[8]

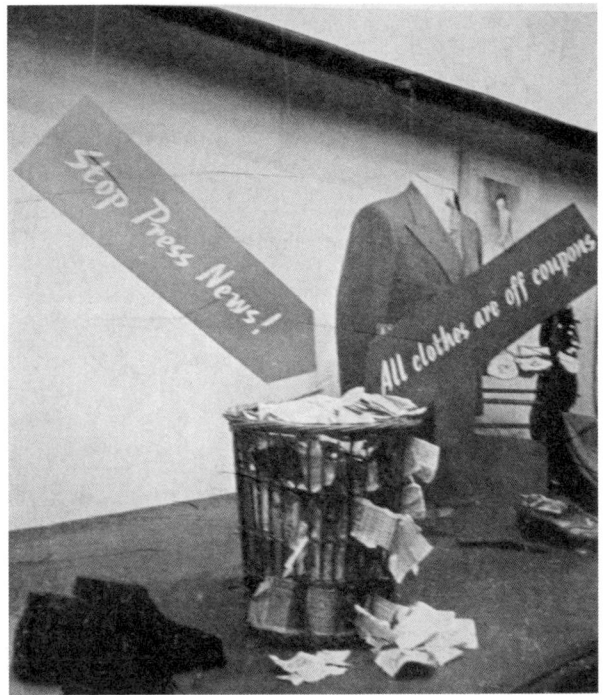

Fig. 5. Window display at Simpson, circa 1936.

Similar to the teaching and practice at the Bauhaus, the work at Simpson was fueled through a sense of an interdisciplinary approach to production, creative exploration and experimentation, and collaboration. The team worked as one cooperative unit in which work was passed on from one designer to be executed and finalized by another.[9]

Designing the window displays [fig.5] and exhibitions often demanded attention to typography, photography, and a creative application and presentation of a variety of ready-made products ranging in material and size. Every artistic medium, "from drawing, sculpture, painting, photography, to engraving"[10] was employed for their various tasks. To Moholy-Nagy, "the problem posed by Simpson's window display was basically no different from a setting for *Madame Butterfly*";[11] similarly, Dahl Collings saw "no difference between planning a poster, an electric iron, an exhibition stand or the scenario for a documentary film."[12]

Altogether, the Simpson studio functioned as an experimental laboratory, essential for developing products of technical and artistic quality. Moholy-Nagy and Kepes encouraged their team of designers to experiment with a variety of materials and tools, including rope, rubber, leather, and metals.[13] Nonconventional materials, such as glass and transparent plastics, were also key elements in their experimentation. As a result, Dahl Collings remarked that at Simpson she experimented "untiringly"[14] and without limit. Under the guidance of Moholy-Nagy and Kepes, whom she referred to as professors, she felt like she was capable of accomplishing anything.[15] She described the Simpson experience as being one of the most significant and challenging events in her artistic career.[16]

Although Geoffrey Collings was never employed at Simpson, he mourned Kepes and Moholy-Nagy's departures from London, proclaiming it a "criminal business" to allow them to leave London for Chicago.[17] The Collingses would maintain a long-term and long-distance friendship with Moholy-Nagy, Kepes, and their respective families for decades while back in Australia.[fig.6, 7]

In 1933, Richard Haughton James, at the time art director of the advertising agency McCann in London, organized an international

Veronica Bremer

The Design Centre in Sydney

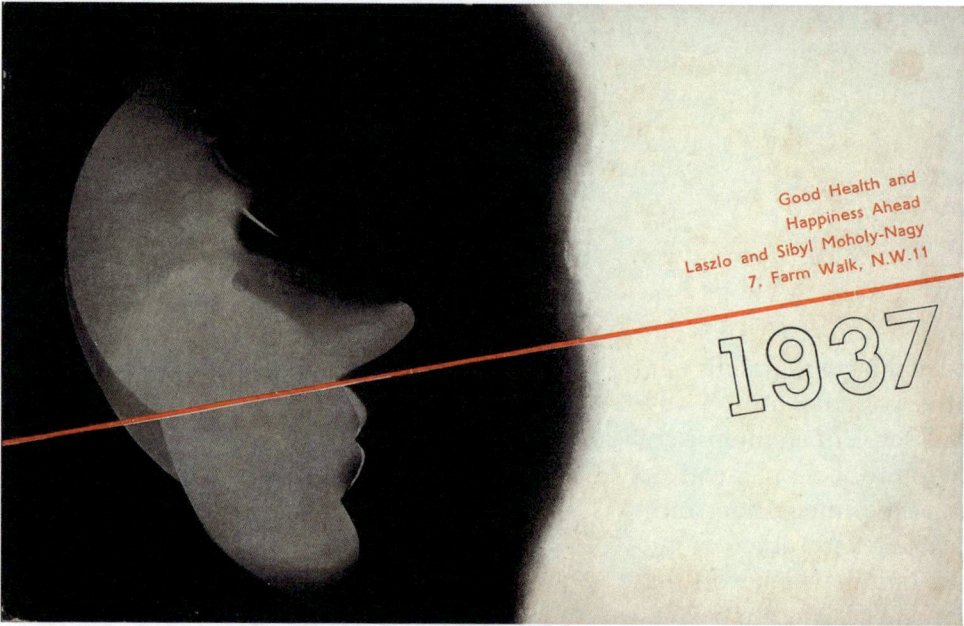

Good Health and
Happiness Ahead
Laszlo and Sibyl Moholy-Nagy
7, Farm Walk, N.W.11

1937

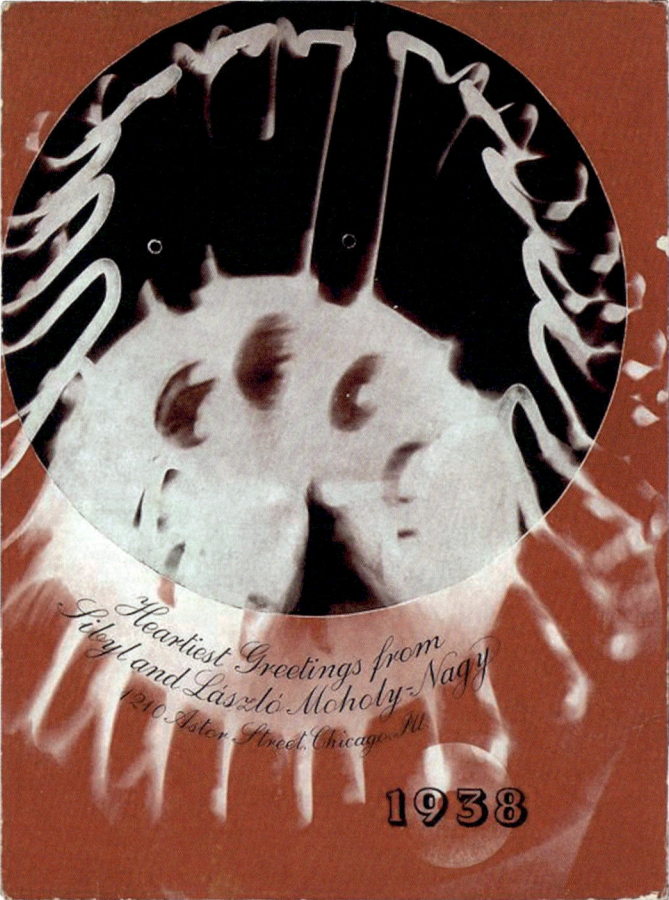

Heartiest Greetings from
Sibyl and Laszlo Moholy-Nagy
1210 Astor Street, Chicago, Ill.

1938

Fig. 6. László Moholy-Nagy, New Year's card from László and Sibyl Moholy-Nagy to Dahl and Geoffrey Collings, 1937.

Fig. 7. László Moholy-Nagy, New Year's card from László and Sibyl Moholy-Nagy to Dahl and Geoffrey Collings, 1938.

show of modern photography in London in which he also included works by Man Ray, and *Bauhäusler* Moholy-Nagy, Hein Neuner, and Herbert Bayer.[18] In 1935, while employed at the American advertising agency Erwin Wasey & Co. in London, James was put in direct contact with Geoffrey Collings, who was also employed there during his time in London. During their work at Erwin Wasey, James and Collings would produce color advertisements for British Celanese and Courtaulds in prominent fashion magazines such as *Vogue*.[19] Furthermore, as a result of James's responsibilities, including publishing book reviews and other writings, he was able to become acquainted with the Bauhaus, its ideologies, and with the *Bauhäusler* themselves:

> *London was full of refugees, brilliant people. Among them were Walter Gropius, founder of the Bauhaus at Dessau, and his colleagues Moholy-Nagy ... refugees from Hitler's Germany. They were very hard up, all of them. Gropius designed a neat cardboard box of knock down bookshelves and did fairly well. Moholy-Nagy was designing packages for Simpsons of Piccadilly. He was a brilliant man, the best of his work being his documentary and abstract photographs.*[20]

James specifically came into contact with Gropius while writing a book review for *Shelf Appeal*, a magazine concerned with packaging, advertising, and design. James's review, "Dr. Gropius and the Bauhaus," focused on Gropius's *The New Architecture and the Bauhaus*, which had recently been published and translated in England in 1935. As recounted in James's autobiography, he and Gropius met in Gropius's apartment at the Lawn Road Flats. This interaction constitutes one of the very few encounters that James chose to extensively discuss in his unpublished autobiography, articulately framing Gropius's theories of education and their lengthy discussion of the Bauhaus. In the book review, James highly praised modern architecture and, most specifically, the work and vision of Gropius, proclaiming: "Dr. Gropius, now settled in England, has exerted a larger single influence on design in Europe than any living man."[21] Gropius's profound influence accompanied James to Sydney when making the long voyage to Australia aboard the *Eridan*, as well as long after his arrival in Australia.

Upon their arrival in Sydney in 1939, the Collingses and James were part of a larger group of artists consisting of émigrés, expatriates, and artists whose overseas travel and exposure to modernism would

Veronica Bremer

The Design Centre in Sydney

facilitate the transmission of modern art.[22] Among this group were designers and commercial artists such as Gordon Andrews, Richard Beck, Elaine Haxton, and architect Arthur Baldwinson. Among the German refugees who were forced out of Germany as they had to flee the anti-Semitic persecution or the hate directed against modernist art were designer Gerard Herbst and photographer Wolfgang Sievers, who had been inspired by the Bauhaus ethos. Many of the German artists and architects who had emigrated to Britain were classified as enemy aliens and were either interned in Britain or deported to Australia. On board the *Dunera* in 1940 and also among those refugees who had been declared enemy aliens was artist Ludwig Hirschfeld-Mack, who had studied at the Bauhaus in Weimar and had become known for his installations and apparatuses that produced kinetic projection with colored light. Through their numerous contributions in the fields of art, photography, design, and art education, these expatriates, émigrés, and Australian artists enriched the cultural and artistic scene in Australia.

In late May 1939, the Collingses and James independently established their business and partnership, the Design Centre, at Sydney's Federation House at 166 Phillip Street. The Federation House was a trade union building and "a hub of cultural activity"[23] as a result of its ongoing activities, including plays and meetings of members of music and writing clubs.[24] As described by Geoffrey Collings, their shared vision for raising industrial and commercial design standards in Australia as well as belief in collaboration formed the foundation of the Design Centre:

> We believed in better design and we propagandized for it. We thought that working together, combining our talents, we might have more effect, and as we knew most of the designers around anyway, we could invite them to work with us on projects that the Design Centre was handling.[25]

Their objective was simple: the Design Centre proposed to consult with any manufacturer on his design problems. In promotional material, the Collingses and James highlighted their specialization in commercial design, packaging, and display, as well as their work experience in Australia and abroad.[26] In a letter written by James to Amalgamated Wireless Australia Ltd., a prospective customer, James outlined the objectives and mission of the Design Centre:

> My partners and I are not inclined to tackle any design problem without being given at least as much information as if we were in our clients' own

employ. We regard our job as that of solving definite selling problems in terms of design, and like the engineer or architect suppose that the solution of any problem lies in the circumstances of the problem itself.[27]
The letter also reveals James's appreciation of modernist design, his indebtedness to Gropius and Moholy-Nagy, and his goal to design goods primarily based on their function and purpose.

As this letter suggests, James was very articulate. He had used writing as a powerful communication tool since his days in England as a way of reaching a larger audience, and he continued to use his writing skills while representing the Design Centre. He also particularly stressed the need for designers who possessed a willingness to experiment with available materials in order to produce durable, functional, and economical products. Similarly, in his 1939 article, "Better Design. Here and Now," James maintained the importance of industrial design education:[28]

The object of industrial design schools is to produce skilled persons to undertake specific tasks in industry, as designers, foremen of workshops and art directors, and to give the ordinary workmen an understanding. It will probably mean importing trained teachers until Australia can produce them herself. The teacher is all-important.[29]

As part of the "£.S." series, the Design Centre published a series of articles on "good design." In "£.S. Display: Creating Store Personality from the Shop Window,"[30] Dahl Collings wrote about her firsthand experience and exchange with Moholy-Nagy, whom she characterized as a "brilliant Hungarian designer and painter" at Simpson.[31] She praised the simple and effective Simpson window displays, and featured a photograph of the window display designed by Moholy-Nagy in the article that was later published in the 1940 edition of *Retail Merchandiser and Chain Store Review*. This not only helped to showcase her international experience and exposure; it also illuminated the relationship and connection between the Design Centre and modern master Moholy-Nagy.

After meeting Sydney Ure Smith,[32] an established publisher, patron, administrator, and supporter of the visual arts, James was offered the opportunity to write an article for the first issue of Ure Smith's *Australia National Journal*.[33] This collaboration led to James's first article on the Bauhaus in Australia, "The Designer in Industry: A Serious National Need," in the 1939 issue of *Australia National Journal*, with the cover design and also a possible illustration by the

Veronica
Bremer

The
Design
Centre
in
Sydney

481

Fig. 8, 9. Dahl and Geoffrey Collings, photographs of *Exhibition of Modern Industrial Art and Documentary Photos*, Sydney, June 6–24, 1939.

Fig. 10. Dahl and Geoffrey Collings, Invitation card for the *Exhibition of Modern Industrial Art and Documentary Photos*, Sydney, June 6–24, 1939.

Collingses.[34] Drawing from his own personal acquaintance with Gropius in London back in 1936, James discussed Gropius's ideas, supplementing them with quotes from Gropius's book. James highlighted the Bauhaus as a unique educational institution and provided a detailed overview of the Bauhaus curriculum, a focal point thoroughly discussed by Gropius in his book.[35] The Bauhaus curriculum presented in the article illustrates the type of educational training that James consistently advocated.[36] Similar to his 1936 book review in which he had praised the Bauhaus, James's article also acknowledged the tremendous influence of the Bauhaus on modernist design through an unprecedented, practical, and conscientious approach: "... the Bauhaus ... ha[s] thereby crystallized theory into a working method of education less arbitrary in its operation and more exactly suited to modern needs than any other we can quote." [37]

The Collingses further utilized exhibitions to achieve their aims in introducing modern art and design in Australia. Shortly after founding the Design Centre, the Collingses held their joint exhibition, *Exhibition of Modern Industrial Art and Documentary Photos*, [fig. 8, 9] in June 1939. The exhibition ran for more than two weeks at the David Jones Gallery on Sydney's Market Street.[38]

The exhibition showcased their new identities as cosmopolitan, modern, experimental, and collaborative artists and designers. To present their recent London experience, the Collingses were very selective in choosing their international contacts. The exhibition, for example, was officially opened by British expatriate Frank Medworth, who had migrated from London to Australia just one and a half years prior to the exhibition and who was working as a lecturer at the art department at East Sydney Technical College.[39] The back of the invitation card for the exhibition intentionally reused the statement written by Edward McKnight Kauffer for the invitation card to their *Three Australians* exhibition, held one year prior in London. Kauffer's statement appeared alongside a quote from Ure Smith:

> *Dahl and Geoffrey Collings, after being successful in London, elected to return to Sydney at a time when their experience, as designers, can be used to some purpose. They are very much alive, eager to express themselves— to a point of impatience. They certainly have something to give as modern industrial artists. Their outlook is refreshing and I am convinced they will make an important contribution to the new movement in industrial design which is waiting to be exploited in our country.*[40]

The Directors of David Jones' cordially invite you to

an Exhibition of Modern Industrial Art and Documentary

Photos to be held at their Galleries, Market St. Store

DAHL AND GEOFFREY } COLLINGS

June 6th-24th. The Exhibition will be opened on Tuesday

June 6th at 3 p.m. by Mr. Frank Medworth·R.B.A., F.S.A.M.

Private View Monday June 5th at 2.30 p.m.

Sydney, June, 1939

Dahl and Geoffrey Collings, after being successful in London, elected to return to Sydney at a time when their experience, as designers, can be used to some purpose. They are very much alive, eager to express themselves — to a point of impatience. They certainly have something to give as modern industrial artists. Their outlook is refreshing and I am convinced they will make an important contribution to the new movement in industrial design which is waiting to be exploited in our country.

SYDNEY URE SMITH.

London, June, 1938

We must get rid of the idea from our minds that Australia stands only for Sheep Farming, the Life of the Open Air, and Sports — especially Cricket. Slowly and surely there are influences at work introducing other aspects of what might be called a more intellectual life.

These Australian artists are symptomatic of this gradual change: their approach to designing and photography is the same as in this country, but it has the added attraction of simple directness, which seems to come from their affinity with the open-air life of their own country. Their work is so interesting that I am glad it is to be shown to the English public. I believe it is the first occasion upon which an exhibition of this kind has been devoted entirely to Australians . . .

E. McKNIGHT KAUFFER.

This statement by Ure Smith, one of Australia's prominent cultural personalities, served as an acknowledgement of their authentic promise as modern industrial artists.

The specifics of the exhibition were also thoughtfully considered with the aim of showcasing their diverse international travels and work experience. The Collingses organized photographs based on the geographical locations where they were taken in order to emphasize their international, exotic allure. The titles and names of experimental works were also listed in the exhibition catalogue with respect to their corresponding geographical locations in Europe, such as "Laguelia, Italy" and "Belver, Spain." To accentuate their work experience in London, most of the design work that was featured was commissioned by British companies such as Austin Reed, Viyella, Harvey Nichols, and Simpson Piccadilly.

Committed to the Bauhaus emphasis on experimentation, the Collingses exhibited what they referred to as "experimental designs" for both the Orient Line and Smith's *Australian National Journal*.[41] The duo also exhibited experimental photographs, referred to in the exhibition catalogue as "excursions in colour, observation and technique." The catalogue referenced "photographs without a camera," [42] alluding to Moholy-Nagy's dominant influence in the production of photograms.[43]

Like Moholy-Nagy, whose work frequently featured hands, so as to uphold "the values of individualism while exploring the new languages of collective bodies,"[44] the Collingses featured two graphic fingerprints on the cover of the exhibition catalogue and on the invitation card.[fig.10] [45] Moholy-Nagy's attraction to "the organic quality found in the manifold lines of the palm and fingers"[46] resulted in the print of his own hand as a present to Gropius. Moholy-Nagy also possessed a set of handprints from his Bauhaus colleagues.

Produced through the Design Centre's broad range of expertise and firsthand exposure to modern art, James's and the Collingses' writings, broadcasts, speeches, and exhibition work possessed an authenticity and assertiveness necessary to demand attention and address the dire need for modern art and design standards in the country. Their articles, lectures, and exhibitions prove to be one of the most, if not *the* most, critical and influential outputs of the Design Centre that served not just to articulate the Design Centre's goals and increase its visibility, but to educate the general Australian public and con-

Fig. 11. AWA table model
radio cabinet in colored
Bakelite, as reproduced in
Australian Timber Journal,
February/March 1940: 91.

sumers about good design, modern art, the need for knowledgeable instructors in Australia, and a better education for industrial designers.

During its brief lifetime, the Design Centre also produced design models for industry and blueprints for radio sets [fig. 11] and restaurant murals.[47] It also provided art direction, graphics, and exhibition design.[48] As part of their cumulative last efforts to gain commission for the Design Centre, James and the Collingses proposed a set of documentary films to the Australian government that ultimately failed to materialize. With World War II approaching, they had seen it as an opportune moment to acquire governmental funding to produce documentary films.[49] In their proposal, they ambitiously argued for "an urgent necessity to push forward with the making of the right kind of propaganda films" and introduced concepts for four documentary films dealing with Australia's war effort; each was to span two reels, or approximately 1,800 feet. The proposal of films was a bold one, for it sought to develop documentary film at a time when documentary film was "completely unknown in Australia."[50] At the most practical level, the film projects would provide some financial alleviation and prosperity to the Design Centre. The films would also explore the link between art and industry, uniting man and machine under a Bauhaus-inspired collaboration. Just as well, the films aimed at demonstrating comradeship among Australia's workers as well as the union between a worker and his tools and the machinery of industry. The further aim of the film projects to dignify all workers and men fueling the war effort, regardless of specialization, promoted the concept of a strong, modern, and industrialized Australia. The films further contained the social considerations inherent in the Bauhaus's concern for housing and design that aimed to "characterize the inner dignity of the method of labor."[51] These proposed film projects deserve acknowledgment, for they boldly offered to explore the uncharted terrain of documentary film within Australia.

While the Collingses and James offered a wide spectrum of training and interests, implementing something as radical as the Design Centre was no small feat in Australia in 1939/40. It was laden with implications that threatened its livelihood and ultimately contributed to its dissolution. With the outbreak of World War II, the eventual demise of the Design Centre drew closer. On the one hand, "the war

Veronica
Bremer

The
Design
Centre
in
Sydney

485

had begun to consume people's attention,"[52] but perhaps just as detrimental to the Design Centre was the conservative artistic climate that denounced modern art and praised the pastoral tradition. A prevailing perception of modernism as "morbid and 'un-Australian'"[53] significantly hindered its aims. Moreover, at the time that the Design Centre was established, modern industrial design in Australia had not yet been established as a distinct discipline. The Collingses' and James's establishment of the Design Centre preceded and/or developed parallel to many organizations that would become active throughout the late 1940s, including the Australian Commercial and Industrial Artists' Association (ACIAA), The Design of Industries Association (DIA), The Society of Designers for Industry (SDI)[54], and the Contemporary Art Society (CAS).[55]

Although the Design Centre was neither viable nor financially successful,[56] its significance also lies in its pioneering efforts to offer industrial design products better suited for modern society during a time when industrial design in Australia had not yet been established as a distinct discipline. The Design Centre certainly was a catalyst that provided James and the Collingses with an institutional base to move forward in transplanting their modernist aesthetic into the modern design of Australia in the decades that followed.

The author wishes to acknowledge the generous support of the Paul Mellon Centre for Studies in British Art for a grant that enabled research at the Simpson/DAKS archive to be undertaken.

1   Another notable example of a design studio that implemented a Bauhaus approach was Prestige Studio, based in Melbourne and run by Dresden-born artist Gerard Herbst (1911–2011). For more information on Prestige Limited and Gerard Herbst, see: Anne-Marie Van de Ven and Veronica Bremer, "The Bauhaus Link in the Life and Work of Émigré Artist Gerard Herbst," in *Electronic Melbourne Art Journal* (EMAJ) 9 (2016): 1–40. For more scholarship that explores the influence of the Bauhaus in Australian art and design, see: Ann Stephen, Philip Goad, and Andrew McNamara, *Modernism & Australia: Documents on Art, Design and Architecture 1917–1967* (Carlton, Vic.: Miegunyah Press, 2006), Ann Stephen,

Philip Goad, and Andrew McNamara, *Modern Times: The Untold Story of Modernism in Australia* (Carlton, Vic./Sydney: Miegunyah Press in association with Powerhouse Publishing, 2008), and Anne-Marie Van de Ven, "Images of the 1950's: Design and Advertising," in *The Australian Dream: Design of the Fifties*, ed. Judith O'Callaghan (Sydney: Powerhouse Publishing).
2   Geoffrey Collings Biographical Information, 2007/30/1-5, Dahl and Geoffrey Collings Collection, Museum of Applied Arts and Sciences (hereinafter MAAS).
3   The department store Simpson was also commonly referred to as "Simpsons" and "Simpsons Piccadilly" and "Simpsons of Piccadilly."
4   Bronwen Edwards, "A Man's World? Masculinity and Metropolitan Modernity at Simpson Piccadilly," in *Geographies of British Modernity: Space and Society in the Twentieth*

Century, ed. David Gilbert, David Matless, and Brian Short (Hoboken: John Wiley & Sons, 2011), 152.

5 Rosemary Ind, *Emberton* (London: Scolar Press, 1983), 32.

6 Simpson Piccadilly Minutes Book, 1936, 24, DAKS/Simpson Archive, London. The Simpson Minutes Book contains details of the directors' meetings regarding financial matters and personnel issues that took place in the early years after its founding. In attendance were board members Alexander Simpson, Sir William Crawford, and Herbert Hollister.

7 For more information on the Simpson experience, see: Veronica Bremer, "Dahl Collings (1909–1988) and her Itinerary: Australia, England, and Back" in MOMOWO: *Women Designers, Craftswomen, Architects and Engineers between 1918–1945*, ed. Marjan Groot, Helena Seražin, Emilia Maria Garda, and Caterina Franchini (Ljubljana: France Stele Institute of Art History, 2017); Geoffrey Caban, *A Fine Line: A History of Australian Commercial Art* (Sydney: Hale & Iremonger, 1983); and David Wainwright, *The British Tradition: Simpson – A World of Style* (London: Quiller Press, 1996). Simpson letter from General Manager W. P. Yates to Dahl Collings, February 21, 1936, 2007/30/1-22/1/1, Dahl and Geoffrey Collings Collection, MAAS.

8 Dahl Collings, "Creating a Store Personality through the Window," *Retail Merchandiser and Store Review* (January 1940): 22, 2007/30/1-14/1/16, Dahl and Geoffrey Collings Collection, MAAS.

9 Dahl Collings, "Creating a Store Personality through the Window," 22.

10 Dahl Collings, "Creating a Store Personality through the Window."

11 Sibyl Moholy-Nagy, *Moholy-Nagy: Experiment in Totality* (Cambridge, MA: MIT Press, 1969), 125.

12 Richard Haughton James, "Exhibition of Modern Industrial Art and Documentary Photos at the David Jones Gallery," (1939), 3, 92/191-22-7, Dahl and Geoffrey Collings Collection, MAAS.

13 Dahl Collings, "Creating a Store Personality through the Window."

14 Caban, *A Fine Line*, 72.

15 Caban, *A Fine Line*, 72.

16 Caban, *A Fine Line*, 71.

17 Richard Haughton James, "Dahl and Geoffrey Collings," in *Commercial Art / Art and Industry* (August 1938): 40, magazines.iaddb. org/issue/CAI/1938-08-01/edition/null/page/8.

18 The *Twenty-Seven Photographers* exhibition at the Wertheim Gallery opened on July 27, 1932, and ran for six weeks. The exhibition also featured the work of Margaret Bourke-White, Edward Steichen, Albert Renger-Patzsch, Tony von Horn, Francis Bruguière, Horst P. Horst, and Anton Bruehl.

19 Richard Haughton James, "'Second Thoughts': The Autobiography of Jimmy Haughton James," unpublished typescript volume, bound in green cardboard covers, circa 1981, 133, 90/944-1/1, Richard Haughton James Collection, MAAS.

20 James, *Second Thoughts*, 142.

21 Richard Haughton James, "Dr. Gropius and the Bauhaus," in *Shelf Appeal* (September 1935), 90/944-5, Richard Haughton James Collection, MAAS.

22 As echoed in the work of Michael Bogle, Richard Haese, and numerous other scholars, travel outside of Australia was crucial for the seed of modernism to be planted, with Europe serving as an ideal and pivotal destination for education and practice.

23 Bernard Smith, *A Pavane for Another Time* (South Yarra, Vic.: Macmillan, 2002), 43.

24 Smith, *Pavane*, 43.

25 Caban, *A Fine Line*, 77.

26 Design Centre document, 90/944-5, Richard Haughton James Collection, MAAS.

27 Letter by Richard Haughton James on behalf of the Design Centre to L. A. Hook, Esq., Amalgamated Wireless Australia Ltd., May 2, 1939, 90/944-5, Richard Haughton James Collection, MAAS.

28 Although industrial design training in Australia was extremely limited during this period, a formal industrial design curriculum was implemented by architect Harold Brown, head of Applied Art at Melbourne Technical College. Through Brown's individual efforts, a four-year "Industrial Design Diploma" was instituted in the School of Applied Art's prospectus in 1939, making it one of Australia's first industrial design curriculums. Its enrolled students focused on drawing, modelling, and illustration. Following the first-year foundation course, the curriculum was comprised of various examinations, including general design, lettering, industrial design, composition of form and color, and the history of architecture. See Michael Bogle, "Establishing the 1939 Industrial Design programme at Melbourne Technical College," www.academia.edu/35956326/ Establishing_the_1939_Industrial_Design_programme_at_Melbourne_Technical_College.

29   Richard Haughton James, "Better Design. Here and Now," 1–2, 90/944-5, Richard Haughton James Collection, MAAS.

30   Dahl Collings, "Creating Store Personality from the Window," MAAS.

31   Dahl Collings, "Creating Store Personality from the Window," MAAS.

32   Being neighbors at the Federation House with Ure Smith had its benefits, and it opened many doors for the Design Centre. Although Ure Smith was already acquainted with the Collingses (who had produced work for his previous magazine, *The Home*, before their travels to London, and had worked with him at the 1939 New York World's Fair), Ure Smith was able to meet James.

33   In 1916, Ure Smith had founded *Art in Australia*, and then in 1920, *The Home*. *Australia National Journal*, similar to *The Home*, had a multidisciplinary focus and featured industry, architecture, interior decoration, travel, and art.

34   Dahl and Geoffrey Collings, "Industrial Art and Documentary Photos," exh. cat. (1939), 92/191-22/7, Dahl and Geoffrey Collings Collection, MAAS.

35   For a discussion of the Bauhaus curriculum, see: Gropius, *The New Architecture and the Bauhaus*, 66–68.

36   See also James's 1939 article, "Relating Art to Modern Life," in which James explicitly calls for the training offered by Walter Gropius at the Bauhaus: "Yet workmen and designer are one. Ought to have same training. We all need some training. Bauhaus. Gropius. National effort needed, here now. New outlook needed, here now;" Notes on "Relating Art to Modern Life" lecture, 2, 90/944-5, Richard Haughton James Collection, MAAS.

37   James, "The Designer in Industry: A Serious National Need," 90.

38   The high-end David Jones department store that oftentimes served as an exhibition platform for many Australian societies and organizations.

39   Medworth was presented as "bring[ing] modern ideas from England." In London, he had served as head of the Drawing and Painting School at the Hull College of Art. *National Australia Journal*, 36.

40   Sydney Ure Smith in Invitation Card 92/191-22/4.

41   *Dahl and Geoffrey Collings: Exhibition of Modern Industrial Art and Documentary Photos*, exh. cat. (Sydney: David Jones's Art Gallery, June 6–24, 1939).

42   Dahl and Geoffrey Collings, exh. cat.

43   While photograms were typical of the avant-garde period, created by artists such as Man Ray and El Lissitzky, it was the Collingses' direct, firsthand exposure to Moholy-Nagy's experimentation with photograms that had resulted in this particular exodus of influence within the exhibition.

44   Sabine Hake, *The Proletarian Dream: Socialism, Culture, and Emotion in Germany, 1863–1933* (Berlin: De Gruyter, 2017).

45   Although the representation of the human hand in the visual arts witnessed increasing popularity and an "elevated status" during the Weimar Republic, it was Moholy-Nagy's fascination with the hand and fingerprints that was, of course, most accessible to the Collingses. D'Alessandro, "Through the Eye and the Hand," in *Moholy-Nagy: Future Present*, ed. Matthew S. Witkovsky, Carol S. Eliel, and Karole P. B. Vail, 66.

46   Moholy-Nagy, *Vision in Motion*, 37.

47   "2 Artists with Jobs and a Family," in *The Sunday Herald*, August 17, 1952, 30.

48   One possible project that the Design Centre handled was the display for the Collingses' modern art exhibition at David Jones. Most of the proposed changes for the display included color adjustments to the text, background, and photo print. "Notes on design for display for David Jones: announcing modern art exhibition," undated, 90/944-5, Richard Haughton James Collection, MAAS.

49   Jenny Allen, "Australian Visions. The Films of Dahl and Geoffrey Collings," in ERAS Journal, artsonline.monash.edu.au/eras/ eras-journal-allen-j-australian-visions-the-films-of-dahl-and-geoffrey-collings/.

50   One of the film projects, entitled *Born to Fly*, was to document Australia's involvement in the Empire Air Scheme. Another film project, *Men in Blue*, aimed at demonstrating the importance of secondary industry to the war effort, "stressing the fact that every man who works a machine in his daily work, is strengthening his nation for victory." The third proposed film project, *Army of Steel*, would showcase "all men from Australia—from the factory, the sheep station, the office desk, the lonely farm, the engine room." *Speed the Plough* further aimed at capturing Australia's vast national resources, "stressing the fact that the man on the land is playing his part in helping to feed and maintain the motherland." "Design Centre," May 11, 1940, 1–2, 90/944-5, Richard Haughton James Collection, MAAS.

51   Walter Gropius, "Monumentale Kunst und Industriebau," lecture held at the Folkwang Museum, Hagen, April 10, 1911, manuscript, Gropius Sammlung 20/3, Bauhaus-Archiv Berlin, repr. in *Ausgewaehlte Schriften*, 31, quoted in   J. Schwartz, *The Werkbund: Design Theory and Mass Culture before the First World War*, 56.

52   Eileen Chanin, Judith Pugh, and Steven Miller, *Degenerates and Perverts: The 1939 Herald Exhibition of French and British Contemporary Art* (Carlton, Vic.: Miegunyah Press, 2005), 209.

53   Chanin et al., *Degenerates*, 89.

54   In 1948, Richard Haughton James would hold a leading role as one of the supporting designers of the SDI.

55   In the early 1940s, the Collingses and James would become actively involved in several early key organizations that supported the related fields of design, the livelihood of artists, and an approach to modern art production. Before the solid establishment of these organizations in Melbourne and Sydney, the working conditions for Australia's freelance commercial and industrial artists were poor and unspecified; no labor code or basic wage existed. These design organizations would later serve as platforms for the Collingses, Morrison, and James to continue promoting the Bauhaus through lectures, writings, and exhibitions. Participation in these various organizations also provided the Collingses, Morrison, and James with a powerful network comprised of Sydney's foremost progressive artists, designers, and architects, some of whom had also come into contact with the ideas of the Bauhaus and the *Bauhäusler* themselves.

56   The Design Centre was under financial strain concerning the ratio of profits. The appointed auditor that reviewed the Design Centre's sales and expenses advised keeping a close watch "so that drawings can be curtailed before the firm becomes financially embarrassed." Letter from "Auditor" addressed to "Mssrs. Design Centre," October 30, 1939, 90/944-5, Richard Haughton James Collection, MAAS.

Veronica Bremer

The Design Centre in Sydney

Anna Vallye

From *Siedlung* to Township: The Martin Wagner – Walter Gropius Collaboration at Harvard in the 1940s

As the world of art and design celebrates the Bauhaus centennial, we do so in tandem with a broad revaluation of the momentous and fraught legacy of the Weimar Republic, underway in multiple fields of scholarship. Long assessed through the lens of political failures that cumulatively led to National Socialist hegemony, Weimar thought and institutions are now being reclaimed as modes of vital democratic invention, state formation, and contestation—ways of thinking and strategies of practice whose legacies bridged the mid-century cataclysm.[1]

Art and architecture historians have often thought of postwar Bauhaus legacies in similarly bleak terms: the various efforts to reinvent the institution itself or its design approaches in the extensive Bauhaus diaspora seen as mired in political compromise, lacking in utopian idealism and creative vigor, subject to commodity culture pressures—an "aftermath."[2] In light of the present, what if we consider instead the historical fates of the Bauhaus as a constituent of the Weimar Republic not in terms of pedagogical models or design principles, but rather in terms of ongoing reinventions of relationships between cultural and political practices? We know that art is always subject to political pressures and that it may be shaped into a tool of the state, but from the creative laboratory of the Weimar Republic emerged the idea that art can also do some of the shaping. And that idea survived.

Through the 1920s, the Bauhaus was but one of the institutions in an increasingly crowded field of cultural and political initiatives aimed at defining new arrangements of state-society and state-economy relationships and reordering existing public and private domains. In that sense, its ultimate end, inherited from the Werkbund, was to accomplish nothing less than a realignment of national economic culture through the refounding of industrial production processes upon vanguard aesthetic principles. That project, furthermore, would proceed, to recall the famous motto attributed to Hermann Muthesius, "from sofa cushions to city planning"—or, as adjusted by Walter Gropius in 1935, "from study of the function of the house to that of the street; from the street to the town; and finally to the still vaster implications of regional and national planning."[3]

Although the concrete products of Bauhaus workshops may not easily lend themselves to thinking at the scale of the urban fabric, we should not forget that the Bauhaus initiative was conceived within that expanded programmatic context.[4] This fact should hardly be surprising, given that since the latter half of the nineteenth century, in Germany as elsewhere, urban space had emerged as perhaps the primary arena for the generation of novel processes of state governance understood as the management of private economic interests, whose instruments were both political and aesthetic.[5] The Weimar social democracy created legislative opportunities for the realization of city planning theories and techniques conceived in the late Wilhelmine period.[6] In the Weimar years, the management of state-economy relations in the urban fabric was also seen to depend on the rationalization of the building industry on the basis of organized mass production.[7] A clear conceptual line led, indeed, from the Breuer chair or the Brandt teapot to city planning.

The career of planner, architect, and urban "engineer" Martin Wagner is an interesting case study of Weimar ideas in urban planning as they relate to the shaping of a Bauhaus legacy in the United States, from the 1930s and into the postwar years.[8] Wagner was the chief planner (*Stadtbaurat*) of the Greater Berlin municipality from 1926 to 1933. After his dismissal from that post and a brief tenure as a planner in Ankara, Turkey, he was hired in 1938 as professor of city planning at the Harvard Graduate School of Design (GSD) at the urging of Walter Gropius, who had been the head of its architecture department since 1937.[9] He served in that capacity until his retirement in 1951 and passed away six years later in 1957. Wagner's innovative approach to the urban fabric as an avatar of rationalized national economy burgeoned in the early years of the twentieth century, was extended, systematized, and applied in the 1920s, and then adapted to altered circumstances in the mid-century United States. Through his work with Gropius at the

*Anna
Vallye*

From
Siedlung
to
Township

491

so-called "Harvard Bauhaus"—though the notion was always painted with very broad (and polemical) strokes—Wagner's ideas about cities became entwined with the Bauhaus legacy in America, contributing to it a thread of reflection on issues like economic policy and administration, not often numbered among Bauhaus practical or intellectual innovations.[10]

"City planning is economic planning," Wagner proclaimed in the late 1920s.[11] The series of residential settlements (*Siedlungen*) built under his direction by the GEHAG (*Gemeinnützige Heimstätten-, Spar- und Bau-Aktiengesellschaft*) cooperative association of building trades in Berlin was certainly the most visible manifestation of that premise. Sponsored by state-industry limited-dividend building societies, the *Siedlungen* put into practice in the area of housing the model of cooperative public-private partnerships that defined the Weimar state's approach to economic management or "rationalization" (*Rationalisierung*).[12] These were settlements of a few thousand inhabitants each, set within park or garden spaces, and provided with the basic social facilities and services necessary to maintain self-sufficient community life.[fig. 1] Its lineage in the international Garden City conception made the *Siedlung* an entirely plausible intervention in American planning discourses of the early 1940s, buttressed by the recent examples of TVA Greenbelt towns and wartime defense housing settlements. Rechristened as "township," the *Siedlung* would form the basic conceptual building block of Wagner's theoretical and pedagogical approach at Harvard.[13]

In Germany, Wagner's acquaintance with Gropius seems to have been collegial, if cursory. Gropius was among the architects who contributed to the design and construction of the Grosssiedlung Siemensstadt (1929–34) in Berlin-Charlottenburg, carried out under Wagner's direction, and the two would have certainly encountered each other frequently through Weimar progressive architecture circles and organizations, such as The Ring and RFG, the National Society for Research in Building and Housing Economy (*Reichsforschungsgesellschaft für Wirt-*

Fig. 1. Siedlung Zehlendorf, Berlin (Bruno Taut, architect). Walter Müller-Wulckow, *Wohnbauten und Siedlungen* (Leipzig: Karl Robert Langewiesche, 1929).
Fig. 2. Walter Gropius, Siedlung Dessau-Törten, general plan (1926–28).

schaftlichkeit im Bau- und Wohnungswesen). Gropius had a general interest in the *Siedlung* model, informed by a communitarian ideal joined to a programmatic concern with modernizing mass housing construction through prefabricated building units and mechanized production processes.[14] He promoted these strategies at the Bauhaus, both through the Haus Am Horn model dwelling developed for the Bauhaus exhibition of 1923 in Weimar, and the Siedlung Dessau-Törten in Dessau (1926–29).[fig.2] [15] With Gropius looking to build a design and planning faculty at the recently formed GSD after 1937, Wagner, by his own account unhappy in Turkey and without prospects in Germany, was a logical choice and an apparent ally.[16] Between Wagner's arrival at Harvard in 1938 as a Gropius recruit and the later 1940s, the two architects often collaborated on student assignments and publications.

In fact, Wagner made a pronounced imprint on Gropius's writings related to city planning in the 1940s. With characteristic agility, Gropius wove this new thread into the tapestry he so influentially associated with a totalizing Bauhaus "idea": "an ever-wider and profounder conception of design as one great cognate whole—the mirror of the indivisibility and immensity and underlying unity of life itself, of which it is an integral part." [17]

For his part, Wagner would confront that assimilation with growing resentment, fueled by his fiery temperament and an all-too-conspicuous difference in professional success enjoyed by the two colleagues. "The longer I am here [in America]," confessed Gropius in 1948, "the more famous I become, and it is sometimes not entirely easy to keep up the pace."[18] "The 'hall of fame' is much too huge for human acoustics!" Wagner bitterly echoed in 1956, "Who would stand up against the cultivated 'big three' [Gropius, Le Corbusier, and Mies van der Rohe]!"[19]

The years of exile that followed his dismissal from the post of Berlin's *Stadtbaurat* never brought Wagner anything close to the short-

Anna Vallye

From *Siedlung* to Township

lived prominence and agency of his youth. In America, he was a dedicated and beloved teacher and a prolific writer, whose contributions on theoretical and technical subjects appeared in both English- and German-language venues. Though sophisticated, passionate, and informed, Wagner's manuscripts tended to be awkward in English— peppered with grammatical errors, odd neologisms, arcane learned references, and overwrought witty flourishes.[20] Those that made it to print failed to garner much attention. Pugnacious by nature ("Like you, I am a 'volcano,'" he wrote to his friend Ernst May, "better yet: a global explosive!"[21]), Wagner confronted his growing isolation with a proportional belligerence, rarely missing a chance to go on the offensive. In 1948, as Gropius was fretting the ballooning demands on his time, Wagner launched a heated skirmish over plans for their latest collaborative publication.[22] Soliciting the reinforcement of Harvard colleagues Joseph Hudnut and G. Holmes Perkins (a typically savvy move by the consummate politician), Gropius had substantially revised and curtailed Wagner's manuscript. The flurry of strongly-worded missives that followed accused Gropius of back-stabbing, grandstanding, and plagiarism. "You know perfectly well that I am a Parsifal of truth and justice," Wagner wrote, "and therefore with a good conscience I speak everything I think."[23] This was, it may be granted, a matter of perspective. In any case, the falling out put an end to any further collaboration, though concepts derived from it continued to resonate in the work of both—Gropius's version well-known today, Wagner's barely.

The ideas that dominated the Wagner-Gropius "township" model of planning turned on issues of political-economic management, rather than those of urban design. The architects strode forcefully into that fraught territory, and the gambit probably resulted in the failure of implementation for their proposals as national planning solutions in the American context. In Wagner's long-standing view, regional decentralization was but a correlate to national economic management through centralized planning ultimately premised upon socialization of the land.[24] In a 1939 GSD lecture, Wagner reiterated his opposition to treating land as a "commodity." The basic economic attributes of commodities—mobility, reproducibility, and interchangeability— were contrary to those of land. Therefore, he called for "a special kind of land politics and an exceptional position for land in ordinary economics and politics."[25] In his "blueprin[t] for rebuilding our cities," co-written with Gropius in 1942, for example, self-contained "town-ships," aggregated as needed into larger cities or regions, would "form the basic units of the new town pattern," premised on a regional conception of "country-cities in city-countries" built on communally owned land.[26] "The land," they wrote, "has been traded across the counter of real estate offices as though it were a commodity. But land is not a commodity; for, unlike buildings, it cannot be produced nor moved nor replaced. Land is of such a peculiar nature that it should be owned by the communities ..."[27] Instead, market demands would be satisfied by a thoroughgoing commodification of the individual dwelling through mass production. "As soon as the non-commodity land," Gropius and Wagner wrote, "can be legally detached from the commodity house, industrial plants producing modern shelter units on the assembly line basis will flourish."[28] Effectively, therefore, the architects proposed to disaggregate real estate as an economic unit of value, normally composed of land and any structures or improvements on it: privately owned dwelling on the one hand, publicly owned land on the other.

As detailed in other contemporaneous texts by Gropius and Wagner, the logistics of carrying out communal land ownership and redevelopment would be very similar to the process established in 1920s Germany: A "Metropolitan Reconstruction Finance Corporation" would be set up and funded through proceeds from imposed "amortization quota" on all existing city structures, publicly and privately owned.[29] This replicates the German model of land acquisition with proceeds from the *Hauszinssteuer* (housing tax), and development by building corporations, such as the GEHAG, to be cooperatively owned and managed by tenants' associations. But, as Wagner and Gropius were careful to point out to American readers,

> [s]uch a regulation would not mean the compulsory expropriation of private property; on the contrary, it would mean conservation of private property, and the owners would be duly credited with the annual quotas but would be entitled to spend them only for the renewal and rebuilding of city structures. [30]

The same point was stressed in a collaborative student problem given by Gropius and Wagner at the GSD in January and subsequently published as an *Architectural Forum* article in July 1943.[fig.3] [31] Assuming increased population mobility as the composition of the workforce changes with the changing needs of industry, the boundaries of the

Anna
Vallye

From
Siedlung
to
Township

495

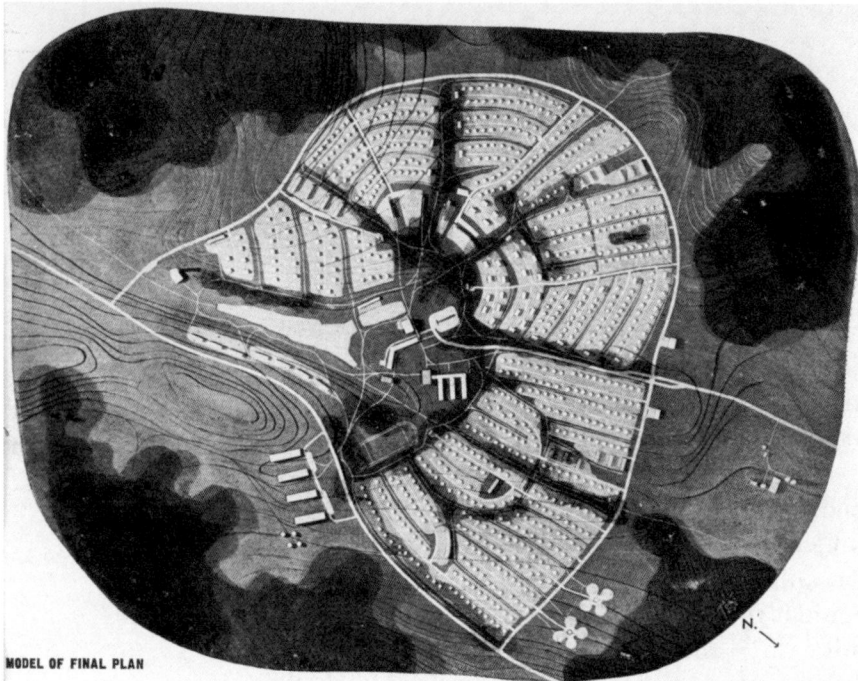

MODEL OF FINAL PLAN

"township" had to be allowed to grow or shrink over time. The necessary flexibility would be satisfied "by making the housing facilities elastic." Different housing types would be offered: permanent units adaptable to the evolution of the family, demountable units, and mobile units (trailer homes) for migratory workers.[fig.4 a, b] [32] The ultimate task was to provide a "maximum of flexibility in housing design" so as to "fit the family in any state of its size, its age-composition, its income, and its other varying demands." [33] Variability extended not only to size and use, but also to appearance. "The more standardization and prefabrication is used," Gropius and Wagner wrote, "the more will be needed the vision of the designer to secure individual variety, in spite of the increasingly limited number of types to be used."[34] Although intimately linked, building and land were autonomous functions both in concept and in practice: the land stable and uniform, the building variable and disposable, both physically and economically. "[T]he building of new settlements," Gropius and Wagner concluded, "will in the future be based on planning principles that emphasize lasting *site values* in contrast to more flexible building values ..."[35] Illustrating these points were student drawings of modular dwelling designs, accommodating a variety of arrangements, as well as future expansions or additions—an approach first broached by Gropius in his *Baukasten im Grossen* (Large-Scale Building Blocks) scheme with Fred Forbát at the Bauhaus in 1922–23, and later elaborated in his contribution to *Das wachsende Haus* (*The Growing House*) prefabricated dwelling design competition, organized by Wagner in 1932.[fig.5] [36] Under Wagner's influence, Gropius's ideas on architectural mass production, born in the 1910s and gestated at the Bauhaus, were now spliced into the broad framework of a public-private economic structure.

TWO-STORY DETACHED HOUSE designed by R. M. Kuhlman. The accommodations include living, dining and kitchen on the first floor, with two bedrooms and a bathroom on the second floor. Open space under second floor overhang is used for the carport.

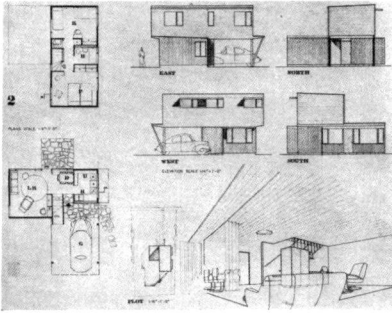

ONE-STORY DETACHED HOUSE designed by F. A. Macomber. Model shows the street entrance side of the dwelling unit. Accommodations consist of living, dining, kitchen and utility areas, plus two permanent bedrooms. One or two demountable bedroom units can be added, together with their toilet facilities.

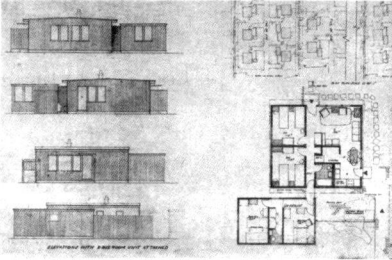

TWO-STORY ROW HOUSE with two-bedroom units designed by K. H. Cheang. The model shows the entrance side of the units. The accommodations consist of living, dining, kitchen and utilities on the first floor; two bedrooms and bathroom on the second floor. Projecting storage units and trellis give privacy from the neighbors.

ONE-STORY ROW HOUSE designed by H. McK. Jones. The model shows the garden side, with the additional, transportable bedrooms projecting from two of the dwelling units. Accommodations consist of living, dining, kitchen, bathroom and utility space plus a permanent bedroom unit, apart from the transportable one.

ONE-STORY SEMIDETACHED HOUSE designed by W. H. Radford. The view of the model is taken from the garden side. The maximum accommodation comprises living and dining room, kitchen, utility room and three bedrooms (alternative: one or two bedrooms only). The link between two units consists of carports on the street side, porches and a storage bin division on the garden side.

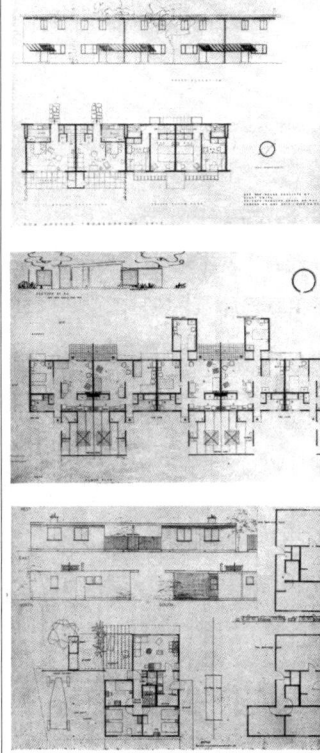

Fig.3. Plan for a proposed "township" in the Boston metropolitan region. Work by Harvard GSD students. From Walter Gropius and Martin Wagner, "A Program for City Reconstruction," *Architectural Forum* (July 1943): 75–86.
Fig.4a, b. Studies of various types of housing units. Work by Harvard GSD students. From Walter Gropius and Martin Wagner, "A Program for City Reconstruction," *Architectural Forum* (July 1943): 75–86.
Fig.5. Walter Gropius, "Copper House," 1932. Martin Wagner, *Das wachsende Haus* (Berlin: Deutsches Verlagshaus Bong & Co: 1932), 66.

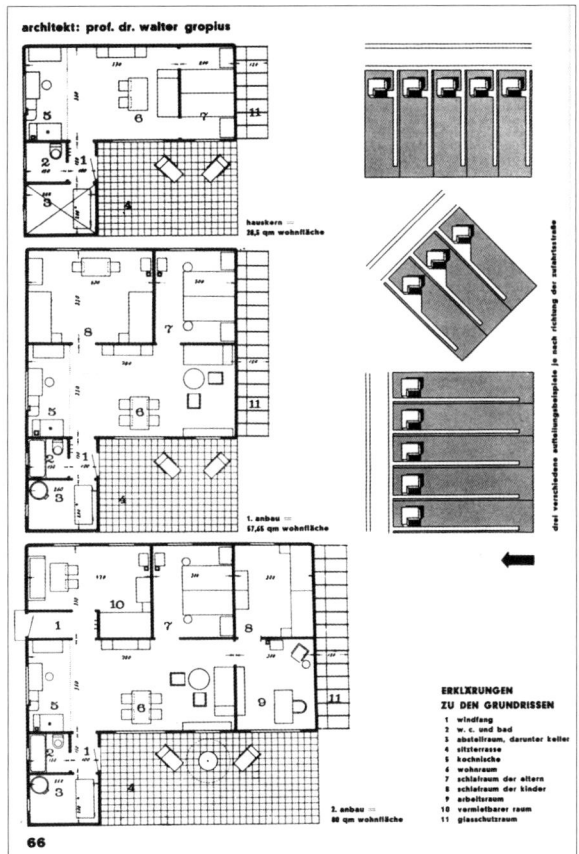

architekt: prof. dr. walter gropius

hauskern
28,5 qm wohnfläche

1. anbau
57,65 qm wohnfläche

2. anbau
80 qm wohnfläche

ERKLÄRUNGEN
ZU DEN GRUNDRISSEN

1 windfang
2 w. c. und bad
3 abstellraum, darunter keller
4 sitzterrasse
5 kochnische
6 wohnraum
7 schlafraum der eltern
8 schlafraum der kinder
9 arbeitsraum
10 vermietbarer raum
11 glasschutzraum

Fig.6. Walter Gropius, *Rebuilding Our Communities* (Chicago: Paul Theobald, 1945). Cover page. Design by Morton Goldsholl.

Gropius's ideas on planning penned independently of Wagner were an iteration of the same conceptual formula, but their communitarian stakes softened and masked by a rhetoric of democratic ideology. In *Rebuilding Our Communities* in 1945, Gropius spelled out his ideas on planning as a product and generator of participatory democracy.[fig.6] Based on a "lifelong conviction that the future of architecture and building stands upon a sound reorientation of the entire community set-up," he declared himself to be part of a "generation of architects who are developing a set of standards focused on contemporary social conceptions, and who have therefore joined hands with the professional planners."[37] His argument was premised on securing a direct relationship between the organization of the urban "pattern" and the quality of "community life," measured by the degree of "personal contact" between citizens and elected officials. This vision of a close-knit or "integrated" community, modeled on the medieval town square or the New England village, proceeded from the ability of "every one of us [to be] instrumental in the formation of his own environment" to the general defeat of metropolitan anomie.[38] Ostensibly based on the New England colonial-era commonwealth, but equally reminiscent of the medievalizing communitarian utopias that fueled the early years of the Bauhaus, the ideal now dictated that effective urban redevelopment must rely first and foremost on the reorganization of the nation's "administrative framework" to enable participatory forms of government.

Thus, the basic urban unit would also be the basic administrative unit of governance: a half-mile radius "neighborhood" with five to six thousand inhabitants. From the neighborhood, the "administrative area" would expand to the county or city precinct, then the state, and finally the federal government. In this way, "the social initiative of the people would ... originate at a local level and gradually reach out into a wider region."[39] Planning proceeded by establishing a direct relationship between a module of the urban fabric—the township—and a unit of government scaled to enable participatory democracy. "We badly lack legal instruments," Gropius wrote, "to channel any development—privately or publicly undertaken—into a controlled and well-balanced communal organism. We cannot blame the real estate man who simply follows his business; it is up to the community to keep him from running wild." The ultimate issue once again was that of situating urban redevelopment as an appropriate instrument for "communal" or public mediation of private interests, a regulatory intervention in the real estate market. Characteristically, Gropius would transcribe this task in terms of his synthetic and totalizing vision: its true ambition would be "to replan society ... and embrace all phases of life."[40]

In practical terms, however, the administrative arrangement advocated by Gropius had as its end goal the gradual elimination of public housing subsidies by "solving the housing problem economically." This meant reducing free-market housing costs through "industrializing" the residential building process in order to make home ownership accessible to "the average income." Individual dwellings should be supplied entirely by the market; only then could society, "without infringing upon individual freedom, eliminate the bugaboo of excessive governmental control."[41] On the other hand, *land* would be gradually taken out of the systems of private ownership and dispersed controls. First, localities should be given the power to zone already developed land and to "regulate subdivisions" on outlying vacant land. The ultimate endpoint, although only suggested as a *possible* outcome, would be socialization of the land. "[W]ithout undermining the basic conceptions of property," Gropius wrote, "the ownership and use of land must be regulated by legislation so that the right of the community gradually rises above that of the individual when vital public problems are concerned."[42]

The severing of the economic link between building and land, central to the functions of real estate, foretold the failure of the Wagner-Gropius intervention as a political blueprint for American territorial development—even as the physical patterns of metropolitan decentralization that they supported broadly took hold through other arrangements, eventually taking the familiar maligned forms of suburban sprawl and inner-city decay.[43] But while their proposals were certainly not economically liberal enough for the postwar United States, they were also not especially socialist. In this, too, they followed the political models elaborated in the Weimar Republic. Socialized land ownership was embraced by Wagner and Gropius because it would facilitate centralized planning, the general goal of which was the increased efficiency of economic administration within a capitalist framework.

In his analysis of the concept of *Sozialisierung*—an approach to national economic management imperfectly translated as "socialization" —in Weimar Republic politics, historian Charles Maier points out the ambiguity and flexibility of "socialism" as a policy objective, which, ultimately, "allowed even conservatives and business leaders to design a socialism that they could accept."[44] In the negotiations leading up to the drafting of the Weimar constitution, for example, the ruling Social Democratic Party (SPD) tended to define socialism as "the maximization of the general welfare," rather than a redistribution of economic power. Correspondingly, the economic policy that would come to define Weimar democracy was founded in the idea of *Gemeinwirtschaft* —common or collective economy—premised upon industrial self-management by associations of labor unions, business leaders, and consumer and government representatives, to the end of the enhancement of overall national productivity. It was economic management for more efficient production, leading to the presumed furthering of communal welfare.[45] Wagner's writings of the period repeatedly engaged the *Gemeinwirtschaft* concept, and his "communal economy," proposed as the model for nationalization in *Das wachsende Haus*, took off from the same ground.[46] In his 1951 magnum opus, *Wirtschaftlicher Städtebau* (*City Planning According to Economic Principles*), the model township became the manifestation of a collective "We-economy" (*Wir-Wirtschaft*) vested with enduring communal values, in opposition to the wasteful and destructive speculative "I-economy" (*Ich-Wirtschaft*) of the free market.[47]

New Deal, and even 1940s, America was not inhospitable to such ideas. As Wagner and Gropius were adapting Weimar Republic models of governance in their proposals for the rebuilding of America's urban fabric, the GSD was reshaping the city planning department to bring it into better alignment with a profession that saw itself gaining increasing influence in the expanding administrative bodies of the state, from the national to the local.[48] In 1950, Chairman of Harvard's Department of Regional Planning G. Holmes Perkins stressed that the "expanding sphere of government activities has made it abundantly clear that the former supposed limits to city planning have become myths."[49] The prospects for comprehensive public control of the urban environment for the "public good," as defined by planning experts, would not have seemed as bleak as they do in historical retrospect. Still, when Wagner outlined his thoughts on "American versus German City Planning" in *The Journal of Land and Public Utility Economics* in 1946, decrying the lack of comprehensive planning instruments in US local governments, historian and political scientist Byrn J. Hovde countered in his (generally sympathetic) published response that "there is no use in demanding that American democracy follow any non-American patterns."[50] America has only started to "develop a strong tradition of public interest as against individual interest," and while "planning and the necessary governmental reconstruction [were surely] not far behind," it would take place according to the structures of American democracy: "We shall not be ourselves with any other."[51] Hovde would remain among the very few to engage in print with Wagner's ideas.

Still, the Wagner-Gropius translation of planning concepts and strategies developed in Weimar Germany did grasp the greater imperative to guarantee the freedom of private enterprise in the American context. In bisecting the land-building economic unit, they attempted to find a solution that could satisfy the need for architectural agency and control over the urban fabric within the constraints of a market-based liberalism. If their strategy was unsuccessful, it stands as a record of sustained engagement with questions of governance in the urban fabric on the part of émigré *Bauhäusler* and fellow travelers—a vital part of the Weimar architectural legacy that remains poorly explored.

1   For a broad interdisciplinary introduction to these recent developments, see Geoff Eley, Jennifer L. Jenkins, and Tracie Matysik, eds., *German Modernities: From Wilhelm to Weimar; A Contest of Futures* (London: Bloomsbury Academic, 2016).
2   See, for example, William H. Jordy, "The Aftermath of the Bauhaus in America: Gropius, Mies, and Breuer" in *The Intellectual Migration*, ed. D. Fleming and B. Bailyn (Cambridge, MA: MIT Press, 1969).
3   Walter Gropius, *The New Architecture and the Bauhaus* (London: Faber and Faber, 1935), 98.
4   City planning concepts and approaches were explored at the Bauhaus after the arrival of Hannes Meyer and Ludwig Hilberseimer in 1928. But the community settlement (*Siedlung*)

model was also pursued by Gropius from the very beginning, for example in multiple iterations of plans for an unrealized Bauhaus Estate (*Bauhaus-Siedlung*) in Weimar (1920–25), as well as the later Dessau-Törten Estate (*Siedlung Dessau-Törten*) (1926–29). See, e. g., Walter Scheidig, "Die Bauhaus-Siedlungsgenossenschaft in Weimar 1920–1925," *Dezennium II: Zwanzig Jahre VEB Verlag der Kunst Dresden* (Dresden: VEB Verlag der Kunst, 1972).
5   For a relevant history of German city planning, see, for example, Brian Ladd, *Urban Planning and Civic Order in Germany, 1860–1914* (Cambridge, MA: Harvard University Press, 1990).
6   Ladd notes, for example, that "German cities had by World War I developed most of the

legal and administrative tools used by planners around the world during the following decades." Ladd, *Urban Planning*, 239. This would reinforce the claim of Eley et al. that the chronology of German modernity might best be dated from 1870. See Eley et al., *German Modernities*.

7 For an analysis of urban space as a cultural register of the mass society in the Weimar era, see Sabine Hake, *Topographies of Class: Modern Architecture and Mass Society in Weimar Berlin* (Ann Arbor: The University of Michigan Press, 2008).

8 For a biographical overview of Wagner's career, see Bernhard Wagner, *Martin Wagner, 1885–1957: Leben und Werk* (Hamburg: Wittenborn Söhne, 1985). The main scholarship on Wagner's career in Germany is concentrated in Ludovica Scarpa, *Martin Wagner e Berlino: Casa e città nella Repubblica di Weimar, 1918–1933* (Rome: Officina, 1983) and Klaus Homann, Martin Kieren, and Ludovica Scarpa et al., eds., *Martin Wagner, 1885–1957: Wohnungsbau und Weltstadtplanung. Die Rationalisierung des Glücks* (Berlin: Akademie der Künste, 1986).

9 For Wagner's work in Turkey, see Esra Akcan, *Architecture in Translation: Germany, Turkey, and the Modern House* (Durham: Duke University Press, 2012).

10 For the "Harvard Bauhaus" formulation, see, for example, Klaus Herdeg, *The Decorated Diagram: Harvard Architecture and the Failure of the Bauhaus Legacy* (Cambridge, MA and London: MIT Press, 1983). See also Jill Pearlman, *Inventing American Modernism: Joseph Hudnut, Walter Gropius, and the Bauhaus Legacy at Harvard* (Charlottesville and London: University of Virginia Press, 2007). Only recently have Bauhaus scholars started to focus in-depth on issues of economic organization and management that may be said to fall within the rubric of state-society relations, such as problems of copyright, national economic policy, and the interplay between industrial leadership and political administration. See Robin Schuldenfrei, "Production: The Bauhaus Object and Its Irreproducibility," in *Luxury and Modernism: Architecture and the Object in Germany, 1900–1933* (Princeton: Princeton University Press, 2018); T'ai Smith, *Bauhaus Weaving Theory: From Feminine Craft to Mode of Design* (Minneapolis: University of Minnesota Press, 2014); John Maciuika, *Before the Bauhaus: Architecture, Politics and the German State, 1890–1920* (Cambridge: Cambridge University Press, 2005); Walter Scheiffele, *Bauhaus, Junkers, Sozialdemokratie: Ein Kraftfeld der Moderne* (Berlin: Form und Zweck, 2003).

11 Martin Wagner, *Das Neue Berlin*, n. d. (ca. 1932), MS, Papers of Martin Wagner, Frances Loeb Library, Harvard University Graduate School of Design, 78. From here on: PMW.

12 For more on this, see, for example, "Socialization and Rationalization of Housing in the Weimar Republic: The Work of Martin Wagner," in *Social Housing in the Weimar Republic*, ed. Architectural Association and Goethe Institute (London: Architectural Association, 1978), 54–74; Homann et al., *Martin Wagner, 1885–1957*.

13 For more on this, see my "Design and the Politics of Knowledge in America, 1937–1967: Walter Gropius, Gyorgy Kepes" (PHD diss., Columbia University, 2011), 138–195. See also Álvaro Sevilla-Buitrago, "Martin Wagner in America: Planning and the Political Economy of Capitalist Urbanization," *Planning Perspectives* 32 (Summer 2017): 481–502.

14 See note 4. There is extensive literature on issues of industrialized building production, a chief concern of many modern architects. For Gropius's pursuit of the prefabricated dwelling from Germany to America, see, for example, Gilbert Herbert, *The Dream of the Factory-Made House: Walter Gropius and Konrad Wachsmann* (Cambridge, MA: MIT Press, 1984); for Wagner's efforts to institute industrial production methods at the settlements planned by him in Germany, see Jörn Janssen, "Produktion und Konsum von Wohnungen sozialisieren? Der Verband sozialer Baubetriebe und die Deutsche Wohnungsfürsorge AG für Beamte, Angestellte und Arbeiter," in *Martin Wagner, 1885–1957*, ed. Homann et al., 25–45.

15 See, for example, Winfried Nerdinger, *The Architect Walter Gropius* (Berlin: Bauhaus-Archiv Berlin and Cambridge, MA: Busch-Reisinger Museum, Harvard University, 1985), 15–19; Wallis Miller, "Architecture, Building, and the Bauhaus," in *Bauhaus Culture: From Weimar to the Cold War*, ed. Kathleen James-Chakraborty (Minneapolis: University of Minnesota Press, 2006), 63–89.

16 See correspondence between Gropius and Wagner in Walter Gropius Papers, 1925–1969, Houghton Library, Harvard University, Folder #1681.

17 Gropius, *New Architecture*, 98–99.

18   Walter Gropius to his sister, Manon Gropius, July 22, 1948, Walter and Ise Gropius Papers, Smithsonian Institution, Archives of American Art, Washington, DC, n. p. All translations are mine unless otherwise noted.

19   Martin Wagner to Lewis Mumford, March 4, 1956, Lewis Mumford Papers, Kislak Center for Special Collections, Rare Books and Manuscripts, University of Pennsylvania, n. p.

20   Many drafts of published and unpublished manuscripts are collected in PMW.

21   Martin Wagner to Ernst May, Istanbul, March 12, 1937, Ernst May Papers, Nuremberg, GNM, DKA, NL I, C-772.

22   See Martin Wagner, *Townlets and Towns: A Study on City Reconstruction Made by the Students of the Graduate School of Design, Harvard University*, 1946, unpublished MS, PMW.

23   Martin Wagner to Walter Gropius, December 6, 1948, Walter Gropius Papers, 1925–1969, Folder #1681, Houghton Library, Harvard University, n. p. Translation by Andro Mathewson.

24   There is a long evolution of this concept in Wagner's writings, culminating before the war in *Das wachsende Haus* (Berlin/Leipzig, 1932), where rationalization of the residential building industry was linked to an efficient urban plan premised upon the eventual socialization of the land. See also Manfredo Tafuri, "Sozialpolitik and the City in Weimar Germany," *The Sphere and the Labyrinth: Avant-Gardes and Architecture from Piranesi to the 1970s*, trans. Pellegrino d'Acierno and Robert Connolly (Cambridge, MA: MIT Press, 1987), 224–229.

25   Martin Wagner, "Is Land a Commodity?" February 25, 1939, PMW, 54.

26   Walter Gropius and Martin Wagner, "Epilogue: The New City Pattern for the People and by the People," in *The Problem of the Cities and Towns: Report of the Conference on Urbanism, Harvard University, March 5–6, 1942*, ed. Guy Greer (Cambridge, MA, 1942), III, 102.

27   Greer, 110.

28   Greer, 110.

29   Martin Wagner and Walter Gropius, "Cities' Renaissance," *The Kenyon Review* 5 (Winter 1943): 28.

30   Wagner and Gropius, "Cities' Renaissance," 28.

31   Walter Gropius and Martin Wagner, *Housing as a Townbuilding Problem: A Post-War Housing Problem for the Students of the Graduate School of Design, Harvard University, February–March, 1942* (Cambridge, MA, January 20, 1942); Walter Gropius and Martin Wagner, "A Program for City Reconstruction," *Architectural Forum* (July 1943): 75–86.

32   Gropius and Wagner, "A Program for City Reconstruction," 96.

33   Gropius and Wagner, *Housing as a Townbuilding Problem*, 31–32, 33.

34   Gropius and Wagner, *Housing as a Townbuilding Problem*, 44.

35   Gropius and Wagner, *Housing as a Townbuilding Problem*, 30, 45. Emphasis in the original.

36   See Miller, "Architecture, Building"; Martin Wagner, *Das wachsende Haus* (Berlin/Leipzig, 1932).

37   Walter Gropius, *Rebuilding Our Communities* (Chicago: Paul Theobald, 1945), 13.

38   Gropius, *Rebuilding*, 16, 26.

39   Gropius, *Rebuilding*, 20.

40   Gropius, *Rebuilding*, 25.

41   Gropius, *Rebuilding*, 34–5.

42   Gropius, *Rebuilding*, 32.

43   The latter point is emphasized in Sevilla-Buitrago, "Martin Wagner in America," although the former is overlooked.

44   See Charles S. Maier, *Recasting Bourgeois Europe: Stabilization in France, Germany, and Italy in the Decade after World War I* (Princeton: Princeton University Press, 1988), 138.

45   Maier, *Recasting Bourgeois Europe*, 138–146.

46   See Wagner, *Das wachsende Haus*, 228. See also Barbara Miller Lane, *Architecture and Politics in Germany 1918–1945* (Cambridge, MA: Harvard University Press, 1985), 250, note 16.

47   Martin Wagner, *Wirtschaftlicher Städtebau* (Stuttgart: Julius Hoffmann Verlag, 1951).

48   For curricular reforms in city planning at the GSD in relation to the Wagner-Gropius collaboration, see Vallye, *Design and the Politics of Knowledge in America*, 138–195.

49   G. Holmes Perkins, "The Planning Schools: 3. Harvard University," *The Town Planning Review* 20 (January 1950), 317.

50   Martin Wagner, "American versus German City Planning," *The Journal of Land and Public Utility Economics* 22 (November 1946): 321–338; Byrn J. Hovde, "Critique: 'American versus German City Planning,'" *The Journal of Land and Public Utility Economics* 23 (August 1947), 242.

51   Hovde, 242–243.

Michael Kubo

"Companies of Scholars": The Architects Collaborative, Walter Gropius, and the Politics of Expertise at the University of Baghdad

Fig. 1. The Architects Collaborative (TAC), University of Baghdad, site plan, January 20, 1960. *The Architects Collaborative 1945–1965* (Teufen: A. Niggli, 1966).

The steady expansion of US architectural practice after the 1950s frequently followed the path of geopolitical and economic interests abroad. As the shifting dynamics of the Cold War implicated new territories as puzzle pieces in the global map of US and Soviet influence, the newly post-colonial states of the Arab and Persian Gulf gained importance both as potential allies within the developmental framework of US technical assistance, and as sources for the increasingly valuable strategic currency of oil.[1] Governmental and financial aid programs such as Point Four sought to embed US influence within national modernization efforts in these states, while pro-US alignments such as the Baghdad Pact—established in Iraq in 1955 along with Turkey, Iran, and Pakistan as a territorial hedge against Soviet incursion into the Middle East—competed with other transnational formations in the region, particularly the Pan-Arabist movement embodied by the rise of Gamal Abdel Nasser in Egypt. In parallel, consortia of US and European oil companies extended their interests beyond the major prewar sources of foreign petroleum in South America and Southeast Asia into the Arab and Persian Gulf states after World War II, exploiting concessions gained by US and British interests in the early twentieth century.

At the same time, these newly independent states, freed from direct British and French control, increasingly contested and renegotiated the terms of prewar concessions on the way to full nationalization of their oil interests, generating lucrative new revenue streams that could be used to support ambitious national programs of modernization and development.

504

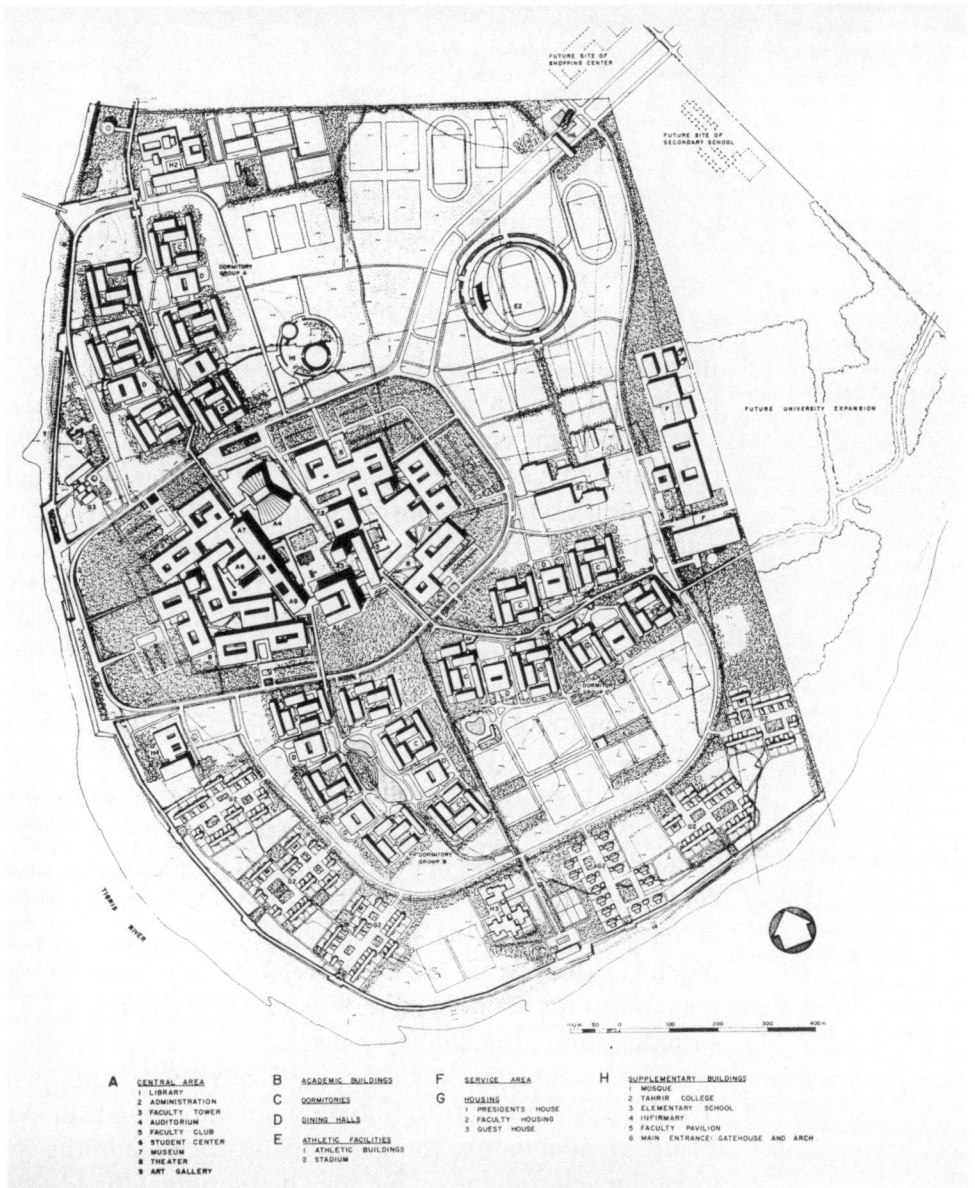

A CENTRAL AREA
1 LIBRARY
2 ADMINISTRATION
3 FACULTY TOWER
4 AUDITORIUM
5 FACULTY CLUB
6 STUDENT CENTER
7 MUSEUM
8 THEATER
9 ART GALLERY

B ACADEMIC BUILDINGS
C DORMITORIES
D DINING HALLS
E ATHLETIC FACILITIES
1 ATHLETIC BUILDINGS
2 STADIUM

F SERVICE AREA
G HOUSING
1 PRESIDENTS HOUSE
2 FACULTY HOUSING
3 GUEST HOUSE

H SUPPLEMENTARY BUILDINGS
1 MOSQUE
2 TAHRIR COLLEGE
3 ELEMENTARY SCHOOL
4 INFIRMARY
5 FACULTY PAVILION
6 MAIN ENTRANCE: GATEHOUSE AND ARCH

By the mid-1960s, many of the US firms established or newly enlarged in the years immediately after World War II had gained significant commissions in the Arab and Persian Gulf states. The expanding presence of US architects in the region within a decade after 1955 included projects by Sert, Jackson and Gourley and The Architects Collaborative (TAC) in Iraq; Brown Daltas & Associates, Edward Larrabee Barnes Associates, and Victor Gruen International in Iran; and Minoru Yamasaki Associates, Skidmore, Owings & Merrill (SOM), Caudill Rowlett Scott (CRS), and Edward Durell Stone in Saudi Arabia.[2] In addressing the problems and the potential of these increasingly competitive territories for architectural work, these firms sought to navigate shifting geopolitical currents in order to stake out forms of practice that would enable them to pursue, and realize, projects commissions in the region. Aspects of the discursive and competitive terrain of practice that had marked prewar competition in the US thus reasserted themselves as US offices sought to understand the cultural, aesthetic, and technical parameters particular to differing national contexts.

A revealing case study for these dynamics of professional and cultural exchange is TAC's design for the University of Baghdad, among the earliest examples of involvement by US firms in the Arab and Persian Gulf states.[fig.1] As an equal partnership of younger architects together with Walter Gropius—renowned as the founder of the Bauhaus in Weimar and later as chairman of the Harvard Graduate School of Design—The Architects Collaborative was uniquely positioned to work across both ends of the discursive spectrum between signature and teamwork in the Iraqi context, gaining the University of Baghdad commission largely through the figure of Gropius but developing the project through more bureaucratic forms of organization.[3] Beyond Gropius's presence as a practitioner and educator of international stature, TAC's success in conducting the project across multiple political regimes lay largely in its self-positioning as an expert practice, a mode well suited to the firm's stakes in shaping the educational and physical structure of the first consolidated university in Iraq—including the first department of architecture in the country—as an infrastructure for national development.

The commission to design the university campus formed part of an extensive modernization program under the Iraq Development Board, created in 1950 to expend seventy percent of the country's expanding oil revenue on national development, first through infrastructural projects and after 1956 through iconic cultural projects by foreign architects including Le Corbusier, Alvar Aalto, Frank Lloyd Wright, and Gio Ponti. The majority of these projects ended in 1958, when public hostility to foreign influences culminated in the coup d'état of July 14, 1958, in which the US- and British-affiliated Hashemite monarchy of King Faisal II was overthrown and military general Abd al-Karim Qasim came to power. Yet TAC's commission for the university continued, proceeding in fits and starts through violent political and economic realignments into the country's second building boom under Saddam Hussein in the late 1970s and early 1980s. Within a decade of the beginning of the Baghdad commission, the TAC office was heavily dependent on work throughout the region, with commercial and cultural commissions first in Kuwait and eventually in Jordan, Saudi Arabia, Iran, and the Emirates from the 1960s through the end of the second boom in crude oil prices in 1983.

Companies of scholars

TAC's commission for the University of Baghdad was gained through contacts formed in the interstices between US professional training, the bureaucratic channels of the Development Board, and the emerging terrain for modernist architectural practices in Iraq in the 1950s. The key interlocutors in this transnational exchange were Ellen and Nizar Ali Jawdat, architects who had studied under Gropius at the Harvard Graduate School of Design from 1942 to 1947—a period when women and foreign students made up a significant portion of the student body during wartime—before returning to practice in Baghdad, where they became advocates of Gropius and TAC for the Development Board commissions taking shape in the 1950s.[4] TAC's ability to navigate the university commission through local constraints additionally relied on the presence of Hisham A. Munir, the associate architect for the project from its early years until 1990, when he left for the US amid the political turmoil of the First Gulf War. In this sense, both the Jawdats and Munir epitomized the elite class of increasingly US-educated professionals, foreign and Iraqi, that comprised the generation of young architects who began self-consciously modernist practices in Baghdad after World War II.[5]

A crucial impetus for instigating the university commission was Gropius's visit to Baghdad in August 1954 to visit the Jawdats upon his return from a Rockefeller Foundation-sponsored trip to Japan following his retirement as chair of the Harvard Graduate School of Design. While there, Gropius gave a lecture on modern architecture at the US Embassy at the request of David D. Newsom, the Public Affairs Officer for the US Embassy and director of the United States Information Service (USIS) in Baghdad.[6] Following his return to Cambridge, Ellen Jawdat expressed her intent to promote Gropius for a role within the architectural development taking place in Iraq, writing to him that "We are more than ever convinced that we must find some way for you to make your contribution to this country."[7] Indeed, the Jawdats subsequently prepared a short essay and information sheet arguing for Gropius's appointment as a coordinating regional planner to oversee the Development Board's expansive building program for the country, instigating a process that eventually led the Development Board to offer Gropius and TAC the commission for the University of Baghdad campus in September 1957.[8]

In contrast to its origins in Gropius's charismatic appearance in

Michael Kubo

"Companies of Scholars"

Baghdad and the Jawdats' personal advocacy on his behalf, the project developed by TAC for the university spoke the professional language of teamwork and expertise from its origins. The first scheme, though commissioned prior to the 1958 coup, was submitted in its *Report on the University of Baghdad* of January 1959, a 104-page technical report accompanied by a pilot plan and floor plans for the campus, model photographs, and six colored perspectives.[9] Following a trip by Gropius to Baghdad the following month to discuss whether to proceed with the project, a revised second scheme of the project was submitted a year later on January 20, 1960, with a preliminary design drawing set supplemented by a detailed 155-page description of the building program.[10]

While there were significant changes to the organization of the campus and the architectural expression of its major buildings between the first and second schemes, including a considerable increase in the program and number of students to be accommodated by the new university, the fundamental task of creating the first consolidated university in Baghdad remained the same across these two phases. TAC was responsible for planning the administrative and departmental structure of the university, as well as the complete design of the campus and its facilities. Unlike European and US campuses that had developed piecemeal over time, the commission for the University of Baghdad offered an "opportunity which has been given to no other similar institution" in either East or West. "For the first time," the anonymous text of the TAC report suggested, "it might be possible to plan a total university—both the physical plant and the philosophy of education—to make use of and profit from the experience of major Western universities and at the same time to cater to the particular needs and desires of the people of Iraq."[11] While the concept of a "total" institution here referred to the chance to unite the spatial and pedagogical structures of the University in TAC's design, the twin ideals of unifying the academic disciplines and synthesizing local and foreign educational models resonated with the Bauhaus sense of creative unity as well as with Gropius's conception of "total architecture," conceived as the result of democratic collaboration by "a closely cooperating team together with the engineer, the scientist and the builder."[12]

The central question in conceptualizing a "total university" for Iraq was its expected role in the country's ongoing modernization efforts, particularly through the expansion of an elite, educated class of graduates that could serve in the future tasks of national development. Among the forms of expertise that would be enabled by the new university was the first dedicated school of architecture in Iraq, established in 1959 as a separate faculty within the department of engineering, coincident with the planning and design of the consolidated Baghdad campus. Unsurprisingly given his pedagogical legacy from the Bauhaus to Harvard, Gropius took a particular interest in the role of an architectural curriculum in addressing a national context in which "Most new buildings continued to be poor imitations of modern western buildings," as "the age-old building traditions of the Middle East ... [were] rapidly being replaced by new materials and construction methods which neither builders nor designers had mastered adequately."[13] According to Fuad Uthman, a member of the faculty of architecture from 1961 to 1969, Gropius recommended as a result that the new school "deal with the development and improvement of local construction techniques," suggesting "that the country needed a school of building construction more than one of architecture."[14] This distinction echoed the Bauhaus emphasis on building (*Bau*) as the highest unity of the arts, a synthesis its third director, Ludwig Mies van der Rohe, affiliated with the German sense of *Baukunst* (the art of building) rather than *Architektur* (architecture) as a tectonic rather than aesthetic pursuit.[15]

A more specific model for the University of Baghdad's pedagogy, including the faculty of architecture, was provided by an official affiliation with the University of Texas at Austin after 1963. Even prior to this formal relationship, the foundational architectural curriculum in Baghdad had been modeled on the five-year sequence of typical US undergraduate architecture programs, as drafted in 1959–60 by Munir, a graduate of the University of Texas in 1953.[16] Kenton W. Keith, a USIS officer in Baghdad in the mid-1960s, later described the alliance between the two universities as "a kind of twinning relationship" that involved exchanges of both students and professors, one that was encouraged on both sides as "of benefit to the Iraqis and of benefit to the long range interests of the US."[17] Such exchanges underscored the degree to which TAC's design was intended to create an expert university for the training of experts, including forms of training fashioned after the same US models of architectural practice that were embodied in TAC's own presence in Iraq.[18]

*Michael
Kubo*

"Companies
of
Scholars"

While its participation in the university as a technically sophisticated office of coordinating experts seemingly reinforced this symmetry between models of pedagogy and practice, TAC cautioned in its initial report against a conception of the future university as dedicated solely to the production of technicians. The firm argued that it was crucial for the government to avoid an exclusive focus on the immediate provision of expertise, in favor of a more flexible, integrated educational program encompassing a humanistic curriculum beyond the narrow scope of professional training.[19] This holistic emphasis echoed the earlier Bauhaus conception of unity across creative disciplines, as reflected in Gropius's declaration upon the school's founding in 1919 that "art is not a 'profession'."[20] In contrast, TAC sought an educational structure that would oppose the technocratic emphasis on specialization that, in its view, increasingly plagued the culture of education in the US as well.

Such problems returned TAC to the question of whether to plan the university's administrative and physical structure according to departments with separate facilities, or with a more integrated structure that would allow for flexibility and change over time. Conceptually, the report asked, "Are [universities] agglomerations of college buildings per se or are they companies of scholars devoted to common professional pursuits?"[21] Partner Robert S. McMillan echoed this terminology in describing the firm's approach to the University of Baghdad, likening the problem to that of designing "a 'single industry town'—the industry being education."[22] In organizing the Baghdad campus around shared facilities rather than separate departments, these "companies of scholars" became the organizing principle for the university as a whole. The terms of this conception of the university bore a specific parallel to the holistic creative model on which TAC itself had been established by the firm's younger partners in collaboration with Gropius, as a company of generalists rather than an aggregation of discrete specializations.[23]

Diagrams of the administrative and physical organization of the university in the 1959 *Report on the University of Baghdad* made clear how TAC sought to relate its pedagogical ideals to the spatial structure of its campus on the Karada site. Dividing the university administration into two major functions, instruction and operations, the report proposed that most university instruction be placed under the aegis of a single Dean of Arts and Sciences, rather than splitting these two

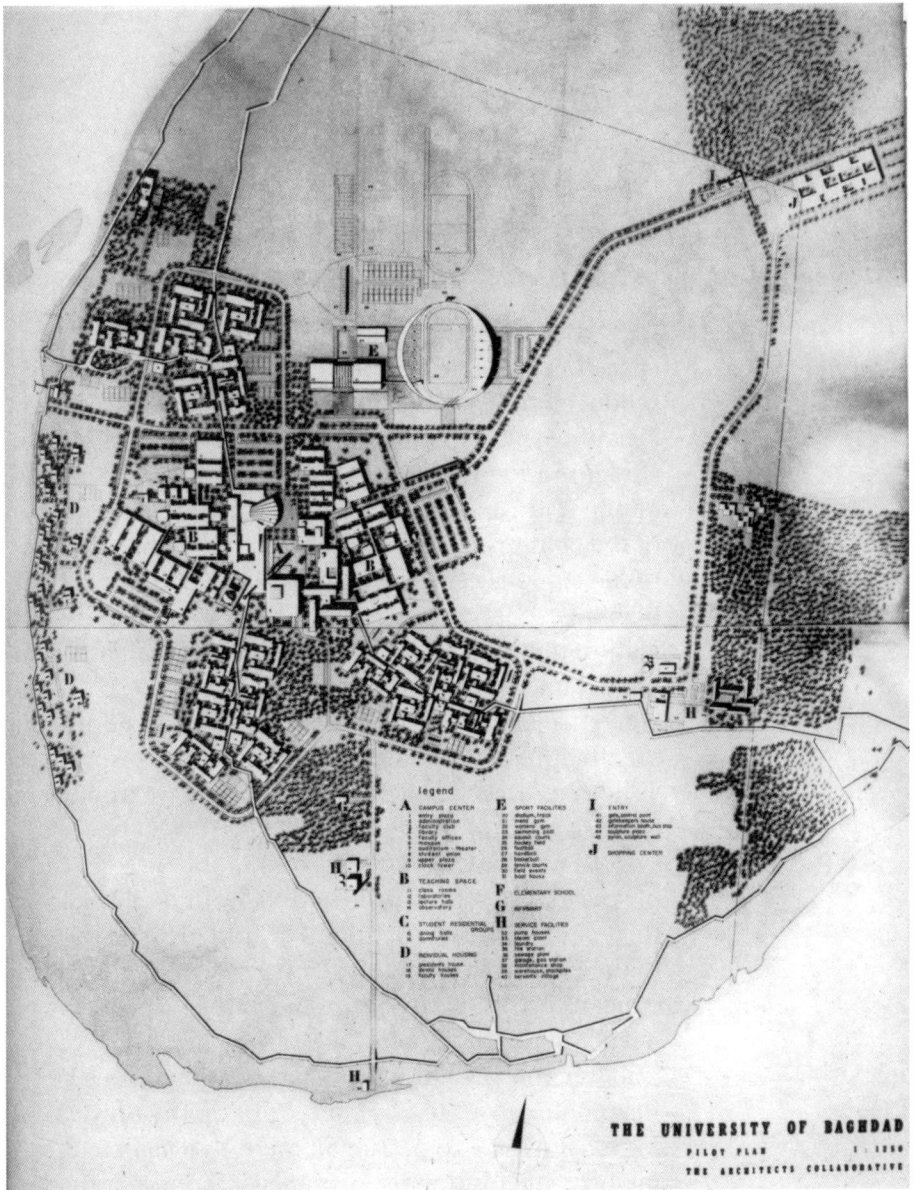

THE UNIVERSITY OF BAGHDAD
PILOT PLAN   1 : 1250
THE ARCHITECTS COLLABORATIVE

domains into separate deanships on the model of the typical US university. This administrative pattern corresponded to a physical structure of shared teaching facilities across departments, rather than a campus based on separate faculties in which each would have discipline-specific classrooms, libraries, and offices.

To these ends, the report proposed that buildings be grouped together essentially by type, in rings extending outward from a campus center toward the river on three sides.[fig.2] The campus center would contain the university library, theater and auditorium, central administration building, faculty club, and mosque, joined by covered passages around an open plaza. This central precinct would be surrounded by a mat of connected blocks of classrooms and laboratory spaces, respectively. While each school would have a permanent headquarters within this matrix, TAC argued that this structure of shared facilities would better accommodate future changes in departmental sizes and

Michael
Kubo

"Companies
of
Scholars"

511

space needs, as well as preventing the effective segregation of different schools into permanent, discrete sections of the campus over time. Teaching spaces would be surrounded in turn by three clusters of student residences served by a ring road, with individual faculty and administrative housing located along the river at the western edge of the campus. The radial pattern of housing clusters connected back to the campus center via paths based on an existing network of 10-foot-high dikes that remained on the site following its reclamation, a feature that was rendered into the pilot plan as a means of providing level changes within the campus. This pattern of "spoke lines" provided a legible symbol of the flood-control efforts that had marked the first phase of the Development Board's work, now incorporated as both a rhetorical device and a primary structuring element within the university plan.[24]

In contrast to TAC's appeals to the broader humanistic character of a new university for the nation, both the Development Board and the US interests that operated in Iraq prior to 1958 were aligned in the expectation that the University of Baghdad would produce an educated class of experts, in much the same terms of "immediate need" that its architects had warned against.[25] Indeed, the desire to train technicians for national development was key among the factors that enabled TAC to continue work on the university project following Qasim's rise to power, an event that signaled the demise of the majority of cultural projects sponsored under the monarchy. Among the commissions that began under Faisal II, only those clearly associated with concrete governmental and social needs were chosen to continue under Qasim, while others, such as Aalto's museum and Wright's opera house and cultural center, were abandoned. The new regime proceeded with Gio Ponti's headquarters for the Development Board itself, now purged of its US and British advisers and reorganized as the Ministry of Planning. So, too, did Le Corbusier's project for a national stadium and sports complex continue until the architect's death in 1965, before its eventual revival and the construction of the gymnasium portion of this complex between 1974 and 1980 by one of Le Corbusier's former associates, Georges-Marc Présenté. The TAC university proposal was the only other of the Development Board projects to continue after 1958, and the only project by a US firm, a particularly difficult proposition in the pro-Soviet context of the Qasim regime.

Fig. 3. Walter Gropius and TAC members with Director General of Baghdad, circa 1965. Left to right: Richard Morton, H. Morse Payne Jr., Walter Gropius, Louis A. McMillen.

Despite its problematic status as a US firm in the post-revolutionary context of the new Iraqi republic, TAC sought to negotiate these political shifts by appealing to the expanded role of education within the new planned economy under Qasim.[26] After delivering the preliminary scheme for the university in January 1959, delayed for four months amid the political turmoil following the coup d'état, Gropius and other members of TAC traveled to Iraq to present the design to the new government in February 1959, unsure of the fate of the project.[27] Qasim gave general approval for the project during the meeting, though not without requesting changes that significantly enlarged the national scope of the university program. These included substantial increases in the number of students to be accommodated by the campus, from 8,370 to 12,000—a figure that would later be expanded to 18,000—and corresponding changes to the sizes of the library, auditorium, dormitory and dining facilities, classrooms and laboratories, infirmary, elementary school, faculty houses, and guest houses to be built for the campus.[28]

More significantly for the form of the new university as a whole, Qasim apparently requested the addition of a tower as a prominent vertical element that would make the construction of the campus visible at a distance—and, more specifically, visible to Qasim from his office within the Ministry of Defense—thus signaling the cultural importance of the university at once to both its client and the general public as a symbol of national progress.[29] This imperative led to the addition of an administrative tower as an anchor for the heart of campus in the revised scheme of the university that was delivered a year later in January 1960, standing on axis with the entry road as it turned toward the ring road that enclosed this central precinct.[fig.3] TAC leveraged its professional expertise in seeking to ensure the continuity of the university commission within Iraq's uncertain political climate, as the firm's June 2, 1959 contract for the university required a deposit of $1 million in the first year and $2.3 million in the second year to a Swiss bank account in order to guarantee regular receipt of payments from the Iraqi government.[30]

Work continued, and by July 1961, international contractors responded to the first tender (or bid group) for the university, one of

Michael Kubo

"Companies of Scholars"

Fig.4. University of Baghdad, construction site, n.d. Left to right: Louis A. McMillen, Umberto Vannini, Walter Gropius, Hisham A. Munir. *The Walter Gropius Archive*, vol. 4 (New York and London: Garland Publishing, Inc., 1990–91).

Fig.5. University of Baghdad campus site, ring road and entry gate as seen from the administrative tower after first phase of construction, n.d.

six phases anticipated to build a campus of some 273 buildings with a budget of $ 80 million.[31] Working drawings were completed by the end of 1962 and construction began early in the following year, with Qasim laying the cornerstone.[32] The visible products of this first phase of building included the administrative tower desired by Qasim, the ring road encircling the campus center, and the entry gate to the campus, titled the "Open Mind."[fig.4, 5] [33] Yet TAC's attempts to ensure the uninterrupted progress of the project remained subject to continued political instability in Iraq, as suggested by communications with the Jawdats about the fate of the project following the Ba'ath coup d'état of February 1963 in which Qasim was killed.[34] While portions of the first phase of construction were completed by 1966, further work all but halted through the violent political shifts of successive regimes. TAC's job files record the resumption of construction only in 1971, proceeding through the decade prior to a new wave of redesign and expansion during the next Iraqi building boom—this time under Saddam Hussein, beginning in 1979 and ending in 1983 with the deepening of the Iran-Iraq War and the first OPEC price quotas on oil production.[35]

Universal and regional aesthetics

"Universitas means 'wholeness'," TAC reminded the Development Board in its initial proposal for the university in 1959.[36] To that end, the firm argued, "the aim of the designers has been to achieve accordingly a 'human pattern' throughout the campus which can offer the creative setting for a full, well-integrated life of the students."[37] For TAC, this design approach to the "total university" was intended to achieve a cultural synthesis that might mediate between foreign and local traditions in creating an educational structure at once regional and global. Yet this notion of universality was weighted unequally between local and imported influences, as the introduction to the firm's 1959 *Report* made clear. "What we are suggesting," TAC explained,

> is that it is all too easy to impose western patterns and social and philosophical values on eastern culture without remembering how much the East has to teach the West ... a step forward in world understanding might be made if a university, situated between East and West, were to be so planned and developed as to provide both the intellectual, emotional, and physical environment to encourage synthesis of both types in the development of a world culture.[38]

Fig. 6. Perspective view of typical dormitories, University of Baghdad, first scheme. TAC, *Report on the University of Baghdad*, circa January 1959. Rendering: H. Morse Payne Jr.

Fig. 7. TAC, Tallahassee Civic Center (unbuilt), Tallahassee, FL (1955–56). TAC, *A Civic Center for Tallahassee, Florida*, August 1, 1956. Rendering: Peggy Eskridge.

In arguing for symbiosis, TAC repeated the affiliation of material and scientific expertise with the US and Europe—an affiliation that encoded its own position as an expert practice in the Iraqi context— opposing this technical capability to the "mysticism, philosophy, and aesthetics" of Iraqi culture.[39] In the concluding section of the 1959 *Report*, a single page dedicated to the architectural character of the university, the firm elucidated the principles of this intended synthesis between foreign technics and local aesthetics. "The architecture of the campus," TAC claimed, would be "both contemporary and re-gional," through the incorporation of "indigenous Arabic elements, flat roofs, patios, arcades, parapets, open staircases, open galleries, arches and vaults—but without imitatively borrowing adornment of the past."[fig.6] [40] Through the employment and patterning of such elements, the firm argued, "The sequence and character of these buildings is meant to represent the national pride and the cultural dignity of the modern Arab."

If the varying brise-soleil facades of the library and other buildings for the university expressed the universal technics of climate and its application to the university campus, other formal elements signaled TAC's attempt to identify what Ernesto N. Rogers described, in a 1960 review of the project in *Casabella*, as "semantic values" that would bind the modern architecture of the campus to national cultural impera-tives.[41] Among these devices was a language of concrete arches, used for structural as well as rhetorical purposes among the buildings that comprised the campus center. In the first scheme for the university, this arched motif was employed in particular for the mosque and the campus theater and auditorium: the spiritual and secular cultural icons, respectively, of the campus. In the second scheme, the theater and auditorium preserved this language in modified form, while the mosque, relocated to stand in isolation outside the campus center, was redesigned as a free-standing dome resting on three points.

By the time TAC began design work on the university in 1957, the use of arches as a regionalist sign had become something of a trope in

designs by US architects for cultural buildings abroad.[42] Such buildings
reflected the growing awareness among US architects of the tensions
inherent in adapting modernist architectural language to satisfy nationalist demands for signification in foreign contexts. So, too, the arch
form had emerged as a motif among contemporary artists and architects in Iraq in this period, as later work by Rifat Chadirji, Mohammed
Makiya, Hisham Munir, and others would attest. Yet this language had
begun to appear as a sign of regionalist rhetoric for commissions
within the US as well, as evidenced by TAC's unbuilt scheme for a civic
center for Tallahassee, Florida (1955–56), the immediate precursor to
the auditorium at the University of Baghdad.[fig.7] [43] While Louis A.
McMillen was known within TAC as a primary advocate for arches as
a regionalist language in the firm's commissions in Iraq and Kuwait,
Gropius was more ambiguous about the signification of the arch form
in Baghdad; in his comments accompanying the publication of the
first campus scheme in 1959, Gropius referred only to "shell constructions—vaults and domes" that would "give dramatic accents in the
silhouette" of the campus.[44]

In developing the Tallahassee arena into an auditorium for the
University of Baghdad three years later, TAC's design underwent a
series of subtle but meaningful modifications, particularly in relation
to the structural form of the auditorium and its position relative to the
mosque and other cultural buildings within the campus center.[45]
In the first scheme for the university, the visual contrast between the
concrete vaults of the auditorium and the arcaded pergolas of the
mosque took on additional meaning in the context of the Develop-

Michael
Kubo

"Companies
of
Scholars"

517

Fig.8. Perspective view of campus center with mosque and auditorium, University of Baghdad, first scheme. TAC, *Report on the University of Baghdad*, circa January 1959. Rendering: George Connelly.

Fig.9. Perspective view of mosque, University of Baghdad, second scheme. Rendering: Helmut Jacoby, circa 1959.

ment Board's modernization efforts, as a display of the tensions between the universalizing language of modernism and the self-conscious attempt to identify traditional forms more appropriate to a national Iraqi architecture.[fig.8]

TAC's university offers no obvious monument to the ambition to produce a class of citizens educated along US lines as a vehicle for national development. A candidate might be the administrative tower that appeared in the second version of the university scheme, placed on an axis with the entry road as this turns toward the campus center and designed to be seen at a distance, following Qasim's request for a legible symbol of Iraqi modernization. For their part, TAC proposed the "Open Mind," an arched gateway to the campus composed of paired cantilevered concrete forms framing a thin, linear gap, as an icon of Gropius's lifelong approach to pedagogy as well as a symbol of the Development Board's ambitions for the university as an infrastructure for national cultural development.

Beyond these metaphorical and bureaucratic totems, a more fitting synecdoche for the history of the University of Baghdad might be its mosque, among the elements that were most significantly altered in their form and meaning between the first and second schemes for the campus. Between these two proposals, the conservative design of courtyard and dome that had originally faced the auditorium was replaced by a self-consciously modernist form, placed in isolation on a site beyond the ring road that encircled the campus center.[fig.9] This reconfiguration corresponded with Qasim's desire for a bureaucratic icon—the administrative tower—as a more fitting marker of the construction of a national university under his rule. The displacement of the mosque effectively secularized the main precinct of cultural buildings at the heart of the university, at the same time that it shifted the meaning of the dome from a marker of regionalist accommodation to a heroic structural form as a sign of national progress. Relegated from the center of the campus to its periphery and radically modified in its form and signification, the mosque stands as a historiographic cipher for the cultural stakes of authorship and signification that marked the development of the University of Baghdad. Heroic in aspirations yet marginalized in its realization, the final form of the mosque offers an ambiguous figure of modernization, one that oscillates between images of spiritual and secular humanism, regionalism and universality, historicism and modernism, and genius and bureaucracy.

Michael Kubo

"Companies of Scholars"

519

In this sense, it stands as an unwitting monument to the transnational processes of professional and cultural exchange in which the university campus took shape.

In the partial form in which it was ultimately built in the 1970s and in its present state of decay, the mosque also emblematizes the larger fate of the University of Baghdad campus in the years after Qasim's death in 1963. In the decades that followed, TAC's efforts remained focused on the continuation of the project despite often violent regime changes and shifting political alignments for or against the US and its interests in the region. In the earliest years of the project, this may have reflected a combination of the pragmatic needs of the large firm (already with more than one hundred employees to support by the early 1960s) with Gropius's earnest desire to erect a lasting educational model—one whose origins can be traced in part to the Bauhaus—in Baghdad. By the time construction of the university resumed in the 1970s, however, TAC's ethical and political commitments were determined largely by the imperatives of corporate practice.

Yet TAC's proposal for the university was also designed from the outset to outlast any specific political structure. Unlike Wright's Plan for Greater Baghdad, which was conceived as a heroic monument to the genius of Faisal II and so perished along with his monarchy, both Gropius and TAC sought to position the university scheme on the supposedly more neutral plane of a national infrastructure, a feature that allowed even diametrically opposed regimes to claim its realization in turn as emblems of their governance. In continuing its construction, TAC's partners were left with the problematic burden of a bureaucratic commission, pursued under drastically different political regimes over a span of three decades, that would inevitably be judged—fairly or not—as a direct translation of Gropius's statements on education and society, originated over a half-century earlier in Weimar Germany and developed in the US, into the post-colonial context of Iraq. In this sense, the question of how to evaluate the ultimate successes or failures of the campus remained unresolved long after Gropius's death. By the 1990s, just prior to TAC's demise, Louis A. McMillen could only look back at the University of Baghdad—even with some three-quarters of the original scheme built—and lament that "a great deal more work must be done to complete this great project."[46]

1   Most of the oil consumed in both the
US and the Soviet Union in the 1950s continued
to be produced from domestic sources. The
strategic interest of the US in the oil resources of
the Gulf lay primarily in ensuring stability of
supply to Europe within the framework of the
Marshall Plan, particularly to avoid the potential consequences of political instability caused
by disruptions or dramatic price fluctuations
in the supply of petroleum. See James L. Gelvin,
The Modern Middle East: A History, 4th ed.
(Oxford and New York: Oxford University Press,
2015), 300–316.
2   These efforts were paralleled by the
involvement of large architecture-construction-
engineering firms in both infrastructural and
architectural work in the Arab and Persian Gulf
states, including the presence of conglomerates
such as Bechtel Group, Frank E. Basil, and
Metcalf & Eddy, Inc.
3   The Architects Collaborative (TAC) was
established in 1945 as an experiment in team-
based design by seven recent graduates of
Harvard, Yale, and the Cambridge School of
Architecture and Landscape Architecture—
Jean Bodman Fletcher, Norman C. Fletcher,
Sarah Pillsbury Harkness, John C. Harkness,
Robert S. McMillan, Louis A. McMillen, and
Benjamin C. Thompson—together with
Gropius, then chairman at Harvard after his
emigration from Germany via England in 1937.
4   Ellen Jawdat (née Ellen Stone Coan)
enrolled at the Harvard Graduate School of
Design under Gropius, where she graduated in
1947. There she met and married Nizar Ali
Jawdat, the son of Ali Jawdat al-Ayyubi, the first
Iraqi ambassador to the US from 1942 to 1947
(and later prime minister during the period
in which TAC was officially commissioned to
design the university). After returning to
Baghdad, Ellen practiced as an architect—the
first woman to do so in Iraq—while Nizar Ali
worked as architect for the Iraqi Railways office
in fulfillment of the five years of public service
that were required in exchange for government
sponsorship of his studies at Harvard.
5   Hisham Munir received a B.ARCH. from
the University of Texas at Austin in 1953 and an
M.ARCH. from the University of Southern California in 1956, in both cases designing buildings
on Iraqi sites as thesis projects. After gaining
experience by working for various offices in

Dallas and Los Angeles, Munir returned to
Baghdad in 1958 to seek the architectural and
infrastructural commissions that were increasingly available in Iraq under the Development
Board. Significantly, these were often highly
technical in both building type and construction technology, as with his first project, a com-
petition-winning entry for a tuberculosis hospital in Mosul, designed in reinforced concrete
and completed in 1964.
6   Bauhaus-Archiv, Werkverzeichnis 151,
Baghdad University. An accompanying list of
guests for a lunch and dinner with Gropius
named a number of young architects trained
in the US and Europe, including Qahtan Awni
(University of California, Berkeley), Jaafar
Allawi (University of Liverpool), and Rifat
Chadirji (Hammersmith School of Arts and
Crafts in London). Harvard University,
Houghton Library, MS Ger 208, folder 956.
7   Ellen Jawdat to Walter Gropius,
October 3, 1954, Harvard University, MS Ger
208, folder 956.
8   Typescript of essay and information
sheet written by Ellen Jawdat, n. d. Personal
papers of Ellen Jawdat.
9   The Architects Collaborative, *Report on
the University of Baghdad Designed by The Architects
Collaborative, Cambridge, Massachusetts, U. S. A.*,
circa January 1959.
10   The Architects Collaborative, *Preliminary
Design Report: The University of Baghdad*, January
20, 1960. The report references meetings in
February 1959 in which general approval for the
project was given and changes and additions
to the original program were specified. Ibid.,
1–2. Ellen Jawdat wrote to Gropius in the same
month from Rome—where she and Nizar had
escaped following the coup—to thank him for
reporting his "impressions of the situation in
Baghdad" while visiting them upon his return
from Iraq. Ellen Jawdat to Walter and Ise
Gropius, February 14, 1959, Harvard University,
Houghton Library, MS Ger 208, folder 956.
11   TAC, *Report on the University of Baghdad*, 1.
12   Walter Gropius, "The Architect within
Our Industrial Society," in *Scope of Total Architecture* (New York: Harper & Brothers, 1955), 80.
13   Fuad A. Uthman, "Exporting Architectural Education to the Arab World," *Journal
of Architectural Education* 31, no. 3 (February
1978): 27.

Kubo*

"Companies
of
Scholars"

521

14   Uthman, 27.

15   See Fritz Neumeyer, *The Artless Word: Mies van der Rohe on the Building Art*, trans. Mark Jarzombek (Cambridge, MA: MIT Press, 1991).

16   Uthman, 29.

17   Kenton W. Keith, USIS Rotation Officer, Baghdad (1966–67), interviewed by Charles Stuart Kennedy, 1998, in The Association for Diplomatic Studies and Training Foreign Affairs Oral History Project, "Iraq Country Reader," adst.org/wp-content/uploads/2012/09/Iraq.pdf, 164.

18   By 1978, of the 200 architects practicing in Iraq, some 180 had been trained at the University of Baghdad, with the remainder having studied in the US, the USSR, and European schools on both sides of the Cold War divide. Uthman, 30.

19   TAC, *Report on the University of Baghdad*, 3–4.

20   Walter Gropius, "Program of the Staatliches Bauhaus in Weimar" [1919], trans. in Ulrich Conrads, *Programs and Manifestoes on 20th-Century Architecture* (Cambridge, MA: MIT Press, 1964), 49–53.

21   TAC, *Report on the University of Baghdad*, 21.

22   Robert S. McMillan, "Visual Problems in Town Planning: The 'University Town' at Baghdad," transcript of paper delivered at "The New Metropolis in the Arab World," an international seminar sponsored by the Congress for Cultural Freedom and the Egyptian Society of Engineers, Cairo, December 17–22, 1960: CAI/15, 3.

23   See Walter Gropius, "TAC's Teamwork," in Walter Gropius and Sarah P. Harkness, eds., *The Architects Collaborative 1945–1965* (Teufen: Verlag Arthur Niggli, 1966).

24   TAC, *Report on the University of Baghdad*, 32.

25   Henry Wiens, responsible for the Point Four program as director of the United States Operations Mission (USOM) to Iraq from 1954 to 1956 and among the guests Gropius had met on his 1954 trip to Baghdad, confirmed that among US aims in this period, "In education, emphasis was placed on technical training." Wiens, "The United States Operations Mission in Iraq," *Annals of the American Academy of Political and Social Science* 323 (May 1959): 142–43.

26   Unlike cultural programs seen to be of dubious value to the post-revolutionary state, like opera or art, education took on greater importance within governmental plans under Qasim, modeled in part on a Soviet-style planned economy as a spur to national economic development. See Phebe Marr, *The Modern History of Iraq*, 3rd ed. (Boulder, CO: Westview Press, 2012): 100.

27   These difficulties are detailed in a letter from Ellen Jawdat to Ise Gropius, May 1958 (Harvard University, Houghton Library, MS Ger 208, folder 956); letters from Walter Gropius to Ellen Jawdat, May 29, 1958, and Ise Gropius to Ellen and Nizar Jawdat, September 9, 1958, Harvard University, Houghton f 2013M-29.

28   TAC, *Preliminary Design Report*, 6.

29   Louis A. McMillen, "The University of Baghdad, Baghdad, Iraq," in John C. Harkness, ed., *Walter Gropius Archive, Vol. 4: 1945–1969; The Work of the Architects Collaborative* (New York and London: Garland Publishing, Inc., 1991), 189.

30   TAC, microfilm of contract, June 2, 1959, with renewals in 1961 and 1964, cited in Mina Marefat, "The Universal University: How Bauhaus Came to Baghdad," in Pedro Azara, ed., *Ciudad del espejismo: Bagdad, de Wright a Venturi = City of Mirages: Baghdad, from Wright to Venturi* (Barcelona: Universitat Politecnica de Catalunya, 2008): 158 and note 15.

31   "Everybody's Baby," *Time* 78, no. 2 (July 14, 1961): 66.

32   McMillen, "The University of Baghdad, Baghdad, Iraq," in *Walter Gropius Archive, Vol. 4: 1945–1969*, 190.

33   McMillen, 190. Less visibly, this first phase of construction also included extensive work in flood control, water, and landscape engineering along the Tigris River.

34   Ise Gropius wrote to Ellen Jawdat on October 27, 1963 of Walter Gropius's concern regarding the continuation of the university project, though cautioning that Walter "is a man who absolutely never gives up and as long as the financial situation permits he will not abandon this scheme." Harvard University, Houghton f 2013M-29.

35   See *Medinaat Al Salaam: Baghdad 1979–1983*, special issue of *Process: Architecture*, no. 58 (May 1985).

36   TAC, *Report on the University of Baghdad*, 94.

37   TAC, *Report on the University of Baghdad*, 94.

38   TAC, *Report on the University of Baghdad*, 8–9.

39   TAC, *Report on the University of Baghdad*, 8–9.

40   TAC, *Report on the University of Baghdad*, 94.

41   Ernesto N. Rogers, "Architecture for the Middle East" ("Architettura per il Medio Oriente"), *Casabella continuità* 242 (August 1960): vii.

42   See, for example, Paul Rudolph's unbuilt design for a US embassy in Amman, Jordan (1954), the entry to Raymond & Rado's US embassy in Jakarta, Indonesia (1953–58), or the warehouse wing of Richard Neutra and Robert Alexander's US embassy in Karachi, Pakistan (1955–61).

43   See The Architects Collaborative, *A Civic Center for Tallahassee, Florida* (August 1, 1956).

44   Walter Gropius, introductory text to "TAC: The Architects Collaborative 1. The University of Baghdad," *Architectural Record* 125 (April 1959): 148.

45   The design for the university auditorium eliminated the parabolic arch that acted as the major visual element of the Tallahassee scheme in favor of a simpler structure of reinforced concrete piers supporting the radial barrel vaults above. In abandoning the dominant structural motif of the earlier project and its explicit homage to Le Corbusier's unbuilt Palace of the Soviets (ca. 1931), the Baghdad design effectively altered the meaning of the arched concrete forms that remained, divorcing them from a modernist visual language of heroic structural form to serve as signifiers of regionalist adaptation.

46   McMillen, "The University of Baghdad, Baghdad, Iraq," in *Walter Gropius Archive, Vol. 4: 1945–1969*, 190. Jack Hepting, TAC's chief site architect for the University of Baghdad from 1972 to 1986, later claimed that three-fourths of the project had been built by 1986, at a total cost of $750 million. Matt Viser, "Design for a Dictator: Local Architect Recalls a Career Building Hussein's Iraq," *The Boston Globe* (March 13, 2005): 122.

Michael Kubo

"Companies of Scholars"

Hamed Khosravi

Obscured Modernism: Revisiting the Legacy of Gabriel Guevrekian

There are two historical group meetings of architects, planners and artists, captured in photographs, through which the history of the Modernist movement unfolds. The first of these, taken in December 1926, shows the Bauhaus masters standing on the roof of the school building in Dessau. [fig.1] At the center is Walter Gropius, embraced like a leader by the masters of his school, noticeably projecting confidence, looking proud of the history he's made. The second photo was taken less than 18 months later, in June 1928, at La Sarraz, during the meeting at which CIAM, the International Congresses of Modern Architecture, was founded.[fig.2] Here, architect Gabriel Guevrekian stands out in the first row, immediately recognizable by his bald head, sharp double-breasted suit and confident, upright posture. He radiates assurance—all the more remarkable given that he was standing shoulder to shoulder with many of the leading lights of the Modernist movement, among them Max Ernst, Mart Stam, Sigfried Giedion, Josef Frank, Gerrit Rietveld and, skulking towards the back of the group, Le Corbusier and the patroness of the meeting, Madame de Mandrot. Not yet thirty, Guevrekian was already recognized as one of the protagonists of the European avant-garde.[1] But other roles awaited him. Before another decade was out, Guevrekian had hopped continents to work on a series of monumental buildings that were designed to present to the outside world the modern face of Reza Shah's Iran. Then, after a career drought coinciding with World War II, he again moved thousands of miles to take on his final guise, as a professor in a Midwestern university in the United States.

The two central figures in the photographs have upheld the flag of the movement during subsequent decades—though while Gropius

Fig. 1. The Bauhaus masters on the roof of the Bauhaus building in Dessau for the occasion of its opening on December 4 and 5, 1926. From left: Josef Albers, Hinnerk Scheper, Georg Muche, László Moholy-Nagy, Herbert Bayer, Joost Schmidt, Walter Gropius, Marcel Breuer, Vassily Kandinsky, Paul Klee, Lyonel Feininger, Gunta Stölzl, and Oskar Schlemmer. Photograph by Emile Gos.

Fig. 2. Official group photograph, CIAM I, La Sarraz, 1928. From left to right, top row: Mart Stam, Max Ernst Haefeli, Rudolf Steiger, Paul Artaria, Friedrich Traugott Gubler (press); middle row: Richard Dupierreux (Institute Cooperation-Intellectuelle, Paris), Pierre Chareau, Victor Bourgeois, Ernst May, Alberto Sartoris (obscured behind Guevrekian), Hans Schmidt, Hugo Häring, Juan de Zavala, Le Corbusier, P. Rochat (press), Henri Robert von der Mühll, Huibrecht Hoste, Sigfried Giedion, Werner Max Moser, Josef Frank; third row: Pierre Jeanneret (hand in pocket), Gerrit Rietveld, Gabriel Guévrékian, Lucienne Florentin, Madame Hélène de Mandrot, André Lurçat (hand in pocket), Gino Maggioni, seated: Fernando García Mercadal, Nelly Weber, Christophor Tadevossian. Photographer unknown.

525

Fig.3. László Moholy-Nagy
standing on the wall of
the Triangular Garden in
Villa Noailles, 1930.

has gained much more attention, Guevrekian remained almost obscured. Although he never formally taught at the Bauhaus, he had a close relationship with the school's directors and masters. It was not surprising when Gropius and Moholy-Nagy included the Guevrekian's project for the Hotel Touring-Club in France (1923) in the first Bauhaus book, *Internationale Architektur* (1925), alongside the works of more established architects and protagonists of the time. A few years later, Moholy-Nagy paid a special visit to Guevrekian's recently built Cubist Garden in Hyères.[fig.3] Excited about what he had seen, Moholy sent a few photos of the trip along with a letter to Carola Giedion, expressing greetings to Sigfried, Max, and Gabriel.[2]

Gabriel Guevrekian is not only one of the most prominent, yet lesser-known, pioneers of the Modernist movement; he is perhaps its most exceptional one. He was a nomadic figure, whose constant movements made possible the first exchanges of ideas between the East and West, but also between various schools of thought within Europe; the French avant-garde, the Wiener Werkstätte, the Russian Constructivists, the Dutch De Stijl, the German Ring, and the Bauhaus. Although few available accounts on Guevrekian's works see the first CIAM meeting as his professional inception,[3] a close reading of the preparatory correspondence and invitations to the first CIAM reveals that most of the guests, including those who participated as well as those who weren't able to join the congress, were contacted through Guevrekian's extensive professional and personal network.

From Constantinople to Vienna

Guevrekian was born on November 21, 1900 in what was then Constantinople, but while he was still an infant, his Armenian family migrated to Tehran to escape Ottoman persecution. This turned out to be a good move, since the Iranian Constitutional Revolution of 1905–07 had opened the way for sweeping social and political reform. Through

Guevrekian's father, Simon, who worked in the Qajar court as a surveyor and registrar of the crown jewels, the family came into contact with the city's aristocratic, cultural and intellectual elites. At the age of ten, after finishing primary school, Guevrekian and his older sister, Lyda, then moved with him to Vienna, where his uncle, Alex Galoustian, was a practicing architect. He continued his studies, enrolling first in a private music school and then, at the age of fifteen, starting his architectural training at the Academy of Applied Arts (Kunstgewerbeschule) in Vienna. Aside from the fact that World War I had broken out the year before, his timing was perfect, as the school was flourishing under the direction of teachers such as Oskar Strnad (his diploma master), Josef Frank, and Josef Hoffmann. It was at the Kunstgewerbeschule, too, that he met Hans Vetter, a fellow student who would become his lifelong friend. The two young men shared a similar sense of self-assurance. Vetter had grown up in a liberal artists' "colony" in the suburb of Kaasgraben, in one of six villas designed by Josef Hoffmann. His father was the head of the National Theater, and among the frequent visitors to his family home were Egon Schiele, Oskar Kokoschka, and Gustav Klimt. After graduating in 1919, Guevrekian and Vetter worked for Strnad and for Hoffmann, mostly on residential schemes. During this time, Guevrekian also occasionally attended the Bauschule of Adolf Loos.

A generation before, when Josef Hoffmann and Koloman Moser had founded the Wiener Werkstätte in radical opposition to the prevailing neoclassicism, fin-de-siècle Vienna had been the epicenter of Europe's artistic and intellectual avant-garde. But the war had robbed it of its luster. By 1922, the cosmopolitan émigré had decided it was time to move on. With a small entourage—his sister Lyda and Hans Vetter, who would soon become Lyda's husband—Guevrekian traveled north to Paris, the glittering postwar capital of the arts, where he would make his name.

Parisian avant-garde

In 1923, architect Marcel Temporal, who later also became known as a puppeteer, was casting ideas for the urban section of the 16th Salon d'Automne, an annual showcase for the less conformist artists and architects of Paris and their friends. Doubtless he was hoping, in his second stint as curator, to match the success of the previous year, when Le Corbusier had caused a stir with a spectacular 100-square-

meter diorama of his City of Three Million Inhabitants and, smaller in scale but equally indelible, a plaster model of his Maison Citrohan, already containing the five points of a new architecture that he would formulate in writing only seven years later.

The brief that Temporal gave to the exhibitors in the group l'Art Urbain was to investigate the hotel industry, which he asked to frame in relation to the various regional identities of France—or, more specifically, as a counter to the right-wing regionalist movement that had spread across Europe in the wake of World War I.[4] Adolf Loos presented his Grand Hotel Babylon (designed for Nice) which together with Guevrekian's Hotel Touring-Club de France—two large-scale structures accommodating more than 500 guests—attracted the highest level of opprobrium from conservative critics.[fig.4]

Guevrekian designed a project that rejected every principle of French regionalism. His Hotel Touring-Club was a prototypical model that could be expanded in any direction, horizontal or vertical, and replicated ad infinitum in any region of France. Spaced along the highways at 300–400 km intervals, the hotels were designed to form a network of minimum habitation machines, reduced to the barest formal expression, and distinguishable from each other only by their two-part identifying code, made up of the road number and a letter: for example, A20-A, A4-B, or A8-C. The Hotel Touring-Club was completely self-sufficient, like a small city. In addition to units of accommodation, it contained restaurants, a cinema, theater, shops, garages, and car-repair workshops. On each level there was a common hall that doubled as a library, with walls decorated with regional maps, and bookshelves laden with publications of potential interest to the motorist. Leading off from both sides of the hall were identical series of rooms: smaller ones on the lower floors for the chauffeurs, and suites with bathrooms for their employers on the floors above. Regardless of type, all were fitted out with the minimum of furniture.

Fig. 4. The model of Touring-Club de France, 1923.
Fig. 5. Gabriel Guevrekian, Perspective Ferroconcrete Villa, 1923.

The critic Gaston Varenne saw in the work of Guevrekian and Loos—who had described the aesthetics of his Grand Hotel Babylon as "Algerian"— an expression of contempt for the venerable traditions of France:

> Only concerned with volumes and forms, excluding all sentimentalities, these architects ignore tradition, preferring instead original solutions ... their buildings are nothing like what we [in France] are accustomed to seeing ... [They] do not realize that, under the pretext of modernity, they have returned to very primitive designs. Their buildings seem to refer back to Nineveh or ancient Egypt.[5]

Ironically, Varenne's xenophobic outburst harbors an aesthetic insight: the architecture of Nineveh and Egypt was indeed inherent in the abstract, Cubist qualities of both projects. A few years later, in the preface to his book *Hôtels et Sanatoria* (1931), Guevrekian—the urbane nomad—would locate the origins of the contemporary hotel in the caravanserais and monasteries of the Middle East, pointing out that a certain idea of collective short-stay accommodation had endured despite the revolution in the means of transportation. Expanding on the theme, he writes: "Recent social changes have given rise to a new way of living inspired by the idea of staying in a hotel, where a minimum private habitation unit is served by common spaces of work, fun and relaxation."[6] This was the kind of collective living embraced by the Hotel Touring-Club de France.

Besides the hotel, Guevrekian also showed two other projects in different sections of the 1923 salon:[7] a realized design for a music shop, *Le Sacre du printemps*, and a hypothetical project for a Ferroconcrete Villa, represented in plans and a low-angle perspective in the style of Mallet-Stevens' *Une cité moderne* (1921), albeit rendered in a rather purist fashion. Raised on pilotis, the villa contained more than a few allusions to contemporary visionary designs for planes and motorcars.[fig.5] One particularly distinctive feature was the external ramp that connected the balcony of the large studio on the third floor with the roof terrace—an idea realized by Le Corbusier only a few months later in his Cité Frugès in Pessac. In a 1932 article on "Deutsche Kunst," Sigfried Giedion claimed that the Ferroconcrete Villa also had some bearing on Le Corbusier's 1924 design for the Villa La Roche.

Hamed Khosravi

Obscured Modernism

Persian garden designer

It was the 1925 *Exposition Internationale des Arts Décoratifs et Industriels Modernes* in Paris that provided Guevrekian with his entrée into the role for which he remains best known—that of a landscape architect, and specifically the designer of the checkerboard garden at the Villa Noailles in Hyères.

The Art Deco Expo—a six-month extravaganza that took over a large swathe of central Paris—was designed to show the impact of modernity in every sphere. Jean-Claude Nicolas Forestier, curator of the garden section—there were 11 other sections, devoted to such themes as architecture and textiles, photography and cinema—commissioned pairs of artists and architects to design "instant" gardens to flank the pavilions: instant because they had to bloom immediately and last for the duration of the fair, from April to October. Mallet-Stevens solved this difficulty together with sculptors Jan and Joël Martel, developing a garden with trees cast in concrete.

Alongside this French modernist take on the garden, Forestier themed other installations according to more conventional geographic divisions—Arabic, Moorish, Spanish, Italian, Japanese, etc. Guevrekian was allocated the Persian garden, which he had to fit into an oddly shaped plot, an elevated corner site that opened onto the main exhibition pathway, just in front of L'Esplanade des Invalides. Titled *Jardin d'Eau et de Lumière* (Garden of Water and Light), Guevrekian's installation was the precise realization of a conceptual painting of the scheme he had produced earlier in the year—an abstract illustration of a flattened axonometric view. With its vivid shades of crimson, green, yellow and cobalt blue forming an abstract yet playful composition of triangles, the painting borrowed both from traditional Persian miniature composition and from the style of Guevrekian's Cubist friends, in particular the artist Robert Delaunay's *Window* and *Circular Forms* series.[fig.6]

The garden was simply a stylized triangular walled space, a piece of landscape contained within a boundary made of concrete and colored glass and designed to be perceived only from the outside. At its center was a tiered fountain, on top of which Guevrekian installed a revolving sculpture by the French glass artist Louis Barillet; "rather a nightclub trick than a serious attempt at garden decoration,"[8] sniped critic Fletcher Steele. The space between the fountain and the walls was geometrically patterned, with triangular patches of flowers

Cl. Rep

JARDIN ET FONTAINE
Par GUEVREKIAN

and grass forming solid colors of orange, purple, red and green, and each panel was also slightly tilted to follow the inclined ground plane. The striking effect of these colors and the geometric composition as a whole meant that the garden immediately became one of the most noticed and debated installations in the exhibition, and would ultimately win Guevrekian the jurors' Grand Prix.

Among the many visitors to that fair in 1925 were Charles and Marie-Laure de Noailles, wealthy patrons of the arts and owners of the legendary hôtel particulier at 11 Place des États-Unis (site of notorious parties with Jean Cocteau, Luis Buñuel and Man Ray, and an extravagant interior designed by Jean-Michel Frank). At the time, the couple was collaborating with Mallet-Stevens on the design of their holiday villa in Hyères on the Côte d'Azur. After seeing Guevrekian's installation, the Vicomte de Noailles (who had earlier commissioned an abstract garden of boxwood and colored gravel for the grounds of his Paris home) wrote to Mallet-Stevens, saying, "I very much liked this garden at the Decorative Arts and would gladly ask [Guevrekian] to design one for here, if you think this kind of thing would amuse him."[9]

Guevrekian gladly accepted the commission to design a 120-square-meter garden on another triangular plot in the southeast corner of the Noailles' Hyères estate. Besides its bounded geometry and the fact that it was designed to be viewed from a terrace, outside its perimeter, the garden had many other elements in common with the earlier expo installation: the plot was framed by crisp concrete walls, the ground plane was tilted, and flower beds filled with brightly colored tulips were arranged in a mosaic checkerboard pattern, again framed by white concrete dividers. There were some differences, though, notably the two orange trees that were planted symmetrically

Hamed
Khosravi

Obscured
Modernism

531

just in front of its entrance, and the sunken pool of water that marked the central axis. In lieu of Barillet's spinning ball, the Hyères garden featured a bronze sculpture by Jacques Lipchitz, *La joie de vivre*—a dancing figure with a large guitar which rotated every four minutes on its mechanized base. The statue was not part of Guevrekian's original design, and after its installation, the perimeter walls of the garden were subsequently lowered, to make both the statue and the geometry of flower beds more visible.[fig.7]

Upon its completion in 1927, the garden immediately became a celebrated modernist monument and even found its way onto celluloid, featuring in a number of sequences in Man Ray's 1929 surrealist film of the Villa Noailles, *Les Mystères du Château de Dé*. Sadly, these stills, together with a number of photographs of the garden taken by Man Ray and by Thérèse Bonney, were soon all that remained of the garden.[fig.8a, b] By 1934 the Vicomte's gardeners had filled the entire triangular plot with low-maintenance aloe, having grown tired of the upkeep the garden required. By the late 1930s, the site had fallen into total neglect. It was only in the 1990s that the city of Hyères—which now owns the estate—renovated both the villa and its garden, even if the troublesome tulips were replaced with hardier marigolds.

Tehran city architect

When the Great Depression took hold in France in 1931, architects began looking for commissions and projects outside Europe. André Lurçat moved to Moscow to work for the Soviet government. Auguste Perret took on projects in Egypt and Lebanon. After nearly abandoning architectural projects for more theoretical urban pursuits, Le Corbusier picked up commissions in South America and the Middle East. In 1933, Guevrekian and his wife set off for northeast Asia, initially planning only to stop first in Tehran to visit family. Immediately, Guevrekian was asked to design two urban villas—one for a family member, the other for some friends, Persian aristocrats. Later that year, Reza Shah Pahlavi, the shah of Iran, appointed Guevrekian as Chief Architect of Tehran. The city was then in the midst of a large-scale urban reconstruction as part of the shah's effort to refashion Iran in a modern image, clearing away all traces of its Qajar past. Guevrekian's first public project was the design of the National Theater He was then asked to prepare the master plan for Tehran, but when city officials asked for numerous revisions, he refused. Preferring to be

Fig. 7. Model of the Triangular Garden at the Villa Noailles, 1928. Photograph by Thérèse Bonney.
Fig. 8a. Triangular Garden at the Villa Noailles, 1928. Photograph by Thérèse Bonney.
Fig. 8b. Stills from Man Ray's *Les Mystères du Château de Dé*, 1929.

his own boss, he redefined his relationship with the government, setting himself up as an independent contractor. With a group of French, Swiss, and Iranian architects and engineers, he designed the Ministry of War and an amphitheater for the military school, and also supervised the construction of the Ministry of Foreign Affairs and the Central Bureau of Records and Archives. Perhaps the most important project to come out of this period, however, was the design and construction of the Officers' Club, a collaboration with the French engineer Pénalié and Iranian-Armenian architect Vartan Hovannesian, a colleague from his brief time at Henri Sauvage's office. Similar to his European projects, Guevrekian designed every last detail of the crisp five-story building, right down to the bricks, which were custom-made to achieve the correct proportions of walls and openings. Lavishly appointed, the club was decked out with the most advanced building services: the elevators, central heating system and sanitary fittings were all imported. To balance construction costs, Guevrekian combined these imports with local skills and materials, developing many innovative construction techniques in the process.

Two years into his Persian sojourn, Guevrekian was invited by the Minister of Finance, Ali-Akbar Davar, to run the technical department of the Société Générale de Construction, which coordinated all public building activities in the city. In this capacity, he designed the Palace of Justice with French architect Marcel Dubrulle and produced two schemes for the Ministry of Industry and Mines with Swiss architect M. K. Akatos.[fig.9] There are some interesting parallels between these austere yet tasteful compositions and Marcello Piacentini's design for the Città Universitaria in Rome, conceived in the same period. However, the use of elements taken from traditional architecture, such as the *iwan* (portal) and *badgir* (wind-catcher), makes the work essentially Iranian. Parallel to all of this, Guevrekian's private office was involved

Part 2

The
Bauhaus
in
Weimar

534

in the design and construction of twenty houses across Tehran, where he enjoyed considerably more freedom to design in the modern style, working with generous budgets.

Private houses

Out of twenty private residences that Guevrekian designed in Tehran, only eight are known today.[10] In two articles, in *L'Architecture d'Aujourd'hui* (1938) and *Art et Decoration* (1946), Guevrekian proudly introduced his works in Tehran, going briefly through the design of the villas and a few of his public works.[11] Among these houses, Villa Khosrovani demonstrates continuity in form and style from Guevrekian's European projects and in particular displays a similarity to Villa Heim, designed and constructed between 1927 and 1929 for Jacques Heim, the famous fashion designer, in Neuilly, Paris.[fig.10] Shahab Khosrovani was a prominent entrepreneur from a noble Iranian family; he was also a member of the Iranian parliament (1947–53) and the economic advisor to the Iranian government. The first villa, built in 1936, was located in a shaggy plot in the northern part of the city. The land was subdivided from an old garden. The villa embodies a cubic form, surrounded by old pine trees. Similar to Villa Heim, Guevrekian designed a series of cascading terraces that connect the interior spaces of the house to the garden.[fig.11]

The building had three zones that were masterfully joined together: a service zone centered around the kitchen that was connected to the maid's room and given separate access, living spaces divided among three floors, and a small office for business meetings that had a separate entrance and vertical access. On the ground floor, the formal living room was placed next to the service zone; a cylindrical staircase led to the first floor which included the family sitting room, dining room, and a reading room. Private spaces and bedrooms were all on the second floor. The house is mostly blocked on the east and west sides; all the openings faced south or north, framing spectacular perspectives of the garden.

Similar to Villa Heim, Guevrekian designed all the interior details, lightings and furniture of Villa Khosrovani. He also designed a second house for Khosrovani in the northern district of Shemiran. Unlike the first house, the latter villa had an austere cubic form covered with brown brick and built on a hilly landscape of northern Tehran. Adjacent to the villa was a terraced garden cascading down the slope.

Hamed
Khosravi

Obscured
Modernism

535

Fig. 10. Villa Heim, Neuilly-Paris, 1927–29. Photograph by Thérèse Bonney.
Fig. 11. Villa Khosrovani, Tehran, 1936. Photograph by Gabriel Guevrekian.

Villa Malek-Aslani was built in 1935 on Shah Reza Avenue, a newly constructed street just outside the northern moat of the city. Unlike Villa Khosrovani, the site did not have any plants or vegetation. Indeed, it became an opportunity for Guevrekian to express once again his never-ending love of garden design. A raised platform separated the villa from the courtyard; along the southern façade, it was used to create an open terrace overlooking the garden. The main access to the villa is from the south; after crossing the garden and stepping up to the raised platform, one could enter the house through the main entrance on the east side. Compared to Villa Khosrovani, the Malek-Aslani was a smaller house, with only two floors; it had a symmetric form facing to the south. Guevrekian adjusted the form by tilting up the projected roof. In this way, he corrected the proportion of the main façade and covered the pitched roof as well. In interviews, he mentioned that he did not favor pitched roofs and that he always preferred flat roofs that could be used as roof gardens and terraces. However, Guevrekian met with technological difficulties in the construction of these houses in Tehran, and he mostly came up with solutions that relied on local expertise and low-cost materials.

Among the other villas, the two houses for Ali-Akbar Siassi (1935) and Asghar Panahi (1934) were the most distinguished. Siassi, by that time, was a professor at the University of Tehran; he later became the university rector (1942–54) and then minister of education (1943). Villa Siassi is one of the few villas by Guevrekian that still exist; most were demolished and replaced by new buildings.

While Guevrekian was in Tehran, his friend Vetter was in Baghdad, working on King Faisal's palace as project architect for Clemens Holzmeister, who had won a competition. After this, Vetter returned to Vienna, but not for long. When the Nazis annexed Austria in 1938, he had to leave not only on account of his left-wing politics—which caused him to be summarily dismissed from his teaching post at the Academy of Applied Arts—but also for the sake of his second wife, Jadwiga Orsul, who was Jewish. Around the same time, Guevrekian's sister and her husband, Carl Einstein, were interred in France after having fought with a German anarcho-syndicalist brigade in the Spanish Civil War.

Back in Tehran, the death of the minister of finance under suspicious circumstances brought the activities of the Société Générale de Construction to an abrupt end in February 1937. Soon afterward,

Guevrekian's wife, Henriette-Aimée, was diagnosed with malaria.
The couple decided it was time to leave. They took refuge with the
Creed family in London, but Guevrekian found the British capital far
less rewarding than Tehran. The bright side was that Gropius was still
in London when Guevrekian arrived. However, Gropius soon left the
UK and started his new life in the United States. Guevrekian decided
to stay in London, joining the firm of Connell, Ward & Lucas, where
he was friends with the partners, and collaborated on several competition entries and a large-scale housing project. None of these were
ever realized, and the office closed at the outbreak of the war in 1939.

Guevrekian's four short years in Tehran proved to be the most
productive period of his professional life. He would later express his
deep regret at leaving behind the country where he had defined a
new style. As he pointed out in the January 1938 issue of *L'Architecture
d'Aujourd'hui*, his Iranian houses could not be directly compared to his
earlier work. The climate and the limitations of local building techniques and materials made it impossible to simply transpose European
architecture onto the urban fabric of Tehran.[12] Instead he initiated
a new movement of Iranian Modernist architecture, defined not by a
top-down imposition of the shah's will but by a desire to respond to
sweeping social change. Guevrekian told his French readers of the
"semi-religious" traditions that were now obsolete: the division of the
house into male and female quarters, the predominance of an uneven
number of openings, the placing of the entrance on the south façade.
Freed from these constraints, Guevrekian opened up the enclosed
forms of traditional Iranian typologies and exposed them to the city.

American professor

Being in Europe during the war was not anything close to what Guevrekian could have expected in his ambitious professional life. He stopped
working between 1940 and 1944 and moved to southern France. Guevrekian reinstated his practice with small commissions in 1944; however, they did not fulfill his dreams. Guevrekian and his wife moved
to the United States in 1949, where he again met some of his old friends
from the Bauhaus and the international circles he had frequented.

In April 1948, Gropius wrote Guevrekian a letter of recommendation to Turpin Bannister, who was still at the Carnegie Institute,
working together with Guevrekian's lifetime companion, Hans Vetter.
It was June 1949, and Guevrekian was now teaching in the US. A job

Part 3

Bauhaus
Architects
in
Exile

at Auburn University in Alabama—secured through Gropius and Vetter—had given him a ticket out of war-torn Europe. But after less than a year in Auburn, he had had enough. Cutting short the preamble, he got straight to the point: "I want very much to change ... to be nearer to an intellectual center which I would naturally prefer. I believe that practicing, even so little, is one important part of teaching, in order to be in touch with the realities,"[13] Guevrekian confided in a letter to Turpin Bannister, a professor at the University of Illinois in Urbana-Champaign. Bannister took the hint, and by the end of the summer Guevrekian had been installed as a professor of architecture at the University of Illinois. He was then close to his friends Moholy-Nagy and Mies van der Rohe, with whom Chicago had just become a unique and flourishing intellectual center.

In Chicago, Guevrekian finally had the space and freedom he needed to try out his ideas in architectural education.[fig. 12] He developed a new design curriculum, which included master classes, and expanded the activities of the school, connecting it to the cultural life of the city by curating exhibitions and hosting symposia. He brought the essence of modernist art and architecture to the US through his design studios and seminars. He wrote effusively of how Chicago was the "place to be": "Things are changing, and Chicago is again becoming a nucleus for art and architecture. It will be more so in the future. It is in the right place. There is now a 'middle-west' movement centered in Chicago, but it is not visible because it is so broad, so spread out."[14] Once again, his instinct for being in the right place at the right time had proved unerring.

Guevrekian became a naturalized American citizen in 1955 and remained at the University of Illinois for a total of twenty years until his retirement in 1969. Well established in the US, he would also spend part of each year in Europe, teaching on the university's first study-

Hamed Khosravi

Obscured Modernism

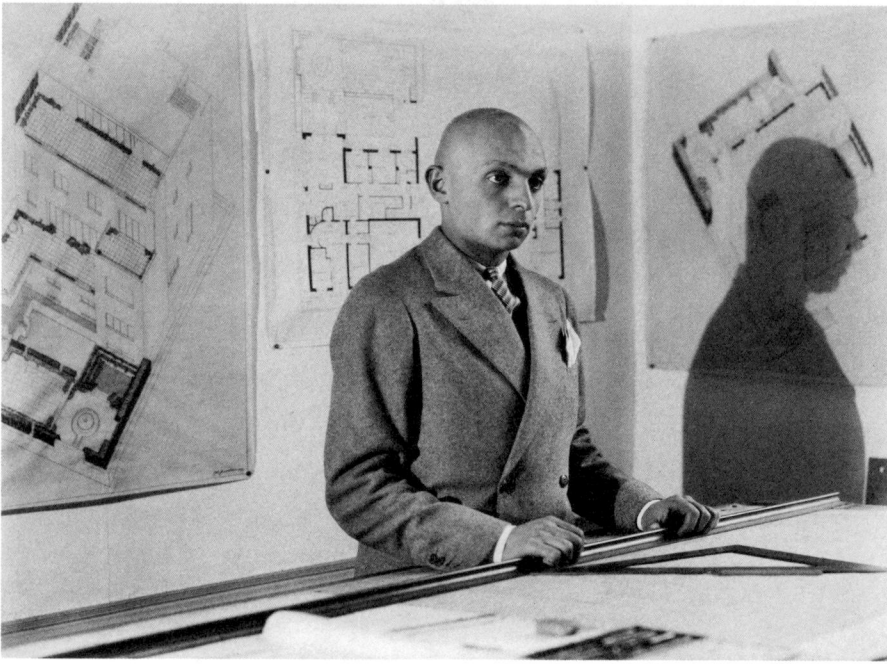

abroad program (another of his innovations), which he strategically based in La Napoule on the French Riviera. He and his wife bought an apartment in Antibes, with views across the rooftops to the Mediterranean. They planned to spend their years of retirement there. Soon after moving back to Europe, however, Henriette-Aimée became unwell. After a protracted illness, she died in Paris on September 15, 1970. Guevrekian died in Antibes six weeks later, on October 29, 1970.

He had consistently collected postcards, many of which are now held in the archive of the University of Illinois. These vintage postcards are all signed and dated. They include no city view, nor any work of architecture, and instead feature mostly just paintings, Rembrandt's *The Night Watch*, Raphael's *The Marriage of the Virgin*, and Manet's *Déjeuner sur l'herbe* among them. Neatly packed together in boxes, their accrual seems to symbolize a certain nomadism, both geographic and professional, in which change was not just a consequence—of crisis, illness or war—but a very deliberate choice.

Of course, the other things that Guevrekian clearly collected, even if he would never have perceived them in these terms, were the various lives that he lived—a serial adoption of personae that was in no sense a form of conceit. Guevrekian was not someone who thrived off the reflected glory of others. Quite the opposite: he made every discipline meaningful, every city central, every period epochal simply by his own very tangible engagement with it. And if there is a single postcard-like image that represents all of these multiples, it is one ironically not found in his collection (even if it perhaps should have been there). In 1927, American photographer Thérèse Bonney[15] took a portrait of Gabriel Guevrekian [fig. 13] that shows him standing at his drafting table, impeccably dressed as ever, his fingers resting on his parallel motion, while he stares ahead intently from under his characteristically darkened brow. Behind him is his axonometric drawing of

Villa Heim, a token of one life already lived, while ahead of him is cast his shadow—its own, more benign, Dr. Caligari-like outline even more precise than his three-dimensional real self—seemingly pointing the way ever forward to yet more lives that still needed to be led.

Gabriel Guevrekian was one of those who seem to be citizens of the world rather than of one particular country. The obscured Modernism has been not only an archaeological inquiry into the life and works of Guevrekian, but also the history of modern architecture—a history that is reconstructed by putting together bits and pieces of archival materials and documents from more than thirty archives and libraries in eleven countries.[fig. 14] Portrayed through news clippings, photographs, audio recordings, drawings, models, letters, and postcards, Guevrekian represents a key figure around whom the contemporary role of architect as writer, practitioner, educator, and public intellectual could be revisited.

Guevrekian Always Ahead, Times Had To Catch Up

By JOANN WATSON
News-Gazette Staff Writer

Gabriel Guevrekian, professor of architectural design, has not had to "keep up with the times." Rather, times have had to catch up with him.

He has been referred to as a radical. In the early 1920's he was designing homes and public buildings which only now are popular with the public.

Although flat roofs are fashionable today, Guevrekian spent a considerable period of time in those early years trying to convince people the flat-roofed houses he had built did indeed have roofs.

He led the movement in Europe for contemporary architectural design. The rejection of a friend's modern design for the League of Nations, prompted him to co-found the International Congress of Modern Architecture at Paris in 1928.

Guevrekian came to the University of Illinois in 1949 and remained until his retirement this fall. With him, he brought a generalist's view of architecture and a strong belief in what he feels is good design.

He recalls his slim days as an architect in Paris. Business was badly needed,. but when a women wanted a traditional house design, Guevrekian could not bring himself to develop one. Instead, when his client returned, he handed her a contemporary design.

Doesn't Want It

"This is not what I want!" she cried.

"Yes, but that is what I design. If you don't like it, there is an architect upstairs who will do what you want," he replied.

His entire life has been marked by this resistance to conform to what he did not believe in. In his words, "I would never prostitute my belief in my work."

Guevrekian hopes that he has taught his students over the years that the human being is the most important consideration in architectural design. Architecture should encompass man's behavior.

For that reason, he believes that architecture must vary from place to place. It should not impose upon men, but give shape to his environment. Culture and climate dictate the type of buildings needed.

"Therefore, one cannot transplant a design which is good for one place to another," he states emphatically. "Very often it will not work."

For this reason, Guevrekian founded the University of Illinois architecture extension at La Napoule France. Approximately 40 students are selected to attend the one semester program. He hopes that these students will come to better understand the way other people live.

Enjoys Freedom

Professor Guevrekian has been very happy at the University of Illinois. "There is so much freedom here," he explains. "Architecture is not bound by governmental dictate as in so many other countries."

He recalls an experience after World War II when he taught architecture at an institute in the Saar. He gave an assignment to a class comprised mostly of Germans. He returned to the class two days later and saw nothing but blank sheets placed before him.

"What is the matter?" he asked the students.

"Professor," they responded, "you forgot to give us the order to begin."

About his students at the Univeristy of Illinois, Guevrekian feels many of them lack real courage in their convictions. He assumes money will be the directing force for many of them.

Professor Guevrekian is retired now. He and his wife, Henriette Aimee, will not remain long at their home of 17 years at 606 W. Mighican, U. They leave shortly for an unspecified stay at Antibes, France.

Looking Ahead

But he is still as concerned with the direction architectural design will take in the years ahead. "This is a transitional period," he explains, "but I cannot give this period a more specific name. That must be left for someone to do 50 or 100 years from now."

The problem he sees as most pressing today, the one which will give architecture in America its greatest challenge,

News-Gazette: Photo by Robert Arbuckle
PROF. GABRIEL GUEVREKIAN
. . . ahead of his time

is city planning.

He feels traffic is the major part of this problem, "Have you ever stopped to think that an average car takes up approximately 400 square feet of space and has 450 horsepower — all to move one small body around?" he exclaims.

For short distances, as in the cities, he believes that a good public transportation system would be available including underground trains and possibly rolling side - walks and modified forms of hover craft.

Professor Guevrekian has left his mark on the College of Architecture and the many students he has instructed. In an article in "The Ricker Render" in 1966, student David Hanser wrote, "He has spent his whole life protesting against misconceptions, defending himself and his ideals . . . protesting now in Vienna, now in Paris, Tehran, London, even in Urbana."

1   In an interview with Alfred Roth on June 3, 1970, Guevrekian recalls the starting point of the idea of the first CIAM. He explains that he had known Madame de Mandrot quite well for many years. She had a nice apartment in the same building, at Rue Champerret in Paris, where Guevrekian's brother-in-law Carl Einstein, the German historian and art critic, lived. They were at the core of the circle of Parisian avant-garde, to which Einstein, Guevrekian, Bataille, Braque, Delauneys, and others belonged.

2   The letter, dated October 27, 1930, was sent by Moholy-Nagy to Max Ernst, Hans Arp, Sigfried Giedion, and Gabriel Guevrekian. Available at the gta Archiv, in ETH Zurich, numbered: 43B-K-1930-10-2.

3   For example, see Eric Mumford, *The CIAM Discourse on Urbanism, 1928–1960* (Cambridge, MA: MIT Press, 2000).

4   See "Au Salon d'Automne," *Gazette des sept arts* 8 (1923), 7.

5   Gaston Varenne, "L'Art Urbain et le Mobilier au Salon d'Automne," *Décoration* 264 (1923): 161–184.

6   Gabriel Guevrakian, *Hotels & Sanatoria, Repertoire de l'Architecture Moderne* 6 (Paris: Editions S. De Bonadona, 1930).

7   After a brief spell working for Henri Sauvage, Guevrekian and Vetter had both joined the Paris atelier of Robert Mallet-Stevens, who was responsible for coordinating the design of the entrance area of that year's salon: a cubist-style park.

8   Fletcher Steele, "New Pioneering in Garden Design," *Landscape Architecture* 20 (1930), 159–77.

9   Charles Noailles to Mallet-Stevens, November 5, 1925. See Cécile Briolle, Agnès Fuzibet, and Gérard Monnier, *La Villa Noailles: Rob Mallet-Stevens* (Marseille: Editions Parenthèses, 1990), 62.

10   Two villas for Shahab Khosrovani, Villa Malek-Aslani, Panahi, Siassi, Firouz, Taleghani, and Nezam-Mafi (Farmanfarmaian).

11   Gabriel Guevrekian, "Habitation à Teheran," *L'Architecture d'Aujourd'hui* 9, no. 1 (1938), 58–59, 78; and Gabriel Guevrekian, "Maisons en Pays de Soleil," *Art et Decoration*, Mar. (1946), 190–96.

12   Gabriel Guevrekian, "Habitation à Teheran," *L'Architecture d'Aujourd'hui* 9, no. 1 (1938), 78.

13   Gabriel Guevrekian to Turpin Bannister, June 13, 1949. Available at the University of Illinois Library Archive.

14   "Tribute to a Radical," unpublished interview with David A. Hanser in 1966. Manuscript is available at the University of Illinois Library Archive.

15   Thérèse Bonney, an American photographer, was one of the young foreigners drawn to the bright light of the Parisian Modern movement during the 1920s. She received her PHD from the Sorbonne in 1921. While in Paris, she found her passion in the austere aesthetics of modernism. She opened her photography studio, designed by Gabriel Guevrekian, in Rue de la Paix in 1923. Bonney recorded the changing face of the city of Paris, documenting architecture, interiors, exhibitions and installations. She photographed almost all of Guevrekian's works in France between 1923 and 1932, including Villa Heim, Garden of Water and Light, and the Triangular Garden in Villa Noailles. See Lisa Schlansker Kolosek, *The Invention of Chic: Thérèse Bonney and Paris Moderne* (London: Thames & Hudson, 2002).

Ines Weizman

Bauhaus Modernism across the Sykes-Picot Line

In September 2015, a massive dust storm swept across the Middle East. In Syria, Lebanon, Israel/Palestine, even in Cyprus, visibility was reduced to only a few meters. One of the scientific reasons for that dust storm was that Syrian farmers, chased out by war and drought, had abandoned their war-torn villages, homes, and fields, which had, like all things abandoned, gradually turned to dust. Then came the easterly wind and raised that dust into the air, gathering it up into an orange cloud system on a continental scale and slowly carrying it through the atmosphere, moving it across national borders. The cloud, larger than any state it crossed, reminds us that this wonderful but tragic war-torn region is a shared space, with a shared ecology, inhabited by a shared humanity.

The image of suspended, transnational dust makes me think of the famous scene of Michelangelo Antonioni's slow-motion blowing-up of a modernist masterpiece in *Zabriskie Point*—perhaps modernism's first on-camera death, the second being the one polemically announced in 1977 by Charles Jencks, the destruction of Pruitt-Igoe.

This essay could only start with dust: the dust cloud of the hundred-year history of modernism in this region and the political and colonial projects in which it was implicated. Dust is matter in motion, and this essay touches upon this dynamic. It tells the story of two buildings, one located in the Syrian Golan Heights, the other in Tel Aviv. Both today are popularly referred to, erroneously but perhaps affectionately, as Bauhaus Modernism, sometimes merely as the *Bauhaus* buildings. Neither, as I will show, was designed by a Bauhaus teacher or graduate, yet through their histories I will follow the story of modern architecture as it is divided and displaced by borders, exile, and war. It is a story that has entangled

544

protagonists, objects, materials, and ideas. In its form and associations, this essay tries to capture something of this entropy.

To do so, I will follow my own methodology in recent years, that of "documentary architecture." This regards the building itself—its material and media palimpsest—as a historical document. Next to the architectural document, the traditional métier of architectural history, "documentary architecture" is a method of analysis that brings the architectural historian closest to the archaeologist.[1] It seeks to make existing materials and textures, whether investigated by plain sight or under the lens of a microscope, tell their stories, the stories of time and transformations. The history of buildings is solidified in a long process of material transformations and adaptations. A formal analysis of buildings, for example merely through photographs and plans, is not able to reveal the possibility that the best records of the history of air quality, the history of pollution, are the external surfaces of buildings, which fold the chemical composition of the air into the first few millimeters of a building. The documentary method—a method that treats buildings as diagrams of site-specific material forces that negotiate abstract architectural intentions—approaches architecture and the story of buildings' patina, adaptation, transformation, and degeneration not "merely" as architectural histories, but reveals what might otherwise remain invisible to architectural history.

This applies to dust as well. As outlined in the introduction, dust is never a single object. Dust is a lived environment in which human materials, building materials, airborne substances, materials from animals, and molecular substances interact.[2] We could describe these as the sediments of layers of history. Dust is the link between an object and its environment: it is neither one nor the other, but something in between. It is a complete record of the environment and its combination into a single substance when collected and compressed. The figure of dust undoes the singular, fetish-like qualities of any object but particularly that of a Bauhaus object, whose fetish qualities seem to have increased exponentially in this centennial. Carlo Ginzburg referring to Marc Bloch's *Feudal Society*, described the historian's gaze shifting between a "constant back-and-forth between micro- and macrohistory, between close-ups and extreme long shots, so as to continually thrust back into discussion the comprehensive vision of the historical process through apparent exceptions and cases of brief duration."[3] It is within this spectrum of micro- and macrohistory that

Ines Weizman

Bauhaus Modernism across the Sykes-Picot Line

545

Fig. 1. Photograph of the 1915 locust plague in Palestine.

I would like to connect the materiality of the two buildings, the two subjects of this essay, to the very beginning of the Bauhaus.

The enormous dust cloud of 2015 passed by the sites ruptured by ongoing historical calamities. In 1915, a devastating locust infestation blackened the sky and destroyed most of the vegetation in Palestine, Mount Lebanon, and Syria.[fig. 1] The great famine that followed was the devastating consequence of political, economic, and environmental factors, the combination of a severe drought, a plague of locusts, and a stifling blockade of goods and food supplies.[4] After the Ottoman Empire joined Germany, the Allies enforced a blockade of the entire eastern Mediterranean in an effort to cut off their supplies. In return, a blockade was introduced by General Jamal Pasha, commander-in-chief of the Turkish forces in Greater Syria and the one responsible for the Armenian, Greek, and Assyrian genocides that began around that time. On May 9, 1915, Ottoman soldier Ihsan al-Turjman, stationed in Jerusalem, wrote in his diary (which was lost in 1917 and only resurfaced in the 1970s in the Abandoned Arab Property [sic] section of the Hebrew University library):[5] "Our lives are threatened from all sides: a European war and an Ottoman war, prices are skyrocketing, a financial crisis, and the locusts are attacking the country north and south. On top of all this, now infectious diseases are spreading throughout the Ottoman lands."[6] Indeed, the region saw epidemics of such diseases as malaria, dysentery, typhoid, and typhus.[7]

It might be difficult to establish a clear line of causality between military violence, ethnic cleansing, genocide, and the epidemics of the time, but they certainly correlated. At the time, the Spanish flu was moving along the front lines of the First World War, as well as the lines of trade and supply that the war spawned. This particularly virulent strain of influenza infected about 500 million people worldwide, killing over 50 million people between March 1918 and March 1920. Despite its magnitude and impact, this horrendous figure has largely been undocumented and unaccounted for, probably because it was mainly viewed from the European continent and Western history tended to trivialize it in comparison to the devastation of the two world wars.[8] But as Laura Spinney argues in her book *Pale Rider*, the history of the pandemic requires a different "approach to telling the flu."[9] The pandemic is generally regarded as beginning with the report of a cook's illness on March 4, 1918 at Camp Funston in Kansas. This was one of the US military camps that recruited and trained soldiers of the American Expeditionary Forces (AEF), which would soon bring the influenza virus to Europe: first to France, then to the trenches of the Western Front, in the last six months of the war, and from there to Germany, Britain, Italy, and Spain.[10] By May 1918, the virus had reached northern Africa and India, and by July, China, Japan, and Australia. In fact, the flu spread in three distinct worldwide waves, and understanding its impact would require a non-European perspective as well as a form of historical narration that cannot be merely chronological. This is because the pandemic, as Spinney states, "is a social phenomenon as much as it is a biological one; it cannot be separated from its historical, geographical and cultural context."[11]

Perhaps it is all too symbolic that Sir Mark Sykes, who in collusion with his French colleague François Georges-Picot drew the fateful line through the Middle East which bears their names, fell prey to this virus in 1919.[fig.2] It happened while versions of the line were being drafted and debated for the Paris Peace Conference in Versailles. He died at the age of 39 on February 16, 1919, in his room at the Hôtel Le Lotti in Paris. As a diplomat of aristocratic upbringing, his remains were not thrown into a mass grave like many thousands of other victims of the malady, but were encased in a hermetically sealed lead coffin and returned to his family at Sledmere House, Yorkshire. This body in the lead coffin contains one of the very few traces of the virus today. In 2008, 89 years after his death, the body of Sir Mark Sykes was unearthed by a team of scientists who in his uniquely preserved remains tried to find the genetic footprint of the 1918 virus which could potentially help to engineer a vaccine against the lethal HINI virus that was then spreading globally. The lead tub contained a dead body, but living viruses. And in a way, the viruses still preserved in the bones of Sir Mark Sykes also contain the information necessary for

Ines
Weizman

Bauhaus
Modernism
across
the
Sykes-Picot
Line

547

A

B

the unpacking of the epidemiological history of World War I and the
complete reorganization of states that have since eroded the bloody
borders of the Middle East through subsequent wars, conflicts, and
requisitioning of colonial empires. The grandson of Mark Sykes,
Christopher Simon Sykes, said in the run-up to the exhumation: "It is
rather fascinating that maybe even in his state as a corpse, he might
be helping the world in some way."[12] Virologic archaeology is indeed
part of the archaeology of modernism.

The Sykes-Picot Line in a hundred-year perspective

The establishment of the Bauhaus School in the same year of 1919 was
a consequence of students and teachers returning from the front lines
of World War I. As presented earlier in this volume in the essay by
Norbert Korrek, the building by Henry van de Velde—who as a Belgian
national himself became an enemy alien when the war began—still
housed a hospital for war wounded when Walter Gropius founded the
Bauhaus and was forced to share the building with soldiers and medical staff. The Germany to which these soldiers returned was different:
the old order removed, a country in ruin, a broken system, broken
bodies, the Kaiser had abdicated, and the empire was giving birth to a
nation-state. People were moving across the continent. Refugees were
everywhere. Europe at the end of 1918 might not be the same as the
Middle East, but it brings to mind the hundreds of thousands of refugees who have since 2011 embarked upon a perilous journey to flee
the wars in Syria and elsewhere, as their cities have been devastated by
bombs and knives, and turned into dust.

The two scenarios might not be the same, but one is a consequence of the other. What happened at the end of World War I determined the contours of conflict in the century that followed. The recent
wars and the images of spectacular violence they generated are in part
a consequence of historical violence whose roots extend to the colonial history of the Levant and the political and cultural occupation to
which this territory has been subjected in the last one hundred years.
Nothing embodies this colonial order and its bloody collapse more
than the Sykes-Picot Line mentioned above, infamously first drawn in
the sand with a measuring stick, dividing the regions dominated by the
British after World War I from those dominated by the French: thus
Palestine from Syria, and Syria from Iraq.[13]

*Ines
Weizman*

Bauhaus
Modernism
across
the
Sykes-Picot
Line

549

Fig.3. Aerial photograph by the Royal Air Force of the British (left) and French (right) customhouses (marked red and enlarged by the author) on the border between the French and British Mandate in the western Golan Heights, RAF PS12 no. 5134, January 29, 1945.

In a 2014 Daesh video, a victorious Islamic fighter explained how he and his army had stormed a customhouse at the Iraqi-Syrian border. After stomping angrily on a metal signpost that had marked the border, the fighter then pointed to a map painted on the outside wall of a building, probably a former French border post, and went on to describe it as the legacy not of local politics and culture, but of Western colonial history. The film ends with a promise that Daesh will take all customhouses along the Sykes-Picot Line and a final scene—as if in homage to Antonioni—in which the building explodes, turning into an enormous dust cloud. This destruction helps to shift attention to the architecture of border and customhouses—not as forensic archaeology, but because these buildings, more than any others, are the manifestation of a border that was, along most of its route, unfenced and unprotected. Their architecture shows how the Levant, from Cairo through Amman to Damascus, has been seen as a screen upon which the development of modernism was projected. Modernism has professed itself to be a movement beyond borders, but along the Sykes-Picot Line it was employed in the service of imperial border-making: part of an imperial infrastructure of oil pipelines, canals, train tracks and airfields.

Bauhaus on the Golan[14]

The customhouses stormed by Daesh are not the only ones made obsolete by shifting borders. There are two abandoned customhouses, one British and one French, about a mile apart, on both sides of the Sykes-Picot Line on the edge of the Israeli-occupied Golan Heights.[15] Immediately after crossing the Jordan River and the internationally recognized border of Israel eastward into the Golan Heights,[16] you can see them along Israeli Highway 91, previously a long-established east-west trade route through the Middle East.[fig.3]

These buildings mark one of several points of crossing on the Sykes-Picot Line. The British site is an improvised clutter of found structures around an old transit yard. The French site could not be more different: a grand modernist ensemble of buildings now referred to by Israelis living nearby and cheekily by the tourist guides as "Bauhaus on the Golan." The establishment of these customhouses mark two important historical geopolitical transformations in the Levant: the division of the defeated Ottoman Empire by European powers as a result of World War I, and the constitutive era of pre-state Zionism.

But what is generously and imprecisely referred to today as Bauhaus on the Golan is nothing but the result of a transfer of modernity to "the Levant"[17]—a transfer that needs to be contextualized and situated within the political context of other colonial European transfers, rather than being promoted as a result of a well-known school. This architecture was both the medium and means of a new political era in the region.

Whereas between France and the southern coast of England, between Dover and Calais, say, there is a thirty-kilometer-wide channel, here there was only the trickle of the Jordan River a few meters wide and a cartographic line clumsily drawn over it, continuing haphazardly through the rest of the Middle East, punctured from time to time by colonial outposts such as these customhouses.

The customhouses are located on a hill just beyond the international border marked by the Jordan River, which two bridges span today. One was built recently to carry the heavy traffic of cars and tanks that are driven up or down the mountain several times a day;

Ines Weizman

Bauhaus Modernism across the Sykes-Picot Line

551

Fig. 4. Drone photograph of the lower (British) custom-house. Photograph by Ines Weizman, 2019.

the other is a disused Bailey bridge[18] that was erected in the 1960s, after the occupation by the Israeli military, over the traces of the medieval Jisr Benât Ya'qūb bridge.[19] This crossing once marked the northernmost point reached by Napoleon's army when he was trying to conquer the Middle East. It is also the same point at which Major Fritz Ludloff, a German officer who had been in charge of drawing and aerial photography as part of the German Samarra Expedition of 1911–13 with archaeologist and orientalist Ernst Herzfeld,[20] failed in September 1918 to fulfill the command of General Otto Liman von Sanders to defend the bridge against the Australian Mounted Division led by British General Sir Edmund Allenby.[21] The German's last gesture in Palestine was to dynamite the bridge that had, since Roman times, connected Jaffa through the *Via Maris* to Kuneitra and Damascus, linking Egypt with the northern empires of Syria, Anatolia, and Mesopotamia. Like its namesake, this literal "road to Damascus" might offer a new turn in our current reading of modernist historiography.

The road is currently lined with fences warning of minefields, Israeli military base after military base, burnt carcasses of Syrian tanks, monuments to fallen Israeli soldiers, stubs of basalt stone walls of forcibly vacated Syrian villages, and tank barriers. Strangely, here, the minefields act as the perfect nature preserve. The landscape is pristine, untouched, full of wildlife and freely grazing cattle and flowers, demonstrating how much more of a violent threat to nature development is than war. It is bizarrely cinematic, in an *Apocalypse Now*-cum-*The Lord of the Rings* sort of meets *The Sound of Music*.

Only a short distance from the bridge, the former British customs building, unlike its developed counterpart on the upper part of the mountain, is completely dilapidated and inaccessible. Surrounded by a fence warning of land mines, it can be studied only through drone photography.[fig.4] [22] While the French mark their pride and power on top of the mountain in a large modernist functionalist building ensemble, the British appropriated an existing khan, or caravansary, an Arab courtyard building that provided stables for animals and resting places for travelers and merchants, and expanded it with a larger

Fig.5. Photograph of the lower (British) customhouse. Photograph by Ines Weizman, 2017.

storage and office building in the British signature orientalist eclecticism of the time. The cows that inhabit this building today might still be reminiscent of this time. No wonder they felt comfortable, as if, thanks to the supposed presence of mines, they were being visited for the first time.[fig.5] In Britain and its colonies, particularly in the Middle East and especially in Palestine, architectural modernism would arrive through European, mainly German, refugees and emigrants throughout the 1930s. The master plans for the garden suburbs of Jerusalem and Haifa were British only on the surface, yet in plan—drawn in haste by Patrick Geddes in 1919 on his way to India, and in 1925 for Tel Aviv—anything architectural extruding from the surface was rather of European modernist influence.[23] One could say that up until the mid-1930s the British were slow to adopt modernism, both at home and in their colonial outposts. The architectural research that would finally unearth the documents that would allow the establishment of the authorship and the dating of these two buildings has yet to be done, but for now we can attempt a stylistic reading of these buildings, one local and eclectic, the other modernist, as they seem to represent the different attitudes to architectural modernism that the British and French had in the mid-1920s and early 1930s.

The French customhouse is now in private hands. It will open as a boutique hotel in autumn 2019 after extensive renovations and an enthusiastic campaign by its owner, Leo Gleser. Also known as Colonel Gleser, he is a former high-ranking officer in the military and the Mossad who more recently has made a name for himself as a leading security adviser for large international events such as the Olympic Games in London and in Rio. After acquiring a lease on the land and the building in 2012, he's wasted no time in transforming the dilapidated, bullet-riddled building, which Israelis remember as a target, a field toilet, and a wall for juvenile graffiti, into what he calls a "Bauhaus Hotel" aimed at tourists coming to enjoy this war-torn, or rather war-preserved, landscape.[fig.6] Despite there being no verifiable link between the building and the Bauhaus school, he seeks to include the building in the international Bauhaus celebrations. With support from the Israeli army as well as the Ministry of Tourism, he has

Ines Weizman

Bauhaus Modernism across the Sykes-Picot Line

553

Fig.6. North façade of the upper (French) customhouse before renovation. Photograph by Edith Tsouri, 2013.

managed to clear an area of 70 dunams (about seven hectares) of land mines that had surrounded the customhouse and its adjacent buildings. A local architectural office and engineering firm developed a plan for the conversion of the remaining buildings (not all have survived) into a luxurious residence and a boutique hotel compound. The owner's daughter, a young interior designer, was tasked with revealing the building's "Bauhaus features," while Gleser himself traveled to Europe to collect historical building materials. Closer to home, he uprooted and transferred dozens of palm trees and—when the palm trees failed to thrive after two years—even a few olive trees from across the region. The new hotel development will include a swimming pool as well as additional buildings to increase the hotel's capacity. [fig.7, 8] 24

The Beit Ha-Mekhes Ha-Elyon, Hebrew for the Upper Customhouse in the Golan Heights, was actually not a single building, but an ensemble of structures of various sizes and functions. Surrounded by a wall, of which traces are still visible, was the main customs office building, the house of the tax office manager, and a building for a stable. Outside of the wall, directly over what is today Highway 91, stood a drive-through, physical customs check that, in contrast to the buildings within the walls, was built from concrete and might have dated from the later 1930s. This building, which was destroyed in the early 1970s, had something that could either be a rounded front cashier's desk, a kiosk, or an outlook. [fig.8] Near that building was a small bunker that blew up unexpectedly on June 15, 1967, when a few days after the end of the Six-Day War the victorious Israeli army tried to handle enemy ammunition stored in it. The explosion killed eleven Israeli soldiers, an incident that in the euphoria over the victory of the war was not reported until about 1990. [25]

The renovation makes it difficult to recognize the original ensemble. Prior to renovation, the bullet holes in the original buildings, more likely the consequence of Israeli military training than a gunfight, revealed the basalt stone walls below the concrete plastering originally painted in a deep yellow/ocher, a testimony to the fact that it was likely built by local masons.

Fig. 7. Advertisement for the renovated upper customhouse in *Hotel Design* Magazine, 2018.
Fig. 8. Renovated upper costumhouse with "Bauhaus" lettering, 2019.
Fig. 9. Photograph of drivethrough border building of the upper customhouse around 1967.

The main building, rising slightly above the rest, is a rectangular two-story building that demonstrates a rather classical sensibility to order and symmetry, hiding within its modernist plain walls. It is typical of what Jean-Louis Cohen described as "militarized modernism."[26] In plan and elevation, the building is rather dull, a seemingly indistinct, yet respectable institution. The central stairwell, as if mimicking a central clock tower, steps forward from the façade, extending one floor height above the roofline.

Right next to that building stands the director's or tax officer's house, demonstrating a more dynamic plasticity. Its most dominant element, following the same logic of "military modern," is again a stair tower, whose tall vertical window spans two and a half floors. On its eastern wall, three round windows are set against six stone shelves that protrude outward from the stairwell structure—Corbusian portholes without a sea—as if *Vers une architecture*, published in 1923, had already been sitting on the desk of the unknown architect in charge of the design of the customhouse ensemble. This was a project so remote, so unlikely to be reviewed by anyone he might consider to be of significance, that it would allow the sin of experimentation, a dry run, before a metropolitan commission were given, even if that metropolis were one of the capitals of the newly occupied Orient. Indeed, it is a specimen of that classical rationalist modernism that was rather common in the French-dominated colonial world spanning from Algiers through Cairo to Damascus between the mid-1920s and 1930s.

The customs building most probably has nothing to do with the Bauhaus, but the insistence of its owners in referring to it as such testifies to the export of its brand name. To understand the power of the Bauhaus name in the region, we would need to travel through this crossing in both directions, to the stations woven together by Route 91—Tel Aviv/Jaffa, Damascus, and later Beirut. The customhouse is the first building that one would see when driving out of Palestine into Syria and Lebanon, but it is certainly not the last modernist building along that way. It is a good gateway. The story of the Bauhaus in the Middle East is most often confined to Palestine, to Jewish migrants and "the White City." The customs building problematizes this conception; indeed, it contradicts it because it is positioned right outside of the borders of what we might consider the space of the "Bauhaus." Seen from Tel Aviv, this building is not *in* Palestine, but it is the first building *after* Palestine.

Bauhaus in the Levant

It is no longer possible to travel the road from Jaffa to Damascus, or from Haifa to Beirut and to Istanbul, and back to Cairo. The space of modernism in the Middle East—Henry-Russell Hitchcock and Philip Johnson thought of modernism as an architectural movement, but also as a movement across borders—seems to be fractured, truncated. But it was not always so. The fact that there was a customhouse meant precisely, border or not, that goods and people went through it, that the space of movement and trade was larger and much more fluid than that which exists today.

One of the architects who exemplified that liquid, connected, navigable space was Antoine Tabet. The architect built in places that today lie on both sides of the customhouse, across the uncrossable borders of the present day. Tabet received a degree in engineering from the École Supérieure d'Ingénieurs in Beirut in 1927 and had even worked at the atelier of Auguste Perret in Paris. His son, Jad Tabet, a Lebanese historian and president of the Order of Engineers and Architects in Lebanon, whom I met in Beirut to research the work of his father, elsewhere reflected on the problem of colonial modernism and local identity: "[Antoine] Tabet refuted the notion of a singular origin of any work of art or nation, in favour of a more hybrid understanding of culture and nationhood." Rather, "he presented a vision of architectural history which was both autonomous and continuous, containing its own internal dynamic and linked to the development of construction techniques and the changing laws of design and production." [27] Though building mainly in Lebanon between 1931 and the 1950s, famously the St. Georges Hotel in Beirut,[fig.9] Tabet had also built a large housing complex for Arab entrepreneur Raja Raïs in Haifa in 1937/38. [28] It was meant to house managers and higher-ranking staff of the Iraq Petroleum Company that was then in charge of laying the oil pipeline between Haifa and Kirkuk, and as such was another product of the Sykes-Picot Agreement.[fig.10][29] In Haifa, like in Beirut, Tabet used reinforced concrete in combination with tinted artificial stones and orientalist or Art Nouveau elements, as if not fully converted into modernism.[30] There is also Lebanese architect Elias Al-Mor, who in 1937 completed the Alhambra cinema in Jaffa, or Bauhaus architect Selman Selmanagić (whose story Ines Sonder began to tell in this volume), who might be the mirror image to Tabet.

The history of Arab, or Levantine, Modernism is, however, largely

Fig. 9. Façade detail of St. Georges Hotel, Beirut, 1931 (architect: Antoine Tabet). Photograph by Ines Weizman, 2018.

untold, or little intersected across today's national borders.[31] Efforts such as those of George Arbid, an architect and also mayor of a village in the Chouf mountains in Lebanon, in co-founding the Arab Center for Architecture in Beirut, to archive the history of modern architecture in Arab societies have only recently emerged.[32] They are an invaluable attempt to resurrect the forgotten history of modernism in the region, especially now that the historiography of modernism is divided across new conflict lines, each history myopic, introverted, self-referential, like the current governments of the region.

I will write about the efforts of Arab historians to resurrect the story of the Arab Modern at another time. This little taster is here to try to make the reader appreciate the fact that the customhouse is a transition point and a potential connector between two histories, of movement and migration—that of cross-border migrations of the self-modernizing people of the Levant and that of a migration of other moderns that will be swept into the region by the storm of a history about to come. These have finally tragically interfered with each other, become entangled, and crashed against one other. But the story of Jewish migration and flight into Palestine and the story of modernism in the Arab world are also the same history; they share the same world. The customhouse is not only the door to modernism in the region, one of the early birds announcing its arrival, but, following the Futurist slogan, we could consider the door *to be* modernism! Modernism is movement and movement is modernism, and a door, any door, leads in two directions.

The Bauhaus in Israel

In 2003, the "White City of Tel Aviv" was declared a UNESCO World Heritage Site. It followed what Sharon Rotbard described as a "twenty-year historiographic campaign" to create an urban narrative. His book tells how the simplified story of the so-called "White City" was used in the 1980s and 1990s to recast Tel Aviv as a modern, metropolitan, and Western city in contrast to what he called a "black" city: the largely Arab/Palestinian city of Jaffa, as well as the traces of Arab villages that had been cleared to create the "White City."[33] Rotbard also critiques the way the "White City of Tel Aviv" campaign was used to establish a

Fig.10. Façade detail of apartment buildings for Raja Raïs in Radak Street, Haifa, 1937/1938 (architect: Antoine Tabet). Photograph by Ines Weizman, 2018.

hierarchy of cities in Israel: Tel Aviv was branded as the young, fashionable, international city; Jerusalem as the ancient one; and Haifa, which still has a sizable Palestinian population and a remarkable urban ensemble of pre-state modernist architecture that included local elements, some stone masonry, partially built by Arab Modern architects, as not quite as purely white as Tel Aviv. The search for the "white," which according to Rotbard is all too often also labeled as Bauhaus Modernism—there are numerous books and exhibitions called Bauhaus Tel Aviv—obstructs a more complex historical matrix in order to reconstruct the European influences on Zionist architecture in Palestine.

Architectural historian Zvi Efrat summarized the phases of Zionist architecture in Palestine as the "Eclectic Period" from 1900 to 1920, the "White Period" of the 1930s and 1940s, the "Grey Period" of the 1950s and 1960s, and the Brutalist era of post-1967.[34]

> *Zionist modernism is an intense and highly instructive instance of the International Style. After all, this American title, which cannibalized the various early-twentieth century avant-gardes, was primarily intended to nullify the previous native and colonial mimetic economy and to trade exoticism of the 'styles' for the authority of an overstyle. The universalist gesture of all-overness and free flow revealed itself as the most conspicuous form of cultural colonialism.*[35]

The historiography of the Bauhaus in Israel is equally contested. Both Rotbard and Efrat, each in their own way, question its myth, but also critique the meaning of the campaign to selectively preserve parts of the city and promote them in the name of the Bauhaus. To say Bauhaus, they claim, shifts the historiography of the modern movement in Israel from its colonial roots to a story of national regeneration— refugee architects escaping Germany and building its socialist dreams on the sands.[36] At the same time the exodus of Palestinians makes way for Bauhaus modernism, dust rises and settles. Further, as Myra Warhaftig has shown in her seminal book *They Laid the Foundation: Lives and Works of German-Speaking Jewish Architects in Palestine 1918–1948*,[37] modernism in Palestine had turned into a style in the 1930s and 1940s, one that related more to the general functionalist movement of *Neue Sachlichkeit* and International Style than directly to the original work and intentions of the Bauhaus in Weimar, Dessau, and Berlin.[38]

Ines Weizman

Bauhaus Modernism across the Sykes-Picot Line

559

Fig. 11. Max Liebling House, Tel Aviv. Photograph by Jannis Uffrecht (CDA), 2018.

Indeed, the architects who locally propagated the values of the version of modernism originating in Germany and the Bauhaus school, including former Bauhaus students such as Arieh Sharon, Shmuel Mestechkin, Shlomo Bernstein, Chanan Frenkel, Edgar Hecht, Munio Weinraub, and Selman Selmanagić, worked across the country with no exclusive focus on Tel Aviv. Tel Aviv was largely built by young architects who were aware of modernism, but one that, as Efrat argues,

came about not in a place of modernity and modernization, but in their place; an architecture that was to devise the missing context, to stage a revolution that never was, to recall processes of modulation and serialization that occurred elsewhere, and to fabricate not the city itself, but the cosmopolitan mis-en-scène and petit bourgeois decorum longed for by the incoming central European Jewish immigrants and the exiles of the fourth and fifth aliyot.[39]

To better interrogate the difficulties that the circulation of ideas, but also other dynamics, the movement of people, building materials, and finance from Germany to Palestine and the larger region implied, I would like to move to another case study, the Max Liebling House in Tel Aviv.

Tracing the materiality of Bauhaus Modernism

In 2019, the White City Center will open after extensive renovations. [fig. 11] The project was launched in 2015 by the Tel Aviv-Yafo municipality and the German government. The center aims "to support the development of a vibrant German-Israeli cooperation" and to increase the familiarity of the UNESCO-recognized "White City of Tel Aviv."[40] The opening might be overshadowed by the fact that in 2019, while the "White City of Tel Aviv" is being recognized for its UNESCO status as a World Heritage Site, Israel has angrily left the international organization. Relations deteriorated gradually. In 2011, UNESCO became the first UN body to admit Palestine as a full member. In response, Israel and the United States stopped paying their annual dues, which in the case of the latter amounted to about 22 percent of the organization's total budget. Following UNESCO's recognition of Palestine, however, several sites within the Israeli-occupied West Bank were added to its list of World Heritage Sites: in 2012, it was the Church of the Nativity in Bethlehem; in 2014, these were the terraces of Battir (just as the Wall was being designed to cut through them, a declaration that contributed to Israel's supreme court canceling plans to build the Wall there);[41] and in 2017, the Old Town of Hebron/Al-Khalil was added. In response to the Hebron listing, Israel's UN envoy, Danny Danon, complained that "ancient Jewish sites were protected as Palestinian heritage sites," and described UNESCO as a "tool for Israel's enemies."[42] Modern, bustling Tel Aviv and occupied and segregated Hebron embody the paradoxical matrix of contemporary Israel.

The Max Liebling House

The history of the White City Center, colloquially also known as the Max Liebling House, is being researched by the members of the White City Center together with the Centre for Documentary Architecture (CDA) that emerged from research I conducted with students at the Bauhaus-Universität Weimar. This historical project includes both documentary and material research. The building's renovations offered an occasion to engage with the buildings' materiality and have a look behind layers of paint. Indeed, within the depth of the (off-)white painted walls lie accumulated material strata, histories of builders, materials, and users. Old pipes and layers of paint, brushed over for 90-odd years, could now erupt onto the surface through the gift of an opportunity. Conservationists, architects, photographers, filmmakers, and historians should always rush to a restoration site of a building under their scrutiny, like geologists who depend on the layers of rock exposed by seismological cracks. This is, as mentioned above, the very basis of the method of documentary architecture: a view of a building that in its very materiality is a document to its own history.[fig. 12]

This multi-apartment building was built by investor Max Liebling and his wife Tony, who had immigrated from Switzerland with Austrian passports in 1935. They commissioned architect Dov Karmi, who had initially studied at the Bezalel Academy of Arts and Crafts in Jerusalem and had then studied architecture and engineering from 1925 to 1930 at the University of Ghent in Belgium. During this time, Karmi as well as fellow students from Palestine, such as Elsa Gidoni and Genia Averbouch, might have come in contact with Henry van de Velde,

Ines Weizman

Bauhaus Modernism across the Sykes-Picot Line

561

Fig. 12. Montage of situation before renovation and digital reconstruction of a staircase of the Max Liebling House, Tel Aviv. Photograph by Anna Luise Schubert, Ortrun Bargholz, Eugen Happacher (CDA), 2018.

who after leaving Weimar in 1915 had moved first to the Netherlands and in 1926 back to Belgium to take up a position as chair of architectural history in Ghent and as director of the Institute Supérieur des Arts Décoratifs in Brussels.[43] This network of relationships not only points to complex trajectories of ideas and discussions that the young architects had before their return to Tel Aviv around 1930—in which the Bauhaus might have been discussed—but also might explain some of the particularly interesting color schemes Karmi had developed for the interior of the Max Liebling House.[44]

Tony and Max Liebling, who co-inhabited the multi-apartment house together with several families of well-known German émigré physicians, bequeathed the house after their deaths to the Tel Aviv municipality with the wish that the building be used as either an orphanage, a residential facility for children, a home for the elderly, a dorm for needy students, or a museum. The municipality seized on the latter. Until the last residents moved out of the building, the municipality used the apartments to house a kindergarten on the ground floor as well as for office space.

Still, before renovation work began, the CDA had the chance to document the building in the condition it was in 2015.[45] Following the premise of the "documentary method," in which we examine buildings as both material and media realities, we documented the work of the international preservationists of the Max Liebling House to reconstruct the material history of the building.[46] To study the "biography" of the building, we used archaeological techniques, looking at the texture of material surfaces for clues to builders and users, and through the depth of the walls in search of buried objects and old infrastructural systems that we corroborated with documents, plans, photographs, notes, and correspondence. The material fact of the building—rather than merely its architect or its inhabitants—thus emerges as a protagonist. Perhaps not surprisingly, some of the findings lead back to Germany.

The controversial Haavara Agreement (Hebrew for "transfer") was arranged in 1933 between the Jewish Agency of Palestine and the German Reich Ministry of Economy (Reichswirtschaftsministerium), following negotiations that had involved private Jewish businessmen in both Mandatory Palestine and representatives of the Jewish Agency in Germany.[47] This agreement enabled German Jews—"encouraged" to emigrate from Nazi Germany but forbidden to take more than a small fraction of their wealth out of the country—to get some of their money when arriving in Palestine.[48]

The system worked in the following manner: mediated through a Berlin-based trust company, the Palästina Treuhandstelle zur Beratung Deutscher Juden GmbH, or Paltreu (The Palestine Trust for Guidance of German Jews (my translation)), German Jews deposited their funds in Reichsmark in special accounts held in two banks owned by well-known German-Jewish banking families— M. M. Warburg & Co. in Hamburg and A. E. Wassermann in Berlin. Meanwhile in Mandatory Palestine—mediated through the office of the Haavara Ltd. in Tel Aviv—local importers could use this money to buy German products. At the time, German industry was heavily subsidized by the Nazis, and through the Haavara agreement these products could be marketed cheaper than similar products produced in Palestine or imported to it from elsewhere. So while manufacturers in Germany were paid through the Paltreu accounts held in the Warburg and Wassermann banks in Germany, importers in Palestine paid for the German products by paying into the Haavara accounts held at the Anglo-Palestine Bank and the Bank of the Temple Society. The money held at the Anglo-Palestine Bank and the Bank of the Temple Society was then used to pay the newly arriving German-Jewish migrants in Palestine in Palestinian pounds, after deducting generous fees.

Between 1933 and 1939, when the boycott against German goods was tightening, the Haavara Agreement provided Germany with some lucrative currency,[49] though eventually it was more of a symbolic victory that helped Germany argue to those boycotting it that Jewish organizations themselves were trading with it. This led to allegations, some of which continue to this day, that the Zionist agency collaborated with the Nazis.[50] This accusation makes the historical error of conflating the motivations and actions of people fleeing for their lives with those facing a consumer choice of whether to buy a product of

Ines
Weizman

Bauhaus
Modernism
across
the
Sykes-Picot
Line

563

a murderous regime. In any case, this sophisticated transfer system, which involved individuals and brokers, had to be operated according to changing processes that needed to be continuously adjusted and renegotiated to respond to the evolving political situation in both Germany and in Mandatory Palestine. Indeed, events were evolving rapidly in both places. At the same time the Nazis tightened their grip on power and escalated their repressions against the Jews, the British authorities, pressed by the Arab opposition to Jewish migration, tightened their control over immigration.

The current condition of the Max Liebling House, "stripped bare" during the process of renovation, presents a precious opportunity to unveil material evidence of a hidden past with the full spectrum of the methods of documentary architecture. Materials have complex stories to tell, details as minute as the constituent ingredients and color pigments of the terrazzo of the floors, the inscriptions on the back of tiles such as stamps for the company Villeroy & Boch, and pipework deep within the walls of the building, but also the house's more obvious façade elements, windows, door handles, fittings, and paints.[fig.13–15]51 To trace the complex history of modern architecture, it is necessary to reconstruct the trajectories of building materials, building elements, and objects as they lead back to German construction factories, manufactures, retailers, and possibly architects. The quality of cement, whether gray or white, or the chemical characteristics of color pigments—information in the very grains of dust—reopens, like the virus buried in the body of Sir Mark Sykes, a history of materials that seems to contain the world.[fig.16]

In Tel Aviv, modern architecture has been presented as a unique form of national regeneration that stands in contrast to both the European past and the orientalist context of the Middle East. While the history of German emigration to Palestine is certainly a core chapter within the history of the Bauhaus and the migration of its ideas, protagonists, and objects, the Bauhaus jubilee currently being celebrated intimates a much larger and more multifaceted regional historiography of modernism in the Levant.

The material analysis of the Max Liebling House reveals a problem in the narrative of the White City of Tel Aviv and connecting its origins to the Bauhaus: a correlation between the time of construction of most of the buildings in the modernist core of Tel Aviv—between 1933 and 1939—and the years of the Haavara Agreement with Nazi

Fig. 13. Tiles in staircase, Max Liebling House, Tel Aviv. Photograph by Jannis Uffrecht (CDA), 2018.
Fig. 14. Detail of wall of balcony in Max Liebling House, Tel Aviv, investigated by preservationist Dr. Norbert Höpfer. Photograph by Amelie Wegner (CDA), 2018.

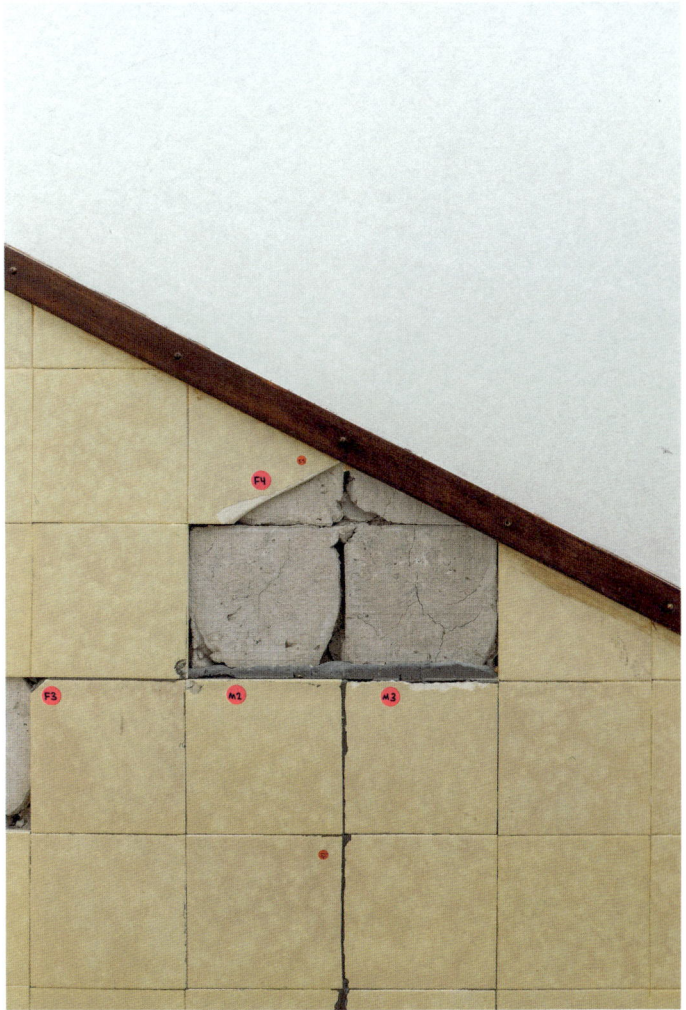

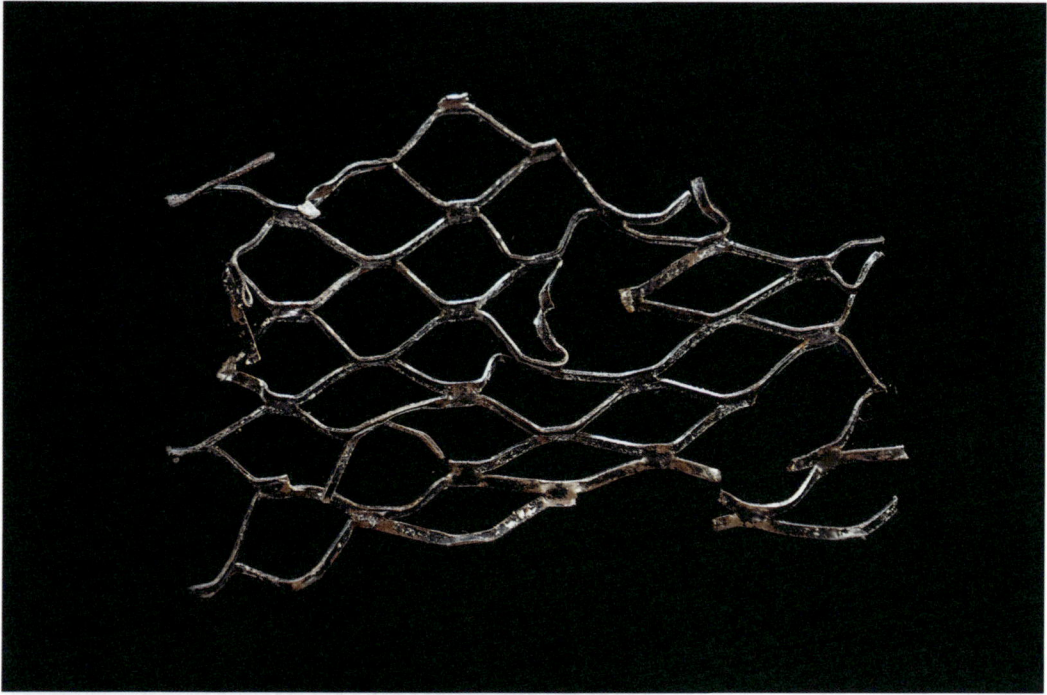

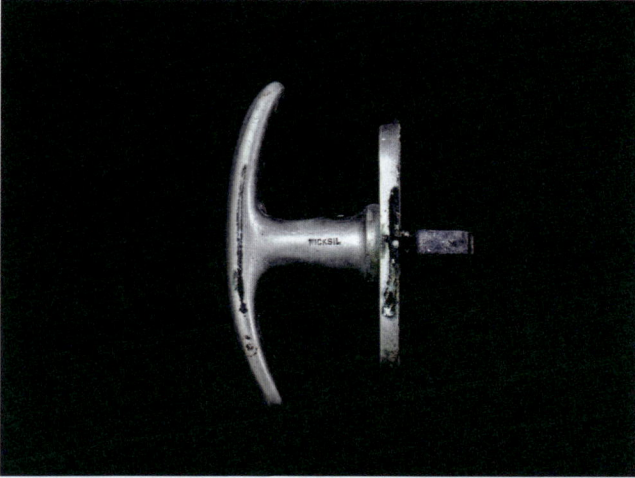

Fig. 15a–c. Material analysis
of building elements of the
Max Liebling House.
Photographs by Anna Luise
Schubert (CDA), 2018.

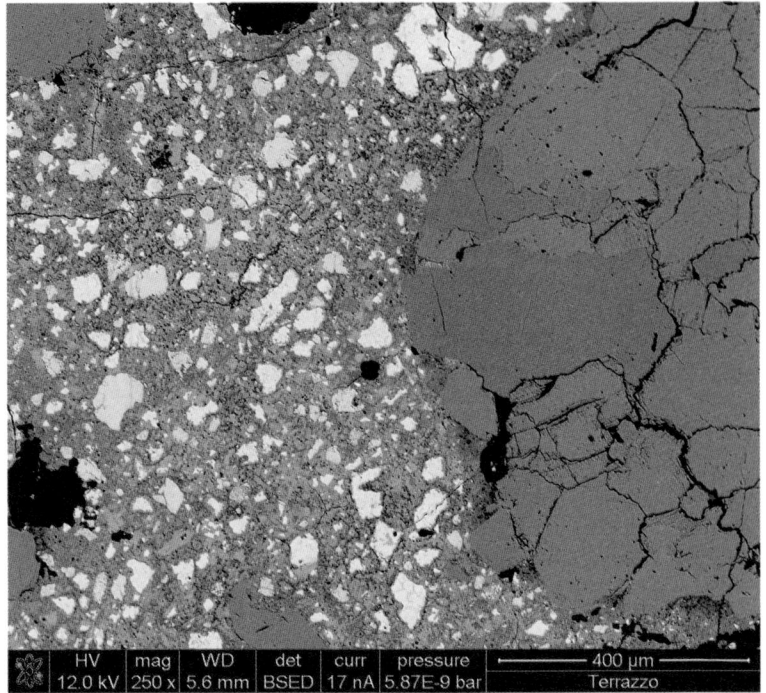

Fig. 16. Microscopic analysis of the terrazzo of Max Liebling House. Photograph by Dr. Bernd Möser, Bauhaus-Universität Weimar, 2018.

Germany. Thousands of migrants and refugees moved from Germany to Palestine during these years, and many products from factories affiliated with the German regime found their way to Tel Aviv, fueling the growth of the so-called "first Hebrew town." The White City, then, has an undoubtedly dark core, given the controversial nature of the Haavara Agreement, but this duality is fully understandable, given the historical circumstances.

Another collateral effect of the Haavara Agreement, one that can only be touched upon here, was the prevalence of economic difficulties faced by factories and local manufacturers in Palestine. Although the causalities of closures cannot always be fully reconstructed, the Phoenicia Glass Works Company in Haifa, for example, was forced to liquidate in 1937 after only a few months of production in light of the robust imports of similar products from Germany. Another historical coincidence is the Arab rebellion in Palestine that broke out in 1936. This protest was largely articulated around a general strike and an economic boycott of Jewish goods and services before it was suppressed by the British.[52]

One of the reasons for the Arab rebellion was economic. In his essay "From Poverty to Revolt," historian Mahmoud Yazbak recounts how, from the mid-1920s, the Arab industries and "mobile wage-workers" that had moved to the non-agricultural sector of the economy suffered a recession under the impact of new Jewish products and productions. In the mid-1930s, cheap imports from abroad, together with the imposition of high import tariffs on goods from Palestine, caused "tens of thousands" to become "[j]obless and destitute." Subsequently,

> thrown back between village and town and ever more desperate because of the deepening poverty in which their families were sunk, they began to form huge pockets of social discontent, especially in the shanty dwellings on the outskirts of Jaffa and Haifa.[53]

It would be too simple to claim that the Haavara Agreement is the cause of these developments, but it is certainly their context, and it is

Ines Weizman

Bauhaus Modernism across the Sykes-Picot Line

567

possible that the agreement contributed to the aggravation of these conditions. This incident might also be a link that connects the two buildings and the two sides of the Sykes-Picot Line.

Proximate sensing and digital tactility

The plain surfaces of modernism are what lead it to its fascination with paint—be it the Pantone colors of Le Corbusier, or the whiteness of the White City—but here, in the Max Liebling House, the white is also a whitening out, a whitewash behind which lie traces of a tragic past. When we peel away these layers, an archaeology of modernism is forced to reveal the strata of a fossilized past. The depth of the wall is the building's "unconscious." Like an architectural version of Benjamin's "photographic unconscious," it is revealed by new digital methods and technologies that can arrest, slow or accelerate time.[54]

That technological unconscious is being explored through a multiplicity of sensors and methods of detection that go into the minute and molecular level of matter. All that remained dormant for more than eighty years—unknown to the people who lived in the buildings and those who wrote their histories and that of the White City itself—is now exposed to the reality of these new findings. It is this "architectural history in the age of digital detection" that permits us to uncover this latent, suppressed history.

Navigating the deep space of architectural history must cross physical and cultural borders, different media, archival practices, and modes of communication. In this new cartography of research, digital media becomes an important tool—one that, in this case, helped the history of modernism in British Mandate Palestine and its frontier zones as a networked set of encounters between people and things in motion. In this task, architectural details, fragments, and material samples enable the unpacking of the "deep memory" of the building.

It is with this new sensibility of documentary architecture, and through a critical use of new technologies, that we can start to make sense of the pulverized molecular fragments of history—the clouds of dust raised by the region's warlords, scattering across borders drawn in sand, then marked in concrete, gathering in the depth of buildings—and compose it into data.

1 Ines Weizman, "Documentary Architecture: The Digital Historiographies of Modernism," *Faktur: Documents and Architecture*, no. 1 (Fall 2018): 6–25 (English); Ines Weizman, "Dokumentarische Architektur. Digitale Historiografien der Moderne," ARCH+ 234: *Datatopia* (2019): 198–209 (German).

2 This reflection on dust builds largely upon Eyal Weizman's reading in relation to an enormous analysis conducted by Forensic Architecture to reconstruct the particularly heavy IDF bombing of the city of Rafah in Gaza on August 1, 2014. In relation to the cloud atlas FA produced to synchronize images and videos of the events from social media, he described these bomb clouds as "airborne cemeteries of architecture and flesh." Eyal Weizman, *Forensic Architecture: Violence at the Threshold of Detectability* (Zone Books, 2017), 193, 133–213.

3 Carlo Ginzburg, *Threads and Traces: True, False, Fictive* (Berkeley: University of California Press, 2012), 207.

4 Part of the reason for the devastating effects of the famine in the Lebanese mountains and in the Golan have to do with the fact that at the end of the 19th century, the French had introduced silk production in Syria and in the Lebanese mountains. For this, farmers, supported by the Ottoman government, replaced their traditional agriculture with thousands of mulberry trees that the silkworms favored. When World War I halted the silk trade, the Lebanese farmers, dependent for their food supply on economic exchange with other areas, were severely affected. Their now one-crop economy, combined with the difficulties involved in making a rapid transition from growing mulberry trees to food crops, led to starvation among the poor. For a more detailed account of the agricultural changes that also led to changes in the form of ownership and maintenance of the land, and hence changes in social relationships among the area's inhabitants, see Kais Firro, "Silk and Agrarian Changes in Lebanon, 1860–1914," *International Journal of Middle East Studies* 22, no. 2 (1990): 151–69.

5 Salim Tamari, *Year of the Locust: A Soldier's Diary and the Erasure of Palestine's Ottoman Past* (Berkeley: University of California Press, 2011), 19.

6 The diary of Ihsan Turjman, in Salim Tamari, *Year of the Locust: A Soldier's Diary and the Erasure of Palestine's Ottoman Past* (Berkeley: University of California Press, 2011), 118.

7 Stefanie Wichart, "The 1915 Locust Plague in Palestine," *Jerusalem Quarterly* 56/57: 29–39; Zachary J. Foster, "The 1915 Locust Attack in Syria and Palestine and Its Role in the Famine during the First World War," *Middle Eastern Studies* 51, no. 3 (2015): 370–94.

8 Laura Spinney, *Pale Rider: The Spanish Flu of 1918 and How It Changed the World* (London: Penguin, 2017), 4–7.

9 Laura Spinney, *Pale Rider*, 7.

10 Paul Klee wrote in November 1918 in his letters to his wife Lily and his son Felix from his service in the Bavarian air force that he had recently suffered from symptoms of the flu: "Ich hatte einen deutlichen Grippeanfall, bekam vorgestern Fieber und Husten. Eine phantasievolle Nacht machte mich aber wieder gesund. Es war zu deutlich, daß es ausbrechen wollte und nicht konnte." ("I had a clear case of influenza, with fever and coughing the day before yesterday. A night of creativity returned me to health. It was all too clear that it wanted to break out, but couldn't.") Letter, November 14, 1918, in *Paul Klee, Tagebücher 1898–1918* (Leipzig, Weimar: Kiepenheuer Verlag, 1990 (Cologne: Dumont, 1957)), 353.

11 Laura Spinney, *Pale Rider*, 5.

12 "Aristocrat's coffin could hold key to bird flu," *The Telegraph*, March 1, 2007, retrieved on May 5, 2019, www.telegraph.co.uk/news/uknews/1544160/Aristocrats-coffin-could-hold-key-to-bird-flu.html

13 As the First World War broke out, Britain, France, and Russia became allies against Germany and hence also declared war on the Ottoman Caliphate that had joined forces with Germany. In 1916, British diplomat Sir Mark Sykes and his French counterpart François Georges-Picot signed a secret agreement on how to divide the Ottoman Empire once the war ended. With the approval of Russia, which was still under tsarist rule, Britain was allocated the coastal strip between the Mediterranean and the River Jordan, Jordan, southern Iraq, and the ports of Haifa and Acre. France was allocated control of southeastern Turkey, northern Iraq, Syria, and Lebanon. Russia was to take control of Istanbul, Turkish Armenia, and northern Kurdistan. Palestine at that stage was reserved for an international

*Ines
Weizman*

Bauhaus
Modernism
across
the
Sykes-Picot
Line

569

administration. This secret agreement became known in 1917 when Russian revolutionary leaders published its terms to the embarrassment of the British and the French. The line nonetheless became a reality after the First World War when Germany lost the war, and the French and British took their share of the Levant. According to Sir Mark Sykes, who in 1915 first presented his proposal, a line had to be drawn through the Ottoman Empire from the "e" in "Acre" to the last "k" in "Kirkuk" on the map of the Middle East. See further: James Barr, *A Line in the Sand: Britain, France and the Struggle that Shaped the Middle East* (London: Simon & Schuster, 2012 (2011)), 12.

14   This essay expands on an earlier version. See Ines Weizman, "Bauhaus on the Golan: Notes towards an Architectural History of the Sykes-Picot Line," in *Bauhaus Magazin*, no. 7 (KOLLEKTIV, 2015): 112–120, Ines Weizman, "Archives Fever – Adolf Loos in Palestine," in: Jörg Stabenow and Ronny Schüler, eds., *The Transfer of Modernity: Architectural Modernism in Palestine 1923–1948* (Berlin: Gebrüder Mann Verlag, 2019), 33–47.

15   In 1923, according to the League of Nations mandate, France was assigned the League of Nations mandate of Syria, which in addition to Syria proper included the territory of present-day Lebanon and Alexandretta. The borders of this mandate, which lasted until 1943 when Syria and Lebanon reached independence, were in accordance with the Sykes-Picot Agreement of 1916.

16   Until the United States concurred in 2019, Israel was the only country to accept its (own) annexation of the Golan.

17   Referring to the architecture of the Levant Fair, which in 1934 was turned from temporary exhibition pavilions into an ensemble of "white" International Style architecture, Zvi Efrat noted the awkwardness of the style of the British pavilion: "In the context of the British patronage of the Levant Fair and British colonial architecture in Palestine, the fair's *sachlich* architecture—including the austere British pavilion itself—seems almost subversive in its outright rejection of masonry techniques, arts and crafts surfaces and Orientalist motifs." Zvi Efrat, *The Object of Zionism* (Leipzig: Spector Books, 2019), 172–183. Interesting as markers for the conditions of trading across the Levant are

also the pavilions of Egypt and Lebanon, which the Jewish architects of the Levant Fair equally subjected to the white architecture of the fair.

18   More on the transportable bridge designed by British engineer Donald C. Bailey in Jean-Louis Cohen, *Architecture in Uniform: Designing and Building for World War II*, catalogue of an exhibition held at CCA (Paris: Éditions Hazan, 2011), 270ff.

19   Hebrew: Gesher Bnot Ya'akov, English: Daughters of Jacob Bridge.

20   In 1917, when the British Mesopotamian Expeditionary Force captured Samarra, they discovered about ninety boxes filled with antiquities that German archaeologist Ernst Herzfeld and Friedrich Sarre had excavated from the site with the intention of shipping them to Berlin. While the Foreign Office initially refused to remove these treasures from Iraq, in 1921 the Colonial Office, personally authorized by Winston Churchill, arranged for their shipment to the British Museum, where they were to be examined and treated by Herzfeld. Eventually, after the contents of the boxes had been catalogued and sent to various international museums, in 1936 only two boxes were returned to the Iraq Museum that had been built in 1926 and that had requested their return. See Juliette Desplat, "The Other Battle of Samarra," retrieved May 6, 2019, blog.nationalarchives.gov.uk/blog/the-other-battle-of-samarra/

21   General Otto Liman von Sanders was appointed Chief of the German Military Mission to Turkey in 1913. In February 1918 he was appointed commander of "Yildrim," Army Group F, an alliance of the German and the Ottoman armies during the First World War, from February 1918 to October 1918. Denied the needed supplies and reinforcements, he failed to stop British General Sir Edmund Allenby's troops and its Australian allies from driving through Palestine. Otto Liman von Sanders, *Five Years in Turkey* (Naval & Military Press, 2015 reprint (1928)), mention of Major Ludloff and the retreat across Jacob Bridge, 286.

22   In truth, the way through these old land mines, as my father-in-law in fact demonstrated, is to walk on the excrement traces of the cattle there. There probably haven't been any live land mines here for a long time, he said, as we made our way to the building in shoes we will never wear again. When we got to the building, we had to laugh aloud in relief, to see that the entire building was the resting place of about 20 cows peeking through its windows. Given that cattle meat is a large part of the Israeli Golan's economy, they must have felt secure behind the land mine signs.

23　Between September and November 1919, Patrick Geddes spent time in Palestine at the invitation of Chaim Weizmann, who commissioned Geddes with the planning of the Hebrew University. See Volker M. Welter, "The 1925 Master Plan for Tel-Aviv by Patrick Geddes," *Israel Studies* 14, no. 3 (2009): 98, 94–119.

24　In 2018 the hotel was advertised in the Israeli magazine *Hotel Design* with the following description: "The project is a Bauhaus building from 1919, unique in the world for being not in an urban context but in a natural one. The hotel is divided into three Bauhaus buildings for conservation that include eleven beautiful suites, each in a different style. The design style combines the modest, simple, and minimalist style of the Bauhaus with its precise historical beauty, together with a Parisian style of abundance and glamor as well as a Mediterranean style." *Hotel Design* (2018). Translation: Eyal Weizman. See figure 7.

25　A memorial to those soldiers killed was installed on the grounds of the future hotel in autumn 2018.

26　Jean-Louis Cohen, *Architecture in Uniform*, 13.

27　Jad Tabet, "From Colonial Style to Regional Revivalism: Modern Architecture in Lebanon and the Problem of Cultural Identity," in *Projecting Beirut: Episodes in the Construction and Reconstruction of a Modern City*, ed. Peter Rowe and Hashim Sarkis (Munich, London, New York: Prestel, 1998), 85.

28　Alona Nitzan-Shiftan, "On the Architectural and Zionist Modern Movements," in *The Transfer of Modernity: Architectural Modernism in Palestine 1923–1948*, ed. Stabenow and Schüler (Berlin: Gebrüder Mann Verlag, 2019), 216–17.

29　In 1934, the pipeline was completed that ran from Kirkuk to Haifa via Al-Hadithah, from where another pipeline ran through Palmyra to Tripoli.

30　Tabet, 84.

31　An important contribution to this field was the conference and publication by Amal Andraos and Nora Akawi with Caitlin Blanchfield, eds., *The Arab City: Architecture and Representation* (New York: Columbia Books on Architecture and the City, 2016), and Anthony Downey, ed., *Dissonant Archives: Contemporary Visual Culture and Contested Narratives in the Middle East* (Tauris, 2015).

32　In 2014, on the occasion of the 14th Architecture Biennale in Venice, at which curator Rem Koolhaas asked the national pavilion to take the 100-year perspective since World War 1, 1914–2014, as inspiration, Arbid in collaboration with architect Bernard Khoury produced an installation at the Pavilion of the Kingdom of Bahrain titled "Fundamentalists and Other Arab Modernisms" that aimed to show 100 buildings from twenty-two countries across the Arab world. See also *Fundamentalists and Other Arab Modernisms*, catalogue of the exhibition at the Pavilion of the Kingdom of Bahrain, 14th Architecture Biennale in Venice (2014).

33　"With its establishment as a local hallmark, the Bauhaus Style began to infiltrate outside Israel's borders, this time as a national claim for an international recognition. Soliciting this approbation internationally involved a certain degree of emotional extortion, as if to say: 'You didn't want us in Weimar—please accept us in Tel Aviv.' After all, the Jews, the Weimar Republic and the Bauhaus were all victims of the Nazis." Sharon Rotbard, *White City, Black City: Architecture and War in Tel Aviv and Jaffa* (Pluto Press, 2015), 12.

34　Zvi Efrat, "Bauhaus Buildings without Bauhaus," in *Die Zeitschrift der Stiftung Bauhaus Dessau*, no. 2 (November 2011): 5.

35　Zvi Efrat, *The Object of Zionism*, 153–60.

36　Sharon Rotbard, *White City, Black City*, 43ff.

37　Myra Warhaftig, *They Laid the Foundation: Lives and Works of German-Speaking Jewish Architects in Palestine 1918–1948* (Tübingen: Ernst Wasmuth Verlag, 1996).

38　*Matter of Data: Tracing the Materiality of "Bauhaus Modernism,"* exhibition of the Centre for Documentary Architecture (CDA) at the Bauhaus-Museum Weimar and the Liebling House, Tel Aviv, 2019. Online platform accessible at documentary-architecture.org

39　Zvi Efrat, *The Object of Zionism*, 152–71, 163.

40　Website of White City Centre, www.whitecitycenter.org, accessed on May 28, 2019

Ines Weizman

Bauhaus Modernism across the Sykes-Picot Line

41   Eyal Weizman, *Forensic Architecture*, 125–127.

42   www.haaretz.com/us-news/u-s-and-israel-officially-leave-unesco-citing-anti-israel-bias-1.6805062, accessed on May 14, 2019.

43   Thanks for assistance in this research to Mrs. ten Hove from the archive of Ghent University and to Vera Heinemann, Anna Luise Schubert and Amelie Wegner, Centre for Documentary Architecture (CDA).

44   In her fascinating study of color pigments hidden under layers of paint in the Max Liebling House, preservationist and color expert Marlu Müller-Ortloff revealed, rather than a white color, a light spectrum of orange, peach, and apricot throughout the house, which she argues could be traced back to van de Velde's color theory that he developed in Weimar in the early 1910s and which he might have taught in Belgium to Dov Karmi. Interviews and film documentation conducted by the CDA in her pigment studio in Weimar, April 2018, and in the Max Liebling House, July 2018, accessible through the Web archive of the CDA: documentary-architecture.org

45   For the inauguration of the Liebling House, the CDA presented an exhibition in 2015 on research about German-Jewish émigré architects titled *From the Second Life: Documents of Forgotten Architectures*.

46   See note 1.

47   Zionistische Vereinigung für Deutschland, or Zentral-Verein deutscher Staatsbürger jüdischen Glaubens.

48   The agreement was a means of solving the bind in which Jews who were trying to leave Germany were caught: due to Germany's currency controls, they could take only 200 Reichsmark (towards the mid-1930s even less) out of the country, while the British Mandate immigration authorities had set immigration quotas that made visas conditional on a certificate that showed that émigrés had sufficient funds to afford life in Britain and in Palestine.

49   Günter Schubert, *Erkaufte Flucht: Der Kampf um den Haavara-Transfer* (Berlin: Metropol, 2009).

50   The Haavara Agreement was already discussed controversially by Hannah Arendt in her book *Eichmann in Jerusalem*; Edwin Black in *The Transfer Agreement: The Dramatic Story of the Pact between the Third Reich and Jewish Palestine*;

Tom Segev, *The Seventh Million* (Picador, 2000), and others. A fundamental study is Werner Feilchenfeld, Dolf Michaelis, and Ludwig Pinner, *Haavara-Transfer nach Palästina und Einwanderung deutscher Juden 1933–1939* (Tübingen: J. C. B. Mohr, 1972). See also Dorothea Hauser, "Zwischen Gehen und Bleiben. Das Sekretariat Warburg und sein Netzwerk des Vertrauen 1938–1941," in *"Wer bleibt, opfert seine Jahre, vielleicht sein Leben." Deutsche Juden 1938–1941*, ed. S. Heim, B. Meyer, and F. Nicosia (Göttingen: Wallstein, 2010), 115–33; Dorothea Hauser, "Banking on Emigration: Reconsidering the Warburg Bank's Late Surrender, Schacht's Protective Hand, and Other Myths about Jewish Banks in the 'Third Reich,'" in Christoph Kreutzmüller and Jonathan Zatlin, eds., *Dispossession: Plundering German Jewry, 1933–53* (Ann Arbor: University of Michigan Press, 2019 (in print)). See also "Material Itineraries: Reporting the Import of German Building Materials in Palestine 1930–1940," unpublished MSC theses of Anna Luise Schubert and Amelie Wegner (Bauhaus-Universität Weimar, 2018) (supervised by the author). The author would like to thank Dorothea Hauser for so generously sharing her insight into the history of the Warburg Bank in relation to the Haavara Agreement.

51   Ines Weizman, "Black Coloured White/ Schwarz Gefärbtes Weiß," in *All about Tel Aviv-Jaffa. Die Erfindung einer Stadt*, ed. Hannes Sulzenbacher und Hanno Loewy, 200–08.

52   G. Walsh, Economic Advisor to Government of Palestine, Jerusalem. Note of an interview with the economic advisor on June 17, 1938 regarding the reopening of the Phoenicia Glass Works, Haifa, dated June 22, 1938, Israel State Archive, File C/13/36.

53   Mahmoud Yazbak, "From Poverty to Revolt: Economic Factors in the Outbreak of the 1936 Rebellion in Palestine," *Middle Eastern Studies* 36, no. 3 (July 2000): 93–113.

54   "Photography … can bring out those aspects of the original that are unattainable to the naked eye yet accessible to the lens … enlargement or slow motion, can capture images which escape natural vision." Walter Benjamin, "The Work of Art in the Age of Mechanical Reproduction," in *Illuminations: Essays and Reflections*, ed. Hannah Arendt (New York: Schocken Books, 1968), 220.

Part 3

Bauhaus
Architects
in
Exile

Onward:
Turning Dust to Data

Bernhard Siegert

Dust to Data: Apocalypses of Territoriality

The images from Austria, Hungary, Slovenia, Croatia, and Macedonia which television broadcast for many weeks in 2015 were dominated by a recurrent motif that showed one of the most archaic and elementary cultural techniques: the erection of border fences and the sorting out of people by gates and locks. Something happened which nobody had expected: Space reported back in a brute, massive, and obtrusive way. "The ontology of the immured space" ("*die Ontologie des ummauerten Raumes*")[1] is not in need of a philosopher; it's writing itself right now. Space reported back in a way that made the so-called spatial turn look rather ridiculous. This is not the space of Michel de Certeau which urban-space-loving literary scholars and architectural theorists cherished for so many years. This is old, ugly, geopolitical space that nobody wanted to deal with anymore, since it unavoidably evokes the "problematic" figure of Carl Schmitt. For decades, legal scholars kept telling us that Europe is not defined by territory, that Europe is a community based on treaties. The law that was enacted by treaties is confronted again by the law that is created by space.[2] Cornelia Vismann, a legal scholar who was a cultural and media historian, never grew tired of pointing out this duality in the history of law.

In consequence, Europe reflects its own conditions of possibility in terms of an apocalypse of territoriality, which resulted for instance in massive re-inscriptions of what Schmitt called the "Nomos of the Earth." The term *nomos* expresses the idea that the law is a unit of ordering and locating, that it is bound to enclosures, to landmarks, to the possibility of demarcation, and thus to the Earth. A crisis of the *nomos* therefore automatically evokes images of the sea. Something can be possessed by someone, wrote the first theoretician of the international law of the seas, Hugo Grotius, in his treatise *The Free Sea*, only if it can be measured, demarcated, and defended by fixed borders.[3] Europe between the southern border of Germany and the western border of Turkey appeared for several months in 2015 as a space that nobody knew how to demarcate anymore. The state of crisis in which the UK, Poland, Hungary, and right-wing populist parties in almost all European countries consider Europe to exist is caused by the hallucination that European territory was flooded, that its legal status was determined by a category that applies only to the ocean: *res omnium*. Several states reacted to this impression with rigorous reterritorialization: border fences cut through Europe for hundreds of kilometers, and a bureaucracy of registration was installed in order to place the passage of migrants under state control as well as to distinguish between legal and illegal subjects.

The hallucination that the continent could turn into a *res omnium* gave rise to another idea that has always opposed the idea of *res omnium*: the idea of a *mare nostrum* or *mare clausum*. *Mare nostrum* signifies the legal idea that an ocean becomes the property of a state or an empire by excluding certain elements from it. The model for this idea had always been the Mediterranean. In antiquity, it was Pompey who turned it into a Roman *mare nostrum* by his victory over the pirates (which was the beginning of the end of the Republic). Later, Venice and Genoa raised the same claim, at least for certain parts of the Mediterranean.

Shortly before the First World War, Gabriele D'Annunzio propagated an Italian *mare nostrum* in verse, drama and manifests. His play *La Nave* (1909), which tells the mythical story of the foundation of Venice as an anti-New Jerusalem, celebrates the apocalypse of territoriality as the origin of a new *patria* on the ships that rule the waves of the Mediterranean. Shortly after World War II, it was Alexandre Kojève who agitated for the founding of a "Latin empire" which was the origin of the French project of an *union pour la méditerranée*, so dear to Monsieur Sarkozy.[4] Today the European Border and Coast Guard Agency, FRONTEX, is oriented towards the idea of *mare nostrum* as it aims to turn the Mediterranean Sea into a militarized border zone by installing an architecture called Eurosur ("European Border Surveillance System").[5]

Bernhard Siegert

Apocalypses of Territoriality

"Historicizing the sea"

Not only law depends on the *nomos*; history does as well. "Every historical development starts from two correlated concepts: property and
enduring settlement." Thus begins a treatise on the *templum* by classicist Heinrich Nissen, published in 1869.[6] This implies contrariwise that
the sea is placed beyond history. For neither is the sea apt for enduring
settlement nor is it possible to acquire property of the sea, according
to Grotius. The sea is *hors de la commerce*; it is the property of all.
A classicist and student of Mommsen like Nissen, for whom the
construct of *templum*, which literally means the "delimitated which is
cut out," is at the origin of history, turns his back on the sea, as the
sea turns its back on history. "The sea," Carl Schmitt wrote, "has no
character, in the original sense of the word, which comes from the
Greek *charassein*, meaning to engrave, to scratch, to imprint."[7]

To historicize the sea has been put on the agenda by postcolonial
cultural studies, which "take issue with the cultural myth that the
ocean is outside and beyond history, that the interminable, repetitive
cycle of the sea obliterates memory and temporality, and that a fully
historicized land somehow stands diametrically opposed to an atem-
poral, 'ahistorical' sea."[8] Against this "predominant Western view,"
cultural studies have taken pains to demonstrate that the sea is a space
that is full of histories, especially histories of the disenfranchised, of
the have-nots, of the deracinated: slaves, pirates, refugees, and other
groups of people who are excluded from justice and civil society. "Sea,"
claims John Mack, "needs to be historicized."[9]

The great historian of the Mediterranean, Fernand Braudel, was
a bit more modest and reflexive about the possibility of historicizing
the sea. "We shall of course have to measure these expanses of water in
relation to human activity; their history would otherwise be incomprehensible if indeed it could be written at all."[10] Historicizing the sea
means to humanize the sea; to measure it in relation to human activity,
which is—for anthropological reasons—oriented towards *terra firma*.
This does not only mean that oceanic deep time or the hydrosphere
and the biosphere enter human history only inasmuch as they become
the subject of exploitation and extraction. It also means that the agents
that "historicize the sea" are means of transportation, mainly ships;
techniques of navigation, such as determination of position and speed,
manuals for pilots, the grid of meridians and parallels, onboard radio,
radar, and space-borne positioning systems such as GPS; and media

of representation, from stories that are told and written to logs, maps, and computer models. The history of the sea, in other words, presupposes media of datafication. For a long time, therefore, a history of the sea could crystallize only at those places where the distinction between land and sea, between re-territorialization and de-territorialization, is constantly re-produced and designed, i. e. ports. There is no history of the ocean as an arena of transnational interchange without the archives of port authorities, migration authorities, and trade houses.

Migrants become passengers become vagabonds

In sixteenth-century Spain, the state had already successfully claimed what John Torpey called the "monopoly of the legitimate means of movement"[11] across the ocean from the Old World to the New. The passenger who traveled from Seville to the New World was a figure produced with great bureaucratic effort. His legal mobility had to be distinguished on the one hand from the dangerous mobility of idle vagrants, beggars, and adventurers. On the other hand, the legal passenger was produced by the exclusion of all persons of "Moorish" or Jewish origin. One might say that this operation pre-figures the basic distinction on which the modern nation-state is founded, whose "development ... has depended on effectively distinguishing between citizens/subjects and possible interlopers."[12] Schmitt's notion that the Nomos of the Earth is something like a culture-historical origin of human law is a myth. Before people settled, they had been in motion, migrating ... "*Multi sunt, qui vagantur et incertas habent sedes*": Thus begins the Decretum Tametsi, by which the Council of Trent decreed in 1563 that all parishes in the Catholic world had to keep a record of baptisms and marriages.[13] It took a long time to turn Europe into a space of settled existences and a space where settledness became a necessary criterion for the legal subject and a precondition of legal migration.

The threshold between land and sea, between Spain and the Americas, is the place where one had to reproduce the difference between the *cristiano viejo* on the one hand and the "New Christian," the *converso* and the *reconciliado*, on the other. Both could be achieved only by subjecting the mobility of the passenger completely to the power of writing, to the agents of writing (the *letrados*) and their institutions. But the process of licensing could always be used as camouflage

Bernhard Siegert

Apocalypses of Territoriality

for the parasitic forms of non-settled life, too. In the seventeenth century there were viceroys in *Nueva España* and officials in the *Casa de la Contratación* who were convinced that the whole process of licensing had only the effect of populating *las Indias* with vagabonds.[14] Therefore, discursive practices and administrative techniques blossomed around this delicate act, practices of authentification that individualized the ordinary people who wished to leave Europe by making them speak of themselves.

Early modern bureaucracy and datafication of human existences relied completely on the cultural technique of writing. "For a long time," Michel Foucault wrote,

> *ordinary individuality—the everyday individuality of everybody— remained below the threshold of description. To be looked at, observed, described in detail, followed from day to day by an uninterrupted writing was a privilege. The chronicle of a man, the account of his life, his historiography, written as he lived out his life formed parts of the rituals of power. The disciplinary power reversed this relation, lowered the threshold of describable individuality and made of this description a means of control and a method of domination. It is no longer a monument for future memory, but a document for possible use.*[15]

The Casa de la Contratación in Seville is one of the first sites in early modern Europe where juridical procedures forced hundreds and thousands of simple existences to deliver a written account of their origin, orthodox faith, and orderly life to a representative of the king.[16] But the screens of the surveillance apparatus that was designed to monitor sea traffic were made of paper, and the practice of "historicizing the sea" was largely restricted to ports and harbors. On the high seas, it was the tragic and pitiful figure of the *escribano de nao*, the ship scribe, who alone in the midst of a slippery world of smuggling and faking had to keep a record of all that took place on board, and especially to register all events of death (in order to prevent some stowaway from assuming the identity of some deceased passenger).

Architectures of the elemental

The maritime space of the twenty-first century is no longer constructed by means of paperwork. Today the ship scribe's records and the captain's log are overarched by an architecture of remote sensing devices (optical and thermal cameras, land-, sea-, air-, and space-borne radar, vessel-tracking technologies, and satellite imaging technologies) that "turn certain physical conditions into digital data according to specific sets of protocols, determining the conditions of visibility of certain objects."[17]

Historicizing the sea is dependent on media which territorialize the sea, which create some kind of infrastructure of the sea. These infrastructures are deployed in the service of colonization, exploitation, stewardship, and surveillance. The sea that is historicized is always already anthropogenic and "anthropocenic." The threshold of description, which Foucault addressed with respect to the bureaucratic recording of individuals in the *Ancien* Régime, is lowered to the level of the dust that everybody is—a dust that can be written down only by technical media of local and global surveillance. There is no maritime jurisdiction and no maritime stewardship without sensor media that trace the course of ships and boats, and whales, and containers, oil spills, icebergs, and plastic garbage. The historicizing (and territorializing) of the sea began in the mid-nineteenth century, when ships were turned into measuring instruments. As ships began to probe the deep-sea floor, and to explore the patterns of ocean currents, ships became centers of datafication.[18]

The deployment of EU external border protection technology in the Mediterranean since 2011, however, means the rise of a new architecture of the sea—an infrastructure that not only opens up a new chapter in the history of territorializing the sea, but that creates a new ocean altogether.

First, this infrastructure of the sea has completely canceled out Hugo Grotius's argument that the sea is free, that the sea cannot be anyone's property because ships leave no tracks in the sea. The opposite is true. Not only are the waters of the Mediterranean completely demarcated by various jurisdictions. The simultaneous existence of different ecological, humanitarian, and border security jurisdictions[19] allows for the strategic mobilization of humanitarian duties like search and rescue, much in the same way as in the 18th century the enemy of mankind served as a legitimization for interventionist "police actions." Gerry Simpson pointed out that the establishment of an international community of states needed the figure of the "enemy of all": "Empire needs pirates."[20] Borrowing an idea from Eyal Weizman, one could say that building Fortress Europe results in the creation of the "victim of all" as a necessary consequence of the strategy of turning the Mediterranean Sea into the EU border zone. It is the "victim of all"—the

Fig. 1. Trajectory of the boat that was "left to die" in the NATO Maritime Surveillance areas, as reconstructed for the Forensic Oceanography report.

Fig. 2. Envisat-1 vessel detection data for March 29, 2011 with a corresponding table of returns documenting the estimated length of vessel and degree of confidence that the data is correct. Analysis by Lawrence Fox III for the Forensic Oceanography report.

illegalized migrant—whose rescue allows for interventionist policing and action in foreign territorial waters for which there would otherwise be little or no legitimization.

Second, the legally striated sea is constantly overwritten by another geometry, by another architecture, projected by the various kinds of land-borne, ship-borne, air-borne, and space-borne sensing devices. This sea is technologically constructed by a geometry based on the orbits of satellites and the vertical paths and surfaces established by the transmitted and backscattered electromagnetic signals.

Infrastructures, Reinhold Martin tells us, are producers of the distinction between the symbolic and the real.[21] They create at the same time dust and data. Forensic architecture and its sub-team Forensic Oceanography, however, demonstrates that in the age of digital electronic media and powerful computational tools of modeling, nearly all kinds of dust can be turned into data. Techniques of representation do not need to construct imaginary walls on the sea surface as was practiced by marine painters in the 17th century; they can make use of the information built into the optical and electromagnetic geometry of digital images to construct places and the histories that occurred at those places. Once it was: "Dust you are and dust you will be" (Genesis 3:19), or in the Christian version: "Ashes to ashes, dust to dust." Today, dust cannot return to dust anymore. Dust to dust has become dust to data. Particles of smoke, ripples on the water, the breeze of air over the surface of the water—in one word: "the elemental"—becomes part of a media system which is the basis for the generation of the cultural history of the sea in the late 20th and early 21st centuries. The elemental is the sublation of the distinction between nature and technology.[fig.1–4]

Alexander Galloway and Eugene Thacker claimed that we need a "climatology of thought," but that is not enough. We need a climatology of media theory, too, because it is literally the media of climatology of which the new architecture of the sea is made. "The elemental," Galloway and Thacker wrote, "is the environmental aspect of networks."[22] This is especially true in the case of images taken by Synthetic Aperture Radar (SAR), which, together with Radar Altimetry (RA), is the standard equipment on board most of the satellites of which the EU external border control agency makes use.[fig.5][23] The specificity of SAR is due to the fact that the original purpose of this remote sensing technology was not only to detect and register ships, but also

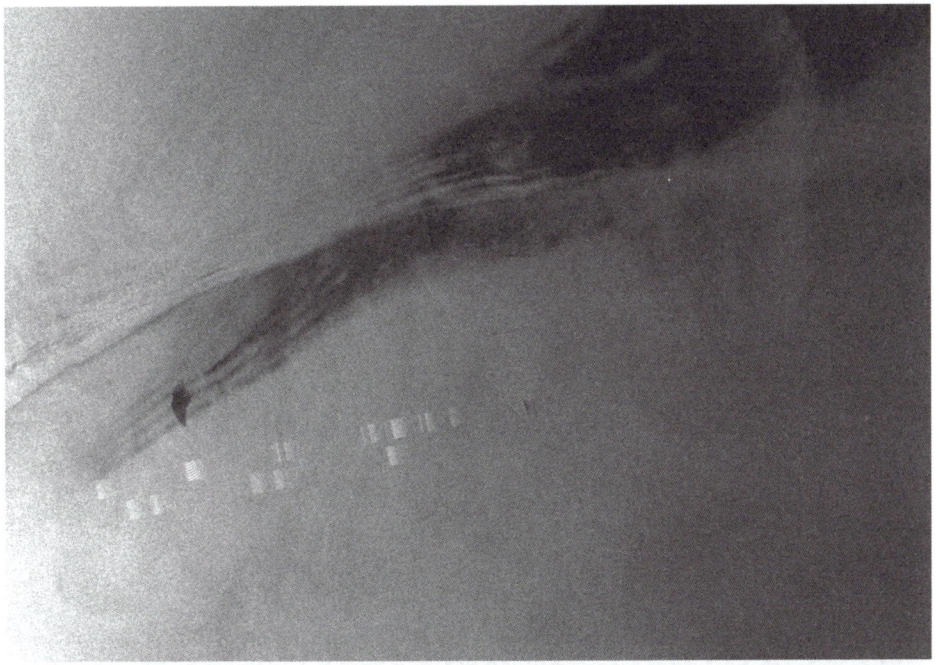

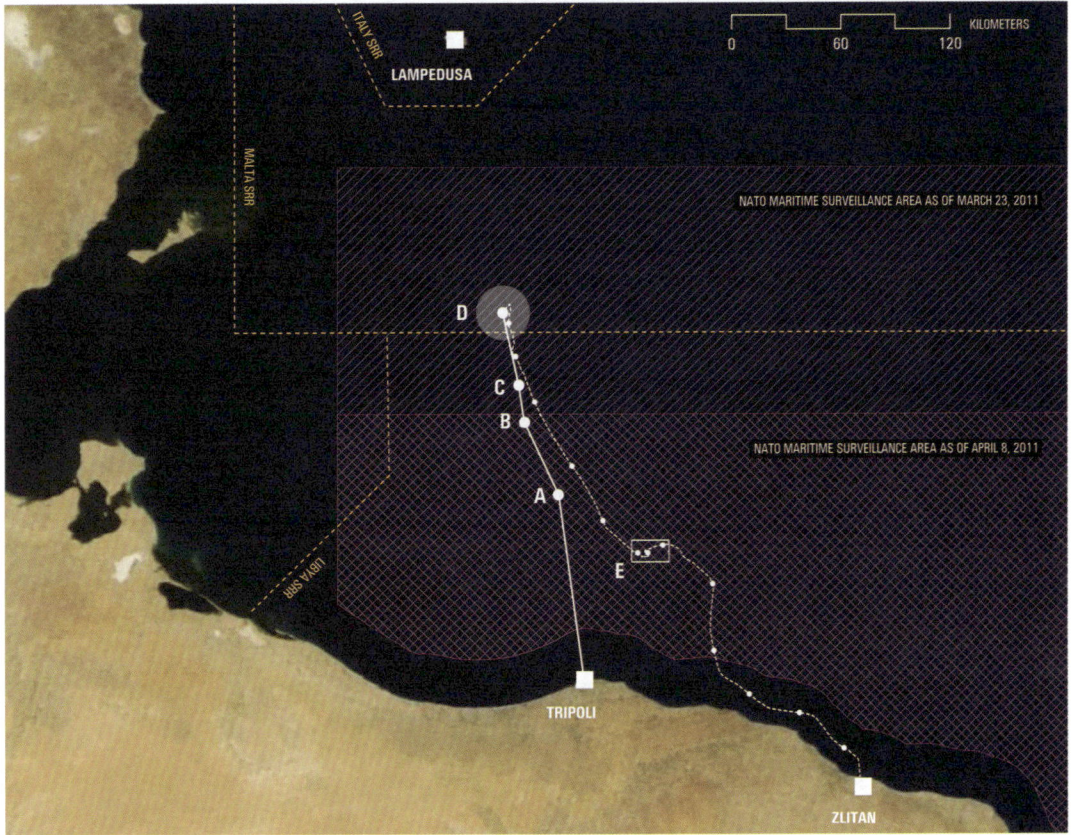

MILITARY SHIPS IN VICINITY

"LEFT-TO-DIE" BOAT TRAJECTORY
MIGRATION ROUTES
COMMERCIAL VESSEL POSITIONS (AIS)
MAIN FISHING AREAS
FRONTEX OPERATIONAL AREAS
SEARCH AND RESCUE ZONES
SINGLE SAR
NATO SURVEILLING AREA
MILITARY SHIPS
DISTANCE OF KNOWN MILITARY SHIPS
SATELLITE IMAGERY
VESSELS CORRELATION
GEOLOCATION
SIGNALS COVERAGE

0   35   70   140   210 KM

NVM CLUSTERS GARIBALDI
Italian Navy
Ground Cover: 148 / 152 Nm
NVM RDSGSXI
Italian Navy
Patrol Boat: 41 Nm

ITNS MENDEZ NUNEZ
Spanish Navy
Frigate: 28 Nm

HMP ETNA
Italian Navy
Auxiliary Vessel: 153 Nm

NATO LETTER TO THE COUNCIL OF EUROPE INDICATING
THE DISTANCE OF SEVERAL MILITARY SHIPS FROM THE
MIGRANTS' BOAT, 02.2012

KING JACOB 21:01

05:39 [19:04]
05:58 [19:04]
08:35 [19:04]

23:46
11:22 [19:04]
10:14 [19:04]
10:27 [19:04]

01:06 [19:04]
23:47
21:15
00:28 [19:04]
22:40
21:31
00:47 [19:04]
21:27
COLLISION

CP 920 BRUNO GREGORETTI

WRECK

21:49

MIGRANTS' BOAT
SIGHTED

CITY OF LUTECE

21:38

11:30 [19:04]

11:24 [19:04]

SPEED (in knots)   0-1   2-5   6-10   >11
BRUNO GREGORETTI
KING JACOB
CITY OF LUTECE

0   1   2   4 km

Waves	Oil spill	Wind field	Current front	Internal waves

Fig. 3. Forensic Oceanography researchers conduct an interview with survivor Dan Haile Gebre in Milan, December 21, 2011. In this still, we see an early sketch of the chain of events map being used to help Gebre recall the events.

Fig. 4. Drift model providing hourly positions of the vessel. Over time, the margin of error in the drifting vessel's track decreases as it is constrained by the known position of landing.

Fig. 5. Marjolaine Rouault, An Introduction to Synthetic Radar Aperture Observations.

to obtain two-dimensional spectra of ocean surface waves to reveal ultra-high-resolution surface wind field patterns, to identify numerous oceanic features, as well as to detect oil spills, ship and detailed sea ice conditions.[24] The side-looking SAR forms an image from the Bragg resonance between the transmitted vertically polarized radar pulses and the short gravity waves. These short waves are formed in response to local wind stress and are further modulated by the orbital motion of the longer waves, by the surface current and by sea surface temperature gradients. Basically a SAR image is a co-production of the electromagnetic microwave radar pulse, the backscattering of the pulse by the rough ocean surface, and the resonances of the backscattered pulses (the constructive and destructive interference during the coherent addition of backscatter from many different scatterers).[25] Hence what you get is an image that is calculated from the backscattered pulses from the rough ocean surface which is modulated by the horizontal wind speed. Thus the ocean is not what is represented here; it instead becomes part of the imaging technology.

SAR imagery relies on the fact that the environment becomes a constitutive factor of image production. SAR imagery is destined to make visible phenomena that are not visible to the eye, but that become visible by turning the ocean surface into an element of surveillance technology. The elemental turns into a hybrid of nature and technology. "Emerging at the intersection of electromagnetic and physical waves, what we see here is not simply a new representation of the ocean, but a new ocean altogether, one simultaneously composed of matter and media."[26]

FRONTEX, the border agency, the European Maritime Safety Agency (EMSA), and the European Fisheries Control Agency (EFCA), as the agencies responsible for coastal and maritime surveillance, merged in 2016. "Stewarding the oceans" acquires a new meaning: control of migrant flows through rescue and pushback operations becomes part of the ecological and economical management of the seas. Intercepting vessels suspected of "engaging in criminal activities," combating illegal fishing, detecting oil spills and changes in the maritime ecosystem from now on belong in the same category. The environment becomes part of the surveillance and policing techniques by which maritime space is constructed.

Bernhard Siegert

Apocalypses of Territoriality

1   Peter Sloterdijk, *Sphären II. Globen* (Frankfurt am Main: Suhrkamp, 1999), 251.
2   See Cornelia Vismann, "Terra nullius," in Cornelia Vismann, *Das Recht und seine Mittel. Ausgewählte Schriften* (Frankfurt am Main: S. Fischer Verlag, 2012), 309.
3   Hugo Grotius, *The Free Sea*, trans. Richard Hakluyt (Indianapolis: Liberty Fund, 2004), 34.
4   See Wolf Lepenies, *Die Macht am Mittelmeer. Französische Träume von einem anderen Europa* (Munich: Hanser Verlag, 2016). As a matter of fact, the dream of a Mediterranean empire under French domination dates back to Napoleon I's Egyptian expedition.
5   It attests to a grotesque Freudian slip when the rescue action of the EU which brought help to the shipwrecked refugees off the African coast was christened "Mare Nostrum." After all, the pronoun *noster* stands in this term not for "us" in the inclusive sense, as if to mean "the sea of all of us," but in the exclusive, and therefore eminent political, sense: "Our sea, not your sea."
6   Heinrich Nissen, *Das Templum. Antiquarische Untersuchungen* (Berlin: Weidmann, 1869), 1.
7   Carl Schmitt, *The Nomos of the Earth in the International Law of the Jus Publicum Europaeum* (New York: Telos Press, 2003), 42–43.
8   Bernhard Klein and Gesa Mackenthun, *Sea Changes: Historicizing the Sea* (New York and London: Routledge, 2004), 2.
9   John Mack, *The Sea: A Cultural History* (London: Reaktion Books, 2013), 17.
10   Fernand Braudel, *The Mediterranean and the Mediterranean World in the Age of Philipp II*, trans. Siân Reynolds (Berkeley/Los Angeles/London: University of California Press, 1995), vol. 1, 103.
11   John Torpey, *The Invention of the Passport: Surveillance, Citizenship and the State* (Cambridge, UK: Cambridge University Press, 2000), 1.
12   Torpey, *Invention of the Passport*, 2.
13   "Canones super reformatione circa matrimonium," in *Concilium Tridentinum: Diariorum, actorum, epistularum, tractatuum. Nova Collectio, edidit Societas Goerresiana, vol. IX: Actorum pars sexta* (Freiburg im Breisgau: Herder, 1965), 970.
14   See Bernhard Siegert, *Passagiere und Papiere. Schreibakte auf der Schwelle zwischen Spanien und Amerika* (Munich: Wilhelm Fink Verlag, 2006), 105.
15   Michel Foucault, *Discipline and Punish: The Birth of the Prison*, trans. Alan Sheridan (New York: Vintage, 1979), 191.
16   See Bernhard Siegert, "Pasajeros a Indias: Registers and Biographical Writing as a Cultural Technique of Subject Constitution (Spain, 16th Century)," in Bernhard Siegert, *Cultural Techniques: Grids, Filters, Doors, and Other Articulations of the Real* (New York: Fordham University Press, 2015), 82–96.
17   Charles Heller/Lorenzo Pezzani, "Liquid Traces: Investigating the Deaths of Migrants at the EU's Maritime Frontier," in *Revue Européenne des Migrations Internationales* 30, 1014, no. 3: 673.
18   See Robert C. Cowen, *Frontiers of the Sea: The Story of Oceanographic Exploration* (London: Victor Gollancz Ltd., 1960), passim.
19   See Juan Luis Suárez de Vivero, *Jurisdictional Waters in the Mediterranean and Black Seas* (European Parliament, 2010), 27.
20   Gerry Simpson, "Enemies of Mankind," in Jennifer Gunning and Søren Holm, eds., *Ethics, Law, and Society* (Aldershot, UK and Burlington, VT: Ashgate, 2006), vol. II: 87.
21   See Reinhold Martin, *The Urban Apparatus: Mediapolitics and the City* (Minneapolis: University of Minnesota Press, 2017).
22   Alexander R. Galloway and Eugene Thacker, *The Exploit: A Theory of Networks* (Minneapolis: University of Minnesota Press, 2007), 157.
23   See G. Duchossois and R. Zobl, "ERS-2: A Continuation of the ERS-1 Success," in *ESA Bulletin* 85: 14, 23.
24   See J. A. Johannessen, B. Chapron, W. Alpers et al., "Satellite Oceanography from the ERS Synthetic Aperture Radar and Radar Altimeter: A Brief Review," in Johannessen et al, *ERS Missions: 20 Years of Observing Earth* (2013), 201.
25   William G. Pichel, Pablo Clemente-Colón, Christopher C. Wackerman, and Karen S. Friedman, "Ship and Wake Detection," in *Synthetic Aperture Radar Marine User's Manual* (Washington, DC: National Oceanic and Atmospheric Administration, 2004), 281.
26   Charles Heller and Lorenzo Pezzani, "Liquid Traces," 666f.

Onward:
Turning
Dust
to
Data

Tom McCarthy and Eyal Weizman in conversation

Cracks, Memory, Clouds, and Data

EW: Hi, Tom! How to begin? Actually, when we had a conversation in preparation for this panel, we thought it would be a great idea to have you read paragraphs from your book and we'd use these readings as a kind of springboard to reflect upon your work, upon issues of common interest. But also, I feel so very enriched by this conference thus far, so we can spend time reflecting on *Dust & Data* and maybe even the Bauhaus, too.

TM: Me, too. It has been a fantastic and incredibly stimulating conference. In relation to our discussion about dust and data, we came to talk about that passage about the crack. The hero of *Remainder* has suffered a trauma: something fell out of the sky and hit him on the head. It is a piece of technology. He never says what it is. Physically, he was injured and had to relearn how to move, how to speak, everything. He can do it, but he feels inauthentic, somehow secondhand. He is not being; he is reenacting—he is copying being. He has gained a huge amount of money in compensation from the responsible parties. But he has lost his sense of authenticity, and so he is drifting around, wondering what to do with his vast amount of money, while feeling somehow fake. So he goes to a party in London, and as he goes into the bathroom, he sees a crack on a wall that suddenly brings up a fragment of his lost memory.

[*Tom McCarthy reads an excerpt from* Remainder.] [1]

Trying to reconnect to this memory, he pays architects to rebuild this crack, even a whole building in which to trigger all his senses; he hires people to fry liver and move around. Desperate and frustrated that he cannot really regain much more of his supposed lost "authenticity," he starts reenacting more and more violent events. He needs violence. So eventually he is reenacting a bank robbery in which people are actually getting killed. This is why, Eyal, you are on my radar and I have been fascinated by your work on forensic architecture. This sense of reconstructing space always within a context of trauma and of traumatic memory, in which some type of version of the real is at stake, even if that itself is a kind of fiction or fantasy. But somehow there's this notion that through these kinds of reenactments we can come to the real. Your work on cracks really investigates the materiality of architecture and things.

EW: Yes. Whenever I reread your story, I keep seeing new elements that are relevant and fascinating. And indeed, I am interested in the physicality of the crack. It is interesting because the Bauhaus is almost 100 years old and it has this image of being perpetually young. The Bauhaus building in Dessau for one, but also the historical buildings here in Weimar, have undergone several rounds of restoration that have tried to bring back their youth. But the decay and the multiple layers of restoration and hence rediscovery should also be considered critically. This is something that I think Ines [Weizman] means when she called this conference *Dust & Data*. So a crack is both dust and its knowledge—in your work, memory.

But let's start with: What is a crack? A crack is not an object. A crack is an event. It is a process of material deformation with the potential for further transformation. It can linger in something for years in a state of potentiality, or it can speed up and tear a building apart. On the other hand, it might be filled. Every restoration is also an act of destruction: a kind of epistemo-logical reduction, or the reduction of the potential for memory. A crack is also an event that erases its own traces, and this is what I find very suggestive. It has the potential to become a kind of erasure of erasure—a double erasure that is something that is important when you are thinking not of forensics but rather of counter-forensics. It is often the erasure of a trace of a crime that would lead you somewhere. You could no longer see the traces of a crime; rather, you could see only the fact of its erasure. And those traces of erasure are what is important.

Many architects here would be familiar with Leonardo da Vinci's notebooks and his description of cracks: pages of pages on cracks and why they are formed in buildings. There are those cracks that are formed because of mistakes in the construction. There are those cracks that are formed because the plaster that has been put on top of stone is facing the sun and is drying up too fast. There are cracks that come out of seismological movement, so they also point to geological time. And you realize that, in a sense, a crack becomes to Leonardo a kind of a hybrid phenom-enon that combines all those things, human and environmental. Human labor, skill, materials, environment, geology—in the sense of seismological influences, the orientation of the building. It is interesting that it is really through the crack rather than

Tom McCarthy Eyal Weizman

Cracks, Memory, Clouds, and Data

through the solid and opaque wall that you can read the reality of that structure. Like geologists going for the wound of an earthquake to examine the buried stratigraphy. So I think, in some other place in his notebook, he does a gesture that is very kind of Tom McCarthyist—well, I think, he must have—where he says looking at cracks is a way of training the imagination about forms and destruction and what might have happened or could happen.

TM: It's migratory. It traverses the border.

EW: Yes, it traverses the border between the rock and the column. Cracks are oblivious to the difference between what we understand as figure and ground: a building and a site. The crack might start moving through bedrock, then through roads, then through columns and then through walls appearing and disappearing as they follow the lines of least resistance where the cohesive forces of matter are at their weakest, where the aggregate forces in rocks loosen. At a place that, let's say, a lizard died seven hundred million years ago, there is a deposit of a mineral in that place in a rock. The crack would find the lizard a million years later. Moving through concrete, it will find a cigarette butt thrown into the concrete mix several decades ago. The crack has a material memory. And that is another thing that I think is incredibly fascinating: that you chose cracks to describe memory and erasure.

TM: The crack is all the things you mentioned, and it is also an opening. It is a space of potential, potentiality. It is an opening to another possibility. Something could come through that crack. Something could be birthed out of that crack, you know? I was so happy to hear Bernhard Siegert mention Heidegger earlier, because I hadn't read "The Origin of the Work of Art" when I wrote this book. But I read it soon afterwards and thought, "Oh, this it is what I mean," because Heidegger, he uses this term "crack"—*der Riss*—the kind of rupture, the cracking open as a kind of a fissure, an opening, and he compares it to—using very architectural language—to a sketch pad, a drawing board, a blueprint for a possible work that could emerge from that. And one other way of thinking about the crack, of course, is as something legible: as a form of writing, if you like—a set of marks that can be read, which is another very Heideggerian idea of literature. The gods have departed and have left all these marks—these scorch marks—on the earth from when they blasted off. They are fault lines, these cracks. The task of a poet is to descend into these cracks and

Onward:
Turning
Dust
to
Data

590

the dust that has fallen from those cracks—almost like a record needle going into the grooves and making them resonate. I mean, I also had in mind Rilke's notion of *Urgeräusch*—this idea of primal sound which to Rilke is totally scriptural. He saw the crack running down the skull when he was a medical student. He remembered a very imaginative teacher at his high school when he was demonstrating acoustic physics by making them put a needle into just anything. You can make a mark in anything and put a needle in with a little speaker and it will play it. You can do it on the streets. You can do it on any surface at all. But Rilke is reminded most of all of the skull and the fissure, the seam that joins us together. So this relation between the archival—between literature as a kind of replay of a traumatic primal trace—and, of course, death, basically, very much reappears in your work. I mean, you did this work on Mengele's skull and the whole kind of forensic recovery of these objects.

    EW: This being in kind of an unfortunate business of working in forensics sometimes takes you to rather extreme situations. In Guatemala, we were at a site of a mass grave where one of the most dedicated citizen forensic groups in Guatemala was acting to represent those victims of genocides. A forensic anthropologist described to me how fragile a skull buried for 30 years could become. He looks at those cracks. And it is from the crack that he would reconstruct whether that skull had been shot and how. Then he described to me something that was so horrific and surprising at the same time that that thought still haunts me. He said, "When a person is executed—and usually the method of execution was a shot in the back of the head—the entry hole is pure and round. But what happens is that cracks start appearing around the entry hole, moving along the circumference of the cranium. So when the bullet hits the skull again as it exits, it hits a surface that is already cracked, meaning that the cracks travel faster than a bullet that travels faster than the speed of sound. Cracks do not move like objects would. They are a space between objects or within an object, so frictionless that the crack can actually accelerate as it moves. So that makes the reading process incredibly complicated. Again, a destruction of destruction.

TM: So the skull pulverizes. The skull becomes dust.

    EW: I wanted to return to memory in relation to sound, vision, and smell as they exist in your book. The idea that external

*Tom
McCarthy
Eyal
Weizman*

Cracks,
Memory,
Clouds,
and
Data

591

objects could function as prosthetic memory. But the more one uses these aide-mémoir, the further you can also get from the original memory. Whenever you reenact from memory, you both get closer to the event and you also erase it, in the same way that a tape that is played again and again gets erased with every play.

TM: Freud called that the secondary revision, an overwriting.

EW: And this is what exists so beautifully in your book. Memory is not simply that kind of huge archive where you just have to open the right drawer and when you find that drawer you get a thing neatly stored there. It's continuously in motion and it's a plastic thing. The process of looking for it transforms it. It's almost like with archaeology: you have one shot at it, because by excavating you also destroy. If you mess it up, that's it. You have one shot at getting at the right layer and documenting things properly. And that reminded me of the critique that a French poet called Jacques Roubaud has leveled at Frances Yates's beautiful and classic *The Art of Memory*. What Roubaud says that Yates neglected to mention or to understand is that when the orator would build a memory palace and would use it several times, in several different speeches, revisiting the rooms and picking up the objects/memories from them, old objects previously stored in these would reappear in the wrong speech. Older speeches delivered from the same palace will be haunting all subsequent ones. There is always a remainder which is the trace of the trace or the trace of erasure, and at some point that building would become so haunted by layers of memories that it has to be destroyed. It cannot be used anymore as a memory palace. Can you speak a little bit about the way that in that book the whole notion of memories you created is a kind of plastic, in the sense that we never get there?

TM: Even my narrator can't remember the original house. Was it in Paris? No. Maybe. Yes. Maybe not. And then he realizes it is a composite memory. It is what Proust describes: you can remember a house that never existed, because you take the staircase from one house and the wallpaper from another and a portrait from a third and you collage them together and you remember that as though it has existed, even though it didn't. What matters is not whether or not it existed; it is the structural situation or it is the desire for pleasure, Freud's pleasure at repetition and reenactment. To Freud, in "Beyond the Pleasure Principle," repetition is never about recapturing an authentic moment, because that is by definition beyond representation. It stands outside anything that can be recuperated. But it is a form of pleasure that drives towards death, ultimately. That would be the end point. I think it's also the driving logic of capitalism. My hero sees people like trendy kids in the street striking certain postures and [wearing] certain clothes, and he notes that they are reenacting certain moments in ads or movies. He recognizes the source: an MTV video or whatever it is. He sees that kind of replay in simulacrum as the kind of cultural logic that we are occupied with: an over-emphasized narrative of authenticity: *Express yourself. Be yourself. Et cetera.* But of course, this is completely fictitious. The aim within capitalism is just to generate these endless circles of consumption and replay, and re-consumption and re-replay. So I think he is living that kind of logic to its ultimate conclusion, which ends up being a form of ultra-violence. Another writer that I was thinking of a lot when I wrote this book and *Satin Island* and that your group's work around the Syrian prison brings back very strongly to my mind in Lawrence Abu Hamdan's very powerful presentation is the work of the Marquis de Sade, who is one of the most interesting—one of the most powerfully architectural—writers. *The 120 Days of Sodom*, which no one's actually read, is not so much a book as I think it is an allegory of narrative. The perverted libertine antiheroes in that book go to a building and they modify the building. It is this castle which is beyond the legal jurisdiction, the border, of Europe. It is extraordinary. They do extraordinary rendition *avant la lettre*. They kidnap all these teenagers. They take them to this castle with four high-class prostitutes and they construct a room which is a kind of auditorium/space of reenactment. It is a room with a central floor and four alcoves—niches built into each corner. Each of the libertines sits in one of the corners, and the teenagers—the captives—are on the floor. And one of the prostitutes stands in the middle of the floor and narrates her sexual escapades.

The rules of the game are such that any one of the four libertines, but only they, may at any point say, "Stop. That's good. Let's do it again. Let's reenact it." The only rule they have is that nothing may be done unless it is a reenactment of a narrative situation. And then they start modifying it, saying: "Well, let's do it. Now we've done it. Let's change it so we do the other bit that we did yesterday from the other

Tom McCarthy Eyal Weizman

Cracks, Memory, Clouds, and Data

story, but we'll combine it." Exactly what you were describing: replay becomes secondary and tertiary, an almost algorithmic reenactment sequence. This situation combines architecture and narrative, or uses architecture to construct what is primarily a narrative space. Within that narrative space, there is a possibility of moving from being a listener or reader, a passive listener or a passive reader, to an active doer or redoer. And this is a move into violence. It is a setup. I think when you see those pictures coming out of Abu Ghraib, for example, I think exactly that type of logic is in play in those pornographic images that are coming out of, you know, the American military personnel reenacting sexual kinds of fantasies on Iraqi prisoners' bodies. I think it is this kind of cultural logic in de Sade that we should now pay close attention to.

EW: Perhaps there is also a moment when various categories may blur the absolute distinction between the senses. In our Saydnaya project—the architectural reconstruction from memory of this notorious and secret prison in Syria—hearing the testimonies again and again, you understand that you experience people in situations of the liminality of all senses, from the liminality of vision. It was totally dark, but not pitch-dark: they did see something. It was incredibly silent, but they did hear, as Lawrence Abu Hamdan so beautifully described, the reverberation, the whispers. It is the kind of liminality where one sense morphs into the other. A whisper is simultaneously the vision of the lip moving, the moisture of breath, and the little you might hear as sound. There are phenomena that exist between the senses, slipping between them. That is the essence of trauma. Lawrence Abu Hamdan was speaking about the sound of the gates closing: one gate after another in seemingly endless repetition. "I don't know if there were actually so many gates," he said, "but that represents truthfully the condition and the situation of the witness." Or another witness, when being beaten, drops his hands from his eyes—they had to press their hands against their eyes firmly at all times— and he glimpses for a split second something of the space around him and describes it in a way that we know was architecturally incorrect. He describes a round hall when we know this space to be a corridor. But the error more faithfully describes a situation of being in a space all surrounded. We ask him if he was sure. Yes, he was. The distortion of memory is so much more significant than an accurate architectural description, because it includes both a faithful description of space and the psychological condition: something else, an excess.

TM: I completely agree with Jacques Roubaud's critique of Frances Yates. Perhaps we can draw a distinction from psychoanalysis, or from cultural thought generally, between the notion of (on the one hand) an archive, which would be the faithful library that we can open to find a document or a record; and on the other hand the crypt. The crypt is a concept that was developed out of the writings of Freud by Maria Torok and Nicolas Abraham in the 1970s, two psychoanalytic writers. Derrida writes the introduction to their book *The Wolf Man's Magic Word: a Cryptonymy*. It is a very interesting notion, because the crypt has a double sense. In architecture, a crypt is a tomb where you bury a body. But in linguistics, there exists the semiotic crypt to describe a place where you bury information that is maybe recovered by the spy at the other end of the telephone wire or the computer on the other end of that kind of keychain: encrypted language. For Abraham and Torok, the crypt is not a place of memory; it is a place of absence and encoded trauma. It is always born out of catastrophe. And it is a place not so much of burial and mourning as of melancholia: an incomplete memorialization where the body that should be in it is somehow absent. The crypt is a non-space. Derrida describes that in his introduction to that book as an "internal prosthesis." It is like a technological prosthesis to the psyche. He talks about it as kind of internal vomiting. It is this kind of polluted, disgusting space that contaminates the whole kind of psychic system. But it also produces a kind of code, and that is then transmitted out into the world. The crypt always leaks. Information travels. The walls of the crypt are porous. It is not the recovery of something. It is a setup, or we can almost call it a fictional or, rather, poetic transformation of an absence: a set of absences into fault lines that form their own network. That network can be a life or a world. I think cryptology is a very good way of understanding the work of art or a literary work.

> **EW:** You discuss the leaks of crypts and the transmission of signals in both of your novels, in *C* and in *Satin Island*. Perhaps we should move to the next paragraph that we've planned to read so that we have more material to work with.

TM: Well, this is a paragraph that I feel could almost have been written by you. The situation here, set in World War I, is that Serge, the hero of this book, is a reconnaissance flight radio operator. He sits in the back of the plane, looking backwards like Walter Benjamin's "angel of history," sending encrypted radio messages back to the ground. He is taking photographs to better assess which parts of German territory to bomb. He has also been reading Arthur Golding's translations of Ovid, in particular a line about carrying "your thoughts ... to all the seas." Or Cs. Serge flies in C Squadron. The novel is called *C*. "C" is the chemical symbol for carbon, which is what carbon paper is: what you put between pieces of paper to make a copy. "cc": carbon copy. It is also, of course, the basic element of life. He's also been reading Hölderlin and the line from *Patmos* about the bird of heaven communicating magnificence and anger. The bird of heaven makes it known. You just need to know that to understand some of these passages. And in this bit, he also discovers, as many World War I pilots did, his chemical box and starts playing with it; and discovering 'C' or cocaine ...

　　[*Tom McCarthy reads an excerpt from* C.][2]

　　EW: What I admire about that paragraph is the way in which you make the earth liquefy. And it seems that what you are making of the atmosphere, of the clouds that are simultaneously meteorology—the weather—and mustard gas, is about two clouds. That's the gas warfare. And there is the line of steam left by the planes that you want to snort, kind of like those cocaine lines at London parties. Do propellers also leave them, or is it more of a jet phenomenon?

TM: There were vapor trails of planes in World War I from the fuel being burned.

　　EW: In Ruskin's *The Storm-Cloud of the Nineteenth Century*, the meteorology of the smoke clouds hanging over Britain's Industrial Revolution cities is about the loss of the skies, but they are also the result of labor and in a sense exploitation. These clouds are the materialization of sets of economic relations. It is the Industrial Revolution cloud. It meets the meteorological cloud and erases it. We can't talk about pure meteorology. It is meteorology that is kind of processed through human activity and, in your case, war. So in your book, we already have three clouds: the weather cloud, the mustard cloud, and the vapor trail of warplanes. Of course, there would be also a fourth kind of cloud, that of the bombs themselves. So we have a spectacle of weaponized meteorology. And this is only the air. The ground itself also liquefies. It is continuously made and remade, the mud in the trenches and the body of the soldier within the mud as a kind of morphing of figure and ground. It is not a person in mud; it is the mud-human tangle that is moving towards the German trenches or towards the British or French trenches. Then they are buried in mud, and it reminds me of that description in Kern's *The Culture of Time and Space* and his description of the way in which the World War I trenches break, fragment and reorder the time-space conception. After World War I, that broken and reordered conception is picked up by the Bauhaus and is rearranged in an amazing creative production that reworks, in a way, the trauma of the war as well. Actually, what you have done here in that piece is to create an image of the Anthropocene, only accelerated—very fast and very violent. Sky and earth are blurred into this kind of insane painting, a hallucinatory frenzy.

TM: Into the skull. Into the cranium.

EW: You liquefy so many borders there between the earth and the sky, between the person and figure and ground, and somehow create a super-intense image of something that I've called on another occasion the political plastic: the kind of enormous plasticity of continuous transformability. This is what conflict does to space. It completely blurs its borders and subjects it to motion.

TM: I was reading accounts of World War I pilots, and I was also reading Marinetti a lot—Marinetti's incredible writing about the aesthetics of being in an airplane. Marinetti loved it, of course. He was a fascist. But what is fascinating is that the aesthetics that he announces become the aesthetics of the avant-garde of modernism and the pictorial and poetic avant-garde, and incidentally also open up like a crack all these possibilities for more radical left-wing thinking. Nabil [Ahmed]'s talk was brilliant, and I love this dual move: you know it is data. It is something that is almost a crime. It is the mark left by an industrial crime, but it also hides it. It does this double move of encrypting again, if you like. When I visited your office, you and your colleagues were talking about thresholds of visibility—you know, how big does something have to be before it can be read by a satellite, for example: as big as a car, as big as a person? Apparently, the American satellites pixelate the entire State of Israel. I mean, that is the size of, you know, what is occluded, clouded—what doesn't

Tom McCarthy Eyal Weizman

Cracks, Memory, Clouds, and Data

597

end at the clouds. I'm very taken by this idea. What can you read, what can you snort into your cranium, in terms of liquefied dust traces or whatever, you know? World as information, as material information, and what resists that—what becomes cloudy? Does that kind of make sense?

EW: It is a kind of state violence that does not bother to hide its tracks. That is the violence that comes to intimidate, to terrorize: that is the opposite. In terror, you want to make a spectacle out of your violence in order to effectively govern the survivors. Terror does not act on the people it kills. It acts on the people it doesn't kill ...

TM: ... to encourage the others, as Voltaire would say.

EW: Yes, to encourage the others. But then there is another form of violence that would seek to be beneath the threshold of detectability, and that violence could be denied. In World War I, it is not an issue of pixels. It is a question of the materiality of the film itself. In World War I, in order to actually capture things in aerial images with the low-resolution film, images had to be shot very early in the morning or very late in the evening with the long shadows. The elements the negative was scattered with, silver salt grains on the film, when you look at them through a microscope, they look like big boulders randomly distributed on the film. But the size of those grains was not fine or small enough to always capture people on the ground, so in fact it almost always erased people from those images. This is the threshold of detectability—and when you arrive at this condition, you need to do two things simultaneously: you need to look at the surface of the earth as if it were a photograph exposed to politics, and then you need to look at the surface of the film as if it were a landscape. So they both become kind of analog surfaces. Both are topographic and in fact blur the differences between presence and representation.

TM: Absolutely. In the book that I've most recently published, *Satin Island*, the motif running through it is of an oil spill. This catastrophic oil spill that's happened, well, it plays out over the two or three months that the book is taking place. The narrator, another kind of antihero, is fascinated by this. I mean, he loves it. He finds it beautiful in this kind of aesthetic way, because what he is seeing is precisely a kind of, well, it is a plasticity. It is a becoming plastic of the earth. It is a becoming synthetic of the earth. But then, of course, oil is ... it is an archive. I mean, oil is dinosaurs and trees from millions of years ago. It is this spilling forth of, you know ... it is the return of the repressed in kind of material form. It is an opening of the crypt in a kind of geological sense. So this sense, it is representation. When a bird becomes covered in oil, the bird becomes a statue of the bird. It is this kind of perverse logic the hero rather ironically—or maybe I am rather ironic—follows to its end, where he says we should celebrate the oil as a kind of work of art. He gives this presentation at a TED talk and he is shouted off the stage or ignored because it is so offensive. But I think, you know, what is interesting there is that the novel in fact actually begins with an image of the Shroud of Turin as — again — an act of staining, a kind of marking, where the object is sustained as itself a part of the event. It is not an abstract kind of record of it; it is a material print. It is a polluted surface. And following this through the narrator of *Satin Island*, he is a corporate anthropologist who mines data for a consultancy. He is totally working within this whole machine of capitalism and so on. But he's read his Deleuze and his Adorno and is feeding this kind of radical theory back into the machine ... Anyhow, he sees the oil spills ultimately as an act of writing. And the moment when the black oil hits the white shoreline is to him the moment when the ink hits the paper. The moments of writing as a kind of ... not as some Hegelian *Aufhebung* and purification of thought, but as the exact opposite. It is a kind of dirty staining, you know? Kafka talks about, you know, putting a stain on silence. And I am very taken with this idea of what writing might be. Ultimately it would not be the photograph of the world. It would be a kind of plasticky stain to partake in this ... whatever: this plain of consistency of pollution.

> **EW:** Yes, half of a circle, less than a semicircle, and at that moment, because when you would write, you would have the candle above [the page], you know, or some sunlight; it would become a mirror. So at that moment, that split second, the writer would see himself or herself. That was considered to be the magic of writing: the moment of self-reflection when the ink itself becomes the room and you see yourself in the text.

TM: Yeah, I mean, Mallarmé describes ... he is also very much into the materiality of writing, but he talks about the abyss of the ink well — this black kind of void. He would write with a mirror in front of him, so he was looking at himself as he wrote. But then he would turn away

*Tom
McCarthy
Eyal
Weizman*

Cracks,
Memory,
Clouds,
and
Data

599

from himself and look at the well ... or he describes turning away from seeing himself reflected back from the desk as a subject to the void, the abyss, the, well, literally, this hollowing out of space which is ink, and this absolute kind of loss of identity. But what is interesting ... I mean, Mallarmé was a huge presence to me when I was writing this book because of his idea of "The Book," the "Book to Come": the idea that everything in the world that exists, exists in order to become a book. But this "book," of course, won't be a book—not a conventional book. It would be some collapsed multimedia network. I mean, he's writing this in the 1890s; he takes his cue from Wagner and his whole idea of a *Gesamtkunstwerk*; but to me it completely anticipates digital culture, Google *und so weiter*: everything becoming data. But what is interesting is that Mallarmé sees this in relation to some kind of void, some kind of negative, some complete abyssal disappearance.

> **EW:** Which could bring us rather neatly, now that we're talking about writing, to the last paragraph that you wanted to read: the one about buffering. And also knowing we are being kind of aware of time, we would have to effectively end with it.

TM: The narrator of *Satin Island*, who identifies himself only as "U"—the letter U—is a corporate anthropologist, and he writes dossiers. He writes reports for a consultancy. The clients might be, you know, a jeans company or it might be a government think tank. He mines data sets. He does ethnographic research and he presents this data. I didn't make this up; there are many anthropologists doing exactly this. But he is also ... he is being tasked by his boss with the idea of writing the Great Report, the ultimate report on our era—this kind of, again, multimedia, multi-platform kind of construct that would sum up our age. But he is continually confronted with this kind of specter of his own redundancy. So Malinowsky, the kind of founding father of anthropology: his first commandment was "Write everything down," turn everything into data, even trivial things, because it's all got to form one massive data set that will somehow reveal the culture to you. But my guy realizes that in the 21st century, of course, everything already *is* written down. I mean, you walk down a stretch of street, you have been filmed by three cameras, your iPhone is tabulating exactly where you were. Everything is recorded. It is encrypted. It is in a black box somewhere. The NSA has a copy, but even they can't read it. So the narrator thinks: What I am here for? What use is the "writer"? I mean, this is of course the way for me to think about what ...

The writer is not the one who writes. Software writes. What does the writer do then? Anyhow, in this passage, he becomes obsessed with what we could call the temporality of the cloud, perhaps. I mean, it occurs to me in light of what's been discussed today. U's consultancy is working on this massive government project that nobody really understands—but it is really important. They are working on this massive project, and there is too much information. Their servers start jamming. Ines asked me to read the passage about data buffering in *Satin Island* to end this intense and unique conference which might indeed have produced a new productive buffering of ideas and information. Thank you, Ines and Eyal, for this conversation.

    EW: Thank you, Tom.

[*Tom McCarthy reads an excerpt about data buffering from* Satin Island.][3]

This conversation took place during the XIII. International Bauhaus-Kolloquium *Dust & Data*, Weimar, on October 29, 2016. The discussion was intersected by Tom McCarthy reading from three of his novels which are not reprinted here, but are indicated in footnotes to the interview.

1   Tom McCarthy, *Remainder* (New York: Vintage, 2007), 64–68: "It happened like this ... When I was satisfied of that I opened them again and left the bathroom."

2   Tom McCarthy, C (London: Jonathan Cape, 2010), 155–158: "On days when they're assigned to artillery patrol ... he could wipe the whole sky clear."

3   Tom McCarthy, *Satin Island* (New York: Random House, 2015), 67–69 (sections 7.6 and 7.7.): "Back in the office, as our work on the Koob-Sassen Project kicked in and the general traffic-levels edged up, we started experiencing problems with our bandwidth. There was too much information, I guess, shuttling through the servers, down the cables, through the air. My computer, like those of all my colleagues, was afflicted by frequent bouts of buffering. ... if the cursor and red section catch up, then buffering sets in again. Staring at this bar, losing myself in it just as with the circle, I was granted a small revelation: it dawned on me that what I was *actually* watching was nothing less than the skeleton, laid bare, of time or memory itself. Not our computers' time and memory, but our own. This was its structure. We require experience to stay ahead, if only by a nose, of our *consciousness* of experience—if for no other reason than that the latter needs to make sense of the former, to ... narrate it both to others and ourselves, and, for this purpose, has to be fed with a constant, unsorted supply of fresh sensations and events. But when the narrating cursor catches right up with the rendering one, when occurrences and situations don't replenish themselves quickly enough for the awareness they sustain, when, no matter how fast they regenerate, they're instantly devoured by a mouth too voracious to let anything gather or accrue unconsumed before it, then we find ourselves jammed, stuck in limbo: we can enjoy *neither* experience *nor* consciousness of it. Everything becomes buffering, and buffering becomes everything. The revelation pleased me. I decided I would start a dossier on buffering."

Biographical Notes

PERSEPHONE ALLEN's research focuses on early twentieth-century European art and design history with an emphasis on gender and photography. She received her MA in design history from the Bard Graduate Center, where her thesis was awarded the Lee B. Anderson Memorial Foundation Dean's Prize in 2017. She has taught design history at the Mason Gross School of the Arts at Rutgers University and currently works in education and public programs at the Frick Collection in New York City.

PEP AVILÉS is assistant professor at the College of Arts and Architecture at Penn State University. He is a historian, architect, and educator. He holds a diploma in architecture, a master's degree in the history and theory of art and architecture from the Escola Tècnica Superior d'Arquitectura de Barcelona, and an MA and PHD from Princeton University. Avilés has taught at Columbia University, The Cooper Union for the Advancement of Science and Art, the Universitat Politècnica de Catalunya, and the Barcelona Institute of Architecture, where he was appointed head of graduate studies. His academic work has been published in journals such as *Footprint*, *Thresholds*, *San Rocco*, *Volume*, *Project Journal*, *Quaderns d'Architectura i Urbanisme* among others. He is the editor of the Spanish translation of Sigfried Ebeling's *Der Raum als Membran* (1926).

PETER BERNHARD is an adjunct professor of philosophy at the University of Erlangen-Nuremberg and a research fellow at the Bauhaus Dessau Foundation. His research focuses on logic, epistemology, and the history of ideas of the artistic avant-garde. He has published extensively in these areas. In 2017 he published a volume about the guest lectures at the Bauhaus in Weimar, as part of the series of *Neue Bauhausbücher*.

ANNA BOKOV is an architect, educator, and historian. She holds a PHD from Yale University and an M.ARCH. from Harvard Graduate School of Design. She teaches at the Cooper Union and Parsons School of Design. Formerly she taught at Cornell AAP, Yale School of Architecture and Yale School of Art, Northeastern University, and Harvard University. Anna has worked as an architect and urban designer with the Office for Metropolitan Architecture; NBBJ; Gluckman Mayner Architects and Polshek Partnership (Ennead); and the City of Somerville Office of Strategic Planning and Community Development. She collaborates with the nonprofit organization Terreform ONE. Anna has been a recipient of the Graham Foundation Grant, Mellon Fellowship, and Beinecke Research Grant at Yale. Her research has been presented at MOMA, Bauhaus Dessau Foundation, Columbia University, Canadian Centre for Architecture, AIA New York, and Venice Biennale. Her upcoming book, titled *Avant-Garde as Method: Vkhutemas and the Pedagogy of Space, 1920–1930* is dedicated to the history of early modern design education, focusing on the Soviet counterpart of the Bauhaus. Anna is currently working on curating events dedicated to the centennial of Vkhutemas in 2020.

VERONICA BREMER received her BA in art history from the University of Houston. She earned her MA in intercultural humanities at Jacobs University in Bremen, where she is currently a PHD candidate. She has served as a research associate for the Australian Research Council project "Bauhaus Diaspora and Beyond: Transforming Education through Art, Design and Architecture," and currently works as an instructor at Leuphana Universität Lüneburg. Her research has been generously supported by the Paul Mellon Centre for Studies in British Art, the Claussen Simon Stiftung, the German Academic Exchange Service (DAAD), and the Klassik Stiftung Weimar.

ZEYNEP ÇELIK ALEXANDER is an associate professor at the Department of Art History and Archaeology at Columbia University. Her work focuses on the history and theory of architecture since the Enlightenment. After being trained as an architect at Istanbul Technical University and Harvard Graduate School of Design, she received her PHD from the history, theory, and criticism program at MIT. Çelik Alexander is the author of *Kinaesthetic Knowing: Aesthetics, Epistemology, Modern Design* (Chicago and London: University of Chicago Press, 2017), a recipient of the Charles Rufus Morey Award from the College Art Association. A second volume, *Design Technics: Archaeologies of Architectural Practice*, co-edited with John J. May (Harvard University) and forthcoming from the University of Minnesota Press in 2019, examines the histories of a series of techniques that have come to dominate contemporary design disciplines.

MARIJA DRĖMAITĖ is a professor at Vilnius University's History Department. She holds a PHD in the history of architecture (2006). Her scientific interest is focused on 20th-century modern architecture, socialist Modernism and industrial heritage. She is the author of *Baltic Modernism: Architecture and Housing in Soviet Lithuania* (Berlin:

DOM Publishers, 2017) and editor of *Architecture of Optimism: The Kaunas Phenomenon, 1918–1940* (Vilnius: Lapas, 2018).

THOMAS FLIERL studied philosophy and aesthetics at the Humboldt University of Berlin, from which he also holds a PHD. After professional engagements in the public administration of culture and in politics, he has since 2006 been a historian of architecture and urban planning. He is a member of the Bauhaus Institute for the History and Theory of Architecture and Planning in Weimar and the author and editor of numerous books, including *Berlin Plant* (ed. 2010), *Städtebau-Debatten in der DDR* (ed. 2012), *Standardstädte. Ernst May in der Sowjetunion 1930–1933* (ed. 2012), *Ernst May und die Planungsgeschichte von Magnitogorsk 1930–1933* (ed. 2014), *Von Adenauer zu Stalin. Der Einfluss des traditionellen deutschen Städtebaus in der Sowjetunion um 1935* (ed. 2016), *Hannes Meyer und das Bauhaus. Im Streit der Deutungen* (ed. 2018). Flierl has been a fellow at the Institute for Advanced Studies at the University of Konstanz.

CHRISTOPHER T. GREEN is a PHD candidate in art history at the Graduate Center of the City University of New York. His research focuses on primitivism of the historic and neo-avant-garde, modern Native American art, and the pressures of the digital mode on culture and art-making. His criticism and essays have appeared in *ARTMargins*, *The Winterthur Portfolio, Art in America*, and *The Brooklyn Rail*, among others, as well as exhibition catalogues for the New Museum, Artists' Space, and the Fondation Fernet Branca. As a 2018–2019 Smithsonian Institution Predoctoral Fellow, he conducted dissertation research on the interrelationship of Euro-American Modernism and Northwest Coast Native art and he is the 2019–2020 Dedalus Foundation Dissertation Fellow.

ZSÓFIA KELM was born in Györ, Hungary, in 1987. She studied art history and translation in Vienna and Madrid, respectively. She also holds a master's degree in urbanism, completed in 2014 at the Bauhaus-Universität Weimar. She has worked for ICOMOS Austria and at the Austrian Commission for UNESCO, first as program specialist for culture and communication and, later, as program specialist for education and science. She is currently a PHD candidate in architectural history and theory at the Bauhaus-Universität Weimar under the supervision of Ines Weizman. Her thesis deals with the legacy of the Hochschule für Baukunst und Handwerk under Otto Bartning, the successor institution of the Bauhaus in Weimar.

HAMED KHOSRAVI is an architect, writer, and educator.
He holds a BA from the Faculty of Fine Arts at the University of
Tehran and a Master in Architecture (MSC) from the Iran University
of Science and Technology. He later studied Urbanism at TU Delft
and the Istituto di Architettura di Venezia. Hamed received his PHD
in "The City as a Project" program at TU Delft/Berlage Institute.
Hamed teaches at the School of Architecture, Oxford Brookes
University, and is a guest lecturer at the Faculty of Architecture,
TU Delft. In 2013, he co-founded Behemoth, a Rotterdam-based
architectural think tank, with whom he curated "Architecture of
Fulfilment" at the 2014 Venice Biennale, "Penelope; the Endless
Loom" for the Supreme Achievement, Rome 2015, and "Cerberus,
the Three-Headed Monster" for the 2016 Venice Biennale. His recent
articles include "Camp of Faith" (2013), "Geopolitics of Tabula
Rasa" (2014), and "Discreet Austerity" (2015).

NORBERT KORREK studied architecture at the Hochschule für
Architektur und Bauwesen (HAB) Weimar, where he set up and
directed workshops for artistic experimentation in the Architecture
Department. In 1986, he received his PHD with the dissertation topic
of the history of the Hochschule für Gestaltung Ulm. From 1986
to 2009, he organized the Internationale Bauhaus-Kolloquien at the
HAB Weimar. From 1990 to 2018 he was a research associate at the
Chair of Design and Architectural Theory, focusing since 2008 on
the theory and history of modern architecture. From 2015 to 2017
he provisionally took over the chair. Today he is a member of the
Bauhaus Institute of History and Theory of Architecture and Planning at the Bauhaus-Universität Weimar. His research focuses on the
history of the HAB Weimar. His publications and contributions to
exhibitions center around the architectonic work of Henry van de
Velde, the Bauhaus and how it was received in the GDR, and National
Socialist buildings in Weimar.

MICHAEL KUBO is Assistant Professor in the History and Theory
of Architecture at the Gerald D. Hines College of Architecture and
Design, University of Houston. He was previously the Wyeth Fellow
at the Center For Advanced Study in the Visual Arts, National Gallery
of Art and Associate Curator for *Office US*, the US Pavilion at the 2014
International Architecture Biennale in Venice, Italy. His books
on twentieth-century architecture and urbanism include *Imagining
the Modern: Architecture and Urbanism of the Pittsburgh Renaissance* (2019),

Heroic: Concrete Architecture and the New Boston (2015), and *Office us Atlas* (2015). He is currently preparing a book on The Architects Collaborative and the authorship of the architectural corporation after 1945.

ANNA-MARIA MEISTER is a historian, theorist, and architect working at the intersection of architecture's histories and the histories of science and technology. Her work focuses on the production and dissemination of norms and normed objects as social desires in German modern architecture. Meister is professor for architecture history and theory at TU Darmstadt after receiving a joint PHD degree in the history and theory of architecture and the Humanities Council from Princeton University, and holds degrees in architecture from Columbia University in New York and the Technical University of Munich. Her writing has been published in *Harvard Design Magazine*, *Volume*, *Uncube*, *Baumeister*, *Arch+* and as a book chapter in *Architecture and the Paradox of Dissidence* (Routledge, 2013). Her research was featured at the Lisbon Triennale 2013 and the 14th Venice Architecture Biennale 2014.

TOM MCCARTHY is a novelist whose work has been translated into more than twenty languages. His first novel, *Remainder*, won the 2008 Believer Book Award and was recently adapted for the cinema. His third, *C*, was a 2010 Booker Prize finalist, as was his fourth, *Satin Island*, in 2015. McCarthy is also author of the study *Tintin and the Secret of Literature*, and of the essay collection *Typewriters, Bombs, Jellyfish*. He contributes regularly to publications such as The New York Times, The London Review of Books, Harper's and Artforum. In 2013 he was awarded the inaugural Windham Campbell Prize for Fiction by Yale University. He is currently a Fellow of the DAAD Artists-in-Berlin Programme.

NICHOLAS DE MONCHAUX is a professor of architecture and urban design at the University of California, Berkeley, where he serves as director of the Berkeley Center for New Media, as well as a partner at modem, an Oakland, California-based architecture practice. He is the author of *Spacesuit: Fashioning Apollo* (MIT Press, 2011), an architectural and urban history of the Apollo spacesuit, winner of the Eugene Emme Award from the American Astronautical Society and shortlisted for the Art Book Prize, as well as *Local Code: 3,659 Proposals about Data, Design, and the Nature of Cities* (Princeton Architectural Press, Fall 2016). His design work has been exhibited widely, including at the Biennial of the Americas, the Venice Architecture Biennale, the Lisbon Architecture Triennial, the San Francisco Museum of Modern Art, the Yerba Buena Center for the Arts, the Storefront for Art and Architecture, and the Museum of Contemporary Art in Chicago. He is a fellow of the American Academy in Rome.

ELIZABETH OTTO is an art historian and the author of *Haunted Bauhaus: Occult Spirituality, Gender Fluidity, Queer Identities, and Radical Politics* (2019) and *Tempo, Tempo! The Bauhaus Photomontages of Marianne Brandt* (2005). With Patrick Rössler, she coauthored *Bauhaus Women: A Global Perspective* (2019) and coedited *Bauhaus Bodies: Gender, Sexuality, and Body Culture in Modernism's Legendary Art School* (2019). Among her other coedited books are *Passages of Exile* (with Burcu Dogramaci, 2017), *Art and Resistance in Germany* (with Deborah Ascher Barnstone, 2018), and *4 "Bauhausmädels": Gertrud Arndt, Marianne Brandt, Margarete Heymann, Margaretha Reichardt* (2019); this last volume was also the exhibition catalogue to her co-curated show at Erfurt's Angermuseum. Otto is Associate Professor at the University at Buffalo (SUNY), where she has also served as the Executive Director of the Humanities Institute. Her work has been supported by numerous organizations including the Alexander von Humboldt Foundation, the Center for Advanced Study in the Visual Arts, the National Humanities Center, and the University at Pittsburgh's Humanities Center.

JÖRG PAULUS studied German literature and philosophy in Heidelberg and Berlin. He was editor at the Berlin-Brandenburgische Akademie der Wissenschaften and has taught at universities in Berlin (TU), Braunschweig, Hannover, and Tokyo. Since 2016, he has been a professor of archival and literary research at the Media Department of the Bauhaus-Universität Weimar. His research focuses on theories and media theories of philology; literature and culture around 1800, around 1900, and in the present day; literary anthropology; and the way archives, letters, and cultural technology are researched. His publications include *Philologie der Intimität. Liebeskorrespondenz im Jean-Paul-Kreis* (Berlin and Boston, 2013); *Umstrittene Postmoderne. Lektüren* (ed. with Renate Stauf and Andrea Hübener, Heidelberg, 2010); "Spezielle Charaktere. Das Habitat der Buchstaben in der literarischen Anthropologie," in *Medienanthropologische Szenen*, ed. Christiane Voss, Lorenz Engell, and Katerina Krtilova (Paderborn, 2019).

ALINA PAYNE is a professor of history of art and architecture at Harvard University and the director of Villa I Tatti, the Harvard University Center for Italian Renaissance Studies. She was trained as an architect (BARCH, McGill University) and received MA and PHD degrees in the history of art and architecture (University of Toronto). She is the author of *The Architectural Treatise in the Italian Renaissance* (Cambridge University Press, 1999; Hitchcock Prize, 2000), *Rudolf Wittkower* (Bollati Boringhieri editore, 2011), *From Ornament to Object: Genealogies of Architectural Modernism* (Yale University Press, 2012), *The Telescope and the Compass: Teofilo Gallaccini and the Dialogue between Architecture and Science in the Age of Galileo* (Leo Olschki, 2012) and *L'architecture parmi les arts: Matérialité, transferts et travail artistique dans l'Italie de la Renaissance* (Louvre/Hazan, 2016). She has published numerous articles on Renaissance and modern architecture, on historiography and artistic theory. She was awarded the Max Planck and Alexander von Humboldt Prize in the Humanities in 2006. She is a fellow of the American Academy of Arts and Sciences.

ROBIN SCHULDENFREI is the Katja and Nicolai Tangen Senior Lecturer in 20th Century Modernism at The Courtauld Institute of Art, University of London. Her research focuses on the subjectivity, materiality, political agency, and social impact of architecture and its objects. She has written widely on modernism as it intersects with theories of the object, architecture, interiors and especially on the Bauhaus. Her publications include *Luxury and Modernism: Architecture and the Object in Germany 1900–1933* (Princeton University Press, 2018) as well as numerous articles, essays and the two edited volumes — *Atomic Dwelling: Anxiety, Domesticity, and Postwar Architecture* (2012) and, co-edited with Jeffrey Saletnik, *Bauhaus Construct: Fashioning Identity, Discourse, and Modernism* (2009). She is currently writing a book on objects in exile and the displacement of design.

KATHRIN SIEBERT is an art historian and architect who teaches and conducts research at the interface of architecture, history, and theory. After studying architecture in Erfurt, she worked as an architect in Rotterdam and Delft. She then completed her MAS in architecture history and theory in Zurich, where she also studied art history, social history, and modern history. Her research centers on the production of architecture, art, and theory in the twentieth century, with a particular focus on housing, urban planning, and rational design from the interwar period to the present as well as on architectural theory in the GDR. In 2018, she finished her dissertation on Swiss architect Hans Schmidt at ETH Zurich.

BERNHARD SIEGERT is a professor for the theory and history of cultural techniques at the Bauhaus-Universität Weimar. He studied German and comparative linguistics, philosophy, Judaic studies, and history at Freiburg University and received his Dr. phil. from the Ruhr University Bochum in 1991. After a position as research assistant at the Chair for Aesthetics and Media History at Humboldt University in Berlin, Bernhard Siegert came to Weimar in 2002, where he was one of the founders of the Graduate School "Mediale Historiographien" in 2004 and initiated the degree program "Media Architecture" (Master of Science) at the Bauhaus-Universität. In 2015 he was Phyllis and Gerald LeBoff Distinguished Visiting Scholar at the Department for Media, Culture, and Communication at New York University, in 2016 International Visiting Research Scholar at the Peter Wall Institute for Advanced Studies, University of British Columbia, Vancouver, in 2017 Eberhard Berent Visiting Professor and Distinguished Writer in Residence at the Department of German, New York University, in 2018 Guest Lecturer at the Department of Culture and Aesthetics, Stockholm University, Sweden, and in 2019 Visiting Professor at Harvard University, Department of Visual and Environmental Studies. Since April 2008, Bernhard Siegert has been, alongside Lorenz Engell, director of the IKKM in Weimar.

FRANK SIMON-RITZ studied history and German literature at the Ruhr-Universität Bochum. From 1990 to 1993, he was a fellow in the postgraduate program of the University of Bielefeld. From 1993 to 1995, he trained as a scientific librarian at the university library of Mannheim and at a school of library studies in Frankfurt am Main, receiving his PHD in 1995. His first position was at the Library of Duchess Anna Amalia in Weimar. There he was the group leader for the "Weimarer Nietzsche-Bibliographie." Since 1999, he has been the director of the university library of the Bauhaus-Universität Weimar.

INES SONDER studied mathematics and physics (diploma), then art history and Hebrew/Israel studies at the Humboldt University of Berlin (MA), before earning her PHD at the University of Potsdam on the Zionist reception of the Garden City in Erez Israel. She is a research associate at the Moses Mendelssohn Center for European Jewish Studies, Potsdam. Her research topics include the history of pioneering female architects, the exile of architects and Bauhaus pupils in British Mandatory Palestine, and German Jewish immigration. Exhibition curator in cooperation with the Bauhaus Dessau Foundation and the Bauhaus Center Tel Aviv. Her publications include *Carmel: The International Style in Haifa* (Tel Aviv, 2015); "Bauhaus Architecture in Israel: De-Constructing a Modernist Vernacular and the Myth of Tel Aviv's 'White City'" (*Handbook of Israel: Major Debates*, Berlin/Boston 2016); and *Lotte Cohn. Eine schreibende Architektin in Israel* (2 vols., ed., Berlin 2017).

DANIEL TALESNIK is a trained architect from the Catholic University of Chile in Santiago. He holds a MSC in Advanced Architectural Design and a PHD in the history and theory of architecture from Columbia University. He specializes in modern and contemporary architecture and urbanism, with a particular focus on architectural pedagogy and the relationships between architecture and political ideologies. In 2016, he defended his doctoral dissertation, *The Itinerant Red Bauhaus, or the Third Emigration*, which studies a group of Bauhaus students who followed Hannes Meyer to the Soviet Union in 1930–31. This dissertation also addresses a previously unrecognized, politically motivated movement of architects from Europe to the USSR, Asia, and South America in the 1930s and 1940s. Many of these architects returned to Europe after the war. Talesnik has taught in the Catholic University of Chile, Columbia University and the Illinois Institute of Technology. He is currently a curator at the Architekturmuseum of the Technical University of Munich where he curated the exhibition *Access for All: São Paulo's Architectural Infrastructures* (June 12–Sept 8, 2019).

JOYCE TSAI is chief curator at the Stanley Museum of Art and associate professor of practice in the School of Art and Art History, University of Iowa. Her curatorial, pedagogical, and scholarly work addresses questions of technology, politics, and philosophy in modern and contemporary art. She holds an MA in German and art history and earned her doctorate from the Humanities Center at Johns Hopkins University. Her book *László Moholy-Nagy: Painting after Photography* (2018) is the winner of the Phillips Collection Book Prize. She was guest curator of *The Paintings of Moholy-Nagy: Shape of Things to Come* (2015) at the Santa Barbara Museum of Art and editor of the catalogue of the same title distributed by Yale University Press. She was recently co-curator of *Dada Futures* (2018) at the Stanley Museum of Art.

ANNA VALLYE is an assistant professor of art history and architectural studies at Connecticut College. Her research explores modern architecture's intersections with the reciprocal politics of knowledge production and state governance in the United States and Western Europe in the twentieth century. Her current book project focuses on the American careers of Walter Gropius, Ludwig Hilberseimer, and Martin Wagner in the interwar and immediate postwar period. Vallye is the author of *Léger: Modern Art and the Metropolis* (Philadelphia Museum of Art and Yale University Press, 2014), as well as multiple scholarly essays and book chapters on modern art, architecture, and urban planning. Her most recent article, on data visualization in the work of Martin Wagner, is forthcoming in the *Journal of Urban History*.

ANSELM WAGNER studied art history, philosophy, and classical archaeology in Salzburg and Munich (MA in 1991, PHD in 2002). In 2010, he was appointed professor and chair of the Institute of Architectural Theory, Art History and Cultural Studies at Graz University of Technology. Since then, he has been the editor of GAM (*Graz Architecture Magazine*) and the book series *architektur + analyse* at Jovis, Berlin, and head of the research projects "The Solar Houses of Konrad Frey" and "Buddhist Architecture in the Western Himalayas." Wagner is the editor of various books, among them *Abfallmoderne: Zu den Schmutzrändern der Kultur* (LIT: Vienna and Berlin, 2010, 2nd ed. 2012), *Was bleibt von der 'Grazer Schule'? Architektur-Utopien der 1960er revisited* (Jovis: Berlin, 2012; with Antje Senarclens de Grancy), *Staub: Eine interdisziplinäre Perspektive* (LIT: Vienna and Berlin, 2013; with Daniel Gethmann), and *Is There (Anti-)Neoliberal Architecture?* (Jovis: Berlin, 2013; with Ana Jeinic). His latest book is *Architekturführer Graz* (DOM publishers: Berlin, 2019; with Sophia Walk).

CHRISTIANE WOLF holds a doctorate in art history. She attended universities in Göttingen and Bochum. Since 1998 she has been at the Bauhaus-Universität Weimar, where she first worked in the context of research projects at the Department of Architecture and Urbanism. Since 2006 she has been the director of the Archiv der Moderne.

EYAL WEIZMAN is the founding director of Forensic Architecture and professor of spatial and visual cultures at Goldsmiths, University of London, where he founded the Centre for Research Architecture in 2005. In 2019 he was elected fellow of the British Academy. The author of more than 15 books, he has conducted research and taught at many universities worldwide. He was a global scholar at Princeton University and a professor at the Academy of Fine Arts in Vienna. He is a member of several managing and advisory boards, including the Technology Advisory Board of the International Criminal Court and the board of trustees of the Centre for Investigative Journalism. He is also a founding member of the architectural collective DAAR in Beit Sahour, Palestine. Eyal studied architecture at the Architectural Association, graduating in 1998. He received his PHD in 2006 from the London Consortium at Birkbeck, University of London.

INES WEIZMAN is director of the Bauhaus Institute for the History and Theory of Architecture and Planning and a professor of architectural theory at the Bauhaus-Universität Weimar. In 2015, she founded the Centre for Documentary Architecture (CDA), which she has since directed. She trained as an architect at the Bauhaus-Universität Weimar and the École d'Architecture de Belleville in Paris, the Sorbonne, the University of Cambridge, and the Architectural Association School of Architecture, where she completed her PHD thesis in history and theory. In 2014, her edited book *Architecture and the Paradox of Dissidence* was published by Routledge. The book *Before and After: Documenting the Architecture of Disaster,* co-written with Eyal Weizman, was published in the same year by Strelka Press. In 2016 she organized the XIII. Internationales Bauhaus-Kolloquium, titled "Dust & Data," and in 2019 the XIV. Internationales Bauhaus-Kolloquium. The CDA exhibition "The Matter of Data: Tracing the Materiality of 'Bauhaus Modernism'" will be shown in 2019 at the Bauhaus-Museum Weimar and the Liebling Haus in Tel Aviv.

Image Credits

— *The Agency of Objects*
Fig. 1. © Harvard University, Houghton Library.
Fig. 4. © Victoria and Albert Museum Library, London.
Fig. 5. © Harvard University, Widener Library.
Fig. 7. © Adam Yarinski, Architecture Research Office, New York.
Fig. 8. © Bauhaus-Archiv Berlin.
Fig. 9. © Special Collections, Loeb Design Library, Harvard University.
Fig. 10. © Alina Payne.
— *The Bauhaus and the Vacuum Cleaner*
Fig. 2. © Bildrecht Wien 2018.
Fig. 3, 7, 8. © Deutsches Hygiene-Museum Dresden.
Fig. 9. © f8 archive / Alamy Stock Photo.
Fig. 10. © Wikimedia Commons 2009.
— Faktur, *Photography, and the Image of Labor*
Fig. 1. Courtesy of Princeton University Library. Rare Book Division, Department of Rare Books and Special Collections, Princeton University Library.
Fig. 8. Courtesy of Collection of the Russian State Library, Moscow / HIP / ArtResource, NY.
Fig. 9. Courtesy of Institute of Design Papers, Special Collections and University Archives, University of Illinois at Chicago Library.
Fig. 10. © 2018 Artists Rights Society (ARS), New York / VG Bild-Kunst Bonn. Image provided by the Bauhaus-Archiv Berlin.
— *Queer Coded Bauhaus*
Fig. 1. © Bauhaus-Archiv Berlin, Archiv Peiffer Watenpul.
— *The Metallic Sphere as Mechanical Eye*
Fig. 1. © The Mary and Leigh Block Endowment Fund.
Fig. 2. © The Thomas Walther Collection; gift of Thomas Walther.

Fig. 3–6, 8. © Bauhaus-Archiv Berlin.
Fig. 7. © Lucia Moholy Estate / Artists Rights Society (ARS), New York / VG Bild-Kunst, Bonn. Photo: Imaging Department. © President and Fellows of Harvard College.
— *Towards a Digital Bauhaus*
Fig. 1. © The Josef and Anni Albers Foundation.
Fig. 2. © The Josef and Anni Albers Foundation, 1976.6.21.
Fig. 3. © The Josef and Anni Albers Foundation, 1976.7.1106.
Fig. 4. © Harvard Art Museums / Busch-Reisinger Museum, Kuno Francke Memorial and Association Funds, BR49.261.
Fig. 5. © Yale University Art Gallery 1977.160.1. Gift of Anni Albers and the Josef Albers Foundation, Inc.
Fig. 8. © Yale University Art Gallery 2016.64.1. Bequest of James H. Clark, Jr., B.A. 1958.
Fig. 9. © The Josef and Anni Albers Foundation, 1976.7.1105.
Fig. 10. © Harvard Art Museums / Busch-Reisinger Museum, Gift of Walter Gropius, BR50.81.
— *Reinscribing Mies's Materiality*
Fig. 1. Bauhaus-Archiv Berlin. Copyright Walter Gropius, Ludwig Mies van der Rohe. © Artists Rights Society (ARS), New York / VG Bild-Kunst, Bonn; Walter Peterhans: © Museum Folkwang, Essen.
Fig. 2. Bauhaus-Archiv Berlin. © Artists Rights Society (ARS), New York / VG Bild-Kunst, Bonn.
Fig. 3 left. Atelier de Sandalo, courtesy of Brno City Museum. © Artists Rights Society (ARS), New York / VG Bild-Kunst, Bonn.
Fig. 3 right. Atelier de Sandalo, courtesy of Brno City Museum. © Artists Rights Society (ARS), New York / VG Bild-Kunst, Bonn.

— *1919: The Turning Point*
Fig. 3. Courtesy of the Münchner Stadt-museum, Sammlung Mode / Textilien / Kostümbibliothek.
Fig. 5. Bauhaus-Archiv Berlin. Photo: Gunter Lepkowski. Inv. 2965/11.
Fig. 6. © 2016 Artists Rights Society (ARS), New York / ProLitteris, Zurich.
Fig. 7. Bauhaus-Archiv Berlin. Photo: Bauhaus-Archiv Berlin. Inv. 603.
Fig. 8. © 2016 Artists Rights Society (ARS), New York.
Fig. 9. © Archive of the Hochschule für Gestaltung Ulm / © Archive of the Hoch-schule für Gestaltung Ulm.
Fig. 10. With permission from the Getty Research Institute, Los Angeles (850514), Box 2. © 2016 Artists Rights Society (ARS), New York.
Fig. 11. Bauhaus-Archiv Berlin. Photo: Bauhaus-Archiv Berlin. Inv. 8057/2_S10. © Estate of Walter Gropius / Sodrac (2016).
Fig. 12. © Estate of László Moholy-Nagy / Sodrac (2016).
— *Epochal Trace*
Fig. 1–5. © 2019 Estate of László Moholy-Nagy.
— *"Reserve Hospital No. 11 Art School":*
Fig. 1–4. Private Collection Norbert Korrek.
Fig. 5. Landesarchiv Thüringen – Hauptstaatsarchiv Weimar, Thüringer Rotes Kreuz, vorl. Nr. 14.
Fig. 6. Landesarchiv Thüringen – Hauptstaatsarchiv Weimar, Thüringer Rotes Kreuz, vorl. Nr. 42.
Fig. 7, 8. Universitätsbibliothek Weimar, SoB 4-241 302, *Thüringen im und nach dem Weltkrieg. Geschichtliches Erinnerungswerk an die Kriegsteilnahme, die politische Umwälzung und Erneuerung Thüringens in Wort und Bild*, vol. 1 (Leipzig, 1921), 379.
Fig. 9, 10. Landesarchiv Thüringen – Hauptstaatsarchiv Weimar, Staatliches

Bauhaus Weimar Nr. 75, Bl. 11.
— *Vkhutemas and the Bauhaus*
Fig. 1. Courtesy of Museum of Modern Art, New York.
Fig. 2. Courtesy of Shchusev State Museum of Architecture.
Fig. 3. Courtesy of Rodchenko and Stepanova Archive.
Fig. 4. Courtesy of Zakhar Bykov Archive. Moscow State Stroganov Academy of Industrial and Applied Arts.
Fig. 5. Courtesy of Museum of Moscow Architectural Institute.
Fig. 6a, b. Courtesy of Museum of Modern Art, New York.
Fig. 7, 8. Courtesy of Museum of Moscow Architectural Institute.
Fig. 9a, b. Courtesy of Museum of Moscow Architectural Institute.
Fig. 10. Courtesy of Bibliothèque Kandinsky. Centre Georges Pompidou.
Fig. 13. Courtesy of Museum of Moscow Architectural Institute.
Fig. 14. Courtesy of Beinecke Rare Book and Manuscript Library.
Fig. 15. Private collection Anna Bokov.
Fig. 16. *Arkhitektura Vkhutemas,* Moscow, 1927. Front cover of pamphlet, design by El Lissitzky. Beinecke Rare Book and Manuscript Library.
Fig. 17a, b. Courtesy of Beinecke Rare Book and Manuscript Library.
— *Fates of Books*
Fig. 1–6. Bauhaus-Universität Weimar. © Tobias Adam.
— *The "Second Faculty" at the Weimar Bauhaus*
Fig. 1. Goethe- und Schiller-Archiv / Klassik-Stiftung Weimar, Nachlass Werner Deetjen, Signatur GSA 132/44. © Klassik-Stiftung Weimar.
Fig. 2. Bayerische Staatsgemälde-sammlungen (Pinakothek der Moderne), Fotothek.

Fig. 3. Bauhaus-Archiv / Museum für Gestaltung. © Bauhaus-Archiv Berlin.

Fig. 4. Bauhaus-Archiv / Museum für Gestaltung, Konvolut "Leben am Bauhaus Weimar," Inv.-Nr. 3098. © Bauhaus-Archiv Berlin.

Fig. 5. Sammlung Magdlung, Signatur K2-232. © Sammlung Magdlung.

Fig. 6. Landesarchiv Sachsen-Anhalt, E 200, Image Archive City of Dessau, Fritz Schade Estate, F 303.

Fig. 7. Bauhaus-Archiv / Museum für Gestaltung, Inv.-Nr. 12635. © Stiftung Bauhaus Dessau. Photo © Andreas Feininger / Getty Images.

— *The Influence of the Bauhaus*

Fig. 1. Otto-Bartning-Archiv, TU Darmstadt, Inv.-Nr. 2006F01730.

Fig. 2. Otto-Bartning-Archiv, TU Darmstadt, Inv.-Nr. 2006P01746.

Fig. 3. Otto-Bartning-Archiv, TU Darmstadt, Inv.-Nr. 2006F01701.

Fig. 4. Otto-Bartning-Archiv, TU Darmstadt, Inv.-Nr. 2006F01672.

Fig. 5. Otto-Bartning-Archiv, TU Darmstadt, Inv.-Nr. 2006F01681.

Fig. 6. Brandenburgisches Landeshauptarchiv, Signatur: Rep. 601, Nr. 3699.

Fig. 7. Brandenburgisches Landeshauptarchiv, Signatur: Rep. 601, Nr. 7627.

Fig. 8. © Centre for Documentary Architecture.

Fig. 9. © Centre for Documentary Architecture.

Fig. 10a. Otto-Bartning-Archiv, TU Darmstadt, Inv.-Nr. 2006F01739.

Fig. 10b. © Centre for Documentary Architecture, Jens Stöbe.

Fig. 11. © Centre for Documentary Architecture, Jens Stöbe.

— *Party Politics and Architecture*

Fig. 1–4. Private archive of Madleen Lamm-Schmidt.

— *The Long Path to the Restoration of the Bauhaus Dessau*

Fig. 1. Archiv Karlheinz Schlesier.

Fig. 2, 3, 15. Archiv Christian Schädlich.

Fig. 4, 16. Archiv Marlis Grönwald.

Fig. 5. SLUB / Deutsche Fotothek.

Fig. 6. Archiv der Moderne / Universitätsarchiv Bauhaus-Universität Weimar.

Fig. 7. SLUB / Deutsche Fotothek.

Fig. 8a–c, 9, 10, 11, 12, 13, 14a–d. Archiv der Moderne / Universitätsarchiv Bauhaus-Universität Weimar.

— *Transcripts of Filmed Interviews* Portraits (screenshots) © Centre for Documentary Architecture.

— *Migrant with a Conflicted Sense of Home*

Fig. 1–2. Bauhaus-Archiv, DAM, gta ETH.

Fig. 3a, 6. gta-Archiv, estate of Hannes Meyer.

Fig. 3b. Source unknown.

Fig. 4, 5. Shchusev State Museum of Architecture, Moscow.

Fig. 7. Sozialarchiv Zürich.

Fig. 8. Staatsbibliothek Berlin.

— *Tibor Weiner's Architectural Design Teaching Curriculum*

Fig. 1. Shchusev State Museum of Architecture, Moscow.

Fig. 2, 6, 7. Miguel Lawner Archive.

Fig. 5. Archiv der Moderne, Weimar.

Fig. 9. Bauhaus-Archiv Berlin.

Fig. 10. FORTEPAN / Sándor Bauer.

— *Bringing Bauhaus Modernism to Lithuania*

Fig. 2, 3. Personal collection of Alfonsas Švipas.

Fig. 4. Lithuanian Central State Archives.

Fig. 4a, 8, 8a, 8b. Raminta Švipaitė-Šinkus's (Švipas's daughter's) personal collection.

Fig. 5, 6. Collection of the M. K. Čiurlionis Art Museum.

Image
Credits

618

Index

Index

623

625

Acknowledgments

My especial gratitude goes firstly to the authors and conversation partners in this book who have responded to its premise in remarkable, thorough, and imaginative ways and have built and supported the argument of this book. It has been an enormous pleasure and a truly rewarding experience. My thanks also go to the speakers, discussants, organizers, and supporters of the two Bauhaus-Kolloquien in 2016 and 2019 in Weimar who have underpinned this collection of essays. Members of the Bauhaus Institute for the History and Theory of Architecture and Planning, particularly my co-director Max Welch Guerra as well as my colleagues and staff at the Bauhaus-Universität Weimar, have offered invaluable insight and advice on research and collaboration. I am grateful to the Archiv der Moderne, the archive of the Foundation Bauhaus Dessau, and the Bauhaus-Archiv Berlin, which have fundamentally helped this research. My colleagues in the wonderful team of the Centre for Documentary Architecture have made this book possible not only through financial assistance, but also through their help in research organization and by always keeping my spirits high.

This project was made possible by a number of generous sponsors: a grant by the Graham Foundation for Advanced Studies in the Fine Arts helped the project develop at its early stages. The Wüstenrot Stiftung has also donated generously to realize the book. The B100 Fund of the Bauhaus-Universität Weimar helped with the translation of texts to make the research of German-speaking authors available to international readers. Financial assistance from the company FSB was coupled with friendly collaboration with its team, particularly with Wolfgang Reul, who has taken interest in the content of the book and has helped to promote it in lectures and conversations. Graphisoft Archicad helped with the actual production of this book. The Rosa-Luxemburg-Stiftung kindly contributed toward the cost of printing. The Bauhaus Institute for the History and Theory of Architecture and Planning helped to cover some of the cost of image rights.

I would like to thank Paul Feigelfeld and Elias Quijada Link for their translations and proofreading at early stages of this book. Simon Cowper did wonderful work in making us all speak the same language. Michael Pilewski, my marvelous copy editor, has worked far beyond his mandate and has, although invisible, become a great partner and friend in thinking about this book. I thank him for steering this book to port. Helmut Völter has produced an original and powerful graphic design for this book, giving a huge multiplicity of forms a single robust framework. Anne König and Jan Wenzel and their team at Spector Books ensured the high standards of book production and printing. They are keeping the lost art of bookmaking alive in Leipzig.

I am indebted to my friends and colleagues who have helped me through valuable discussion and by reading part of this collection, and who have given me support at various stages of this book. I would like to thank Nora Akawi, George Arbid, Pep Avilés, Ariel Caine, Tony Chakar, Amy Chung, Zeynep Çelik Alexander, Ortrun Bargholz, Franca Beer, Katharina Benjamin, Magdalena Droste, Jurga Dubaraite, Moritz Ebeling, Zvi Efrat, Thomas Flierl, Eva Franch i Gilabert, Manuel Herz, Waleed Karkabi, Bernard Khoury, Vera Heinemann, Wolfram

Höhne, Nina Katchadourian, Sonja Kettel, Eva Maria Körber, Meira Kowalski, Simon Heidenreich, Lena Lorenz, Rebecca Mead, Anna Maria Meister, Shourideh C. Molavi, Sina Najafi, Sarah and Nessie Nankivell, Erkka Nissinen, Ana Paula Nitzsche, Martin Pohl, Jorge Otero-Pailos, Eduardo Rega Calvo, Angalika Sagar, Hrair Sarkissian, Elizabeth Otto, George Prochnik, Sharon Rotbard, Charlotte Samtleben, Markus Schlaffke, Anna Luise Schubert, Robin Schuldenfrei, Adania Shibli, Ines Sonder, Annette Stenger, Markus Stenger, Mara Trübenbach, Jad Tabet, Joyce Tsai, Volkmar Umlauft, Eline van der Vlist, Xenia Vytuleva, Robin Weißenborn, Amelie Wegner, Tracey Eve Winton, Sebastian Wrong, and Jonas Žukauskas. I also thank my students throughout the years for having heard versions of my arguments and for giving me invaluable feedback.

Having studied at the Bauhaus-Universität Weimar from 1992 to 1998 and having returned to teach there, as well as being connected to Thuringia through family there, I also regard this book as a testament to my involvement with this place, both personal and academic. In the early 2000s, as part of my doctoral research, I looked back at the effects of the political transformation of East Germany in 1989 and tried to map the historiographical gaps of architectural and urban practices in a reunified Germany in which a Western reading of East Germany has ignored important reform movements, gestures of dissidence, and sensibilities in communication and exchange across disciplines and borders. Interestingly, some of those gaps remain today. This book cannot fill them, but it is dedicated to a radical shift that occurred in an era involving changing ideologies and a transformation of material culture and personnel of which little is recorded.

My grandmother from Eisenach passed away in 2019, shortly before her 100th birthday. I thank her and my parents in Leipzig, and my family in London, and in Haifa for tolerating this work done between family duties and festivities and for the wonderful help in balancing the demands of work and life. This book would not have been possible without their unquestioning support and their acceptance that I stop dusting and move on to data. Little Alma and Hannah were wonderfully supportive in the way that only they could be. They were the real junior professors! Finally, Eyal, my private eye and rock, has followed me through the ups and downs of my own Bauhaus history. Thank you for standing by me with your wisdom, wit, and love.

Imprint

Concept and editing: Ines Weizman
Graphic design: Helmut Völter
Lithography: Scancolor Reprostudio GmbH
Translation: Simon Cowper, Michael Pilewski
Copyediting: Michael Pilewski
Typefaces: Starling, Monotype Grotesque
Paper: Munken Lynx 90g, Materica Pitch
Printing and binding: optimal media GmbH

Published by:
Spector Books
Harkortstraße 10, 04107 Leipzig
www.spectorbooks.com

Distribution
Germany, Austria: GVA, Gemeinsame Verlagsauslieferung
Göttingen GmbH & Co. KG, www.gva-verlage.de
Switzerland: AVA Verlagsauslieferung AG, www.ava.ch
France, Belgium: Interart Paris, www.interart.fr
Southern Europe: charlesgibbes@orange.fr
UK: Central Books Ltd, www.centralbooks.com
USA, Canada, Central and South America, Africa, Asia:
ARTBOOK | D.A.P. www.artbook.com
South Korea: The Book Society, www.thebooksociety.org
Australia, New Zealand: Perimeter Distribution,
www.perimeterdistribution.com

First edition
Printed in the EU
ISBN 978-3-95905-230-6